Travels in North America, 1832–1834

Travels in North America, 1832–1834

A Concise Edition of the Journals

of Prince Maximilian of Wied

Edited by MARSHA V. GALLAGHER

Translated by
WILLIAM J. ORR, PAUL SCHACH, AND DIETER KARCH

Foreword by JACK F. BECKER
Introduction by MARSHA V. GALLAGHER

University of Oklahoma Press : Norman

In cooperation with the

Margre H. Durham Center for Western Studies,

Joslyn Art Museum, Omaha, Nebraska

Library of Congress Cataloging-in-Publication Data

Names: Wied, Maximilian, Prinz von, 1782–1867, author. | Gallagher, Marsha V., editor.

Title: Travels in North America, 1832–1834 : a concise edition of the journals of Prince Maximilian of Wied / edited by Marsha V. Gallagher ; translated by William J. Orr, Paul Schach, and Dieter Karch ; foreword by Jack F. Becker ; introduction by Marsha V. Gallagher.

Description: Norman : University of Oklahoma Press, 2017. | Includes bibliographical references and index.

Identifiers: LCCN 2016028710 | ISBN 978-0-8061-5579-1 (hardcover : alk. paper)

Subjects: LCSH: United States—Description and travel. | Missouri River Valley—Description and travel. | Wied, Maximilian, Prinz von, 1782–1867—Diaries. | Germans—United States—Diaries. | Naturalists—Germany—Diaries. | Natural history—United States. | Frontier and pioneer life—United States. | Indians of North America—History—19th century. | Indians of North America—Languages—History—19th century.

Classification: LCC E165 .W6413 2017 | DDC 917.304—dc23

LC record available at https://lccn.loc.gov/2016028710

Copyright © 2017 by Joslyn Art Museum, Omaha, Nebraska. Published by the University of Oklahoma Press, Norman, Publishing Division of the University. Manufactured in the U.S.A.

1 2 3 4 5 6 7 8 9 10

Contents

Illustrations

All artworks reproduced in this volume were originally drawn, painted, or printed on paper. All are from the Maximilian-Bodmer Collection in the Margre H. Durham Center for Western Studies at Joslyn Art Museum, Omaha, Nebraska.

FIGURES

PLATES

Foreword

JACK F. BECKER

Executive Director and CEO, Joslyn Art Museum

On 4 July 1832, a ship arrived in Boston Harbor from Holland, carrying as passengers Prince Maximilian of Wied-Neuwied, his hunting guide and servant David Dreidoppel, and the young Swiss painter Karl Bodmer, whom Maximilian had engaged to document his travels. Over many months, the trio would make their way down the Ohio River to St. Louis. Setting out from that city in April 1833, they began a 2,500-mile journey by steam- and keelboat up the Missouri River, traveling as far as Fort McKenzie, in present-day Montana. After wintering at Fort Clark near the Mandan villages, they completed their trip downriver the following spring, having spent over a year in the wilderness of the upper Missouri. Maximilian's journal from this voyage is one of the critical primary documents of the American West. He captured the frontier on the cusp of the mass emigration along the Oregon and California Trails and before the industrialization that followed the Civil War forever transformed the western landscape. Seen alongside Maximilian's *Journals,* Karl Bodmer's watercolors and drawings remain among the most perceptive and compelling visual accounts of the nineteenth-century American interior and its native peoples.

The Maximilian-Bodmer Collection has been closely associated with Joslyn for over five decades. When this collection was purchased by M. Knoedler and Company in New York in 1959 from the descendants of Prince Maximilian, Eugene Kingman (then director of Joslyn) understood its significance. In conjunction with a December 1961 exhibition, the museum mounted a major campaign to purchase this treasure, remarkable in the fact that so much of it had survived intact. A few months later, Northern Natural Gas Company of Omaha, under the leadership of John F. Merriam (corporate chairman) and Willis A. Strauss (corporate president), purchased the collection and placed it on long-term loan at Joslyn. The company (at that time called Enron) donated the entire collection to the museum in 1986. A transformative gift to the Omaha community, the Maximilian-Bodmer Collection quickly became an internationally renowned cornerstone of Joslyn's collection of American Art.

The translation, editing, and publication of the original three-volume edition of *The North American Journals of Prince Maximilian of Wied* was made possible by generous gifts from the Arader Galleries, Anne and Steve Berzin, Robert Daugherty, Charles W. Durham, Judy and Terry Haney, Susan and Michael Lebens, Pinnacle Bank, Marlene and J. Joe Ricketts, Phyllis and Del Toebben, and Dorothy and Stanley M. Truhlsen, as well as the museum's Bodmer Society and Margre H. Durham Center for Western Studies. The National Endowment for the Humanities awarded the project a substantial grant in 2006, and generous gifts from Howard and Rhonda Hawks and the Hawks Foundation allowed Joslyn to bring the project to completion.

While dozens of Joslyn staff members and outside colleagues and advisors contributed to the original publication, Stephen S. Witte, editor of the *Journals,* and Ruby C. Hagerbaumer, former coordinator of curatorial projects, deserve special mention. Finally, Marsha V. Gallagher, former chief curator at Joslyn and director of the project, took on the challenging task of editing the three complete volumes of the *Journals* down to this more practicable scale without losing the character and resonance of Maximilian's voice—her ongoing dedication is much appreciated.

We hope this concise edition of *The North American Journals of Prince Maximilian of Wied* brings his remarkable story to new audiences, who will be equally captivated and enthralled by Maximilian and Bodmer's journey. We are certain you will continue to find inspiration in the landscapes and peoples that drew them to the American West nearly two centuries ago.

Acknowledgments

Many scholars and specialists contributed their time and expertise to making the complete three-volume edition of *The North American Journals of Prince Maximilian of Wied* a reality. Of these, the project's advisory board members were arguably the most important: Philip J. Deloria (University of Michigan), Raymond J. DeMallie (Indiana University), Dieter Karch (University of Nebraska–Lincoln), Robert B. Kaul (University of Nebraska–Lincoln), Gary E. Moulton (University of Nebraska–Lincoln), James P. Ronda (University of Tulsa), and W. Raymond Wood (University of Missouri). Dieter Karch, Bob Kaul, and Ray Wood continued to offer guidance during the production of this new, shorter edition, as did my editorial colleague on *The North American Journals,* Stephen S. Witte (South Dakota State Historical Society Press).

Other individuals who aided in various ways with the production of the concise edition include Deb Covert (Omaha, Nebraska), Sabine Fleishner (Omaha, Nebraska), Theodore W. James (Bellevue, Nebraska), and Susanne Koppel (Hamburg, Germany). At Joslyn Art Museum, which houses the Maximilian-Bodmer Collection, Jack F. Becker, executive director and CEO; Toby Jurovics, chief curator and Richard and Mary Holland curator of American western art; Kay Johnson, registrar; Sarah Haines, assistant registrar; and Ruby C. Hagerbaumer, former coordinator of curatorial projects, provided much-appreciated support and assistance. The University of Oklahoma Press is justly renowned for its ongoing commitment to important publications on the American West; particular thanks go to Steven B. Baker and Charles E. Rankin.

Photographs of artworks by Karl Bodmer illustrated in this book and the color photograph of Maximilian's journal (pl. 1) are by Malcolm Varon of New York City; all other photographs of the prince's drawings are by Lorran Meares of Tucson, Arizona.

A final note of sincere appreciation to Ted, who tolerated having Maximilian in my life far longer than either of us would have believed credible.

Editorial Procedures

The purpose of this condensation is to provide, in one easy to hold and read book, a concise version of the original large-format, three-volume *North American Journals* (or *NAJ*) publication. As published in 2008, 2010, and 2012, the journal entries and footnotes (both Maximilian's own and those of the editors) amount to about 700,000 words. The reduced version contains a little more than 200,000. Neither figure includes any front matter (such as tables of contents and introductory essays) or appendices (assorted informational tables, indices, and so forth); those are additional. The condensed book therefore represents less than a third of the original, but we can confidently say that it gives a good overview and understanding of where Maximilian went in North America, what he saw, and what he thought was significant about both. The following observations are for readers who want to know what is *not* in the book they now hold.[1]

Maximilian wrote a journal entry for almost every day of his two-year sojourn. A very few daily entries have been entirely deleted, a few consecutive days have been combined (indicated in the entry dating), and, obviously, most have been condensed. He regularly recorded temperatures (often more than once per day), wind and water current directions, and weather descriptions; these have typically been deleted except where necessary for understanding his subsequent comments or the day's events.

Geographical observations are a key element of any travel account. Maximilian was an avid user of maps and published guides and described the course of his journey in great detail, recording both what he saw in his guides and what he personally observed. Key place- and feature names have been retained in the condensation, sometimes in bracketed modern terminology. Interested readers can generally find named locations by looking them up in readily available printed sources (such as road atlases) or online through search engines like Google; for obscure or no longer extant sites, the large map that accompanied Maximilian's *Reise* in 1839–43 ("Route of Prince Maximilian of Wied in the Interior of North America from Boston to the Upper Missouri . . . in 1832, 33 & 34") is useful, and there is a digitally available, easy to explore reproduction on the David Rumsey Map Collection website (www.davidrumsey.com; see "Cartography Associates" in the bibliography). Many geographical changes have occurred since the early nineteenth century as a result of dam building, river channel shifts, etc.; only major differences have been footnoted here.

It would be difficult to overstate Maximilian's interest in and dedication to the science of biology. He minutely explored his biological surroundings, recording everything from mosses to mammals, and collected and preserved multiple specimens thereof. He generally used Latin names, most of which have changed from his day to ours, sometimes radically. For the reader's convenience, a flora and fauna cross-reference list has been provided at the back of this condensation with contemporary (as of 2008) scientific binomials for the Latin and common names used by Maximilian; these should allow the reader to do further research if desired. Maximilian's sharp-eyed land formation descriptions are prized by today's geologists, but the descriptive terminology and analytical framework have changed and are not easily updated without the extensive footnoting of the larger *NAJ* volumes, which the interested reader is encouraged to consult.

Maximilian was a great linguaphile. He read, spoke, and/or understood several languages other than his native German, including French and English; his handwritten journals, though done mostly in German, reflect that knowledge and usage. To illustrate his familiarity with English, most words and short passages he penned in that language (except for place-names and certain proper nouns) are indicated as shown here. Maximilian saw linguistics as an important aspect of his ethnological studies of South and North American peoples, and he carefully recorded vocabulary, pronunciations, and, when he had sufficient time for field study, notes on grammar as well. The nearly two dozen different Indian language vocabularies in *NAJ* could not be included here, but examples of the prince's usage of French and Indian place- and object names remain to add color and meaning to the condensation text. Tribal names vary in Maximilian's manuscripts and publications; in *NAJ* and in this condensation they have been standardized, generally to those used in the Smithsonian's *Handbook of North American Indians* (edited by William Sturtevant).

On his first exploratory expedition, to South America in 1815–17, Maximilian—a fairly accurate but unpolished amateur artist—did his own illustrative work in the field, which became the basis for the more elaborate printed plates that accompanied the 1820–21 publication that summarized his journey. In 1832 he hired a young professional artist, Karl Bodmer, to accompany him to North America and produce field sketches and compositions for the prince's anticipated later publication. On the expedition, Maximilian nonetheless continued to make his own drawings for his own reference. There are nearly five hundred of his ink or ink and watercolor sketches in or associated with the three manuscript journals at Joslyn Art Museum, ranging in size from tiny to full page; most are reproduced in the *NAJ*. A few of his best and most informative images are included in this condensation, which is additionally beautifully illustrated with several of Bodmer's best landscapes and Indian portraits.

Aside from the above-noted exceptions, this shorter version of the *NAJ* generally follows the guidelines outlined in the editorial procedures essays in *NAJ* (1:xix–xxiv; 2:xxiii–xxvii; and 3:xvii–xx).

The translation of the manuscript journals into English took place over a long period of time (one version was apparently begun in the 1940s) and involved many individuals. This work presented many challenges, including the script Maximilian wrote in, a form of Sütterlinschrift, which has not been in general German use for several decades and requires special knowledge to read. The nearly two centuries that elapsed between the prince's pen and this volume also means many differences in the meanings of words and phrases, as well as in punctuation styles. For the *NAJ* publications, the editorial team preferred a fairly literal translation approach, keeping as true to the letter of Maximilian's prose as proved readable, preserving content and tone for interested researchers to interpret. In this condensation, a more liberal approach seemed necessary and appropriate for a broader readership. By its very nature, condensation requires judiciously eliminating words, sentences, and paragraphs and shortening or combining the remaining phrasing. To avoid word repetition, alternative translations have often been employed here. For example, *niedlich* is often translated as "pretty," but it can also mean "nice," "sweet," or "winsome"; *hutte* can clearly mean "hut," but in the Native American contexts within which Maximilian uses the word, it is more likely to refer to a "tipi" or "lodge." For ease of reading, Maximilian's frequently almost bewildering use of several tenses (including present, past, and past perfect) in a single descriptive passage has been made more uniform. Although such changes may modernize Maximilian's text, the editorial intent has always been to represent his style and interests as truly as possible; this condensed account is still very much his own.

Brackets are used liberally in the condensation and represent editorial insertions, sometimes serving as a bridge between phrases originally separated by several clauses or even sentences, sometimes adding information the prince must have intended but did not include, and frequently correcting or updating a place-name or other term to one more familiar to a twenty-first-century reader.

Maximilian's expedition to North America was an adventure, with all the excitement of experiencing new places, meeting new people, seeing new things. It was also a well-planned scientific undertaking, intended to enlarge our understanding of "the natural face of North America and its aboriginal population,"[2] and Maximilian's published findings include a wealth of early, firsthand, unusually objective information. While the compression of a condensation heightens one's sense of sharing in the prince's discoveries and commiserating with his disappointments, it has required the elimination of much data. Readers of this shorter version may also enjoy the larger volumes of the *NAJ*, and anyone interested in using Maximilian as a research resource should consult not only the *NAJ* but also the *Reise* or its shortened nineteenth-century English edition; although there is duplication of data, there are interesting, sometimes surprising differences in content and tone, and neither source can be considered more complete than the other. It is my hope that whichever of these you study, you will come to know, as I have, a most remarkable man.

An Introduction to Prince Maximilian of Wied and His Expedition to North America

[Prince Maximilian's 1832–34 manuscript journals] clearly demonstrate the dramatic changes to the Missouri River valley in the decades after Lewis and Clark. The American presence had . . . spread its influence throughout the river valley. Everywhere Maximilian noticed the changes: to native peoples, flora, fauna, and landscape. Being a man of science with a keen eye for the natural setting, he brought a store of knowledge and a professional bearing unmatched by the American explorers. . . . His desire was to document a remnant of the West that was fast disappearing. And he did it so well.[1]

Gary E. Moulton, 2005

Little . . . has yet been done towards a clear and vivid description of the natural scenery of North America. . . . The vast tracts of the interior . . . are, [in particular,] but little known, and the government of the United States may be justly reproached for not having done more to explore them.[2]

Maximilian, Prince of Wied, 1839

Maximilian Alexander Philipp (1782–1867) was the eighth of ten (some sources say nine) children born to Friedrich Carl Graf (then addressed as count; later *prinz,* or prince), ruler of the small sovereignty of Wied-Neuwied on the Rhine River near Koblenz in today's Germany.[3] He was tutored at home as a child, spent a great deal of time outdoors, became a skilled hunter, and by the age of six had already begun a collection of natural history specimens. Aside from voluntary service in the Prussian army against the French (1800–1808; 1813–14), he devoted most of his long life to the study of natural history. He enrolled at the University of Göttingen, where his most influential teacher was Johann Friedrich Blumenbach, often called the father of physical anthropology; Blumenbach's cranial research led him to one of the earliest classifications of the races of mankind. Maximilian also greatly admired Alexander von Humboldt, whom he first met not long after the older explorer and naturalist's return in 1804 from five years of travel in Latin America; a Wied family member stated in 1954 that Maximilian's "paramount interest in the American continents derived from the influence [of Humboldt,] his model, friend, and mentor."[4]

At the conclusion of his last military service in 1814, Maximilian refocused on scholarship and made plans for a scientific expedition to Brazil, a location choice likely influenced by Blumenbach and Humboldt. He spent two years there, often working under uncomfortable, difficult field conditions in the dense eastern rain forests, yet nonetheless amassing thousands of floral and faunal specimens, observational notes, and drawings. These later formed the basis for several well-received publications, particularly his *Reise Nach Brasilien in den Jahren 1815 bis 1817* (Journey to Brazil in the Years 1815 to 1817), which appeared in two volumes in 1820–21. That he was even then seriously contemplating a similar expedition to North America is evidenced by his statement in the Brazilian *Reise* that it would be particularly interesting to compare Brazilian tribal peoples to those of North America, and he therefore planned to undertake a journey there someday.[5]

Maximilian's preparations for his North American exploration were characteristically thorough. He sought letters of introduction from European colleagues to individuals in the United States who could assist him on his travels and in his studies. He also asked for friends' advice on what supplies he should take with him; some items were evidently more expensive in America, where wages were high, while others were not—"artists' materials and paper [could] be bought as cheaply in New York or Philadelphia" because taxes on them were greater in Europe.[6] One of his most consequential decisions was to hire a professional artist to accompany him on this new expedition. Maximilian had done his own sketching in Brazil, and the illustrations in his subsequent publications were based on those drawings, which were accurately detailed but somewhat stiff and lacking aesthetic appeal. Perhaps Maximilian recognized this, or one of his more artistically inclined siblings (two were amateur painters) may have suggested the idea, and he began to search for a suitably talented assistant. He was again aided by his collegial network, one of whom wrote, "Serene Prince. . . . I forward to your Highness herewith the sketches I received today from [a] young master artist. . . . They show . . . his artistic talent and how much can be expected from him for our purpose. . . . [He] would like very much to participate in the journey and since he is not demanding [and is] able to stand the strain and difficulties of such an expedition . . . [then] if your Highness considers his talents satisfactory . . . nobody is as apt. . . . What the master lacks . . . is a little knowledge of the art of hunting, but that he can learn."[7] The young master was Karl Bodmer (1809–93), who had just turned twenty-three at the time this recommendation was made. A native of Switzerland, Bodmer studied watercolor and engraving with his uncle, the painter Johann Jakob Meier (1787–1858), before moving to Koblenz in 1828. By 1832 he (with his brother, Rudolf [1805–41], also an artist) had already published numerous engravings of the Rhine River and landscape; these may have caught the eye of Maximilian's colleague. A contract was negotiated between Maximilian and Bodmer. The prince would own the artworks produced, though Bodmer would be given some freedom to do additional studies. The artist would receive a modest salary (forty-five thalers monthly),[8] and his expenses would be paid, but he was warned that they would live very frugally—which, in the freezing winter of 1833–34 at Fort Clark, proved all too bitterly true.[9]

By the spring of 1832, Maximilian was ready for his new journey. When he departed his home in Neuwied on 7 May, he was accompanied by Bodmer and David Dreidoppel, the Wied estate huntsman.[10] They traveled by river steamboat to Rotterdam and Hellevoetsluis, from whence they sailed on the American brig *Janus* on 18 May, bound for Boston. The *Janus* was a small merchant ship, and their accommodations were spartan; Maximilian remarked that the booking agent "must have considered [them] easy to please" when he chose this ship.[11] (Even so, his records show that he paid 750 Dutch guilders for his party's passage, equivalent to over 7,000 euros in 2014.)[12] The voyage took longer than anticipated, nearly seven weeks, and was marked by violent storms as well as long periods of frustratingly calm or contrary winds. Maximilian was frequently confined to quarters by weather but stayed on deck when he could, measuring air and water temperature and wind direction and force, as well as identifying creatures of the sea and air. He routinely recorded this type of data along with other facts and observations in often quite lengthy journal entries on virtually every day of his two-year expedition. After arriving in Boston on 4 July, the prince spent two days exploring the city and nearby sites, describing the places and the inhabitants in detail; these descriptions included enumerations of the dozens of plants and animals observed, by both scientific and common names. He went to Providence to board a steamer for New York City, where he had business to conduct and supplies to purchase, as he did in Philadelphia. After a short side trip from the latter to Bethlehem, he decided to return there for a longer stay before embarking on his western exploration. There were likely many reasons for this pause in the expedition, but two of the most pressing were the cholera epidemic then spreading through large cities and along major travel routes and the loss of much of the party's considerable baggage, "a most unpleasant [situation] since many essential instruments, guns, books, etc., were in those cases";[13] the trunks and boxes were not found and delivered to the prince till early September.

From almost the moment of his arrival in Bethlehem on 2 August, and on nearly every day of his six-week stay there, Maximilian set out on excursions into the countryside, sometimes by carriage but mostly on foot. He was interested primarily in the local flora and fauna and meticulously recorded the Latin and common names of hundreds of species in his journal. His daily entries usually included observations on the weather (he repeatedly complained of the summer heat) and on the occupations and foibles of town and country residents. The prince's September journey on public conveyances from Bethlehem to New Harmony in southwestern Indiana seems arduous by twenty-first-century standards: six days in crowded horse-drawn coaches on less than turnpike-quality roads, plus eight days on steamboats almost as crowded and in constant peril of damage by collision or boiler explosion; the same trip would take a modern traveler a very leisurely two days in a comfortable automobile. Neither the discomforts of travel nor the continuing specter of cholera deterred Maximilian from making a detailed record of what he saw, naming small towns passed by, inns stopped at, hills and mountains crossed, crops being raised, and the industry or crudity of the citizenry.

New Harmony was founded in 1814 by the German George Rapp (1757–1847) as a theocratic commune; the land and buildings were sold to Robert Owen in 1825, when Rapp and his followers moved to Economy, Pennsylvania (Maximilian visited that self-sufficient settlement on 29 September on his way from Bethlehem to New Harmony). Owen, a British social reformer, and his partner, William Maclure, envisioned a different utopian society than Rapp's, one based on science and education. To that end, several learned scholars were brought to New Harmony, and though the community did not thrive, in 1832 two eminent scientists, Thomas Say and Charles-Alexandre Lesueur, still resided in the village. There was also an excellent natural history library, which delighted the prince. Neither Maximilian nor Dreidoppel was feeling well at the time of their arrival in New Harmony on 19 October, having suffered periodic digestive complaints for many months. The prince's lengthy convalescence prolonged an anticipated short stay into a four-month residence. Even when ill, Maximilian daily recorded the temperature at least once and sometimes more often. Whenever the weather allowed, he, Bodmer, and/or Dreidoppel went on hunting excursions to identify and, where feasible, to obtain specimens of the flora and fauna of the area. They particularly enjoyed the wildlife abundance of Fox River and Fox Island — between 5 and 13 December they hunted there seven times and did so again on many occasions in the new year, often staying from morning till dusk. The prince meticulously entered in his journal the Latin and common names of the many dozens of species observed and collected. He commented (sometimes positively, sometimes acidly) on local inhabitants and economic activities, describing the cultivation and harvest of crops (maple sugar "sold here for seven to eight cents a pound")[14] and the husbandry (or lack thereof) of livestock. When Bodmer returned from a seven-week trip to New Orleans, where he had transacted business for the prince, Maximilian had the artist recount everything he saw and then studied every related sketch, specimen, and document brought back; the latter included broadsides advertising slave auctions and a table of the distances between the twenty-five landings between Louisville and New Orleans, a total of 1,423 miles. Although this condensation contains little more than 20 percent of the original chapter 5 (the longest in the three manuscript journals), it amply illuminates Maximilian's scientific and personal predilections and how the prince's sojourn in this intellectual community prepared him well for the western explorations and encounters to come.

In Boston, New York, Pennsylvania, and Indiana, Maximilian was dismayed by the lack of interest in the native peoples of North America, who had been largely eliminated or forced from their homes in the eastern United States. He was eager to get to St. Louis, where he knew he would begin to accomplish the real scientific purpose of his journey: to study the upper Missouri region and thereby experience "the natural face of North America and its aboriginal population," as he phrased it in the preface to his later published work, *Reise in das Innere Nord-America in den Jahren 1832 bis 1834* (referred to in this condensation as the *Reise* [*Travels*, in English]).[15] He left New Harmony on 16 March 1833 and rode down to Mount Vernon on the Ohio, where he and his party boarded a downriver steamboat two days later. His detailed journal entries contain comments on the settlements, landmarks, and shipping traffic on the Ohio and Mississippi rivers; he also carefully copied related information and river maps from a published guide, Samuel Cumings's *The Western Pilot*, as part of his account. Once he arrived in St. Louis (on 24 March), his excitement becomes almost palpable, particularly in his descriptions of his first encounters with Native people; no element of physical appearance, clothing, ornament, weaponry, personality, music, or language escapes his pen. St. Louis was a rapidly growing frontier town, and while there the prince met many of its most prominent figures. None other than General William Clark, then U.S. superintendent of Indian affairs, advised him how best to undertake the next portion of his exploration, and arrangements were made for Maximilian,

Bodmer, and Dreidoppel to travel up the Missouri River under the protection of the American Fur Company (AFC). The prince purchased supplies in St. Louis for his anticipated botanical and other studies, as well as articles to trade with the Indians for ethnographic items for his collection. On 9 April, his substantial baggage was taken aboard the AFC steamboat *Yellow Stone*, and on the following morning, the passengers—including several Fur Company and Indian agency officials and numerous boisterous engagés (hunters, woodcutters, and other AFC workers), as well as Maximilian's paying party—boarded the steamer and set off upriver, waved on by a crowd of bystanders. The AFC's *Yellow Stone*, the year before, had been the first steamer to ascend the Missouri above Bellevue, Nebraska, in an experiment to see whether such ships could supplant the smaller sail- and man-powered vessels traditionally used for trade on the upper river. That trade was booming in the 1830s—tens of thousands of hides, skins, and pelts obtained from the Indians in return for trinkets, kettles, guns, and liquor—and the AFC had become the dominant mercantile force in the region.

On the first days of this voyage, steaming through the sparsely settled, relatively new state (1821) of Missouri, Maximilian met no Indians but did see evidence of their recent habitations and recorded tribal information from the company and government representatives on board, each of whom had long associations with Native residents of the region. Once they passed the mouth of the Kansas River on 21 April, they were officially in Indian territory, and soon they came to Cantonment Leavenworth, the most remote American western military outpost at the time. After concluding official business there, the *Yellow Stone* proceeded on through increasingly treacherous waters: groundings on sandbars in shifting channels and damage from huge snags caused many delays for reconnoitering and repairs. Maximilian took advantage of the downtime to explore the adjoining forests and meadows, remarking on their spring freshness (he was particularly impressed by the brightly blooming redbud trees) and collecting specimens for later research. His first significant encounter with Indians was at Jean Pierre Cabanné's trading post, just north of present-day Omaha, Nebraska, on 4 May, where he witnessed a striking, moonlit Omaha tribal ceremonial dance. In the following weeks he stopped at a succession of posts and government agencies and met Poncas, Sioux, and Assiniboines. At one place, Fort Clark, near modern Bismarck, North Dakota, he marveled at the "powerful," "handsome," and beautifully attired crowds of Mandans, Hidatsas, and Crows, who had gathered there to trade.[16] Bodmer later recorded their meeting with some of these remarkable men in *The Travellers Meeting with Minatarre* [Hidatsa] *Indians near Fort Clark* (see pl. 32). By 24 June, Maximilian's party had reached Fort Union, the AFC's largest post at the time, beyond which steamer travel was deemed impossible. River voyages to the two posts farther upstream (Fort Cass on the Yellowstone and Fort McKenzie on the Missouri) required navigation in smaller vessels. Our travelers continued on a company keelboat, the *Flora,* carrying men and goods to Fort McKenzie, estimated by the prince as about 650 river miles from Fort Union.[17] This was arguably the most spectacularly scenic portion of the Missouri journey, but it was a five-week, laborious upstream struggle. The *Flora* had a sail, but progress more often than not required the crew to pole and pull the heavily laden boat against the current. The slowness of the passage allowed the prince time to hunt for more specimens. When they went through what Maximilian called the Mauvaises-Terres (today's Missouri Breaks), the generally stoic scientist was astonished; he remarked that it would take a painter years to record what they saw,[18] and he could not find sufficient words himself to describe the wondrous stone pinnacles and buttresses and other "unusual formations" before them.

The Wied party spent seven weeks at Fort McKenzie, the AFC's recently and still not-well-established foray into luring the lucrative Blackfoot trade away from their northern competitor, the Hudson's Bay Company. The Blackfoot had a well-earned reputation as mercurial allies to traders and as dangerous enemies to all their foes. They were also generous hosts and almost as curious about these strange European visitors as the visitors were about them. Maximilian took full advantage of his extended stay to study Blackfoot culture in carefully recorded detail. He had originally hoped to strike out overland for the Rocky Mountains as the next segment of his journey, but the rapidly changing September weather and seeing firsthand the violence of Plains warfare (when six hundred Assiniboines and Crees attacked the Blackfoot camp at Fort McKenzie) convinced him to return downstream instead. On 14 September, in a small boat built and manned by the Fur Company for his use, he set off downriver for Fort Union; with the current in their favor, this time the voyage took only about fourteen days. He spent a comfortable but brisk fall month at Fort Union before setting off downriver again, headed for Fort Clark, where, on 8 November, James Kipp—the clerk or manager of Fort Clark—welcomed Maximilian, Bodmer, and Dreidoppel for a long winter's stay. Their drafty, hastily built quarters offered less than ideal protection against the increasingly cold weather; on 3 January, "the mercury [froze] in the bulb, meaning [the temperature was] lower than −30°F." Maximilian noted that everything in their room turned to ice: boots and shoes were frozen; ink and watercolor paints had to be thawed by the fire before they could be used. Food was in short supply; game, usually the mainstay of the men's diet, was scarce, and rats decimated the stored corn that, in dwindling quantities and (to the prince) unappetizing preparations, became their major sustenance.

For Maximilian, these privations were gratifyingly offset by the opportunity to become familiar with Mandan and Hidatsa culture and individuals. He explored nearby villages, attended ceremonies, and entertained a steady stream of visitors in his room, among them many chiefs and respected elders. Several of these men became his friends, and their conversations lasted till late into the night, carried on with the help of Kipp or old Toussaint Charbonneau (who had traveled with Lewis and Clark and now lived with the Hidatsas) as interpreters and likely with Maximilian's growing knowledge of the two native languages as well as sign language. While the prince recorded quantities of verbal data, Bodmer executed studies of villages, dances, and especially people. His portraits fascinated their subjects and others who viewed them; sometimes the likenesses made those who gazed at them uneasy, for they seemed dangerously magical, but more often they were admired—a few men asked for depictions of revered animals, and others attempted to copy this new, realistic style so different from their own pictographic paintings.

Maximilian, whose health throughout the expedition had been less than perfect, now became increasingly ill. He complained of, among other afflictions, a swollen leg, which by March 1834 confined him to bed. One can judge the severity of his deteriorating condition by the length of his journal entries, which gradually become more and more brief and acquire an almost querulous quality, very unlike that of the enthusiastic scientist of previous months. Fortunately, the fort's cook recognized symptoms similar to the scurvy that had decimated a Missouri River garrison some years before; he saw to it that the prince got some early spring greens, which rapidly alleviated his illness. On 18 April, with the river finally free of ice, the prince records, "[A]t about three o'clock, we took leave from Mr. Kipp and the inhabitants of the fort. . . . [Our Indian friends] shook our hands." Then, "I was led onto the boat, still quite lame. A few cannon shots were fired in our honor." With that, they glided away down the Missouri. When Maximilian arrived in St. Louis on 27 May, he settled his accounts with the AFC, made arrangements to ship his many crates of specimens to Europe, had new traveling cages made for his live bears (which he had acquired on the upper Missouri and took all the way to Neuwied), and explored several large prehistoric Indian mounds near the city. By 6 June he was back in New Harmony to bid farewell to Messrs. Say and Lesueur. This accomplished, he set off by carriage and stage to Louisville, where he resumed steamboat travel to Cincinnati and then Portsmouth, where his party took passage on 20 June on one of the horse-drawn boats that plied the recently (1832) completed Ohio and Erie Canal to Cleveland on Lake Erie; the prince was especially interested in canal locks, aqueducts, and other engineering feats, the observation of which may have been a factor in planning his return route. At Cleveland they boarded a lake steamer to cross "the oceanlike expanse" to Buffalo. They made a brief side excursion to Niagara Falls, which Maximilian found "more grand by far" than he had imagined from published descriptions, and then continued on via the Erie Canal to Albany and down the Hudson River to New York City, arriving on 5 July. He spent several days visiting notable scholars in New York and Philadelphia, making and renewing acquaintances that became part of his future natural history network.

On 16 July, Maximilian and his traveling companions (including the live bears) set sail from New York on the sizeable packet boat *Havre*. Their return voyage to Europe was much shorter and more pleasant than their 1832 adventure; it was considerably less stormy, and the accommodations almost luxurious by comparison—there was even time and space for shipboard games, such as shuffleboard, which the prince described but evidently did not choose to play. Meals seemed sumptuous; perhaps motivated by the memory of his starving winter at Fort Clark, the prince devoted quite a bit of journal space to rapturously recounting the availability of fresh and cured meats, fruits, vegetables, nuts, sweets, milk, and fine wines. After landing at Le Havre on 8 August, Maximilian proceeded homeward at a leisurely pace via riverboats and carriages, stopping at various points to visit collectors and dealers of natural history specimens; "about noon" on 25 August he arrived in Neuwied, where he "surprised [his] family, [who were] all completely healthy." This day marked the official end of the prince's expedition but also the beginning of his work on the publications that shared his experiences and scientific findings with his far-flung colleagues. The foremost of these was his two-volume *Reise,* published in German by J. Hoelscher in Koblenz between 1839 and 1841, followed by a French (1841–43) and a shortened English (1843) edition. All were illustrated by woodcuts and a portfolio or atlas of engravings after the originals by Bodmer, who personally supervised the print production in Paris in accordance with Maximilian's directives.[19]

Although this book recounts the same expedition as the *Reise,* it is not drawn from that publication. It is a condensation of *The North American Journals of Prince Maximilian of Wied,* volumes 1–3 (University of Oklahoma Press, 2008– 12), a translated and annotated edition of three manuscript journals now in the

Maximilian-Bodmer Collection (MBC) in the Margre H. Durham Center for Western Studies, Joslyn Art Museum, Omaha, Nebraska. The MBC comprises hundreds of artworks and archival items related to Maximilian's 1832–34 expedition and his subsequent publications on North America.[20] The art is principally that of Karl Bodmer, including approximately four hundred beautifully rendered original works in pencil, ink, and watercolor and over five hundred examples of the prints he produced (largely based on those original works) to illustrate Maximilian's *Reise*. There are also numerous drawings by the prince and artworks by others that he obtained to further his North American studies. The archival collection is even more extensive, containing Maximilian's correspondence planning the expedition, letters written to his siblings during that sojourn, and dozens of reports from Bodmer and Hoelscher as the *Reise* illustration production and publication slowly progressed.[21] But the archival holding of most significance is the three journals referenced above. They were written by Maximilian as a detailed, chronological account of his 1832–34 expedition that he called his *Tagebuch* (usually translated as "journal" or "diary" but literally meaning "day book"; see pl. 1 for an illustration of the first manuscript volume). The bound journals, each containing about three hundred closely written pages, were clearly not field-produced, for they are not only neatly penned with comparatively few errors (especially considering the field conditions at times) but also contain phrases and references indicating that they were written later. For example, in his entry for 23 March 1833, passing by Jefferson Barracks on his way to St. Louis on a Mississippi steamboat, the prince writes, "I shall describe this installation later"[22]—two days before he meets and is invited by William Clark to visit this military post. Although similar to the *Reise* in organization and content, the manuscript journals are far from being identical and do not appear to be the material sent to Hoelscher to set into print; for example, chapter numbers are different, some subjects are covered in more detail in the journals, and a number of scientific names are given in later nomenclature in the *Reise*. There is also the matter of voice: in these journals, evidently made for his own reference and use, his tone is more personal, while in the *Reise*, it is understandably more formal, more that of the scientist.

The production of the *Reise* and its French and English editions consumed nearly a decade of Maximilian's and Bodmer's time. They remained in occasional contact thereafter and collaborated on one more project years later, in 1865: a monograph on North American reptiles and amphibians, written by the prince and illustrated by Bodmer. The painter remained in France, where he established residence in Barbizon, a noted artists' community not far from Paris; neither his work for Maximilian (so prized today) nor his European paintings and prints brought him the recognition he hoped for, and he died at the age of eighty-four, poor, ill, and nearly blind. The prince continued to live with his family at Neuwied until his death in 1867. He maintained an active international correspondence and specimen exchange with fellow students of natural history, published numerous articles, and received recognition in the form of election to membership in scientific societies, such as the Academy of Natural Sciences in Philadelphia.

What do we know about Maximilian as an individual? His scientific self is everywhere evident in his writings, published and private; the prince's journals and letters are as replete as his published works with sharp-eyed, coolly stated observations and data. There are passages, though, that reveal other elements of his character and personal interests. He was very close to his family, making note of his correspondence with them and of their birthdays and notable events, such as the birth of a grand-nephew.[23] He clearly was comfortable with and enjoyed the company of a wide range of men, from fellow scholars like Thomas Say and Edwin James, to frontier fur traders and Indian warriors and elders, to American businessmen such as the Astors, father (John Jacob) and son (William Backhouse). Class or social standing generally seemed less important to him than experience and knowledge, that is, the capacity to contribute to his research interests. But his aristocratic heritage is occasionally discernible in his irritation at what he saw as crudity or bad manners (such as American eating habits, idleness, and poor taste in clothing). Perhaps a more subtle indication is his use of titles. Dreidoppel and Bodmer were both Maximilian's employees, and he appears to have been fond of both men. In his journals, Maximilian generally refers to the former, a Wied family retainer for decades, by his given name (David) or his surname (Dreidoppel) but never as "Mr. Dreidoppel." For the artist, although sometimes calling him "Bodmer," the prince typically wrote the name "Mr. Bodmer," giving the young artist the same respectful address as other professionals and gentlemen of his acquaintance.[24]

Maximilian's American contemporaries may have found him eccentric but likeable and interesting. Alexander Culbertson, a young AFC clerk who came to know the prince at Forts Union and McKenzie, said,

In [1833] an interesting character in the person of Prince Maximilian, from Coblentz on the Rhine, made his first appearance in the upper Missouri. The Prince was at that time nearly seventy [actually fifty] years of age, but well preserved, and able to endure considerable fatigue. He was a man of medium height, rather slender, sans teeth, passionately fond of his pipe, unostentatious, and speaking very broken English. His favorite dress was a white slouch hat, a black velvet coat, rather rusty from long service, and probably the greasiest pair of trousers that ever encased princely legs. The Prince was a bachelor and a man of science, and it was in the latter capacity that he had roamed so far from his ancestral home on the Rhine. He was accompanied by an artist named Boardman [Bodmer] and a servant whose name was, as nearly as the author has been able to ascertain its spelling, Tritripel [Dreidoppel], both of whom seemed gifted to a high degree with the faculty of putting their princely employer into a frequent passion, till there is hardly a bluff or a valley on the whole upper Missouri that has not repeated in an angry tone, and with a strong Teutonic accent, the names of Boardman and Tritripel. The Prince . . . at every opportunity [ranged] in quest of new objects to add to his collection of small quadrupeds, birds, botanical specimens and fossils; [and kept] his artist as busy as his easy nature allowed in making sketches of the scenery.[25]

Kenneth McKenzie, a partner in the AFC and head of its upper Missouri operations, came to know Maximilian well in 1833–34 (he also visited the prince in Neuwied some years later) and referred to him as "a fine old gentleman" whose company he enjoyed. He said, "I trust the public will some day have an opportunity of judging how judicious & indefatigable his researches have been relative to the manners & customs of the natives, in procuring an extensive collection of objects in Natural history hitherto unknown or undescribed, a vast number of new plants, a ponderous cargo of mineralogical specimens & a portfolio rich in Indian portraits and the peculiar and unrivalled scenery of the Upper Missouri."[26] Seventy years later, the distinguished librarian, historian, and editor Reuben Gold Thwaites (1853–1913), in the preface to his 1906 reprinting of Maximilian's *Travels*, remarked, "A traveller of today, gliding across the plains and along the windings of the Missouri in a [railway carriage], may follow the pages of Maximilian and the plates of Bodmer, and thus obtain as clearly as words and pictures can express, an accurate presentation of the trans-Mississippi region in 1833."[27] The country that Maximilian experienced then is today very different in many ways, the land and particularly the lives of its Native peoples markedly altered by settlement, commerce, and social change. The prince's publications, including this newest addition, a condensation of his *North American Journals*, add greatly to our understanding of what we can no longer see for ourselves.

Abbreviations

AFC	American Fur Company
ANB	*American National Biography*
DAB	*Dictionary of American Biography*
DCB	*Dictionary of Canadian Biography*
DSB	*Dictionary of Scientific Biography*
EWT	*Early Western Travels* (Thwaites)
JAM	Joslyn Art Museum
KBA	*Karl Bodmer's America* (Hunt et al.)
KBNAP	*Karl Bodmer's North American Prints* (Ruud et al.)
KBSA	*Karl Bodmer's Studio Art* (Wood et al.)
MBC	Maximilian-Bodmer Collection, Joslyn Art Museum
ODNB	*Oxford Dictionary of National Biography*
USGS	U.S. Geological Survey

Cast of Characters

These brief biographical notes are intended to provide basic information, where known, of individuals not sufficiently identified in Maximilian's text.

Ajanjan (d. ca. 1834). Assiniboine warrior commonly known as The Light and as General Jackson. George Catlin painted a double portrait contrasting Ajanjan's Assiniboine clothing with the military uniform he received on his 1831–32 Washington trip. Ajanjan's fellow tribesmen did not accept his account of what he had seen there as credible; he was killed following an argument over the veracity of his claims. Ewers, "When the Light Shone in Washington."

Ashworth, Charles Howard. English traveler who met Maximilian on the *Yellow Stone* in 1833 and joined Nathaniel Wyeth's Oregon-bound party at the 1834 Green River mountain man rendezvous. Little else is known of him. Jackson, *Voyages,* 89–90.

Astor, John Jacob (1763–1848). Founder of the Astor family fortune. Controlled much of the fur trade through his American Fur Company (1808–34). *DAB.* His son, **William Backhouse** Astor (1792–1875), studied at the University of Göttingen at the same time as Maximilian. *DAB.*

Atkinson, Brevet Brigadier General Henry (1782–1842). Held several military commands west of the Mississippi River after 1819. Supervised construction of Jefferson Barracks in 1826; served as its commander until his death. Atkinson was in charge of the Regular Army troops engaged in the Black Hawk War of 1832. *ANB.*

Badollet, Jean (or John) (1758–1837). Swiss immigrant. Served as register of the government land office at Vincennes (1804–36) and as a member of the Indiana constitutional convention in 1816. Thwaites, *EWT,* 24:138n138.

Barrabino, Joseph (d. 1834). Italian-born druggist and naturalist in New Orleans. Friend of Lesueur and Say, who published descriptions of insect specimens provided by him. Bodmer was his guest in New Orleans, 1833.

Barton, Benjamin Smith (1766–1815). Botanist and ethnographer as well as a physician and professor of medicine at the University of Pennsylvania. In *New Views of* *the Origin of the Tribes . . . of America,* Barton argued (using linguistic evidence) that North American Indians had origins in Asia. *ANB.*

Bean, Jonathan. Government subagent for the Sioux, 1827–34. Thwaites, *EWT,* 22:235n171.

Beauchamp, Robinson Pemberton (1788–1833). Government subagent at Bellevue Agency. Died when cholera struck there in 1833. Barry, "Kansas before 1854," 332.

Bennett, Andrew. Captained 1833 Missouri River voyage of the *Yellow Stone* and took command of the *Assiniboine* in autumn of the same year. Jackson, *Voyages,* 27, 84, 110.

Berger, Jacob (or Jacques) (active 1809–47). French Canadian. Once an employee of the Hudson's Bay Company, Berger was important in establishing trade between the American Fur Company and the Blackfoot Indians in 1830–31 because of his fluency in the Blackfoot language. Thrapp, *Encyclopedia,* 4:42–43.

Bernhard, Duke of Saxe-Weimar-Eisenach (1792–1862). Visited United States and Canada, 1825–26. In 1831–32 correspondence, Maximilian sought his advice on traveling in North America. For Duke Bernhard's travel account, see Jeronimus, *Travels.*

Big Elk (Óngpa-Tánga). Principal leader of the Omaha Indians from about 1811 to 1843. Visited Washington in 1837–38. U.S. authorities had a positive view of Big Elk because he accepted the idea that Indians should take up settled, permanent agriculture. Wishart, *Unspeakable Sadness,* 78.

Bijou, Joseph and Louis. See Bissonet.

Bird, James, Jr. (ca. 1798–1892). Son of Hudson's Bay Company trader and Cree woman. Lived among the Blackfoot for much of his adult life, having married a Piegan in the 1820s. Worked for various fur companies but apparently preferred to operate as an independent trader, trapper, guide, and interpreter. American Fur Company officials regarded Bird as untrustworthy in 1833; he had rejoined the Hudson's Bay Company that summer. Wickman, "James Bird, Jr."; *DCB.*

Bissonet, Joseph (b. 1778) and **Louis** (1774–ca. 1836); brothers. The former served the 1820 Long expedition as a guide; he often used his stepfather's surname, Bijou. Louis was an active trader in the upper Missouri in the early nineteenth century. Hafen, "Joseph Bissonet, dit Bijou"; Luttig, *Journal of a Fur-Trading Expedition,* 34, 56, 148–49.

Blackbird. See Waschínga-Sáhba.

Black Hawk (1767–1838). Sauk warrior. Led a band of Sauk and Meskwakie Indians trying to return to their former Illinois lands in April 1832. He soon realized that the government would not tolerate this and attempted to negotiate a withdrawal back to Iowa. After several armed clashes that proved disastrous for the Indians, Black Hawk and the remnants of his band surrendered in August 1832. *ANB*.

Blumenbach, Johann Friedrich (1752–1840). Professor of medicine at the University of Göttingen and author of *De generis humani* (Göttingen, 1776), a pioneering study in comparative anatomy and physical anthropology. Blumenbach collected human skulls from around the world. *DSB*. Maximilian attended Blumenbach's lectures during his own studies at Göttingen. In an undated postexpeditionary set of notes on North American Indians (JAM, MBC, Acta 8, 4–8), Maximilian refers to Blumenbach as his "never to be forgotten teacher."

Bodmer, Karl (1809–93). Swiss-born artist who accompanied Maximilian on the 1832–34 expedition and later produced the prints that illustrated the prince's published account of the journey.

Bonaparte, Joseph (1768–1844). Elder brother of Napoleon, who made him king of Spain (1808–13). Fled to the United States after Napoleon's defeat. Purchased an estate called Point Breeze near Bordentown in 1816. Stroud, *The Man Who Had Been King*. **Charles Lucien Bonaparte** (1803–57), a nephew of Napoleon, was a respected zoologist and ornithologist. *DSB*.

Bradbury, John (1768–1823). English botanist. Traveled up the Missouri River to the Mandan villages in 1811, amassing a large collection of plant specimens. Unfortunately, many of his specimens were first described in print by others, notably Frederick Pursh (1774–1820). Taylor, "John Bradbury."

Cabanné, Jean Pierre (1773–1841). French-born; moved to St. Louis in 1798. His long fur trade career was split among several different companies and partnerships. At the time of Maximilian's Missouri River journey, he was a partner in the Western Department of the American Fur Company. Mattison, "John Pierre Cabanné, Sr."

Campbell, Robert. See William Sublette.

Catlin, George (1796–1872). Painter, writer, and impresario; dedicated most of his professional life to the portrayal of American Indian life. Traveled widely in the West, including an 1832 venture up the Missouri as far as Fort Union. Catlin, *Letters and Notes; ANB*.

Charbonneau, Toussaint (ca. 1758–1840?). Served as an interpreter on the Lewis and Clark expedition; best known as husband of Sacagawea. Maximilian met him several times during his sojourn on the Missouri. Hafen, "Toussaint Charbonneau."

Chardon, Francis A. (d. 1848). Active in the Missouri fur trade; best known for the journal he kept while in charge of Fort Clark after 1834. Mattison, "Francis A. Chardon"; Abel, *Chardon's Journal,* xxxvii–lxviii.

Chouteau, Jean Pierre (1758–1849). Influential figure in the St. Louis–based fur trade. A founder of the Missouri Fur Company in 1809. His half-brother **Cyprien** (1802–79) managed an American Fur Company post on the south bank of the Kansas River (near the later community of Muncie, Kansas) for many years. His son, **Pierre Chouteau, Jr.** (1789–1865), also a successful businessman, was a partner in the American Fur Company at the time Maximilian was in St. Louis. *ANB;* Thwaites, *EWT,* 22:251n200.

Clark, William (1770–1838). Served in several federal and Missouri territorial government positions after the Lewis and Clark expedition of 1804–06. At the time of Maximilian's visit, Clark was superintendent of Indian affairs, headquartered at St. Louis. He was called "General" for his service as a brigadier general of militia. *ANB.*

Cooper, William (ca. 1798–1864). Close friend of Charles Lucien Bonaparte; founding member of the Lyceum of Natural History of New York (now the New York Academy of Sciences). Fairchild, *History,* 70–73.

Culbertson, Alexander (1809–79). 1833 marked his first voyage as a clerk for the Upper Missouri Outfit of the American Fur Company. Had a long fur trade career; built Fort Benton in present-day Montana in the 1840s; and served as an interpreter at the 1851 Treaty of Fort Laramie negotiations. After retiring from the frontier, his uncle, "Captain" **John Craighead Culbertson** (fl. 1791–1857), lived in Cincinnati, where Maximilian met him in 1834. Wischmann, *Frontier Diplomats,* 33, 82; Mattison, "Alexander Culbertson"; Jones, *In Memoriam,* 138–40.

Cuvier, Georges (1769–1832). French scholar of natural history; a founder of paleontology. Maximilian met him in Paris in 1814. Noll, "Prince Maximilian's America," 33.

Dougherty, John (1791–1860). Missouri Fur Company trapper before 1812. Later served as interpreter and Indian subagent under Benjamin O'Fallon. Indian agent for the upper Missouri from 1826 to 1839. Thrapp, *Encyclopedia*, 1:420. His brother, **Joseph L. Dougherty**, served as clerk for the Sublette and Campbell Hidatsa post at the time of Maximilian's journey. Thwaites, *EWT*, 23:218n167.

Drake, Daniel (1785–1852). Prominent Cincinnati physician, medical educator, and natural scientist. *ANB*.

Dreidoppel, David (1793–1866). Wied family hunter; accomplished taxidermist. Assisted Maximilian on both his South (1815–17) and North American (1832–34) expeditions. Schmidt, "Hofjäger David Dreydoppel."

Dubuque, Julien (1762–1810). Namesake of the Iowa city of Dubuque; first Euro-American to undertake large-scale lead mining operations in that region. *ANB*.

Dunklin, Daniel (1790–1844). Governor of Missouri, 1832–36.

DuPonceau, Pierre Etienne (Peter Stephen, 1760–1844). French immigrant; settled in Philadelphia after the Revolutionary War. Became a successful lawyer and earned a reputation as a scholar of Indian languages. President of the American Philosophical Society at the time of Maximilian's journey. *ANB*.

Eyriès, Alexandre (dates unknown), and **Jean-Baptiste Benoit** (1767–1846). French brothers; the latter translated into French Maximilian's published account of his 1815–17 Brazilian voyage. Larousse, *Grand dictionnaire*, 1235. Maximilian visited Alexandre in Le Havre in August 1834.

Floyd, Sergeant Charles (ca. 1782–1804). The only member of the Lewis and Clark expedition to die en route, near present-day Sioux City, Iowa, where a memorial has been erected in his honor. Holmberg, "Life, Death, and Monument."

Fontenelle, Lucien (1800–ca. 1839). New Orleans–born fur trader active first in the Missouri Fur Company and later the American Fur Company. Trottman, "Lucien Fontenelle."

Fretageot, Achilles (1813–73). Achilles and his mother, an educator at New Harmony, are both mentioned in Pitzer, "Original Boatload of Knowledge."

Gardner, Johnson (fl. 1824–34). Led the trappers who captured and killed the two Arikaras in the incident described in chapter 8, 21 May 1833; a slightly different version is given in the 8 May 1834 entry. Maximilian's account likely minimized the brutality of the revenge exacted by Gardner and his associates for the deaths of their peers. Haines, "Johnson Gardner."

Garreau, Joseph. Interpreter and trader among the Arikaras and Mandans for about forty years. Moulton, *Journals*, 3:315–16n2.

Gebhard, Frederick (d. ca. 1835). New York merchant who assisted Maximilian with his shipping needs and visited him in Pennsylvania. Scoville, *Old Merchants,* 131–32.

Glass, Hugh (d. 1833). Mountain man of near-legendary reputation. Maximilian obtained his information about Glass from James Hamilton Palmer, q.v. Biographies include Myers, *Saga of Hugh Glass.*

Godman, John D. (1794–1830). American naturalist. Studied, practiced, and taught medicine. Principal work: *American Natural History,* published 1826–28. *ANB.*

Hamilton, James. See Palmer, James A. Hamilton.

Harlan, Richard (1796–1843). Philadelphia physician. Author of *Fauna Americana* (1825), *American Herpetology* (1827), and several articles on subjects including anatomy and paleontology. *DAB.*

Harvey, Alexander (d. 1854). Employed by American Fur Company in various capacities in the 1830s and 1840s; formed his own company in 1846. Notorious for vindictiveness and explosive temper. Mattison, "Alexander Harvey."

Hoboken, Anthony van (1756–1850). Prominent Rotterdam shipping agent and ship owner. Maximilian booked passage on the *Janus* through van Hoboken's firm. *Nieuw Nederlandsch Biografisch.*

Humboldt, Alexander von (1769–1859). German traveler/scientist. Visited the United States in 1804 on his way home from over four years travel and fieldwork in South America. Elected a member of the American Philosophical Society that year. *DSB.* Maximilian's 1815–17 Brazilian voyage may have been inspired in part by von Humboldt's scientific tour.

James, Edwin (1797–1861). Trained physician; served as botanist and geologist on Major Stephen Long's 1820–21 expedition to the American West. Compiled the published record of that expedition. *ANB;* James, *Account of an Expedition.*

Keokuk (1790–1848). Sauk chief who advocated accommodation with whites after 1821 visit to Washington in an Indian delegation. Opposed Black Hawk's return to Illinois in 1832; persuaded most Sauks to stay out of the ensuing conflict. The U.S. government subsequently spared Keokuk's village from land cessations in Iowa, but they were later obliged to go to Kansas. *ANB.*

Kipp, James (1788–1880). Born in Nova Scotia of Dutch ancestry. In the 1820s, he was a member of the Columbia Fur Company; joined the American Fur Company after the merger of the two companies in 1827. Built at least five trading posts for these companies during his long career. In charge of Fort Clark during

Maximilian's stay in 1833–34. Wood, "James Kipp."

Krumbhaar, Lewis. W. and L. Krumbhaar's Philadelphia drug supply firm was on Market Street (advertisement, MBC, JAM). Mr. Krumbhaar provided assistance to Maximilian at both the beginning and the end of his North American journey.

Lachapelle, David (d. 1843). Served the Upper Missouri Outfit of the American Fur Company as a hunter and interpreter. Abel, *Chardon's Journal,* 297n354.

Laidlaw, William (ca. 1798–1851). One of the principal partners in the Columbia Fur Company, along with fellow Scots Kenneth McKenzie (q.v.) and **Daniel Lamont** (ca. 1798–1837), who each had an important position in the American Fur Company after the latter absorbed the former company in 1827. Mattison, "William Laidlaw"; Abel, *Chardon's Journal,* 219–20n67.

Lea, Isaac (1792–1886). Partner in the Philadelphia publishing and bookselling firm Carey and Lea; published descriptions of over 1,800 mollusk species. *DAB.*

Leavenworth, Colonel Henry (1783–1834). American military officer. Led 1823 military expedition to punish the Arikaras for attacking fur-trading party. Held several important western commands following the War of 1812; Fort Leavenworth, Kansas, is named for him. *ANB.*

Lesueur, Charles-Alexandre (1778–1846). French naturalist and scientific illustrator. Traveled to Australia with Nicolas Baudin, 1800–1804, later through the United States and West Indies with William Maclure. Resided in the United States from 1815 to 1837; went to New Harmony in 1825. See Hamy, *Travels.*

Lisa, Manuel. See Mitain.

Long, Stephen H. (1784–1864). Served in U.S. Army Corps of Topographical Engineers for nearly five decades. Led two important exploring expeditions: on the Great Plains to the Rockies in 1819–20, and on the Minnesota River and Red River of the North in 1823. Wood, *Stephen Harriman Long.*

Maclure, William (1763–1840). Scottish-born merchant and geologist. Robert Owen's partner in the unsuccessful venture to establish an ideal community at New Harmony, Indiana, in 1825–27. President of the Academy of Natural Sciences of Philadelphia from 1817 until his death. See *DSB.* His brother, **Alexander,** lived at New Harmony for many years. Thwaites, *EWT,* 24:133n.

Maskepetoon (ca. 1807–69). Leader of a Plains Cree band that mainly hunted in Alberta but made occasional trips into southern Saskatchewan and northern Montana. While visiting Fort Union in 1831, he was invited to Washington by

Indian subagent John Sanford. He became known as friendly to whites and as an advocate of intertribal peace in the Canadian West. *DCB.*

Mató-Tópe (Four Bears, ca. 1795–1837). Prominent Mandan chief, respected among his people as a warrior and religious leader. Much of what we know of him comes from the writings of Maximilian and Catlin and portraits by Bodmer and Catlin. Died in a smallpox scourge that decimated many upper Missouri tribes. Catlin, *Letters and Notes,* esp. 145–54; *KBA,* 317, 318; Truettner, *Natural Man Observed,* esp. 178–80.

McKenzie, Kenneth (1797–1861). Scottish-born trader known as the King of the Upper Missouri. His Columbia Fur Company competed successfully with John Jacob Astor's American Fur Company, which led to a merger in 1827. After that, McKenzie led the AFC's Upper Missouri Outfit and was in charge of company operations in the region through which Maximilian traveled. Lamar, "Kenneth McKenzie," 671.

Miller, Alfred Jacob. See Stewart, Captain William Drummond.

Mitain. Daughter of Omaha leader Big Elk. Manuel Lisa (1722–1820), an active fur trader and Indian subagent, married Mitain in 1814 to strategically ally himself with the tribe. Oglesby, *Manuel Lisa,* 153–54.

Mitchell, David Dawson (1806–61). In charge of Fort McKenzie during Maximilian's 1833 stay there; went on to become a full partner in the Upper Missouri Outfit in 1835. Later served twice as superintendent of Indian affairs at St. Louis (1841–43, 1849–53); government's lead negotiator for the 1851 Treaty of Fort Laramie. *ANB.*

Moncravie, Jean (or John) Baptiste (1797–1885). Surname spelled various ways by Maximilian and others. Fur company clerk at Fort Union and amateur artist. Hanson, "J. B. Moncravie"; Ewers, "Folk Art in the Fur Trade," 151–53; see an example of his artwork in *NAJ,* 2:509.

Morton, Samuel George (1799–1851). Philadelphia physician, paleontologist, and physical anthropologist. Like Maximilian's mentor, Johann Friedrich Blumenbach, Morton collected human skulls and attempted to describe differences among racial groups based on cranial measurements. *ANB.*

Nuttall, Thomas (1786–1859). British-born naturalist who spent considerable time in the United States from 1808 to 1842. Collected plants in the Missouri and Arkansas river valleys and along the Pacific coast. Most notable publication: *The Genera of North American Plants. ANB.*

O'Fallon, Benjamin (1793–1842). Appointed in 1817 by his uncle, William Clark, as

Indian agent for the Sioux, headquartered at Prairie du Chien; remained in government service until 1827. Noted for zealous enforcement of government regulations, including those banning alcohol from the Indian trade. Accompanied the Stephen Long 1819 expedition as far as the Pawnee villages in present-day Nebraska. *ANB.*

Ortubise, Pierre. Mixed-blood Sioux interpreter; worked for the American Fur Company at Forts Pierre and Clark during the 1830s. Lecompte, "Charles Autobees," esp. 22.

Owen, Robert (1771–1858). Born in Wales. Made a fortune in Scottish cotton mills during the first two decades of the nineteenth century Devoted remainder of his life to social reform, including the attempt to establish a science-driven utopia at New Harmony. *ODNB.* Maximilian spent time with three of Robert Owen's sons during his stays at New Harmony in 1832 and 1834: **William** (1802–77), **David Dale** (1807–60), and **Richard** (1810–90). *DSB, ANB.*

Palmer, James A. Hamilton (d. 1840). American Fur Company clerk at Fort Union. Maximilian obtained much information about the fur trade and fur traders during his two stays at that post. Mattison, "James A. Hamilton (Palmer)."

Paul Wilhelm, Duke of Württemberg (1797–1860). Made three voyages to the New World, traveling extensively in the United States, Mexico, and South America. Maximilian knew his publication, *Reise in Nordamerika . . . 1822, 1823 und 1824.* See Lottinville, *Travels.*

Peale, Charles Willson (1741–1827). Philadelphia artist, naturalist, and museum pioneer. Founded the Philadelphia Peale Museum about 1784. His son **Rubens** (1784–1865) established a New York Peale's Museum in 1825; P. T. Barnum acquired that collection for his American Museum in 1843. Another son, **Titian Ramsay Peale** (1799–1885), accompanied Major Stephen H. Long's expedition to the Rocky Mountains in 1819–20; he was the curator of Peale's Philadelphia museum when Maximilian visited there. Sellers, *Mr. Peale's Museum,* 21–22, 238–39, 249, 251, 258, 260–64, 305.

Petalesharo (ca. 1797–ca. 1858). Skiri Pawnee. Rescued a Comanche captive from a ritual sacrifice in 1817, leading the Pawnees to abandon the practice of human sacrifice. For this and his commitment to warm relations between the Pawnees and the U.S. government, he was lionized during his 1821 visit to Washington as a member of a Pawnee delegation. Numerous spelling variants of his name and that of his father, **Lateleseha,** are known. *ANB.*

Picotte, Honoré (1796–1860). Joined Upper Missouri Outfit in 1830. In 1833–34, appears to have wintered well below Fort Clark, near the mouth of Apple Creek, North Dakota, where he traded with Yanktonai Sioux living in the area. Gray, "Honoré Picotte, Fur Trader."

Pilcher, Joshua (1790–1843). Early business partner of Manuel Lisa. Joined American Fur Company in 1833; later served as an Indian agent (1834–38) and as superintendent of Indian affairs at St. Louis (1839–41). Sunder, *Joshua Pilcher.*

Pratte, Bernard Sr. (1771–1836). A partner in several fur-trading firms, along with Jean Pierre Cabanné and the Chouteaus. In the 1820s his firm joined forces with John Jacob Astor's American Fur Company. *DAB.* His son, **Bernard Jr.** (1803–87), was captain of the *Assiniboine* on Maximilian's upriver voyage in 1833; he later served two terms as mayor of St. Louis. *DAB.*

Rafinesque, Constantine Samuel (1783–1840). Much of this eccentric's wide-ranging scientific work was rejected by his contemporaries, but his reputation has been somewhat rehabilitated with the passage of time. Warren, *Constantine Samuel Rafinesque.*

Riley, Brevet Major Bennett (1787–1853). Commanded the first U.S. military escort of a trading party on the Santa Fe Trail in 1829 before assuming command at Fort (Cantonment) Leavenworth. Fort Riley, Kansas, is named for him. Thrapp, *Encyclopedia,* 3:1221–22.

Robidoux, Joseph (1783–1868). Operated trading post at what later became St. Joseph, Missouri. Mattes, "Joseph Robidoux."

Ross, William (ca. 1760–1842). Militia general and Pennsylvania state senator. Thwaites, *EWT,* 22:112n45.

Sanford, John F. A. (1806–57). Pierre Chouteau, Jr.'s son-in-law. Government subagent for several upper Missouri tribes from 1826 to 1835. Hill, *Office of Indian Affairs,* 187.

Say, Thomas (1787–1834). Founding member of Philadelphia's Academy of Natural Sciences (1812). Accompanied Stephen Long's 1819–20 and 1823 exploration expeditions as a naturalist. Moved to New Harmony in 1825. Major publications include *American Entomology* and *American Conchology. DSB.* His wife, **Lucy Way Sistaire** (1801–85), prepared the majority of the plates for *American Conchology.* Bailey, *American Women in Science,* 346.

Saynisch, Dr. Probably the Lewis Saynisch mentioned in the 1897 *History of Tioga County, Pennsylvania* as the first doctor to settle permanently in the town of

Blossburg, a "native of Germany" who moved to Pennsylvania from New York and died between 1856 and 1858.

Schmidt, J. W. Prussian consul in New York City; entertained Maximilian during the prince's 1832 and 1834 visits to the city. Schmidt resided in or near Manhattanville, then an independent village located near the intersection today of Broadway and 125th Street. *Longworth's American Almanac.*

Schuchardt, Frederick (b. ca. 1808). Nephew and business partner of Frederick Gebhard, q.v. Scoville, *Old Merchants,* 131–32.

Schweinitz, Lewis David von (1780–1834). A native of Bethlehem, Pennsylvania, where he was a Moravian Church clergyman. Maintained large herbarium; wrote numerous books on botany. Thwaites, *EWT,* 22:78–79n33.

Seidel, Charles (d. 1861). Native of Saxony. Principal of Bethlehem's Seminary for Young Ladies (later called the Bethlehem Female Seminary), 1822–36. Served as a pastor and executive board member for the northern province of the American Moravian Church. *Historical Sketch of the Moravian Seminary for Young Ladies,* 18–19.

Seymour, Samuel (ca. 1775–ca. 1832). Artist. Accompanied Major Stephen H. Long's 1819–20 and 1823 exploratory expeditions. *Who Was Who . . . Art.*

Silliman, Benjamin (1779–1864). Yale professor of chemistry and natural history. Founding editor of the *American Journal of Science and Arts,* now published under the title *American Journal of Science. ANB.*

Skenandoah (ca. 1706–1816). Oneida Indian; war chief of the Wolf Clan. For a discussion of his life, see Hauptman, *Conspiracy of Interests,* 42–47.

Stewart, Captain William Drummond (1797–1871). Scottish nobleman, retired British officer. Traveled extensively in the Rocky Mountain region from 1832 to 1843. Hired American artist **Alfred Jacob Miller** (1810–74), to accompany him to the 1837 fur trade rendezvous on the Green River. Stewart's 1833 encounter with Maximilian and Bodmer may have inspired him to seek artistic documentation of his own travels. Tyler, "Alfred Jacob Miller," 19–45.

Sublette, William (1799–1845). Operated fur-trading firm with partner **Robert Campbell** (1804–79) in opposition to the American Fur Company. Thrapp, *Encyclopedia,* 1:216. William's brother, **Milton** (ca. 1801–37), was a partner in the firm of Sublette and Campbell. Nunis, "Milton G. Sublette."

Tappan, Benjamin (1773–1857). Politician, jurist, amateur scientist. Served as first president of the Historical and Philosophical Society of Ohio; represented Ohio in the U.S. Senate from 1839 to 1845. *ANB*.

Taylor, James (1796–1848). Kentucky militia brigadier general during the War of 1812. Founded the city of Newport across the Ohio River from Cincinnati. Cousin of Zachary Taylor, twelfth president of the United States. *Appleton's Cyclopedia*.

Tecumseh (ca. 1768–1813). Shawnee leader. Tried to organize trans-Appalachian Indian groups into a grand confederacy to resist further white encroachment. Killed while fighting for the British during the War of 1812. *ANB*.

Tracy, Edward (d. 1851). Prominent St. Louis merchant; first president, St. Louis chamber of commerce, 1836. Beckwith, *Creoles of St. Louis,* 133; van Ravenswaay and O'Connor, *St. Louis,* 300.

Treviranus, Ludolph Christian (1779–1864). Botany professor, University of Bonn. *DSB*. In an undated letter to Maximilian, probably written in 1833, Treviranus acknowledged receipt of seeds Maximilian sent to him in 1832 (JAM, MBC).

Troost, Gerard (1776–1850). Dutch geologist. Came to the United States in 1810; resident of New Harmony, 1825–27. Served as Tennessee state geologist, 1828–50, as well as professor of science at the University of Nashville. *ANB*.

Twigg, William Augustus (1794–1877). Born in London; moved to the United States in 1818. In 1828, married Virginia DuPalais, a niece of Charles-Alexandre Lesueur. Became a brigadier general of Indiana volunteers in 1830. Indiana Historical Society, "New Harmony Collection."

Volz, Charles L. Listed as a merchant, at 24 Wood Street, in *Harris' Pittsburgh Business Directory for the Year 1837.*

Wabokieshiek (White Cloud, ca. 1794–ca. 1841). Known to whites as the Winnebago Prophet. A religious reformer of Sauk-Winnebago ancestry, Wabokieshiek advised Black Hawk that the Winnebagos and Potawatomis would support his efforts to retain Sauk lands in Illinois, but most remained neutral in the 1832 Black Hawk War. Surrendered with Black Hawk in August 1832. Waldman, *Who Was Who in Native American History,* 380–81.

Waschínga-Sáhba (Blackbird, ca. 1750–1801). Powerful Omaha tribal leader in late eighteenth century. Reputed to use poisons obtained from white traders to dispatch his enemies until his own death (attributed to smallpox). His grave was a familiar landmark on the river for many years. For varying views of Blackbird, see Liberty, Wood, and Irwin, "Omaha"; Fletcher and La Flesche, *Omaha Tribe;* and Thorne, "Black Bird."

White, Henry (1788–1860). Superintendent of the Utica and Schenectady Packet Boat Company at the time of Maximilian's North American expedition. Wager, "Whitesboro's Golden Age," 75.

Wied, Hermann zu (1814–64). Son of Johann Karl August, nephew of Maximilian; succeeded his father as the ruler of Wied in 1836. **Johann Karl August** zu Wied (1779–1836), Maximilian's elder brother (known as August), was the ruling prince of Wied and head of the family at the time of Maximilian's North American expedition. **Karl Emil Friedrich Heinrich** zu Wied (1785–1864) was another of Maximilian's brothers. **Louise** (1773–1864) was Maximilian's only living sister at the time of his 1832–34 expedition. **Luitgarde** Wied (1813–70), Maximilian's niece, the daughter of his brother August, married Count Otto zu Solms-Laubach (d. 1872) in 1832.

Wilson, Peter (1797–1826). Indian subagent, 1824–26. Wilson's first post was among the Sioux; he was transferred to the Mandan villages in 1825. Morgan, *West of William H. Ashley,* 246n183.

CREE

BLACKFOOT Fort
McKenzie ASSINIBOINE
Great Falls   Fort Union
                                              HIDATSA
GROS VENTRES   Fort Clark   *Bismarck*
des PRAIRIES   MANDAN   YANKTONAI SIOU

Yellowstone River

                                                    Missouri River

                                    Fort Pierre   YANKTON SIO
                TETON SIOUX
                                            PONCA

                                        OMAHA   *Omaha*
                            Platte River   Bellevu

```
The Journey Westward
━━━━━━━━━━━━━━━━

The Return
▪▪▪▪▪▪▪▪▪▪▪▪▪▪▪

0      100     200     300     400 miles
```

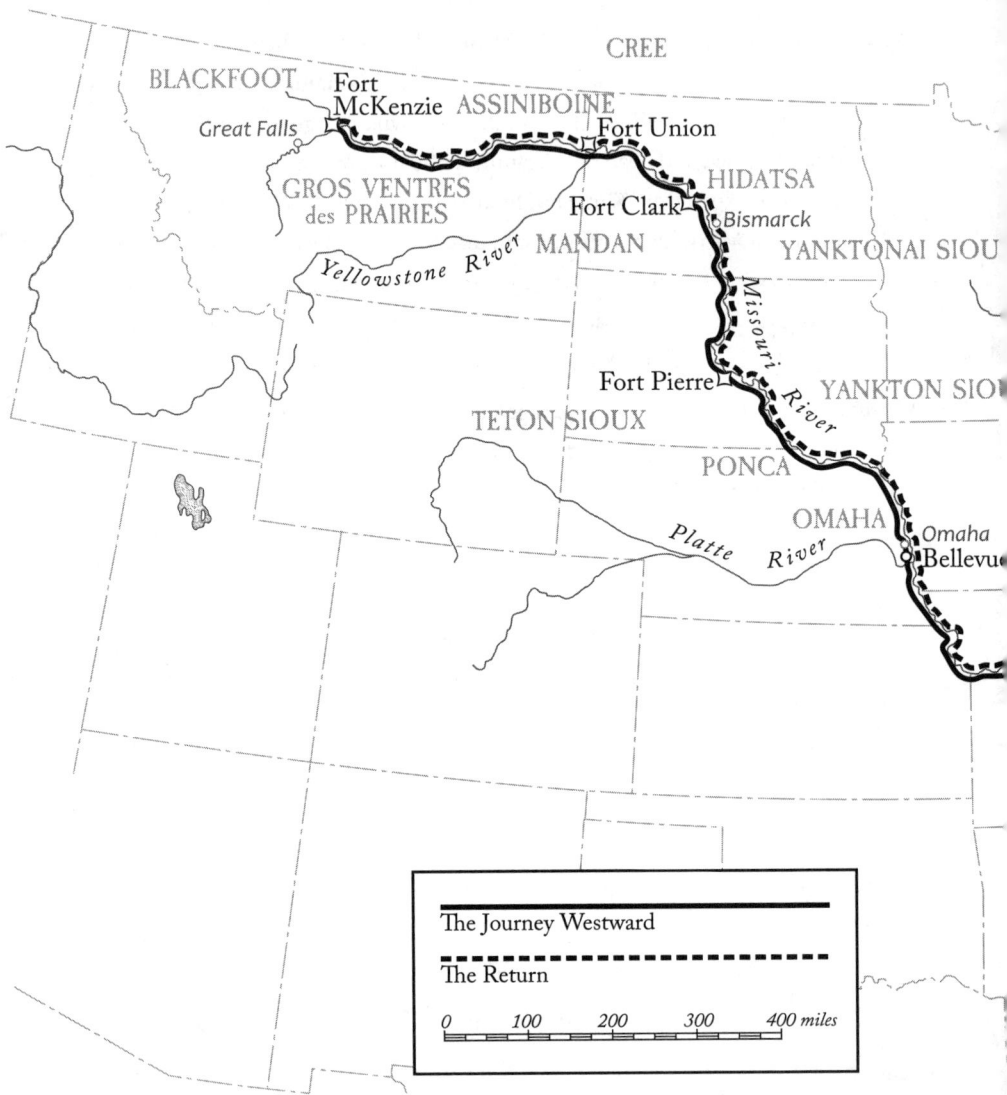

Routes of Prince Maximilian's party from Boston to Montana and from there
to New York City. Map drawn by Tom Jonas, 2016, based on a map by Staple &
Charles Ltd., 1984. Copyright © 2017 by Joslyn Art Museum, Omaha, Nebraska.

SAUK &
MESKWAKI

Wabash River

St. Louis

Vincennes

Cincinnati

Louisville

New Harmony

Mississippi River

Ohio River

Pittsburgh

Cleveland

Buffalo

Bethlehem

Philadelphia

New York City

Boston

Hudson River

New Orleans

Travels in North America, 1832–1834

I

[Journey] from Europe to Boston

7 May: At two o'clock, departure from Neuwied on board the steamboat *Concordia*. Evening at the Rheinberg [Hotel] in Cologne.

9 May: At five o'clock, arrival at Rotterdam. We took lodging at the Hôtel des Pays Bas [with a] beautiful view of the city. Many large ships: a war brig; five or six American ships; the beautiful new Indiaman *(Prince of Orange)*. Six hundred men work on these docks. Became acquainted with Mr. Hoboken. He owned fourteen ships, was always building new ones, [had] his own dock [and a] country home close to the city, [with a] garden [and] greenhouses.

13 May: Dinner at Mr. Hoboken's home. Preserved Indian fruits, good wines, strawberries, melons; afterward, coffee with pipes and cigarros. In the evening, music; dancing near the piano.

15 May: In the morning, business. Wine and baggage brought on board. At ten o'clock, departure on the steamship *De Zeeuw* to Hellevoetsluis, [where] we went ashore and took lodging.

17 May: In the morning, wind and torrential rain; gulls, especially *Larus ridibundus,* with attractive plumage and black heads, flocked together above the turbulent water, looking for refuse. In the afternoon the brig *Janus,* [our passage to North America, was sighted.] We completed our affairs on land, boarded the ship at nine in the evening, [and] slept very quietly on board that night.

[18 May:] At two or three o'clock, the *Janus* weighed anchor and the pilot steered out to sea. The weather was nice. The shores disappeared [and] toward noon we could no longer see land. The sea was rough, all of us somewhat seasick; Mr. Bodmer was very sick; he slept on deck that night since our ship's cabin [had] an unpleasant odor [that] caused the sickness to be worse.

19 May: During the night we were becalmed. At nine thirty a view of Calais. On the opposite side we could clearly discern Dover Castle with a telescope. No wind all day; the ship sailed very slowly. At six in the evening we were about opposite the French coast between Calais and Boulogne. We saw neither

marine animals nor marine plants, only a few birds. Today Mr. Bodmer felt well and finished several sketches.

21 May: Good weather but contrary wind; we tacked. The *Janus* is a brig of 170 tons, built in Plymouth near Boston, very durable and sound. Lengthwise the *Janus* measures 41 to 42 of my paces, and in width, at the mainmast, 9 to 10 paces. Cabin small, no windows aft, six bunks. Capt. Robbins was a native of Plymouth; the second was Master Gooden; the steward and cook, a mulatto; five sailors in addition.

24 May: In the morning, almost calm; the ship moved slowly forward. [Great Britain's] Land's End was already somewhat behind us. Toward noon the sun's heat became intense, 13½° Réaumur in the shade.[1] In the evening, light on the Scilly Islands.

25 May: A [barn] swallow (*Hirundo rustica*) flew aboard. In the afternoon an English battleship (probably seventy-four cannon) proudly sailed northward past us and hoisted its flag; we did the same. Several porpoises. In the evening a Dutch brig from Havana, which had made the voyage in forty days. We conversed with it.

26 May: During the night the wind shifted to an easterly, hence very favorable, direction. At noon we drank to the health of my eldest brother [August], whose birthday was today. Brisk wind during the afternoon; [at] night the sea raged fiercely, tossing the ship.

27–30 May: At nine o'clock [on 27 May] a large Dutch brig; [its Bavarian] skipper came on board and requested news from Europe. Took a letter [to brother Karl] along for me. In the afternoon, very high seas; during the night, [and for the next three days,] torrential rain and storms. We remained in the hatchway. Mr. Bodmer and Dreidoppel were a little sick.

31 May: Fierce gale from the northwest; dark squalls toward sundown; very high, obliquely rolling sea; the [*Janus*] listed enormously but luckily recovered. The sea beat against the ship and even [came] into our cabin.

1 June: Weather a little better [but] toward evening, torrential rain and storms again. With the sea rolling like high mountains, we plunged from crest to trough; we seemed to be sailing in a deep valley and could not see even 80 paces. The waves broke violently against the ship, and whoever ventured on deck was thoroughly drenched. The scene was dreadful but terribly beautiful! I had never seen anything like this, [not once] on [my] entire [1815 and 1817] Brazilian voyage; in this respect the [northern] Atlantic Ocean is far worse than the more southerly seas. We mostly lay in bed; for several nights

[we did] not sleep; [we] could not stand on our feet in that foul-smelling, crowded cabin. Five persons were housed there [in] dismal captivity. The sailors worked terribly hard. Every evening I gave them some *Genever* (gin), of which they were very fond.

2–4 June: Weather even fiercer. The big foresail was ripped into shreds [one] night [but] in the morning a new one was spread. [Finally] the clouds parted somewhat, and the wind shifted to the north and became gentler and more favorable to us.

5 June: Toward morning, a strong northern breeze blew us [briskly] forward. [We] saw several varieties of petrels soaring above us the previous stormy days: *Procellaria pelagica;* another species, white like a gull (perhaps *Procellaria glacialis*) but black and white; another one grayish brown above, rust-red underneath. We saw no fish at all.

Today, for the first time in nine days, I could again think about my journal and add what is written here, but the motion was so strong that one could write only poorly [and] crookedly.

Afternoon very nice. The sailors repaired torn rope ladders [and] greased the masts with tallow, so that the sails would slide up and down more easily; they also smear their rain gear with boiled oil, so rain cannot penetrate it. Beautiful moonlit night; we slept peacefully.

6 June: After breakfast we examined the charts and books belonging to the ship. These included Elford's *Marine Telegraph,* a book [about numbered signal flags]. The *Janus* had these flags. All American ships carry this book.

At about ten or eleven o'clock, the first Portuguese men-of-war *(Physalia)* appeared, about three or four of them, with several jellyfish or related [creatures] of bluish violet color, some of them yellowish or yellowish red on the bell or umbrella. In the afternoon, very little wind; in the evening, calm; innumerable *Medusa pelagica* and Portuguese men-of-war floated by. We caught several of the former.

7–8 June: We examined the ship's charts: the best one for the northern coast of America is that by Blunt, *Northeastern Coast of North America from New York to Cape Canso including Sable Island.*

9 June: Toward morning, calm; the sea had a heavy ground swell [and] a somewhat more greenish color. The sounding lead with a 140-fathom line was tossed out but did not reach bottom. The men were busy repairing several sails. At about three o'clock a very threatening mass of clouds appeared in the northwest. This immediately prompted Robbins to lower all the sails.

What luck! For suddenly a violent storm squall with pelting rain broke upon us from the northwest; the captain assured us that never in his long career had he experienced a more furious one. The wind howled as [if] hundreds of bass viols were being stroked; the ropes flew about and emitted sounds like aeolian harps. The loosened sails fluttered and sounded terrible until they could be bound up: the sailors worked for several hours during the worst of the storm and finally accomplished the task, at the risk of their own lives.

The sea was frightfully wild; [waves] like high mountains broke on board and inundated the *Janus;* the leeward side was continually underwater [and] whoever came on deck was drenched. The ship plunged from the crests into the troughs of the waves; it groaned and creaked mightily, which sounded [increasingly] violent to us, in our small cabin down below. Robbins had lashed the rudder firmly in the correct direction and was clinging to the foredeck of the ship. The terrifying storm continued until nine o'clock in the evening, when the wind subsided somewhat. The ship, to my great astonishment, had maintained a constant uprightness [through it all]. [That] night a gale howled, which seemed mild after the previous storm, although [it] was severe enough.

10 June: [The stormy weather continued and] the ship struggled against the contrary wind. We were confined to our beds the whole day. Mr. Bodmer was sick, Dreidoppel somewhat less so. With such turbulent motion, there could be no thought of working.

12 June: In the morning, nice. The entire deck was scrubbed. On the ocean [there were] numerous round spots, which reflected all the colors of the rainbow. The sailors maintained that these are composed of fatty material spewed out by whales and other cetaceans. A school of porpoises swam ahead of the ship. Someone reached for the harpoon, but they moved away. Temperature of the air 14¾°R, of the water 14°R, the warmest day until now.

14 June: One ferocious storm squall followed hard upon another. Robbins prepared for it by taking in all the sails; he was extremely cautious [and] constantly on deck, steadfastly observing the wind, so his eyes were red and inflamed from the spraying salt water.

15 June: The ship was turned in a southerly direction. We had adverse weather the entire voyage; if the wind was favorable, it was very weak; if it was contrary, it became a gale and the sea towered up against us.

16 June: Weather a little better; we could sit on deck. Temperature of the air (a

cold wind) 11°R, of the water 14°R. Skipper Robbins explained this great discrepancy between the temperature of the air and water as a result of the warmth of the Gulf Stream, flowing from the Gulf of Mexico. That may well be correct, for this warm current extends as far as the region south of the [Grand Banks], exactly where we were [then].

All afternoon a strong northwest wind blew, which drove the sea ahead very hard against us. Behind the ship, above [our] smooth, white-streaked wake, as many as twenty small petrels *(Procellaria pelagica)* hovered incessantly and often came very close. Unfortunately, we [were unable] to get a single bird since it [was always] impossible to lower a boat.

17 June: Beautiful, clear weather, but again, no wind, [so] the ship lay virtually still. Water temperature much colder than yesterday, probably because we were getting closer to the banks. Today the large storeroom on the deck of the ship was opened to obtain zwieback. I had my gun case removed and a double-barreled shotgun made ready to shoot storm petrels. During the noon meal, the comment was made that we had now eaten breakfast, lunch, and dinner together at the mess table ninety-two times, yet we will certainly not get to Boston in less than two weeks. We amused ourselves [that afternoon] by tossing small pieces of fat to the storm petrels, which devoured them instantly.

18 June: Dense fog covered the ocean. It was extremely wet on board; the sails dripped. At three thirty there was thunder in the west and northwest, directly before the ship. So that we should indeed learn all the joys of life at sea, a dark, ominous thunderstorm came closer and closer, a long streak of black clouds on the horizon. The thunder rumbled more hollowly and not as sharply as on land; bolts of lightning struck the water. The necessary precautions were taken: all studding and other sails without exception were taken in; the yards were set against the wind. Without sails the ship rolled violently and unpleasantly. Then the thundershower came. Several thunderclaps resembled cannon shots [but] the lightning did not come very close. [In a short while], several sails were again hoisted. The rain continued to pour down heavily.

About five in the afternoon, dolphins (porpoises) appeared. Gooden, the mate, [grabbed] the harpoon, and before I had reached the prow of the ship, someone called out that a fish had been caught. The head of the harpoon had passed completely through it, and the heavy animal, 6 French feet in length, was gradually hoisted.[2] It struggled violently, and the iron of the harpoon was on the point of tearing out when a rope was thrown around it below the pectoral fins, and the prize was successfully brought on board. This dolphin *(Delphinus delphis)* is not the porpoise *(Delphinus phocaena)* found in the European ocean; it [is] very different. It was 6 lines short of 6 feet; dark steel gray above, white underneath, and with some long gray stripes and cloudy markings along its side. The animal bled profusely. Someone cut it above the caudal fin, and within five minutes it was dead. It rained steadily while Mr. Bodmer made a sketch of the dolphin and I measured it. Afterward the skin of the animal was removed along with the fat (blubber), which covers the entire inside of the skin to about the thickness of a finger, and under it lay the dark-red muscle meat, neat and clean. It is said to be very tasty, but the blubber is stripped away as soon as possible, since otherwise the meat takes on the taste of train oil. We examined the internal organs of the dolphin as evening approached.

[19 June:] For breakfast today we had fried dolphin liver, and all of us found it very tasty, as good as venison liver. In addition, we had salt beef, half moldy American cheese, and coffee. The lead was tossed out—the same line used recently—but did not touch bottom; therefore we were not yet on the [Grand Banks] of Newfoundland. At noon for lunch we had a dish of dolphin meat, pork, potatoes, and dumplings in a whitish sauce; the dolphin meat, quite black, was boiled [and] somewhat stringy, but tasty.

20 June: A brisk wind drove the ship [while] fog covered clothing as though it were hoarfrost. Many birds [were seen, so] we knew we were close to the [Grand Banks] and coasts of Newfoundland. About seven o'clock [that evening], a calm; the ship rolled to [such] an extraordinary degree [that] one could scarcely keep one's footing. We saw a fishing boat (a two-masted schooner) [and] realized that we [must be] on the [Grand Banks]. The lead was thrown out and touched bottom at 35 fathoms, proof that we were [indeed there]. The night was calm.

21 June: Overcast sky, wind northwest, contrary; our course, unfortunately, southwesterly again. The [Grand Banks] of Newfoundland [are] 570 miles long from north to south and 180 miles wide at [the] widest point. The water is 30 to 40 fathoms deep, and the [Banks are] said to be completely overgrown with *Fucus* (rockweed), in which live countless fish, especially codfish *(Gadus morhua),* halibut, and other varieties. These fishing grounds are very well known. Every year about 150 schooners, ships of 70 to 80 tons and crews of eight to ten men, go there from the American coast, stay for

several months, and fish [until] they have a full cargo (probably 33,000 fish or more [per ship]). In America these fish sell for two to three dollars (five to seven and a half florins) per hundredweight. Many French ships also come here to fish.

In the afternoon, almost calm. A guillemot *(Uria troile)* swam beside the ship. The captain shot it and had it fetched with the boat. It was incorporated into [my] collection.

24–26 June: I had a long discussion with Master Robbins about nautical observations on board a ship. Measuring the altitude of the sun [to determine latitude] at noon is very easy; I had learned it almost perfectly, and it provided much pleasure and entertainment. [On the 25th] we were south of Sable Island [and] our bowsprit was directed toward Nova Scotia.

27 June: In the morning, dreary, overcast sky. Many indications of nearby land: grass, *Fucus,* and other flat greenish objects, which we could not distinguish clearly, floating more deeply in the sea. Several birds not seen before. We were now at the western end of Sable Island Bank and approximately 60 miles from the coast of Nova Scotia. The various tacks that we made since yesterday afternoon, [because of unfavorable winds, totaled 124 miles].

28 June: A head wind blew straight from the west and the sea rolled against us. Last evening we were no farther than 25 miles from the coast of Nova Scotia; now we ran in a straight line toward Roseway Bank. The ship made [many more] tacks. [That night] the powerful, unfavorable west wind that had been blowing uninterruptedly for the past three days developed into a violent gale.

29 June: The ship made slow progress, since the sea surged very high against us. [But by noon] we were directly southwest of and not very far from St. George's Bank.

At lunch today we had no more wine; forty-three bottles had been emptied [and] we still saw [no] harbor. We made up for this lack as best we could with a beverage [made of] water, vinegar, and molasses, which is heavily consumed in America when cider or apple wine is lacking.

Various objects on the ship, such as water casks and the like, were painted today. Some of the sailors worked on the ropes, always in need of repair. We observed much *Fucus* [and] a few *Procellaria pelagica* inspecting an old meat cask thrown into the sea.

30 June: Nice, clear, and sunny morning; sea smooth as a mirror. Today we had been at sea for forty-four days; [we] were only one and a half days from

Boston but could not get there. About ten o'clock the boat was lowered, and Mr. Bodmer made a very accurate sketch of the *Janus*. The captain and Dreidoppel accompanied him. Dark-brown fish played around the rudder.

Noon observation: latitude 42°10′ north, longitude 66°4′ west. Temperature of the air at twelve o'clock, 10½°R, of the water 9°R. [Later] in the afternoon an unfavorable wind became so strong, and the movement of the ship also, that we forgot to read the thermometer.

1 July: The sea was very wild and pounded the bow of the ship violently. Snow-white foam and spray struck the deck. The evening was pleasant, the sun set amidst clouds, [and] the waxing moon had a halo. Little wind during the night, always from the same unfavorable southwest direction.

2 July: In the morning, pleasant weather, calm sea, unfavorable wind. An American dove (undoubtedly *Columba migratoria* [passenger pigeon]) alighted on one of our yards, where the captain shot it. Unfortunately, it fell into the sea and we could not get it.

Since yesterday noon we had made [two long] tacks [for a total of 79 miles]. At four thirty we saw ships on all sides, five in number, including small schooners out to catch mackerel; [they] often remain at sea for three to four weeks. The wind shifted a little more to the south; this immediately allowed us to steer correspondingly more to the west.

3 July: After midnight the wind returned to its old, contrary southwest position. We continued all night in the same direction. Tack at eight o'clock. It was very pleasantly warm, the horizon hazy. Consequently, we could not discern with certainty the coast of America, which was close to us to the west, while our course was southerly. Someone climbed the mast to see better, but from there, too, land could not be discerned with certainty. Our impatience was great at being so close to land and yet not being able to reach it. We were now located approximately opposite Cape Ann, the northernmost cape of the Bay of Massachusetts, and were sailing toward Cape Cod, the southernmost promontory of the bay. A streak of fog concealed [the coast, but] suddenly, we caught sight of Cape Cod, 15 miles south of us. At one thirty, [after considerable tacking], the ship sailed up along Cape Cod, a long, low strip of land. We could clearly distinguish the white sandy coast, alternating with low, dark-green thickets, perhaps juniper or the like; the lighthouse, a moderately high tower; a tall building beside it; and, not far away, a windmill and several dwellings.

[In] incomparable weather, the *Janus* hastened ever closer to its destination. The sailors were occupied all day repairing the rigging and cleaning [in preparation] for the approaching landing. From six to seven o'clock, the evening was splendid; the heat disappeared; the dark-blue surface of the sea shone serenely, moved only by a gentle wind. Individual fishermen's sails, brown or dazzling white, gleamed near the American coast, already veiled by the haze of the evening. Peace prevailed on this broad panorama. A butterfly *(Papilio plexippus)* came on board and was captured.

We calmly continued our set course when suddenly the wind veered to the north, becoming extremely favorable. Everyone set to work to turn the ship, and all faces shone with joy. The wind blew briskly a while but [then] subsided somewhat. The moon shone very brightly; the ocean, smooth as glass, glistened from its light.

4 July: Shortly after daybreak we were assembled on deck. All around, the thunder of cannon resounded, for today was the famous Day of Independence, highly celebrated in the United States, on which, by chance, we reached the harbor—an interesting moment! After about an hour, the ship turned and we approached the low coast that extended scenically before us on both sides. In the center, in the direction of Boston, stood, on a small rocky island, the snow-white Boston Lighthouse, with its black roof; beside it were several small, picturesque islands. In the distance there were a few high, blue mountains [and] many towns. More and more beautifully, the islands and the coast emerged, like decorations on the dark-blue surface of the sea.

On the [mainmast] of the *Janus* [we] hoisted the number of our ship (45. 53.) with four of the blue-and-white signal flags. These signals were immediately relayed by a telegraph located on a nearby island [to] give the ship's owner the good news that his ship [was safe]. All the ships that sailed around us, even the fishing boats, [flew] the colorful national flag today.

[Our] pilot approached in a small boat and boarded the *Janus.* Ships were sailing in all directions; many others lay at anchor. The wind [was] weak [so] we tacked in between the islands. Picturesque glimpses of attractive homes, trees, and the imposing city of Boston with its reddish brown roofs. A magnificent view!

A high smoke cloud rose on shore from the first houses of the city; finally, a very large flame. We learned upon our arrival in Boston that this was a fire in a warehouse for salted mackerel; the fire had been caused accidentally by melted tar. Nearby, a large brig also caught fire and was completely destroyed. We were able to verify this from what we saw during our walk that evening, when the stench of burnt fish was still quite unbearable. At about one thirty, the *Janus* dropped anchor at the India Wharf among many large, imposing ships from various parts of the world.

II

Stay in Boston, New York, and Philadelphia

[FROM 4 JULY TO 1 AUGUST 1832]

[4 July (cont.):] At [that] time the heat was very great. We went to the Commercial Coffeehouse [and] took lodging. My baggage had to remain on board the ship [to undergo customs].

Boston generally impressed me [as] an English city, [with] some differences: long streets, good sidewalks, very pleasing houses, no lack of impressive buildings [and graceful] churches. Boston has various parks and avenues and, as in the largest European cities, very fine and diverse shops.

The Americans are mostly tall, often lean. Generally one does not see very many Negroes, and all of them are free, whereas in the southern states some are still slaves. Not far from the public promenade there was a small street that, for the most part, was entirely inhabited by Negroes and their mulatto or freed descendants. I looked in vain for the original American race, the Indians; they have disappeared from this region.

After we had made [lengthy] observations in the very lively streets of Boston, we proceeded to the inn, where, in a long room, we found a table set for sixty to seventy persons. On the door a sign was fastened stating that no one may enter the dining room until a bell is rung, and this rule was closely observed, for scarcely had the bell rung than a crowd of hungry gentlemen stormed in, hurled themselves at the table, and immediately helped themselves. The food—roast beef, potatoes, green peas, salmon, and a few additional vegetables—was devoured in very short time. Then there were strawberries with cream and sugar, everything served very quickly and in meager quantities. The knife was [the principal tool] for eating, because the fork had only two tines and was thus merely a stabbing weapon. Cider and water, mixed [together], were served as the beverage. Wine had to be ordered. The guests scattered very quickly.

5 July: In the morning we left for the customhouse and the *Janus* [and arranged for the shipment of our baggage to New York]. Later we visited all the booksellers and engravers' stores throughout Boston but found nothing at all

about Indians—a matter of great consequence to me—and very few natural history books.

6 July: After [an early morning carriage drive to see the countryside and the Bunker Hill monument, then under construction], we went to the stagecoach office of J. Barker at the Marlboro Hotel. We had to wait a long time [for] our [stage], a spacious coach for nine [passengers]. The road from Boston to Providence, where one boarded steamships to New York, [was] 41 miles. At first one saw pretty, stylish country homes in large numbers. [As] they become more and more infrequent, [one saw instead woodlands, farms, fields, and occasional towns]. We changed horses at three different places, ate lunch at Dedham, [and in the evening] reached the pretty, busy city of Providence, located on a narrow inlet of the ocean extending into the mainland.

[7 or 8 July:] Providence is a lively place that maintains brisk commerce with the countryside. The luxury in this city is significant. The female sex paraded about on the streets in the most elegant finery; [even] the country and field ladies, often from small, wretched cottages, [wore] silk and large hats with veils like the most genteel ladies. Prosperity must exist here, for one never saw beggars or poor, idle people. Negroes were more frequently seen in Providence than in Boston and the more northern regions. The considerable number of ships lying at anchor here also indicated significant commerce.

[8 July:] This morning, at eleven thirty, the [steamship] *Boston* arrived from New York. The master told me that there was indeed cholera in that city.[1] Yet we had no choice [but to] go there. At three thirty, we boarded [the *Boston*, along with] probably one hundred [other passengers]. The ship was excellently equipped. In size it resembled a frigate. It was very wide and had three decks [and quite elegant dining and sleeping arrangements]. As soon as the steam pressure began to rise, the heavy engines were started up by first unthrottling one engine and then gradually releasing several ropes. The vibration was especially severe in the stern of the ship. The ship sped off as swiftly as an arrow. Presently a large metal bell, which almost deafened us, was rung to summon the passengers to pay their fare, which, to New York, amounted to six dollars, including meals. Before dusk we no longer saw any coastline to the left but instead had a view of the open sea; [that] did not last long, since after a few miles [we turned] to the right between Long Island and the mainland. At seven o'clock the bell was rung for tea.

9 July: Very early in the morning we came on deck. To the left one no longer saw

the sea but, instead, the coast of Long Island, [with] dark forest, steep sandy banks, [and] several wide, picturesque bays. A narrow [strait] was called [Hell Gate]. We rounded a cape to the right [and saw] beautiful trees and a thousand other plants, sheltering in their shade the most elegant country homes. In short, a harbor entrance so splendid that none other ever seemed more lovely to me. [When] the *Boston* docked I took [a carriage] to the American Hotel.

New York is a big, imposing commercial [center] like the largest cities of Europe. It has 220,000 inhabitants. Broadway, the finest street, is several miles long and very impressive. The houses are made of brick, very elegant, with gas lighting in the evenings. Here one could find all the luxuries and fashionable goods of Europe and the entire world. But the copper engraving shops were very poor and deficient; people here did not seem to have much appreciation for this field. New York has many stately buildings and churches for all religions.

[10 July:] On the tenth we undertook a walk. New York offers several [vantage points] where one can observe the large, [impressive] city [and] countless ships, especially on the two waterways, the North and East Rivers, which enclose it on the north and east sides. The latter is an ocean inlet; the former is the Hudson River. The city is actually located on an island.

[There were theaters] and similar entertainments; however, very little has been done for the sciences. Several natural history collections were exhibited for a fee, but they were mixed with art objects of all kinds. The so-called American Museum, bordering the park, had a rather impressive collection of animals: elephants, lions, tigers, and many other large and small animals, as well as rare birds, but they were very poorly displayed. This was accomplished better in Mr. Peale's museum, where there were fewer but far better mounted animals.[2] Here a Bengal tiger was exhibited in absolute perfection [and] an especially fine specimen of *Cervus virginianus*. There were also several dealers in natural history objects here, where, among other things, one found very nice conchylia. All the specimens were expensive. Naturalists often find interesting animals in the very substantial fur businesses there. I could buy black (American) bearskins for three dollars and a fine mountain lion skin for five dollars.

The most extensive fur trade is conducted by Mr. [John Jacob] Astor. Originally from Mannheim on the Rhine, he came to the United States a poor man and is now said to be the richest person in the United States. The

[American Fur] Company belongs to him. At this time I did not get to see Mr. Astor's fur warehouse, but we did visit another storeroom, where the owner gave me a beautiful Indian otter fur medicine bag [and] showed us a complete Mandan Indian costume, which included a necklace [made] from the claws of the *Ursus ferox.*

On [15] July we were invited to the country home of Mr. Schmidt, the Prussian consul, seven miles from New York. We drove into Mr. Schmidt's garden, [which had] beautiful plants. At one thirty, we sat down to dine. Negroes and mulattoes waited on us. Ice was always on the table here; all beverages were [iced]. It is only natural that people should catch cold in this hot country in summertime, since they generally continue to eat ice even during the occurrence of cholera. A doctor who dined with us had me eat ice with ginger, although I suffered constant abdominal pains.

After our meal we took a walk to the nearby lunatic asylum, of which the aforementioned doctor was the administrator.[3] It was situated in a kind of park on a gentle rise and enclosed on all sides by thickets, country homes, and gardens. The main building was impressive, made of brick, [with] several floors, and maintained neatly and elegantly throughout; distinguished patients obtained nice, well-furnished rooms. We walked through the tidy cells of the patients and viewed the building in which the worst of these patients were kept. A man with a long beard and a thick cudgel entertained us with stories about Ohio steamboats; we had to shake hands with him. Others were securely confined or sat in introverted melancholy. The [surrounding] deer park was more cheerful, [with] nice, tame animals [and] beautiful plants.

We returned to the city late, and on the way I acquired some additional interesting information about this region. In addition to the lunatic asylum, the institutions for public welfare in this city include an institute for the deaf and dumb and a prison for crafty old criminals as well as one for young offenders, who are separated in order, perhaps, to reform them; there are many good, useful institutions in this country.

On 16 July I left the inn early. Mr. Bodmer stayed behind to wait for Dreidoppel, who was supposed to [arrive soon with the bulk of our baggage]. I left New York at six o'clock on a steamboat completely filled with passengers; one could hardly find a place to sit. Our ship followed [the Raritan River] as far as [New] Brunswick. [From there we took a large stage to] the Delaware [River], where the steamship *Trenton* was waiting to take us on board. We sailed down the beautiful Delaware, [and] at about four or five o'clock we docked near Chestnut Street in Philadelphia.

[At my] hotel there was no room available because of cholera refugees from New York, [so] I was quartered for the night with a gentleman from that city in one of the parlour[s]; in inns in this country, a big distinction is made between the living room and the parlour, where no one sleeps. I went to many bookstores that afternoon, particularly to Carey and Lea, where there were nice things, but nowhere did I find [the natural history references] I was looking for.

On the 17th of July I visited Mr. Krumbhaar, [who] received me very cordially and, with his cabriolet, showed me the city and the interesting Fairmount waterworks. I spent [the] evening at his home. Philadelphia is a beautiful, large city of 160,000 inhabitants and in overall appearance is rather different from New York and Boston. The houses are not so tall, [and] all streets intersect at right angles. A characteristic feature of this city are the poles, erected on both sides at the edge of the very fine broad, brick streets [and] provided with awnings, so that on most streets one can walk in the shade.

An entire section of the city is inhabited by Germans; one hears much German and French spoken. There are even sermons in German in the German churches. The Quakers are very numerous. Quaker is a derisive name; they call themselves Friends. They do not practice baptism. There are rich people among them. There are also Catholic churches here, and freedom of religion is completely unrestricted.

Of the natural history institutions in Philadelphia, [the Peale Museum] is certainly the most interesting. Since the [curator, Titian Peale,] was with Major Long in the interior of the western states, as far as the Rocky Mountains, and had also been in South America, he had assembled a very large collection of interesting objects, from which, however, many things, even the large European animals, are still lacking. One can see the elephant, the rhinoceros, the bison (buffalo) very nicely displayed here, as well as the wapiti (elk) with enormous antlers, the North American antelope, the [bighorn sheep] from the American mountains—many interesting animals. Well worth viewing are the costumes and finery of various peoples, including the North American Indians, of whom [there were] several complete figures. As in all the American museums described thus far, this collection was actually a hodgepodge—paintings, models, art objects, and natural history specimens all displayed together.

In order to learn more about the Indians of North America, I made considerable efforts to find some drawings and illustrations, without success. The most important work of this kind ever to be published, however, was [said to be imminent]: a book with 120 color lithographed portraits of the famous chiefs of all the Indian tribes.[4] These are from the Indian Office in Washington, where oil paintings of all of them are kept. This work is to appear in some twenty installments, each with six illustrations, at a price of six dollars, and will contain an excellent text with the history of these peoples. I saw a few sample sheets at a local bookdealer's shop.

On 18 July I left Philadelphia at noon and boarded the steamship *Burlington*, on which we sailed up the beautiful Delaware and had lunch. At about four or five o'clock, the ship docked at Bordentown, [where] I took lodging.

[19 July:] Early on the nineteenth, I undertook a walk to the country home of [Joseph] Bonaparte, ex-king of Spain, [who had lived here for about fifteen years but was not presently in residence]. It is located 300 paces from Bordentown. On the right side of the path, I went botanizing [and saw] magnificent rhododendron shrubs blooming, ten to fifteen and more feet tall, [and] thickly entangled by wild grapevines. I took these [and many other] plants with me. As the day began to cool, I went to Bonaparte's country home. The gardener, who was working in the large garden, nicely planted with all sorts of European vegetables and fruits, opened the door for me. The home itself was simple, moderately large with three floors, a [railed] terrace, and a [glassed-in] pavilion. After returning to the inn, I prepared [my] collected plants.

20 July: Today it was so hot that one could scarcely leave the [inn]. It was warm even at dusk but pleasant on the elevation above the river. The catbirds flew back and forth across the river. Swallows also put in an appearance, [and] crickets chirped repeatedly [and] more rapidly than in Europe. I took a walk along the high bank of the Delaware and saw *Datura* and pokeweed *(Phytolacca decandra)* blooming in all the wild, uncultivated places.

[21 July:] I had expected to receive letters from Mr. Bodmer in New York, but nothing arrived. Again the heat was great. At about ten o'clock, the Fahrenheit thermometer in the shade of the cool passageway in the inn stood at 73°. Today I engaged in a botanical conversation, something that is probably infrequent here: a well-informed man told me a good deal about the plants of this region. He was the governor of the province of New Jersey, [Mahlon] Dickerson.

22 July: During the night Mr. Bodmer woke me. He had written me two letters, neither of which I received. In order to conclude our affairs quickly, he had appeared in person. Much to my chagrin, I learned that our chests and trunks still had not arrived in New York from Boston and that there was no prospect of them for a long time.

Since today was Sunday, when neither steamships nor stages went to New York, Mr. Bodmer stayed here, and after breakfast we took a walk to [Joseph] Bonaparte's garden. We viewed the nicest places, Mr. Bodmer sketched [the] residence, and I once more took back many interesting plants. It was very hot in the afternoon.

On 23 July at nine o'clock, Mr. Bodmer left for New York on the stage. I took the steamship *Philadelphia* to the city of the same name, where I arrived at about six o'clock in the evening. [I intended] to travel to Bethlehem and look for a place [to] begin our natural history work.

On 25 July, at three thirty in the morning, the stagecoach arrived [at my] inn to take me aboard. It was [so] warm that morning that one could hardly endure a coat. We drove through Germantown and at eight o'clock reached Chestnut Hill, where we took another stage with fresh horses and had breakfast in the meantime. From here on, and all through this region until past Bethlehem (56 miles from Philadelphia), almost all the planters and farmers were of German descent [and] preferred to speak German.

We drove [past farmsteads, fields, and meadows and] through magnificent lofty woods. We broke an axle beam on the coach, which we repaired only after working for a long time.

The beautiful redheaded woodpecker *(Picus erythrocephalus)* was extremely common, [and we saw] many other interesting birds, [among them] *Sylvia sialis*, the robin, [and] the fox-colored thrush *(Turdus rufus)*. So far I had not seen any birds of prey.

[When] we reached the beautiful, rather broad Lehigh River, spanned by a bridge, [we] were in Bethlehem. Bethlehem is a colony of the Moravian Brethren in North America and one of the more outstanding ones. It is situated on the slope of a hill, has an impressive-looking church with a cupola supported by several columns and several handsome buildings such as the boarding school. At present the town consists of only a few streets, still unpaved in the center but provided with good stone sidewalks. The English [inn] of Zenas Wells was very good; there was a German inn on the canal below. Stages departed from [Bethlehem] daily for Philadelphia, Mauch Chunk, Easton, and Reading.[M1]

[26–27 July:] My first errand was across the street to a young doctor, who also had the pharmacy. For some time I had not felt entirely well, and I wanted to cure my ailment. Dr. Staud, a pleasant young man [with] a flourishing practice, gave me some medicine that kept me home until that afternoon.

On the morning of the twenty-seventh I met by chance a German doctor from New York, the son of a pharmacist from Dierdorf near Neuwied, who had been in America for some time. Dr. Saynisch was a fine, friendly man who was uncommonly delighted to get to know me by my real name.[5] He had a good knowledge of natural history, [and] he took me to the local minister, Mr. Seidel, a lively, pleasant, very well-educated man [whose extensive] library [had] works in natural history—Wilson, Catesby, and other very valuable ones—[and an] interesting mineralogical and shell collection. Mr. Seidel was so kind as to show me the girls' school first of all: a spacious, well-ventilated, cool, and bright building, where fifty to sixty children of the female sex are educated. In each room there was a pianoforte (ten in all). The church [was] large, inviting, and [well lit]. On the second floor there was a hall with an organ built in New York; very good concerts were given there. In Bethlehem, as in all colonies of the Brethren, one could find artisans and stores of all kinds. On the streets one usually heard German spoken.

In the afternoon I visited Dr. Saynisch in the lower inn, where he had been living for a considerable length of time. [He had] some very good works on natural history as well as various natural history specimens, several of which I received as a gift. Later Pastor Seidel arrived, and we took a walk up along the eastern bank of the [Lehigh River]. We [crossed] the canal that [went] from Mauch Chunk, past Bethlehem, to Easton about fifty miles away. Anthracite coal from Mauch Chunk is transported on the canal. In the high mountains around Mauch Chunk, there are very significant deposits. [Along the Lehigh] bank, Pastor Seidel had transformed a path into a pleasant promenade, along which benches and tables had been set up. [It] was very picturesque. We returned over the ridge of the mountain and

---

M1 About 1,000 persons live here now. [The "impressive-looking church," Central Moravian Church, still stands at 73 West Church Street. The church is a central feature in a Bodmer watercolor view of the town of Bethlehem; see pl. 2.]

found [a] young botanist, Mr. Moser, who was traveling here for German scholars; [he] was highly skilled at collecting plants. Today he had some beautiful [sedges and ferns]. We went home for a short while, and then the Reverend Seidel came and took me to Mr. von Schweinitz's home. He had once visited me in Neuwied. At that time he was working on a large study of North American fungi, [a] work [that presently included] 3,000 species. Mr. von Schweinitz was the first superintendent and clergyman of the colony at Bethlehem and also a distinguished botanist, [with] a very complete herbarium; [he] knew the area around his home perfectly.

On 28 July I returned by stage to Philadelphia, [which] I reached in the evening at about the same time that Mr. Bodmer and Dreidoppel arrived from Bordentown by steamboat. [On the following day,] Mr. Krumbhaar introduced me to Mr. [John] Vaughan, a secretary of the [American Philosophical Society]. In their library and collection [there were] fine works, [including] the most extensive one by Audubon [and others by] Catesby, Comte de Buffon, [and Alexander] Wilson. In another room they displayed a collection of Mexican and Peruvian rarities, including several remarkable grave objects, such as idols and ornaments. I [met the physician and student of herpetology] Dr. [Richard] Harlan, who was then very occupied with his cholera patients, among whom he had observed another severe case today.

30 July–1 August: We traveled [by crowded stagecoach to Coopersburg], where [we] took lodging for several days [and engaged in several productive hunting and botanizing expeditions with local residents].

III

Sojourn in Bethlehem, Pennsylvania, and Excursions into the Surrounding Region

[FROM 2 AUGUST TO 16 SEPTEMBER 1832]

On 2 August, we left [Coopersburg] at nine o'clock and drove to Bethlehem in a small open carriage called a dearborn. In the noonday heat, we reached the lower inn at Bethlehem, where we took lodging for a while. The young botanist Moser was still here [and] had already assembled a significant botanical collection, especially of rare aquatic plants from the Delaware and the [Lehigh]. In the afternoon we—Dr. Saynisch, Mr. Moser, Bodmer, and I—made a short journey by boat to the two river islands situated near Bethlehem, which were overgrown with tall shady woods. We [searched particularly for] turtles and bullfrogs; of the former there were as many as nine different species here. A thundershower drove us into a dead, burned-out *Platanus* trunk, in which ten persons could easily have found standing room.

3–6 August: We undertook walk[s] of several miles along the canal in the direction of Easton [and] to a nearby mountain, where we shot some most interesting birds, including the *Icterus baltimore,* with its magnificently fiery color, as well as the *Fringilla tristis, Muscicapa ruticilla, Sylvia sialis;* [on 6 August, I finally] bagged the beautiful blue finch *(Fringilla indigofera).*

7 August: Today we received many bullfrogs, some of them very large. Mr. Bodmer sketched two of them. We also [got] a live young skunk, which was killed and stuffed that afternoon. Several new turtles and tree frogs increased our collection. Today it was so hot in my room that, with windows and doors open, I still recorded a temperature of 22½°R at five thirty in the evening. I was delighted today to receive [my] first letter from Neuwied.

8 August: Dreidoppel went hunting and brought back some interesting birds. Mr. Bodmer completed the drawing of an old female bullfrog, of which I had obtained a large number and compared and described the different genders. It rained heavily today and was very warm besides. All the windows and doors of the houses are open, even late in the evening. Perspiring bodies

catch cold easily as a result, and today that is just what happened to us.

9 August: A day of prayer proclaimed because of the cholera. Dreidoppel had caught cold; during the morning his vomiting and diarrhea were very severe. I, too, experienced the latter along with abdominal pains.[1] The sky was cloudy and overcast; the air very humid. Our plant [specimens] and stuffed animals dried poorly in this weather. At ten thirty we went to church. It was rather full. Mr. von Schweinitz delivered a sermon on present prospects for the approach of cholera and drew a moral about how religion must and can touch our lives in such situations.

10[–11] August: Dreidoppel still sick; my condition somewhat better. Dr. Saynisch and I undertook a hunting excursion into the forest along the road to Pittsburgh. We returned about twelve o'clock, when the heat was already great. Our landlord, Mr. Wöhler, brought me three tortoises, and in the afternoon I received a splendid specimen of *Ondatra* (muskrat), a female; we dissected [it the following day].

12 August: Mr. Bodmer sketched a general view of Bethlehem with a cross section of the [Lehigh] Valley and the canal, a most beautiful overview. No natural history excursions were undertaken today, since in this country nothing of this kind may be pursued on Sunday. Today I wrote to Mr. Gebhard in New York and to Mr. Krumbhaar in Philadelphia to urge the expedition of the chests and cases that had been loaded on board the schooner *Sun* at Boston and were still missing.

14 August: My condition was better, although I still had not fully recovered. Using Wilson's *Ornithology*, I made a list today of the [37] bird species we had bagged here so far. In the evening we received a nice snake *(Coluber saurita)*.

17 August: Rain. Dense mist and fog. We could not go out today. Mr. Bodmer sketched several toads with great accuracy. In the afternoon, we went to Pastor Seidel's and accompanied him to the church, where we had been invited to a love feast. All the children sat up front, just as they do in Neuwied on such occasions, the clergy and elders beside the altar. With the bishop at their head, they entered when we were all seated. First the clergyman, Pastor Seidel, sang a verse, then the choir, afterward the children, then the congregation. English and German hymns alternated. Soon the customary cakes were brought in, just as in Germany, as well as small faience cups of coffee, which were passed around.

18 August: In the morning, an excursion along the Monocacy to get *Quercus*

chincapin and *heterophylla,* two beautiful oak species growing here. Along the brook we found large tracts of common cattails *(Typha latifolia)* and several beautiful plants. Old oaks *(Quercus alba, coccinea, tinctoria);* tall walnut trees as well as sassafras, beeches, and many other trees. In the dense brushwood along the bank, the white-and-black tree creeper *(Certhia varia)* and the *Muscicapa ruticilla* crept; on the willow thickets, the *Icterus phoe-niceus,* which we could not reach because of the swamp. Farther on, along the wooded bends of the brook, we found several small herons *(Ardea vi-rescens).* In the tall, airy oak forest, we bagged several young specimens of *Trochilus colubris* and then returned in the rain to our dwelling. When we arrived we found much to do, for neighboring farmers had supplied us with all kinds of animals, including a hare *(Lepus americanus)* and the so-called woodchuck *(Arctomys monax).*

19 August: Sunday. In the morning, an osprey *(Falco haliaëtus)* was brought in. A young bird from this summer, it had been winged along the [Lehigh]. Last evening I received word from Mr. Gebhard that my baggage had left New York for Philadelphia.

22 August: A morning walk down along the canal, where large numbers of hum-mingbirds flew around the beautiful *Impatiens fulva* down along the bank of the [Lehigh]. I shot several. Finally I bagged a *Picus auratus,* a very beau-tiful bird we had not yet obtained. It sat motionless on the tip of an acacia tree *(Robinia pseudoacacia),* and I brought it down with fine bird shot. In the afternoon I obtained the largest bullfrog I had yet seen, for with out-stretched hind legs, it measured 12 inches, 6 lines in length. That afternoon Dr. Saynisch drove to Nazareth to make several natural history acquisitions for us.

Today we prepared for a five- to seven-day journey to the Delaware Gap and Mauch Chunk. Our landlord, Wöhler, will drive us with his horses. He knows the entire region with its rarities of nature and is himself a hunter. It was far preferable to travel this way [rather] than on the stage, [because] we could stop whenever we wished, hunt, collect plants, etc. At five o'clock, temperature of 20°R. If this summer is any indication of what others are like, summers here are hotter and more uniform than in Europe.

23 August: Early in the morning at five o'clock, we — Dr. Saynisch, Mr. Bodmer, and I — boarded our carriage. Dreidoppel remained behind, [ready] to pre-pare immediately [any] animals we sent back. We drove up through Beth-lehem and followed the road to Easton [and] saw densely cultivated, gently

hilly land alternating with field and forest far and wide. This entire region is part of a limestone formation. One frequently comes upon limekilns, particularly in the woods, and on the fields one sees heaps of quicklime, often very large, piled up in rows as fertilizer [to be] spread over the fields. Because cattle always grazed out in the open, the fields, pastures, and every piece of property were all enclosed by wooden fences.

In the clover fields, we heard the call of the partridge *(Tetrao virginianus),* which consists of two whistling sounds abruptly expelled one after the other. The fence mouse *(Sciurus striatus)* ran on the fences. Redheaded woodpeckers flew from tree to tree. Several different kinds of flowers, including *Antirrhinum linaria, Phytolacca decandra, Verbascum thapsus, Rhus typhinum,* a tall *Eupatorium purpureum,* and many other plants, were abundant along the way. Large orchards usually surrounded the dwellings. The trees were laden with rather small yellow apples. Cultivation of fruit lags far behind here. After we had gone 12 miles, we reached Easton with about 2,000 inhabitants, at the confluence of the Delaware and the [Lehigh]. At the square, on which the rather small courthouse was located, we stopped at the inn for breakfast. First, however, we took a short walk to the Delaware River, which glides past the city between beautiful banks overgrown with tall trees. The main street led directly to the Delaware, over which a large, long, very fine covered bridge with three arches (600 English feet, or 243 of my paces in length) had been constructed. It was painted bright yellow and [had] fifteen windows on each side. This structure, like all similar things in the United States, was a private undertaking; a fare was paid for each crossing.

We continued [our] journey, [following] the western bank of the [gleaming] Delaware. The road was very pleasant, [shaded by] tall forest trees. Somewhat farther on, we turned away from the Delaware for a while to climb over rather impressive elevations to Martin's Creek, [but] we soon left this brook, too, and the region lost its charm as we moved away from the streams. In a side ravine leading up toward the mountain, the area had a bare appearance. The path over the hills led gently uphill and downhill, until we reached [a] plateau [with] a view to the west of the first chain of the Allegheny Mountains (here called Blue Mountains), a long but not very high, picturesque mountain chain [that] extends from the north to the southwest and has a deep gorge on the horizon and a little to the left, called Delaware Water Gap or, simply, Delaware Gap, where that river cuts through the mountains. This place was our destination today. It is 23 miles from Bethlehem, and we were just a few miles away from it.

Our gray horses trotted along briskly [till] we caught sight of the Delaware. We soon reached its bank. The shining surface of the river reflected the surrounding forest in a most picturesque way, like a camera obscura. We followed the bank of the river upstream; the road was not far from it. To the left there were cornfields and habitations with fences, but [then we reached] the foot of the Allegheny Mountains, from which the river issued through [the] deep gorge [of] the Delaware Gap. The mountain range boldly rose on both sides of the river, and the valley became more and more narrow. Immediately before the Gap, there was an inn, the mountain [face] behind it, barely a few hundred steps away.

The Delaware Gap Inn, as I was told, had an elevation 600 feet higher than Philadelphia, and the mountain behind this house [was] 600 to 700 feet higher [yet]. We could have spent the night [here,] but we preferred another [inn] located beyond the Gap. The road ran along the bank of the river; the mountain rose abruptly beside our wheels. Here was a primeval wilderness, tall forest with a densely crowded, varied understory. In the gorge, which we followed gradually upward through the Gap, I noticed [dozens of] plants we had not seen before, a dense jungle that was already being refreshed by the [cooling] evening temperature.

The river passed through a gorge only as wide as the river; the mountains forming the Gap [were] high and steep. Mr. Bodmer sketched this extremely wild and interesting view. We continued to drive gradually upward. On an eminence [above] the valley, a lone house was located, in which there lived an old Frenchman, Mr. [Antoine] Dutot, who was formerly a planter in [Santo] Domingo and was now impoverished. From here the road led over several gradual elevations [to] a large open area in the woods, [where] several persons had settled. Here we found quarters at a fine inn, managed by a certain Broadhead. There were about twelve or thirteen wood houses, of rather uneven construction, scattered along the road; [together these] bore the name Dutotsburgh.

24 August: We were under way by five o'clock and roamed about with our shotguns. Mr. Wöhler and the son of our innkeeper had gone into the large mountainous forests to hunt for squirrels and other animals. We went down the road toward the Gap.

The old Frenchman Dutot, who had largely forgotten his mother tongue, invited me into his house, where his son and family lived. I was shown various roots to which great curative powers were attributed. One of them, called lion heart, was said to be an infallible cure for snakebite. The plant, *Prenanthes rubicunda,* [has] a tall shaft with many flowers and large, arrow-shaped leaves. The root contains a milky sap. It is cooked in milk; two tablespoonfuls are taken at a time. The swelling is said to disappear even if the root is merely chewed. An old man still living in the vicinity provided the information about this remedy, which he had received from the Delaware Indians, who left this region sixty years ago. (The river and the Indians [are called] Delaware [after] the English Lord Delaware. The original name of those Indians is Lenni-Lenape.) I was shown yet another root said to immediately staunch the most profuse flow of blood from every type of wound; I believe it was snakeroot *(Aristolochia serpentaria).*

We bought a live fox *(Canis vulpes americanus),* which at first we tried to lead home alive on a rope but soon killed and carried. Mr. Wöhler returned home with three nice big squirrels *(Sciurus cinereus).* Then he went out again and returned with a magnificent beetle *(Nicrophorus grandis),* black with orange-colored spots, as well as many salamanders *(Salamandra aurantia),* which he had caught on rocks and tree trunks in the woods. He shot several golden-winged woodpeckers *(Picus auratus)* and a large hairy woodpecker *(Picus villosus).*

[25 August:] We made ready to travel early. A man from the neighborhood brought us a white-tailed deer *(Cervus virginianus)* antler, which I bought. I had obtained three of this kind yesterday. Deer and other large animals had already become rare in these regions, [so] today we intended to go to the Poconos to search for [them]. Our way led in a southwesterly direction, up along Cherry Creek in a gentle, beautiful valley with intermittent [farmsteads,] meadows, thickets, and woods in which one gradually climbed higher and higher. The farmers were occupied with various tasks. All spoke German; only a few individuals were of English descent. Near the farms, many cattle and horses of very good quality, as well as fat hogs, large sheep, chickens, turkeys, geese, and ducks, even guinea hens not infrequently. Turkeys are no longer found here in the wild state; too many hunters comb the forests everywhere.

Today we saw the beautiful large passenger pigeon *(Columba migratoria)* and several birds of prey in a nice oak forest but did not bag anything. We were told that there were many ruffed grouse *(Tetrao umbellatus)* in the forests here. Though elevated, this region was cultivated everywhere and in some areas closely resembled our homeland.

We drove past a pretty lake, about a mile long, surrounded on both sides by beautiful woods. Then we went up a mountain through a shady forest of deciduous timber and pines mixed with hemlock. We followed the wagon on foot with our hunting rifles, but not a single bird could be seen. When we were past the summit, we caught sight of the Poconos. Unbroken forest covers this entire mountain region. We came into continuously higher and more rugged areas; pines and hemlocks more and more gained the upper hand in the deciduous woods. On an elevated plain, we were surrounded as far as the eye could see by woods. Most people [in this area] earned their living from woodworking. We saw a large number of sawmills, which consume the main product of the region. We crossed [a creek with] a very twisting course about five or six times. At one place we found a tanner's house, [with various] hides hung outside. Upon inquiring, we learned that deer were numerous here [so] hunting was productive. Rattlesnakes were very common in this region. We saw the skin of [one] hanging outside a house, and somewhat farther on two stuffed skins of this dangerous snake. They are eaten here to some extent; people believe that, if preserved and prepared in a special way, they are an effective remedy for certain illnesses.

We [proceeded toward] the uninhabited higher, wilder regions, climbing through magnificent dense forest; [the road was] partly overlaid with wood and covered with earth and required a wagon with good springs.

[At] the crest, one perceived an imposing panorama: high ridges rising one after another [all] darkly covered with forest. We soon reached the home of a physician, who showed us a rattlesnake preserved in spirits and sold [it] to us. A half mile farther on we found the inn of a certain Sachs, whose father came from Saxony. We stayed [there] overnight.

26 August: We dispersed early in the woods. Dr. Saynisch stuffed our birds. Mr. Wöhler and a good hunter from the neighborhood, whom we had fetched from 4 miles away just last evening, hunted deer and heath hens. Mr. Moser, [who had accompanied us from Bethlehem,] and I undertook a walk toward a nearby lake, Long Pond. We followed the turnpike road upward, turned off [on] an old [seldom-used] path, [and eventually] found the lake, overgrown with short swamp and reed grass, situated among pine forest and several kinds of beautiful plants. We found no waterfowl at all; the [creek-fed] lake was about a mile long and did not have much open, clear

water. In its vicinity there were only small birds, a sparrow hawk, several swallows, and especially *Fringilla erythrophthalma,* which frequented the low shrubs.

Mr. Moser suddenly called to me; he was close to a rattlesnake. I quickly went over, and he insisted that he had heard rattling sounds, [but] our search [for the source] was futile. Because of dangerous snakes, one must walk with some caution in this thick vegetation; sturdy boots are very necessary, because snakes cannot strike through them.

Upon returning with a large vasculum full of plants, we learned that a black bear *(Ursus americanus)* had been caught in a trap today 6 miles [away] and killed with two shots through the head. Our hunters had found [just] a deer and many heath hens. After lunch they went off again [but bagged little else]. We decided to leave here early in the morning and drive to the inn where the bear had been caught.

27 August: We left Sachs' house at seven o'clock. The so-called turnpike road leads upward directly through the forest but in this region was very bad. We paid a highway toll not far [from] the house where the bear had been caught yesterday. We were shown the hide, which had been nailed up to dry on a gable of the barn; the head had been placed in the trap again as bait; the claws had been thrown away. They regretted not having known that we wanted a bear, and we decided to take a look at [nearby] bear traps early the following morning.

As soon as we crossed a gentle elevation in the forest, we reached a swift brook, the Tobyhanna, over which [there was] a covered bridge 20 to 30 paces long. This stream meanders among lofty woodlands of old Canadian hemlocks intermingled with several kinds of deciduous trees and a dense undergrowth of enormous *Rhododendron maximum* [and] *Kalmia latifolia;* how magnificent it must be when these plants are in bloom! Scarcely a few hundred paces beyond the brook [was the] inn where we stayed today. We sent several hunters out to shoot a bear or a deer; just last week two of the former had been shot quite near this place. We saw the hide of one of them; it measured more than 7 feet in length. We were also offered two live young bears. A hunter brought in several deer antlers, which I bought.

We had not been long in the house before all of us left for the woods. Mr. Bodmer sketched the Tobyhanna bridge and its picturesque surroundings. The rest of us looked for birds and plants, [but] there were very few birds near the house, and none of our four hunters brought in anything. We were delighted, however, to walk though the wild, primeval forest.

In the afternoon Mr. Moser joined us. He had found several salamanders of a variety of *[Salamandra] aurantia* and brought some nice plants along. The hunters brought several birds, [including] an old pheasant hen *(Tetrao umbellatus)*, so far advanced in molting that we could not use it for the collection.

28 August: In the morning, drizzling rain. At eight o'clock the hunters went out to check the bear traps. At ten o'clock we went to the house where the bear had been caught the day before yesterday to see the bear trap. The owner of the house took his rifle [and] led us to the trap. After struggling through [a dark, wet forest and] several areas with blackberries and other bushes, we came down to the place where the bear had been caught. On a somewhat cleared spot, the trap stood between young hemlocks. It was a genuine deadfall made of heavy trunks in such a way that a young bear [could] be captured in it alive. The trap was [completely] concealed with branches, and all [its] parts retained their bark. The head of the recently caught bear had been placed in the trap as bait. We wanted to have it, and the man therefore took it out and fastened the animal's lungs in its place. Then we returned, delighted by our excursion into this bear wilderness [so near] human habitation.

In the afternoon our hunters returned but brought nothing with them. Later, for two and three-quarter dollars, I bought another hide of a bear that had been killed 15 miles from here last week. The hunters found four bears together in the blueberries and shot two of them, the old female and a young one; if they had had dogs, they would have gotten all of them. That morning we had eaten some of the bear meat and had found it similar to mutton.

29 August: At about nine o'clock in the morning, we left [our] inn and began our journey to Mauch Chunk. The entire region, far and wide, was nothing but beautiful, wild forest, a very dense mixture of hemlocks, pines, maples (already [turning] red), [and] beautiful tall beeches; nothing was lacking but a good black bear to perfect my delight [in] this sublime [country]. After a few miles we reached a sizable clearing in the forest, where the village Stoddartsville on the Lehigh was situated, [with] several attractive houses. One then again climbed a hill and continued through dense, lofty forest, where several small, nameless creeks flowed among picturesquely wild tree trunks. At an inn, called Bock's Inn for its former owner, we refreshed ourselves

and watered the horses. [Later] we reached Shades Creek, where there was a sawmill. On the house we saw [many] white-tailed deer antlers hanging. We stopped and bought four antlers, which were immediately tied below the carriage.

We traveled over considerable elevations, [viewing] peak after peak and ridge after ridge succeeding one another. The highest of these Pocono peaks is the so-called Pimple Hill, near Sachs' house, where we spent the night of 25 August.

We presently reached a place that, to a certain extent, is a dividing line, for here one suddenly has a view far into the deep Wyoming Valley in which the Susquehanna flows, and to the rear, a wild mountain and forest view of the Allegheny Mountains far into the distance. Unfortunately, this grand panorama has not been sketched. [At this point] one begins to descend the slope toward the Susquehanna, a very long declivity with great variety, where the forest becomes more and more intermingled and inviting [as] pine trees give way to deciduous timber.

Descending somewhat more than halfway down the mountain, [we] reached a place where travelers [look down on a] magnificent panorama! The broad, extensive valley was full of villages and individual habitations alternating pleasantly with forest and field. The river flowed through its entire length. Right at our feet, at its midpoint, [was] the inviting town of Wilkes-Barre, into the streets of which one could see. One easily understands that this valley was once a dense primeval forest, for everywhere fields [are] intersected by strips of forest; one can only regret that scarcely a trace of the earlier primeval condition of the land and its inhabitants exists.

After we had enjoyed the grand view for a while, we continued our journey and soon reached a lone inn, where we purchased a live rattlesnake. This snake had been in a box for three weeks and had eaten nothing at all; therefore, its rattling, when provoked, was very feeble. We bought it for two and one-half dollars—it was very large and beautiful—and placed it in a pot filled with grain spirits in which it was transported to Wilkes-Barre.

The hamlet or town [of] Wilkes-Barre has about 1,200 inhabitants, three churches, and rather regular, unpaved streets. [There are] farmers, artisans, storekeepers, merchants, and colliery owners ([the mines were] located west of the road we followed down the mountain). The coal formation extends for 14 miles along the course of the Susquehanna Valley and then stretches across other mountains. A new canal for shipping coal has been [begun] but is not yet completely finished. Its purpose is to connect the mines with [larger waterways. Eventually] the Pennsylvania Canal will [have] Baltimore as its main port. The inn in Wilkes-Barre, where we stopped, was run by a German, a certain Christ, who called himself "Doctor." It seemed just as inadvisable to entrust oneself to his medical knowledge as to his cuisine.

In the afternoon we continued our journey after we had placed our fine rattlesnake in a cask. Instead of following the usual road on the valley floor, we turned left toward the wooded mountains and scarcely an hour later reached a wild, densely wooded ravine where Solomon's Creek, rushing wildly over rocks in the dense, dark forest, came roaring down. Since there was no inn here, we still had 3 miles to go that evening, [to] the crest of the mountain, which proved to be very trying.

The road climbed along the left mountain wall of Solomon Creek in dense forest over rocky ground. To the right, one was always close to the precipice. Two coaches could not pass each other. Fortunately wagons travel infrequently in this wilderness. We climbed higher and higher. The road was very overgrown [and] we found rocks and large stones on [it]; it required all the alertness of our driver, Wöhler, to keep from turning over. We continued driving upward, and to our delight, the moon emerged to illuminate our lonely dark path.

When we were rather near the summit of the mountain, the road divided and we had to make a choice. Fortunately, we succeeded in taking the correct road. At nine o'clock, in a small clearing, we caught sight of a friendly light glimmering. We found a shabby house where two women, one old and haggard, the other somewhat younger but very thin and tall, sat smoking small clay pipes. They were astonished not a little by our late visit, but the fire was immediately rekindled [to heat] water for potatoes and coffee. The owner of the house was named Wright, and only English was spoken there. He was away. Our supper was finished in an hour, and then, with our clothes on, we lay down on beds in a large atticlike room; [they] were double beds, as was almost always the case in this country. The night passed quickly.

30 August: At six o'clock, while it was still cool, we continued our journey through the wooded mountain range. Our host's brother, John Wright, lived 3 miles [away] in a wild little valley in a large wilderness. We [planned] to have breakfast there. The dew had thoroughly moistened the plants, and the coolness was pleasant. Frogs and toads were moving about. We caught three

tiger frogs *(Rana halecina)* and also some common toads, mostly young ones, a few of which were put into the vascula, from which some of them later escaped in our carriage, where they hopped about with large leaps.

At John Wright's house, his wife was at home alone with their small boy. She made us excellent coffee and breakfast. In this remote area everything was very clean and neat. We learned through conversation with her that she was of German descent and born in Tamaqua (part of the coal region, not far from Tuscarora). She lived in a rather roomy log house, where there were a fireplace and an iron stove, yet she said it was sometimes very cold in the house during winter, since it was still not finished properly on the inside.

We reached the Nescopeck Valley, 11 miles distant from our overnight quarters, in five hours. The approach to this valley was a poor, partly stony, seldom traveled road [with] several small plank bridges over [creeks]; some were very dilapidated and dangerous for the horses. We [saw no] human beings or habitations. We looked for animals but caught sight of only a few birds and several frogs. *Gerardia quercifolia* and *pedicularia* grew here abundantly; several varieties of *Rhus, Vaccinium,* etc. We could travel only slowly in these wooded mountains, [so] the journey in this monotonous region lacked variety and was boring.

We finally descended into the Nescopeck Valley and found ourselves at the mill of the miller Bug, who was of German descent. Here we were refreshed with milk and brandy. We watered the horses and conversed somewhat with the miller. Then we traveled straight across the valley and, on the other side, up a wooded mountain, where, [at] the top, we reached an inn that was 18 miles from Wilkes-Barre. From there one crossed a gentle valley and Little Nescopeck Creek [and] climbed a tall mountain wall, [Buck Mountain]. [We] soon reached the highway (turnpike road), which our road joined at a right angle, leading from Berwick in the Susquehanna Valley to Mauch Chunk.

Scarcely a quarter of an hour [later] we found ourselves at the inn of a certain Anders, of German descent. We had lunch and the horses received fodder. It was here that someone recently owned a live young bear, which had been sold to a traveler only a short time ago. We had hoped in vain to find it still [there]. The innkeeper had caught the old bear in an iron trap and then, on three successive days, had caught the she-bear's three cubs.

From here the road led straight through woodland, past Pismire [Ridge].

Farther on we noticed a beautiful rattlesnake lying in the middle of the road, but too late, since one of our wagon wheels had already crushed its head. It had, to be sure, already been killed but would have provided an interesting head for our collections, if our wheel had not accidentally destroyed just that part of it. Dr. Saynisch placed the snake in a natural position, coiled up on the side of the road [where] it would certainly fool a passerby, and presumably it was killed again. [We eventually ascended Broad Mountain,] the highest of the area's mountains. The road led at an angle upward, and [we] climbed for a long time. At the top, the road continued on the ridge of the mountain until descending to just as great a depth into the Nesquehoning Valley. The [valley] is broad, surrounded by high, mountain walls, [its] floor covered everywhere with dark forests, except for small cultivated patches. On the southern wall, [in the distance,] a railroad descended from one of the collieries of the Mauch Chunk Company into the valley of the [Lehigh] and then turned to the right, toward Mauch Chunk.[2] As [we] approached the floor and end of the valley, [we] passed Nesquehoning [Creek] and turned left into the picturesque Lehigh Valley. The [Lehigh River] emerges on the left from an extremely wild, deep mountain valley with dark forests. [Its] surface gleams, hidden beneath tall picturesque oaks, beeches, and chestnuts; this view is one of the most attractive wild forest scenes in Pennsylvania.

[We headed for] the town of Mauch Chunk on the [Lehigh, with its] well-known anthracite collieries. All the buildings [there] belonged almost exclusively to the [mining] company. The [river was] filled with small rafts and boats intended for the use of the colliery. On the banks, large supplies of beams, boards, etc., all of it material for the mines. Buildings of various kinds, such as warehouses, stores, stables, an inn, and the like, had been erected. Barges were being built there to carry away the coal on the Mauch Chunk Canal, which begins near this town and flows past Bethlehem. In short, the production of coal provides a most interesting drama for travelers. It was already dark when we arrived [and] took lodging at the inn, which the coal company had also had built.

31 August: At eight o'clock our group set out to [see] Mauch Chunk. Only the smallest part of the town was located in the [Lehigh] Valley, where our inn was. The largest section was a narrow street of small wooden houses extending for about a mile into the lateral valley from which Mauch Chunk Creek emerged to join the [Lehigh]. Various day laborers and other persons

lived there. This whole town [had] developed since the local coal deposits—9 miles away on the mountain top—began to be worked.

Because coal removal at that elevation was difficult, a railroad was built down to Mauch Chunk. On this railroad, coal wagons, fastened together [and] controlled by a driver, coasted down and then were pulled up again by mules. [There were] three trains of fifteen cars [each]; forty-five cars [total]. Behind these three groups was [another train] of seven cars; in each of these there were four mules. The mules descended as rapidly as the coal; when the coal cars were emptied, [the mules] were hitched up to pull them back up again. This was done five times a day. The 9-mile railroad had iron rails fastened to parallel wooden ties. There was one disadvantage: to limit expenditures, [only] a single track was laid, so ascending and descending cars used the same track, [and] accidents could easily occur. In order to lay a double track—one for ascending and another for descending cars— one would have to remove [more] of the mountain face, since the road is cut into the mountain wall, and this would have greatly increased costs. At several wide spots, where the area permitted, turnouts were constructed. Double tracks were found there.

From the Mauch Chunk Creek valley, we climbed [a] steep path in great heat and found the railroad stages standing in readiness on the track about 150 feet above the town. These were light, four-wheel carriages with eight seats, open at the sides. They ran on the rails [on] small, [grooved] iron wheels. The driver sat up front and had a horn to give signals. In his other hand he gripped a rod; [when] he pulled back on it, the rod firmly pressed a wooden device against the wheel, [and] the friction became so strong that the wagon was first slowed down and finally, if so desired, brought to a stop. Since the coal cars were expected at any moment from the mines, we had to wait, for one must avoid meeting them on the track. We sat on our seats

Fig. 1. Maximilian. Mauch Chunk railroad carriage or stage; view of wheel flange ('b'). Ink.

on the stage. Two such carriages are attached to each other by means of a short iron bar, and two horses were hitched up [to] pull them, [not] from the front but from the side of the wagon beside the track. Finally we heard, "They're coming. We hear them." And soon we, too, heard a distant sound of rolling wheels and saw the black train approaching in the distance. Four to five hundred paces after the first train of cars, the second one followed, then the third, equally distant, and [then the] seven wagons [carrying the] mules, standing very calmly with their heads forward.

A [coal] car [can carry] 2 tons of coal. Forty-five cars carrying 90 tons of coal travel each time, and this, five times daily, amounts to 450 tons or 25,200 bushels of coal a day.

It made a strange impression when the cars and the mule-troop train approached and rolled past extremely rapidly. As soon as [the train] was gone, our grays started out briskly, and we traveled upward at a fast trot, something that can be accomplished only on rails. The railroad follows the high mountain wall through woodland, [and] the valley to our left afforded a wild romantic view: high [forested] mountains enclosed it everywhere.

At midpoint we stopped to wait for cars assumed to be approaching. Having arrived on the summit, we immediately went to [the] inn, where we cooled off [with] some refreshments. As soon as we had rested somewhat, we again boarded the stages and [went] down the slight slope of the railroad to the colliery, about ten minutes from the inn. Near a deep excavation of the upper sandstone layer one enters the pits, [each measuring] perhaps 300 [by] 150 paces [and] about 30 feet deep; completely open on top. One hundred and twelve men work in these mines. One can see the coal, glistening and gleaming, of better quality in some places than in others. Some of it is dislodged with [gun]powder, some with crowbars, [and it is] broken up with pickaxes and scooped into coal cars (wagons). All around the pit, high heaps of rubble have collected; like promontories, [the heaps have] extended farther and farther outward.

In some places there are impressions of prehistoric plants, perhaps palms and ferns, among which we found some interesting specimens. Dr. Saynisch took great pains to find good samples of local fossils for me; he is a mineralogist, [and] we [were soon] laden with beautiful anthracite and rock samples. We boarded the stage again to ride down to Mauch Chunk. We did not need horses; the driver pushed the wagon forward a few feet [and] swung himself onto his seat, and [we went] faster than a horse can run at its swiftest gallop. In a period of seventeen minutes, we covered a large part of the distance without stopping. We had to halt to let the returning coal cars pass [and] then continued rapidly.

At about six o'clock, we left Mauch Chunk [and] rode for a long time on a road along the [Lehigh. We] finally reached Lehighton, a village located very close to the mouth of the Mahoning Valley. The [Moravian] Brethren founded a small settlement [nearby in 1746] that bore the name Gnaden-hütten. The Indians later attacked this town, burned down the houses, and murdered [eleven] of the Brethren. Even now one can see the gravestone that bears their names. The congregation at Gnadenhütten was not reestab-lished, but there were still individual farmers living on the land that belongs to the Brethren.

We continued driving along the side of the mountain through wild forest. [When] night fell the moon revealed a deep cleft [to our right], the Lehigh Gap, where the inn was located in which we wished to spend the night.

1[–4] September: At about eight o'clock, we left the Gap and drove a mile away from the river, over intermittently gentle hills. Several miles farther on [we came to] Berlin [or Berlinsville], a village. One is amused and surprised to see the names of European metropolises in these regions, when one sees how wretched such towns are by comparison. [We continued on, through] Cherryville, the valley of Hokendauqua Creek, [and then] the village Kreidersville, named for the first settler. From here to Bethlehem there were still 7 miles. In a sparse woods to the left of the road, there was a one-story meeting house of a religious sect [called Mennonites]. Buckwheat was in bloom everywhere in this area. At one o'clock in the afternoon, we safely reached Bethlehem again. Dreidoppel had been sick again but was on the way to recovery. We prepared to pack [our] natural history specimens [by] ordering crates and doing the necessary preliminary tasks. On the evening of the fourth, my cases and trunks finally arrived, of which we had been deprived for so long and the lack of which had been so palpable; they were all in good condition.

5–6 September: I was surprised by the visit of Mr. Gebhard from New York; he had persevered there during the cholera but had suffered some indisposi-tions. Cholera was still present in that city, but of a far milder character. I rode to Nazareth, 10 miles away, with Mr. Gebhard and Pastor Seidel. The road led through cultivated areas, woods, and Hecktown, which bears that name for a peculiar reason, which Bernhard of Weimar has already related.[3]

Nazareth is a friendly town with several streets, unpaved, and houses built rather close together. The Brethren had a school for young people here. [There were] 350 inhabitants, an inn, stores, etc., and about sixty young people in the school. [When] we had viewed the main objects of interest in Nazareth, Mr. Gebhard took leave of us to return to New York. We drove back to Bethlehem after buying several additional amphibian rarities.

[10 September:] On Monday, we packed five crates with natural history specimens to be sent to Germany. They contained 34 mammals, 170 birds, 43 turtles, between 40 and 50 snakes, about 40 frogs and toads, etc.

12–13 September: After lunch Mr. Bodmer [retraced some of] the interesting route we had recently taken, [mainly] to complete [unfinished sketches. He] returned from his excursion with a badly injured hand. He [had gone] hunting with a young doctor, because there were many wild doves in the vicinity, and he actually shot one of them. But the powder chamber of the left barrel of the freshly cleaned gun burst and damaged Mr. Bodmer's hand. The ball of his thumb was completely torn open and his hand burned black. The young doctor, [Daniel Broom], bandaged him and brought him back to Bethlehem [that] evening.

14 September 1832: Mr. Bodmer slept somewhat during the night but still had a high fever. Dr. Broom stayed with us until afternoon, and though he had bandaged Mr. Bodmer's hand only three times, he still charged us ten dollars (25 florins).

In the evening, a visit at the home of Pastor Seidel, where I received books in the Delaware language.

15–16 September: Mr. Bodmer spent another night without sleep and in great pain. The bandage had to be removed from his hand. [We continued] preparations for the journey [and made] farewell visits to Mr. von Schweinitz and Pastor Seidel. We agreed that Mr. Bodmer should follow with Dr. Saynisch. I myself intended to depart with Dreidoppel on the 17th.

IV

Journey from Bethlehem in Pennsylvania

to New Harmony on the Wabash

[FROM 17 SEPTEMBER TO 19 OCTOBER 1832]

17 September: [Well before dawn, we boarded the stage from Easton with] several other passengers. It was fully daylight when we reached Allentown, where we changed horses and coaches. From Allentown it was 36 miles to Reading. The region was beautifully cultivated, [with] extensive fields of corn as well as clover and buckwheat. We stopped often at post offices; the large leather mailbag was tossed down, and whatever was supposed to be sent was placed inside. [There were] always a large number of persons sitting in front of the houses, their feet on benches; whoever wished to draw conclusions from this would have to think that Americans were idlers.

Papilio plexippus flew about the fences, and several flights of birds appeared to be getting ready to join the migration south; they were perched together on dead trees. We passed several creeks or small brooks, the names of which elude me. Beautiful white and violet asters; untilled fields completely overgrown with yellow *Solidago* or *Hypericum*. One sees beautiful farmsteads in this region of Pennsylvania. The barns, in particular, are massive, made of limestone, [and] very large; they have stalls underneath with eight to twelve doors and windows, and the upper story of the barn juts out above them. [There were] all kinds of livestock, especially fat pigs with very broad, drooping ears, most of them speckled with round black spots. Rarely did one see rust-red hogs, but they do occur. We saw several beautiful woodlands—oak and walnut trees, also many hickory *(Juglans alba),* which provide the best American wood. Next best is the wood of the white oak *(Quercus alba).* This region has the general appearance of Germany, [but] the ubiquitous, zigzag fences, as well as the tall, slender shape of the trees and the structure of the dwellings, differentiate this landscape from the German.

Toward noon we reached Reading, a rather attractive city of 6,000–7,000 inhabitants on the Schuylkill. There were about 400 Negroes and colored persons here. In the entire state of Pennsylvania there are 37,930 free Negroes and 403 slaves.[1] Cholera had already carried off several persons here, but most of the residents I spoke with did not want to admit this.

I saw the return of a funeral procession in which at least ten women (ladies) rode on horseback. They had saddles with a pommel in front, over which they rested one leg while seated very much to the rear, and wore large hats: a comical caravan. Because the stage that we intended to take to Harrisburg had left two hours ago, I decided to remain here today. One of the ladies who had come with us had given me an orange and a peach, which I imprudently ate and immediately felt abdominal pains. I still felt unwell when I left by stage the following morning at eleven thirty.

[18 September:] The crowding inside the coach was great, for we had eleven passengers, including two women and four children, whose screaming in the very oppressive heat was unbearable. Since I had much baggage, I had to pay a dollar more. The region from Reading onward had beautiful farmsteads with large barns, big orchards (often with clover in them), and [livestock] resting in the shade. The trees were heavy with apples. These thrive, but not plums. Peaches do well. In Reading I saw whole wagons full of them, with people crowding around while children stole some.

We passed Cacoosing Creek and reached the village of Womelsdorf, where we ate lunch. On the way to Lebanon we crossed Swatara [Creek], which empties into the Susquehanna. The region around Lebanon was pleasantly varied, [with] forests [and] wooded mountains in the distance. When evening came, I joined the driver on the coach box. The lanterns on the stage were lighted. Cicadas and crickets were chirping loudly. Several hours later we saw a large number of lights shining ahead of us in a shallow hollow: Harrisburg, our destination.

Harrisburg is a small city of 5,000 inhabitants, with broad streets that cross at right angles. The houses were very diverse, some attractive and made of brick, others low and made of wood. At the inn where we stayed, there was a large square, where the market building was located, as in most Pennsylvania cities. The statehouse, with two adjacent buildings, was located on a slight incline near the city by the [Pennsylvania] Canal, and everything around it was neatly trimmed and enclosed. The building [had] a dome on top supported by columns; from that dome one had a beautiful view.

Harrisburg is the capital of Pennsylvania and the residence of the governor, at the present time [George] Wolf. There were [about] 500 blacks, i.e., colored persons, in this city. There were Germans everywhere, including a skilled German physician. Because of our indisposition, I turned to an English doctor, since I did not know about the other one, and we spent three days here quite indisposed and fatigued.

21–23 September: At nine o'clock in the evening, we left Harrisburg on the stage and continued our journey in the usual manner until daybreak, [when] we found ourselves in the hamlet of Mexico, forty miles from Harrisburg. We soon reached the [Juniata] county seat, Mifflintown, a market town or large village, where we delivered the mail to the post office and changed [horses]. Several persons spoke German. A rather impressive courthouse was just being built. The town [was close to] the Juniata, the valley of which we followed. [The river] had wooded banks and about the same volume and form as the Lehigh. After passing Kishacoquillas Creek, we [were] near a gently widening area of the valley [and] Lewistown, where we had breakfast. The place was a significant market town with several very attractive homes. The fields were being plowed and harrowed. All through Pennsylvania farmers used only horses for field work; I never saw oxen used for this purpose. Very many fine horses are raised here. Beyond Lewistown [was] a hilly region [with] alternating forests and fields. The woods were already markedly changing color: the maples, several *Crataegus,* the dogwood, and the *Rhus typhinum* were the first to turn red. The wild nut trees, particularly the hickory, beautifully yellow, [added] picturesque diversity. The oaks were not yet changing color so markedly. There was forest all around the mountains, and [in it, we began] to climb the first ridge of the Alleghenies.

The road angled upward along a splendid mountain face, [the forest] beginning to display beautiful autumn colors. The grapevines were really large, [their] foliage already light yellow, the small blue grapes a pleasing contrast. The *Hedera quinquefolia* [was] especially magnificent, its scarlet red, decorative tendrils creeping along the white rock rubble on the forest floor. Near the road a beautiful *Tetrao umbellatus* flew away. Otherwise we saw almost no birds at all here; most of them had migrated.

The narrow, rocky road led us down into the Juniata Valley. The [Pennsylvania] Canal, which flowed on the opposite side at a higher level than the river, was [at this place] conveyed across the Juniata [on an aqueduct]; just a little water seeped out through its floor. The canal continued to run beside the river, now on this side, now on that. Somewhat farther on was the town of Huntingdon, located 90 miles from Harrisburg. The stage stopped there. We had supper at a rather good inn on the bank of the [Little] Juniata [and] then proceeded on. So many new passengers got on here that the seating was most uncomfortable; furthermore, we had to travel all night, through dense forest, an open field along the [Pennsylvania] Canal, on which work is still being done, [and] then over the highest ridges of the Allegheny Mountains (about 2,400 feet above sea level). We suffered greatly in the coach, because of the crowding. As day approached, we [came to] the market town Ebensburg, where I stayed to await [Dr. Saynisch and Bodmer and] to recover from the fatiguing night journeys.

On 24 September we went hunting in a true primeval forest: enormous hemlocks, beeches, chestnut trees, birches, and tall maples formed a dark wilderness so full of fallen, rotting, ancient tree trunks that one [had to] make wide detours and great leaps in order to make any progress. On [the] old rotting trunks there was a world of mosses, fungi, *Oxalis,* and ferns; even young trees—beeches, maples, tulip trees, and others—had sprouted on top of them.

In the afternoon I [went] toward the south where there were said to be many pheasants, [although] I found only woodpeckers and small birds. Several swampy ditches and small streams traversed this forest. I had to clamber or scramble over them on fallen trunks, sometimes with great exertion, in the course of which, articles of clothing did not remain in the best condition. I wanted to obtain the pileated woodpecker, and I succeeded, too; their call was audible at a great distance and echoed far and wide in the lonely wilderness. I spent the evening, [as] always, writing by candlelight. Dreidoppel went pheasant hunting with a local resident [on 25 September].

26 September: The morning stage was delayed quite a while, but it finally brought us Messrs. Bodmer and Saynisch. Since they were tired, they took our rooms while we departed with the mail coach in their place. The forest in this elevated region was wild and mostly unbroken. The road crossed it in a straight line. Here and there we came to small log cabins where settlers not very long ago had cleared the forest and planted small fields. Raccoon hides hung outside their cabins, pegged and stretched out to dry. Seven miles from Ebensburg, still on high hills, we reached the boundary of the so-called Alleghenies. The forest changed in character; oaks, chestnuts, black locusts, and other trees replaced hemlocks and beeches. The region

became more open, the forests less dense. We proceeded up and down size-able hills [and] noticed several new trees. In the valley, green alder (*Alnus* [sp.]) and aspen *(Populus tremuloides); in the thickets, gum trees (Nyssa sylvatica)* with scarlet red foliage. The cucumber tree *(Magnolia acuminata),* completely green, still retained its large leaves; its fruits were a beautiful red.

Many freight wagons moved along the road. Before us a broad, deep valley in which the Conemaugh River flowed. [We traveled] through in-termittently open areas, [passed] Armagh, a village, [and] soon saw the [Conemaugh Water] Gap, through which the Conemaugh and the [Penn-sylvania] Canal pass. From here on, the road was bad: stones, deep ruts, and tree trunks [often] in our way. Farmers' habitations were not numerous, small, and poor besides. Many Irishmen were said to live here; they were not praised, because they were not good farmers and often drunkards. The Germans, who often had well cultivated fields here, were [more admired].

Eight miles from Armagh we watered our horses [again]; they had done very heavy pulling in the mountains. In the woods we saw [locust damage] everywhere, on all kinds of trees. Four weeks ago, *[Cicada septem-decem]* were so numerous here that people say a human voice could barely be heard above their din. After a while we reached a gradual elevation from which [we could] see Blairsville ahead, [in a] wide, beautiful valley.

Blairsville is an attractive little place with some very nice homes and good inns. We obtained fresh horses and quickly departed. The region is hilly, much of it cultivated. We met many gentlemen on horseback, as well as farmers' wives with big black hats. Some were smoking pipes. At nightfall we reached [Delmont] and, after midnight, Pittsburgh.

[27–28 September:] Pittsburgh, on the Ohio at the junction of the Allegheny and Monongahela, is a rather old, sprawling, but not particularly handsome city. Since there were extensive bituminous coal deposits in the immediate vi-cinity, this fuel was very inexpensive here and everyone burned it. [So] the whole region, the entire Ohio Valley, lay in a dark haze of smoke, and over the city it was as dense as in England. The smoke gave the buildings a dark, gloomy appearance. The streets were dirty and poorly illuminated at night. Pittsburgh had many imposing buildings and was a very busy, lively man-ufacturing and commercial city. There were iron rolling mills (one of these was located close to our inn), glassworks where glass panes were made, cot-ton-weaving mills [powered] by steam engines, etc.

I [stayed] at the Exchange Hotel. I had letters of introduction [to several prominent, helpful citizens, one of whom] suggested a journey to Economy, a remarkable separatist colony from Württemberg, which was presently established 18 miles from here on the [east] bank of the Ohio.[2]

29 September: We left Pittsburgh at eight o'clock in the morning [and] traveled over the large Allegheny bridge. First there were suburbs, then brickworks and other industrial plants, and finally country homes, including some very nice ones surrounded by pretty trees and gardens. We drove along the right bank of the Ohio Valley [until] we reached the district of Economy, which we recognized from the well-cultivated fields. The pleasing town, with neat, pretty houses and a church made of brick, [was] on the broad, level floor of the beautiful valley. Beyond it, there were wooded mountains with the Ohio flowing before them. We took lodging in a fine, attractive inn. Everyone greeted us in a very cordial and friendly manner, and we felt at home among our countrymen. Several large factory buildings were being constructed, including a cloth manufacturing plant powered by a steam engine, as well as a mill and a cotton factory. Silk, too, was cultivated here, [and] people wore clothing made from homegrown silk as well as from other materials. All necessities were produced here, and a significant agricultural undertaking, including farming and essential livestock production, was also carried on.

[In 1804] Mr. Rapp came from Swabia to America with 600 to 700 immigrants and at that time had very little wealth. He founded three settlements, one after the other: the first, Old Harmony [now Harmony, Pennsylvania], not far from the Ohio; the second, New Harmony, on the Wabash River, which flows into the Ohio, [was] sold to a certain [Robert] Owen. [Then they] moved back to [Pennsylvania], where they founded their present settlement. The entire society is said to own this land and all its produce in common, but old Rapp and his adopted son [Frederick] manage it all and never give an accounting of their administration. This seemed somewhat dictatorial, but everything appeared well ordered and practical. During the day, one saw no one, not even children, on the streets. Everyone was engaged in a useful occupation. They received no wages but, on the other hand, got all they needed free, and nowhere did one see want. Mr. Rapp erected a large building with a sizeable assembly hall located on the second floor [for communal] festivities [and] musical entertainment. On the lower floor of this building, a natural history collection was displayed in three rooms. It contained very interesting things, including minerals and shells;

among the former, pure gold from Carolina, as well as native and foreign fossils. The animals included a huge elk [and] white-tailed deer; [as miscellanea,] Indian objects, Chinese illustrations, etc.

After we had examined all these noteworthy things and had been conducted through the factories, we proceeded to Mr. Rapp's house and were received in a very friendly manner by his family, all dressed in customary Württemberg rural fashion. They told us they never deviate from the old German customs: "We want to remain Germans." The elder Rapp, of venerable appearance, [had] whitish gray hair and a long beard but [also] a brisk, vigorous bearing for his age. We had supper with them, drank very good wine produced here in America, and then were entertained with an evening of music provided by six or seven young girls who sang to the accompaniment of a young man, a schoolmaster.

30 September: Sunday. At nine o'clock we attended church. The men sat to the right of the preacher, women to the left, old people in front, younger people more to the rear. Mr. Rapp's family sat at the very front.

The church had neither organ nor pulpit. When we were all seated, the elder Rapp entered with firm stride. He wore a dark blue suit, a robe, a pointed blue cloth cap on his head, and a hat over that. With a Bible under his arm, he strode firmly down the aisle and sat down at his table, on an elevated platform. He put on his glasses, announced a hymn, and the singing began without organ accompaniment. After [that], the congregation stood for prayer, and then Mr. Rapp delivered a sermon on a passage from the Bible, delivered quite prosaically and in a manner suitable for rural people, with dramatic images and expressions and accompanied by powerful, fiery gesticulations. When [the service was] concluded, the congregation filed out, first the women, [then] the men.

We ate lunch in the inn and then visited Mr. Rapp's garden, where he cultivates beautiful varieties of fruit and excellent wine grapes, as well as several citrus plants, including lemons and Seville oranges. [Gardenias were] still blooming; a magnolia bore ripe seeds, which I took with me. We had a very cordial farewell from the Rapp family, and in the afternoon, at about six o'clock, we again arrived in Pittsburgh. In the meantime Dr. Saynisch [and] Mr. Bodmer [had arrived and] had acquired some noteworthy natural history specimens.

On 1 October an excursion was made on the Ohio with a fisherman (a German from Swabia who had completely forgotten his native language) to look

for the pretty river mussels *(Unio);* Dr. Saynisch brought back at least sixteen different species of [them]. The fisherman brought [us] two species of
most interesting animals: the softshell turtle *(Trionyx* or *Aspidonectes)* and a
big, dark-brown aquatic salamander from the Ohio (listed by Dr. Harlan of
Philadelphia [as] *Menopoma alleganensis*), of which we obtained young and
old specimens so that I could prepare a complete description. Mr. Bodmer
[made] very good drawings of them.

2–5 October: Cool, damp weather; almost all of us had head colds or rheumatic
sensations because of [it]. We worked on the descriptions and sketches of
the [salamanders, mussels, and other specimens collected by or for us].

6 October: This morning, beautiful, bright sunshine. Today we packed 900 river
mussels *(Unio)* from the Ohio, eight softshell turtles, thirty-four salamanders *(Menopoma),* four proteus *(Menobranchus),* one sturgeon *(Acipenser),*
and several birds, which Dr. Saynisch will take back to Bethlehem. In the
afternoon Mr. Bodmer went to Economy with Dr. Saynisch. I accompanied
them to the opposite side of the Allegheny and then went into a nearby
forest, where I collected seeds.

7 October (Sunday): In the evening Dr. Saynisch and Mr. Bodmer returned; they
had seen many interesting things. We made preparations for our departure.

On the morning of 8 [October], at five thirty, the stage arrived, and we took leave
of Dr. Saynisch, who [was] returning [to Bethlehem] and from there to
Europe. We drove to the bank of the Ohio, and the coach, with its four light
grays, was [ferried across] the river. Having arrived on the other side, we
found ourselves at the base of a high, wooded mountain, which the road
climbed at an angle. *Hedera quinquefolia,* with its scarlet red leaves, climbed
tree trunks and made red columns of them. The forest was beautifully colored. The slender beeches were bright green with yellow tips; the maples
vermilion red or yellow; the gum tree *(Nyssa)* vermilion red; the dogwood
beautifully adorned with red berries; the walnut trees lemon- or orange-yellow; many other trees still a bright green—a magnificent mixture of color,
much more vivid and varied than in Europe!

On the summit we emerged from the forest [and passed by croplands
and flimsily built houses]. Seven miles from Pittsburgh, we changed horses,
[and again at] Canonsburg, a town where we were gaped at by curious onlookers. We drove on, sometimes through fields, sometimes through forests.
The region was flatter. [At] Washington, a market town, we ate lunch [and
then went on to] Claysville, a small market town. [We] soon crossed the

Pennsylvania border and were in [West] Virginia; a fence running straight across the valley and up along the hill marked the boundary. The valley became deep and narrow. [As] we drove downward along a creek, dusk fell, soon replaced by beautiful moonlight. The evening was very warm and pleasant. Farther down we crossed a bridge [near a] monument built in honor of Henry Clay, who is famous in the United States because he was very instrumental in building this road.[3] We could see to our left into a valley, where [we] caught sight of the Ohio, on the bank of which Wheeling was situated, where we took quarters for the night.

Wheeling was a city growing very fast, [with] businesses and stores of all kinds. One saw many Negroes and mulattos. The river was very narrow here, somewhat like the Moselle, though not so wide. Several steamboats were being built, and on the morning of 9 October, two ships arrived, one of which would depart that afternoon. We [booked passage]— twelve dollars per person to Cincinnati (400 miles).

The [Nile] had two decks. On the upper one aft, the ladies' cabin. Before it, the large room, where there were now only immigrants. Underneath this was our cabin, the gentlemen's cabin, with sixteen bedsteads. Small steamboats like these are dangerous. They are stoked heavily, and [with] high pressure, there is always the danger that the boiler will explode [when] the ship is stopped to take on passengers.

Our departure was delayed until five o'clock, when we finally left. The channel was narrow, very little water now, [but] everywhere we saw uprooted *Platanus* trunks, lying since the big flood in March, when there was water standing in the lower floors of houses in Wheeling. The evening was pleasant after the great heat of the day. Magnificent moonlight. After supper we sat for a long time on the stern deck of the ship, where one is safest. It was not very pleasant to sleep that night in the cabin with fifteen persons in two rows, one above the other.

10 October: During the night we had lain at anchor; at dawn we continued our journey. Along the bank there were small individual cottages. We stopped and took on wood, [which] was piled up in many places for the steamships. Traces of Ohio floods: broken trunks, piled-up trees, deeply eroded clay banks. The sandbars were yellow from a plant that I could not examine. Floating wood bumped against the ship. The region was beautiful, and the view up the river was excellent. Here several beautiful round islands appeared ahead, all of them covered with tall, picturesque forest. The left bank

is [West] Virginia; the right one, the state of Ohio. The wind that had arisen blew leaves down from the trees and into the river, which became covered with them. Tall *Platanus,* birches, elms. Small habitations in the old forest. Entire mountain walls where the timber was stripped away, then other places completely reddened by sumac.

Extremely narrow channel of the Ohio between the right bank and a sandbar.

We put in on the right side along the bank and took on wood. Mr. Bodmer and Dreidoppel went ashore, and when the bell gave the signal, they returned with the fruits of the pawpaw. [It] grew copiously here, 20 to 40 feet high, with a large leaf and a fruit like a small cucumber. Inside it [were] 12 thick black seeds and a whitish, juicy pulp, which did not taste bad. Many persons find its odor unpleasant. After lunch there was a heavy downpour, very desirable for us, [hoping] the river might rise. The hamlet or village [of] Marietta, [lay] to the right, where the Muskingum River emptied into the Ohio. The place was small but [had] several good brick houses [and] two churches. The March flood of the Ohio must have been terrible; steamboats docked at the third story of houses in Marietta.[MI]

We anchored off the right bank for the night; after supper I made some entries in my diary. During the night, a violent storm with heavy rain. It rained into the upper bunks in the ship.

11 October: In the morning the weather [was] better but very cool. The appearance of the banks was the same as yesterday: constantly dense forest, settlements here and there. We soon reached the Little Hocking River, [on] the Ohio side. Ducks, particularly teal, flew past. Flocks of birds were moving south. We met several flatboats, rectangular boxes made of planks [that] go

---

[MI] Unfortunately, our stay was too short for me to get out and see the largest feature worthy of note in this region: the old Indian ruins, of which [Benjamin] Smith Barton, in his [1787] work *Observations on Some Parts of Natural History,* part 1, [30–35,] London, provided a description and diagram. At that time they still stood out in the open on the plain between the Muskingum and the Ohio. Since then, Marietta has been built right on this spot; a part of the old remains was located in the town, but part of it had been plowed under, and with each passing year, more of it will be [lost]. It is sad that the government does not have sufficient appreciation to preserve such things. It has likewise permitted the extermination and expulsion of still-existing Indians. The Americans have an appreciation only for money or corn and hogs. [The complex of Marietta earthworks and mounds is prehistoric, probably of late Adena to Hopewell construction. For a modern description, see Morgan, *Prehistoric Architecture,* 14–15.]

from Pittsburgh to New Orleans, loaded with all kinds of goods. [They] are often wrecked [but] are insured.

The river channel [at this point] was no wider than 40 paces. The state of Ohio was said to be so fertile that there was no need to fertilize the fields. [Its] valley was very wide here. Large cornfields.

The ship lay to off the right bank. We went ashore for a short while [and] brought back pawpaw branches, a pretty *Aster,* and *Asclepias* pods. Mr. Bodmer, whose hand had scarcely healed, went out with the shotgun and found a splendid bird of prey, which he did not get.

[Later that day] we came to Gallipolis, an old French colony where French was still spoken. An attractive little place, which, however, could only be called a village. Right behind [it], magnificent tall beech forest; along the water, more *Platanus.* Pawpaw trees formed a brushy thicket 20 to 30 feet high under the *Platanus,* [like] the rhododendrons in Pennsylvania. Willows *(Salix)* grew in some places in front of and among the *Platanus.* The sun set behind the mountains; beautiful, magnificently clear evening sky! Gleaming surface of the Ohio! We traveled all night long.

12 October: In the morning, dense fog. At eight thirty, sunshine; we weighed anchor. Our poor old ship was only four or five years old but already condemned; the engine [valves] no longer closed. The lower deck measured about 50 to 51 of my paces. It had no room for walking [and] it was dirty.

To the right, Burlington, a small village with a sawmill. The ship struck large rocks along the shore and listed somewhat. The shuddering caused by the ship's engine was so strong that it was almost impossible to write.

To the left, Catlettsburg [and] Big Sandy Creek, the border of [West] Virginia and Kentucky. Banks on both sides, forest with individual settlements [like] Hanging Rock, a small village with few houses [from] where most of the iron implements for the entire river are shipped. Pretty location, wild, with rocks and forest. Wagons drawn by eight oxen pull the iron implements up and down along the high bank. In the evening we cast anchor. We learned that our ship had caught fire near the steam engine [but it] had been quickly extinguished. In the dark several steamships moved past us. They looked magnificent: lights everywhere, sparks flying about as though from a tall furnace. Toward morning our ship ran aground and remained motionless for a long time. At daybreak, rain.

From here on, farms increased. We [landed at] Portsmouth, an attractive market town with a large warehouse for merchants' supplies; many nice brick houses. A crowd of people stood ready with their baggage to join us immediately. On the other hand, many persons went ashore, as we did for a short while. Immigrants arrived with all their possessions. Peasants carted their beds and sacks, but their greatest wealth consisted solely of small children. One saw very comical scenes: Negroes in ridiculous costumes, [like one with] huge earrings [and] a colorful cloth wrapped around his head. Another [had] a large number of chickens, which suddenly got away from him; one was chased into the water and leaped onto the ship.

Several interesting mountain formations rise in this region. Most of the peaks are round, some broad, [a] few pointed. The mountain chain extended down along the river, [which] made numerous bends and afforded scenic views. Woodlands everywhere; extensive farmlands [within them].

13 October: During the night we passed [several] towns [including] Manchester, Aberdeen, [and] Augusta. While we were sitting at the breakfast table, the ship again forcefully struck bottom. The water [was] very shallow. The Little Miami River, 6 miles from Cincinnati, was almost dry. [At] the beginning of the city [there were] intermittent rows of white, mostly attractive houses along the river. Nice, individual farmsteads with weeping willows, gardens, [and] fruit trees. Several factories, workshops, and stores — much life and activity. Many steamships were anchored here, including *Poland, Sylph, Falcon, Baratavia, Champlain, Atalanta, Farmer, Magnolia, L. Rock, Portsmouth,* etc. The city was growing and crowded together.[M2] Because cholera was so prevalent in Cincinnati, we did not stay there but immediately boarded the *Portsmouth,* which departed at once.

After lunch we [crossed] the boundary between Ohio and Indiana. Banks with cultivated fields or forest. On the right bank, 38 miles from Cincinnati, we [saw] the village Rising Sun with several attractive dwellings. During the night we passed Big Bone Lick, where large mammoth bones have been excavated in the black soil. In Férussac's *Bulletin* there was [recently] a notice

---

[M2] I very much regretted being unable to see the various sights of Cincinnati: for example, the museum of Mr. Dorfeuille, in which there were said to be interesting natural history objects. It is really unfortunate that American museums, like European amusement halls, are obliged to acquire often ridiculous and trivial items. Here, for example, [was] a depiction of hell. The Yankees from the country would not come for a visit unless [there were such absurd] objects. [A reference to the Western Museum owned by Joseph Dorfeuille (ca. 1790–1840). Kellogg, "Joseph Dorfeuille." Maximilian visited this museum later; see entry for 17 June 1834.]

regarding a 60-foot-long animal [having been] discovered there, but the entire report was concocted to lure spectators for their money. In Silliman's *American Journal of Science and Arts* [there is] a correct description of these bones as a refutation.

14 October: Very nice morning; bright sunshine. The town [of] Jeffersonville, [Indiana, soon appeared] on the steep right bank. On the left bank, approximately opposite [that] town, the imposing city of Louisville, with 12,000 inhabitants. The *Portsmouth* docked next to the steamship *Rambler*. Negroes took our baggage to the inn (Washington Hotel), where numerous strangers and, as is usually the case here, idle gentlemen filled all the lower rooms and were encamped around the fireplace with their legs up in the air and their hands clasped behind their necks. We were assigned to a miserable little bedroom with two beds; there was no more room anywhere in the house. Because it was too late to leave here today, we [would] depart the following morning.

Louisville has long, straight streets [that] intersect at right angles but are poorly paved and very dirty. The houses were [varied in] size and architectural styles. Most [were] two stories; the newer ones three stories and made of brick. There were fine shops and stores everywhere; here, as in all the United States cities, elegance was a primary concern of the residents. Today was Sunday, and one saw elegant society streaming into the churches, of which there were many, of quite a few different sects. [There were] pretty little coaches for rent here. Among the coachmen for hire, several were Negroes, some of them still slaves. [On the following page] I shall list the number of Negroes in the various states of North America, according to one of the most recent newspapers.[4]

The city of Louisville had only one tolerably good inn, but a company was constructing a large new one (Louisville Hotel) that will cost 50,000 dollars but will not be completed for several years. Cholera had been here but had not yet carried off many victims. In Cincinnati it was further advanced. There was great terror among the residents, who pressed into the pharmacies, had large pitch poultices applied to their abdomens, sniffed camphor, etc.

15 October: In the morning after breakfast I drove in a gig to the [new Oakland] racetrack, about a good half hour from the city. A company had bought the place, was having it equipped, and would hold horse races from time to time, the first of them next week. The place was a mile in circumference and

	Free Negroes	Slaves		Free Negroes	Slaves
Vermont	881	0	Arkansas territory	141	4,376 [4,576]
Indiana	3,629	3	District of		
Massachusetts	7,045	4	Columbia	6,152	6,119
New Hampshire	602	5	Florida territory	844	15,501
Maine	1,171	6	Missouri	569	25,091
Ohio	9,675 [9,657]	6	Mississippi	519	65,159 [65,659]
Rhode Island	3,546 [3,564]	14	Maryland	52,938	102,994
Connecticut	8,047	25	Louisiana	16,710	109,588
Michigan			Alabama	1,572	117,549
territory	261	42 [32]	Tennessee	4,555	144,693
New York	44,869	76	[141,603]		
Pennsylvania	37,930	403	Kentucky	4,917	165,213
Illinois	1,637	747	Georgia	2,486	217,531
New Jersey	18,303	2,245 [2,254]	N. Carolina	19,543	245,601
Delaware	15,885	3,292	S. Carolina	7,921	315,401
	[6,867]		Virginia	47,348	469,757
					2,009,050

[2,009,050] slaves in the land of vaunted liberty!!!

enclosed by tall planks; in the center [there] was a building open above and on the sides for the stockholders of the company and their families. Several other isolated buildings were for the spectators—one for ladies, another for gentlemen, and another for the judges. For the most part, the horses were not big, [and they] seemed partly Arabian but [were] not outstandingly beautiful. They were fed with oats [and] dried corn leaves instead of hay. Negro boys took care of them. These horses belonged to outside owners, [who] paid [fees] according to the number of [horses and] races run. Even though these races are not comparable with the great English races (everything is done in the English manner), they provide a source of entertainment for Louisville.

In the afternoon we went to Portland, the place of embarkation one-half hour from Louisville, where numerous steamboats lay in readiness. The *Water Witch* was the one we boarded. Since the steamboat could not reach shore, we drove into the water in our carriage to reach the ship, as did the baggage carts. The onrush of passengers, carriages, and freight wagons was very great. One had to keep a watchful eye on the baggage.

The captain, Fleischmann, was a very sensible, prudent man of German descent. He no longer spoke much German, but he understood it well. His ship had good, careful engineers. The *Water Witch* was a nice ship of medium size with two decks. On the lower one, the engines and many deck passengers; on the upper one forward, the place where the barkeeper sold his drinks. Behind that, rooms for cargo, the stewards, and the steamboat officers. Then the large cabin with twenty-four beds and long mess tables; [the tables] were taken away at night, and [additional] beds were made on the floor. Behind this cabin, two others for the ladies [and] the captain's family. It was demanded of those (like us) who wished to travel only as far as Mount Vernon that they surrender their beds to passengers who had booked for the entire voyage [to] New Orleans. Mr. Bodmer protested, and we kept our beds. The evening was warm and pleasant, the heat in our cabin very great.

16 October: At eleven thirty we finally departed, after various additional things had been loaded and all kinds of arrangements made. We sailed down the Ohio past New Albany. We halted just a quarter of an hour below [New] Albany; it had been discovered that [something] had broken on our steam engine, and the captain said that we had barely escaped having our ship blown to bits. [While repairs were made,] we went ashore.

The upper half of the rather steep, fifty-foot-high bank incline was overgrown with *Datura,* whose seeds were now ripe, yet there were still some light-violet blossoms. Several beautifully blue *Eupatorium coelestinum* and *Lobelia siphilitica* were blooming among the *Daturas.* On top, among several cornfields with log cabins, was the beginning of a splendid primeval forest of tall beeches, maples, oaks, walnut trees, etc., which extended inland. In the forest [there] were huge trees, especially maple and *Platanus,* which three or four men could not encircle. Twining plants, *Vitis* and *Hedera,* formed long, thick dangling vines and ropes. There were some interesting birds. Mr. Bodmer shot a splendid pileated woodpecker *(Picus pileatus),* a red-bellied *(P. carolinus),* and the smallest one, a downy *(P. pubescens).* There were wild turkeys everywhere. We would have stayed in this beautiful forest for a long time if rain had not driven us back to the ship. Mr. Bodmer and I passed the time by playing casino until eleven o'clock; three other whist games had begun. At seven o'clock in the evening, the ship was again under way.

17 October: Early in the morning [we] reached Brandenburg, a village on the left

bank. [We passed by] fine, dark forest, cultivated fields picturesquely set in clearings surrounded by tall trees like colonnades and pillars, [and] beautiful long islands, partly overgrown with willows. In the afternoon we [went by] Stephensport on the left; opposite, a village named Rome. Cloverport was situated on the left bank. [That] night, we anchored near the bank until the stars came out, since the moon rose late. In the cabin, card games were organized. [There was] great heat and innumerable cockroaches, which [swarmed over] the beds and fell down on the table.

18 October: In the morning, very warm, [at] six thirty 16°R, wind, overcast sky. To the right we saw Rockport, Indiana, a small town situated on three undulating rocky hills separated by small defiles. From here on, the banks were low, with wooded hills everywhere. After breakfast at eight thirty, we [stopped at] Owensboro, a village with several imposing houses, [to take wood] on board. Many passengers went ashore. An urubu flew above the town. We had observed this bird species approximately since Cincinnati. Half an hour later, departure again. Despite its low level, the Ohio was now very broad and beautiful.

This forenoon, at eleven o'clock, a man died of cholera on our ship. Yesterday he was completely well; during the night he played cards and toward morning began to complain. I saw him at about eight o'clock. Mustard poultices were placed on the back of his neck [and] on his chest, calves, and abdomen, but he died very quickly. Two hours later a box was ready; he was taken ashore in it. His hands and forearms were said to be as black as ink. Many [passengers went ashore and] watched the burial. A hole had been dug at the top of the bank. The box was placed inside it after the dead man's veins had been opened, out of which, however, the black blood did not flow. The name of the deceased was written on a white board set up at the grave.

Scarcely a half hour from the above-mentioned place, we reached Evansville on the right bank, and [later] the market town [of] Henderson on [the] Kentucky side, [where] a great store of provisions was taken on and many passengers went ashore. There [were] more than a thousand young chickens, which had been brought in large crates for sale [at] a dollar a dozen. The sunset was splendid. The wide river was as smooth as a mirror, the thickets magnificently reflected in it, and the sky, completely clear, ranged from splendid lilac to fiery yellow. Toward midnight [we] landed at Mount Vernon, where we disembarked. The night was very dark and so warm that one perspired at the slightest movement. We went into the town of 600 inhabitants and knocked for a long time on the door of the inn, where we finally succeeded in bringing a black to the door. Finally the landlord's son, a pleasant young man, also woke up, and we obtained some very dirty beds, on which we slept in our clothes.

19 October: Early in the morning, a gentleman who had disembarked with us [said he] intended to walk to New Harmony, 15 miles from here. I rented a small wagon, on which we loaded our baggage, and at nine o'clock left for Harmony with Dreidoppel while Mr. Bodmer took the shotgun and began the journey on foot with our companion.

At first the road led alternately through woods and cultivated areas with scattered habitations. The road was very [rough], [and we] drove slowly. Finally we reached magnificent lofty forest where *Platanus, Liriodendron,* maple, storax *(Liquidambar),* the gum tree, willow oak *(Quercus phellos),* and many other beautiful trees grew straight, tall, and dense. Thick trunks rotted on the ground. For the first time I saw persimmon trees *(Diospyros virginiana),* with ripe fruit, near several habitations. A rather deep brook, Big Creek, meandered through the tall forest.

We [finally arrived at] the friendly town of New Harmony on the bank of the Wabash [and] stored our baggage at the inn. Not until several hours later did the foot [travelers] appear. They had seen quite a few interesting things, particularly a flight of [Carolina] parakeets. These pretty birds were said to live here all year; Mr. Say had observed them at −25°R. Because I did not feel very well, I did not go out any more today.

V

Four-and-a-Half Months' Stay in New Harmony

20 October: Today I took medicine to improve my condition. Mr. Thomas Say had heard that I had a letter for him and came to see us. I made the acquaintance of this interesting man, who had undertaken significant journeys to the Rocky Mountains and into the westerly countries with Major Long and was well known and highly regarded as a writer on natural history. Dreidoppel went out in the afternoon and found interesting *Unio* species and several blossoming plants along the Wabash [River].

21 October (Sunday): It rained heavily all night, and there was water everywhere on the broad, unpaved streets of [New] Harmony. We went to visit Mr. Say, who showed us some interesting works on conchology. He was currently editing a description of the North American Testacea, [to be] printed and lithographed here. His wife, [Lucy,] illuminates the plates.

In the afternoon we visited Mr. Say again and went with him to see Mr. [Charles-Alexandre] Lesueur, a well-known [illustrator] and writer [who had accompanied a number of scientific expeditions]. He [was] rather old, with a deeply lined face, and despite the long time he had lived here had still not learned to speak English. He was delighted to converse with us in French; his entire being came to life. His studio was most curious. Directly before the entrance there was a view of New Harmony, painted [like] a theater set; Mr. Lesueur could change this view into one of Market Street in Philadelphia. On pillars [flanking] this small theatrical [scene], a *Grus americana* and an *Ardea herodias* hung on one side, hunting equipment on the other. On the walls, all kinds of instruments; natural history objects on benches, tables, and chairs. A squirrel was being stuffed. Here, rows of enormous *Unios* from the Ohio, Wabash, and Mississippi; there, beautiful bird skins. Elsewhere the owner's drawing and painting equipment and the [portfolios of drawings] he had accumulated on his journeys around the world and on North American rivers. We richly enjoyed looking over [those] sketches.

Abundant material for a most interesting work on natural history was afforded by [his] collection of fishes and turtles. Of the latter Mr. Lesueur had drawn the three varieties [we] acquired at Pittsburgh and had printed them in [French] and American publications. His fishes were beautifully and distinctively sketched in large format, though only a few were completed.

22 October: At nine o'clock I went to see Mr. Say to view his collections of insects and shells. He corresponded extensively and had a very good library at his disposal. He was expecting [more] books from Europe, costing several thousand dollars.

In Mr. Say's garden I found several intriguing plants, [including] *Macelura aurantiaca,* bow-wood or yellow-wood, a prickly tree from Arkansas with very tough wood from which the Indians make their bows. Mr. Say told me that the true homeland of the catalpa is here in the Wabash woodlands, where the tree grows very thick and tall. The wood is used for posts [and is] said to last a long time. *Quercus macrocarpa* also grew here; I obtained some enormous acorns. Dreidoppel went hunting and brought back [four bird] species and a whole basket of various *Unios.*

Mr. [Richard] Owen, the son of the former owner of Harmony, paid us a visit and invited us to come to his house that evening. At five thirty he called for us with his carriage. The weather had cleared, and the sun shone brightly. The carriage was a kind of cart; the horses were poor. Mr. Owen rode along beside us on horseback. This young man was educated entirely in the European manner and spoke German well; he and his brother acquired [the language] during their three-year stay at the Fellenberg Institute [in Switzerland]. His wife, [Martha Chase Owen,] was English, vivacious and talented—she painted very well and had musical ability. We spent a very pleasant evening at Mr. Owen's house, a mile from Harmony, and did not return until ten o'clock.

23 October: The day was pleasant but somewhat cool. Dreidoppel went out in midmorning and shot several birds. Mr. Bodmer [began] a view of Harmony [see pl. 3]. Mr. Say and I visited Mr. Lesueur, who showed us his sketches of the West Indian islands and North America.

24 October: At ten thirty, Mr. Say and I took a short walk to the hills, where one had a nice view overlooking the town and the river. The Wabash is a rather imposing river flowing through level, wooded regions. The woods had lost their beautiful multicolored appearance; most of the leaves had fallen, [and] only some of the oaks still had yellow and brown foliage. Mr. Say persuaded

me to call the doctor [and so] I spent the evening with my medicine.

25–26 October: Cold in the mornings. Mr. Bodmer sketched on the island, where he saw parakeets *(Psitt. carolinensis)*. These birds usually stayed all winter and plundered ripe fruits, especially apples. Since I was still indisposed, I did not leave the house [either day]. Mr. Bodmer was also taking medicine. Mr. Say, [who] sent us engravings for our diversion, was ailing too, as was our landlord.

27 October: State of my health somewhat better. In the morning Dreidoppel went to Wabash Island, where he shot an urubu in flight (the species with the reddish head) and fetched it home alive. Messrs. Say and Lesueur visited; the latter brought me a special species of *Equisetum,* which [grows] up to six feet high; it was said to occur frequently along the Mississippi [and] on the islands of the Missouri.

28 October (Sunday): Dreidoppel and a local resident [went] 4 miles to the Fox River. He killed a young male *Anas sponsa* and saw many ducks, several of which he winged but did not get. I still did not venture far, only for a short visit to Mr. Say. In the evening a *Falco haliaëtus* and a large *Strix* were brought to us. Today Dreidoppel saw a large number of turtles at the place where the Fox River emptied into the Wabash. They were sitting in groups of about thirty on a trunk in the water, [all] piled up, little ones sitting on top of larger ones.

29 October: The sun shone brightly. We prepared to pack the natural history objects we had [recently] collected, for which purpose a crate was ordered. I dismissed the physician.

A few observations about New Harmony. [It] was built here by Mr. Rapp (now at Economy) in a flat, wooded region,[MI] on the Wabash in Indiana about 15 to 20 miles away from all other villages or towns. [When] Rapp [decided] to move to another area, a wealthy Scot, Mr. [Robert] Owen, bought the entire property, which was quite substantial. [Mr.] Owen had his own unique religious and philanthropic views. He wished to found a community that would own everything in common. He did not have a high regard for religion, so Rapp's church was now used as an amateur theater. One can read more about Owen's society in the writings of Duke Bernhard of Saxe-Weimar. It cannot be denied that [Mr. Owen] had good intentions. [But] the [project] did not turn out well financially, [and] Mr. Owen sold

---

[MI] In Posey County, which numbers 6,000 persons.

about half of his property to [another] wealthy Scot, Mr. [William] Maclure, who now lived in Mexico but had established a [substantial] library, printing press, and engraving and print shop in Harmony.

Mr. Say, that famous traveler and active scholar in the fields of entomology and conchology, supervised Mr. Maclure's properties and used the fine library, [with] many excellent, distinguished volumes in the field of natural history. The engraving shop constantly produced small plates for dissemination; Mr. Say was having his shell illustrations (for a work on North American species) engraved here, [and] his wife looked after [their illumination] with great care and enthusiasm. To help Mr. Say, Mr. Maclure had substantial shipments of books sent from Europe every year. Mr. Lesueur owns additional works. Apart from the persons just mentioned, the family of Mr. Owen is perhaps the most interesting one here. We were given a very friendly reception in all these homes.

Harmony, [with] about 600 inhabitants, [was] built in a regular manner with broad, unpaved streets. The buildings were often [set] far apart. The following factories, trades, and artisans were here: two jurists (lawyers); three doctors; six stores; two grocers selling groceries and spices; a steam sawmill; two spirits distilleries; four whiskey distilleries; one clockmaker (bad); two smiths; one hat maker; two joiners; four master cobblers; one master tailor with five workers; two master coopers; two wheelwrights; two master saddlers; one cigar factory; two inns; one beer brewery; two tanneries; two butchers; three or four [seasonal] flatboat builders. The remaining inhabitants were mostly farmers. Much whiskey, pork, beef, [and] Indian corn were shipped to New Orleans. Most craftsmen's [products] were expensive, particularly sawed boards; the carpenters demanded two to two and one half dollars (five to six florins) for a poor, flimsily constructed crate of poplar wood.

The site [of New Harmony] is completely flat. The [Wabash] inundated the adjacent lowlands every winter. The river [had] all kinds of interesting islands. Its bed nourished remarkable, large bivalve mussels (*Unio,* etc.), which Mr. Say described superbly. [According to David Thomas,] the tribes living along it were the Piankashaws and possibly others. Several years ago the Miamis still roamed the Wabash prairies.

The prairies—the level, open grasslands of western America—began about 20 miles from Harmony: [more] about them elsewhere. The region around Harmony was quite built up, yet large forests, in which solitary settlers lived, were not far away. Land in the vicinity of Harmony was very fertile but no longer inexpensive. Private land could not be purchased for less than fifteen dollars an acre, but [public domain lands were] less costly. Food was cheap. Indian corn — seven dollars on the Canadian border — sold [at Harmony] for six and one-fourth cents a bushel.

30–31 October: [On Tuesday] we learned from Mr. Hall that the cholera was not yet [in Mount Vernon]; on the other hand, it was said to be in St. Louis. [Wednesday] I went out with Messrs. Say and Lesueur to see the Indian mounds near Mr. Lesueur's house. They [were in] Rapp's cemetery; several could still be seen quite clearly. In these shallow burial mounds, the Indians constructed graves by placing stones on edge; many bones have been found in them.[1] Several Swabian farmers from Rapp's society lay buried among the old Indians. Mr. Bodmer and I were invited to Messrs. Owen for lunch. After our meal we watched threshing [done] with horses, which was the general practice. The wheat was piled up in the field on a small, round threshing floor [with] no outer barriers. Three men rode six horses in pairs behind one another in a circle, and they trampled out the kernels. A fourth worker [had] a pitchfork and repeatedly tossed [any] escaping stalks under the horses' hooves. Care must be taken that horse droppings do not fall on the grain.

Today I saw an excellent book for travelers on the Ohio and Mississippi that contains a map of the entire course of the rivers with all [their] islands, rivers, creeks, and towns: [Samuel Cumings's] *The Western Pilot for 1829,* Cincinnati, Ohio, N. and S. Guilford.[2]

1 November: Mr. Hall, our traveling companion and associate since Louisville, left today. We wrote to St. Louis to have any letters for us there forwarded here. Cholera was now said to be [even] more severe there.

In the afternoon we visited Mr. Lesueur, and with him and Mr. Say [we] climbed the high loft on what had once been the church, the tallest building in town. From here we had an interesting view: to the south and west, [an overview] of the meandering Wabash; around Harmony, a beautiful plain, cleared by Mr. Rapp's Germans and now covered with fields of tall corn, enclosed by forest. From there we went into Mr. Lesueur's house and viewed until evening the superb collection of drawings of mollusks, frogs, and mammals that he made during his journey around the world with Captain Baudin.

2 November: In Mr. Say's yard we examined a stout storax tree (*Liquidambar styraciflua*), the resin of which has a peculiar odor that I do not find very pleasant. Mr. Lesueur gave me his essay on *Trionyx*, which was printed in [France]. I still lack Say's essay on turtles and Le Conte's on the amphibians of North America.

At four o'clock in the afternoon, I went with Mr. Owen to his whiskey distillery, which was driven by a steam engine. A mill for grinding wheat, rye, and corn was set into motion by steam. On an adjacent floor there was a pump, which filled a large mash vat with boiling or very hot water. Various kinds of grain were quickly shoveled in by four men with scoops. Four iron rakes constantly turned in the vat and mixed the mass. [That was then] drained into other large cauldrons [to] ferment. Steam was let in; as the vapors passed through a copper coil in a vat filled with cold water, they were condensed [as] whiskey. The residue was used in several ways, especially for fattening [hundreds of] pigs [for butchering]. Mr. Owen leased [the distillery] to someone familiar with its operation in return for a portion of the spirits. About 1,500 barrels of whiskey were produced yearly, and the price of a barrel was ten dollars (the whiskey was of poor quality).

During the evening Mr. Say told us interesting things about his stay among the Indians when he traveled up the Missouri with Major Long.

5 November: Rainy weather; we worked at home. Because voting for the new president took place today [Andrew Jackson versus Henry Clay], all the nearby settlers were in Harmony on horseback. It was as though a cavalry squadron had moved into town; there were horses everywhere, at times twenty to thirty tethered [in one place]. Everywhere one saw the dirty farmers riding about in the rain in their ridiculous attire. After these crude individuals had registered their votes, they did ample justice to the whiskey; it was asserted that there would be no lack of brawling and disorderly conduct. Toward evening most of them rode home.

8 November: In the morning the grass was covered with white frost. At nine thirty I took a walk to the hills where Mr. Bodmer [was sketching] a view of the Wabash and of Harmony. I stalked far over the hills, covered by densely entangled undergrowth, but saw nothing except for some tits (*Parus bicolor* and *atricapillus*), a yellow woodpecker (*Picus auratus*), crows, and urubus. At the edge of the forest, I came upon a flight of *Fringilla hudsonia*; these seemed to have come southward from the north. Mr. Bodmer could not continue to sketch, because it was too cold; I gave him my shotgun and

went home. In this country it was really very bad during the winter; the houses were quite flimsily constructed. We could not endure the whole winter in the house where we were living, [so we planned] to travel south by steamboat as soon as possible. [But] I was still sick.

9 November: I went walking with Messrs. Say and Lesueur; afterward they came to my place, and we spent the evening at home. [A] young man from the Fox River brought us a deer and five wild turkeys, [but] they were too poorly preserved to use for our collection.

10 November: Mr. Bodmer and Dreidoppel returned [from hunting] at four with an *Anas sponsa* and a parakeet. They had shot several parakeets, which, however, had remained hanging high in the trees. They had seen five turkeys, which had flown across the river, and also wild geese but not many ducks. My complaint had worsened after half a glass of wine that afternoon.

11 November: During the afternoon I went for a walk [and] obtained a native coot (*Fulica*). Today I sent a messenger on horseback 50 miles for a physician, Dr. Dake, who lives 15 miles from Shawneetown, [Illinois], and is said to be competent. Since I had been very careful about my diet today and had eaten nothing but rice boiled in water and some chicken, I felt better. The cool weather may have helped. Today at Mr. Lesueur's I saw excellent illustrations of invertebrates from the South Sea.

14 November: In the morning, colder. Mr. Bodmer went hunting with Russel, the young hunter who [had brought us so many turkeys]; they will not return until tomorrow. During the afternoon Mr. Say and I took a walk up along the Wabash. We found various interesting seeds, especially the ten-inch-long flat pods of the *Bignonia crucigera*.

15 November: Dr. Dake [came] and gave me his advice. Mr. Lesueur gave me the bark of the *Ulmus rubra*, the tree called slippery elm here. When boiled or chewed, this bark provides a viscous, slimy liquid that is excellent for drawing inflammation from wounds [and] as an internal remedy alleviating diarrhea. This forenoon I was surprised to receive a voluminous letter from Germany, dated the 1st of September (which brought very pleasant news, except for the advance of cholera to the Rhine), [and] letters from Mr. Volz and Dr. Saynisch in Pittsburgh.

At dusk Mr. Bodmer and his hunting companion returned home; they [had] three turkeys, one splendid wild goose (*Anser canadensis*), two large owls, and four parakeets. They had seen about fifty turkeys. Mr. Bodmer could not bring down the turkeys with a shotgun. With his rifle, which was over four feet in length, the hunter shot extraordinarily far and never missed. [He] shot down one turkey, loaded again, and shot a second.

Very crude, inhospitable people lived where the young hunter dwelled. Their log hut was wretched and small. The wind blew through the [chinks in the] walls—[even though] the people were well-to-do, since they owned eighty acres of land. In the evening Mr. Bodmer was given a piece of bacon and a small container of sour milk. He and the hunter had to sleep in the same bed. On the following morning, he got no breakfast; he had to leave hungry and get breakfast at another house. For two days [they] roamed the forests along the Fox River [and] found the trails of deer, raccoons, turkeys, etc. The reeds *(Miegia)* were often very troublesome; the hunters had to force their way through, making their hands sore.

17 November: Mr. Say gave me some old Indian skulls that had been removed from the burial mounds [in the cemetery] near New Harmony. Only the top sections were preserved: the facial bones were missing, and everything was extremely fragile and weathered. I intended these heads for [Professor] Blumenbach's collection.

18–19 November: [Cold,] dreary weather; it seemed that winter was beginning early this year. Mr. Say came to my place to identify my Wabash mussels; he knew [many] species, and his descriptions and identifications were certainly very correct.

Mr. Bodmer purchased a fine otter skin for one and one-half dollars; [it] had a very dark blackish brown color. Mr. Say gave me a small cask of amphibians from the Harmony region, [including several species of mud puppy, skinks, and snakes].

20 November: It was very cold in the large room where Mr. Bodmer and I were staying, and we were chilled through when the breakfast signal came. In this house, that was always given with a large triangle, struck twice (the triangle was rung at mealtimes in all three Harmony inns; Mr. Owen had the privilege of selling these triangles, [and] every innkeeper was obliged to buy from him). It is the prevailing custom in North America that no one has breakfast or dines in his room; a bell is rung, and then everyone comes storming in.

In the afternoon, a stroll with Mr. Say. In Mr. Maclure's big orchard we found *Picus villosus* and *pubescens* on the apple trees and *Certhia familiaris* along the Wabash. Dreidoppel and Mr. Bodmer returned in the evening from their hunt and brought back a parakeet that had been shot in the wing and seemed to be growing tame. They had [also] bagged a beautiful blue jay *(Corvus cristatus).*

21 November: Our tame parakeet seemed to be holding up and healing. In the afternoon, during my stroll with Mr. Say along the Wabash, [in] a tangle of trunks that had floated [downstream, we found] a domestic [sow] consuming her dead piglets. It had farrowed too late, and the piglets were scarcely several days old. Four had died, most certainly of cold—in this country people do not concern themselves about livestock—and the remaining three young ones were stiff from the cold. I picked up one of them, but it squealed and the mother left her dismal repast to run to the aid of her young one, whereupon I let it go.

We saw no additional birds, except for gray-and-white finches. On one of the lower branches of a tree, we found the cocoon of the beautiful big nocturnal moth *Bombyx cecropia.*

22–24 November: Mr. Bodmer finished a pretty sketch of the church and Mr. Lesueur's house. Mr. Say paid us a visit and related interesting things about his journeys to the Rocky Mountains. [He gave me] various books, including Lahontan's *Nouveaux voyages* [in America] and Bullock on Mexico. Mr. Bodmer rode with Mr. Twigg [on a three-day journey] to the prairies near Albion to shoot prairie hens. [I got many birds and] Russel brought me two nice raccoons, a very large rust-bellied squirrel, and a handsome wild goose; I paid a dollar for them all.

25 November: We had much work to do describing, measuring, and preparing our animals. Yesterday, at Mr. Lesueur's, I met a gunsmith who lives 4 miles from here; he was exceedingly well pleased with my Morgenroth rifle-shot-gun. He could not stop praising it and declared that in his entire life he had never seen anything like it and wished to be allowed to take it apart.

[My] afternoon stroll was pleasant; I visited Mr. Say in his little house in the garden, where he usually worked. He kept his shells and insects there, and [it] was his favorite place. Dreidoppel became sick today, suffering the same ailment that had been afflicting me for six weeks.

26 November: All night long, a violent storm and drenching rain. Late last evening I had to have the doctor called for Dreidoppel, who developed an intense fever and had severe diarrhea with a bloody discharge all day today. He was given a laxative of calomel with rhubarb [and] was somewhat better [but] still had diarrhea. With extraordinarily severe changes of weather, illnesses are not unusual, and abdominal troubles are very common. Otherwise,

New Harmony on the Wabash is an extremely healthful place; one heard little about significant illnesses, and there were many old people. Visitors yesterday told me about health conditions in St. Louis. In one day (in a population of 5,000–6,000), thirty persons died of cholera, although there had been no deaths reported in recent weeks.

27 November: At about noon Mr. Bodmer and Mr. Twigg returned from Albion, a small town on the boundary of the so-called prairies in Illinois (fringes of forest could be seen everywhere in the distance—the genuine prairies beyond the Mississippi have almost no trees at all). The travelers received a friendly welcome everywhere. People promised to send us all kinds of animals from that area. There were wolves there, red, gray, and black ones; [also] gray and red foxes. [Bobcats] were not uncommon, likewise the rat with pouches in its cheeks (gopher). White-tailed deer *(Cervus virginianus)* were numerous. There were various bird species not found in the forests. During the migratory season, for example, *Grus americana* (whooping crane, a splendid bird); the prairie hen *(Tetrao cupido);* the beautiful white-and-black kite, *Falco furcatus;* [and] a large earless owl *(Strix nebulosa).* Mr. Bodmer had drawn some very nice sketches, including the head of a white heron. On the way back, they were told that, during the migration season, there were swans, geese, ducks, and cranes in such numbers that one could not hear gunfire because of the clamor.

28 November: Our tame parakeet died suddenly yesterday evening; undoubtedly it had burned itself by the fire; these birds have very sensitive beaks. Stroll in the afternoon with Mr. Say. It was so warm that in my [still ill and] fatigued state I was weary to the utmost degree. [But we nonetheless collected] black *Gryllus* and the local earthworms.

29 November: At seven thirty, temperature of 11°R. It was so warm that one could hardly endure the fire. Mr. Bodmer went out at nine o'clock to sketch the Fox River. I received from Russel, the hunter, a female opossum that had excellent winter fur and was extraordinarily fat. We spent the whole morning packing because we [planned] to move on 1 December. Mr. Bodmer returned at dusk. He had bought a hunting dog. Today Mr. Lesueur was sick; he had a fever [and was also] suffering from an injury to his shinbones, which were very inflamed. There was a good plaster here for such wounds: slippery elm bark. When chewed or soaked in water, [it] swells and becomes viscous, cooling, and refreshingly mucilaginous, relieving inflammation and keeping wounds smooth and moist. Michaux includes a sketch

of the tree in his *Sylva Americana.*

Several [other] plants were used as home remedies here, such as an African [one] called Benin-plant; the leaves, soaked in water, produce [a curative for] diarrhea. Here and along the Mississippi, especially in the summer, they steep [*Mentha* sp.] in water with some sugar to produce a cooling, stomach-fortifying beverage. For the very frequently occurring cases of diarrhea here, some doctors prescribed enemas of flaxseed and cornstarch boiled in water [with] a grain of opium. Most of the unskilled country doctors, however, knew nothing about those remedies and relied on calomel and castor oil.

A letter arrived today from New Orleans with sad news about the ravages of cholera in that city and environs. The inhabitants had fled in all directions, the stores were closed, and all business [had ceased]. The devastation was said to be frightful, especially among the lower classes and the Negroes. We deeply regretted that, under such circumstances, we could not visit those interesting regions. It was advantageous for us that the Wabash was too low for steamboat navigation [and] we remained more isolated from communication with the Mississippi.

30 November: Today I made my first attempt to drink a cup of coffee again. We got our baggage ready for moving. During the night Mr. Bodmer had had such a strong nasal hemorrhage that he became quite exhausted. He is very prone to nosebleed. Before noon I visited Mr. Lesueur and found him better.

Today the town was filled with large numbers of farmers; there was an election for the municipal council. The local country people wore all sorts of clothes, [just as] in the cities (round felt hats, caps of all colors, frock coats, plaid coats, etc.), but [they were] all extremely dirty and disheveled, with long beards and hair hanging wildly from their heads. Horses were tied up in large numbers everywhere, because here everyone rode and pedestrians were rare. [But] if one asked a farmer how many horses or cows he had, he replied, "Such and such a number, if I can find all of them." No one knew how many hogs he had.

Mr. Say frequently sent me all kinds of things, especially books, through his young Mexicans. He had two of them, Cavallos and Lopez, both of Indian descent but no longer of pure race. Unfortunately, during my entire North American journey, I had not yet seen one native Indian. To find them one had to cross the Mississippi. This winter, they [intended] to drive the last settled remnants of these nations [beyond that river]—the Cherokees,

Choctaws, and others—an act of sheer brutality![3] Such is the vaunted liberty of America![M2]

1 December: This morning we moved into the New Harmony Hotel ([of] Mr. [Samuel] Arthur), diagonally opposite from Mr. Say's house. The landlord was an Englishman. Our lodgings were far more pleasant and the food better. The landlord and landlady [were] very friendly, agreeable people. [But] the table company was [often] unpleasant: shabby, dirty farmers who [came in, said nothing,] wolfed down their food, and left as quickly as they came.

2 December: This morning Russel, the hunter, [had] six wild turkeys, but they were not of good quality. The old toms were very shy now and hard to shoot. Today I gave our friendly landlord a list of all the animals I should like to have from this region, which he intended to [share with] acquaintances in the Illinois prairies.

3 December: Early in the morning, surroundings white with hoarfrost. We worked at home all forenoon. Our landlord traveled to Albion and hoped to bring back some natural history specimens for us.

4 December: Mr. Say visited us, and we identified several turtles and other amphibians. [He] lent me Gmelin's [book on the] Linnaean system. Indeed, [in Harmony] we had convenient access to all the important works of natural history, a matter of great significance when identifying natural history objects. In the evening our landlord returned from the prairies with many deer antlers.

5–6 December: Mr. Bodmer and I left the house early to hunt along the Fox River. In the morning the weather was cool, clear, and nice. At noon it became very warm. We went out on the Wabash in a boat but had to do the work ourselves, because in our haste we could not find an [oarsman].

At the place where we set out, the Wabash divided into two branches, the main, or northern, branch, [and] the southern one, [called] Cutoff River—the island between the two branches is called Cutoff Island. We passed Cutoff Island to our left and followed the main branch of the Wabash with Fox

---

[M2] [A] newspaper recently listed the tribes still living in the territory of the United States: l) Choctaws 20,000. 2) [Shoshones] 20,000. 3) Crees 20,000. 4) Cherokees 15,000. 5) Blackfoot 15,000. 6) Chippewas 15,000. 7) Sioux 15,000. 8) Pawnees 12,000. 9) Assiniboines 8,000. 10) Potawatomis 6,500. 11) Winnebagos 5,800. 12) Sauks 6,800. 13) Osages 5,000. 14) Menominees 5,200. 15) Crows 4,500. 16) Kansa [——].

Island to our right.[4] The banks were covered with lofty, beautiful forest in which tall, huge *Platanus,* with their broad branches, gleamed snow-white in the densely entangled thicket. After rowing for one-half or three-quarters of an hour, we got out on the right bank and fastened our boat behind some thick fallen trunks. From [there] it was several hundred paces across Fox Island [to] Fox River. This stream was quite scenic, with romantic banks, wildly toppled tall trunks, huge *Platanus* with white bark, splendid oaks, hickory, shellbark, etc. The *Gymnocladus,* with its large thick pods, grew there. Beautiful catalpas, with their long, narrow, legume[-like pods]. *Bignonia radicans* and *crucigera,* as well as enormous grapevines, *Rhus, Hedera quinquefolia,* and *Smilax* species entwined the forest giants. The *Platanus* trunks, which six to seven men often could not span at the base, were remarkable. At a height of 20 to 30 feet, the trunks usually forked into many massive branches, covered with an almost dazzlingly white bark [that] shone forth in the brownish gray forest stripped of its leaves by winter.

This quiet, solitary brook was visited by numerous ducks. [We shot multiple times, but] unfortunately, we did not have any dogs and therefore lost many of the ducks we hit. Mr. Bodmer searched for the location, discovered earlier, where he had begun a beautiful view of the stream. On the island, I crept farther along the Fox River [and] found a beautiful ash-blue kingfisher *(Alcedo alcyon),* a species we had not yet [bagged]. I shot it, and it fell into the brook, but I could not reach it, so I fetched Mr. Bodmer [to help]. When we came to the spot where the bird lay, the air was filled with turkey buzzards, which [arrived] in a second if one shot even a single bird. They hovered over us and sat in groups of five or six on the tall, dry *Platanus* branches. I fired at them, whereupon they scattered. The kingfisher had already been carried [off] by those assembled guests.

Forcing my way through dense cane and climbing over countless fallen trees, I scoured the tall, wild forest almost until evening. I found especially many woodpeckers and brown creepers *(Certhia familiaris), Sitta carolinensis,* titmice, cardinals *(Loxia carolinensis),* several finches, and winter wrens *(Troglodytes hyemalis),* and shot several of these. The urubus often hovered above me. There were *Picus pileatus,* very large [and] black as a crow, with several beautiful white markings and a blood-red crest. I shot three of [them] since they were not very shy. When the sun had set, we got into our boat again and, with no little difficulty, rowed up the Wabash against the current toward New Harmony. We did not arrive home until dark. [We repeated this hunting excursion the next day,] with somewhat less exertion, for we took a rower along.

7 December: Rain and densely overcast sky. It was exactly seven months today since we left Neuwied. Today [the] weather prevented us from making a hunting excursion to the Fox River. In the afternoon at the home of Mr. Lesueur, I met a certain Mr. Nohl from New Orleans, who had just come from there. He had been traveling for twenty-one days. One of the boilers on his steamboat had burst and had killed seven persons. Fortunately for the passengers in the large cabin, of whom there were twenty to thirty, there was a large pile of bags of salt between the cabin and the boiler; they absorbed and broke the main force of the steam and boiling water. In New Orleans as many as 500 persons had died in one day from cholera, but now the number was only twenty to thirty.

9–10 December: Dreidoppel rode to Mount Vernon on the Ohio to buy some cotton and blotting paper, which we could not obtain here anywhere. A live opossum, [a gift from the hunter, Russel,] drank water and ate pastries. Russel [also] delivered two female raccoons; another man brought in nine [turkeys]. An extraordinary number of these birds had been brought to Harmony since we [arrived].

14 December: Before daybreak, a violent thunderstorm. The thunder was so powerful that the windows rattled continually. After ten o'clock, better weather. We worked at home and, with the description and preparation of our collected specimens and Mr. Bodmer with his drawings, had quite enough to do.

16–17 December: Rain deteriorated into large snowflakes [that quickly melted]. In the streets, endless mud. Our landlord returned from Albion and brought me a nice skunk, the delightful odor of which soon spread throughout the entire house. I made a description of it and carried the smell with me for a long time.

19 December: Bright weather; the most penetrating cold up to now [about 19°F]. In the afternoon I took a walk [and saw a recently farrowed sow as well as a cow with a new calf]. It was remarkable how animals were indifferently [allowed to] roam about here; the cold weather must have killed many a young animal. Russel arrived on a horse, from which ten turkeys were hanging, one of which I kept. Another man brought a young mink. Mr. Say spent the evening with us.

20 December: This morning we dissected a skunk, a task that requires considerable

resolve. We collected the stinking matter from the glands in a glass in order to have it analyzed in Europe, for I assumed that this had not yet been done. In our room it was so cold all day that one had to get up every few minutes and go to the fire. Visit in the evening at the home of Mr. Lesueur. He told us of the arrival of Mr. Fountleroy from Nashville, who comes here every winter to shoot large numbers of turkeys, which he salts and takes home.

24 December: Last evening we talked at great length with Mr. Say about Indians and various travel accounts of North America. Mr. Say named several that I did not yet know, including the works of DuPonceau (in Philadelphia) about North American Indian languages.

Today the first prairie hens *(Tetrao cupido)* were offered to me for sale, but [they were] too expensive. A backwoodsman, who had ridden 12 miles, brought us a fine [bobcat], for which I paid two dollars; [it] was nice but extraordinarily slender and thin-bellied—apparently it had not caught prey for a long time. An hour later Russel appeared with a splendid eagle that he had shot from a tree with his rifle. These creatures [seemed like] Christmas Eve gifts [for me].

As soon as it grew dark, Christmas Eve was welcomed with heavy charges of powder by young people on the streets of Harmony. This unpleasant surprise took place directly beneath our windows. Otherwise, however, there was no trace of an observation of these days, because there was no church; the somewhat coarse population of this area celebrated the most solemn festivals of Christendom by drinking, hunting, singing, and dancing.

25 December: People welcomed Christmas by shooting in the streets. Mr. Owen visited us early and invited us to dine with him that afternoon at five o'clock.

A crowd of people from Albion gathered to attend a dance in this house this evening. Our landlord frequently brought [such] guests up to us to show them the strange, marvelous creatures and their zoological collection. To be sure, these guests were often a nuisance, but it was my policy to let them in and show them things, since they were often hunters and occasionally later sent us interesting animals.

Since I did not feel very well, Mr. Bodmer conveyed my apologies to Mr. Owen. I spent the evening at home. Underneath me a wild dance—a large drum and several violins and pipes or flageolets created an uninterrupted music that resounded in the ears; the huge kettledrum did not remain silent for one moment. Mr. Bodmer attended the dance for a while.

28 December: We worked at home and packed cases with natural history

specimens, which Mr. Twigg will take to New Orleans. These were [crate] numbers IX, X, XI.

29 December: Mr. Twigg left for Mount Vernon early today with my three natural history crates to embark for New Orleans, [where] he will have them sent to Europe. Mr. Bodmer decided to go along to New Orleans to make sketches and collect some natural history specimens; they would board the first steamboat in Mount Vernon and be back here in four to five weeks.

31 December: Early in the morning, on the last day of the year 1832, densely overcast sky and an extremely mild temperature. I went to see Messrs. Say and Lesueur. The latter was preparing a deer. That evening, the last one of the year, I spent in pleasant conversation at the home of Mr. Say.

1 January [1833]: Toward midnight there had been some shooting to celebrate the new year, but I did not hear much of it. After breakfast, while occasional shooting was still going on, I took detailed measurements of the fish otter (*Lontra canadensis*) I obtained yesterday, which I found most interesting. At six o'clock the New Year's Dance began in our house. The noise from the big drum was thunderous. I sneaked up to the door and saw dancers executing a square dance according to the old triple-time step, grasping hands in all directions. They danced without putting on gloves, some of them in their overcoats, young and old together.

3 January: I measured a truly enormous, very old opossum, which had been brought to us yesterday; it weighed 11 pounds. During the afternoon I took a walk with Mr. Say. We perspired and felt exhausted; it was warm, springlike weather. In the evening I was at his home, [and] the conversation turned to garden vegetables and fruits. [Dozens] of them were grown here, [but] Indian corn [was] the primary product of the region (it grows to be 10 to 15 feet tall here and matures in October, November, and December; often some of it is left standing throughout the winter until needed). Not much wheat, rye, [or] barley. Substantial amounts of oats for the horses. Some buckwheat. Among the useful plants, tobacco should not be forgotten. Cigarros were made in Harmony, which, however, were of poor quality.

6 January: I gave Mr. Lesueur a muskrat from the three [brought to us] yesterday. In the afternoon, a short walk with Mr. Say, then a visit at his home. He showed me his shell collection and observed that he was missing the common European *Ostrea edulis,* which I shall send him. Today we talked about cattle breeding in this region. It is still very primitive, [and] that was why beef here was such poor quality.

8 January: In the afternoon we went to Fox Island with a resident of Harmony. In the canebrakes it was very easy to go astray, and we twice came back to the same spot. Our guide had [asked] me to bring along a compass, but I forgot to do so. After tramping for a long time [we reached] the pond we were looking for. Our guide, equipped with a hoe and a basket, sought the roots of a yellow-blooming *Nymphaea [advena]*, which he wanted to use as a remedy for a facial tumor. While he was digging, we looked for birds and near the corner of a cornfield found a whole flock of parakeets *(Psittacus carolinensis)*, which flew about with a loud cooing call and perched on the high, white branches of *Platanus* trees. They darted about as swiftly as arrows; the bright green flock afforded a most delightful sight.

9 January: At eight thirty it began to snow heavily, and a powerful wind blew from the northeast. [By] noon, the snow had stopped, [and] in the afternoon, [I] walked to the Wabash ferry landing.

Country people rode in and out of Harmony in large wagons loaded with corn or pigs, which they sell in town. Then, in the Harmony taverns, they fortified themselves with whiskey, which often went to their heads so that they became noisy, their crudeness revealed in the most glaring light. They knew nothing of schools and instruction and grew up like savages. In Harmony there was one school, where children learned to read and write. People paid tuition in the amount of two dollars quarterly [for this instruction]. In the countryside, [however, there was no such instruction].

10 January: A powerful wind blew. In our rooms — doors and windows severely drafty, fire of wet wood in an open fireplace — it was so cold and unpleasant that we could neither work nor write; even in bed we were freezing. [So] an additional small stove was placed in our [quarters]. Farmers brought us four raccoon skins for sale.

11 January: Our [new] stove served its purpose very well; it was now tolerably warm in its vicinity. Yesterday Mr. Say and I talked about American naturalists. Here [are] a few words about [some of them]. Thomas Say is certainly a very modest, conscientious, and well-informed man, and he seems to me to be the leading zoologist. Harlan is a superficial compiler. Rafinesque seems to be a charlatan who tries to make himself important by [naming] new genera and species. Nuttall is a well-informed young man, his merits well known. In Godman, America lost a promising young naturalist. [William] Cooper, a zoologist in New York, assisted [Charles Lucien] Bonaparte; [both] fine naturalist[s].

13 January: Everything was covered with snow, [and] it was still snowing. To-day, in Silliman's *American Journal of Science and the Arts*, I found a [statement] that it is necessary to stuff amphibians because it is too expensive to preserve them in spirits. But everyone knows how unsatisfactory stuffed amphibians are and that the only good way to preserve these animals in collections is with alcohol or spirits.

14 January: Yesterday I talked with local residents about the value of land around Harmony. The conclusions were more or less the following. The soil was black and so rich that one [often] did not have to fertilize it to grow corn. In the vicinity of [Harmony], land was no longer cheap, but several miles away along the river there was still much [public domain land] which could be bought for one dollar [and] twenty-five cents an acre; this [land, however], had the disadvantage of being inundated frequently by the river, [although that] did not occur every year [and] fertility was thereby improved.

15 January: Heavy rain, [but] we had many animals and birds, so we had suffi-cient work at home. [Then] we received another large male mallard *(Anas boschas)*, a young tom [turkey], and three black crows, which I was very pleased to have.

16 January: The fires in my stove and fireplace were vigorously fed and tended, whereby the temperature rose to a tolerable level. I was happy to receive a letter from Neuwied dated 26 October in response to one I had sent from Bethlehem on 5 September. In the letter [there was] a description of [my niece] Luitgarde's wedding.

18 January: I took my walk and saw seventeen prairie hens, large flights of *Columba migratoria,* [and] many ducks *(Anas clangula)* on the Wabash. I shot several birds, and a man brought me a wolf [that] seemed completely identical to the European one. I paid four dollars for it, [and] in the afternoon Messrs. Say, Lesueur, and Nohl called to see [it].

20 January: Genuine, beautiful spring day. The windows were open, and for the most part [we had] no fire. Word was received that cholera had again bro-ken out in New Orleans. Dreidoppel finished [stuffing] the wolf. I stuffed a squirrel. In the evening, visit from Mr. Say until ten o'clock.

22–23 January: In the afternoon we went out with Mr. Nohl [hoping] to find foxes but found only a hare. In the evening a stranger arrived who gave interest-ing news from St. Louis. A Mr. [George] Catlin, who lived for a long time among the Indians high up on the Missouri above the Yellowstone River [and] painted many portraits of them, had [recently] left [St. Louis] for

New York, [intending] to write about his journey. [Later] we talked [with Mr. Say] about the Missouri and its numerous Indians, in which he still maintains a very strong interest.

25 January: Dreidoppel and I left Harmony early to shoot some parakeets. We crossed the Wabash and saw two splendid *Aquila leucocephala* but could not get close to them. They hovered over the river looking for fish.

Dreidoppel found flights of parakeets, of which he killed fourteen, sometimes several of them with one shot. Then they came toward me, and I shot three. These most delightful creatures are not at all timid and alight immediately after they have been shot at. When winged, they very quickly become tame.

29 January: [After five days of hunting expeditions and specimen preparation,] I spent this evening at the home of Mr. Lesueur, who gave me shards from the Indian graves he had excavated; all [had] markings on the outside, mostly parallel stripes. Others looked as though they had been made in a cloth or basket, the impressions of which they [retained]. They were [formed] of dark-gray clay. Mr. Lesueur had seen large flat containers with somewhat figured handles still [intact].

30 January: Today I preserved swamp plants from Fox Island; I hoped Professor Treviranus in Bonn would quickly identify [these] and other plants. I placed a *Scalopus* in spirits in order to have its skeleton prepared in Germany.

I consulted [Benjamin] Smith Barton's work *(New Views of the Origin of the Tribes etc. of America)*. He lists [more than thirty] nations and compares their languages. A letter, dated 14 January, from Mr. Gebhard in New York informed me that my first eight crates of natural history specimens had been sent to Europe. Mr. Say received news from Boston that a ship, which was supposed to bring him a chest with natural history specimens, had been wrecked.

31 January: In the evening Mr. Lesueur paid me a visit. We talked about the natural history of fishes, a field in which he has done much work, and about the method of stuffing fish. He immediately pastes the fins with paper [and] then lets the fish dry for twenty-four hours (not in the sun), so that the scales no longer drop off. He leaves the eyes in, and for smooth-skinned, eel-like fish he makes a round opening in the mouth and draws the body through this aperture.

2 February: [At] Mr. Say's I met Mr. [Alexander] Maclure. We talked at length about the Indians and their strong, vigorous characters.

This evening the first steamboat from Shawneetown came up the Wabash. They sail from New Orleans and Louisville to Logansport on the Wabash, about 200 miles [above] Vincennes, and back again. They sail only when the water is high; sixty to seventy (a year) pass Harmony.

3 February: Regarding the conversations last evening about the Indians, I should note that Mr. Maclure, a very sensible man and a calm observer, told me that when he came here in the 1790s, he saw many different tribes of Indians and noted very diverse facial features. This interesting observation conforms with what I saw in Brazil. We also talked about the [old] Indian burial mounds [that] exist in many places: Harmony, Economy, along Grave Creek near Wheeling, near St. Louis, etc. (About this see David Thomas and other books.)

Unfortunately, the Indians have now been driven so far back that anyone reluctant to travel very far can hardly see any of them. Yesterday Mr. Maclure said, very rightly, that because of the settlements here in America, it is just as impossible for the original inhabitants to maintain themselves as it is for native wildlife, for the first undertaking of the colonists is always to destroy everything within reach. [Their] destructive rage is a sickening sight.

Thus the Indians disappeared. Big-game animals are so depleted that in ten years neither deer, wolves, nor wild turkeys will be found here. The elk, bear, and beaver have already disappeared; the remaining animals will soon follow. The government deserves to be severely reprimanded for not putting an end to these excesses. If one part of the year were set aside when no one was allowed to hunt, and if hunting rights were more restricted, then at least some of the animals would be preserved. This also holds true for forest trees. Soon there will be no usable trees, only completely devastated forests, in the inhabited parts of North America. One can feel only disgust and revulsion at the sight of such a coarse population streaming in with [neither] humanity nor moderation in their treatment of Indians, [and] mistreatment of the animal [world].

4 February: I received word of Mr. Bodmer's [imminent] arrival in Mount Vernon. At three o'clock Mr. Twigg [appeared, and] we learned that Mr. Bodmer would probably come with the next steamboat. Mr. Twigg [had brought me, and left temporarily in Mount Vernon,] thirteen live turtles, several nice crabs, some enormous frogs, [and] a live coati. Mr. Barrabino in New Orleans had sent several bottles of interesting snakes.

5 February: Early in the morning, I sent a wagon to Mount Vernon to bring back my [specimens and] live animals. They consisted of three varieties of turtles *(Testudo clausa* [and] *Emys serrata* and *concentrica)* and the live coati, which was very tame. While I was writing, a turkey buzzard, a coati, and fourteen turtles were moving about in our two large rooms. Mr. Lesueur and others came to see [them].

6 February: Mr. Say examined my turtles and took pains to identify them. Arthur drove to Mount Vernon to fetch [the remaining] natural history specimens: five glass containers with Louisiana amphibians [and] many snakes, among them two specimens of the water moccasin.

10–11 February: At 10°R we could not tolerate any fire in the room. I reviewed lists of the various species of turtles discovered up to now in the United States and found that I lack only five or six of [the seventeen species].

Mr. Maclure informed me that two deer heads with tangled antlers had arrived for me, although I had not yet heard anything about them. We talked about the arrangement of the United States by states. There are twenty-four states, but there will soon be a new [one]: Michigan. (When the population reaches a certain size, the people have the right to form a state.)

12 February: I received the two deer antlers tangled together. They had been found north of Evansville on the Ohio. One deer had still been alive. I received a letter from Mr. Nicolet, my banker in New Orleans, which informed me that Mr. Bodmer had withdrawn 3,000 dollars for us.

14 February: The tall forests bordering the Wabash [and] the fruit trees in the gardens and fields of Harmony were covered with ice or heavy hoarfrost. During a walk in the afternoon I saw only small birds, [but then] an entire flight of bluebirds *(Sylvia sialis)* in Mr. Maclure's orchard. I spent the evening at Mr. Lesueur's, where we perused Férussac's *Bulletin des sciences naturelles,* which had recently arrived from France.

15 February: In the morning, the entire countryside covered with a beautiful, deep, tracking snow. I went to the duck creek, followed fox tracks half covered by snow, shot three times at ducks, and bagged a nice mallard drake. At three o'clock in the afternoon, Mr. Bodmer returned from his journey to New Orleans. We spent the evening at Mr. Say's, where Mr. Bodmer gave us the following account of his journey.

[He] had to wait five days in Mount Vernon for a steamboat. Repeatedly during the night they went to the bank and called out to steamboats. Once someone on a ship asked what kinds of passengers there were, and the reply was: two cabin passengers with 150 barrels of whiskey (which Mr. Twigg had with him). But the captain continued on. Finally, on 3 January after midnight, the steamship *Homer* arrived, the finest plying the Mississippi, and the travelers embarked. At the confluence of the Ohio and Mississippi, the region was flat. The banks of the Mississippi lack variety up to the vicinity of Iron Banks [near Columbus, Kentucky]. Memphis, on a high bank, is a rather important town. Natchez is situated on picturesque elevations; Natchez-under-the-Hill, a dirty town notorious for gamblers and dissolute women, [is located] on the bank below. [At this landing] there was lively trade. The steamship stopped there for an hour and took on wood. Roses bloomed out in the open in profusion, [and] much *Tillandsia usneoides* hung from the trees in long strands. The sudden climatic change made a most pleasant impression: in two days [they] passed from deep winter into beautiful spring.

Fort Adams, [Mississippi], on the left bank of the river, is a town of about twenty houses, but the actual fort no longer exists. The travelers passed the mouth of the Red River at night, as well as Bayou Sara or St. Francisville, [Louisiana]. Very early in the morning, they arrived in Baton Rouge. The town has an attractive location on the left bank. On the following morning at about eight o'clock, they arrived in [New Orleans]; thirty to forty steamboats were tied up at the quay.

Mr. Bodmer was given a friendly reception by the Italian druggist Barrabino and invited to live in his home. Mr. Barrabino was a friend of Lesueur and a correspondent of Mr. Say. A generous, pleasant, well-to-do man [who] spoke many languages and was well versed in and made collections of natural history (he sent me that fine present of Louisiana amphibians). Mr. Barrabino provided Mr. Bodmer the opportunity of drawing several Indians from the tribes of the once powerful Choctaws, Cherokees, and Chickasaws, now frequently in a sad state of drunkenness and degradation.

The different races of humanity were most interesting, for this city has people of all nations, especially Negroes [in] various degrees of mixture. The quadroons were praised as being especially handsome. Several ships lay at anchor, including a packet boat full of Negro slaves bound for Mobile. Depressing scenes of how this class of humanity was treated. Mr. Bodmer saw them being sold and punished. A Negress was led to the gallows to be hanged because she had struck the slave overseer. A Spaniard and a Negro boxed with bare fists. The white man knocked one of the eyes out of the

Negro's head and then fell down on his knees before him to beg forgiveness.

After a stay of about a week, [when] our financial affairs had been settled with Mr. Nicolet, Mr. Bodmer embarked on 22 January on the steamship *Arkansa* for Baton Rouge.

[They passed many plantations,] the planters' homes usually barely a gunshot away from the bank. Broad paths led through lanes of orange trees and gardens to the houses. The [main] dwelling was usually large [and] built of brick, with verandas, galleries, [and a] red roof. In rows on both sides, small board houses painted white, where the slaves lived. A certain general was said to own a plantation with 1,200 Negro slaves near Baton Rouge.

Mr. Bodmer stayed at Baton Rouge for three days and did several sketches, including one of the barracks located up the river, where about 150 men and five or six officers of the regular military were stationed.

[Mr. Bodmer took] the steamboat *Napoleon* [to] Natchez, [where he remained] for a week. He saw [and] sketched many Choctaw Indians. [Natchez has] a significant cotton trade. The streets were frequently choked with wagons coming from the plantations, often drawn by five pairs of oxen harnessed in tandem. About six bales of cotton, each weighing 400 pounds, were loaded onto one wagon. Several steamships go back and forth between New Orleans and Natchez exclusively [to service the cotton trade], some carrying 2,730 bales of cotton.

In Natchez Mr. Bodmer boarded the steamboat *Cavalier,* [which] had many passengers. [The *Cavalier* docked at Mount Vernon on the morning of 15 February,] and Mr. Bodmer immediately rode to Harmony.

16 February: In the morning, Mr. Bodmer worked on the interesting sketches he had brought back; [I] showed them to Messrs. Lesueur and Say [that afternoon].

17 February: In the evening I paid a visit to Mr. Say. We talked at great length about Indians, [especially] the famous Chief Petalesharo, who is poorly depicted in Godman's *Natural History.* On the other hand, that work includes a picture of Óngpa-Tánga (Big Elk) that, according to Mr. Say, is [a] good likeness. [In March 1820] Mr. Say [told Big Elk] not to go to the military post at Council Bluff,[5] [because] the mortality from scurvy was high there (and because they were not eager for this chief to learn about the sad, weakened condition of the fort). When warned, Óngpa-Tánga stood up and [declared vigorously] to Mr. Say that he feared nothing in the world, for he

was in the hand of Wacondá (the Great Spirit), who completely guided his destiny; he would not stay away for fear of contagion. If, however, Mr. Say did not wish him to go there, then he would not do so.

18–20 February: [Went hunting on Cutoff Island and in the woods around the Wabash.] In our lodging the carpenter made crates in which to pack our collections. I described a beautiful bird of prey, *Falco borealis,* which Russel brought me. It was a resident [species in this area].

22 February: I wrote letters to Mr. Nicolet (banker) in New Orleans, to send him receipts for the money received there by Mr. Bodmer, and to Mr. Barrabino. The cooper arrived, and we packed nine turtles from New Orleans in a small cask. Afterward I took my walk. The sun was shining, and it was very warm and pleasant. The glow from the swollen Wabash was especially beautiful. I heard Bodmer shooting over on Fox Island, where he had gone with young Duclos; [they] returned with ducks, [including] *Anas rufitorques* and *crecca.* [They] had seen an extraordinarily large number of ducks, returning from their southern migrations.

23 February: Our second collection of natural history specimens, made during the second half of our stay here, was almost packed. It filled five crates, for a total of eight Harmony cases. Today, for the first time in a long while, Mr. Say visited us; he had been indisposed for several weeks. In the evening we went over to his place [and] met the Harmony postmaster, Monsieur Gex, a Swiss [immigrant].

24 February: In the morning at daybreak, snow, [but] only an inch.

Today I attempted to draw up a list of birds [observed] during my four-month stay in Harmony: nonmigratory [resident] birds [and those passing through; all told, about 60+ species]. In the evening Mr. Say and I went to Mr. Maclure's. We had a discussion about the constitution and government of the United States, which was quite interesting and instructive for me. The Chamber of Deputies [the Senate] is the first; each state sends two deputies [senators]. The second chamber is that of the Representatives, which corresponds to the House of Commons in London. Behavior is somewhat tumultuous there, [and] far more decorous in the [first] house. An Indian chief [observed and described] it very well; he said [that] in the first chamber there were men, in the second, boys.

25–28 February: I put together a list of the principal trees and shrubs here, as well as I could identify them in their defoliated state. There are approximately [eighty-two trees, shrubs, and woody vines.] The vegetation near Harmony is quite different from that of Pennsylvania.

[Afternoons spent on pleasant walks near the Wabash, hunting for ducks.] I heard cranes flying high up in the sky. I found a small plant already in bloom *(Arabis rhomboidea* or *bulbosa)* and others of the same variety with buds, even though it was very raw and cold, the small pools still covered with ice. [On 28 February] it began to snow; [by] five o'clock [it] was three inches deep. We stayed at home to work. Dreidoppel packed crates; we sketched and wrote. In the evening, a visit in the evening to Mr. Say.

1 March: In our room it was cold; the wood was not dry, [and] green wood yields no heat. Today I labeled our five crates, which were ready to go to New Orleans and Europe. A sixth small one was filled with bones from old Indian graves and intended for [Professor] Blumenbach; in it there were [also] seeds for Professor [Heinrich Adolph] Schrader and a letter for [my nephew] Hermann, who was studying at Göttingen.

The cold weather delayed our departure, since Mr. Bodmer still had to finish his view of the Fox River, and when the weather is cold and the ground wet, sketching out in the open is impossible. In the evening, we went to the home of Mr. Lesueur. We spoke much about the limestone formations of the Ohio and Mississippi, where many [fossils can be] found. Near Natchez and other towns, Mr. Lesueur had made significant collections of [these; he] precisely depicted and sketched the various strata, as well as the shells, animal teeth, fish bones, and the like occurring in them. At St. Louis, Lesueur found some very nice big [fossil crinoids,] pentacrinites and encrinites, on the steplike limestone ridges near the city.

2 March: During the night we shivered in our beds. [In the] afternoon I went to the creek near Harmony, which was almost completely frozen over; [the ducks] anxiously sought small open brooks and did not seem to want to remain on the Wabash. [That evening, at] Mr. Say's, we talked about Peale's Museum in Philadelphia. The collection was established by the late [Charles Willson] Peale, who was a saddler and an enthusiastic portrait painter. He did numerous pictures of outstanding men from the American Revolution [and also of] distinguished scholars, including [Alexander] von Humboldt, Messrs. Say, Lesueur, etc. He was a rather poor painter. The museum, [which] still belongs to his family, [had natural history] material from various quarters, a significant collection, [but Peale] was not a naturalist.

7 March: I rode with Mr. Bodmer and Mr. Lesueur to the Fox River. At Cutoff

Island we got out. Woodcutters were cutting wood for the steamboats. They had felled heavy trees, and their blows and the crashing of the falling trees resounded through the lonely wilderness. At noon we met near the place where Mr. Bodmer was finishing a sketch. I had just shot a nice wood duck *(Anas sponsa)*. We enjoyed our frugal lunch of salt pork and bread, with which we drank Fox River water with some brandy. I could not persuade old Lesueur to sit down; [even] at his age he was very active and nimble from morning till evening.[6] While we were occupied with our meal, two large wild turkeys came streaking over the river and alighted near us on trees. Mr. Lesueur and I ran toward them, but my haste caused me to forget about the safety catch on my gun, and it failed to fire.

I had dinner at Mr. Maclure's, [where] we had interesting conversations about the great usefulness and importance of the maize plant (Indian corn) [and the] buffalo (bison), once numerous in [nearby] forests; men who had come to this place while young had seen them. Mr. Say spoke of the excellence of the bison meat he had eaten west of the Mississippi.

9 March: I crossed the Wabash and lay in wait for ducks. The weather was as warm as in May. In the evening, visit to Mr. Say. We talked about the various religious sects in the United States, of which there are a very large number, the names of which can be found in *Darton's Pocket Tablet of Christian Sects,* London, 1816. These include Independents, Glassites, Episcopal[ians], Dunkers (Mennonites), Dissenters, Calvinists, Baptists, Arminians, Arians, Antinomians, Shakers, Lutherans, Quakers or Friends, Unitarians, Swedenborgians, Separatists (Rapp), [and many others].

10 March: Early this morning two [young Frenchmen,] the Duclos, took us to the Fox River. I got out first, but since it was Sunday [and] people [were] everywhere, one was almost unable to shoot because of the hunters. I saw a large number of turtles sitting on old trunks and logs in the water. They were large and small and in groups of four or five. They were very shy and immediately dove into the water when they saw people. I fired; one remained, [others] escaped. The one I hit was alive but severely wounded; it was [a] specimen of the beautiful species with two red spots behind the head. Mr. Say described it under the name *Emys biguttata.* I saw a flight of parakeets, heard an owl calling inside an enormous tall *Platanus,* [and] saw a wild turkey streak across the Wabash. We returned to Harmony at dusk.

13 March: We worked at home; Dreidoppel went out. Someone brought us a muskrat, and I talked with Mr. Say about measuring elevations. Mr. Lesueur gave

me copies of his etchings of fossil shells and petrifactions along the Mississippi. We spoke further about the museums in the larger American cities. Given the Americans' general lack of appreciation for the proper study of nature, public collections have been able to maintain themselves only by including organs, bands, and various kinds of frivolities, such as poor-quality wax figures, a representation of hell (in Cincinnati), etc., for the entertainment of boorish country folk. These draw crude crowds of spectators, and [the owners'] incomes greatly increase. There was steady attendance [after] the hell scene was set up in the otherwise interesting natural history museum at Cincinnati. Previously Mr. Dorfeuille could hardly pay the building rent with the revenues from the twenty-five-cent admission.

14 March: Beautiful weather. We saw buds on several trees, bees swarming, grass sprouting. In the evening, a dance at our house. The delightful music began with the big drum at six thirty; other amenities did not fail to appear. Backwoodsmen arrived on horseback to grace the dance with their presence. Because we had not attended the earlier dances, to which we [had] received invitations with various odd distortions of our names, we had not been invited today.[7] [Instead,] we visited Mr. Say [for] our next-to-the-last evening in New Harmony. We spoke much about regions along the Missouri, and Mr. Say promised me several additional letters to acquaintances in those regions. [At home] they were dancing fiercely in time with the big drum and diligently fortifying themselves with whiskey.

15 March: We worked at home, packed, and made parting visits to Mr. Owen, Mr. Maclure, Mr. Twigg, Mr. Lesueur, and Mr. Say. After a stay of almost five months in New Harmony, we took a very heartfelt leave of good friends, especially Mr. Say and Mr. Lesueur, who had shown us ample kindness during our stay here. The sojourn in Harmony, in spite of the unfavorable time of year, nevertheless taught us much about this part of Indiana and was of great value for our collections.

VI

Journey from New Harmony on the Wabash to St. Louis on the Mississippi and Stay There

16 March: After breakfast Mr. Bodmer and I mounted our landlord's two light bays and rode ahead of the wagon that [carried] Dreidoppel and our [belongings]. The morning was glorious and very warm; the sunshine was pleasant. We puffed our cigarros as we rode from Harmony up the hills, [through] tall woodlands [and past] cultivated fields scattered throughout the forest. The road, which ran between hills and small valleys following endlessly one after the other, was rather good. At twelve thirty, in quite hot weather, we [saw] Mount Vernon before us as we came out of the forest. This small town, with scattered houses and [a] red courthouse on an open area (see Mr. Bodmer's sketch), had about [600] inhabitants, including five physicians. About a third of its houses were brick. The town was more lively now than [at] our arrival last October. We took lodging in the Mount Vernon Hotel, and soon our baggage arrived. My zoological collection, sent here earlier, had gone off to New Orleans the day before yesterday.

The Ohio had a far more imposing appearance now than it did last autumn. It is much broader than the Rhine and sometimes rises 30 feet higher, until it reaches the thresholds of the wooden houses of Mount Vernon built along the bank, a level at which the river must be extremely impressive. It was now broad, high, and much closer to the houses than in the fall.

Since we wanted to go to Shawneetown [for a short stay], we asked to [be notified] of the arrival of [any westbound] steamboat, day or night. Dreidoppel [also] stood by for embarkation, [but he was to take our baggage straight to St. Louis].

17 March: [Next morning, a Sunday,] Mr. Bodmer went hunting for birds and frogs. I went into the courthouse, which was always open, and paced off the interior. The building had two stories. The assembly chamber, on the ground floor, [measured] 14 steps on each side. A long court session lasting several weeks had recently been held here.

Years ago, Meskwaki Indians lived in this region. They were not numerous and stayed near the mouth of the Wabash and along Big Creek. They were strong, handsome people, with breechcloths, bows, and arrows, [and] about 30 to 40 shabby guns. They were experts with the bow. Their [lodges] were built of thick bundles of cane and lined on the inside with deerskins. Their heads were shorn except for a tuft of hair in the middle of the head. They painted themselves red. I spoke with one of the first settlers of this region, who moved in 1806 into the Wabash woodlands, where there were then no white people. The year before the battle of Tippecanoe, [fought in 1811], the Indians left this area and never returned.

Morning of [18 March]: Dreary, heavily clouded sky. During the night two steamboats had gone upstream, but none had come down. In Mount Vernon we [had] scarcely anything to do and were bored in this miserable place, from which we hoped every moment for deliverance. At ten o'clock two steamboats came down the river. The first one, the *Conveyance,* lay to and took on wood. The second one, the *Napoleon,* on which Mr. Bodmer had traveled [in February from Baton Rouge to Natchez], did not stop. Thus, we had to board the *Conveyance,* [which] was small and much slower than the large, swift *Napoleon.* At eleven o'clock our boat departed. We paid three dollars' passage for two persons to Shawneetown. The ship's cabin had sixteen berths. Four gentlemen were playing cards [there]. Though well dressed, they blew their noses after the fashion of German peasants, chewed tobacco, and spat on the rug. We watched the *Napoleon,* [which] had a long lead. Our course closely [followed] the southern bank. When we sat down to eat, we could already see the white buildings of Shawneetown at the end of a long, straight stretch of the river. After our meal we disembarked in the ship's boat, and the innkeeper led us to his house while an old Negro took our luggage there.

Shawneetown, a miserable place constructed parallel to the river, had 700 inhabitants, several stores, a post office, taverns, etc. It looked even more wretched than Mount Vernon. The inn was rather good.

Indians of the Shawnee tribe and some Delawares once lived [in] villages in [this] vicinity. Recently a brook or the river washed away a bank [and exposed] a large number of skeletons. Flint arrowheads were found everywhere.

We had intended to stay here for several days to sketch the cavern of Cave-in-Rock but learned we had been misinformed and this place was 25 miles [downriver]. Since there was no reason to remain, we decided to leave on the next steamboat.

[19 March:] At daybreak the pleasant, friendly innkeeper wakened us to announce that two steamboats were coming down the Ohio. We jumped out of bed, quickly got ready, and had the inn's blacks take our luggage to the *Paragon,* [which was] not large but said to be fast. A much larger ship, the *Brunswick,* had just departed. We boarded the *Paragon* and found Dreidoppel on board with the baggage. Estes, the captain, a friendly, agreeable man, had established a farm near Prairie du Chien about a year ago. The Menominees and Winnebagoes, with whom he was on very friendly terms, lived close by. He provided me with some interesting information. According to him, the Winnebagoes build long lodges with rounded tops and are large, handsome people. The Menominees are not so tall but very well built, about 5' 8", and have handsome, round faces.

The total length of our ship was about 51 of my paces. It had sixteen beds in the men's cabin. Families lived above on the second deck. We departed early [and soon] approached the most beautiful section of the Ohio, where it has higher, rocky banks, wooded hills, [and] picturesque valleys. Flatboats floated by. The buds already lent the *Platanus* a reddish brown tinge on top. Before us a beautiful view into the distance, where a steamboat gave off smoke. I sat on the stern gallery of the ship next to [a] hanging piece of meat and wrote with [Cumings's *Western Pilot*] of 1829 in hand. The Americans, in their great indolence, stared in astonishment at my activity.

We [passed] Cave-in-Rock Island, [Kentucky]; Cave-in-Rock, [on the Illinois bank, lay] directly opposite the end of [the island]. [Then] Hurricane Island, [Kentucky], appeared; from now on, gentler, frequently undulating banks. [*The Western Pilot* map] no. 18 directed steamboats to the right of Hurricane Island, [which] was very long; it took at least half an hour to sail past it. On the river a man in [a] boat waved his hat vehemently. The engine stopped; the red-haired passenger was taken on board. To the right, rugged hills with rocky debris and individual trees; wherever there was limestone, one saw single cedars. The strata were often noteworthy, the hills mostly gently conical; sometimes the tops were stratified. At eleven o'clock a Negro rang for luncheon, consisting of crackers, cheese, ham, raisins, and almonds, with which people drank cider.

Golconda appeared behind an island to the right, in an inlet behind lofty wooded hills where Lusk Creek emptied. This town was the seat of the judicial courts of Pope County, Illinois. A new courthouse was being built [in] exactly the same architectural style as the one in Mount Vernon: rectangular, three windows on each side. We caught up with the *New Brunswick,* a large New Orleans boat; all the people, black and white, gathered to watch [our ship,] the *Paragon,* pass [by and] leave that steamboat far behind. We stopped [at Smithland, Kentucky,] for a half hour; the *Brunswick* followed our example [and] also took on some wood. Chickens from this ship ran into the town and prompted a chase.

The Ohio [was] very broad and imposing. To the left, picturesquely wild forest scenes; hills in the tall timber on which there were small, white log houses (unpainted but made from new lumber). The Tennessee River discharged to the left, [an important river with a] course 1,200 miles in length. [Then,] the town of Paducah, where the steamboat *Samson* lay at anchor. We stopped to discharge passengers. This town had developed only recently, for *The Western Pilot* of 1829 did not mention it. We stopped near [a] clearing with several dwellings and took on wood. Our ship needed eight cords of wood daily, [assuming the wood] was good and dry. In the evening, uniform land overgrown with tall forest. We lay to at the bank for the night.

20 March: [Early in the morning we came] to the mouth of the Ohio [and a] point of land to the right between the Mississippi and the Ohio with several houses, a tavern, and a store. We stopped and loaded wood. [I] visited the store, where many animal skins were piled up, and bought a fine black bearskin for two dollars. This bear had been killed in the vicinity just recently and her three cubs captured. We saw one of them. It was still very small and had no teeth, [but] its claws [were] powerful. It was not for sale. The large antlers of an elk *(Cervus canadensis)* hung outside the store; they asked too much for them.

We sailed into the Mississippi and followed its left bank upstream. Here it was wide as the Ohio, its water the same color. Snags in the water; one could navigate here only by day because the river was low; the lead was tossed out continually. In an hour the ship covered 5 to 6 miles against the current. At eleven o'clock, luncheon. To our left the steamboat *O'Connell* had firmly run aground and had unloaded its cargo on the flat sandy shore. After lunch, we put in at the right bank to take on wood, for which we paid [a farmer] five dollars ([for] two cords). We went into the [nearby] dense, beautiful forest [and] became keenly aware of spring. There was undergrowth [everywhere], 10–15-foot-tall spicewood (*Laurus* [—]) every-where, covered with yellow blossoms; the cut wood has a very aromatic fra-grance, like [bayberry]. On the ground, pretty [yellow] *Fumaria* bloomed everywhere. In front of the house, which was right on the bank, stood a tree wildly entwined [by] a beautiful *Bignonia radicans.*

After a half-hour stop, we continued. The river soon formed several branches and surrounded several islands. [One could see] how islands were sometimes formed in these rivers. At one place the bank had caved in and revealed piled-up layers of huge tree trunks with their crowns peering out. On such accumulations sand is deposited and, gradually, earth, on which willows grow first, then cottonwoods, and finally hardwoods.

We sailed close to the banks, terribly eroded by the current. The wind drove the ship still more to the side, and suddenly we were aground, even though the *Paragon* had a draft of only five feet. The engine stopped. A sounding was taken. They pushed with poles, let [the ship] drift backward, finally let it swing sideways, and ten minutes later we were afloat. Pieces of limestone lay on the bank like ruins. Twilight [presently] fell, and we took shelter from the raw night air below deck. At nightfall we lay to on the Missouri [side] near a recently built house. A stairway of roughly hewn wood led up to the top of the steep, 50- to 60-foot-high bank. A big fire was kindled on top, and we warmed ourselves by it. The captain sat on the steps. The tall forest trees, especially *Platanus,* [were] splendidly brightened and reddened by the flames. Afterward we entered the small but clean [dwell-ing], which was well caulked on all sides, and conversed with the lady of the house.

21 March: [In the morning], after a journey of about one or one and a half hours, a gradual bend to the right, within which, on the left side, Cape Girardeau was located, an old French settlement that people said was growing — [hard to believe] from the shabby appearance of the place. The river now divided around the broad Devils Island, [Missouri], the tip of which was shaped like a broad bastion. In the river a steamboat lay; [it] sank (was snagged) three months ago. It was already totally destroyed. The river was beautiful and wide. Tobacco was cultivated on the left side. Limestone walls with trans-verse strata, horizontal layers and vertical cleavage, steep, and overgrown above with woodlands. At about one o'clock, Hanging Dog Island, [Illinois], linked to the right bank by a large sandbar.

After lunch, sparsely wooded hills to the left. Many [pines] interspersed among the deciduous trees. The ship ran aground but was immediately free again. It turned to the left but was stranded again for about half an hour. The engine was reversed, [the boat] turned, and finally a passage was found to the left along the land.

[Apple] Creek to the left; immediately behind it, a settlement with much piled-up firewood [and] a large wooden signboard on which the grade of the firewood and its price were written: Ash $1.25.

Soon strange rocks appeared to the left [and right, such as] the Grand Tower, an isolated roundish, drum-shaped formation, 60 to 80 feet high, in magnificent evening illumination.[1] We were delighted by this scene. Directly opposite, to the right along the bank, stood three or four extremely odd rocks full of fissures and clefts. They were remarkable. The one in front was called Devil's Bake Oven. A short distance beyond this rather narrow, rocky passage, [Brazeau] Creek poured into the river on the left side. Here we put in and took on some wood at about five o'clock in the afternoon. Near the creek to the north several habitations were located, in one of which a Negro family, undoubtedly slaves, lived. Between the houses and the bank were a large number of long beds planted with cotton *(Gossypium)*. We sailed on. The river soon made a turn to the left. At suppertime we put in on the Illinois bank and took on wood.

22 March: Splendid morning. View of the sunrise from the stern of the ship. Magnificent colors in the wake of the steamboat as the glowing disk of the sun rose above the Mississippi forest. After several miles, the pilot had a sounding made. Just as the captain announced 6 feet of water, the ship ran aground. The engine pushed backward; we turned left and soon were free again. To the right, [Mary's] River emptied from densely wooded banks. Soundings continued. The depth varied from 7 to 8 or 9 feet of water.

At the village of Chester, [Illinois], we put in for a quarter of an hour. [I saw] a beautiful lizard with carinate scales, dark angular stripes on its back, and two areas with a metallic sheen now underneath its body *(Agama* [—]).

[That afternoon, we came to the vicinity of Ste. Genevieve, located upstream on Gabarre Creek.] We went ashore [for a few hours]. Ste. Genevieve, a large village of 600 to 800 inhabitants, was about 20 minutes away from the [river] landing. An old French colony, it appeared to be in a state of dilapidation. The houses were mostly one story with verandas on posts. Many Negro slaves. People spoke mostly French but also English. [There were] several Germans, too.

Rana halecina were in [Gabarre] creek in large numbers for spring mating; we caught several of them. I [also] collected several blossoms.

In April or May, caravans depart [from] here for the interior (the upper Missouri). They were now getting ready. Somewhat farther inland [there] were important lead mines. At about six thirty we boarded and had supper. As night fell, we ran aground. I worked on my diary.

23 March: The disk of the sun rose magnificently over the forest; it glowed like fire in the Mississippi. To the right, strange walls of rock alternated with bottomland. On the opposite bank, tall forest [with] no hills, [a] partially eroded bank [with] sandbars before it.

[A little later, we passed the site of] Fort [de] Chartres, once a strong garrison, on the land to the right. Our course was north[ward]. This morning we [had] covered 10½ to 11 miles. To the left [there] now appeared a most remarkable towerlike rock turret, resembling one of our old castle ruins on the German Rhine.

[Farther on, past Plattin] Creek, [Missouri], one saw Herculaneum, in a shallow inlet. Gray wooden cottages, several painted white, only one brick house among them, lay scattered about, with tall *Platanus* and cottonwoods among them. Near those miserable huts, several elegant ladies walked along the shore, the veils on their large hats fluttering fantastically in the wind!!

A brisk, favorable wind from the south today. In the afternoon, striking cliffs to the left again. On the sandbar of an island, a troop of wild turkeys walked contentedly. The steamboat *Michigan* moved past us, a big, beautiful ship, its name painted in red. We continued [past the mouth of the Meramec River], a broad view before us. [Later, we spied] the Jefferson Barracks, [where] the United States flag waved. In the barracks, the famous Sauk chief Black Hawk was being held prisoner with eight to ten [other] chiefs, including the Winnebago Prophet [Wabokieshiek. We passed the barracks] at five thirty in the evening. The river made a tight bend to the right; to the left of that bend lay Carondelet, a French settlement, built about a hundred years ago by French Canadians. We continued somewhat farther and lay to for the night near a single house.

24 March: In the morning at daybreak, we sailed back somewhat, around a sandbar, to get into the channel [and then] around the upper tip of [a] willow island, and St. Louis appeared on the bank. [Initial] view of the city rather unattractive, [but] as we approached more closely, the city presented itself more favorably, beautifully illuminated by the rising sun. We landed and

took lodging at the Union Hotel, [where] I found a letter from Neuwied, [dated] the 21st of November.

25 March: In the morning a steamboat arrived with many Indians from the two tribes of Sauk (Sac) and Meskwaki (Fox) [who] came to appeal for the release of their compatriots in the barracks. We hurried to the building that had been assigned to them as temporary quarters. On the riverbank we saw a crowd of people, and among the Europeans, strange-looking figures wrapped in red, white, and green blankets. When we reached them, they were already in the building. My first view of them astonished me greatly [but] nevertheless revealed to me their great similarity to the Brazilians; they are absolutely of the same race. Strong, well-built men, some at least ten inches [(approximately 6 feet)] tall.[2] Most had broad faces and sturdy features. Hair and eyes black, teeth mostly very white and strong, arms not thick, calves usually thin. Skin often dark brown [and] heavily smeared with paints. Their heads were mostly shaven [except for] a tuft of hair on the back of the head, which they braided [as a base for] an ornament of red and black horsehair, [to] which they fasten single feathers, black at the tips or completely black, the white section often dyed red.[M1] [See pl. 1.] Their ears were pierced along the upper edge with three or four holes and hung with short strings of blue and white wampum, like tassels. They wore similar strings of [wampum] around their necks. The women had large heads; their hair [was knotted] in back [and] wrapped in green [and] red material.

All of them had painted their faces more or less red, mostly in the following ways but differing according to individual taste. [Sometimes] the area surrounding the eyes and ears was red, often the cheeks, too. With others, the entire head was completely red, except for a white spot on the forehead and a black one around the mouth and chin, giving them a fearsome appearance. Some had the [upper] face painted red, the lower part black; or, on each side of the chin, a black or yellow hand with outstretched fingers.

A tall, handsome Sauk man named Massica (Turtle; see [pl. 1]) had a height of [approximately 6'] and a nice bold face, sometimes wild, sometimes very expressively friendly. His black eyes sparkled and his snow-white

---

[M1] They shave or pluck out all their body hair, as well as their eyebrows and beards, after rubbing them with hot ashes. They use a coiled piece of wire to pull out their facial hair.

teeth gleamed in the dark brown face, which was partly painted red. On his forehead he wore a long, beautiful band of otter skin that hung in double strands over his shoulders down to his heels. All of them were wrapped in woolen blankets, mostly red, [some] green and white. [Under] their blankets, some had [shirts] of green or multicolored calico, the sleeves with a kind of ruffle [on] the wrist, neck, and chest. The pants (leggins) [were deerskin], as were the shoes, [which were] made in the Indian manner [and] often artistically adorned with needlework on the instep. Most wore brass necklaces and bracelets.

In their hands, the 30 to 40 men all carried their weapons, such as tomahawks (battle-axes made of steel [and] manufactured by the whites, [with an] attached pipe; the pipestem also served as a handle). We saw no bows and arrows in this group; on the other hand, [there was] a kind of lance, a long sword blade [attached to] a pole covered with red woolen material, with feathers and other ornaments, and often [also] decorated with little bells and animal hides.

The principal Sauk chief was Keokuk, a good-looking man of medium height with an intelligent, pleasant expression and features differing little from those of Europeans, though of a darker color. He had a calico jacket, a large medallion hanging on his chest, a multicolored ornamented cloth around his head, and was wrapped in a green woolen blanket. In his hand he carried a peace pipe decorated with feathers and other objects to which, among other things, a woodpecker's beak was attached, though not one from a *Picus principalis,* which I saw on another Indian. His face was not painted; his ears had their natural shape. This chief was not of purely Indian descent; his father or his mother was said to have been European.

The languages of these two tribes differ little from one another and do not sound very barbaric. They have no velar sounds or any real nasal sounds. The words, however, are often pronounced somewhat indistinctly, so that sometimes it is not easy to record them, yet less difficult, as I have discovered, than many [other] Indian nations. I recorded [a vocabulary] directly according to the Indian pronunciation while the interpreter, a French-Canadian and half Indian, stood by and assisted me. These languages are easiest for a German to record because there are sounds and syllables in them that are difficult for English and French speakers, such as the German *ch,* as in the word *ich* and others like it.

It was most interesting to observe large numbers of these Indians together. They were anything but quiet and serious; on the contrary, one often witnessed hearty laughter and vigorously expressed merriment. On the steamship, they often sang, generally not entirely unharmoniously. If one approached and addressed them in a sincere manner, they usually had very cordial, friendly expressions; they were pleased to provide words of their language and willing to be sketched, [which] they seemed to enjoy. There were several men of graver temperament among them, especially Watapinat (Eagle's Nest), a Meskwaki [who] usually sat, serious and still, observing everything.

These Indians lived on the western bank of the Mississippi opposite Rock Island, a journey of about two days north of St. Louis. Some lived along the bank, [but] the main group [was] about 20 miles inland, where they hunted herds of bison in fall and winter. They were rather numerous; the Sauks could put 1,600 warriors in the field.

Our dealings with the Indians that morning were quite absorbing. Toward noon I went to several distinguished St. Louis [citizens] who were acquainted with Indians and the regions in which they lived. I had letters from [Duke] Bernhard of Weimar to General Clark and Mr. [Jean Pierre] Chouteau, [Sr.]. General Clark (called "the Redhead" by the Indians) was Superintendent of Indian Affairs and a fine man whom they respected. Under him were several Indian agents for the western territories, and under them there were several subagents. [General Clark] owned a collection of all kinds of Indian utensils, weapons, and the like, most of which he collected during his journey with Captain Lewis across the entire breadth of America to the Pacific Ocean. He said there would be a small council with the Indians that afternoon, [where] the chief would deliver a speech, and he invited us to it.

At two o'clock we went [to his house]. The Indians, about 30 in number, were sitting in several rows along the walls, the chiefs on the right side. General Clark sat in the middle, Mr. Bodmer and I at his side. Behind the general stood a table [at] which the secretary recorded the parley. All [the] Indians were painted and adorned. General Clark first had them told why he had called them together. The interpreter, a heavy man with a very brown face, translated his address. Then the Indians' leading chieftain stood up before the general, his peace pipe in his hand. He gesticulated with his right hand and moved it in accordance with his various thoughts [as] he spoke loudly and briefly, each sentence followed by a pause. [The chief's] statements were translated and written down, so the discussion lasted over half an hour. [The Indians] were told that they should persevere [in] their good attitudes as in the past. [If] they wished to see their captured brothers freed soon (at home the [prisoners'] wives and children were suffering hunger), the general would intercede for them with General Atkinson, the troop commander, about this matter, [but] they [must then] keep a watchful eye on the captives when they were released.

That afternoon I looked up Mr. McKenzie, who was the principal associate of the [American] Fur Company, and made his acquaintance, since he was an important man for our journey up the Missouri. He was expecting his steamboat *Yellow Stone* to arrive [soon] from New Orleans; [he intended to] travel up the Missouri on it, and we hoped to go along.[3] General Clark invited us to accompany him the following morning on the steamboat *Warrior* to Jefferson Barracks, where all [the visiting] Indians were to see their captive friends.

[26 March:] On the morning of the 26th at seven thirty, we found the Indians already on board the *Warrior*. We had provided ourselves with a supply of cigars and, with small gifts like these, gained their friendship and trust. When General Clark and later the interpreter arrived, we weighed anchor and sailed down the Mississippi. The Indians occasionally sang on this journey; they gathered near the bow of the ship for this purpose. Many, who beneath their woolen blankets were completely naked above the waist, were thoroughly chilled in the raw, cold, penetrating wind, yet they [remained]. Below deck in the stern of the ship, [some] had a fire [on which] they cooked and roasted [provisions]. They attentively examined the steam engines, the hissing and roaring of which entertained them.

At ten o'clock we approached [Jefferson] Barracks, [and we saw] many of its residents on shore. We landed and marched in a procession, the chiefs at the head of the Indians, up the hill to the barracks. General Clark introduced us to the commanding officer, General Atkinson, and after a short pause at his house, [everyone] met in a large room of the barracks, where the Indians had already taken their places in rows. General Atkinson sat [opposite] them, General Clark beside him; spectators, including many women, made up the audience.

When all were assembled, Keokuk, with the help of the interpreter, addressed a speech to the general, and the latter replied that he could [now] see the prisoners, who were brought in. At their head was Black Hawk, an old man, not very large, rather light yellow in complexion. [He had] an almost completely Chinese face, an impression to which his shorn head, with a small lock behind, contributed. None of the captives were painted.

They entered, at least Black Hawk [did], with rather dispirited expressions. Although no Indian betrayed any sign of emotion, in most of them one could very clearly sense a feeling [of depression]. The prisoners shook hands one after the other with all of us and then sat down in the inner circle of the assembly. Two of the prisoners, the Winnebago Prophet and another Indian (they were characterized as evil men), had chains and large iron balls fastened to their legs; none of the others were shackled. [A] guard led them about for several hours every day.

The speeches began, as yesterday. Keokuk spoke several times and pleaded for the prisoners. The general always answered in short phrases that he would intercede for them but demanded that they keep a watchful eye on the prisoners, especially the two evil men. The Indian assembly, as usual, expressed its approval [loudly]. After General Atkinson had emphasized a number of matters for the Indians' observation and consideration, we departed and left the Indians to speak among themselves, so they could freely vent their feelings. The sight of old Black Hawk and his fellow sufferers was touching, and most of those gathered here may well have felt sympathy for them.

We proceeded to the general's dwelling. Later [we] took a walk with General Clark, on which we viewed the long, low barracks (from the outside [only], since General Atkinson did not offer to show us [more]). There was a permanent parade ground in the square formed by the buildings. The hospital nearby was of medium size. From the [hilltop] elevation where the barracks were located, the view was very attractive, especially that of the beautiful Mississippi.

We were invited to General Atkinson's for lunch. At three o'clock we again boarded the *Warrior* with the Indians; General Clark returned by land. We had a tedious voyage up the Mississippi and did not arrive in St. Louis until late that evening. In the meantime the Indians had provided much entertainment. They sang now and then [and] had repainted themselves. I recorded words of their languages.

27 March: Because our itinerary for the coming summer had not yet been determined, I went to see Mr. McKenzie, [who soon] will go upriver [on his steamboat *Yellow Stone*]. This ship never took passengers, [so] whether we

would travel on it was still uncertain. At Mr. McKenzie's I made the acquaintance of Major Dougherty, who had traveled with Major Long to the Rocky Mountains.

Later we had Indians in our house who were sketched. We served them apples, almonds, and cigarros and also paid them for [posing]. They were quite happy to be sketched.

28 March: A [Scotsman, Captain Stewart,] who was planning a major overland expedition to the Rocky Mountains, came to my place. He brought news from Mr. McKenzie and told me that the principal reason for hesitation about our traveling on his ship was that we might not always abide by company prices. I told him that I would always do so and hoped the matter could be arranged. We finished our work with the Indians today and bought some of their ornaments.

29 March: During the morning I made various purchases and orders. At eleven o'clock Mr. Bodmer and I went upriver to [see] Major Dougherty, [an] Indian agent Mr. Say had recommended. He was at Major O'Fallon's, [where] we were invited for lunch. Both men were well known because of their journeys with Major Long into the interior of the western territories.

Major O'Fallon was not well educated, as he himself immediately said. [He] did, however, have much practical experience in the regions of the Missouri and thus was helpful to us. His house was attractive, decorated with Indian implements and paintings that the [artist] Catlin painted for him in exchange for numerous Indian artifacts. O'Fallon's Indian pipe bowls were remarkable. After lunch we were taken into [his] well-tended garden [and] found some interesting things there, too, [such as] several shrubs from the upper Missouri [and] sweetgrass, which the Indians wore around their necks because of its pleasant scent. We also saw the petrified skeleton of a large crocodile-like animal that Major O'Fallon had found on [a Missouri] riverbank. O'Fallon lent me [maps] of the Missouri (covering at least the greater part of its course) for our journey; Lewis and Clark had drafted these on their expedition.[4]

30 March: Stewart (the Rocky Mountain traveler) came at nine o'clock to say that Mr. McKenzie was ready to talk with us. I went with Mr. Bodmer to the fur [company] office. Mr. Chouteau, Jr., was also there. Our course was determined: we were to travel with Mr. McKenzie up the Missouri to their fort [near] the Yellowstone River and winter there. We discussed the things we needed to take along and the long preparation for such a journey. Major

Dougherty would make the first part of the journey with us. Later we walked about in the city with Captain Stewart and ordered tomahawks and large knives. Visit in the evening at the home of Captain Stewart.

31 March: Sunday, and elegant society made its appearance. A large number of persons strolled about the city. Even the Negroes, of whom there were very many here, almost all slaves, were seen dressed in the best possible manner; they complained, however, that they must also work on this day. There were many Catholics here in St. Louis, but one did not hear church bells on Sunday as in Europe; probably [there] were no bells here.

1 April: This morning Mr. Bodmer saw several large swallows. From our windows we [watched] a neighbor beat his slave, again and again. A crowd of spectators stood around. These are the free Americans! A Negro slave who waited on us expressed his displeasure loudly. A German who lived about 80 miles up the Missouri visited us. That region is very fertile, [with] wild turkeys in large numbers and not at all shy.

We proceeded to the office of the American Fur Company. Mr. McKenzie was there and told me he could vouch for nothing more than that we could come along as far as the *Yellow Stone* was able to forge ahead. I agreed to this. Fare and baggage would be calculated accordingly. Later I met Captain Stewart and, in his company, made various purchases. At ten or eleven o'clock, the heat was already great, with dust in the street. I sent a letter to Mr. Say in Harmony. The tomahawks that had been ordered for us were finished today, for five dollars each.

In the afternoon I paid a visit to General Clark, who told us we should make written application to him if we wanted passes for the journey on the Missouri, [so] later we wrote the [required] letters to [him]. We made a large number of preparations, and I made the purchases needed for our planned work. These include the following articles: 1. A new double-barreled shotgun with powder horn and shot bags. 2. Good tomahawks. 3. A large cleaver. 4. Small knives. 5. Lead for bullets and casting ladles. 6. Four different sizes of shot. 7. Powder. 8. Tobacco of two different grades and cigarros. 9. Tinder. 10. Flints. 11. Wire and wire pliers. 12. Twine. 13. Cotton. 14. Tow. 15. Four reams of botanical paper. 16. Spirits for [preserving] amphibians. 17. Fishing tackle. 18. Ink and sealing wax. 19. Mercury. 20. Medicines such as rhubarb, linseed, quinine, and the like. 21. [—] lbs. of alum. 22. Arsenic soap. 23. Colors and drawing paper. 24. Pencils. 25. Several books. 26. A new sketch case. 27. Several metal containers for amphibians. 28. Whitish gray felt hats. 29. Several white books. 30. Soap. 31. Sewing needles, thread, and silk thread. 32. A hand ax. 33. Cardboard. 34. Bags. 35. Portfolio. 36. Towels. The evening was warm and the night very dark; we [stayed] home.

2 April: Dreidoppel went out to buy various things. Mr. McKenzie, whom I spoke with before lunch, advised me to come to the office at nine o'clock the following morning, [and] he would sell me trade goods for the Indians. In the afternoon we again made purchases. General Clark sent me my passport for the Indian territories along the Missouri. These passports are useful only at military posts and with Indian agents; of the former there is now only one, and of the latter, three on the Missouri: Major Dougherty, Major B[ean], and [—]. The first is in charge of the district on the lower Missouri. I [looked for] the younger Mr. Chouteau, the chief official in the American Fur Company, and again did not find him at home.

3 April: At nine o'clock I was at Mr. McKenzie's office to discuss various necessary arrangements for the journey. We agreed that I should buy merchandise for [trading with] the Indians at the [company's] fort[s], where they could be purchased more cheaply than elsewhere. In the afternoon we made many [more] purchases, especially of powder and lead, which are so necessary. Captain Stewart told me he would probably depart today, perhaps within the next several hours, and took leave of me. It was too bad that we had to take all the taxidermal materials (cotton, tow, and the like) with us. Mr. Bodmer went out to buy the spirits we needed, and Dreidoppel to buy tobacco. During the evening we were busy at home. Later, heavy rain, thunder, and lightning.

4 April: It rained all night and was therefore very muddy. Again today we hunted for necessary supplies, particularly spirits, tobacco, tow, and the like, [at] no small effort. I exchanged money at the bank and walked a half mile through deep mud to a rope maker [with] a large supply of fine tow, of which I bought 33 pounds for 1 dollar 98 cents. Then I went to the office of the American Fur Company, where I found Messrs. Chouteau and McKenzie, who told me that the steamboat would probably leave on Monday, but they could [not be] definite. They were currently occupied with repacking all the goods received from New Orleans. These gentlemen told me that it was better to leave my money here since I would not be able to use it in the wilderness.

That afternoon, too, purchases and searches were made. The carpenter arrived, and I ordered a packing case. In the three and a half bookstores of

St. Louis, I looked for works relating to the natural history of this region and the Indians but found nothing of significance and everything about a dollar more expensive than in the East. I learned that a steamboat on the Missouri had run onto a snag and had sunk. Navigation on the lower part of this river is said to be difficult and dangerous.

I had letters from Duke Bernhard of Weimar to several distinguished residents of the city, including General Clark and Chouteau *père*, and though I delivered these letters in person, no one returned my visit. Discourtesy and rudeness seemed to be the order of the day here, something that must be attributed to their [distance] from good society, their commercial spirit, and their [dedication] to making money. [On the other hand], in view of our many urgent tasks, it was pleasing not to be annoyed by visits.

[It should be noted that] St. Louis is a productive, lively place [situated] along the Mississippi on a gently sloping bank. [There were two major streets parallel to the river], one of which [featured] many quite imposing houses; that of the younger Mr. Chouteau, massive and made of limestone, was one of the most beautiful.

The best inns were located on Main Street, [but they were] only mediocre, and in them one dined badly with all kinds of persons, often poorly dressed. Blacks and mulattos were the only servants; they were numerous, almost all of them slaves. The streets were still under construction, yet [there were] very nice individual buildings, several attractive churches, a statehouse, a college, various factories and workshops ([including] an ironworks where, among other things, steam engines were built), [and] two market halls—one on a [town] square; the other, on the northern edge of the city, was not in use.

There were a large number of French in St. Louis, also many Germans. Many persons speak French, even a large portion of the Negroes. There were several wealthy merchants, especially the owners of the American Fur Company, who were extending their trade north and west, up the Missouri into the interior of this country and toward the English border. About this, see [information given later in] this diary.

Numerous merchants from the East, North, and South come here on business, to which the excellent communication on the Ohio, Mississippi, and Missouri (three major rivers flowing through a vast stretch of the country) contributes greatly. Steamship navigation was flourishing, [from] here to New Orleans or to Louisville.

Among the most remarkable features near St. Louis are the old Indian fortifications, or ramparts and mounds, located above the town on the bank of the river.

5 April: I went to the office of the American [Fur] Company, where I found Messrs. Chouteau and McKenzie. I deposited 2,500 dollars, for which I received a receipt and a letter of credit. These gentlemen were very courteous, and Mr. Chouteau invited me to his house tomorrow evening at seven o'clock to [meet] his family.

After [lunch] we went to the *Yellow Stone* and inspected it. It was moderately large [with] a wide gallery on all sides on which one could take walks. Its boiler was being repaired and other necessary preparations made. Afterward we bought several additional articles to trade with the Indians. We now have: 1. Calico (colorful fabric). 2. Knives of various kinds. 3. Brass bells. 4. Burning glasses. 5. Red dye (vermilion). 6. Red ribbons. 7. Colorful plumes. 8. Iron and chemical lighters. 9. Tobacco pipes. 10. Tobacco. 11. Yellow nails. 12. Quids. 13. Glass beads of various colors. Value about 24 dollars, 36 cents, or about 61 florins. Later I received a new crate for natural history specimens, for which I had to pay 3 dollars. It was immediately packed [and sent] via New Orleans to [New] York, where it will be shipped [to Europe]. In the evening we worked and packed and finished writing letters.

6 April: After breakfast we attended to various matters. I took care of my correspondence: sent a letter to Europe; wrote others to Mr. Nicolet in New Orleans, etc. The day of our departure was approaching; our baggage was ready, and on 9 April we sent it aboard.

VII

Journey from St. Louis to the Borders of Settlements along the Missouri

On 10 April at 10:30 in the morning, the steam engine on the *Yellow Stone* was started after [we] had assembled on board. Mr. Chouteau, his daughters, and other ladies accompanied us on the journey today, [as did] Messrs. Sanford and Pilcher and several employees of the company; Messrs. McKenzie and Dougherty joined [us] later. The *Yellow Stone*'s flags were fluttering, an American one aft and [a triangular] one forward, with the initials of the American Fur Company. At least twenty Canadians (engagés,¹ or trappers), some of them drunk, were sitting on the upper deck of our ship; they fired a running volley from their muskets and rifles [as a signal of our imminent departure]. We quickly sailed past the city [as] an [onshore] crowd jubilantly shouted a farewell.

The river formed a broad, brownish gray expanse. The name of this stream is derived from the language of the Ojibwe and related tribes: Meschi-Sipo (Sipo, "river," and Meschi, "large"). Beyond St. Louis, single dwellings, factories, etc., appeared along the western bank. The drunken engagés continued making a lot of noise; they shouted, fired their guns, drank. They were as coarse as the Indians [and] spoke French; some were half-breeds, dark brown. One such small fellow was very unpleasant; he [had] an Indian scalp stretched on a circular frame. All of them kept big scalping knives in sheaths on [their] belts. At eleven o'clock we had a small creek to the left; on the Illinois bank, [a] tall forest with high white *Platanus*, [everything] turning green. [We saw] groups of turtles, undoubtedly *[Emys] geographica*, sunning themselves on trunks lying along the bank; lofty cottonwoods [and] redbuds *(Cercis)*, covered with little flowers. Soon, before us to the left, [we spied] the wooded promontory dividing the Missouri from the Mississippi. In the river [there was a] very striking distinction between the water of the Missouri and that of the Mississippi: the former was yellow-brownish and murky; the latter, clear and greenish. At noon we turned into the Missouri;

our Canadians fired some shots to greet [it]. Navigation is very dangerous on the Missouri: on both [banks], large piles of [driftwood] in the water leave only a narrow channel.

On the southern bank, we [passed by Fort] Bellefontaine, formerly a military post for protection against hostile Indians. Urubus (turkey buzzards) flew above the forest. Beyond [Bellefontaine], a wooded hill was reddened by the blossoms of the delightful redbud. It is characteristic of North America that most trees bloom before they produce leaves: for example, oaks, cottonwoods, walnuts, *Prunus, Cerasus,* [etc.]

We moved along the right bank. The Indian agent Sanford told us about [Duke] Paul of Württemberg, who twice made a journey up the Missouri. He published an account of his first journey, with lithographed plates, [a book] just for his friends. He is said to have lied terribly and to have spent much money. On the right bank we saw several men near a firmly anchored fishing rod, [with] which they pulled in a big fish. A sounding was taken.

Another sandy island, [one of many seen today]. They were mostly pointed at the ends, [their] banks 8 to 10 feet high [with] young willows on top, as slender as whips, growing crowded together. Rushes (*Equisetum* [sp.]) grew among them in a few places. Large deposits of driftwood at the upstream tips [of the islands] as well as along the [river] banks. A kingfisher (*Alcedo alcyon)* perched on a cottonwood on an island, ruffled its crest, and flipped its tail up.

The river soon made a sharp turn to the left. Before sundown, magnificent blood-red sun, [its] reflection in the water indescribably beautiful. About a mile farther, a recently sunken steamboat on the left bank. A large group of people had built shacks there, likely [intending] to salvage as much as possible from the wreck. In the evening we put in at the bank.

11 April: Pleasant weather. Endless forests; attractive prairies were said to [lay] behind them. Our morning wash water was completely brown, as was the drinking water, [but it was] very cool and healthful. Along the left bank, white dogwood blossoms contrasted beautifully with those of redbud. [After breakfast,] we approached St. Charles, a town of about three hundred houses; [a] massive limestone church with [a] short steeple stood out attractively. On the elevation behind the town [there was] an old, short tower, [the type that] formerly served to protect towns against Indians; in St. Louis there were five such towers. It is 25 [river] miles from St. Charles to the mouth of the Missouri.[2]

We put ashore on the bank opposite [St. Charles], to take on wood and wait for Mr. McKenzie and Dougherty, who were coming by land from St. Louis. In the woods there were several houses with fenced-in fields; in their gardens, a very pretty *Ribes* with yellow, fragrant blossoms, which we added to our collection. We undertook a short excursion into the forest, and although we could not go far, we found redbud *(Cercis),* box elder *(Acer negundo),* plum trees *(Prunus* [—]), yellow and sky-blue *Viola* blooms, a yellow plant similar to *Ranunculus,* [and] a rose, the small leaves of which were just opening.

After about two hours, Mr. Chouteau and his ladies took leave of us; Mr. Chouteau walked along the bank to watch us move off. On board we now had Messrs. McKenzie, Dougherty, Sanford, Pilcher, and several employees of the Fur Company, mostly of French descent. Mr. Pilcher was famous for his long journeys through the Rocky Mountains, to the Columbia, and around the sources of the Missouri. Sanford was subagent for the Indian nations of the Arikaras, Mandans, Gros Ventres, and Blackfoot. Major Dougherty was in charge of the Pawnees, Otoes, and Omahas, and Major Bean, who would soon come aboard, of the Sioux and Poncas.

[Later,] we had [a rapids, Ramrod Eddy,] to our right, and we sailed along close to the [opposite] bank. During lunch the ship was made fast to the bank because of an ever-increasing wind; [it] was blowing to such a degree that we could not continue all afternoon, [so Bodmer went hunting] with Dreidoppel; they brought back several interesting plants, butterflies, and *Picus carolinus.* We [remained] there until about five o'clock, then sailed on. At dusk we put in for the night. From here to the mouth of the Missouri it was 37 [river] miles.

12 April: In the morning, very cool, overcast sky, moderately strong wind. To the right, wooded limestone hills. In the river and along shore, snags in large number. Several islands, also sandbars. [All] very interesting.

As on the Mississippi, the rocks formed round tower shapes and tall, ascending pinnacles, like old ruins, [the] valleys between them filled with green trees in young foliage. [Later,] we sailed close along the right bank, which was steep and 20 feet high. Redbud painted the woods beautifully red. We steered over to the left bank and sailed rapidly upstream. There were several settlements here and cultivated fields where there was always firewood stacked. I bought from the rowdy young engagé the Blackfoot scalp he was carrying. He had been wounded in the back by one of those Indians and was lame.

This morning Major Dougherty gave me the following information about Indians of the Missouri, the western wilderness, and the Rocky Mountains. The Hidatsas live in three villages near the Mandans. The Mandans live in two villages. The French call the Hidatsas Gros Ventres. The Crows (Corbeaux) live near the mountains southwest of the Blackfoot and probably have one thousand warriors. The celebrated [Pawnee,] Petalesharo, known from Long's [expedition], died of illness, like his father, Lateleseha. The Pawnees consist of four bands: the Loups [Skiri] Pawnees, Republican Pawnees, Grand Pawnees, and [Papaye] Pawnees. The Otoes and Missourias are now mixed. The latter speak the language of the Otoes (the same words but with a different accent). [The] Omahas, Poncas, Osages, [and] Kansa (as they are called by the Americans, or Cans, as they are called by the French—they call themselves Kånzä)³ speak the same language. The more northern peoples—the Sioux, Assiniboines (they speak the same language), Arapahoes, Cheyennes, Kiowas, Blackfoot, Crows (they call themselves Apsarukä)⁴—differ greatly from the former in their customs and practices, for they do not plant corn. The Hidatsas are like the Pawnees, Otoes, and Omahas in that they raise corn. The Sioux and related tribes, who live exclusively from hunting, do not shave their heads. On the contrary, they let their hair hang down long and often wear artificial hair [as well], from the forequarters of buffalo or from slain enemies. They attach this hair to their own with pine resin. In September the Pawnees, Otoes, and Omahas usually return from their hunting expeditions and harvest the maturing corn. At the end of October, they leave, hunt during winter, and come back to their villages in March. Then they sow corn and stay until the end of May or middle of June, when they again leave.

At 1:30 we put in [at] a settlement [and] took in a large load of firewood. Beautiful plants grew [nearby]: [blooming] redbud; *Claytonia virginica; Hydrangea,* [its] leaf buds just opening; a pretty phlox. After lunch, we were fully occupied preparing specimens. [Then] we hastened on. There was not much wildlife left in these regions; turkeys and deer were said to be rather rare, as the area was too heavily populated. Most of the [local] inhabitants lived on the elevations, because it was more healthful there than on the lower riverbank. The river sometimes, although not often, overflowed here, [forming] lowland marshes and pools [that], because of the shade of the dense forests, did not easily dry up and therefore produced fevers.

Something broke on the steam engine so that we drifted backward; fortunately, there were no snags in our way. The matter was soon repaired, and we sailed close along the steep right bank. Before us, a very beautiful view of the river in the bright evening sunlight. To the right, limestone hills rose again in the forest; cedar shrubs grew on them. This tree with black berries *(Juniperus virginiana)* was [also seen] along the Ohio and Mississippi. It provides aromatic wood of which pencils are made. It is said to be extremely durable; posts made from it last sixty years and more in the ground.

The port side of our ship struck many snags here, but [the vessel] was built sturdily for dangerous voyages on the Missouri. The Fur Company has had another steamboat, the *Assiniboine,* built for the same purpose. We soon put in at [the right] bank to spend the night. After supper we went [ashore] where a high fire of sturdy tree trunks was burning near the fringe of forest. Our Canadians came to the fire [and] carried on a lively conversation in French. Messrs. McKenzie, Dougherty, and Sanford arrived soon afterward, and we spent a while here under the beautiful canopy of stars while men on the *Yellow Stone,* the lights of which shone toward us, played a Scottish tune on clarinets.

13 April: We set out at dawn. At about seven o'clock [on the] broad river, we had a beautiful view into the region of the Gasconade River: many broad sandbars; scenic hills; woodlands; bright morning sunlight over everything. After breakfast we halted at the left bank near a settlement, took in wood, and botanized. Ironwood, the sugar tree, redbud, spicewood (almost done blooming), a beautiful violet phlox, a blue *Viola* without scent, the fork-shaped flower *[Dicentra cucullaria], Claytonia virginica,* and several additional plants were in bloom.

At eight o'clock we moved on. To the left, the Gasconade River emerged from low-lying hills [with] many [pines that] supplied St. Louis with boards and lumber. [By ten thirty], we reached the hamlet of Portland on the right bank. In the forest to the left, *Pavia lutea* (buckeye), already very green, grew abundantly. While lunch was being served, many islands and sandbars [passed] before us, several of them covered with driftwood. After [a while, we saw] the Osage River, a beautiful and powerful brook, emerging from banks with tall woodlands. It was said to have a stronger current than the Gasconade.[5] To the right a wooded hill appeared with several houses before it: Cote Sans Dessein, an old French settlement. [Andrew] Bennett, our skipper, lived [there]. A boat was sent to bring him and his wife on board. He brought along two small half-breed children he was rearing. While they were fetching the captain, we put in at the left bank and collected [several familiar] plants in the nearby forest, and also a bulbous plant that people here called Adam-and-Eve, said to provide a good medication for wounds.

Half an hour later we moved on. [After some time, we reached] the capital of the state of Missouri, Jefferson City, a village or town of about one hundred scattered houses. The home of the present governor, [Daniel] Dunklin, rested on the eminence [and] faced the river. It was not large [but] was made of brick. The three hills on which the town, begun about ten years ago, was situated were crisscrossed with fences, and the stumps of felled trees were still standing everywhere. As we approached the town, two cannon were fired, and the population stood on the elevations as the *Yellow Stone* hurriedly steamed past. We continued until dusk and put in on the right bank for the night.

14 April: Beautiful, bright day. The river formed a broad expanse with islands and sandbars; to the left [Sugar Loaf Rock,] a high, isolated boulder, stood like a tower in the forest. Major Dougherty once came down the Missouri with [some] Iowas. [They] told him there had been a legend among their ancestors that this boulder arose from dung dropped [here] by a large breed of buffalo living in the sky; they themselves no longer believed this legend.

[At midmorning we saw] the steamboat *Heroine* at the left riverbank, taking on wood. To the left, a long island [and then] a treacherous spot full of snags; we sailed through and brushed against them. About an hour later, we passed rock walls along the left bank; [still] later, very interesting limestone walls [at] the right, separated into broad towers by ravines; falcons (*Falco peregrinus*?) nested in those rocks. The ravines were often very rugged and picturesque. *Picus pileatus* (called woodcocks) flew [about] in one of the gorges.

Immediately after lunch we reached Rocheport on Moniteau [Creek]; the hamlet was just two years old. [Directly] behind [and] above the village there were rocks with red drawings, certainly by Indians (thirty years ago this entire region was still inhabited by Indians); [one drawing appeared to be] a male figure with raised arms.[6] [That afternoon we halted at] Boonville on the left bank and bought cigarros made from locally cultivated tobacco.

I had hoped to obtain botanical paper at Boonville, but since it was Sunday, the stores were closed. The town had forty to fifty houses. The inhabitants came to the riverbank to see the steamboat.

At five o'clock we struck bottom solidly but were not grounded. The river was very wide; along the bank, several islands on which rushes *(Equisetum hyemale)* grew underneath the cottonwoods and willows. This type of shave grass is good for polishing, and livestock like to eat it. We put in [at the town of Arrow Rock] for the night, [and there we] went into a store and bought several reams of botanical paper for five dollars.

15 April: In the morning, after breakfast, we put in at a settlement and took on wood. This whole region, as far as the Mississippi, is very fertile and heavily populated; good farms.

[In the afternoon] we came to a place where the Missouri made an enormous bend that took us at least one and a half to two hours to get through. It was full of large sandbars and so [many] snags that we could [proceed] only with danger. Forward, the lead was continually tossed on both sides,[7] and thus we were able to get through. When we had left the big bend behind us, we [saw] cornfields to the left [and,] perched on withered cornstalks, parakeets *(Psittacus carolinensis)*. Later we reached areas where the big sandbars had angular banks, like bastions and entrenchments, [and] enormous deposits of driftwood. Remarkable riverbank destruction: large masses of land had slid down; young, 30- to 40-foot cottonwoods [and] cornfields entirely torn away except for small remnants. In June, with the next flooding, the river will [again] come roaring down [and the banks will] collapse on all sides, often with trees and wood floating in every direction, [in] eddies, whirlpools, and multiple torrents.

At five o'clock in the evening, we reached the mouth of the Grand River, a beautiful river about the size of the Wabash but now very low. Forest and greening willows bordered it. The Iowas lived up along the Grand River until 1827, when they moved to the Platte River.[8] They call the Grand River Nischna-Honjä, the Missouri Nischu-Djä. In their language, nischna is "river."

Before dusk we steered over to the right bank and put in there to take on wood and spend the night. We immediately dispersed into the forests, the nearby homes and cultivated fields. In the latter we found a flock of parakeets, six of which Mr. Bodmer shot; [the others] did not fly away after they had been shot at (regarding the tenacity of this bird see Drake, *Picture of*

Cincinnati, page 118). We also found some interesting plants [and] pursued a squirrel without success. We all returned to the ship for supper and then carried on our usual evening occupations.

16 April: We set out early. Islands and sandbars to our left; to the right [there were] as many large trees in the river as in a whole devastated forest. Three large gulls *(Larus)* flew downriver. After breakfast, big bends in the river; its water very cold. Exceptionally large [quantities of] earthy sediment were [carried by] the strong current. After nine o'clock, a violent collision with a piece of wood, [and then] we became totally entangled in a huge mass of driftwood. The ship rose up and was jolted; the engine often stopped. Finally, we pulled free again, [but we] ran aground several times.

After lunch we found ourselves near Fox Prairie.[9] At one time the Meskwaki and Sauk [Indians] joined battle here with the Missourias and [almost] completely exterminated them. The Missourias came down the river in many canoes close to shore. The enemies had concealed themselves along the bank and at close range shot [the Missourias] in their vessels, then sprang up with their war clubs and knives and killed the wounded. Only a few escaped. This remnant now lives along the [opposite] riverbank with the Otoes and other tribes. We went to the upper deck of the ship [to] view the prairies, but the weather was too hazy and we could not see far.

About three o'clock in the afternoon, we put in at the left bank near Webb's Warehouse to take on wood. We looked for plants and found [only] ones we had already observed. The stop lasted a quarter of an hour. Soon we were again without sufficient water; the engine was not running, [so] the current drove the ship to the side. For a long time we lay motionless near the shore while the boat was sent out for a sounding. Until about evening we slid, more or less on the bottom, covering about 7 miles from Webb's Warehouse. When night came, we were not in a favorable situation.

On 17 April we departed early but put in off the left bank about six o'clock to take on wood. Because of my severe head cold, I did not go ashore [at this short stop]. In the region [of Tabo Creek] our ship ran over several big trunks lying on the bottom. [We] crushed and broke some of them; a huge trunk with [a] cluster of roots came up writhing like a snake that had been stepped on. A very bad [stretch] followed, a narrow passageway between large trunks with jagged points lying left and right in the water. A paddle on one of the wheels broke, requiring a short stop. A bald eagle alighted on the shore. Its nest, built of sticks and twigs, rested in a fork of three thick branches on a tall *Platanus*. We assumed that there were already eaglets in it.

With a writing tablet in hand, I recorded every major change during the journey, and from time to time Dougherty gave me words of the Otoe language and others, which I wrote down; we smoked a large number of cigars. The ship [again] moved over snags, one of which lifted the rudder up into the air. We [saw] a steam sawmill and several other buildings on the left bank, about half a mile from the town of Lexington. When Major Dougherty first traveled up the Missouri twenty-four years ago, [none of] this existed. People knew nothing about steamboats. The settlements reached 12 miles beyond St. Charles and no farther. There was no town at Cote Sans Dessein; only huts [that] French hunters used for hunting. The Osages roamed and lived in the region where Lexington is now located.

Upstream from the sawmill we reached the tip of a large island [and] followed the river through a very large bend full of dangerous snags; the engine often stopped. After lunch the channel ran along the right bank; to avoid a sandbar, we came so close to it that the ship brushed it and I could reach cottonwood blossoms with my hand.

After a good stretch of the river had been free of wood, we [came to] a channel [in which] nowhere, [for] a stretch of 500–600 paces, did there appear more than 10 feet of space between [snags]; the pilot twisted like a skilled coachman through these dangerous [places], which [have brought] disaster to many a steamship and boat. About an hour later we took in wood, but our stop was short. We soon reached several islands to the right, separated only by narrow channels. The water was too shallow [so] we halted and pushed the ship [with sturdy poles] and continued [our] voyage. We stopped for the night on the right bank about 5 miles from Fort Osage. Mr. Sanford went out with a rifle, bagged a rabbit, and wounded a deer. We found a new tree in bloom, which seemed to me to be *Zanthoxylum*.

18 April: We could not immediately continue our journey [this morning], because the engine was broken. Dreidoppel heard wild turkeys in the forest near the ship; he and Bodmer went out to hunt them. I went botanizing [and] found many trees with fresh foliage; the spicewood was rather green, as [were] several other shrubs. A blue and a sea-blue *Viola* were the only flowers. The air was filled with the cries of sandhill cranes *(Grus canadensis)*; they were moving in a northeasterly direction. Their call sounds like that of European cranes but is usually clearer and more whirring or chirring. The men shot

often at these beautiful birds without getting any of them.

Sanford and Dougherty went ahead to hunt; we [would fetch] them on board farther upstream. The boat was sent out to take soundings. [Mr. Bodmer and Dreidoppel] returned [with] a wood duck, a rabbit, and a live, 5-foot-long black snake (Coluber constrictor).

At a quarter to twelve, we finally set out, after repeatedly ringing the bell to summon the scattered crew back from the woodlands. We were scarcely a short distance from our night quarters when we ran into great peril. The water was so densely filled with so many snags that we could barely get through; we paused, took soundings, and cut off several dangerous trees. Twenty-six men were put onto a sandbar to the left to pull the steamboat. They all exerted themselves [and] pulled in line, but the rope broke suddenly, and the entire crew fell flat on the ground. As a precaution, the ship was fastened to a large tree; this was our salvation, for soon afterward the rudder was dislodged and rendered useless; we would surely have drifted onto the snags and foundered.

Not until about two o'clock, when the rudder had been repaired, were we able to continue our journey, yet not even a half hour had gone by before we were firmly aground on a flat sandbar, and despite all efforts, we remained there the entire night. Our situation was [precarious], for there was a very strong current on the sandbar where we were stranded. Since the ship could not be secured, [we might have been] swept away during the night, but everything remained unchanged, and the level of the river fell even more. [See pls. 4 and 5.]

On 19 April: In the morning the ship still lay on the sandbar but gradually moved a little. We [needed to] unload half [the cargo], since we had no hope of making headway without this measure. We were [still] about 3½ miles from Fort Osage. Messrs. Dougherty and Sanford had not returned. Our black snake had fully revived, and we kept it alive. A flatboat arrived, and goods were loaded onto it, taken ashore, and piled up in the forest. Full boatloads like these, one after the other, left the ship all day. Propelling the loaded flatboat over the sandbars and shallows required great effort.

In the afternoon Mr. Bodmer went ashore with a gun. Most of the animals had been frightened away by the noise [of] our large crew, for we had one hundred men on board and today all but a few of them were moving about. At 3:30 the crew succeeded in pushing and pulling the Yellow Stone free from the sandbar, whereupon we started the steam engine and put in at the right bank, somewhat below the mouth of Fishing [River]. The wares that lay on shore belonged partly to the Fur Company [and] partly to the government—goods sent for the Indians, intended for Dougherty's agency (gifts and other disbursements made to the Indians are said to amount to about one-half million dollars yearly). Three men were left there to guard them. A party of about thirty men returned the [borrowed] barge to its owner on Fishing [River]. Somewhat farther on we took these people on board again; one of them had been drinking in the heat; [a] clerk gave him a strong dose of calomel.

Before dusk we reached [the abandoned] Fort Osage, located on a pretty, level ridge on the [south] bank of the river. One can still see the old, demolished ramparts close to the water. The Osage Indian tribe call themselves Wasaji.[10] They were still at Cote Sans Dessein just ten years ago, but they were forced farther back into the prairie toward the Arkansas River: another example of the beneficence of the Americans. They are said to be one of the handsomest Indian tribes: tall, well-built men [who] shave their heads, paint themselves, and are generally ornamented like Sauks and Meskwakis. The whole region through which we were now traveling was primarily their territory; many of them lived along the Osage River. Now they have been forced so far back that we had no hope of seeing any of them along the Missouri. [A few] travelers have provided some information about this people, but no very detailed descriptions. Several were put on display in Germany for money; on their return the poor Indians [did] not have much good to relate about their trip. They had to sing, dance, and display other skills, solely [to profit] their French guide and interpreter.[11] Their place of habitation now is along the Arkansas River near the sources of the Osage River; sometimes they roam as far down as the Red River.

We put in on the left bank [near] Fort Osage and spent the night there.

20 April: The river had fallen another inch during the night. The [Little Blue] River [was] to our left, hidden behind a long island. Scarcely had we left [that] behind us when the ship struck a sandbar. The engine was put in reverse; the current caught the steamboat and drove it past [a] promontory so closely that it [sheared] off the columns of the lower gallery that supported the upper deck on [the left] side. The carpenter was able to set most of them upright again except for two, which were broken to bits. After breakfast the river was very broad and beautiful but very shallow; we struck bottom several times.

Mr. McKenzie gave me a gift of beautiful Indian artifacts: a pair of Cree

Indian moccasins and a shot bag, which is worn over the shoulder and fastened in front with a belt. They were made of deer or antelope leather and delicately ornamented with colorful porcupine spines or feather quills.[12] The dyes for these quills are quite beautiful and vivid; the Indian women boil them from European fabrics and from roots. These women do extremely neat work, colorful figures smoothly stitched [on] leather.

About 9:30 a brisk, favorable wind arose. The bank to the right was 15 to 20 feet high and steeply eroded. Several settlements. [Then] a very wide spot in the river [and] an island with a promontory of willows; we steamed along beside [it]. Farther on we found Mr. Sanford, who had shot a rabbit. He was brought aboard with the boat. Dougherty had traveled ahead to [Fort] Leavenworth. At noon a violent storm with heavy rain, hail, thunder, and lightning.

We soon reached the landing place that led to the village of Liberty; [there was a] one-hour stopover. [The] location [was] very picturesque; [there were] small houses [where] colorfully attired people had gathered. Ten Germans here had taken employment with a Rocky Mountain fur company, [that of] Messrs. Sublette and Campbell. They received eighteen dollars a month here; farther upstream, fifteen [dollars]. Two keelboats were here, which had come up from St. Louis; a large number of the men on shore were passengers or members of their crew.[MI]

We continued [up the river and] took on wood not far from Blue River. There were several habitations in front of the hill, and we [saw] small, narrow canoes with several French engagés from the upper Missouri who had just come down from there to await the *Yellow Stone*. Several of these men were half-breeds of brown color. They had Indian utensils as well as partly Indian dress; one of them, a small swarthy Frenchman, wore a fur cap with a short ostrich feather.

From [the Blue River] on, there was a gradual bend in the river and sandbars in several places; we pressed ahead slowly [with] occasional jolts

---

[MI] These keelboats belonged to a fur company competing with Chouteau and McKenzie, that of Messrs. [Campbell] and Sublette, which will probably not last very long, for the former has already crushed many a similar enterprise along the Missouri and conducts the most far-ranging business. Along the Missouri several fur companies existed: one of them perished; the others merged, forming the present one, which has an extensive range of undertakings and will probably not be [outdone] by any other. More detailed information needs to be collected on this subject.

from the shallows and bars. We saw a cow sunken in quicksand so deeply that it inevitably had to perish there. It had been lying in this condition for perhaps several days; with the approach of our ship it exerted itself in vain. Evening came upon us; we spent the night off the right bank.

21 April: We set out after dawn; one and a half hours later we stopped at the left bank and took on some wood at a settlement near wooded hills, which were turning a picturesque green. From this place it was about 1 mile to the mouth of the Kansas River, which was now very low. Its clear, green water contrasted sharply with the brown of the Missouri. Here, on the point of land between the Kansas and the Missouri, is the boundary of the United States, [where] one enters the territory of the free Indians. The boundary runs from south to north.[13] Along [the Kansas] River and, to some extent, in the vicinity of its mouth, is where the Indians driven from the eastern states were assigned land, and some of them settled here. Remnants of the Lenni-Lennape (Delawares), the Shawnees, Miamis(?), Peorias, Kaskaskias, Piankashaws, Weas, and possibly of other tribes now lived here; villages of the Kansa nation were located about 90 to 100 miles upriver [on the Kansas]. We stopped at the [Kansas] mouth for a half hour [and then] continued on. Three to four hundred paces [farther, on] the left bank, there formerly was a trading house for the Kansa nation; [it] has been closed. From here Mr. Pilcher began his fur-trading ventures to the Columbia and the Rocky Mountains. He traveled through all these regions and endured great hardships, but his fur company failed and now he was going to [run the] trading post [north of the Bellevue agency].

A chain of beautifully green hills arose in the forest to the left. Along the bank, for the first time on the entire trip, we saw a free Indian approaching, wrapped in his woolen blanket, but we moved away too quickly. To the right on shore we once again saw piles of cut wood near a settlement. From now on, we will probably not find any like that. We had run into a dangerous area densely filled with snags; the ship steered around [them], reached the better channel of the river, and made [some] progress. [Then] we struck bottom and ran over [more] trees; [something] caught between the paddles of the left wheel and broke [several] with a loud, cracking noise. [Thus] we proceeded by fits and starts. All the underbrush in the forest on the [high bank] was tinged red from redbuds; individual redbud trunks were 30 to 40 feet high. [Many men had taken advantage of our slow progress to go hunting.] Finally we saw [them ahead of us]. Upon our approach [some] jumped down from the high bank, [while] others slid down a diagonally inclined tree; in all there were forty-two men. Mr. Bodmer and Dreidoppel brought a parakeet *(Psittacus carolinensis)*, a squirrel, a young rabbit, two nice *Heterodon* (hognose) snakes, and a passenger pigeon *(Columba migratoria)*. [The hognose] snake varies greatly in its primary color. The two specimens were equally large; one had a gray-brown, the other a nearly black basic color.

The Platte River [of Missouri] emptied here on the right side. The Iowas lived along it 6 to 7 miles upstream. They have already been mentioned. The region [they] inhabit and in which they hunt are the environs of the [Missouri] Platte, the Nodaway, and [the] Nishnabotna rivers. They call themselves Pa-ho-dji, Dusty Noses,[14] a name they received from other Indians because they lived along a sandy bank of the [Upper] Iowa [River].

On the left bank we now had beautiful wooded hills, dotted with young foliage and blossoms. To the rear we had a magnificent view in the beautiful, clear evening illumination; the various gradations of the elevations and woodlands were very picturesque; the majestic surface of the water gleamed beautifully. On the bank [we] saw several Schawano Indians ("Shawnee" of the Americans), who waved to us.

We stopped [later] for the night.

22 April: In the morning, we reached denuded hills to the left with tall stumps from felled trees; [at] the top, a sentry stood. A large group of people sat and watched us; this was the landing place for Cantonment [Fort] Leavenworth, situated on the elevation. Cantonment Leavenworth, the last military outpost [we would encounter], was designed for four companies of regular military, which, however, altogether numbered only 120 men. They were commanded by Major Riley. To reinforce them, another hundred rangers (mounted, nonuniformed but well-armed men) had been added; they had a motley appearance. There were seven houses for the officers and men; about seven additional dwellings were located on the other side of a hill. The major's house was at the top and rather imposing.

Since the military here controls the importation of whiskey, our ship was unloaded and the casks were searched. A certain number were confiscated from Mr. McKenzie, and they also wanted to take a small cask from me, but Dougherty recovered it [since it was necessary for the scientific preservation of specimens]. Whiskey [could] not be brought into Indian Territory. This [United States] law had been in effect since last year. Several officers went back and forth all day; our cabin was like a dovecote. Major Bean (Indian agent) came on board with his baggage.

Close to the bank where the ship lay at anchor, the limestone strata had interesting shells, several of which we took along. On the bank, black oak and other trees were blooming, as [were] several interesting plants, including a small *Oxalis* with a bulbous root and pale violet flower. Mr. Bodmer saw a blackbird with a yellow head and caught a small species of tree frog. At twelve o'clock, 82°F on the ship. The summer heat is said to be [so] terribly intense on the prairies [that] people often lie down in the water.

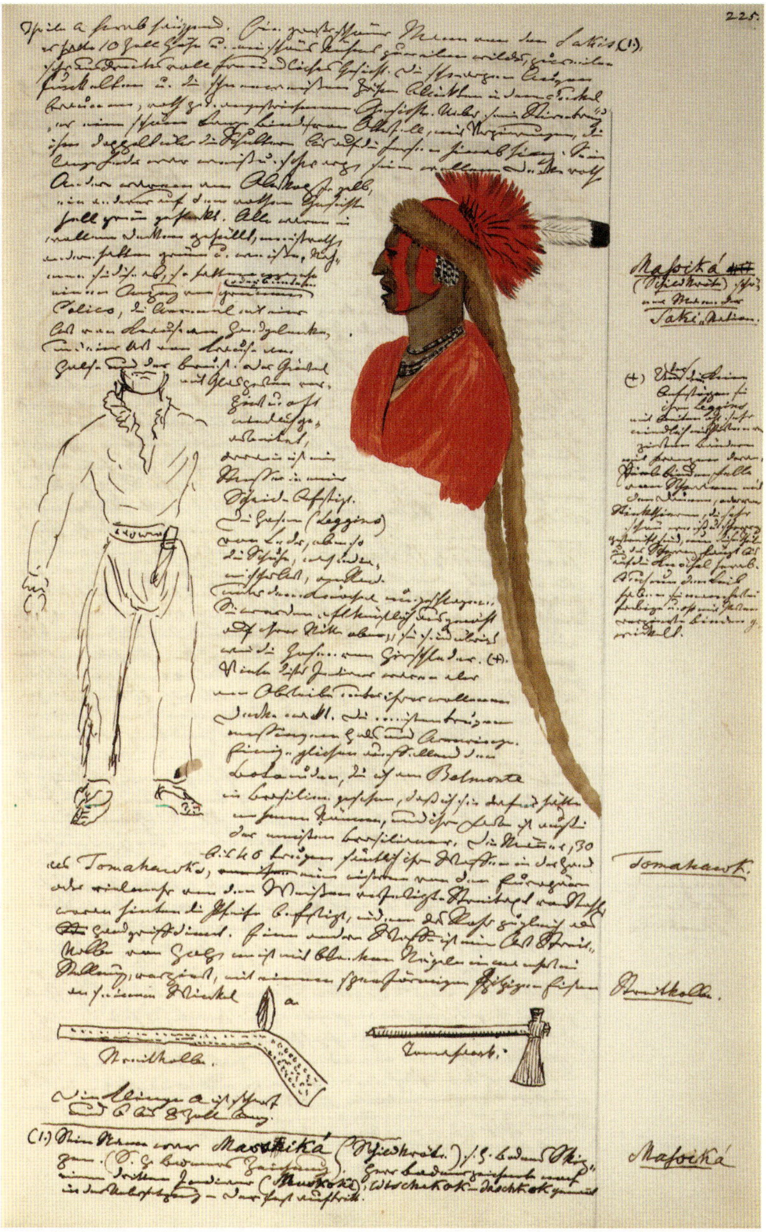

PLATE 1. Maximilian. A page from the prince's handwritten *Tagebuch*, or journals (manuscript volume 1, page 225), containing part of his entry for 25 March 1833, St. Louis, describing Sauk and Meskwaki Indians encountered there. The color profile is of Massica, a Sauk man. Ink, watercolor. Page size approx. 13 × 8 in.

PLATE 2. Karl Bodmer. *View of Bethlehem on the Lehigh*. Watercolor. Chapter 3 is devoted to Maximilian's stay in this eastern Pennsylvania town in August and September 1832. The handsome "church with a cupola" still stands. 11 ⅞ × 17¼ in. 1986.49.27.

PLATE 3. Karl Bodmer. *View of New Harmony.* Watercolor. Maximilian's party spent the winter of 1832–33 in this southwestern Indiana community of about 600, happy in the company of New Harmony residents and fellow scientists Thomas Say and Charles-Alexandre Lesueur; see chapter 5. 6¼ × 10¾ in. 1986.49.368.

PLATE 4. Karl Bodmer. *The Steamboat Yellow Stone.* Watercolor. Steamboat travel on the Missouri was difficult and sometimes dangerous in 1833; damaging snags were a constant threat, and vessels frequently had to be partially unloaded, as in this scene of 18–19 April, to lighten them sufficiently to be floated off sandbars. 8¼ × 13¼ in. 1986.49.131.

PLATE 5. Karl Bodmer. *Snags on the Missouri.* Watercolor and pencil. "Our roaring steamboat twisted dangerously among the many snags peering out of the water." 26 April 1833. 8⅜ × 10¾ in. 1986.49.150.

PLATE 6. Karl Bodmer. *The Missouri below the Mouth of the Platte.* Watercolor. On 3 May 1833, as the *Yellow Stone* passed by its mouth, Maximilian remarked that the Platte River was running quite high, its waters visibly distinct from those of the Missouri. 8¾ × 10¾ in. 1986.49.149.

PLATE 7. Karl Bodmer. *Bellevue Agency, Post of Major Dougherty*. Watercolor. The site of this government outpost is marked today by only a few stones within the nature preserve of Fontenelle Forest in Bellevue, just south of modern Omaha, Nebraska. 6¼ × 9½ in. 1986.49.371.

PLATE 8. Karl Bodmer. *Wahktägeli, Yankton Sioux Chief.* Watercolor and pencil. "He was a big . . . man about sixty years old . . . tall, with large, lively eyes and a sharply aquiline nose." 16¾ × 11¾ in. 1986.49.245.

PLATE 9. Karl Bodmer. *Chan-Chä-Uiá-Te-Üinn, Teton Sioux Woman.* Watercolor and pencil. The colorful geometric pattern painted on the robe, commonly called a box and border design, was popular on the central plains, particularly among the Sioux. 17 × 11⅞ in. 1986.49.246.

PLATE 10. Karl Bodmer. *Noapeh, Assiniboine Man.* Watercolor and pencil. Noapeh posed patiently for a long time for Bodmer's portrait, a finished version of which appeared in Tableau 12 in the atlas of prints that accompanied Maximilian's *Reise.* 17 × 11⅞ in. 1986.49.253.

PLATE 11. Karl Bodmer. *Pitätapiú, Assiniboine Man.* Watercolor and pencil. This young warrior carries a shield, likely made of tough bison rawhide covered in a softer painted leather (his protective medicine pouch is attached to the cover), and a tall bow-lance with a metal spearpoint. 16¾ × 11⅞ in. 1986.49.254.

PLATE 12. Karl Bodmer. *Assiniboine Medicine Sign*. Watercolor. Shrinelike arrangements like this were offerings or magical devices honoring the bison herds so crucial to tribal survival, providing meat for sustenance and hides, bone and horn for shelter, clothing, and tools. 9⅞ × 12¼ in. 1986.49.172.

PLATE 13. Karl Bodmer. *Assiniboine Camp.* Watercolor. Among the two dozen or so tipis Maximilian saw that day near Fort Union, this one stood out, and he deemed it "probably a chief's." The owner, chief or not, must have obtained the spiritual protection of the bear, an image painted on the sides of this dwelling. The bear was seen as a strong supernatural power with resources to aid in battle or in healing the sick. 7⅞ × 10⅜ in. 1986.49.379.

PLATE 14. Karl Bodmer. *Junction of the Yellowstone and the Missouri.* Watercolor. Located just above the mouth of the Yellowstone, Fort Union (left of center, near the river) was the farthest limit of Missouri River steamer traffic in 1833 and served as a major post for the American Fur Company. 10⅞ × 16¾ in. 1986.49.376.

PLATE 15. Karl Bodmer. *View of the Stone Walls.* Watercolor. "Remarkable," "unusual," and "strange" are just a few of the adjectives Maximilian employed to describe the fantastic rock formations they saw along the Missouri between Forts Union and McKenzie in July and August 1833, culminating in "the region called Stone Walls" (now more commonly called the White Cliffs of the Missouri). 9⅞ × 16⅞ in. 1986.49.392.

PLATE 16. Karl Bodmer. *Mexkemáuastan, Gros Ventres des Prairies Chief.* Watercolor. This forbidding-looking man had a bad reputation among the AFC traders; he once threatened the life of David Mitchell, who was in charge of Fort McKenzie at the time. 16½ × 11¼ in. 1986.49.391.

PLATE 17. Karl Bodmer. *Kiäsax, Piegan Blackfoot Man.* Watercolor. A resident of Fort Clark at this time, Kiäsax wears a Spanish or Navajo blanket and Spanish-style cross, both valuable trade goods. He carries a long, flutelike pipe over his shoulder; his music was not pleasing to the prince's ear. 12¼ × 9½ in. 1986.49.395.

PLATE 18. Karl Bodmer. *Mexkehme-Sukahs, Piegan Blackfoot Chief.* Watercolor, ink, and pencil. Although this chief preferred the European-style, brightly colored fancy dress uniforms given out by the AFC to their Indian trading partners, the prince insisted on Mexkehme-Sukahs's more impressive (to Maximilian's eye) native garb for Bodmer's portrait. 12½ × 10⅛ in. 1986.49.284.

PLATE 19. Karl Bodmer. *Ihkas-kinne, Siksika Blackfoot Chief.* Watercolor and pencil. This man's otter pelt garment is lavishly decorated with metal buttons and bits of pearly shell, the former, and perhaps the latter as well, likely obtained in trade. 17 × 11⅞ in. 1986.49.285.

PLATE 20. Karl Bodmer. *Stomíck-Sosáck, Blood Blackfoot Chief.* Watercolor. Bodmer's portrait of this man was reproduced in Tableau 46 of the *Reise* atlas of prints. It was so accurate that a century later Weasel Tail, an elderly Blood Indian, recognized it as the respected chief, saying, "I knew his son. He looked just like that picture" (Ewers, "Appreciation," 92). 12⅜ × 9¾ in. 1986.49.286.

PLATE 21. Karl Bodmer. *Pioch-Kiáiu, Piegan Blackfoot Man.* Watercolor. Maximilian found the blue face paint interesting and later, in Europe, had a sample analyzed; it was "an earthy peroxide of iron" mixed with clay (Thwaites, *EWT,* 23:99). 12⅜ × 10⅛ in. 1986.49.296.

PLATE 22. Karl Bodmer. *First Chain of the Rocky Mountains above Fort McKenzie*. Watercolor. These are actually the Highwood and Little Belt Mountains, though Maximilian consistently refers to them as the Rockies. The view is no less real or spectacular for being misnamed. 11¾ × 16⅞ in. 1986.49.210.

PLATE 23. Karl Bodmer. *View of the Bears Paw Mountains from Fort McKenzie*. Watercolor. A companion piece to the preceding plate. Fort McKenzie was located between the two views and could have been portrayed as the center scene in what might have served as a triptych (see Wood et al., *KBSA*, 17). 11½ × 16⅜ in. 1986.49.209.

PLATE 24. Karl Bodmer. *Mandan Shrine.* Watercolor and pencil. Shrines like these were sometimes used as fasting grounds for those seeking supernatural assistance or powers. 8 × 10⅞ in. 1986.49.168.

PLATE 25. Karl Bodmer. *Mih-Tutta-Hangkusch, Mandan Village.* Watercolor. In chapter 17, Maximilian mentions the constant traffic on the frozen Missouri in 1833–34, as villagers traveled between their winter quarters in the sheltering forests below one bank and their principal residences high on the opposite shore; the rounded lodge roofs are visible to the far right of the Fort Clark palisades. Bodmer's image conveys the brutal cold of the setting. 11¼ × 16⅝ in. 1986.49.382.

PLATE 26. Karl Bodmer. *Mató-Tópe, Mandan Chief*. Watercolor. Four Bears posed for this portrait on 15 January 1834. Maximilian admired his attire, especially the carved wooden emblems (colored cylinders and a red knife) and painted symbols of his victories over various enemies; the yellow hand on his chest meant that he had taken captives. 13¾ × 11¼ in. 1986.49.260.

PLATE 27. Karl Bodmer. *Péhriska-Rúhpa, Hidatsa Man.* Watercolor and pencil. Two Ravens posed for at least two Bodmer portraits; here he is dressed in the regalia of the Dog Society—he was a leader of that organization in his village. The impressive headdress includes magpie and wild turkey feathers, as well as colorful strands of dyed horsehair, all of which would have been in constant motion as the wearer danced. 17 × 11¾ in. 1986.49.275.

PLATE 28. Karl Bodmer. *Leader of the Mandan Buffalo Bull Society.* Watercolor and pencil. Maximilian describes the Buffalo Bull and other Mandan men's societies in chapter 18; he saw them dance at Fort Clark on 9 April 1834. 16¹⁵/₁₆ × 11⅝ in. 1986.49.264.

PLATE 29. Karl Bodmer. *Addíh-Hiddísch, Hidatsa Chief.* Watercolor. This highly respected leader was the keeper of an important medicine bundle and had an impressive war record. He is mentioned many times in the journals and was doubtless a principal source of information for Maximilian on Hidatsa history and culture. 16½ × 11⅝ in. 1986.49.388.

PLATE 30. Karl Bodmer. *Interior of a Mandan Earth Lodge*. Watercolor and ink. The myriad details of Dipäuch's comfortable home were sketched over a period of many weeks, from early December 1833 to April of the following year. Maximilian describes the construction of earth lodges and enumerates their contents, from bedding to weaponry — but Bodmer's skill makes them all beautifully real. 11¼ × 16⅞ in. 1986.49.261.A.

PLATE 31. Karl Bodmer. *View of Niagara Falls*. Watercolor. Niagara Falls was a well-established tourist attraction by 1834 and, as Maximilian observed, had been "endlessly written" about. On their return journey eastward, he and Bodmer visited nonetheless, in late June, and found the experience "splendid" and "awe-inspiring"; it was a fitting near-end to their North American adventures. They sailed for home from New York harbor a little over two weeks later. 12¼ × 20 in. 1986.49.396.

PLATE 32. After Karl Bodmer. *The Travellers Meeting with Minatarre* [Hidatsa] *Indians near Fort Clark*. Engraving with aquatint, hand-colored, Vignette XXVI in the atlas of illustrations that accompanied Maximilian's *Reise*. The gesticulating figure, possibly Toussaint Charbonneau, points to Prince Maximilian; Bodmer, wearing a top hat, stands to the prince's left. The man in a cap, whose head can be seen between and behind the two travelers, is believed to be their companion, Maximilian's able huntsman, David Dreidoppel. $11^{15}/_{16} \times 13\frac{1}{2}$ in.

VIII

Journey from Cantonment Leavenworth to the Grand Bend and [Fort Pierre]

[FROM 22 APRIL TO 30 MAY 1833]

[22 April:] At a quarter to five we left [Cantonment Leavenworth and soon] ran into such a large number of snags that a fortunate outcome seemed problematic. Some snags were cut off underwater with the axe; the ship was gradually forced through [the obstacles]. We halted on the other side for the night.

23 [April]: Early in the morning, a large snag struck the ship, and a thick branch forced itself into the cabin, [breaking] the framework of the door. To the left, several sandbars and then, following a narrow stretch, the large Isle aux Vaches (Cow Island), where in 1818 troops destined for Council Bluff spent the winter; [although the season] caught them here by surprise, they had so much game in the vicinity that they could live on it entirely. The Kickapoos [by treaty] will be settled here along the left bank; the Iowas, Sauks, and Meskwakis roam and hunt in these woodlands. To the right there was a particularly beautiful wild forest; redbuds in great splendor; many white blossoms; large quantities of buckeyes, likewise sugar trees—the Indians used its sap to make sugar. Numerous small, rugged paths and animal trails everywhere along the shore. The river made a big bend to the left around the end of [the six-mile-long Cow Island. Later, the] river [flowed] in a broad and stately straight line. Its forests, a soft green color on all sides, were most picturesque; wherever the bank was low, one saw green willows. *Podophyllum peltatum,* with its large leaves, grew all over the forest floor, and the color of the redbuds was absolutely beautiful. Ducks everywhere on the river, mostly the very common wood duck, which the French call *canard branchu.*

At lunchtime we halted and cut great amounts of wood. Imprinted in the soft soil on the bank [were] wolf and deer tracks; the black bear was [also] numerous here [and] the wild turkey. Above, on the tall bank, the forest soil was densely blanketed with thick, tall rushes; short plants could not grow

[here] because the rushes (*Equisetum*) left them no room. One and one-half hours later, we continued on. Off the right bank, snags appeared [and] damaged the ship's right wheel cover. Moreover, we drifted so swiftly from here against a deposit of trees in the water that the boat and the rudder were endangered. We turned in every direction, received severe jolts, did not find enough water anywhere, and struck bottom. Finally, after perhaps an hour, we found [our] difficult way over a sandbar. To the left Independence [Creek] emptied into the Missouri from beautiful wooded banks. There was once a Kansa Indian village in this region, [but] nothing more is to be seen of [it]. After supper and shortly before dusk, we halted to cut wood. Our hunters found another *Heterodon* snake. At night a violent thunderstorm.

24 April: Early in the morning, rain, but pleasant, then slightly overcast. We received violent jolts, ran onto sandbars [and] finally [were] almost completely aground. [We had to] take soundings all around, let the ship drift far back and then find a passage more in the middle of the river. To the right, willows, and behind them, cottonwoods, all of them already green. To the left, beautiful, rough, somewhat rugged hills. Ravines full of various kinds of timber; yellow limestone walls. We again had a very bad passage with many snags [and] hard jolts [but] successfully worked our way through. We put in, and axes were heard striking from every direction. For the first time, Dreidoppel brought back completely open pawpaw tree blossoms and a small species of *Equisetum*. The overheated woodcutters came leaping down from the high banks, lay down flat on the shore, and drank from the cold river (a Spaniard who had recently done this experienced severe abdominal pains afterward, which one of the clerks relieved with a Spanish fly [cantharides] plaster). [After all this,] we cast off, and about an hour and a half later, the Blacksnake Hills (Wåkán-Se-Uä of the Iowa Indians) appeared before us, very scenic, moderately high, [and] wooded, with open green areas on them. Mr. Bodmer made a sketch of the hills and the white trading house situated in front of them. A few men in the service of the Fur Company lived in the house.[1] We put in for a moment.

The men, all French, came on board and related that a raiding party of the Iowa Indians (they lived 5 or 6 miles from the house) had attacked several Omaha lodges on the other side of the river a few days ago. [They] killed two men, four women, and children, wounded several persons, and took a woman and a child prisoner, whom they [later] offered for sale at the trading house. Dougherty, whose agency includes the Omahas, took charge of the matter and remained behind to claim the woman. Bodmer and Major Bean accompanied him. We sailed on for about a quarter of an hour, [then] put in near the high bank, cut wood, and stayed for the night. Our traveling companions did not return until about eleven o'clock. The Indians had assumed they would be reprimanded, and all of them, not excluding the chief, had intoxicated themselves. The prisoners were also drunk. They had sold their wool blankets and [other] things for whiskey. Dougherty [decided] to have the [inebriated] squaw fetched [later].

25 April: Yesterday Bodmer brought back from the prairie near the trading house a pretty, orange-colored flower *(Batschia canescens)* that we had not seen [before]. In the region of this trading house, [there were said to be] settlers as far as 15 miles inland. After breakfast we reached an ugly place full of snags [and large sandbars] along the right bank. Big, broad accumulations of soil, washed up and deposited by the river, filled the bends of its course; they were overgrown with grasses and other plants. About nine o'clock, we were jolted several times by snags [and,] somewhat farther [on, came to] a place where we could not find any channel at all. We turned around [and backtracked more then once] to where we had come from, until we had somewhat more [navigable] water.

The hill to the right was covered with sparse forest; *Podophyllum* with its big, bright green leaves covered the ground. The redbuds and *Crataegus (azarolus?)* or *Pyrus* mingled their red and white blossoms. Ducks in pairs everywhere. Farther [on], to the right in the forest, there was a fire. Smoke rose in several places, and along the ground, the forest was scorched black for a great distance. Indians or river travelers had done this. If Indians wanted to make their tracks unrecognizable or conceal them, they lit the grass and shrubs behind them.

[Then, another] island. River channels very shallow; we ran aground [more than once]. Before twilight we were at the mouth of Wolf River.

26 April: The river was rather favorable today, and we ran fast. On both sides of the bank, sandy shores [with] large fallen tree trunks. A wild goose *(Anser canadensis)* on the shore with four downy goslings. Shots were fired at her; she returned to her young. [A] remarkable hill chain. Dangerous bend in the river, full of snags. Beautiful view of the Missouri before us; it seemed to flow through a narrow gorge. [In] a low-lying area covered with willows, a nice river, the [Big] Nemaha, joined the Missouri. The Iowas, Otoes, Omahas, and Yanktons (a branch of the Sioux) gave the region around this

river up to the Little Nemaha to their half-breed Indians, of whom there are about 150 to 200. The land belonged to the Otoes; the other Indians paid for it to accommodate their half-breeds (offspring of Indians and whites).[M1]

To the left, extensive sandbars; low water. For a long time we could not get away from this spot and often struck bottom, but [we] finally moved on. Strong wind whipped the sand into the air everywhere and into our eyes. The river turned to the right. To the left and ahead, the hill ranges appeared very low [but then higher] as one came closer to them. In the river, snags and sandbars; we often ran aground [but without damage]. Before the picturesque hill chain to the right stretched a narrow prairie, which extended from the nearby mouth of the Nishnabotna toward Council Bluff.[2] We soon found ourselves near this outlet, [where,] one winter, Dougherty shot twenty elk from one herd in the tall woods. The lovely Nishnabotna was once rich in beavers that have [since] fallen prey to European avarice and expert devastation.

In the evening, the sun sinking deep behind the forest illumined the area in an indescribably beautiful manner. We had a magnificent view back toward the gleaming violet-red and purple hill chain; before us, the broad surface of the river [shone as if] on fire, [as did] the vividly green woodlands on shore. The wind had subsided. Our roaring steamboat twisted dangerously among the many snags peering out of the water. [Then the *Yellow Stone*], unable to move forward, drifted with the force of the current against piled masses [of] wood, upon which a large group of men immediately jumped and pushed and held [the steamboat] off. We continued on and, after about half an hour, lay to on the left bank. The whippoorwill, a bird we had not yet seen, was common here, and often heard.

On the morning of 27 April we moved on. To the right along the bank, we saw again the prairie of the Nishnabotna. The [right bank] strata were very distinct; good earth, in part very black, alternated with layers mixed with sand. The river was very narrow here. We struck bottom violently just as we were

---

[M1] It has been two years now since they received this land, but they are not yet using it. [The Treaty of Prairie du Chien (1830) created such a reserve, approximately 138,000 acres, in southeastern Nebraska. The Otoe-Missourias ceded the designated lands, for which the other tribes would pay out of their respective treaty annuities. The government failed to allot any land to mixed-blood individuals until 1860. Virtually all of the acreage was in the hands of white settlers within a few years after allotment. Johansen, "To Make Some Provision," 8–29.]

opposite the Little Nemaha River. About noon, we ran onto a sandbar, [and] the wind, which was beginning to blow violently, drove us more and more firmly onto the sand, and the ship [had to be] fastened with good ropes to the snags in the river.

After eating, our hunters went ashore, but hardly had they left when such a storm broke that there was grave concern for the ship. Several objects—chicken cages, for example—were blown from the deck [and] floated [away]. Some of the chickens drowned. One smokestack was [toppled] by the wind, [which] we were afraid might tear the deck off the steamboat. Fortunately our ropes held firm. The first squall abated, but soon afterward another one arose. The captain hoped to be able to lay the ship beneath the steep bank on our windward side, about 20 feet in height, but that could not be attempted in this storm; we were blown still more firmly into the sand. Rain intermittently accompanied this unpleasant gale. Mr. McKenzie and others very familiar with the Missouri unanimously declared that they had never experienced such a violent storm on these waters. The boat was sent around to fish out various lost objects that had drifted against the sandbars. The ship's carpenter patched things up here and there. After about two to two and a half hours, the storm subsided.

Crows came flying along the sandbar. We trained our rifles on them but [did not] hit any. In the tall woods surrounding the prairie, in the distance, we heard several shots from our hunters. [When they] returned, Mr. Bodmer had killed a beautiful yellow-headed [blackbird], *Icterus icterocephalus,* which we came upon [for the first time] near [Fort] Leavenworth, along with the red-shouldered variety and *Quiscalus versicolor.*

At 4:30 we were able to leave [and] succeeded in moving through the snag-filled area. After a while Messrs. Sanford and Dougherty appeared [and] wanted to be brought aboard by boat. They had killed a raccoon and a mouse for me [but] had had seen no game at all.

We continued along the left bank. When we arrived at a channel (slew) separating [an island] from the mainland, the sun was just setting. We saw [the] magnificent red sunset glow between the island's sparse cottonwoods, whereupon we were told that this very island bore the name Isle au Bon Soleil (Good Sun Island). We put in [there], and the crew left to cut wood. The island was large, 4 to 5 miles long.[3] [By] evening the raccoon killed by Sanford made an appearance in disrobed form on the gallery of the stern of the steamboat, where all kinds of meat were always hanging: chickens, turkeys, and rabbits appeared beside beef and pork. Marmots and raccoons were not disdained by the Negroes and Canadians.

28 April: Early in the morning we proceeded somewhat farther along [Good] Sun Island and lay to there again, since we found no [navigable] water for continuing the journey. The boat made soundings around us but found no passage; [the crew] therefore began to unload the ship to lighten it. After [that], the engine was started and an attempt was made to move on, but we soon ran aground again. It seemed as though we were not to get away from here [this day, so] we dropped anchor [for the night]. [In 1832] the steamboat was stranded here five days because of [low] water.

About five [that] afternoon, a flight of at least one hundred pelicans passed over us in a northerly direction. They formed a wedge and occasionally a semicircle and sometimes broke into two flocks but always reestablished the old formation. One could distinguish their black pinions very clearly, as well as the doubled-up neck and the crooked beak. Since I had never observed pelicans in their natural state, I took them at first for cranes.

29 April: In the morning, mist, fog, even rain. They found more water early, and we left rather quickly. The hill chain [near] the Nishnabotna was remarkable. The hills had extremely odd limestone ledges, now and then shaped like sharply protruding bastions, partially overgrown with green [or] dry yellow grass, or covered with reddish or reddish yellow stones and earth. Before them, a splendid, fresh green carpet of grass, from the Nishnabotna to the Missouri, on completely level alluvial soil. The Otoes, Iowas, Sauks, and Meskwakis hunted [around here]. The number of species of trees that make up the [riverine] forests in this region has already greatly decreased; they include approximately [sixteen species or types].

Along the bank to the left, in the direction of the picturesque hill chain, many snags; sandbars to the right. We ran (or rather crept, since we used only half power) along [the left] bank, where the row of hills remained very close to us for a while. On [them] we observed dry grass and a large number of oaks with yellowish or brownish green blossoms. In places along the bank, phlox, blooming abundantly, colored everything sky-blue.

[After noon we saw] high, steep banks or bluffs of a yellowish red or ashy blue color, on which landslides [sometimes] occurred. At several places these banks were reddish brown, and Dougherty told me that the Pawnee Indians painted themselves with a similarly colored clay, since they had no red clay.

We turned [toward] the right bank, where we soon landed to cut wood. The forest floor was densely covered with *Equisetum hyemale,* on which there were large numbers of insects, probably young ants; one could not reach around without getting his hands stained violet-red with their juice. Otherwise one noticed few live animals in the vicinity—only the bluebird. When I was ready to return to the ship, a man shouted out to me to be careful: there was a rattlesnake *(Crotalus tergeminus)* near [a] fallen tree; he heard it rattling. I found [and] stunned it, and placed it in a tin canister with a *Heterodon* and a black snake, where it soon became very lively again. Later it was placed in spirits. [It] had not bitten the other two snakes.

In the afternoon the weather was very pleasantly warm. We passed many perilous places with snags. The river formed a beautiful broad expanse, [but] the passage, though wide, was too shallow. We remained motionless, and the boat took soundings all around. In the forest on the bank, a few thrushes were singing. We moved to an extensive sandbar in the river onto which wood, boards, and many barrels were unloaded to lighten the ship. [We] investigated the sandbar [and] found tracks of wild geese and sandpipers, a broken, white wild goose egg, [and] driftwood everywhere. We stayed there for the night.

30 April: The wood and the barrels were reloaded with great effort, and after seven o'clock the journey continued. We were soon aground again [and] remained for several hours [in] one place. Sanford and Dougherty had themselves put ashore to go hunting. About 11:30 an attempt succeeded; we came free and immediately steamed along the left bank. To lighten the ship, about thirty men were put ashore, but suddenly we were aground again. The boat took soundings everywhere and returned with the sad news that nowhere was there enough water for our ship. Mr. McKenzie had already sent a man upriver to procure a keelboat on which to unload part of the cargo. Since no one saw any way of going [ahead], the ship was [secured and] everyone went hunting. Shots were soon heard from all directions—most of them [aimed] at ducks. I found horse dung near the shore; it could only be that of Indian horses. I saw few birds [and] no amphibians at all [but] found some blooming elms, willows, and *Prunus padus virginiana* as well as *Crataegus* (probably *azarolus*). Several species of *Vitis, Rhus,* and *Smilax* were on the verge of fully unfolding their flowers. Rain [threatened]; I returned to the ship, several hunters followed, [and] a heavy downpour began. Messrs. Sanford and Dougherty did not return until shortly before dusk; they had

shot several ducks and a wild goose; they also brought me [an owl] and a *Coluber constrictor;* they were soaking wet. In the evening the rain ceased. One of our engagés had handled poison ivy *(Rhus radicans).* His whole face was swollen and distorted, but in this country such a poisoning is not taken seriously, because it soon disappears of its own accord.

1 May: Early in the morning, rain; the forest dripped with water. Despite the extraordinary wetness, one heard shots from our hunters ringing throughout the forest. The river had fallen even more during the night. The clerk soon returned with four wood ducks he had shot. About noon, no more rain, but dark overcast sky.

At 12:30 a big white catfish got caught on one of our fishing lines; [then] a second catfish, somewhat heavier (the first weighed 60, this one 65 pounds), got caught; and then the largest of all (an *Ictalurus furcatus,* blue catfish), weighing about 100 pounds. In its stomach and in those of the others [we] found large pieces of pork, chicken bones, goose feet (refuse from the ship), the extremities of a raccoon, big bones, and the entire gill system of a large fish. The white catfish grows this large only on the lower Missouri; farther upstream, only smaller ones are caught. The length of the largest fish caught was 53¾ inches. Its body was very thick, the belly swollen, and the head very broad and smooth with eight whiskers around its mouth. A great many leeches had attached themselves by suction to its gill openings.

In the afternoon a new storm came up in the west. Dreidoppel returned at just the right time. He had shot a rabbit, saw a shrew, and heard a new birdcall. The face of the man who had touched the *Rhus radicans* was still very swollen today. Mr. Bodmer returned from hunting soaked by the rain; he had not been able to shoot anything. Toward evening the sky cleared somewhat in the west; we [could] expect good weather tomorrow.

2 May: The river rose a little during the night. Mr. Bodmer went out with the woodcutters. I was on land for a short while. Several small birds sang their soft, meager song, but in these [spring] forests, nothing like the invigorating singing of the birds in our German fatherland was to be heard. The local songbirds included a thrush (I did not see it) as well as the *Fringilla erythrophthalma* and a lemon-yellow songbird, perhaps *Sylvia aestiva.* I looked for snakes but found none.

At five minutes before eleven o'clock, the engine was started; steam had been building up for a long time. Again we moved, as we had been doing lately, in a diagonal direction across the river as far as the sandy islands located to the left, but the water began to diminish again and we were stranded. A very strong southwest wind had risen. Mr. Bodmer returned and brought beautiful plants [and] an interesting live snake, *Coluber flaviventris*.

After lunch we [began to find] more water and hence made rapid progress. About an hour [later], we had open, grass-covered prairie hills to our left, with tall forest farther ahead near the water. Here, on a broad stretch, the river was shallow. [Then] Weeping Water Creek emptied to the left; the bank here was steep, 10 feet high, the forest growth very vigorous. The view was illuminated by an extremely bright evening sun, which gave the spring foliage an incomparable splendor.

After supper we saw a canoe paddling toward us; in it was a certain [Lucien] Fontenelle, in the Fur Company's service, [and] another man. [Fontenelle] lived at the post where Major Dougherty owned a house that he used when he traveled as the Indian agent for the Otoe, Omaha, and Pawnee nations. Mr. Fontenelle [planned] to undertake a journey from the [Bad] River to the Rocky Mountains with a party of engagés. He stayed with us today. We soon put in on the left bank.

3 May: [Early this morning] we approached the big Platte River. Four to 5 miles from the mouth, one [could] distinguish its clear, blue water from that of the Missouri flowing separately along our left bank. A mile farther on, the Platte water was covered with white foam; this river had risen, and thereby we got more water. Beyond the Platte, according to Mr. Fontenelle, the Missouri was said to be very low. We halted to cut wood [and then] sailed on. A half hour later, we reached the Platte River on the left bank; it was very high, its bluish water a very distinct semicircle [on the Missouri; see pl. 6]. Twenty minutes farther [on,] Papillion Creek emerged from willow thickets. Before us we saw the green prairie hills on which Bellevue, Dougherty's agency, was located. [See pl. 7.] This place was formerly a Missouri Fur Company trading post; [it] failed and was sold. Mr. Fontenelle acquired it and sold it to the government, which transformed it into the agency for the Otoes, Omahas, and Pawnees, of which Dougherty was now in charge. A subagent, Major [Robinson Pemberton] Beauchamp, and several blacksmiths lived here. Mr. Fontenelle settled about 400 to 500 paces farther down. The government purchased from the Indians the entire right Missouri side as far [north] as the Big Sioux River but to date had left them in possession of it.[4]

About two o'clock, we reached Mr. Fontenelle's residence, consisting of several buildings with fine cornfields situated before pleasantly green, sparsely wooded hills. Some of those cultivated fields belonged to the government. Behind the hills the vast prairie extended. The land here is extraordinarily fertile: a poorly cultivated acre produces one hundred bushels of Indian corn, far more when carefully farmed. The Bellevue Agency [was] very nicely located on an elevation, [along with] the dwelling of a smith and his family and other buildings.

Several men who lived here had Indian wives of the Otoe and Omaha tribes. They came on board, in red and blue [cloth dresses], with characteristic broad faces and large features; round heads; pendent breasts; small hands and feet. Their children had dark-brown hair, nice faces, and snow-white teeth. It was here that twelve Iowas recently crossed the river and pursued a group of unarmed Omahas who had just left [this place], caught up with them on the prairie 3 miles away, and killed and plundered all but a few. Dougherty left [us] now with the intention of clearing up this matter with the Omahas.

We halted here to inspect the site and its beautiful [vista] of the river. On the hill, huge quantities of blue phlox and *Staphylea trifoliata* as well as red *Aquilegia* were blooming. Indian corn, [in] beautiful, varied colors—black, red, etc.—was taken on board. I obtained a nice snake *(Coluber eximus)*, which was regarded as poisonous.

About four o'clock or 4:30, we left [Bellevue] and steered along the wooded left bank. We suddenly caught sight of three Omaha Indians: an old man, a younger one, and a woman. They were wrapped in buffalo hides; the young man had a bow in his hand and on his back a hide quiver with arrows. He was painted white around his eyes and nose. The woman was the well-known Mitain, of whom Say relates in [Edwin James's account of] Long's expedition (vol. 1, p. 223). Recently she was stabbed in the chest by Iowas and only by chance avoided being scalped; her son, likewise wounded, is also on the path to recovery.

This region is the true territory of the Omaha Indians, who roam on both sides of the Missouri, from Boyer River up to the Big Sioux River and the [James] River. They also hunt between the Running Water [(Niobrara)] and Platte rivers. Their nearest village is about 25 miles away from Bellevue. They plant Indian corn, as already mentioned and, when not occupied with its cultivation, devote themselves to hunting buffalo. The nation is not numerous now; smallpox and other diseases have greatly reduced them. They have few young, vigorous people; on the contrary, they have many old people.

Toward evening we put Messrs. Dougherty and Fontenelle ashore at the left bank, [which was] covered with dense cottonwood forests. [They] returned from there to Bellevue, to which [it was] only a few miles on foot. The bank was very rugged [and] heavily timbered. These prairies are favorable for raising livestock. Cattle thrive [and] provide much milk. Mr. Fontenelle said he would have five thousand swine in a few years if the Indians did not shoot too many of them. Tomorrow Mr. Pilcher will also leave us. Toward dusk we lay to on the left bank. The evening was very warm and pleasant.

4 May: At 7:30, 69¾°F. The river had risen an inch. Much driftwood on extensive sandbars; wild geese fled before the steaming monster. [At] a very low-lying spot in the river, the ship violently struck bottom. The boat made soundings, and [we] found a deeper channel. [After many river bends, sandbars to be maneuvered around, and a stop to collect wood, we saw] tall yellow bluffs [and] somewhat farther ahead the white buildings of Mr. [Jean Pierre] Cabanné's trading house. Mr. Cabanné, a partner in the Fur Company, was no longer young and [planned] to leave here in about two weeks to retire in St. Louis. Mr. Pilcher will take his place.

When we arrived we saw, to our delight, a crowd of Indians: Otoes, Omahas, and one Iowa who lived with the Otoes. Most had buffalo hides around their shoulders with the hair turned outward; some had blankets, mostly white, [occasionally] painted with colorful stripes. Their facial features did not particularly differ from those seen earlier. Many were scarred by smallpox; several [had] one eye—a patch on the other one—probably from smallpox. Their faces were painted, some with red chins and foreheads; others [with red] stripes [on] their cheeks. (That evening, at the dance, their faces were painted white.) [A] few had aquiline noses. Some of their eyes were small, some [not]. Their hair hung down to their necks in disorderly fashion; [it was] never shaved off. Some of their leggins were very nicely stitched. Their war clubs were fitted on top with a round ball of white wood studded with yellow nails; the skin of a skunk [hung from] the end of the handle [along with] a bundle of teeth from slain enemies. They had pierced their ears with several holes along the rim, in which they [fastened] strings of blue and white [beads]. Their bows were about 3 feet long, made of white wood, simply and smoothly finished. The quiver was a simple leather bag. The women's faces were not so smooth and flat as [those] of the Sauks and Meskwakis; their noses were longer.

Mr. Bodmer sketched an Omaha, at least [5 feet] 10½ to 11 inches tall, and his pretty child, whom the father had painted, since he was to be sketched (he spit in his hands, where he held cinnabar, made a paste, and painted the child's head with it). He had shaved [the boy's] head and had left a tuft of hair in back and in front; a large white feather was fastened [at] the middle of his head. From an Iowa living here, I bought a bow and arrows, a pair of beautifully decorated leggins, and an interesting whip made of elk bones, on which Indian figures were sketched. This man had an attractive, friendly face; he lived here near the Omahas, who recently made war on his people, but was not worried because they knew that he did not live with his tribe. [His] name was Nih-yu-ma-nih, "Rain that goes or passes over." All of them had black and red Sioux pipes decorated with tin or lead, which they [would not sell] cheaply.

Mr. Cabanné had lunch with us. Later I called on him; his house, which included the store for Indian goods, had a balcony with a fine view of the river. He showed me the nearby cornfields, where fifteen acres produced two thousand bushels of corn every year; the fertility was said to be quite exceptional. Someone brought us a live beaver, still very young, about ten to twelve inches long, already shaped just like the adult animal. Under different circumstances I would certainly have bought it. Later, when the Indians were at the ship, I showed them a rattlesnake in whiskey, and they said that recently a child had been bitten by one and had died.

The ship stayed here today because many things had to be taken care of.
5 May: We were called late last evening to Mr. Cabanné's to see an Omaha dance. About twenty Indians had gathered under bright moonlight in front of the house. The main dancer, a large man over [5 feet] 10 inches (Prussian measure) tall, wore on his head a huge feather crown made from very long tail feathers and pinions of owls and [other] birds of prey; in his hand he carried a bow and arrows. His trunk was bare except for a whitish hide that covered his right shoulder and chest. His arms and naked parts were painted with white stripes. He had his breechcloth around his hips; his leather leggins were painted with dark transverse stripes and [fringed] below. He looked savage and warlike, an image to which his athletic figure contributed. A second dancer, with a muscular body completely bare [and] painted white

on the upper part, [had] a similar feather crown on his head and [a] war club with skunk hide in his hand.

These two, [with] several younger men and boys, formed a line, opposite which other Indians sat in a row. One [of the latter] beat a kind of drum in rather rapid time; others had war clubs decorated with little bells, which they shook and moved in time with the drum; [everyone chanted loudly]. The dance consisted of jumping with both feet simultaneously [but not very] high, the trunk poised somewhat forward, weapons held [aloft]. They sprang toward each other [this way] for about an hour until [sweat] was pouring [profusely], whereupon tobacco was tossed to them, [the] present usually given on such occasions.

Seeing this dance was most interesting, especially [on such a beautiful] American evening. The moon was shining as fully and clearly as if it were day over the vast Missouri wilderness [and with] the din and bustle of the Indians, [an altogether] exquisite scene. It was late when we took leave of Mr. Cabanné and returned to the ship.

At daybreak on the 5th, the *Yellow Stone* [departed]. Mr. Pilcher stayed behind [at] the trading house, and a young Englishman, Mr. Ashworth, [came] along in his place. The river turned right; on its left bank, large alluvial bottoms covered with willows and plant growth. This [remained] the case for a long distance, [till we] navigated past Boyer [River] to our right [and then] saw [on our left] the ruins of Council Bluff. Of the fort abandoned here in 1827, there now stood just the stone chimneys and, in the middle, a stone supply house. The Indians had taken away all other useable objects. The military post at Council Bluff was established in 1819 and equipped for one thousand men, even though the 6th [Infantry] Regiment (now garrisoned in Jefferson Barracks), which was stationed here, comprised only about five hundred. In 1827 these troops were withdrawn, and the [Fort] Leavenworth post was established.[5] People maintain that the site at Council Bluff is far more favorable for observing [regional] Indian tribes than the one at Leavenworth, and some surmise that troops will be transferred here again.

[Near Council Bluff], down along the river, Mr. Sanford once found large mastodon molars, which he gave to General Clark in St. Louis, where I saw them. Presumably they had been exposed by the river.

A very strong wind had been blowing since nine o'clock today; sand from the sandbars flew around everywhere. We struck a sandbar exactly at the time of our twelve o'clock pause. The region [later became] low-lying and monotonous until we again reached the surrounding hill chain; [the hills,] to be sure, were somewhat bare but had unique shapes covered with pleasing vegetation. Wild ducks in large numbers; many treacherous snags. [We spied] an engagé on shore, bringing a letter from the steamboat *Assini-boine;* he was taken on board.

Half an hour later, Soldier River emerged picturesquely to our right [from] wooded banks. The voyage proceeded until evening, [when] we ran aground; the [crew] fastened the ship to the bank.

6 May: They worked all night long with great exertion to windlass the *Yellow Stone* from the sandbar. The dawning morning was pleasant. On both sides, alluvial land with willow and cottonwood, in some places mixed with other forest trees. We saw two large [gray] wolves trotting on a sandbar.

The young Englishman, Ashworth, claimed to be a midshipman from the English Navy and [to have] visited many countries, especially their coastlands. Today [he] told me about his stay among the Sauks along the Missouri. He saw them riding [at full gallop], naked and bareback, without saddle [or] bridle, shooting at targets with bows.

[We came to] a spot frightfully studded with snags; then a vast prairie to the left; [and next,] wildly collapsed banks with willows lying about in crisscross confusion. Farther on to the right, a beautiful forest, dark, shady, and, since it was airy, [an undergrowth of] luxuriant plants snarled with vines. The wild grapevines *(Vitis)* were beginning to bloom, [and] sarsaparilla abounded here.

To the left, large sandbars, and behind them, interminable prairie. On the right bank, the Little Sioux River emerged. About two o'clock we landed on alluvial prairie [to cut] cottonwoods. The prairie was blanketed [in] luxuriant green from all manner of grasses and plants, but not a single blossom. Only a few birds. I shot *Muscicapa tyrannus* (kingbird), which nested here; we also saw a red bird, perhaps *Tanagra rubra,* which we did not get. After half an hour, we continued. The region became more smooth and level. Ducks and geese everywhere in abundance. [Somewhat] farther on, the river made a wide bend around sandbars near magnificent forest. Before dusk we put in for the night, [which] descended so [quickly] that we could not shoot anything.

7 May: Today we have been gone from Neuwied for exactly a year. Early in the morning, excellent weather, bright sunshine. About 7:30, bluffs, yellow clay

and limestone on the left bank, with beautiful thickets. [At a spot where] we were surrounded by sandbars, the boat was set out; the half-breed Chippewa (Defond), one of the Spaniards (Hernandez), and three engagés [went] out to make soundings. The shallow water detained us [a long time, but we eventually moved] slowly along the sandbar off the left bank [and] saw the beginning of Blackbird's Hills [sic], [where] the famous Omaha chief, Waschínga-Sáhba (Blackbird), was buried. On [one of them there was] a small pointed mound: Blackbird's grave.[6] Waschínga-Sáhba was the mightiest chief along the entire Missouri, and his people, the Omahas, were then very numerous. Smallpox and their enemies, the Sioux and the Sauks, have reduced [the Omahas] to the weakened state they are now in. Blackbird was so powerful that traders unconditionally gave him what he demanded. His people dared not waken him loudly when he slept but rather tickled him [awake] with straws. He stabbed one of his wives to death because she had displeased him. He arranged to be buried on [the hill just mentioned], sitting on a live mule. The principal chief of the Omahas is now Óngpa-Tánga, [Big Elk]. He lives on the [Elkhorn] River, which empties into the Platte River about 20 miles above its mouth. The Omahas were said to be able now to muster about 300–400 warriors

At twelve noon, [more] bluffs on the left; on these elevations, we observed for the first time a mixture of conifers and deciduous trees. That morning, on a small, insignificant creek, we saw the first traces of beaver: a tree lay there as though snapped off—the bark and wood had been gnawed through all the way around. We put in before dusk on a sandy shore, cut wood, and remained there for the night. A large fire was soon blazing; we investigated the region and got some exercise. The forest was dense, full of dried plants, and completely devoid of open blossoms. The mosquitoes soon grew very annoying. The call of the whippoorwill sounded forth incessantly in the woodlands on both sides of the river (in America the name of this bird is usually written and pronounced "whippoorwill," but if one listens closely, it sounds like "wipp-per-wipp").

8 May: In the morning, beautiful, clear, pleasant weather. The region rather uniform. On one of the hills to the right, which we reached twenty minutes before ten o'clock, Sergeant [Charles] Floyd, of the Lewis and Clark party, who died here at that time, is buried. The grave is right on the top of the ridge and marked with a short staff, often replaced by the whites [after] being consumed by prairie fire. Somewhat farther upstream, Floyd River,

or Creek, emerged, [and] a half hour [later], the Big Sioux River: willows and cottonwoods along its banks; ducks on its surface. Along a small river, [Pipestone Creek,] that empties into the Big Sioux about 40 miles upstream, the red stone [catlinite] from which the Sioux make their pipes is quarried. People who have been at the site have assured me that [the pipestone] appears in colorful strata alternating with whitish, yellowish, bluish, and variously colored clays. Indians from different tribes come here [to] acquire the stone. It is said that they do not harm each other at the site itself but must be careful when approaching or leaving it.

About 120 miles [up the Big Sioux River] lives a band of the Sioux (or rather Dacotas, as this nation calls itself),[7] known by the name Wáhch-Pekúteh ("Those Who Shoot at a Leaf"). They and another [Dacota] band on the Mississippi plant Indian corn; the others do not. The land of the Sioux begins here along the Big Sioux River. Before 1830, when the above-mentioned land purchase was concluded, it extended even farther down.[8]

After lunch the wind was so strong and the air so full of dust that one could not see. All clothing, even in the cabins, was full of sand and dust. We continued our voyage, [but finally] the [high] wind clouded the distant horizon and so violently agitated the water that the pilot could not readily discern sandbars and logs. We put in before dusk, [and] the woodcutters began their work in all directions. After we climbed the steep bank (with forty to fifty woodcutters, it looked like the scaling of a fortress wall), we plunged into the forest of cottonwoods [and] narrow-leaved willows, [with] very few other tree species. The understory [had] no great diversity. We followed the riverbank and came onto a small prairie, where we tracked elk (*Cervus canadensis*) as well as ordinary deer.

In the north, lightning was very intense, [although] the wind was no longer so powerful. Wild geese called on the river. Dreidoppel shot *Tringa pusilla* on the shore, and in the dark Mr. Bodmer went so far that he could hardly find his way back to the ship. At 8:30 several [violent] thunderstorms arose; the rain poured down [and] the lightning bolts were majestic—they illuminated the [sky] as bright as day [with] long, zigzag lines that encompassed half the horizon.

9 May: The thunderstorm last evening [had] such a powerful wind that, at midnight, we would have had to worry about the ship, had it not lain protected by the forest and the bank. The wind often tore open the doors of the upper cabin and inundated us with rain. Toward daybreak [it] returned with

renewed force: at dawn one burst of thunder followed the other and everyone [believed] that the ship [would] be struck.

As the thunderstorm moved away, the ship left its position. The magnificent springtime verdure [had been] refreshed by the rain. On [a] hill [we spied] several thickets [of species] not [previously] seen, especially buffalo berry, with bluish green foliage, and cedar trees among the conifers. On the lower section of [this] hill, argillite seemed to show on the surface, divided into narrow horizontal layers, blackish blue underneath, yellow-reddish above.[9] Immediately behind the bluffs, [Aowa Creek] emptied, a brook filled with broken trees. We halted [nearby]; the woodcutters and hunters left; the fishermen set out their lines. They saw very fine fish but did not catch anything. It began raining again. We stopped only twenty minutes. After ten o'clock the sun emerged; it became pleasantly warm. At noon we put in at the right bank and cut wood. The forest here was very wild and extraordinarily entangled. Elms, ash, oak (particularly those with rough, corklike bark), box elder, *Rhus, Vitis, Smilax,* currants with yellow flowers (the berries are said to be black), gooseberries, red willow *(Cornus sericea),* and several other plants made up these thickets, mixed with cottonwoods and several varieties of willow. Beautiful birds uttered their cries: a yellow songbird and several others. Big swallows hovered in the air. We looked for snakes, particularly rattlesnakes, but the latter were said to occur mainly in the prairie.

After lunch the steam engine was started and we departed, [navigating from bank to bank to avoid obstructions]. Soon we had no water; the boat took soundings, [and] after a long time we finally got away. As the sun was setting, we passed beautiful hills. Somewhat farther on, we halted off the right bank. There was tall, sparse timber near the river; behind it extended an endless prairie, completely overgrown with yellow, dry grass. When it was dark, we set the prairie grass afire for our pleasure, a magnificent scene. There was no wind, and the fire did not burn long.

10 May: In the morning, dreary sky, wind, rain. The river had risen [and was] very turbulent. About eight o'clock we put in on the left bank, where the *Assiniboine* had left large amounts of excellent firewood for us. Someone had blazed the trees on the bank as a sign.

As [we progressed], we had a beautiful view back toward the hill chain, the character [of which] had gradually changed. They were already far more barren, the forests not as tall. Soon they would be [even] more bare [and] overgrown with short grass, which also [eventually] ends. Not far beyond the spot where [this hill chain] comes close to the Missouri, a small river emptied, the Vermillion River (White Stone River on Lewis and Clark map). Wild geese and ducks in abundance. It is said that one can easily catch very fine fish at the mouth of the Vermillion.

It rained incessantly until one o'clock and then cleared up. The sun shone for a short time, but the sky remained overcast. In shallow water, we made a long halt [and then] proceeded by fits and starts [and] severe jolts. [The landscape alternated from hills to bluffs to flat regions, most with forests of mixed trees and understory.] We landed at a level, narrow area before the hills at 5:30 and took in wood, which stood there in readiness. On the darkly colored hills, the fresh, bright green vegetation was most picturesque. Down below, before the hills, among the cottonwoods and willows grew *Cornus sericea, Aquilegia* [—], with red flowers, an *Aralia* [—], a *Viola* with a white flower (light violet inside), *Prunus padus,* etc. At six o'clock we continued our voyage. We steamed to the right across the river, where there was a tall, shady grove of slender, spreading cottonwoods with a beautiful green carpet beneath them. We sailed somewhat farther and then lay to for the night.

11 May: Extensive prairie to the right, [a smaller one] to the left. Two prairie hens *(Tetrao cupido)* sat on the bank and were not shy; they did not fly away at all. At the place where the prairie ended, the Jacques [James] River emptied behind a sandbar.

To the left on shore, a strange limestone hill appeared like a devastated turret with rubble and transverse strata. The bottom was full of sandbars; [a large snag] came under the ship and lifted it, whereupon [we] drifted into a second one, which broke into pieces. [On] the right prairie, we saw [our] first antelope on the gently sloping green hills. They quickly hurried away over the elevation. Farther on, beautiful green hills to the left, then steep limestone bluffs, in the ravines of which stood short forest and dry trees mixed with conifers. These bluffs—Calumet Bluffs [on] Lewis and Clark's map—were ash-blue [at the base], yellow above, and had deep gorges.[10]

[At midmorning] we halted [while] wood was cut. We found the small flesh-red *Oxalis* with bulbous roots. In the gorges, ash, *Prunus padus,* cottonwood, elm, [etc.]. Mr. Bodmer shot a shiny blackbird *(Quiscalus versicolor).* Thrushes and several other birds inhabited the wooded ravines. We sailed on after an hour.

After lunch we saw the *Assiniboine* ahead; we reached [it] half an hour later. It did not have enough water to proceed. This boat had a much larger, lighter cabin than ours and no passengers at all. The crew had killed a female bear and had two live cubs on board. Yesterday they had seen elk, and they also had several nice fox pelts and a beaver skin. While we were still [examining] the ship, Indians appeared on the opposite sandy bank, probably fifteen to twenty of them. People had seen them coming, riding down over the hills. No one, however, seemed inclined to send them a boat or to sail over to them. We therefore had to content ourselves with looking at them with the telescope.

The prairie beside us was damp, [with] puddles and mud holes. We made excursions [there] and found several varieties of plants with long turniplike roots. The big yellow-breasted lark *(Sturnella)* uttered its short, chirping call, and then a short, pleasantly flutelike [song]. Dreidoppel saw eight prairie hens [and] a variety of curlew *(Numenius)*. We found bison skeletons, [including] a very large skull, which, however, was not quite complete.

When I returned home, I found, to my great delight, three interesting Ponca Indians on our ship: the chief of the tribe, his brother, and a third man. All of them [were] tall [and] well built, with very pronounced features, high cheekbones, large aquiline noses, fiery dark brown eyes, hair hanging down to and even over their shoulders—[in] the case of the chief, somewhat shorter; he wore it in back twisted together in a braid. They were completely naked above the waist, except for a decorated band around their necks. In [the chief's] earlobe [was] a large opening in which [he] wore an ornament made of mussel shells (wampum). Around their wrists each one had a narrow bracelet made of white metal. Apart from their very simple leggins, they wore only large buffalo hides; the chief, however, was in a white woolen blanket. The chief's name was Schudegácheh, that is, "He who smokes." His brother was called Passítopa, which means the number four; [he] was well known because he killed an Indian who attempted to kill a white man [staying] with them. Mr. Bodmer drew both men.[M2]

The Poncas are originally of the same tribe as the Omahas and speak the same language. They have been separated for a long time and live on both sides of the [Niobrara] River. Like the Omahas, they formerly lived

---

[M2] The third Indian, a brave warrior, was Hä-chá-gä, or Deer Antlers with Velvet. [The modern orthography is *He Xá·ga* 'Elk', literally, 'Rough Horns'.]

Fig. 2. Karl Bodmer.
Schudegácheh, Ponca
Chief. Pencil and wash.
The large peace medal
worn by this man
confirms Maximilian's
opinion of his status; large
medals were generally
given by the government
only to principal village
chiefs. 11¾ × 8⅜ in.
1986.49.241.

in earth lodges. But their enemies, the Dacotas and the Pawnees, destroyed their lodges, and since then they have adopted the Dacota way of life, that is, they move about more and live in leather tipis. Their dress and appearance are almost identical with [that] of the Omahas. They have suffered greatly from smallpox and from their enemies; although [they] are said to have been brave warriors, they could now put no more than three hundred warriors in the field. Major Bean was the agent for these Indians; they came, therefore, to speak with him about certain official matters. The chief had once received from Bean a large silver medallion, in the name of President Madison, which he wore on his chest. This man had a fine, manly bearing and an intelligent, thoughtful face. Pipes soon circulated among all of us, in accordance with Indian custom. We took the Indians, after they had eaten their pork, bread, and tea, [with] which Mr. McKenzie had them served, to our rooms, and they were sketched. One of them presented me with his wooden war club; the other, Passítopa, gave me a pair of moccasins made of elk leather, dyed blackish with walnut juice. They presented a second fine pair to Major Bean, who later gave [them] to me. These Indians were not armed. The interpreter told us [they] had been separated from their comrades for a considerable period of time and did not know their whereabouts but presumed that they were hunting at the sources of the [Niobrara] River.

12 May: Beautiful, clear morning. The Indians appeared, wrapped in their buffalo hides, and the chief was sketched. At eight o'clock, the *Assiniboine* moved far backward in order to bypass the sandbar; Messrs. McKenzie and Sanford were on board. We stayed behind on the *Yellow Stone;* this was agreeable to us, since Mr. Bodmer wanted to finish sketching the Indians.

The place we lay at anchor afforded an interesting view: all around us the beautiful, pleasant region [and] the broad river in the brightest splendor of the sun; many people on shore; one steamboat at anchor, one steamboat in motion, and a large keelboat on the river. This isolated wilderness [was] everywhere full of life.

Dreidoppel went out with a gun. Later the chief spoke with the agent, Major Bean. The point of all these discussions was always [their desire] to receive various gifts from their great father (the president). They demanded, for example, hoes for cultivating the fields in order to raise corn. The chief's propriety during his speech was excellent. His noble face had a manly expression. He kept his right shoulder and often his entire upper body free [and] gesticulated vigorously with his right arm and hand. He was not wearing leggins, [and we could see that] his calves were rather sturdy and marked with several short, crisscross, bluish black stripes; otherwise [he was] neither tattooed nor painted. Some of these Indians had been inoculated against smallpox. (The previous year, Major Bean [had brought] a doctor who inoculated 2,600 Indians from different tribes. Many had no confidence in [such a preventive measure] and remarked [that] if they became ill, then they would be willing to undergo the operation.) [Today] they received as presents tobacco, powder, lead, and a red woolen blanket for the chief.

Toward noon the keelboat *Maria* anchored beside our *Yellow Stone;* the fathoming boats returned. Mr. Bodmer had had time to make very accurate sketches of two Indians. Dreidoppel returned empty-handed; several plants were the sole take of his excursion.

The crew worked intensely until about one o'clock to lighten [our] steamboat by transferring part of its cargo to the keelboat *Maria* lying beside it. About two o'clock we weighed anchor and moved backwards and around a sandbar in order to navigate upriver along the other bank. The vessel was carried downstream so swiftly by the current that the Indians, who had never experienced anything like this, became dizzy. [Once we were around the sandbar, we proceeded upriver, and in] twenty minutes, [on our] left, the entire band of Ponca Indians was assembled and awaiting us.

It was amusing to see how the colorful throng came together, wrapped in brown hides [or] white and red blankets, otherwise naked. Small children with fat bellies and thin legs, dark brown, their bows in hand, ran along the bank or cowered down like little monkeys. The men strode gravely, toma-hawks or battle-axes in hand. In the tall, shady cottonwood forest behind [them] were [their] lodges, of which I counted six; one could not see all of them. They were conical and yellowish in color, [these] so-called skin lodges, or leather huts, made from bison hides. Our three Indians were put ashore by boat, and the boat brought back an otter pelt and a beaver pelt. As the steamboat continued on, the Indians returned to their lodges.

The river became very narrow, [with] many snags. Dry grass still covered these hills, because no one had set fire to them. Somewhat farther away, it was beautifully green, like a carpet, because the Indians had burned off the old grass. Toward evening we [saw] the *Assiniboine* ahead of us; we caught up in the darkness. We halted near Bazile Creek, where Poncas formerly lived; [their] graves could be found on the hills in large numbers. The cap-tain of the *Assiniboine* spent the evening with us.

13 May: Early in the morning, we passed the mouth of the [Niobrara], a pretty river. Beautiful bluffs, rounded on top, alternated on both sides of the Mis-souri. If one saw bluffs on one side, then the other was level and had none. The cliffs of the bluffs were crumbled and weathered, full of rubble, with horizontal layers and fissures, in which there were rows of swallows' nests.

[We passed Ponca Creek], flowing diagonally along the hill chain down toward the Missouri. Upstream along [this creek], there were many prai-rie dog villages; large numbers of rattlesnakes lived in these burrows as well. It was said [that the two species] lived together peacefully, but Mr. Sanford thought otherwise, since he often saw abandoned villages full of rattlesnakes.

Some time later we struck bottom, but the ship continued onward. The wind was so strong that the steamboat did not properly respond to the rud-der. We halted about noon to [get] wood. Only red cedars were cut; the red, fragrant wood lent a pleasant aroma to the whole region. They were still full of black berries. In the ravine that I entered grew elms, ashes, *Prunus padus, Celtis,* cedars, *Celastrus scandens, Vitis, Clematis?,* buffalo berries, *Cornus sericea,* and others. On the prairie hills [there were] a large number of beautiful plants, [including] one with long, bright yellow clusters of flowers *(Stanleya pinnatifida),* which we had recently found on the prairie, as well as the wild turnip *(Psoralea esculenta)* with [its] thick, knobby, edible roots, which the Indians eat. We did not see many birds.

In the afternoon the region at first was more flat: low bluffs, the hill chains more flattened off, not so attractive and not so beautifully green. The water was often shallow, and we received severe jolts; various objects were smashed. Between the hills one occasionally glimpsed gentle green valleys. Several small runs emptied into the river; widely scattered sandbars [and] beyond them a long row of red bluffs, which in the distance looked like an American city of brick. On the bank, peculiar woodlands of thick, old, low trees, all broken off stag-headed, the result of storms and severe winters. The soil here, like the character of the region in general, was totally transformed—it had been black and very fertile downstream, here it was infertile.

On the hills beautiful 40- to 50-foot-high cedars *(Juniperus virginiana)* grew, as thick as a man, shaped like old spruce trees, many [of them] withered, with dry branches and crowns. Later, a fine cottonwood forest, with willows before it.

Toward evening a tree hidden in the water broke our right paddle wheel in two; it cracked violently [and] a thick beam snapped off. We put in to the left near a tall forest, went into it, and started big fires while the woodcutters felled trees right and left. Some of the green foliage, mostly from ash and box elder *(Acer negundo),* fell into our fires, [and] the green, sap-filled foliage crackled as it was consumed. [That] evening, lightning bolts and sheet lightning.

14 May: In the morning, pleasant, slightly overcast; [by] nine o'clock, strong wind again. The river was so shallow that we were hard aground less than a half hour [upstream] from our night quarters. The boat made soundings [and] found somewhat more water nearby, and an attempt was made to get away [by] swinging the steamboat around [and moving] along the right bank. [But] soon the engine stopped again, [so] we put forty men out on the right bank to lighten the ship. During the noon meal, we succeeded in moving across the sandbar; the *Assiniboine* stayed behind.

On land along the bank, someone caught a soft-shelled turtle *(Trionyx muticus)* in the grass, which I received alive. Someone also brought in complete specimens of the wild turnip, the roots of which were nearly as thick as a goose egg; it is said to occur only here along the Missouri.

The region before and behind us was most delightful: beautiful hills, several [quite] high. Farther on to the left, along the bank, there were very steep, barren gray hills, almost devoid of vegetation. Sandbars detained us again [until] we finally found [a] channel. Last year the prairie here [was] covered with bison herds, [but] we had not yet reached them. We caught sight of a canoe coming down the river with four men [in it]. Well armed, Mr. McKenzie went to see who it was [and] brought back the report that Indians up along the Yellowstone River had killed seven of his men.[M3]

Before us there was now a large willow and cottonwood island; in the background, an amphitheater of beautiful hills—a scenic landscape. [There was] tall timber on the left bank and then a prairie with traces of Indian lodges. Last fall Mr. McKenzie came upon a Ponca Indian encampment here. Later, a long series of steep, black, [stratified] bluffs. At six o'clock, pelting rain and strong wind; [although] the evening turned calm and pleasant, we found so little water that we had to go back. [We] fastened the ship to the left bank for the night.

15 May: On the bank where we lay at anchor, there were thickets with prairie behind them [with] many traces of Indian horses and a Dacota hunting camp; numerous skulls of deer, elk, and smaller animals lay about.

At seven o'clock we sailed backward to circumvent the sandbars. The *Assiniboine* approached. We frequently ran aground [and] remained motionless until noon. About two o'clock the *Assiniboine* sailed past us; the keelboat *Maria* was far ahead, near the right bank; both ships soon disappeared from view. [By] four o'clock we had drifted so [much] that we lay exactly opposite the place where we had spent the night. A thunderstorm arose, and at that moment the ship began to move. The *Assiniboine* sent [back] the keelboat to reduce our weight, but that was no longer necessary, and it was fastened [to our ship].

Soon we were sailing along the steep right bank [and saw] infertile hills of clay and argillite, mostly covered with dry grass; sometimes thickets in

---

[M3] This report should be corrected. Only three persons were shot to death, including a certain [Hugh] Glass, an old man who spent his whole life as a trapper in the dangerous Indian regions and was often wounded by them. Two of the Arikara murderers were killed. I brought back the scalp of one of them. [This is one of several references to Glass by Maximilian; see especially entries for 6 October 1833, and 8 May 1834.]

the ravines, [especially] cedar *(Juniperus);* it was said that Indian women ate the berries to prevent pregnancy. [Other plants there] included ash, red willow *(Cornus), Prunus padus,* and buffalo berry. We caught up with the *Assiniboine* again; [she] lay close to the bank, and her woodcutters were climbing the hills, felling cedars, [and] tossing the wood down to the shore. We landed 300 paces farther ahead, and our crew, too, cut cedars on the hills. Meanwhile we undertook an excursion [up the ravine of] a small creek with soft, wet soil, along [which] grew bushes and short trunks of *Celtis,* ash, *Prunus padus, Ulmus,* and several others. We caught a pale yellowish bat, saw several snakes, found big animal leg bones [and] several bison skulls, and [observed] various kinds of birds. From this creek we climbed the singular prairie hills surrounding us and found some nice plants, including the wild turnip *(Psoralea esculenta).* [The root] tastes like a turnip [when] it is cooked and roasted; it is nourishing and tasty. The Canadian French call it *pomme de prairie* or *pomme blanche.* From [a high] peak above the river we had, in the midst of [a] dark thunderstorm, a magnificent view of strange hilltops [and] at our feet, the beautiful river, on which two steamboats gave off smoke and steam. [Also] numerous sandbars, separated by narrow channels, affording us no good prospects for our journey.

While we were absorbed in observing this interesting scene, the ship's bell called us back; [it] is always rung twice to call back men scattered far and wide. We hastened down the hills and continued our voyage. A fierce thundershower came at the right time. We found a channel with 5 feet of water, just [what] our ship needed; we nevertheless struck bottom several times. At nightfall we halted at the right bank. The night [was] very dark, the evening very warm.

16 May: In the morning, we reached Cedar Island,[11] put in, and cut [cedar] wood, some of it [a] beautiful violet-red color with white-yellowish veins running along the edge. These conifers were mixed with [a dense variety of other trees, vines, and flowering plants on the island]. In the wild, dark entanglement of this primeval forest, [we] heard only a few bird calls; one of them was that of Wilson's *Turdus aurocapilla,* which crept around in the thicket, most often in pairs. We bagged several of them. We found many elk and deer tracks [and] saw where they had been rubbing against the cedars. A bison had decayed here; we found all its bones lying together.

We remained here for a long time because of a strong contrary wind. I went out with my gun and in the dense forest found some very interesting small birds, including *Muscicapa ruticilla* and the striated songbird with the yellow-red legs *(Sylvia striata)*. The rusty-brown wood thrush was singing, in a manner very similar to our song thrush; it was difficult to find [this bird in] the dense foliage. Doves *(Columba carolinensis)* were also here, but I saw no woodpeckers at all.

At twelve o'clock we still had an unfavorable wind, which agitated the waves so much that the pilots [could not] discern the signs of sandbars, [so] we remained at anchor, and several of the ship's crew went out with muskets or rifles. It can be assumed that the range of the wild turkey reaches up to about here. An occasional turkey might be shot farther upstream along the Missouri, even on the Yellowstone, but [beyond that] there are no wood-lands [to] protect these big birds. The Indians in the regions where these birds are not found like to barter for their beautiful tail feathers and wings to make fans and other things with. Mr. McKenzie [had a large supply] of them on the steamboat.

[That night] the wind abated somewhat. The boat was sent out to take soundings so that we could depart early in the morning.

17 May: [Next] morning we steamed past Cedar Island, several miles long; its tip and end were pure cottonwood forest, the middle almost wholly cedar. [Many animals observed there.] We saw six antelope running on the left bank. [Later, another] antelope, the first that I saw clearly, stood not far from us near the hills. Its back was brown, belly and hindquarters com-pletely white. It seemed frightened by the noise of the steamboat, stopped, and trotted over the hill. The Indians do not shoot as many of these animals as buffalo but like to make their leggins from the skins.

[Low] water. We repeatedly struck bottom; the lead was continually tossed out. In the river, several islands surrounded by sandbars and many snags. Soon a somewhat flatter region [lay] before us; on the right bank, steep bluffs of argillite or sandstone, here and there with towerlike, colum-nar formations. Redheaded woodpeckers *(Picus erythrocephalus)* every-where in great numbers, which I almost never observed along the lower Missouri. We remained motionless for a long time. After our noon meal, the [sounding] boat returned. [It] had not found more than 4 feet of water; nonetheless, an attempt was made, and we sailed to the right across the river, [where] our boat found even less water. We therefore secured the steamboat to the willow bank and undertook excursions into the prairie. After I had worked my way through thickets of dense young willow and cottonwood, I entered the level prairie, which extended to the hills 400 to 500 paces away. It was covered with thick, fresh grass and clusters of other plants. In the small ravines of the hills or where there was more moist soil, [there] were copses of *Celtis, Ulmus,* and the like with roses and other understory, not yet in bloom. I found turtledoves in pairs, redheaded woodpeckers on individual old trees, the towhee bunting, [and] *Fringilla erythrophthalma* in the prairie thickets, as well as *Fringilla melodia* and several others with which I had not yet become acquainted. In the hills I saw dens, probably of badgers, and smaller holes, which a species of striped ground squirrel, likely a suslik *(Spermophilus),* was said to make. Our men crossed the prairie in all directions; shots rang out everywhere and bullets whistled through the air. Many were looking for the [wild turnip], which grew abundantly here. I returned to the ship before sundown; the evening was very pleasant.

18 May: After we had eaten breakfast, we had the pleasure of seeing [our] first buffalo on the hills. There were three of them—bull, cow, and calf—and we observed them with the telescope. The boat was sent out with Mr. Sanford and a few hunters to stalk and hunt the big animals. The young Englishman, Ashworth, accompanied them. They rowed down the river and landed in a ravine a few miles from the bison; we observed their movements from the ship. [After] we lost sight of [them], I went hunting in the willow thickets, [and] in the afternoon I went onto the prairie, shot [a] *Sylvia aestiva,* [and saw many] beautiful plants. I saw [a] *Coluber flaviventris* but could not catch it; it crawled into a stump hole. When I came back, the hunters were returning. They had shot a large antelope and numerous prairie dogs *(Arctomys ludoviciana),* [but their] heads were missing. The antelope had been cut up on the spot. The mosquitoes on the prairie and in the thickets were so unbearable that one could hardly load a gun; this vexation is said to be very bad in midsummer.

19 May: We [still] could not move from this spot and waited for a boat to [offload and] lighten the steamboat. I spent several hours among the tall, shady trees that edged the prairie. Sitting in the cool shade, I was able, despite the heat, to quietly observe the world of nature surrounding me. I saw urubus soaring above the prairie hills and struggling against the strong wind; a pair of falcons pursued and attacked them several times. Several [small birds] flew about in the vicinity. At three o'clock, [in] a powerful thunderstorm, the wind drove the dust into the air and shook the whole ship. It is a peculiarity of these regions that rain and thunderstorms usually develop during spring;

summer and fall are usually very dry—water shortages are common when one moves away from the larger rivers. The thunderstorm passed quickly, the evening was windy and cool.

20 May: This morning the *Assiniboine* came to the spot near the bluffs where we recently lay aground. After eight o'clock we could see its boat taking soundings, and since the water had risen somewhat, ours was launched for the same purpose. We had hoped we [might] leave this place today. Nothing came of this hope.

I undertook [another] long walk into the prairie hills. In the afternoon the woodcutters went out. Toward evening they brought back numerous live bats, *Vespertilio ursinus,* and several snakes, [including] a nice *Heterodon.* Mr. Bodmer went out later but found nothing new or particularly interesting.

21 May: In the morning, widespread heavy rain. At 7:30, 56°F, so cool that we had fire in our stoves. At 8:30 the [rain slackened but] later began again.

Captain Pratte of the *Assiniboine* came over, and a boat came down the river with a [man named] May, who had departed from the Yellowstone River in March. He reduced the number of whites killed there from seven to three; they had been killed by the Arikaras, or Rees, and not by the Blackfoot. On the other hand, the Blackfoot had killed thirteen white men in the Fur Company's service. Thus in one year sixteen men had been killed by Indians. About the death of the three men killed by the Arikaras: [these] men, [including Hugh] Glass, were dispatched from Fort Cass on the Yellowstone [downriver] to Fort Union. In the forest at the Missouri, they met a war party of eighty Arikaras, and all three of them were killed. At the same time another party of eighteen whites with a sizeable number of horses had moved to the sources of the Powder River and were camping there. The same Arikaras spied them out. The whites had shot buffalo cows and made several fires in the fort that [they] had built from felled trees for the horses. During the night they heard wolves howling, but they quickly realized that Indians were imitating these howls and were therefore on their guard. Suddenly all the Arikaras stepped into the fort, pretended to be friendly, [and] seated themselves at the fires. At first they were taken for Crows but were soon recognized as [Arikaras]. A Hidatsa woman who was with the whites hid herself. Suddenly, [the Arikaras] ran out, scattered the horses, and stole most of them. Three of the enemies [were] seized, thrown down, and bound. One of them had a knife, freed himself, and escaped. The two others asked the Hidatsa woman, who had come out of hiding, whether they would be harmed; she answered that they most certainly had to die, [because] the whites had seen the rifle of old Glass and the knife of another of the three slain [whites]. The captives stated their names, declared that they were brave men, chanted their death songs, and were killed.

During our [five-day] stay here I observed [thirty-five bird species, seven mammal species, and seven reptile species].

Toward noon it was still raining; we could not leave the ship. The keelboat of the *Assiniboine* removed part of our cargo.

22 May: In the morning, clear, pleasant weather, warm sunshine. Major Bean had ordered riding horses, which had [just] arrived from his agency; he [planned] to go there by land, and Bodmer [would] accompany him. During the night the river had risen greatly; at 8:30 we were [sent] ashore [with] a large part of the crew in order to lighten the ship. The ship was successfully moved over the sandbars, [and] the bell called us back. [We] had to clamber several miles in deep mud along the bank [and] wade through willow and cottonwood swamps to follow the ship, where we arrived several hours later, bathed in sweat.

[That afternoon we came to a region of] strikingly formed hills, called Bijou Hills, because a certain Bijou, now an old man and Fur Company clerk, spent several winters here.[12] He lives [today] in the vicinity of the Mandans. We were soon hard aground; the boat took soundings; finally we inched forward a little along large sandbars, [but] several hours later, [we] had not moved even a mile farther.

23 May: During the night, [a] storm had blown down one of our smokestacks, the repair of which now detained us. The *Assiniboine* had moved forward this morning and lay at the foot of [the] Bijou Hills. During the night the *Yellow Stone* [could not] be brought to a safe bank; it lay near a sandbar in the middle of the river. We had long been in the territory of the Dacota nation but had the misfortune of finding few bison and hence few Sioux either.

In the meantime we discussed this interesting people at length. Two [stories] were related to me regarding the chiefs' power and love of justice, as well as their high regard for courage and determination. During the hunting season, the Sioux and Ojibwes met from time to time at [a particular] place on [the Minnesota] River, and although they are enemies and kill each other wherever they meet, there [is] a convention according to which they [can] smoke their pipes together in peace. This was the case [in the incident now related], and the Ojibwes had left the Sioux and returned to their camps. When everything was quiet, a young Sioux who could not suppress his natural hatred stealthily made his way to the Ojibwe [lodges], shot and killed [a man], scalped him, and came dancing home with the scalp. Next day, when the chief of the Sioux learned this, he summoned ten or fifteen young warriors and ordered one of them to shoot the wrongdoer, even though he was from [their] own nation. This was done; the young man was killed at the fire in his own [lodge] by two bullets. On the following day the chief invited the Ojibwes and told them that although [the two tribes] were always at war with each other, they must not believe that the Sioux did not know how to uphold their treaties [or] that their word was not sacred, and [he] handed over the body of the Sioux, which they took and were completely satisfied.

A similar story reveals the Indians' esteem for acts of bravery and determination as well as the good result of resolute behavior on the part of whites. Fort Snelling, where Colonel [Josiah] Snelling and a few companies of the regular army were stationed, is located on the [Minnesota] River. A small [acreage] had been purchased for this fort from the Sioux nation. Here, in the vicinity of the fort, the hostile nations of the Sioux and Ojibwes, as mentioned above, sometimes met in peace and smoked and ate together. One evening, four Ojibwes were shot by a like number of Sioux. Colonel Snelling correctly judged this violation of the neutral area. He invited the Sioux chiefs to visit him, had them taken prisoner, and demanded that they surrender the four murderers; [they] were surrendered, and the chiefs were set free. [Next] Snelling invited the Ojibwes, handed the murderers over to them, [and] demanded that they shoot them [immediately]. The large crowd of Sioux and Ojibwes who were present waited in tense expectation; finally a young [Ojibwe] stepped forward and shot the four Sioux. The dead were handed over to their enemies. The Sioux were angry with Snelling, but things remained calm; the Indians [had to] respect [his] strong show of resolve.

The *Assiniboine*, secured to the bank opposite us, was much better situated today than we were; its crew and passengers could go ashore when they wanted to, whereas we sat stranded in the middle of the river, captives who could not leave the ship. At 11:30 we finally departed [and] passed the sandbar with difficulty. Behind us the Bijou Hills gradually disappeared. Mr. Bean's groom, Seroux, was put ashore to fetch his riding horses. He looked like a wild man, with his bare neck, an old hat, and a rough coat. He was tanned and had a long beard, Indian shoes and leather leggins, a leather belt, a broad knife, and over his shoulders a powder horn and a shot bag. This is how most of the engagés looked; they often wore coats made from woolen blankets.

We had scarcely gone a few miles before we were again aground. [There were] such large sandbars extending into the river that our hopes [of an easy passage] vanished. The boats were sent out (the *Assiniboine* was close behind us) but returned with unfavorable [water depth] reports. Therefore, both steamboats were anchored near [an] island, and we immediately visited the dense forest (about which, more tomorrow). When I returned to [the] ship, someone had found a live prairie dog *(Arctomys ludoviciana)* several miles from here. This little animal was very pretty; [it] usually sat like a squirrel on all fours with its head [held] rather high and was not at all timid.

24 May: We waited for keelboats [to arrive and unload us]. Major Bean and Mr. Bodmer [left] to ride overland to the agency. I went into the forest, which began with an extraordinary thicket of willows entangled with vines. We cut a path for ourselves with machetes. In this thicket [we found several species of trees and shrubs]; several crows; *Turdus rufus, felivox, aurocapilla; Columba carolinensis; Picus erythrocephalus; Sylvia striata, aestiva; Muscicapa ruticilla; Vireo olivaceus; Vireo solitarius; Troglodytes aedon; Parus atricapillus;* and several others that I [did] not recognize. A beautiful duck was shot near the bank but immediately plucked, since these pitiful people have no other idols but their stomachs and their moneybags. Every day I found confirmation of the sad observation that they do not do the slightest thing for the sake of science. When I returned to the ship, I found the crew on the sandbar beside it; some were bowling, others had set up a target at which they were shooting, etc.

At eleven o'clock the men were called back by the bell, and an attempt was made to get away. We sailed several thousand paces down the river and then tried to cut across to the left riverbank but reached our goal only after many jolts. After several hours, we met the keelboat ahead of us, brought [it] alongside the steamboat, and loaded [it] with cargo from our ship. While this was being done, Mr. McKenzie and I climbed the highest of the nearby hills. We soon reached grassy elevations and finally the rough, bare domes. On these barren hills [there was,] in large quantities, the cactus cited by Nuttall under the name *Opuntia*, sometimes 1½ feet high, with arms about 5 inches long and white spines often 2 inches long. Its flower is said to be yellow or whitish. The domes were also very interesting from a mineralogical standpoint. There was clay in various colors, [somewhat] similar to kaolin, [and] a kind of isinglass or mica, which seemed to be an outcrop of the clay. The only birds I saw were Say's *Fringilla grammaca,* which seemed to live contentedly on these strange, barren elevations.

Sometime after four o'clock, the keelboat was sent ahead, and [the *Yellow Stone*] followed along the bluffs of the right bank. A half hour later we passed the cargo, covered with white cloth, that the *Assiniboine* had brought to land. Farther on, we found so much water that we did not have to put in until after nightfall.

25 May: We set out early; at five o'clock the mouth of the White River [was] to the left. We stopped [later, for an hour and a half,] to cut wood and make soundings of a shallow stretch of the river. We detoured around extensive sandbars, were aground for a long time, [but finally] came afloat and caught up with our keelboat, *Maria,* which was secured [to our ship]. Twenty minutes [later, we came to] Big Cedar Island [on] our left, at least a half hour in length.[13] [That afternoon,] on an elevated green ridge, we caught sight of several Sioux graves. Most consisted of a scaffold of four long poles, on top of which the dead person lay [on a platform], tightly wrapped [in hides]. [Or] the dead person was buried in the ground, [the burial surrounded by a brushwood] enclosure as protection against wolves. [A little later, on a] promontory to the left, we caught sight of the Sioux Agency, [or Fort Lookout,] and about forty to fifty persons, white and red, assembled there. Several welcoming cannon shots fired by the *Yellow Stone* were answered by the raising of the flag on the flagstaff. We then sailed about a mile farther to a forest, where we took on wood and halted for the night. In order to get to know these interesting Sioux, I returned while it was still dusk to the agency, where Major Bean received me in a very friendly manner. The fort contained several rooms, where we slept very comfortably on buffalo hides and woolen blankets.

26 May: The Sioux Agency (or, as one also says here, the fort) was a square area about 50 to 60 paces on all sides, [enclosed by a] 20- to 30-foot-high wall of posts and planks. Inside were three log houses of several rooms.

About ten Sioux tipis were pitched around this white settlement; their pointed conical shapes presented a singular view. The Dacota Indians we saw here usually lived in the vicinity of whites, since they were poor—none owned more than two horses. The foremost Dacota at the agency, their chief, was the one the whites called Big Soldier—in the Dacota language, Wahktågeli (Valiant Warrior).[M4] He was a big, elderly man about sixty years old, between [5 feet] 10 and 11 inches (Prussian measure) tall, with large, lively eyes, and a sharply aquiline nose.

There were several other interesting [Dacota] men here. For the most part, they had somewhat elongated faces; long, narrow, dark brown eyes; and rather long, gently arched noses. [Some] wore their hair long, braided behind. The older men wore it naturally, usually cut at the neck or somewhat longer, and brushed back from the forehead. The young men went about naked, [each] wrapped only in a large buffalo hide, white and painted on the outside. All of them wore long strings of blue and white wampum in their ears [and] one to three feathers on their heads.

Mr. Bodmer had begun sketching Big Soldier yesterday. [The chief] appeared in full regalia, his face painted completely red with cinnabar, with short black, parallel transverse lines on his cheeks. [Atop] his head he wore [several] long feathers from birds of prey, fastened with a red ribbon. In his ears, long strings of light-blue beads; around his neck, hanging on his chest, a medal he had received from the United States president, with his picture [on one side] and two hands joined together on the reverse. His leather leggins [were] painted with dark transverse lines and crosses and adorned on the outer seam with a [strip] embroidered [in] porcupine quills with yellow, red, and sky-blue figures; his moccasins were attractively decorated in the same manner. He wore a large buffalo hide, tanned white on the outside and wrapped around his body; in his hand [was a pipe-]tomahawk, which he smoked. Thus he stood and sat all day long, [posing for] Mr. Bodmer; [see pl. 8]. The other Indians were not wearing their best clothes but went about quite simply wrapped in buffalo hides.

The Indian tipis were high cones of poles covered with hides, scraped [to] a wholly transparent parchment that let daylight in superbly. On top, where the poles met, the [tipi was] open to let out smoke; they could maintain only a small fire inside. We visited Big Soldier in his lodge. The entrance was a narrow, low opening before which a hide hung on a frame so that the

---

[M4] Wahktågeli was the foremost Dacota (Yankton) Indian at the Sioux Agency. [Although Maximilian identifies this man as a Yankton, his name is given here in the Teton, or Lakota, dialect (in modern retranscription, *Waktégli* 'Returns from War Victorious').]

[entry] could be closed. Inside, the tipi was about 10 paces in diameter; we sat on buffalo hides. The lady of the house was present; their children were married. As a gift I received what the French call a *chichikué*, an instrument rattled while dancing, [made] of narrow pieces of horn fastened by straps to a leather sheath; when a stick is placed in the sheath and moved, the [horn] pieces rattle against each other. These small pieces of horn are cut from antelope hooves and are very decorative.[14]

When making calls on Indians, it is customary to step in quietly, whereupon one is invited to sit down. The host immediately circulates the pipe, which is smoked with solemnity, the smoke ceremoniously exhaled. One is [generally] offered food; our host apologized [for its absence]; he probably did not have much.

Some Dacotas were rich and owned as many as twenty horses. These useful animals were now common among the Indians of the West and Northwest; they bred [and also] stole them wherever they could. [Horses were] probably first obtained from the Spaniards in New Mexico and along the Mississippi. Dogs, which they ate and used as pack animals, were important, too.

A powerful nation, the Sioux even now can still muster fifteen thousand warriors. They live [and hunt in a vast territory extending] east [and west] of the Missouri, from the mouth of the Big Sioux River [to the] Heart River below the Mandan villages. They are a nomadic nation of hunters who follow buffalo herds; along the Missouri one could see four to eight hundred [or] more tipis scattered over the prairie when [bison] happened to be there. [Some] Dacotas also cultivate plants, but as I have already stated, not along the Missouri. The Indians who lived [near the Sioux Agency] belonged to the tribe of the Yanktons; the Tetons lived farther up the Missouri.[M5]

[A] characteristic feature of the Dacotas was the way they treated their dead. It was their custom to place those who died at home on tall, [pole-supported] scaffolds. [The deceased] were wrapped in full regalia in colorfully painted hides with their weapons and equipment [and left] until everything decayed, whereupon the remains [were buried]. Those who died violently,

---

[M5] The Dacotas consist of many tribes. Only the Yanktons, Tetons, and occasionally the Yanktonans [Yanktonais] live along the Missouri. Along the [Minnesota] River and the Mississippi, [the following]: 1. Mende-Wakan-Toann; 2. Wahk-Pe-Kuteh; 3. Wahk-Pe-Toann; 4. Sisi-Toann. The above-mentioned tribes in turn have various bands and villages, which are called by various names.

facing the enemy, were buried on the spot. [Sometimes] they placed their dead on the thick forked branches of trees. There was one [such burial] near the agency. Under the tree there was a small bower, or screen, made of cottonwood branches, which the relatives built [for mourning; they] wept and spent several days at the site. As signs of their grief, they cut their hair, smeared themselves with clay, [and] gave away their [own] good clothing and belongings as well as those of the dead; [these] were distributed to all [persons] present. A young woman wrapped in hides and placed on a support of about six pieces of wood between the branches of a tree had been there for about eight to fourteen days; somewhat higher up on the same tree there was also a child.

We viewed the noteworthy features of the [agency] in the company of Cephir, a friendly interpreter of French descent, who explained everything to us. I had so many interesting things to see that 26 May passed very quickly. In the afternoon, Messrs. McKenzie, Sanford, and Captain Bennett visited us, and toward evening I returned to the *Yellow Stone* with them.

27 May: The *Assiniboine* had arrived at the agency last night and [was] anchored near the *Yellow Stone*. Our woodcutters worked all morning and returned shortly before noon. Mr. Bodmer brought me Big Soldier's leather [clothing] as a gift from Major Bean: an interesting souvenir. Big Soldier visited us once more before our [afternoon] departure; today he had no feathers on his head, just a red ribbon. After he had eaten, he had to leave since the boat was beginning to move; we saw his singular figure on shore for a long time.

[We had not traveled far before we saw] the *Assiniboine* [ahead of us,] hard aground; because the water was [so] shallow, we stayed here today. The men fished and caught several olive-brownish catfish. We went hunting in the nearby forest. The evening was very cool.

28 May: It was 15 miles from our night quarters [up] to the Big Bend; [we] moved on [after eight o'clock]. We passed the *Assiniboine* [and] at one o'clock halted at a prairie to cut wood. From there we sailed straight across the river to an island [and presently] saw an unusual hill chain [ahead]; before the prairie lying between us [and the hills], the river turned right and made the large curve called Big Bend. If one [were to walk] directly across the hill chain, one would come to the river again after 1½ miles, whereas the steamboat [must travel] 25 river miles. According to Lewis and Clark, it is 1,200 miles from the mouth of the Missouri to Big Bend. As we followed the curve of the river, a vast, attractive wilderness view opened up: a level,

green prairie, the hill chain, now green, now dark gray, now violet, illuminated by individual bright flashes of sunlight. We continued to sail until dusk and put in at an island on the right bank.

29 May: Pleasant weather. At seven o'clock we halted about 1 mile from the end of the Big Bend and cut wood. We climbed very high hills here, some of them bare on top, black, and burned; from them one could survey almost the entire Big Bend. The view was very interesting—vast prairies bounded by hill chains. After three-quarters of an hour, we moved on [and] passed the end of Big Bend. In the ravines to the left, the cedars increased [till] they covered the slopes and even several hilltops. [Some time later,] Medicine Creek emptied to the left from wooded banks. Three antelope came out of a ravine and fled across the hills. [Later], heavy, persistent rain darkened the region. After twelve o'clock we saw four men land in a boat on a sandbar. Two of them were brought [to the *Yellow Stone*]. One was Mr. [Daniel] Lamont, a partner in the Fur Company, who had just come from the [Bad River]; the other was Major [David] Mitchell, who had charge of Fort Piegan, or McKenzie, near the falls of the Missouri. The travelers [intended to go later] to St. Louis [but for now] stayed on the steamboat [with us]. We passed Cedar Island; from there it was 30 miles by land to the [Bad] River; by boat approximately 35.

At dusk, we put in at the right bank and spent the night. Wolves howled in the wilderness.

30 May: Early in the morning, dreary rainy weather, cool, windy. Several hundred horses belonging to Fort Pierre grazed in this region, [looked after by] three white men and several Indians; they had put up a leather tipi close to the bank. We obtained fresh meat from them; they had shot three antelope.

The keelboat was untied from our steamboat [so that] we would sail faster. Between eleven and twelve o'clock, we halted at the right bank and cut wood. A plant with somewhat pulpy leaves, called lamb's quarters, grew everywhere; we ate [this] every day, cooked as a vegetable. After lunch we moved on. About one and one-half to two hours [later], cultivated fields to the right in the forest and piled-up wood, much of which we loaded. On the left bank, extremely striking, blackish hills [and] strange vegetation with all kinds of foliage colors: green, bluish, yellowish. At 5:30, after running aground several times, we reached the mouth of the [Bad] River; it rises in the Black Hills, has a long course with many bends, [and then] flows in a straight direction for 150 miles to its outlet. Before us, on the left bank, [was]

Fort Pierre, where Mr. [William] Laidlaw, a partner in the Fur Company, resided. The fort peered out from the trees on the bank and was impressive. A small Sioux village of thirteen tipis was located near it to the left, a singular sight. Our small cannon were fired, and the fort responded with a powerful running volley. The vast, beautifully green prairie was bounded in the distance by hill chains; closer to us, horses and cattle were grazing; still closer to shore stood several Dacota graves. Ten minutes later we [reached] the Fort Pierre landing, on the fifty-first day after our departure from St. Louis. The entire population—several hundred persons, including many Indians—stood on shore; the greeting began. Some of the Indians had their guns in hand; they had joined in the firing. We saw Mr. Laidlaw and also Mr. Fontenelle, who had ridden here comfortably in eleven days from Bellevue by land. After the steamboat landed, we proceeded with a large escort to the fort. We entered Mr. Laidlaw's house, where we relaxed before a good open fire, and then climbed the small tower of the only blockhouse finished [to date]; from [this], or from its gallery, there was a beautiful view over the vast prairies. We spent several hours at Mr. Laidlaw's [and] saw interesting Indian pipes and implements. We returned with a large escort to the ship. The evening was magnificent, and the full moon shone clearly over the broad prairie.

IX

Journey from Fort Pierre on the Teton [Bad] River to Fort Union on the Yellowstone River

[FROM 31 MAY TO 24 JUNE 1833]

31 May: The fort [had an] outer plank enclosure built entirely of wood, which had to be brought downriver from 40 to 60 miles [north of here], since little timber grew nearby. The buildings inside were arranged in a square. In the western corner there was a blockhouse [that] commanded two sides, with two tiers of firing slits. (A similar structure was being built on the diagonally opposite corner.) The lower-level [embrasures were] for cannon, the [upper] for musket fire. On the roof, next to the flag, there was a gallery from which one could survey the whole region. Mr. Laidlaw's house had [only] one story but was very well built, paneled inside, and quite comfortable.

We [next] visited the Indian tipis; dog harnesses and weapons, including shields and spears, hung on poles in front of them. Large numbers of big dogs, most with their tails chopped off, lay around the tipis. They did not bark but bared their teeth as we came closer.

The prairie did not have many flowers now; *Tradescantia virginica* was blooming, as was a yellow-flowered plant of the Tetradynamia. Wide swaths of silver-gray *Artemisia* were also not yet blooming. In the nearby, partially cut forest and in the thickets along the bank, *Fringilla erythrophthalma, graminea; Sylvia aestiva, trichas; Fringilla grammacea, melodia;* and *Falco gutturalis.* The thickets consisted primarily of roses (not yet blooming); willow; cottonwood; ash; elms; *Asclepias; Amorpha; Cornus sericea; Rhus; Vitis;* and others. In the afternoon, I went out and saw [several more species of plants and animals]. On the plains stood a withered tree with a bundle of twigs; at the foot [was] a pile of bison skulls; and all around there was a circle of holes where poles had apparently stood, the whole thing evidently a medicine arrangement of the Indians.[1]

We spent the rest of the day on ship, where there were many Dacotas, mostly slender, rather tall young persons. Many had long wampum strings in their ears, and sometimes very nice necklaces. From one of them I bought a pair of moccasins decorated with the figure of a grizzly bear track.

1 June: Today we packed natural history and other specimens to send back [to Europe via St. Louis]. A large number of Sioux came to the ship. Their faces were painted red; several had a white circle on their cheeks with a black spot inside; [others], a black spot on their foreheads. Teeth white as ivory; I saw no bad teeth among them. Cheekbones mostly quite prominent. Their ears [were ornamented] with long strings of blue and white glass beads. Many, especially the women, wore pretty, wide neckbands densely adorned with white [or] blue beads—they seem to like these two colors [best]. The woman whom Mr. Bodmer was drawing, a Teton—her name was Chan-Chä-Uiá-Te-Üinn—[M1] had a very nicely painted hide [robe].

Major Mitchell presented me with a [handsome] Blackfoot saddle, consisting of two parallel bolsters or rolls of leather, bent upward in front and back, and decorated with colorful rosettes. Such saddles were commonly used here. All the Indians living on the prairie had large numbers of horses. The local [Fort Pierre] Indians belonged to the Yankton, Sisseton, Teton, and Yanktonai tribes.[2]

2 June: The Indians visited us early. Later we went to several of their tipis. I bought various articles from them, including bows, arrows, quivers, a saddlebag of painted parchment, a pipe, a hoop game with four sticks, and the beautiful [robe] worn by the woman Mr. Bodmer had painted. In the tipi that we entered first, we passed our pipe around to smoke. Several tall, impressive men made their appearance. The head of the house was a handsome, rather lightly colored man with a friendly expression. His wife was attractively dressed in ornamented leather, and her summer hide [robe] was handsomely painted. She wanted too much for these things. We got one shield and a pipe, for which we traded glass beads and several other items. All the tipis had iron kettles [for cooking]. At one tipi we saw tanned skins being [further] scraped and also pulled to and fro over a stretched line to make them [even] more pliable. Some of the old women were exceptionally ugly and dirty. In general, the women had to do all the work, and the men led a very easy and comfortable life once they had provided food. They sat around all day, smoked their pipes, or walked about leisurely.

Today bales of bison hides [were] loaded onto the *Yellow Stone* all day

---

[M1] In German: "Woman of the Crow Nation." [In modern orthography, *Khağí Wíi̧ya thawí* (lit., 'His wife Crow Woman'). See Bodmer's portrait of her in pl. 9.]

long, probably 7,000 hides; [this] ship [would head] downstream tomorrow.

3 June: Early in the morning, very cool and windy; heavy rain. The *Assiniboine* tried to cross over early this morning, but the attempt did not succeed and it returned to its previous position on the bank opposite Fort Pierre. We suffered boredom all day, because our things had already been transferred to the *Assiniboine.* At five o'clock, six Dacota Indians came riding up; [their] band, two hundred tipis in all, was camping in the prairie one day's journey from here. They told us that there were large bison herds two days' [distant]. They call the bison tatánka. Some of these Indians were elderly. One saw from their more muscular and well-fed appearance that they suffered less hunger than the Dacotas at the fort. They paid a visit to the ship first, then to Mr. Laidlaw's, where we saw them again. They smoked and ate supper there and thoroughly enjoyed the food. We also ate supper at Mr. Laidlaw's: fresh buffalo meat, potatoes, and coffee. Later, after the *Yellow Stone,* with Mr. Lamont and several company employees [aboard], had taken leave of us [with] a few parting cannon shots, we crossed to the *Assiniboine* in a boat. Messrs. McKenzie, Sanford, and Mitchell stayed at Fort Pierre [that] night; they seemed unable to part from their Indian beauties as yet.

4 June: In the morning I undertook an excursion into the countryside [and collected plant and bird specimens]. I returned to the ship at 11:30, very warm (it was 72°F). Messrs. Sanford and Mitchell had lunch with us. In the afternoon Mr. McKenzie, the interpreter Dorion, and six or seven Dacota Indians [arrived]. After viewing the steamboat with amazement, [the Dacotas] smoked their pipe [and] then were given something to eat, just zwieback and bacon; as a rule they did not like bacon, but to [avoid] giving offense, they bolted it. A remarkable man among them, a Teton of the Brulé tribe—his name was Wáh-Menítu (Spirit, or God, in the Water)—ate [voraciously]; his jaws worked unceasingly. His face, with a strikingly prominent upper lip and gently bent nose, was painted red. His hair hung about his head in disarray, and on top [he wore a raptor] feather in a horizontal position. His leggins were beautifully embroidered with quills and covered with long fringes and braids of human hair;[3] I bought them from him.

Like all North American Indians, the Dacotas have an especially high regard for bravery. [To symbolize] outstanding deeds they wear braids of human hair, first on [their] leggins, then on one arm, [then] on both. This also [applies to] the feathers on their heads. [A warrior] who touches a slain enemy under hostile fire sticks a feather horizontally into his hair;

Wáh-Menítu was entitled to wear three feathers. This [touching] is an outstanding deed, for often nine or ten bold men are killed before one [man] touches the dead body. Whoever kills an enemy with his fist sticks a feather into his hair in an upright position; if he kills him with a gun, he sticks a small piece of wood symbolizing the ramrod into his hair. For truly outstanding bravery, they receive the big warbonnet with buffalo horns, which, at most, two men in a village [may] wear. Its value is as high as that of a horse, and it greatly distinguishes [a] warrior, especially on horseback. If the bearer of this distinction does not behave well, even [just] once, he forfeits the honor of the adornment. This feather [headdress] is really very beautiful; the Arikaras, Mandans, Hidatsas, Crows, and all the other northwestern nations have them, too. The one I saw at Fort Pierre had been given to Mr. Laidlaw by Mató-Tópe, [Four Bears], a Mandan chief who later will often be mentioned.

Dacotas are wealthy when they have good horses and can kill many buffalo. They [might] have as many as thirty to forty horses [and] fine lodges. These usually consist of fourteen hides, each valued at two dollars. The Cheyennes often have as many as sixty horses. Men who are able to support them sometimes have [up to] eight or nine wives. They do not cure diseases very well but [can generally] heal wounds. Often they are very successful at healing those who have been shot through the body or whose knees have been shattered by shot; I saw a hand that had been terribly injured and very beautifully healed. On their deathbeds they usually determine how they are to be buried, whether placed on a scaffold or underground. This I learned from the interpreter Dorion, who grew up among the Dacotas, has always lived among them, and has had several Dacota wives simultaneously. He provided the following names for the five Teton tribes: [Brules; Oglalas; Saones; Blackfeet Sioux; and Hunkpapas].[4]

Wáh-Menítu spent the night with us; he sang and conversed; unfortunately, we no longer had an interpreter. Messrs. McKenzie and Sanford returned to the fort. Beautiful sunset, evening cool.

5 June: Our departure [on the *Assiniboine*] was delayed until ten o'clock. Mr. McKenzie had stayed on land and rode after us. Three cannon shots were fired, the flag was hoisted, and we cast off. At twelve o'clock we had too little water; soundings were made. Mr. McKenzie, with two horsemen, came riding over the hills and dismounted at a ravine down near the water. He was brought over; Mr. Laidlaw was with him [but] left after lunch.

In the afternoon we made very little progress, because the water level was too shallow. In the evening we put in near dense willows and spent the night there.

6 June: Yesterday iron and other merchandise were taken ashore and piled up to our left. This morning loaded keelboats [took even more] cargo from the steamboat. It was very pleasant on the *Assiniboine,* [which] had bright, airy rooms. Its aft cabin had eight beds; the large one, twenty-four. The crew's quarters were on deck. We had about sixty persons on board. The *capitaine* was a reputable man whose name [was] Pratte; his father was a co-owner in the Fur Company, which consists of Messrs. [John Jacob] Astor in New York, Chouteau, Cabanné, McKenzie, and Pratte. Messrs. McKenzie, Lamont, and Laidlaw are partners in the fur trade along the upper Missouri. Our quarters on the *Assiniboine* had a dangerous foundation: there were about two hundred barrels of gunpowder in the ship's hold.

An attempt was made to navigate over to the left bank during the afternoon, but there was not enough water. If the river did not rise, we would stay here a long time. After lunch we left our position, went several miles downriver, [and] navigated around sandbars—all in vain. We often ran aground, sometimes listed to one side for a while, and after several hours returned almost to [our] previous spot. At six o'clock Mr. Bodmer and Dreidoppel returned [from their hunting excursions]. Dreidoppel had shot a splendid *Falco gutturalis* near its nest and obtained its three eggs, which were already well incubated. He also saw the striated finch *(Fringilla graminea);* the black-tailed flycatcher *(Muscicapa melanura);* the alpine lark *(Alauda alpestris);* and the large gray shrike *(Lanius septentrionalis).* They [also had] many interesting plants. Evening on the river was very pleasant. Singing rang out, as well as the violin of our Negroes.

7 June: Mr. Bodmer and Major Mitchell [went] to visit the prairie dog village and shoot some of [them]. I had so many birds to describe that I could not possibly get away. Today one of our young bears, still very small, was put on a tree on shore; seeing how rapidly and agilely it climbed, like a monkey, was interesting. Mr. Bodmer returned early; his companions had gone not to the prairie dogs but to the Indian women of the fort; all these gentlemen have women or girls here whom they "marry"—that is, visit them once a year or every two or three years and then leave them unhappily in the lurch, whereby they turn to prostitution, which is of no great significance here. [They often have] children of these women.

Water [of sufficient depth for travel] had been found, and we cast off after twelve o'clock, succeeded in squeezing through [a] channel between extensive sandbars, moved into deep water, sailed to our [offloaded goods, and retrieved them]. I went with Mr. Bodmer onto the prairie hills [and spent the afternoon exploring the hills and gullies, observing plants and animals]. Nothing of importance presented itself to our double-barreled guns; we turned back.

8 June: We continued our journey early in the morning. The region appeared far more barren and naked here than farther downstream; it was much grayer, [with] little verdure.

About eight o'clock we put in at the left bank and cut wood. [We botanized and] tracked antelope. [The voyage resumed, and around one o'clock we saw] an abandoned log house in which people stayed when cutting wood (lumber [for] building was brought from here down to Fort Pierre). [We were] 15 miles [below] the Cheyenne River. The water began to diminish. The boat went far ahead to take soundings, and we lay idle for a long time. Scraping bottom, the ship was pushed over the shallow spots with the help of the engine and long poles. After six or 6:30 in the evening, we reached deep water near the left bank and sailed along a dense willow and cottonwood forest. When we [tried] to cross the river, however, we struck large sandbars. [We] could go no farther and hence moved back to the just-mentioned forest and spent the night.

9 June: After breakfast we saw the green region of the Cheyenne River before us. The Arikaras once lived at the mouth of the Cheyenne and farther upstream on both sides of the Missouri but were driven away by their enemies, the Dacotas. They now lived somewhat farther upstream. The hills to the right were greener now. Sandbars left us only a narrow channel along the right bank. Here we saw the first magpie *(Corvus pica);* [it] flew out of the cedars. We ran aground [twice before two o'clock] and lacked wood besides; we sent the boat to land to fetch some.

After a good half hour, we saw the boat returning. The men told us they had seen ten Indians, probably a war party, and they did not want to cut wood there. [We] armed ourselves. Twenty-six men in two boats—twelve of them with guns and rifles, the others with axes—shoved off for land. The Indians, probably Arikaras, had taken flight, and the woodcutting proceeded smoothly. [When] one of the boats returned, loaded with wood, it brought back a hunter and an interpreter who had killed an antelope

(*Antilope furcifer*), which was [taken] on board, unfortunately without the hide. It was female, and I obtained the fine head, which demonstrated that females here also have horns, even though I had been told the contrary; the horns, however, [were] short.

10 June: In the morning, [we made] a halt about seven o'clock to take on split wood; about 7:30 we continued on. Far ahead of us we saw Pascal Island.

[A] boat tore loose; we put in at a ravine and sent another boat after it. The men who went ashore with their axes looking for wood saw elk, [so] several hunters left immediately with rifles and muskets. As it turned out, the supposed elk were actually antelope. A good hour later, when the wood-cutters had felled many cedars and two antelope had been brought in, we continued on. It was twelve o'clock. We sailed for a long time along [Pascal Island] (it had large sandbars at the upper end) [and came to] a second island as it began to rain. To the right the hills were flat and unimpressive; to the left, gray bluffs of clay, sand, or argillite. In the gorges, all the trees were dry, gray skeletons: rugged, desolate, barren nature! After [a while], sand hills appeared to the left; [on] the right, Little Cheyenne Creek [emerged] from thickets. The [Missouri] now had a lengthy, beautiful stretch straight ahead. [The] bluffs on the left bank were colored blackish violet by rain. After about an hour, sandbars. The sun set. We halted for the night; the mosquitoes [were] very tormenting.

11 June: In the morning, a raw north wind and heavy downpour. The whole region turned dark and gloomy. A herd of about thirty elk fled over the hills; one saw much more wildlife than previously. Farther away we saw the [effect] of ice-drift on the [trees] along the bank: the bark, especially [on] the thick cottonwoods, was torn off 8 to 10 feet above the water.

At 7:30, 60°F. To the right and left, bluffs and green wooded banks alternated. [Everything was] fresh and invigorated from the rain. The water was shallow; we often ran aground; soundings were constantly taken. The interpreter [David?] Lachapelle gave me words of the Arikara language. At twelve o'clock, we halted for several hours. [A] fine, big male antelope was brought in, and I took its measurements. [Eventually] the steamboat hastened on.

In the dense forest on the left bank, one saw many cottonwoods gnawed by beavers. Somewhat farther on, a beaver lodge on the bank [looked] like a heap of large twigs. These animals seemed rather numerous here, undoubtedly because the trappers did not like to operate in the territory of the hostile Arikaras. Our hunters went out, and the interpreter Ortubise shot two large elk with first-year antlers as large as a European male deer with twelve points. The hunters stayed out until after nightfall; finally they returned with four elk (that is, the venison, [plus] several heads and a whole calf, which were to be incorporated into our collection). Today we thus had six elk and an antelope.

12 June: In the morning, bright sunshine [and a] strong, cool wind. We were now approaching the Grand River (the Wetarkoo [of Lewis and Clark]). Cannons and muskets were loaded, because we were [near] the principal residence of the Arikaras. At noon we made fast at the thickets and cut wood. One and one-half hours later, after lunch, we moved farther along the left bank. To the left the forest soon came to an end. Several miles from the wooded area, on steep banks about 30 to 40 feet high, one could see two Arikara villages of about three hundred earth lodges, abandoned less than a year ago. Both villages lay in the green prairie like ash-gray heaps of huts. The Arikaras left these villages because the corn harvest failed and there were no buffalo in the vicinity. Since the inhabitants left, other Indians, especially the Dacotas, have demolished some of the lodges, yet many provisions are said to be still hidden *en cache* there. Such provisions can remain unspoiled for several years. The names the builders gave these villages are Hóhka-Wirátt or Achtárahä for the southern and Nahokáhta for the northern village.

The Sáhnisch, as they call themselves—or Arikaras, as the Mandans call them, or (as misinterpreted by the whites) the Rikaras or Rees (Les Ris of the French)—are a tribe of the Pawnees, from whom they separated a long time ago.[M2] They now number about 4,000 persons, [including] 500 warriors. Some of them have four or more wives. Brackenridge, who visited them [in 1811], provides exact information.

In outward appearance they do not differ much from the Dacotas. They [are] often tall and well built. The men frequently have coarse features, but the women are reputed to be the most beautiful along the entire Missouri and are often rather light in color. [On the prairies] they are very dangerous to white people, and everyone was very cautious of them. But they are

---

[M2] In their language, sanihsch means "men." Sáhnisch, on the other hand (with the last syllable short), is the name these Indians give themselves. [The modern orthography is *Sáhniš* 'men, Arikaras'.]

said to be hospitable in their homes. The interpreter Lachapelle spent seven years among them.

They plant corn and hunt as well, but because they had no harvest last year, they moved away. They have horses and dogs but rarely eat the latter, since [these] are not big. They hunt buffalo, elk, and antelope. They collect wild fruits and roots, including sweet *poires* and cherries, which they dry, as well as the *pomme blanche,* etc. They plant beans, squash, and watermelons. They wear the same leather clothing as the other Indian tribes [although] the men often go about naked and are said to wear no covering for certain parts of the body.

Most of their customs [are] identical to the Pawnees. They are enemies of the Dacotas, who are very dangerous because [they] are far superior in number. The Arikaras [once] lived on the other side of the Missouri; the Dacotas, however, have driven them to the opposite side, where they now roam the prairies.

Between three and four o'clock, we again put in to cut firewood. We remained for nearly an hour, and Ortubise knocked a very fine large bat (probably Harlan's *Taphozous rufus*) out of the air with his hand. Toward evening the wind subsided; it became very pleasant. And, as the sun neared the horizon, [a] magnificent landscape! A series of steep bluffs on the right bank was colored purple. Right and left, green thickets along the bank, [and] before us, in the beautiful evening illumination, attractively varied hill shapes, including several distant conical domes. The river was rising, carrying tree trunks, branches, and the like downstream.

13 June: During the night the river rose 3½ inches. At seven o'clock we put in at the right bank and cut wood; here another kind of *pomme blanche,* with a beetlike root that fattens the grizzly bears, grew copiously. When humans eat too much of it, it causes stomachache. The much greener prairie and the beautiful domes peeking over it gave the region here a more interesting appearance than yesterday. Bleached buffalo bones remained as remnants of Indian meals. After lunch someone suddenly called out that there were Indians in the vicinity. In the prairie, we saw a man who fired three times with his gun. [We] thought he was a hostile Arikara, but soon a canoe appeared with still another man. [These] company men had come from the falls of the Missouri with letters for Mr. McKenzie. They were taken on board, and they left their small [bullboat] lying on the bank.[5]

We halted after two o'clock near a beautiful cottonwood forest to cut wood. Mr. Bodmer and Dreidoppel went out, found numerous bison and elk trails, and saw blackbirds, the yellow woodpecker *(Picus auratus)*, and the catbird *(Turdus felivox)*. We continued and to the right saw long prairie hills, steeply slanted in front like fortress ramparts and marked with perpendicular furrows; before them, extensive lowlands again with cottonwood and willow, where there were many elk. A dead bison floated past the ship. Prairie hills covered with a soft green carpet [and] dense woodlands alternated on both sides of the river. To the left in the distance, a hill chain with many high domes in the vicinity of the Cannonball River. At six o'clock a dark thunderstorm arose in the northwest; after seven it was black and threatening. A very heavy rain poured down as night approached.

14 June: Early in the morning, slightly overcast sky; powerful, raw wind. At six o'clock we saw a large, white-yellowish wolf on the hills along the bank, trotting beside us about 80 paces away; it was so lacking in shyness that it did not even look at the roaring steamboat. [After] eight o'clock, several rather isolated short, tablelike hills to the left [and] close to the Cannonball River [mouth. Arikara] territory was believed to extend to about this [area]. The Mandans seldom came down so far, [except perhaps] their war parties. At ten o'clock we were not farther than 60 paces from [the Cannonball] mouth. Along its banks lay round, yellow sandstone balls [or concretions] that had rolled down; the river got its [English] name from them. Along the Missouri, rust-yellow sandstone bluffs followed, and in them were actually round, reddish yellow stone spheres, perfectly regularly formed, of various sizes, some with a diameter of several feet, but mostly smaller. They protruded halfway out of [strata in the] steep walls; others had fallen down or had washed out and lay along the bank. Many were broken in half; most were intact. A half hour beyond the mouth of the river I no longer noticed any spheres.

About 12:30 we put in at the right bank near a narrow border of prairie forest and cut wood. *Tradescantia virginica,* with its red flowers, grew abundantly here, [as did] a beautiful, tall plant we had not seen [before], with leaves as thick as a cabbage's [and] beautiful big lilac flowers. *Caprimulgus americanus* (nighthawk) flew about, probably roused by the woodcutters, and there were numerous redheaded woodpeckers. A very black mass of clouds rose on the southwest horizon; it soon thundered and rained. One of our boilers needed repair, [meaning] we would probably have to remain here a long time, [so] about three o'clock we went out onto the prairie. In the grass and in various bushes at the prairie [edge], we found the beautiful ricebird *(Icterus agripennis)*. The male has handsome black and white and melon-yellow plumage; the female [is] very plain—lark-gray, yellowish underneath. In the thickets I found the catbird, the kingbird, *Muscicapa crinita,* the large yellow-breasted lark whose song is heard everywhere, and several additional small birds. There were no larger animals in the vicinity. We stayed [at this anchorage all day] and night. The water level of the Missouri rose more and more; with poles, the men [constantly] fended off large trees that the river washed down; we nevertheless received such jolts that the entire ship trembled.

15 June: In the morning, fair weather. The river turned in a westerly direction toward a beautiful hill range, rather tablelike on top [with] numerous vertical clefts and ridges. After nine o'clock we put in at the green wooded bank to the left to make a few necessary repairs on the ship. Our hunters took advantage of the stop to go out a few miles. I went into willow lowlands, which soon turned into a [dense] thicket so full of withered trunks and branches that we exposed our clothing to great danger, [and] *Xanthium strumarium* burrs continually clung to [us]. We tracked elk *(Cervus canadensis)* everywhere, particularly cows with calves; the former often make deeper tracks than cattle and have a much longer stride than our European stag. Mr. Bodmer and Ortubise had gone with the hunters, intending to return to the ship farther upstream.

About eleven o'clock we moved on. The right bank became more bare; there were prairie hills, low and without any distinctive features; the river, however, soon turned left toward a beautiful hill chain before which [a] Mandan village was [once] located. The river had risen so much that the willows on the right bank were standing under water. This was caused by melting snow in the Rocky Mountains; one [can] always count on two high-water stages of the Missouri in the month of June. The current was very powerful; we could push forward only slowly. At 12:30 we approached the hill range [and] were now in the true territory of the Mandans. The river raged at a sandy point on a bend of the river, caving in the banks and [toppling] willows. We navigated along the right bank; [eventually, in the] lowlands to the left, we saw four of our hunters sitting.

Ortubise had killed a two-year-old buck *(Cervus virginianus)* and wounded a bull elk. Somewhat farther [on], Mr. Bodmer and [Alexander]

Harvey joined us; the latter had killed a black-tailed deer buck (*Cervus macrotis*). Mr. Bodmer had caught two fine specimens of *Coluber proximus*, including a very nice, orangey-red speckled variety, which I described in [my] zoological notebook and [preserved] in whiskey.

After four o'clock we put in at the right bank at a narrow strip of woods not far [below] Apple Creek and loaded wood. Half an hour later we continued on. Shortly before dusk a dead bison floated past, and we saw a big beaver running along the shore; [it] plunged into the water after someone shot at it and missed. We halted off the left bank a short distance [below] the Heart River. During the night, thunderstorm.

16 June: In the morning we [passed] the mouth of the Heart River, [but] before six o'clock the wind and the strong current drove the ship sideways against the bank and forced us to remain there. It was still 50 more miles to the Mandans, about as far as from the Cannonball River to here. The motion of the ship moored at the bank was so strong that it created an unpleasant sensation. I used the time to have the interpreter [Jacob] Berger tell me words of the Blackfoot language. All our hunters went out despite the bad weather. Dreidoppel found three elk and shot the cow, [which we went to fetch; it] was as big as one of our red stags. As we were returning, we saw [that] the river [was] as rough as the ocean. Toward evening the wind subsided somewhat, and we therefore sailed upstream at 6:30. At nightfall we made fast at the right bank.

17 June: At 5:30 the area was flat and devoid of attractive features; half an hour farther on, we saw Square Hill (la Butte Carrée) and several unique sections in the hill chain.[6] Two magnificent, gigantic bison bulls to the right in the prairie; their beards hung far down, and the wind ruffled their manes. [Bison] are rather easily startled into flight.

At eight o'clock, the Missouri was at least half a mile wide, [but] it soon narrowed. Very fresh grass on the prairie to the right, [with] traces of prairie fire. White buffalo skulls and bones glistened everywhere. A Mandan village once stood on the promontory to the right. The Dacotas (from the [Minnesota] River) totally destroyed [this settlement] about forty years ago and killed most of the people.[7] Farther away to the left, beautiful prairie with short bushes, good places for buffalo. [Here,] about a year ago, Lachapelle and several other white men came upon a war party of Mandans and Hidatsas who fired on their mackinaw boat, since it would not land. Such war parties are never to be trusted. Even if they do not kill, they plunder. The even worse Arikaras always kill whites.

[We] halted to the right near the forest along the shore at ten o'clock. Elk antlers of ten and fourteen points were found. Wide, heavily trodden bison paths crisscrossed the forest in all directions; hair hung on the bushes. Dreidoppel pursued a new bird *(Icteria viridis)* with a beautiful bright yellow throat and breast. The mosquitoes were more troublesome. After about an hour we continued. The river turned [left]; we sailed toward the Butte Carrée, a strange hill chain, smooth on top, with clefts and domes and hills like fortresses, everywhere uniformly covered with short grass.

At noon, 70°F. Very warm air, portending thunderstorms. We had a beautiful view back toward the Butte Carrée hills. Time lost because of sandbars and shallow spots. Half an hour later, many beaver slides and gnawed-off trees in the beautiful forest along the bank. An Indian hunting hut. [Later,] in the twilight, we heard several shots [from] the right bank and saw flashes in the dense willow thickets. We were concerned that this might be a Mandan war party and deliberated about what [to] do. War parties are always dangerous. We [drew] closer, saw figures standing on shore in the willows, [and] waited with tense anticipation; [then] they shouted to us, saying that they had peaceful intentions and wished to come on board. Ortubise spoke with them and told them we would land somewhat farther upstream. When we put in, the Indians were [there, and] within ten minutes twenty-three sat in a row on one side of the cabin. Mr. McKenzie and the rest of us gathered and sat down beside them.

They were mostly strong, slender, good-looking men with long, wildly disheveled hair. Some had buffalo-hide robes, others [had] blankets; most were dressed simply, because they were on a hunting expedition. Their party had [come] from three hundred [Yanktonai tipis] in the vicinity; [they] had shot buffalo nearby. During the winter they often came to the Missouri. They were once on good terms with the Mandans, but for about a year [there had been] a rift [between] them, because the Mandans had shot [and killed] a Dacota. Now they wanted to make peace and had sent three of their men to the Mandans with proposals to this effect.

The principal chief among them, dressed in a red uniform with blue shoulder straps and white braiding, his hair bound into a big knot on his forehead (which the Dacotas often do), was Dead Buffalo (Tatánka-Ktấ), [a man with] a characteristically dark brown Indian face. The principal chief

Fig. 3. Maximilian. Dead Buffalo, Dacota chief. Ink. The bound knot of hair above the forehead was a frequent Plains male hairstyle; in some groups, it designated the wearer as a medicine man or sacred pipe keeper.

of the three hundred tipis had stayed home; his name is Jäwitscháhka.[8] After we had been sitting for a long time, the chief stood up, shook hands with each of us in turn, and then, in [a speech of] short, broken-off sentences and many gestures (during which he often paused to deliberate with thoughtful expression), stated [that] they were here by chance, and when they saw their father coming up the river, they [decided] to greet him. They wished to make peace with the Mandans so that they could better trap beaver along the river. They hoped that Mr. McKenzie would take them along to the Mandan villages tomorrow and assist them in their plans.

Mr. McKenzie responded [by saying that] if they would behave well [and] never kill white men, he would be happy to do what he could. He asked them to consider whether it would be better for them to go to the villages on foot or by ship. He was willing to take them along, but he did not know how they would be received by the young [Mandan] men. After they had spoken for a long time, they showed [us] a large, beautiful, tanned whitish bison hide (a great rarity), which they wished to present as a gift to the Mandans, who prize white buffalo hides highly. They had [already] sent a white bison calf there.

The Indians were taken later to another room, where they received something to eat, and they slept on board. The next day, however, they went ashore and followed the ship on foot. There were several big handsome men among them. One [was] dressed in a very old-fashioned uniform, blue with red lapels and collar [and] white braiding and borders. [Such uniforms looked] comical on their bare bodies.

18 June: In the morning, gloomy sky, damp, light wind. In the distance we saw the Dacotas following us over the hills on the right bank. It was about 12 miles [to] the Mandan villages [from the place] we had the meeting with the [Dacotas]. As we came closer, [we had an] attractive view of the reddish village [and] the fort, [silhouetted] against dark blue-green hills. The American flag waved on top of the fort. Cannon and gunfire. We landed at a rather high bank on top of which Fort Clark was located.

[It was] built in a square, in the same manner as Fort Pierre, but scarcely half as large.

At least two to three hundred Indians [were] on the bank, including characteristically tall, handsome men. Their leather robes [were] mostly reddish brown on the flesh side, whitish in a few cases; they also had many woolen blankets. Assembled here were Mandans, Hidatsas (Gros Ventres), and [many] Crows. The latter had only recently arrived from their distant habitations, because their subagent, Mr. Sanford, had informed them of his forthcoming arrival.

In dress, these three nations differed little. They wore their hair long, in some cases hanging down over the hips, cut bluntly on and beside the forehead, above the eyes and on the cheeks, but divided in back into many flat, broad queues, which were kneaded with white or reddish brown clay; this hair was usually lengthened with cutoff human hair. Others bound their hair together in a thick knot. In their ears they wore strings of glass beads and, frequently, above each corner of the forehead, a similar long, ribbonlike pendant fastened to their hair, which [sometimes] hung all the way down to the chest. Necklaces made from grizzly bear claws were not uncommon. They valued these highly and [only] gave them up for a gun or a horse at the very least. Their bodies were mostly naked, painted dark reddish brown; the faces, vermilion. [They had] iron bracelets and rings, also many of brass. Their leggins and leather jackets were ornamented in the Dacota manner,[9] and their buffalo hides, on the reddish brown or white flesh side, [were painted] with [either] colorful figures of men and animals or merely with arabesques.

Many of them were mounted: the saddle like the Hungarian seat, the bridle colorfully decorated with cloth. The stirrups [were] like Turkish ones, covered with leather. Their bows [were] like those already described, but I saw a very big one [with] a lance on top, the whole weapon decorated with feathers and colorful cloth. Most carried battle-axes, beautifully and colorfully decorated on the handles.

Soon, several chiefs and distinguished men came on board, [including] Chárätä-Numakschi, Mató-Tópe, Dipäuch, and Beróck-Itaïnú, from Mih-Tutta-Hangkusch, and the Hidatsa Péhriska-Ruhpa. Mató-Tópe, in German Vier Bären [Four Bears], was especially neatly dressed. They sat around in the small cabin, and the old interpreter of the Hidatsas, [Toussaint] Charbonneau, told them about the Dacotas we had seen yesterday, who wished to make peace. The chiefs discussed the matter pro and contra for a long time; they agreed that [although] they did not want to [harm these men], an agreement was out of the question, because Dacotas were very unreliable people.

All the Indians in our cabin were robust men. They carried war clubs or tomahawks in their hands, [and] a few even had guns; an Indian never goes anywhere without his weapons. In their hands most of them carried eagle fans. On their heads they wore such a mass of long hair [that it] must [have been] very troublesome during the summer (and heavily populated besides). It appeared [to have] never been thoroughly combed. Over [their robes], some carried bows and arrows in quivers; others, powder horns and bags (if they had guns). On horseback they always had whips in hand, because they did not wear spurs. They often rode small, poor horses but often, too, very handsome, impressive ones of all colors. It was a noteworthy sight to see these chiefs speak with gesticulations [that is, signs,] unique to the Indians and understood everywhere by all nations.

Behind the fort were seventy tipis of the Crows, or Corbeaux, whom I visited in the afternoon. The tipis were entirely like [those] of the Dacotas, but one could see small pennants of colored material on top of every single tipi pole. I did not see any scalps here. A striking sight in this camp were the packs of large wolflike dogs of all colors, certainly three to four hundred. They attacked me, barking and howling, and I could scarcely reach the tipis.

From there I went to the [nearest] Mandan village, which was built northward along the river on the high bank, 300 paces away. [Within its surrounding outside fortifications or] palisades there were large earth lodges standing about in no definite order. This village [had] about sixty-five lodges. The second Mandan village was located three miles away; [it had] about thirty-eight lodges. These are all the Mandan villages. The Hidatsa villages were located several miles from here. Most of their inhabitants were at the fort today. Outwardly they did not differ from the Mandans, but their languages were different.

We had a most interesting view of the flat prairie around the fort and the village. Large numbers of horses grazed everywhere. Indians of all ages and both sexes, on horseback and on foot, moved back and forth; the black-haired figures in colorful dress and red-painted faces were most singular. We also saw tall poles erected near the villages, on top of which various objects such as cloth, hides, and the like were suspended: medicines, as the

Americans call them, superstitious protective or sacrificial devices.^{M3}

Returning to the ship, I found a horde of Indians on board. All our acquaintances were there; they smoked, talked, and lay sleeping, wrapped in their blankets, around the fireplace. A crowd had converged near the village; one of the Indians from the peace-seeking Dacota band had been brought over from the other side in a [bullboat]; he was half Mandan. In the evening the Crow agent, Mr. Sanford, had a discussion with the chief of that nation, Eripuáss (Rotten Belly), an important man with a good-natured physiognomy, very intelligent and with great respect in his nation. He had cut off his hair, wrapped [himself] in a miserable old woolen blanket, and smeared his face, since he was in mourning. Mr. Sanford counseled the continued good treatment of whites, hung a medal around his neck, [and] gave him a fine present of cloth, powder, and tobacco on behalf of the government. [Eripuáss] accepted it all without the slightest sign of gratitude (these people regard [such gifts both as a] weakness on the part of the white man and as tribute due them). After dark, we visited him in his tipi with old Charbonneau. The whole camp was filled with horses standing around in the open, some of them with foals. Inside the lodge a small fire was burning in the middle. The chief sat opposite the small door. All around [were] as many men as could find room, [arranged] according to their rank; all [were] naked, only scantily covered by breechcloths. After we had seated ourselves on buffalo hides, the chief lit a long Dacota pipe of red stone [inlaid] with pewter [designs]; [he] let each of us take a few puffs while he held the pipe. Then he passed it around, and it circulated until it was finished. With the help of [Charbonneau], who spoke only the Hidatsa language, we talked with this chief and then returned to the ship.

Today the gentlemen of our group experienced the readiness with which Mandans and Hidatsas offer their wives and daughters; several of us were approached twenty times; men even came and offered [their] wives. No

---

^{M3} We did not yet understand the purpose of all these arrangements; they [are] explained later in a special chapter dealing exclusively with this nation. [Chapter 18 contains the prince's ethnographic essay on the Mandans. The term "medicine" appears frequently in Maximilian's writings about Indians and in accounts by many other European and American authors, often with the dismissive phrasing used here by the prince. Lakota scholar Vine Deloria, Jr., has defined the word as "power," a complex spiritual concept he explores at length in *The World We Used to Live In*, xxiii, 1–214.]

other Indian nation is believed to [outdo those] mentioned here in this respect; exactly the opposite is true of the Dacotas.

The Mandans can put 250 to 300 warriors in the field. They call their nation Númangkake, that is, "people, human beings."[10] The names of their two villages are Mih-Tutta-Hangkusch for the first one and Ruhptare for the second, smaller village. As mentioned, they live in comfortable, secure earth lodges, which are permanent. Most spoke the language of the Hidatsas, although the latter did not speak that of the Mandans. They were enemies of the Dacotas and the Arikaras.

The Hidatsas call their nation Biddahátsi-Awatíss.[11] They lived several miles from the Mandans in three villages. The first is now called Eláh-Sá; the second Awatichai; the third Awacháhwi. They got the name "Minatarris" from the Mandans. They are even more handsomely built than the Mandans, particularly the women, among whom we saw many very pretty ones; their eyes gleamed, snow-white and black, from vermilion faces. Their dress was especially beautiful, richly embroidered with vividly colored beads and feather quills. [The Hidatsas, who] numbered about 350 warriors, lived along the Knife River. They were friends of their close neighbors, the Mandans, [and] enemies of the Arikaras and Dacotas.

The Crows lived along the Yellowstone River, their northern boundary, up to the Rocky Mountains. They [had] about 1,200 [warriors] and 6,000 people in all. They roamed, hunted buffalo and all kinds of game, lived in leather tipis, [and] had many dogs (which they did not eat) and very many horses (9,000 to 10,000), more than the Missouri Indians. They made very fine garments from bighorn hides. [They fought] the Cheyennes, Blackfoot, and Dacotas. They were friends of the Mandans and Hidatsas, whom they seldom saw, however. They traded horses with the latter for European goods. They were well-built men, with slightly aquiline noses, like most Indians. Their language is related to that of the Hidatsas. The Crows despise the white man more than all other Indians, yet in their tipis, they are very hospitable to them. Their trading post [was] Fort Cass on the Yellowstone River. Everything they [produced] was attractive and well made—their weapons as well as their costumes. From the horns of elk and bighorns, they made bows that one did not see [in] any other tribe. They covered [these] with snakeskins, just as I saw among the Piegans.[12]

19 June: Departure at daybreak. The chiefs and several Indians came on board very early. There was a Blackfoot among them, [Kiäsax], whom we [were]

to take with us to the Yellowstone; other Indians wanted to travel with us [only] just beyond the Hidatsa villages. Also on board were Mr. Kipp and Charbonneau, the interpreter. At ten o'clock we reached the second Mandan village, Ruhptare, on an elevated plateau. The dark brown, black-haired inhabitants had all assembled on the bank and on top of their [lodges]. The entire prairie was full of people and horses; in the short willows on the bank, a crowd of naked brown children. Most of the men carried [bird] wing [fans] in their hands and were wrapped in their buffalo robes. The entire village population accompanied us on foot and horseback along the high bank and on the shore below it. A vast, flat region and broad, beautiful river before us; in the distance one [could] see the lowest Hidatsa village, a reddish mass of huts along the left bank, [at the Knife River mouth]. We reached it after a half an hour: Awacháhwi, le Village des Souliers. It was small; we counted about eighteen lodges. The two other villages of this nation lay somewhat farther inland along Knife River. The interpreter Charbonneau, who accompanied Lewis and Clark on their journey to the Columbia, lived in the second, Awatichai, or Little Village. The third, largest, village, somewhat farther upstream, was called Eláh-Sá (Village of the Big Willows).

For us foreigners this trip was most interesting, whereas our Indians calmly continued to smoke their pipes by the fire. Among them was Dipäuch, a tall, strong man with hair tied together in a thick queue hanging halfway down his back. Another huge Mandan, nearly 6 feet tall, had bound his hair together in a huge bundle on his head; he was the inseparable comrade of [Dipäuch], and his name was Beróck-Itaïnú (Bull's Neck). Several of the [men] had their fingers continually in their great supply of hair and usually put their catch between their teeth. Our food greatly pleased them; they liked to drink coffee, and sugar was a dainty morsel for them.

At twelve o'clock, along the left bank, we saw a large number of Hidatsas. They were on foot and on horseback and wanted to see the steamboat. The sight of this reddish brown throng was arresting: more than one hundred of them, all ages and sexes, [including] the most handsome, powerful men we had seen, in the most attractive, highly imaginative, and characteristic [attire]! Their faces painted red, long braids hanging down their backs. Feathers on their heads and, hanging down [beside] each eye, long strings of azure and white beads. Their upper bodies were mostly naked, beautiful brown arms adorned with broad, shiny metal bracelets. With guns, bows, or battle-axes in hand, gracefully decorated quivers on their backs, leggins beautifully embroidered with quills and glass beads in vermilion, azure, or yellow, these energetic, laughing men gave free rein to their feelings. They had beautifully bedecked and ornamented themselves in their finest, and they had not failed to achieve their ultimate purpose: we could not stop admiring them. It is well known along the Missouri that the Hidatsas [and] the Crows create the most beautiful objects of this kind, and [along] with the Mandans, they are probably the strongest, most handsome Indians I saw here. The Dacotas were, to be sure, also tall, but more slender.

It is impossible to describe the variety of people, costumes, and facial expressions we saw here. Among the mounted Indians were men who drove their horses down to the water with whips, [even as their steeds] shied at the frightening hissing of the steamboat. One saw magnificent horsemen with savage vermilion faces, guns, bows, quivers, and all manner of [people wearing] the most beautiful garments. A painter would have found the richest opportunity for his art. Unfortunately, there was no time for drawing [then, though] later that winter we did find some opportunity for this.

The chiefs made a brief visit to the ship [but] had been on board for scarcely a quarter of an hour when Mr. Kipp, Charbonneau, and the Hidatsas left the *Assiniboine*. As we departed, [the throng] gazed with astonishment at the roaring *Assiniboine,* and [the] whole population followed us along the bank [for a time]. They called farewell to [two Blackfoot] friends on our ship [and] waved to them. [Kiäsax] played on his pipe, a long, hollow stick, widened somewhat at the bottom. For ornamentation, a single eagle feather hung on a string at the end of the instrument, [which] was about 2½ to 3 feet long; [Kiäsax] did not let go of it all day long.

[A long passage through strange hills, meadowlands, and broad sandbars.] The evening was very cool and windy, as was the night. [See p. 17.] 20 June: In general this region was rather flat, the hills low; to the right, everything covered with yellow grass. At ten o'clock we tied up at the left bank near a sparse, tall forest to cut wood. Bodmer and three other men went hunting, intending to return to the ship farther upstream. Extremely strange hills behind the forest, flattened off on top and [called] l'Ours qui danse; people say the Indians held a medicine festival here, the bear dance, to ensure good hunting.[13]

After one o'clock we reached a bend of the river to the left. [The Missouri] was broad and magnificent, [with] green borders of forest on [its] banks. Our hunters [appeared]; they had killed two Virginia deer, an antelope, and a prairie hen. Bodmer returned flushed; he had to run a great distance to reach the steamboat. His catch was an Indian stone [tool] he had found in the prairie; [it] had the shape of a battle-axe, rounded off and used by the Indians to crack open heavy buffalo bones.

About one and a half hours later, we [came to some] extremely odd elevations—cones and pyramids [on both sides], like haystacks, one in front of the other. Toward dusk, after being driven by the current against the bank several times, we put in at the right. Fresh, deeply trodden buffalo trails were everywhere in the nearby prairie, [where] we went for an evening walk; the grass [was] wet from dew.

21 June: Early in the morning, fabulous clay hills to the left, domes and peaks of all kinds. *Artemisia* in abundance. The river had risen enormously [and was] covered [with drifting] trunks, wood, chips, [and] branches. The hills had a sad appearance, yellow and nearly devoid of vegetation. Before us, a rather flat, green, spot where the Little Missouri emptied, 1,670 miles from the mouth of the Missouri. We arrived [at] the Little Missouri [around 7:30]; about an hour later, we were in Assiniboine Indian territory.

After twelve o'clock we halted at a prairie on the right bank about 3 [river] miles below Goose Egg Lake. Last year, the steamboat met a large number of Assiniboines here. [Numerous elk, deer, and geese sighted.] A beautiful evening and sunset.

22 June: The keelboat stayed behind; we were making better progress now, [although] wood washed down by the river [gave us] powerful jolts. Several tablelike hills. [Many game sightings.] The region to the left, flat; to the right, dry, rough hills. Fire on deck; fortunately it was extinguished. Drifting trees shattered the right wheel; we anchored at ten o'clock [and] three hunters went out.

Strong west wind. [So] much wood in the water [that] it [was] very difficult to navigate around [a big bend], and we were delayed for two and a half hours. [At first] every effort to overcome [our] obstacles was in vain; the current drove us against the left bank three times, the first time so violently that the gallery at the lower end of the steamboat broke apart. The second [attempt] was no better: [part] of the left wheel housing shattered, fell into the river, and drifted away. We were compelled to have forty men leap ashore [and] pull the ship with towlines. Trees [blocked our] way, and the boat brushed so forcefully against the bank that the lower deck [was] full of earth. After great exertion—while [some] people pushed us away from the bank and [others] (even Mr. McKenzie, Dreidoppel, Mitchell, and our Blackfoot Indians) pulled on the hawser—we finally surmounted the [problems] and proceeded onward.

The hunters had killed two elk cows; [they] carried the meat and were covered with blood from head to foot. We continued on. Far ahead we saw a big bear on [the] prairie and set Ortubise and a hunter ashore. The grizzly bear occurs from this region on. Along the Missouri [its range] does not extend much farther south; it becomes more and more common to the north. Hunting this bear is very dangerous. We anchored about 6:30 for the night near the forest of the left bank.

23 June: Harvey had set beaver traps last night and caught a young beaver, which he was trying to keep alive; the trap had crushed its forefoot. Both our Blackfoot Indians had become accustomed to us. Mr. Bodmer sketched the taller one, something he was willing to permit right away. His name was Kiäsax (L'Ours Gaucher, Bear on the Left). The smaller one was called Matsókuï (Beautiful Hair).[14] The former had adopted the Gros Ventre custom of parting his hair in back into many long strands smeared with clay, which he usually twisted together with a green ribbon at their midpoint into a thick queue. He wore a Spanish blanket with black, white, and blue stripes and a brass cross around his neck, proof of contact with that nation; [see pl. 17]. His jacket was white bighorn *(Ovis ammon)* leather with very long white fringes on the arms; [the bighorn's] range began about where we were now. [Matsókuï] was also supposed to be drawn, but he [refused]. When the interpreter asked him why, he declared that he did not wish to be sketched, for he then would surely die.

At eleven o'clock we put in at the left bank near a forest [to] cut wood. Assiniboines appeared on the shore. Mr. McKenzie sent the dinghy, [which] soon returned [with] eight of them. The chief, a strong, rather tall man, was well known. His name was Stassangä. He wore his hair bound together in back in a short, thick queue; in front, around his face and above his nose, it was cut off bluntly. In his ears he had two perforations [hung with] blue and white glass bead strings; around his neck, a fur neckband with grizzly bear claws. A red wool shirt covered his upper body. His legs were bare, but he had beautiful leather leggins with him, decorated with colorful glass beads, which he put on later, after his comrades had left. The remaining Indians were neither handsomely built nor well dressed; their disheveled hair hung around their heads like broom twigs twisted out of shape, [although some] wore braids. Several had two parallel, blackish tattooed stripes that extended down the sides of the neck [to] beneath the chest. All had bare trunks and were covered with buffalo hides. Most had guns; all had bows and arrows. They spoke a dialect of the Dacota language; therefore, Ortubise could translate their words. [They] smoked the pipe that was on the ship, [since] they had none with them. They were generously fed, [which] pleased them, for they said that since spring, they had often gone hungry because buffalo were scarce. The chief wished to travel to the fort with us; the other Indians [soon returned to shore].

The river turned [a number of times]: beautiful, wild, scenic valleys and ravines or gorges with rock walls, shrubs, and clusters of trees; the hills [just] naked heaps of earth, as though tossed up by moles. On a high, steep bluff, three bighorn, the first of these animals we saw: a ram and two ewes. At dusk we put in near a beautiful forest.

24 June: At [about 8:00] we saw smoke rising along the border of the prairie to the right and then several Indians as well. One stood on the bank and fired three shots from his gun; nine others came running. Several had reddish leather jackets colorfully [embroidered] with porcupine quills. They all came aboard, wrapped in buffalo hides, [with] bows and arrows in hand, [as well as] three or four guns; [one had wound] his fringed rifle sheath around his head.

At 6:30 we reached the mouth of the [quite broad] Yellowstone River; farther [ahead] we saw Fort Union on the green prairie. The American flag flew brightly in the waning sunlight [and] herds of horses grazed all around the fort. [As] we came closer, the cannon of Fort Union thundered [and] ours answered.

Mr. Hamilton (an Englishman who had lived here several years), some company clerks, and about one hundred engagés from all nations—Americans, Englishmen, Frenchmen, Germans, Russians, Spaniards, and Italians—[were] assembled here. Most were with their Indian or half-breed wives and children. We dropped anchor at Fort Union 75 days after our departure from St. Louis.

X

Stay at Fort Union, Description of the Fort and the Surrounding Area and the Assiniboine Indians

[FROM 24 JUNE TO 5 JULY 1833]

[24 June 1833:] Fort Union was begun in the fall of 1829; it was presently complete except for the improvements of several buildings built in haste. It was located [opposite the mouth of the Yellowstone River] on an elevated sandy bank scarcely more than 50 to 60 paces [from] the Missouri, [which] flowed past from west to east, wide and impressive.

The fort was built in a square, the outer sides of which were 84 of my paces in length. On the southwest and northeast corners there were small blockhouses with pointed roofs. The [surrounding palisade] consisted of sturdy poles, placed close together, 15 to 16 feet high [plus] small [spikes] to prevent climbing over. The main entrance faced the river. The superintendent's house, at the rear of the courtyard, was one story with four glass windows on each side of the door. [It] was quite nicely built of cottonwood lumber; [nothing else] was available here. The other buildings were located all around the courtyard along the [palisade]. In wet weather the yard was muddy because fifty to sixty horses (which could not be left outside because of the Indians) were driven in every night. Mr. McKenzie intended to construct a separate enclosure for the horses so that the courtyard would remain dry and firm.

This place [supported itself and] two [other] trading posts: Fort Cass, 200 miles up the Yellowstone, and Fort McKenzie, 650 miles up the Missouri. During the summer, keelboats—long, sturdy boats with a small cabin in the rear—were sent from Fort Union to these posts, with the goods needed for barter with the Indians; [the keelboats] stayed there and brought the furs downriver in spring. A goodly number of whites lived [at Fort Union], employed in the service of the Fur Company; most had Indian wives.

Food available here included the meat of buffalo, antelope, deer, and bighorn. All other articles came up the river from St. Louis. Garden produce could not thrive here, neither potatoes nor corn, for the region was too dry.

Fig. 4. Karl Bodmer. *Fort Union at the Mouth of the Yellowstone River;* detail. Pencil.
This view of the trading post and surrounding Indian encampments is from the north,
looking south toward the Missouri, which flowed not far below the fort. 10⅞ × 17 in.
1986.49.171.

Several kinds of [wild] edible berries and roots, [like] *poires (Mespilus)* and
cherries *(Prunus padus),* were preserved. Hunters on horseback were sent
out for buffalo meat. [They] shot ten to twelve or more buffalo, loaded the
meat onto packhorses, and brought it to the fort. The river provided good
catfish. There was also milk [from] several well-nourished cows, a bull, pigs,
chickens, a male goat, and a considerable number of horses as well as several mules. Essential craftsmen [included] blacksmiths, joiners, carpenters,
[and] tailors. People mostly used Indian moccasins: twelve pairs cost one
dollar, if the leather was provided. Most people dressed partly in leather;
other articles of clothing were expensive, since the company charged higher
prices for its goods [here] because of the long and difficult transportation.
    A certain number of Assiniboines usually lived near the fort [in] leather

tipis, [but] because of the lack of bison, [they] were now farther away. The Assiniboines are genuine Dacotas, and they call themselves that.[M1] They separated from the Dacotas years ago (after a battle against each other near Devil's Lake) and moved more to the north. The borders that designate their present territory are from the Missouri [north] to the Assiniboine River and westward to the Saskatchewan [River], Lake Winnipeg, and Milk River. They are divided into several bands.

They live comfortably in leather tipis and exclusively from hunting; they never cultivate fields. They derive their primary nourishment from the buffalo, which they follow—in the winter, along the Missouri, [where] these animals seek forest [shelter]; in the summer, on the vast prairies. They have few horses but many dogs, which do major work and greatly lighten the women's chores.

In appearance they differ little from the Dacotas, although those we saw were not so slender or tall. Their faces were broader, with very high cheekbones, and they did not wear their hair as long; it scarcely hung over the shoulders, although some had two or three braids. They painted their faces red or reddish brown and often smeared their hair this color on top and in front.

Most of them carried short guns [that] the company sold them (at a price of 30 dollars). They decorated them with [bits of red cloth] and yellow nails, which they drove into the stock. They carried a ramrod in their hands; a powder horn and hunting bag [hung] around their necks. An ammunition bag [was slung] over the shoulder or tied to the belt: it was quadrangular, made of leather, and decorated with fringes, colorful cloth, and porcupine quills. They all had bows and arrows—[some had only] this weapon. Most also had a head breaker [war club]. Their leather jackets were decorated with big, round rosettes in vivid colors, usually one on the back and one on the chest, [with] braids of human hair on the arms. The edges of the leggins [were also] adorned with braids of hair. In summer [most] went without leggins and barefoot, [with] just a bison hide wrapped around them. Others, more concerned about their outward appearance, wore beautifully ornamented jackets and pants.

M1 They pronounce their name a little differently than the Sioux and call themselves Nakota. [In modern orthography, *Nak,óta* 'Assiniboine; Indian'.] The Crees call the Assiniboines "Assinipoatak," from which "Assiniboine" probably came.

The Assiniboine language is essentially that of the Dacotas, altered here and there by separation and time. Like the Dacotas, they place their dead on scaffolds and trees. Near Fort Union [we] saw several dead bodies on trees, tightly wrapped in hides—an unpleasant way to dispose of bodies!

Upon our arrival we called on Mr. Hamilton, who lived here, and we inspected Fort Union rather thoroughly. We were given quarters in the superintendent's house, and our baggage was brought there.

25 June: During the night they began unloading [and reloading] the steamboat. Eight hundred bales (ten pieces each) of buffalo hides were loaded, but during the afternoon, while this work was going on, a heavy storm broke; many hides got wet [and] had to be taken back [to the fort] and dried. Moisture is very harmful [to] such hides. However, there were no moths at all; hides could be left lying for fifteen years without detriment. Besides bison, many hides of beaver, wolf, etc. were loaded: sixty-two packs of wolf and fox pelts, about one hundred pieces in each. The number of bison in these inland plains is enormous; in one year the Missouri [Fur] Company received 42,000 such hides at its various agencies. The number of buffalo consumed along the Missouri and its vast prairies [each] year is enormous. In some years Fort Union alone consumed perhaps 600–800 head. The Indians' consumption cannot be easily calculated [but is] surely about three times as many as the number of hides sold. [Once,] near Fort des Prairies on the [Saskatchewan?], 1,800 buffalo drowned in that river. Every year huge numbers sink in the mud in all the rivers and perish. The species [is] certainly significantly diminishing, especially since only cows are shot. The Indians mostly [blame] the whites for the decrease.

There was much activity and movement in the fort this day; things were carried back and forth in small wheelbarrows, for which the weather was rather unfavorable. The [Indians] were everywhere, constantly demanding things. They particularly [wanted] Indian tobacco (called kinnikinnick by the whites), made from the finely ground or cut bark of the red willow and about one-third tobacco. [They] were too lazy to make any for themselves. The tobacco that the Fur Company supplies them is strong and rolled into 6- to 8-inch-long black twists. Most of these Indians did not even have pipes. They looked rather wretched and dirty, which is the general reputation of the Assiniboines.

Today we ate in the fort; [the] food, very plain and suitable for the wilderness, [was] a strong contrast with that on the steamboat, where we had good white bread, crackers, various kinds of meat and venison (all fresh), vegetables, beans, potatoes, and preserved fruit. During the afternoon we went for a short walk on the prairie behind the fort. Few plants were blooming. *Cactus opuntia* was very numerous. Buffalo bones lay about everywhere. About 1 mile behind the fort, a low hill chain ran parallel to the Missouri. On the most [noticeable hill], the Assiniboines had erected a kind of medicine device. Large, oblong-shaped rocks stood upright; at their base, other, rounder ones; and on top, a bison skull. They built these pyramids to attract the buffalo; Mr. Bodmer sketched one of them; [see pl. 12].

Early in the morning of the 26th we sent case No. XIX, which was packed yesterday, on board the *Assiniboine* [to be sent eventually to Germany]. Hides were loaded until noon. The morning was beautiful, the day very hot. We had breakfast in the fort; afterward I went out. In a small prairie and in a hollow between the hills, I found pairs of blackbirds *(Quiscalus ferrugineus)* in a small bush and shot several of them. The big lark *(Sturnella)* was everywhere, the kingbird too.

At noon we ate on the ship, which then departed. The entire population of the fort stood along the bank. The cannon were brought out, and shots from both sides echoed in the hills. The *Assiniboine* first moved upstream past the fort, then turned and swiftly pursued its destination downstream. Mr. Sanford and several Fur Company employees left with [her]. The evening [was] very pleasant. We walked along the forest above the fort, found about three species of new plants, and could barely ward off the large swarms of mosquitoes that assailed us on the open prairie. When we returned home, several Assiniboines had come to announce the [imminent] arrival of at least one hundred Indians.

27 June: About nine o'clock, ten men [arrived]. A few had skin caps, one with an entire prairie hen tail in front and several ornamented feathers in back. They were not Assiniboines but Crees, or Kristenaux. They had come from a distance of about four days[' travel]. Their appearance was not significantly different from the Assiniboines. They wore their hair hanging naturally around their heads, often long [and] over the shoulders. In front they had a tuft [of hair] down over the nose and cut bluntly across; on one man this tuft hung all the way down to his mouth. Faces painted red, some with black stripes. Clothing made of leather, ornamented with round rosettes of porcupine quills. The chief, Maskepetoon (Broken Arm), wore a medal. He had been to Washington with Sanford.

The Crees call themselves Nahíâak.[1] They live in the same district as the Assiniboines, bounded by the Missouri and the Saskatchewan [Rivers and] Lake Winnipeg. [Like] the Assiniboines, [they] live in leather tipis, do not have many horses, [and use] dogs for pack animals. They are poor and live very scattered about. They are estimated to be six to seven hundred tipis strong, [perhaps] three men to each tipi, thus about 1,800 to 2,100 men in all. They came here to see Mr. McKenzie, [but] they did not bring hides, because it was not the season for them. They live entirely from hunting and, like nearby nations, follow the bison. They make large parks, where they kill many of these animals at a time.[2]

Because it was very warm today, [several] Indians had wound thick wreaths of green foliage around their heads. They looked overheated and fatigued, and their vermilion-painted faces suffered from the perspiration.

The Cree language is related to that of the Ojibwes [and is] completely different from Assiniboine or Dacota. At Fort Union there was an interpreter, Halcro, for the Assiniboines and another, Lafontaine, for the Crees.

[Despite] the noonday heat, the Indians went about in their large buffalo hides. We traded for various small items of theirs, and from Mr. McKenzie's stock I obtained a fine Crow costume: shirt, leggins, moccasins. A clerk in Mr. McKenzie's service, Mr. [Francis] Chardon, presented me with an Arikara scalp. The man from whom this scalp was taken had murdered an old white man, a certain [Hugh] Glass; the scalp was taken as a souvenir and is now in my possession.

Early in the afternoon, we learned that Assiniboines were approaching, and everybody ran in front of the fort. The sight was arresting. To the northwest the prairie was covered with Indians and dogs pulling baggage [on travois]. At the head, about 250 to 300 armed warriors strode like companies advancing side by side. In [military terms], they moved at a rapid pace in rather close formation. They were not more than three to four men deep and thus formed an imposing front. Three to four chiefs went ahead of the center, somewhat as standard-bearers march in front of a Prussian battalion. Shots rang out everywhere from the multitude. They all sang a peculiar chant [with] abrupt, broken tones, similar to that of the Russians.

This interesting throng pushed nearer and nearer, and the closer they came, the more striking the features that unfolded. All were wrapped in buffalo hides but [also] decked out in manifold ways. Most had red faces; some were completely black. Feathers from birds of prey [were] on their heads; on their feet, fox or wolf tails as marks of honor for slain enemies. [They carried] guns in their arms; on their backs, bows and arrows. Some had large wolfskin caps on their heads, which certainly were not cool in the great heat. They looked martial to the highest degree—their proud, erect bearing [and] rapid stride lent them a manly, military appearance. Wild music resounded from the ranks of these savage, rough warriors; they were beating a kind of drum. They advanced to about 60 paces [from] the fort and halted there. The chiefs stood in front. Both interpreters were sent out to meet them. The gate of the fort was closed, and a guard let in only as many persons as were permitted. [Most of the] Indians went to the river to drink, then stood or sat down in the shade. The chiefs and about thirty of the principal warriors were admitted, and they seated themselves in the big room [reserved] for Indians. They sat down all around the walls, and their big, thick stone pipes with unwieldy bowls were passed around. They had with them a fine pipe stem, ornamented with yellow horsehair tufts and yellow nails, intended as a gift for Mr. McKenzie. The warriors spoke little and enjoyed their pipes, the exquisite vapors of which they inhaled in deep drafts. A pail with diluted whiskey was brought in, from which the interpreter gave each of them a certain amount to drink. Before they drank, most of them sprinkled this whiskey five to six times in the air with the first fingers of the right hand, probably as an offering to the Great Spirit (I was also told that they sprinkle this into the air [for] their deceased kinsmen).

Meanwhile, on the level prairie to the west of the fort, hunting or traveling huts—only some covered with hides, most with green twigs—were [being] set up. Horses were grazing, countless dogs lay or moved about, and the Indians were sitting [or] occupied in various ways. The sight was indescribably colorful and absorbing. The interpreter called a particularly striking Indian to me; his name was Noapeh. On his head he wore an ornament with antelope horns, and a crest of black, clipped feathers.

In the evening we went to the camp again. Their way of packing [and transporting baggage by travois] was very practical. The dogs [each] had a skin pad on their backs on which rested two long poles connected at an acute angle [at the top]; at the lower end they were [widely] separated. [Attached to] the middle of these poles was a [flat,] elliptical, netted hoop, on which hide-wrapped [bundles] were tied.

[Numerous] women and children sat around small fires. [When] one visited them, they asked for whiskey and tobacco. If one wished to exchange something with them, they demanded whiskey. Many had [already] bought some, and a few had drunk too much. As soon as night fell, they sang and shouted loudly; the commotion lasted all night, yet nowhere did unpleasant scenes of any kind take place.

28 June: The Indians besieged the [fort] quite early. They were prepared to sell all their hides and belongings for whiskey, and I purchased many interesting Indian objects. The interpreter sent us the Indian with the horn ornament on his head; we had selected [him] yesterday for drawing. As already mentioned, [his name was] Noapeh (Troop of Soldiers).[3] His face was yellowish, his eyelids painted red. His leather jacket or shirt had large [round] rosettes embroidered with [bright] porcupine quills, 8 or 10 inches [in] diameter, on the chest and back. [He] stood patiently for a long time for the painter. [See pl. 10.]

In the afternoon we visited the Indian camp, where most of the foliage huts were already empty. In the distance one saw Indians moving off in three directions; [one of those groups,] about one hundred in number, [intended to join] a war party against the Mandans and Hidatsas. Several Indians remained here, [though,] and thirty-one new tipis of the Assiniboines were [expected] tonight or tomorrow.

29 June: The ground [was] completely saturated by violent rain during the night. One could scarcely step outside. The [anticipated] new band of Indians would [be delayed] because they could not travel when their leather tipis were too heavy, [having been] drenched by rain. [When] a few Assiniboines [appeared] later, they were [wet through and through], something they were completely accustomed to.

It continued to rain until evening, when the sky cleared up. The yard in the fort was a lake. Several Indians arrived, including some remarkable figures. One wore his hair very long and plain, with a clipped tuft in front [that hung] down to his mouth; the hair on the sides covered [and nearly obscured] his face. He had fastened a small white shell [to his hair] above each eye. In his hand was a bow-lance, as high as a man and draped with long bands of grizzly bear intestines smeared with reddish paint. On his back this slender young man carried a round shield (*parflèche* of the Canadians), which was painted green and red and covered with whitish leather.[4] His name was Pitätapiú, of the tribe of the Gens des Roches (Stone Indians). [He] promised to let himself be sketched the [following day; see pl. 11].

30 June: Early in the morning, rain; fierce, cold wind. The fireplaces were lit

in the rooms. It was horrible to watch the Indians, their legs completely bare, wading around in deep mud in this cold weather. It was unusual to have such weather at this time of year, for this season is typically very dry, [while] spring is wet, fall usually beautiful, winter severe and long lasting. One makes use of dog sleds then, but the snow is often too deep (four, five, six feet) for traveling. The past winter was unusually mild along the upper Missouri; the river was frozen for scarcely three days. In general the climate was exceptionally healthful. There were few diseases, and this [was fortunate], since there were absolutely no doctors here. Various persons whom I asked about this matter remarked, "We don't need doctors, because there is no sickness."

Today Mr. McKenzie gave me information about the fur trade of the American Fur Company. Game and fur-bearing animals have extraordinarily decreased along the Missouri in [just] a few years—in [a decade] this business will be insignificant. [As] the number of animals decreased, the American Fur Company extended its [circle of] activity more and more, and thereby increased its profit. They now employed about four to five hundred persons—primarily engagés, French Canadians, but also individuals from all nations. At each fort and for every Indian nation, they kept interpreters, largely half-breeds, most of whom spoke French. Besides the company's paid employees, there were [many] trappers and hunters in the Rocky Mountains and other interior regions, [all of whom] caught animals on their own initiative. They delivered their beaver, buffalo, and other hides to the company [in return] for being provided with [necessary supplies]. Such persons [were] often highly enterprising [and] carried out their tasks at the risk of their lives. In summer, parties of well-armed men on horseback, sufficiently strong [in numbers] to face hostile Indians, went out with supplies on packhorses to various stations. Such a group, led by Mr. Fontenelle, was mentioned earlier on the [Bad] River. [I] have occasionally referred to forts maintained by the company as permanently established trading posts along the Missouri. It had many other smaller ones, however, [each just] a poor log house manned only in winter, [where] neighboring Indians brought [in] their hides for sale. At present, twenty-three trading posts in all, including the forts, are occupied along the Missouri and in the interior, including the Rocky Mountains, wherever trappers and hunters roam about.

Here is a list of the various species of animals according to the value of their skins, as well as the number of hides obtained in the course of one year.

Beaver: about 25,000 hides. These are separated into packs, each one weighing one hundred pounds; usually 60 large beavers [to] one pack. If they are small, the number increases. A large beaver hide weighs 2 pounds.

Otter: about 2,000–3,000.

Bison hides: about 40,000–50,000. There are about 10 hides in one pack of buffalo robes.

Fishers: about 500–600.

Marten: (stone marten) about as many.

Lynxes (the northern): about 1,000 to 2,000.

Wildcats [bobcats] *(Felix [rufus])*: about as many.

Red foxes: about 2,000 hides.

Cross foxes: about 200–300 hides.

Silver foxes: about 20–30 hides (often bring 60 dollars a hide).

Mink: several thousand.

Muskrats: from 1,000 to 100,000. In 1825 the Indians caught about 130,000 along the Rock River; next year half as many; the third year (1827), about 10,000. In the fourth year, it was not worth the effort to catch them.

Deer *(Cervus virginianus* and *macrotis)*: from 20,000–30,000. From Council Bluff on down, almost nothing else is bartered by the Indians; game is decreasing rapidly there, too.

Elk *(Cervus canadensis)*: Its skin is too thick and heavy, [so] it is more for personal use than for sale and export.

Buffalo hides were taken entirely from cows; [those of] bull[s were] too thick and heavy. Antelope and bighorn played little part in trade; the hides were used for clothing; the meat eaten. Wolf hides were not in demand by the company, [so] no hunters were sent to procure them; on the other hand, those that the Indians brought were accepted to keep them in a good mood and [were] then sold cheaply, about a dollar a pelt. The Indians frequently had nothing to trade except their leather shirts and robes. These, too, were accepted in large numbers in exchange for merchandise, but there was little profit in this.

The members of the Fur Company are Messrs. Astor in New York, Chouteau, Cabanné, Pratte, McKenzie, Laidlaw, and Lamont. Messrs. McKenzie, Lamont, and Laidlaw have a share in the fur trade on the upper Missouri above Council Bluff.

Indians sat in our room [and] smoked all day, while it rained and stormed. About noon the weather cleared up somewhat, [so] after lunch we went out and, near the fort in an easterly direction, found a camp of twenty-five Assiniboine tipis. The women—all small, some not [unattractive], with vermilion-painted faces—were very busy [making camp]. One tipi stood out, probably the chief's. It was painted ochre-yellow [with] a broad, reddish brown [band] at the bottom. On each side a big grizzly bear was painted in black [(see pl. 13)]; on the head above the nose, a small, scarlet scrap of cloth fluttered in the wind, probably a talisman, or medicine, as the English call it, a magical or protective device that people highly prize; they never surrendered such things to us unless [we] made a very generous offer. Young Pitätapiú, who was painted today, said a small package fastened [to] his shield was his medicine. When he went to steal horses, it protected him and brought him luck.

We had not been in the camp very long when, [to] the west, we saw the whole prairie covered with Indians. The men, about sixty in number, advanced in a closed column, without music, both chiefs at their head; [they] came as far as the fort gate. There were many old people among them, including one who moved along rapidly with two canes. The chief of the newly arrived band (named General Jackson [or Ajanjan])[5] was an ornately dressed, handsome, well-built man of dark color. Over his beautifully embroidered black leather shirt, he wore a new red wool blanket. A medal hung on his chest; he had been [to] Washington. The entire column marched into the fort and smoked their pipes, whereupon whiskey was distributed to them.

At seven o'clock we went to view the new camp of forty-two pitched tipis, [which] lay in a crescent; fires gave off smoke; life and activity everywhere. We saw extremely entertaining scenes. Boys shot their arrows high into the air. A small, brown, monkeylike child sat on the ground, and a circle of hungry dogs stood around. A very sick man lay in one of the tipis; medicine men were inside, chanting with all their might. A crowd of people peeked in through small openings, and we did the same. [Then] we went to the other camp and bought an attractively made cradleboard; women carried their children [in these] on their backs. It was very neatly decorated with colored porcupine quills and embellished with long, colorful strings.

1 July: During the night the Assiniboines shot to death the Blackfoot [named Matsókuï, whom] we had brought from the Hidatsa villages. He had been warned and hitherto had [stayed] at home, [but last] evening he went out to look for a squaw. He was barely inside a tipi when a shot was fired; [his companion] looked inside the tipi and saw the poor Piegan on the ground, shot in the chest and dead instantly.

At twelve o'clock an Assiniboine deputation, General Jackson at their head, brought Mr. McKenzie a horse. They carried several splendidly decorated pipes, one of which had a large feather fan and numerous green-dyed horsehair tufts. [This was] a genuine calumet, and they presented it to Mr. McKenzie. They stayed about half an hour, during which time General Jackson is said to have spoken very well.

In the afternoon we went into the Assiniboine camp, where an old man was being treated in a tipi by conjurers, or doctors (medicine men). Several men sat in a circle. The sick man had a small white leather cap on his head, which he lowered toward his chest. Two of the magicians had drums shaped like a flat Swiss cheese, which they struck without interruption in rapid time. A third conjurer held a small stone-filled calabash on a stick; he shook this instrument (*chichikué* in French) continuously in a revolving motion. They perspired profusely, chanted, and occasionally uttered short shouts. They sucked on the patient's sore spot, alleging that they were extracting the evil demon. The patient pays greatly for this cure [with] tobacco and [other] valuable things, which these gentlemen never give back, even if the patient is not healed.

2 July: Bodmer and Dreidoppel rode to the hills to sketch a view of the fort; they took their guns along, and an interpreter accompanied them—because of war parties, the vicinity of the fort is always dangerous. At 11:30 the horsemen returned; [from a hilltop] Mr. Bodmer [had recorded] a spacious view [of] the confluence of the Missouri with the Yellowstone.

In the evening we walked about a mile behind the fort [and found] beautiful plants. Only a few were in bloom: a bright yellow [flower], resembling *Helianthus;* the *Cactus* that is called *opuntia* in North American botanical books but which seems a different species to me; [and] *Cactus mammillaris.* The view from these hills was beautiful in the evening light—the fort, the Assiniboine tipis, the mountain chain, the river, and a rainbow in dark clouds. When we returned home, the keelboat had arrived, so we will probably depart in a few days.

3 July: The chief of the Assiniboines (General Jackson) came early to take leave; most of these people would leave today [to] follow the buffalo. Yesterday Mr. Bodmer sketched the tipi with the bears painted on it. I bartered for several items—feather fans, a decorated buffalo hide, and the like. Mr. Bodmer went out to draw the fort [and] brought back numerous cactus flowers. After more exact observation, it appears that what I hitherto called *Cactus opuntia* is *Cactus ferox,* something that the fruit will [later confirm,] if it has thorns.

This afternoon [Fort Union] hunters left on horseback for a bison hunt. During the last [one], they killed nineteen bison. A large number of persons in the fort must be fed, and because there is nothing here but meat, one can imagine how many bison are consumed. In one year three hundred are sometimes killed here just for food. There were some very good horses here for this kind of hunt, although several were quite skittish. Today I received a Crow Indian bow, covered on its outer surface with rattlesnake skin. These Indians make beautiful, strong bows.

The evening was calm and pleasant. After the gate of the fort had been closed, several young people entertained themselves with a kind of rustic music by torturing the drum and clarinet for a long time. Nowhere in America is music at home; the music is mostly bad, and [from what] I have seen, there is little appreciation for it.

4 July: One year ago today we landed at Boston. I went to the prairie early in the morning, equipped with short notched pegs to mark a cacti of each variety, so that next spring I can take them along to Europe. The red(-flowering) kind was marked with a single-notched, the yellow with a double-notched stake.

Temperature at twelve o'clock, 76°F. It was exceptionally hot in the courtyard of the fort. In the afternoon Berger and Harvey rode off to Fort McKenzie; they expected to cover the distance in nine days. They had nothing with them but their blankets to sleep [in], their weapons, and some dried meat.

Today I took fourteen pounds of tobacco from the local store for bartering with the Indians; for [tobacco] everyone here had to pay one and a half dollars a pound, but Mr. McKenzie gave me that amount for only seventy-five cents. Six gallons of whiskey cost ninety-six dollars; Mr. McKenzie gave them to me for forty-eight. All articles are expensive in the company stores; they sold [goods] to their own people at enormously increased prices. The Indians [bought] whiskey at [a markup of] 3,000 percent.

5 July: Our keelboat was [readied] today so that we could leave tomorrow. This morning the interpreter told me a large number of Assiniboine words and provided me [with] considerable information about this nation. These people, as well as the Crees, believe that thunder is created by a big bird, which some claim to have seen. They attribute lightning to the Great Spirit, and whenever there is intense lightning, they believe he is angry. They say the dead go to Heaven, that in the other world the good and the brave will find a land [with] many women and buffalo; the bad or cowardly, however, go to an island where they [will] go hungry and find no women. They believe in an evil spirit who torments people with various diseases, against which their doctors and magicians employ the drum, the *chichikué,* and other remedies. The Crees are not numerous; Assiniboines are.

Toward noon our keelboat was completely loaded; we worked all afternoon arranging our baggage. Mr. Culbertson, [a company clerk,] received instructions today to accompany us to Fort Piegan [to assist] Mr. Mitchell. This young man spoke Dacota because he [was] at the [Minnesota] River a long time. He was good-natured and obliging, though a little negligent. [After] dark, for those assembled in front of the fort, Mr. McKenzie entertained us with firecrackers and rockets. The former were aimed into the crowds of engagés and others unfamiliar with [such] things; one can imagine the resulting panic and laughter.

XI

Journey from Fort Union
to Fort Piegan, or McKenzie

[FROM 6 JULY TO 9 AUGUST 1833]

6 July: At seven o'clock in the morning the keelboat *Flora* took leave of Fort Union; the men started pulling the rope, and we moved along the right bank. The *Flora* was [60 feet] long, [16 feet] wide. The length of our small covered cabin, 10 paces, width 5 [with] a small shuttered window in back; on each side, an entrance, which also provided light. Besides Mr. Mitchell and the three of us, the crew consisted of Mr. Culbertson, a half-breed hunter (Deschamps), his brother, and forty-three men, sixteen to eighteen of whom [usually] pulled the boat [at any one time] with a towline (cordelle) for two hours [while] the others rested [before] relieving the first group. In addition to the crew, there were two Indian women. The boat was heavily laden [with] goods intended for the Indian trade at Fort Piegan, [plus some] food for the long journey. A few shots were fired in farewell [there were two cannon on board]; the flag was hoisted at the fort.

The river turned north. The rope, at first pulled by twenty-six men, caught on a tree in the water; a man waded over and chopped off a branch [to free it]. Forest on both banks. We halted for a while, loaded some wood, and cooked on an iron cookstove on deck. To the right, prairie, with grass, *Artemisia,* an abundance of blooming roses, *Xanthium strumarium,* and other plants.

We rowed across the river, [where] Mr. Bodmer, Dreidoppel, and I, with three other hunters, went ashore. We [hoped] to shoot game, because we had no provisions on board other [than] salt pork and biscuit. We roamed through an old forest of elm, ash, cottonwood, and *negundo,* [then] prairie [and] thickets, [but] saw no game; we were still too close to the fort. We climbed the [bluffs] and the view was remarkable. We [could see] the wide bends [in] the river, green lowlands with forest and willow thickets, prairies, and, behind them, high, strange chains of clay hills, whitish gray with a few dark transverse strata and perpendicular clefts.

We had not been [back on board] very long when [the keelboat] scraped against fallen tree trunks [on the bank], which crushed one of the cabin doors. The men [on the cordelle] were taken in. [Two] large oars were placed into iron [oarlocks], and three to five men [worked] them by walking forward and backward on the deck. A tree swept the deck because the workmen did not hear the warning. The mast stays were torn loose, and I received a [severe] blow. Later the men [had to] struggle forward with the cordelle [over a] forested bank. We heard our hunters shooting on the other side. We ate lunch after four o'clock: salt pork, pemmican, hard zwieback, and coffee.

Evening, beautiful but a little cool. Somewhat before sunset our hunters brought aboard a two-year-old black-tailed buck. In the evening, powder and bullets were distributed among the crew, and they were divided into watches. Two men stood guard for two hours, with three watch periods throughout the night. Mr. Mitchell notified the crew that whoever fired a shot after the evening halt would be fined five dollars. If an Indian war party were in the vicinity, any shot would immediately attract them.

7 July: Beautiful, bright morning. We moved on early. Part of the crew pulled [on] the cordelle; [others] pushed the boat with long poles tipped with iron. We had our little cabin in better order now. Guns hung on the ceiling and walls; the traveling bags and chests were moved to the side, [and] we slept very well on our buffalo hides with blankets. The cabin contained two bedsteads: one for Mr. Mitchell and his Indian woman, who sat or lay in bed all day; I slept in the [second] one. The three other cabin passengers slept on the floor.

After [a few] hours, the forest came to an end to the left, and high, whitish gray bluffs, 150 to 200 or more feet high, precipitously adjoined the river. The heat on deck was very intense; one could not stay there long. On the bank pretty butterflies flew, including the big yellow *Papilio turnus,* common in Pennsylvania. Several ducks; one saw few of them now but many in fall and spring. Shady forest to the right, with tall, dense cottonwoods; on [some], the bark [had been] torn away by ice, a good 15 feet above the river (the bank was 10 feet high).

When we [saw] the remarkable bluff wall at close range, [there were] whitish argillite layers [in] the clay [and] one could see hollow areas, archlike on top, like the gates or windows of old castles. We crossed to the left bank, and the men were put ashore to pull. Mr. Mitchell, Culbertson, and

Bodmer [went] hunting. The river turned left, [and] the forest soon came to an end, followed [by] a prairie covered with *Artemisia,* [where] our men found a large, 3½-foot-long rattlesnake (we could [hear it] rattling); it was brought to me still alive. Deschamps had shot a deer and had seen four elk. About evening we stopped at a forest to the left, [and] our hunters went out [again]; we soon heard them shooting. Evening very pleasant. Our hunters [returned with] a fawn; that was their entire take. In the dense rosebush thicket, Bodmer suddenly found himself quite close to a rattlesnake and caught it. Mr. Mitchell said that he had seen an Indian boy die within an hour and a half from the bite of such a snake, [which] struck him below the ankle.

8 July: We left our position early and sailed [until] the keelboat ran aground near a sandbar off the right bank. The men, in water [up] to their hips, pushed and freed [us] after great exertion. We followed the left bank, where the half-Indian Deschamps (with a clubfoot badly maimed by frostbite) brought back large quantities of scraped-off cottonwood [inner] bark. The pulp, or sapwood, beneath the bark of this tree is soft, extremely succulent, [and] eaten by people here. Its taste is sweet, [somewhat] resembling watermelon; the Indians subsist on [it] if they have nothing better.

Our men often could not advance; the loose, sandy bank frequently [crumbled, putting them] in danger of falling into the river. Several years ago three Assiniboines, [resting] under [a similar] bank, perished [when it] collapsed and killed them. [Several hunters had gone out earlier, but only] Papin had shot a fat deer *(Cervus virginianus);* we did not have lunch until [it] arrived [at] three o'clock [and was] chopped into pieces and prepared for us. [Later, the men] struggled to get over [sandbars and] compacted driftwood with the cordelle, sometimes falling into deep water. When these obstacles had been surmounted, we came to a level prairie on a high bank where, about 150 to 200 paces from the shore, the strangest clay pyramids were piled up like pastries. We continued on beneath high clay bluffs [with] black horizontal strata. It was remarkable to see how our men, in a long row, clambered over the high, sometimes very steep, clay walls. [Finally, we] could proceed no farther here, so we crossed the river [and,] after sunset, tied up for the night on the right bank. The hunters came in; Deschamps had shot a cow elk. Our catch today: one elk and one deer. On upstream journeys one often took no more than three days' provisions and relied entirely on hunting. This could still be done in the upper regions of the river, where there was yet much game; farther down, this was probably no longer possible.

9 July: In the morning, some rain; warm. The mosquitoes tormented us early and greatly. We had to navigate around a very bad spit where the current was quite strong. With great exertion, twenty-six men succeeded in overcoming the current and pulling [the keelboat] around the bend of the river; the wind was against us. We had a beautiful prairie to the right, and when we looked to the left, we caught sight of two deer swimming across the river; a large number of rifles and muskets immediately went into action, but [despite being] greeted by a hail of bullets, [the deer] escaped. Somewhat farther [on], we saw two buffalo in the forest to the left.

[The earlier success of our hunters, however, meant] our deck had venison hanging all over it; one elk provides nourishment for some time. The men break open the leg bones, eat the marrow, and lubricate their gunlocks with it. The hides of the bagged game belonged to the company, which used them to have shoes made for the men. From a large elk hide, one [could] make about twelve pairs of moccasins, for which the maker received one dollar. A deerskin provided not more than five or six pairs.

As we were navigating along the left bank, a tree shattered our cabin door for the second time. Papin brought in a deer and [then], shortly afterward, two even larger ones. The sky became overcast, and it rained heavily. The wind became very strong; we anchored to the right by the forest and remained there for several hours; [the] severe wind was succeeded by [more] rain.

From here on, the bank along the forest was very soft and eroded in various ways; large masses of it were caving in. The forest was so dense that the men had to clear their way with axes [and] great exertion. Beautiful black and white butterflies alighted on the skins of game spread out to dry without our being able to catch any. The wind had driven off the mosquitoes a bit, and we were somewhat more at ease.

10 July: Beautiful, bright, warm day. Our journey was proceeding slowly because of the difficult navigation; we covered no more than 10 miles on either of the previous two days. Our hunters went out early to hunt. Fresh meat was needed, for after one and a half days, little was left of the elk and deer. [When] the hunters returned, they had shot three buffalo [far out on the prairie; some men] left to cut [them] up and bring in the meat. I stayed in the forest with Dreidoppel and shot a magpie *(Corvus pica)* for the first

time. There were two fully grown young ones; Dreidoppel shot the other one. *Icteria viridis,* that lively bird, was not uncommon in this forest. The undergrowth of roses and red willows with *Symphoria* was dense and thorny, the heat was intense, and there was no breeze. In the nearby prairie, we found *Cactus mammillaris;* insects in large number sat on the blossoms.

At 11:30 we returned to the ship at the same time [as] the men with the buffalo meat. At twelve o'clock, 74°F. [We continued our journey, the men arduously working the cordelle. On] the Missouri, navigation with keelboats was once the sole [form] of any importance; only in the [past] three years has anyone tried steamboats for this purpose. [A keelboat] journey from St. Louis to Fort Piegan usually lasted eight months and was dangerous. Shipping by steamboats goes well when the water is at [a] medium level but is not without danger. When there is high water, downstream navigation [is] swift and easy.

Messrs. Mitchell and Bodmer went out to comb the forest. Because of today's heat, we drank a lot of water; in the Missouri it is mixed with so much sand or earth that if one scoops out a glass of it, [there is] a great deal of sediment. Despite this, it is healthful and cool. The [sediment comes from the] Missouri's continually eroding banks. Above its confluence with the Musselshell River, [however,] the Missouri has clear water.

Messrs. Mitchell and Bodmer had found many wild doves *(Columba migratoria),* the fresh, large track of a bear [and] its droppings, and the remains of an Assiniboine in a tree. The forest had thickets of rather ripe gooseberries; the ship's crew eagerly ran to [gather them].

Toward six o'clock a slight breeze blew, and the mosquitoes were less troublesome. The river turned left toward the hill chain, which was not very high or distinctive here. We did not travel much farther; dark clouds were gathering and a severe wind arose, and we therefore remained for the night near a prairie on the right bank. At 9:30 a faint northern light appeared on the northern horizon, [but] the [cloudy] sky [obscured] the full phenomenon.

11 July: To the left, [a] chain of clay hills [of] uniform grayish brown color, with strange cones and domes; forest along both banks. A swamp [blocked our progress], so several [men] were sent out in a dinghy into the willows beyond [it]. They fastened a rope there [and] to the boat in order to pull it [to that place]. The men moved along the deck in a row and hauled; we made it over successfully.

In the north a black storm arose, advancing with thunder and violent bolts of lightning. We moored the boat behind a tall cottonwood forest, where it was fairly well protected. Heavy rain poured down. [When] the storm passed after half an hour, the temperature had cooled, the mosquitoes had disappeared, [and] we continued our journey after two o'clock. We passed a place where the river had broken straight through one of its big bends; one always follows a new Missouri channel. Above this bend the river was very wide and majestic, high and full.

Somewhat farther [on], Deschamps, who had killed an elk cow *(biche),* returned. We [waited] about twenty minutes, until the elk venison had been brought in. To the right we passed a small river, which the English [called] Porcupine [or Poplar] River. [A little farther on,] I got out with several hunters. The forest here bordered on an extensive prairie, overgrown at this spot with *Artemisia.* Numerous isolated, dry, silver-gray trees. In one of them was a *Falco sparverius* nest; I heard the chicks chirping, [and] the parents flew anxiously about. There were many big flycatchers and fresh elk and deer tracks. Dreidoppel roused a deer, and Saucier, our carpenter, shot it. The prairie [here, called] à la Corne de Cerf, [or Elkhorn Prairie], extended as far as the eye could see. In this prairie there was a pyramid of elk antlers, about 500 to 600 paces from the bank, which the Indians (Blackfoot) had piled up. One could see this pyramid, about 15 to 16 feet high and 12 feet in diameter, quite clearly from the river, since it stood completely isolated on the plain. Mr. Bodmer, Dreidoppel, Saucier, Deschamps, and I went [to see it]. Every Indian war party, [by] custom, placed antlers on this heap, indicating the number of warriors in their party with red transverse stripes on the antlers. Mr. Bodmer [sketched] this monument. We took along a good antler with four red stripes as a souvenir; it [was] hard work to get it loose.[1] The pyramid consisted [primarily] of elk antlers, some cast off, others [with] skulls attached, [all] bleached white. [There were also] several buffalo horns among them; the whole thing was probably a medicine [for] good luck in hunting.

[Storm later;] better weather at nine o'clock.

12 July: In the morning, we navigated along the steep bank with much exertion, and even danger, [through two whirlpools]. [When] the wind increased there could be no thought of continuing the journey, so the anchor was cast and the boat secured as well as possible to await the [abatement of the gusts].

The [place] where we lay at anchor was farther up [along] the [Elkhorn Prairie]; one could still see the antler pyramid we visited yesterday. In a small buffalo berry bush I found young, almost fully grown magpies; in the *Artemisia* shrubs, *Fringilla grammacea.* Where the ship lay there were four shelters, [either] hunting huts or those of a war party, made of dry trunks and limbs laid together in quadrangular fashion; several of our men made a fire inside and cooked their meat. I shot several birds and returned. Mr. Bodmer pursued a very large rattlesnake, which slipped away from him into a hole in the ground. He saw the beautiful orange *Icterus,* as well as many *Falco sparverius,* and brought back several plants, including a beautiful, fragrant, large-flowered *Asclepias,* which grew nearby in the forest. There were so many elk antlers scattered [in] the area that one could easily have erected several more pyramids like that of the Indians. The [one we saw] certainly had over one thousand antlers.

At noon the wind increased and drove water into our cabin. [By] six o'clock [it] had abated a little; we continued on and, toward dusk, anchored at the right bank. The change of temperature between yesterday and today was striking—yesterday hot, today cold—but we had a total respite from the mosquitoes.

13 July: We [attempted to proceed] but soon came to shallow water; [this, and strong wind, caused several delays]. I [disembarked] and followed the river upstream for a short distance. The thicket of willows, cottonwoods, roses, and other plants was so dense that I could barely penetrate it. I finally entered a somewhat more sparsely grown area where there were good green areas suitable for grazing by game animals. I found a pair of prairie-hens *(Tetrao phasianellus)* [and] shot the female. Later, on the way back, I got so far into the thicket that, for over one and a half hours, I completely lost direction and only after great exertion and many vain attempts reached the river and our ship. At a quarter past four, the wind had subsided considerably; we lifted anchor and pushed up the middle of the river, but we ran aground [twice, finally] reached the left bank [at] twenty minutes past six, [and] remained [there].

14 July: The region through which we navigated now was low on all sides; forest and willow thickets everywhere. We traveled upstream along the left bank [and] at eight o'clock reached a prairie, where we found a deer and a skunk hanging on a dead tree; our hunters, who had gone out early today, had left [them] there. The skunk was big and old; they had cut out its scent

glands. I hardly had it on deck [when] an engagé came and wanted to eat it. Navigation in this region was made more difficult [by] high water [and] swampy, half-flooded points [with] brushwood and trees piled up before them. People assured me that they never had so unfavorable a journey as this one. Papin shot one more [deer] and Deschamps, two: [so,] altogether, four head of *Cervus virginianus* this morning, all does.

At nine o'clock we ran aground on a sandbar not far from shore. We were there for at least one and a half hours, [struggling to get free]. The men undressed and tried everything: they pulled, pushed, [and] finally unloaded many barrels and other things, [and finally] succeeded in getting afloat again. [A] light wind blew across the water, which allowed us to hoist the sail for a short while. We went back a stretch, then upstream in another channel, where we put in about two o'clock at the left bank to take in venison that the hunters had ready here.

We had scarcely departed when we saw three buffalo over on the bank. We sent out the boat with Papin, Deschamps, and Dreidoppel. The three animals did not wait for them but swam across the river ahead of us. Mr. Mitchell and four or five men with rifles went toward them on this side of the river, and the boat approached them from the rear. As the first one came ashore, it was struck by a bullet and turned around; ten or twelve shots were fired from our boat at the swimming animals, and five or six from shore. [Two] were killed, and Dreidoppel gave one of them the fatal shot. The buffalo that had been hit first reached the opposite bank, climbed ashore with difficulty, disappeared into the willow thickets, and was not pursued. Both dead buffalo were lying so deep in the mud of the bank that one [of them] was left untouched and only a small part of the meat from the other was brought back. This is how they deal with animals here: they kill everything they can reach and thereby destroy their own future.

We continued navigating until about seven o'clock and then stopped at a forest on the right bank. The evening was splendid, a faint aurora borealis in the north.

15 July: [Today] very hot—at 7:30, 75°F. During the night [we heard wolves howling and] buffalo bellowing mightily. The bison mating season was beginning; the bulls shortly become very lean, malodorous, and unpalatable, [and then] only cows are shot.

In the morning we navigated through a flat region [of] mostly woods and meadows. Buffalo had quite recently trodden broad trails everywhere, in all directions; their wool hung on the shrubs; their droppings lay in the paths. I pursued several attractive birds: blackbirds, the kingbird, *Turdus rufus,* the turtledove, the [splendidly] yellow goldfinch *(Fringilla tristis),* the *Icteria,* with [its] many different calls, the beautiful blue finch *(Fringilla amoena),* and the yellow warbler *(Sylvia aestiva).* But [my gun's ammunition], designed for buffalo, spared the beautiful little birds for the time being.

In the afternoon we navigated along the sandy edge of the left bank. At four o'clock or 4:30, Mr. Mitchell returned [from hunting]. He complained greatly about the exceptional heat in the prairie hills; even in our cabin, ventilated by openings on all sides, the thermometer registered 84½°F. [That] evening, [after we had put in for the night,] the mosquitoes arrived and drove us into the cabin, where we closed all the shutters and were prey to the great heat.

16 July: [On] a chain of moderately high hills we saw a herd of many buffalo. Hunters were put ashore: Mr. Mitchell, Culbertson, Dreidoppel, Deschamps, Papin, and I. We followed the forest along the bank through dense, blooming rose thickets as far as the dry, rocky, [almost] flowerless hills. Urubus hovered high in the air. We looked for [bison] cows for several hours, without finding [any]. Shortly before twelve o'clock, feeling as though I had been roasted, I returned to the ship, which was still far back; [I] had to go through hot sand and low willows along the river to reach it. The welcome refreshment of grog soon brought me back to a state in which I could describe this excursion. We navigated upstream until five o'clock, when we found Dreidoppel. He had shot a very large antelope and had prepared its hide for the collection. He had made a fire and roasted the liver for lunch, and while this work was going on, two wolves appeared and stationed themselves without shyness 10 paces away. He could have shot both of them if he had not broken his ramrod. We were in sight of the place where Mr. Mitchell lost his keelboat last year [in] a storm; dark clouds now rose again over this spot, and our helmsman [was apprehensive]. The woods where we took Dreidoppel aboard were full of blackish blue, bristly gooseberries *(Ribes)* with a sweetish sour, pleasant taste, which our men [craved] as refreshment.

The evening was beautiful but too warm. [The] men splashed around in the water.

17 July: Mr. Mitchell and I went 100 paces across driftwood to the place where,

on July 15 last year, the keelboat *Beaver* had been wrecked. We found the exact spot. It had been moored 800 paces farther upstream; a storm tore it loose during the night. Two men drowned and Mr. Mitchell escaped by a tremendous leap from the deck onto land.

We followed the left bank alongside a beautiful prairie with a whitish overgrowth of *Artemisia*. We [passed] the [place] where our hunters had shot a buffalo cow yesterday and then spent the whole day in the shade of the nearby forest and roasted venison. These hunters were often coarser than savages. When they shot an animal, they usually ate the liver raw. Often one saw them cut a calf out of its mother's body and stuff it along with the placenta and all the membranes into a kettle [to] boil, [or they] ate the unborn calf's legs and nose raw; others ate the external sex organs of the buffalo cow raw.

[Later, we saw] a beautiful beaver lodge [beneath a steep bank], a conical, 4- to 5-foot-high pile of dry wood and twigs, [with] a small entrance on top. Unfortunately, we could not stop to inspect this interesting structure. After noon, when it was very hot (86° or 87°F), we followed the wooded right bank. At four o'clock dark clouds appeared and a wind came up. We again crossed the river [and] sent the men out with the cordelle. Deschamps and Papin returned [from hunting with] a large bull elk. They had scarcely arrived when a thunder-and-lightning storm [with high] winds forced us to halt, cast anchor, lay out ropes, and take down the mast. [It] lasted about an hour. The sunset was magnificent, the whole sky red.

18 July: We navigated through low-lying regions: forest, sandbars, and willow thickets along the bank. Driftwood here and there. The low hill chain before us in the distance. Our hunters went out very early in the cool of morning. Twenty-five fish were caught, mostly catfish of the whitish or ash-blue variety and several [whitefish]. The former were tastier.

At eight o'clock a very strong current along the left bank drove us against wood lying in the water; we had to use great force to ward off the branches. I could not cease thinking of my Brazilian river voyage. There, where nature was so luxuriant, grand, and abundant, one heard the cries of the [macaws], parrots, [trogons], and monkeys, where here, as a rule, everything was still, dead, and solitary. The vast prairies have hardly any living creatures, that is, those one could hear or see from a distance, except the huge bison and the antelope, and in the low [woods] along the river, the dangerous bear, three deer species, wolves, and farther upstream in the hills, the bighorn. [When] one meets buffalo herds in the prairie, then it is indeed animated, but more often one finds it desolate and dead. I believe that these arid, withered, and, in winter, frozen prairies bear a strong resemblance to African scenes. One cannot call them luxuriant grasslands or savannas; they are dry plains alternating with ranges of hills. Luxuriant grass is found in only a few isolated spots, [yet] interesting plants [occur] in most places.

At nine o'clock we found [our] hunters on the bank. [They] had shot a big bison bull, [and] we sent men to bring the meat aboard. We [then] navigated through a [side] channel 50 to 60 paces wide, which shortened our route by several miles. Before us on the hills and in a distant prairie, we saw buffalo; Deschamps and Papin went out immediately to get close to them [and later] returned [with] the meat [of another] large bull.

Not long after four o'clock, on a sandbar before willow thickets up ahead in the river, we saw a big bear, and soon another one, which we observed [closely] with the telescope. When wounded, this dangerous animal usually attacks the hunter immediately in a fury. [Bears have] torn many whites and Indians to pieces. If anyone [surprises a bear] in a thicket, it usually attacks, but if it scents someone earlier, it flees. Along the upper Missouri there is no wooded area of significant extent where one does not find these bears. [Grizzlies] are the only bear species in this region; the black bear (*Ursus americanus*) is not found here at all. Hunters generally do not like to shoot at [grizzlies], because they fear them. An inaccurate marksman (unable to hit the animal's head or heart) must look around beforehand for a tree, so he can flee up it, for the grizzly bear does not climb, although the black bear does.

[Then] we saw one of the bears galloping on the sandbar. Mr. Mitchell, Dreidoppel, Bodmer, and Deschamps jumped into the dinghy and hurried over there. At that moment we saw a large bear coming out of the willows and going toward the shore, where a dead buffalo cow lay, on which it sat down and began to eat. With [a] loud splashing of the oars, the keelboat navigated in the middle of the river toward the bear; the dinghy went closer along the bank. Deschamps—a bold, experienced bear hunter—got out and crept low across the sand directly toward the bear. It stood up several times; we saw its huge head with pricked-up ears. It glanced around and then went on eating. The entire crew watched with tense anticipation, [as] Deschamps boldly crept, bent down to the ground, along the sandbar right up to within 80 paces of the bear, his gun always ready for the shot. This bear is said to have poor eyesight, [so] one can get very close [in] a favorable wind. The boat with the riflemen came to about 50 paces from the predatory beast without it being the least concerned. Suddenly the rifles were [raised], and Mr. Mitchell fired at the monster. The bullet hit; we saw the bear roll back [and] heard it utter dreadful cries. When several more bullets struck, it tumbled forward about 10 paces, scratched the spots where it was wounded with its paws, and fell again and again. Deschamps went up and dealt it one and then a second, fatal shot. The majestic animal lay stretched out in its own blood. Ropes were fastened to its heavy body, and it was attached to the dinghy, [which] returned to the keelboat with its catch. I was delighted to see this majestic animal stretched out; I took its measurements, and Mr. Bodmer made a sketch of it. This bear had a length of 6 feet 2 inches and 2 lines; its head was 15 inches 8 lines long; the tail 8 inches. Occasionally one [might] encounter animals nearly twice as big as the one measured here, something confirmed from the length of claws I have measured.

In the north a heavy thunderstorm was gathering; therefore, we hastened to find a good place for the night, under the steep bank of a pretty prairie. The bear was taken by means of ropes, on which several persons pulled, to the prairie and skinned there. It was rather thin, and nobody wanted to eat any of the meat. We were scarcely finished with this work when the storm [arrived]. Thunder and lightning were intense, and at ten o'clock a heavy rain poured down [and] flowed into our beds and threatened papers, plants, and books, for we had little room on this small ship. The rain subsided, and the night was calm and pleasant.

19 July: At seven o'clock the wind picked up, [and] for the first time, we could sail ahead rapidly, [but] because of the river's many bends, [we] did not long maintain the direction needed for sailing.

We prepared the skin of our bear, which I bought from the company for two dollars. Deschamps helped with this task and told many stories about these dangerous [animals]. Once Papin was on foot in the prairie with his rifle when several buffalo hunters on horseback wounded a huge bear. The bear pursued one of the horsemen, overtook him, and was just about to tear the croup off the horse when Papin brought it down with a well-aimed rifle shot [to] the throat. In spring one sees these bears continually along the riverbank [and] among the ice floes, where they eat drowned buffalo lying there. Carrion and meat are this bear's staple food, but it also digs many roots and eats all kinds of berries; [at these times a hunter] can often get very close to one. Lewis and Clark provide numerous examples of the dangers [of] bear hunting.

We reached the mouth of the Milk River at one o'clock. The Milk has a very winding course, and its water is mostly clear.

Our hunters had shot another bear and a big buffalo bull. We halted [nearby] for the night. The bison, already mostly cut up, [was] huge. Mr. Bodmer sketched its head. The hair on [its] crown was somewhat wavy, very thick, coal-black, woolly, [and] 18 inches long. I cut off the entire scalp and kept it. The bull had a strong rutting smell. This is the mating season, and the cow carries the calf until the following April.

20 July: Early in the morning we navigated about 2 miles along a strange chain of nipplelike smooth, round hills, dark, grayish brown [in] color, devoid of plants. The river turned right here and made a bend of 15 miles; the keelboat sailed swiftly [in a] strong, favorable wind, [but only for a short time].

We crossed over to the right [to] follow the steep bank of the prairie. The current there was quite powerful, and [although] the cordelle was heavily manned, we struggled ahead only slowly. As soon as we came into the shelter of the hills, the wind changed, [and] we halted to wait for calmer weather. We remained near a thicket on the narrow prairie, where I found the big shrike, the magpie, and several [other] birds; I hunted them [and] butterflies.

Fig. 5. Karl Bodmer. *Head of a Buffalo*. Ink and wash. 10⅝ × 14⅝ in. 1986.49.338.

Our helmsman, Henry Morrin, shot a big antelope, the skull of which we prepared for our collection. Its meat, as well as that of the bison bull killed yesterday, provided our lunch. Some men went hunting; at three o'clock [when they] were fetched, they had shot twelve bison along the riverbank: four bulls, five cows, and three calves or heifers. They [took] only the meat of the cows; bears, wolves, and bald eagles would benefit from the rest. Today [we] covered just a short stretch, [and] we lay at anchor only a few miles by land from the Milk River.

21 July: We departed early. [It was] the dry season here, which begins in the middle of July and lasts through the entire autumn. Almost all the creeks dry up then; the entire prairie has a yellow, burnt appearance, and dust is stirred [just] by a wolf running across it. The [presence of] buffalo can be recognized at a distance from the dust. In the fall the weather is beautiful and clear, but the river is low and navigation slow. In spring, rain and wind [make] the river high [and] navigation good. Winter, usually five months, is very severe. Last year it was milder than anyone could recall: the Missouri was frozen over for scarcely three days; the snow did not last long either.

[After an afternoon of sailing and cordelling,] on a high hill before us, we saw several large elk; through the telescope [they] proved to be big bulls. [Then,] on the [opposite] bank, a large, dark-colored bear appeared, walking slowly toward the shore. We immediately [gave chase] in the dinghy—shots rang out, and three bullets, the last one in the head, cut the bear down. It was not as big as the male killed recently [and] was very dark colored. We had to be content with cutting off its head and forepaws.

22 July: In the morning, at six o'clock, we reached the hill chain on the left bank: high, rounded, almost blackish clay hills, completely bare. In the gullies between them there was vegetation; otherwise, not a blade of grass. We pushed the ship forward with poles in the middle of the river and, after navigating around a river bend, put out the men on the cordelle and pulled [ourselves] along the left bank. [Later,] we crossed to the right bank and found ourselves opposite two clay peaks resembling the ruins of a mountain castle at Bornhofen on the Rhine. The river made a wide, majestic bend here. We sailed a good stretch until the river again changed direction, [and we] then saw a big bison bull in the young willow thickets on the bank. We sprang into the boat and landed: Mr. Mitchell (who wanted to let me shoot first), [me], and Deschamps. We crept to within 40 paces. The bison was wallowing in the sand, [and] the dust flew around our heads. I was

somewhat overly eager and fired before [it] stood broadside to me. Both of my bullets hit it, and it stood wounded for a while but then ran away; it would perish, but we did not get it.

We pulled on the cordelle to round a point, again got [a] sailing wind, [and thus] moved swiftly past a prairie [and] oddly shaped hills. I received a small young specimen of *Coluber proximus*. [It was] strange that along the entire Missouri we had not seen one specimen from the Sauri or lizard family. We found very few frogs, [though] toads [were] numerous. We continued sailing; the evening was very pleasant, the view of the bare, colorful hills on the left bank most singular. We anchored for the night at a sandbar to the right. We had made good progress today.

23 July: The hunters left early, Dreidoppel with them. [When he] returned, [he] had found [an] *Unio*, the first mussel we had seen on the Missouri. In the Musselshell River farther upstream, we will probably find several [more].

I had [hoped] to have the hide from a bear's forepaw tanned by our Blackfoot woman, something the Indians do very well, but she declined because she could not work on anything from a bear.[2] The Indians are exceedingly superstitious; each has an animal that is medicine, or sacred, to him.

We navigated [along] the prairie to the right where [we] found several buffalo killed by Papin; we loaded the meat. Farther on, a beautiful view before us: unique mountains or hill chains, gray with small black patches of cedar.

Mr. Mitchell went hunting with Bodmer, [and we saw] hunters climbing over the heights. The men on the cordelle killed a rattlesnake *(Crotalus tergeminus)*. [At] twelve o'clock they were relieved. The heat [was] oppressive.

On the right bank, [there] was prairie [beyond] the 12-foot-high, steep clay bank. The left bank [had] willow and cottonwood forest, behind which rose extremely strange, ash-gray clay hills. A light wind arose [about] 2:45. The river was shallow; we ran aground. The men all went into the water and pushed in every possible way. In the end the boat could only be moved backward; we lost 6 miles. We [found an alternative channel,] hoisted the sail, and ran swiftly against the current. The river made a big bend around wide sandbars along the left bank. We halted for the night along an extensive prairie completely overgrown with bluish green *Artemisia* and thorny shrubs. Our hunters brought a doe. The evening was windy, the sky overcast, the mosquitoes very annoying.

24 July: [This morning] we had very strange clay mountains before us, including a pointed pyramid that was supposedly the halfway point between the Milk and the Musselshell River. We navigated across the [Missouri to an old cottonwood] forest, where I got out with Dreidoppel to go hunting. We found [a place] where buffalo had just wallowed, [and we] saw beautiful plants: a purple *Monarda*, a lovely shrub with vermilion berries, etc. Behind the forest a vast prairie extended as far as the eye could see: bare, whitish gray, dried-out clay soil on which three kinds of bushes grew—bluish *Artemisia*, a thorny, fleshy-leaved shrub, and another one with narrow leaves. Here and there, *Cactus ferox*. Wind alleviated the heat a little. Bones of buffalo, deer, [and] elk [everywhere]. Several sparrow hawks and a small bird resembling a lark were the only [large] living creatures we saw here, [although] farther on we found a gaggle of wild geese. Thousands of grasshoppers covered the prairie, hopping around. [Some] made a clicking and clacking noise when they flew up; others whirred. [There were] many butterflies in these grassless, African-hot, dried-out clay steppes, but only of three or four species. Anthills were numerous; mosquitoes and large horseflies swarmed. In a gully we found young magpies *(Corvus pica)*. I shot the old one, since the young ones were already grown, but it fell into a deep cleft.

Dreidoppel felt sick and exhausted [and] sat down by the side of a bare clay hill. I went down to the riverbank to look for the keelboat, when suddenly he shouted something to me. A bison bull had appeared at a great distance, [moving] toward us. We hid behind bushes at the edge of a deep ditch. It came along the trail, as we had assumed it would. The enormous animal, with a long beard, looked most splendid. [Its] forward motion was slow, yet [its] feet created much noise. Finally it went through the ravine below us; the wind was in our favor. As it climbed the opposite bank, I fired a well-aimed rifle shot, and Dreidoppel then shot twice with his gun, whereupon [the bull] stopped, faltered, and lay down. I gave it a coup de grace to put [it] out of [its] misery. [Then] Dreidoppel saw a second, younger bull, crept up on it, and shot it. Meanwhile the dinghy had shoved off from the ship [to fetch us]. I led the men up the ravine; the tongues were removed and very little meat, which we took along to the ship, where we arrived under great heat at two o'clock. The ship had been waiting a long time for us.

Meanwhile Mr. Bodmer sketched indescribably strange clay mountains. This entire chain has thousands of elevations, domes, gorges, [and] small hollows; a sculptor [could not] create [works] with greater singularity—the whole region, with its fresh green forest and willow lowlands alongshore, has a completely unique character.

[With no sailing wind,] we pushed the boat with poles and pulled it upstream with the cordelle. The thermometer at 3:45 registered 84½°F; the heat was intense. Toward sunset we navigated to the left bank, and at dusk [we] halted before several small green islands. Our men cooled off in the river. In the distance there was severe lightning and the sky was covered with dark clouds.

25 July: We went out early [and] crossed over to the right in the dinghy to a narrow wooded promontory, behind which a vast prairie extended. There were blackbirds, woodpeckers, and *Fringilla grammaca* in large numbers. By chance we found a covey of the mountain or prairie cock *(Tetrao urophasianus)*—magnificent, big birds. Unfortunately, we had loaded with ball and did not get any. We found no game; I saw only a young rabbit and shot a great horned owl *(Strix virginiana)* from an old cottonwood.

[We returned to the keelboat.] On the left bank, the strange clay hills close to shore had incredible domes, some just like mountain castles on the Rhine. The wooded promontories became smaller and smaller; soon the unusual clay mountains also came to an end; boulders took their place; and then the forest ceased entirely. Farther upstream [we would come to] the mountains the French call les Mauvaises-Terres (Badlands), where the bighorn *(Ovis ammon)* was not uncommon. While we paused for a short while to load dry wood, two buffalo were sighted ahead of us in the prairie; the hunters crept close and shot both of them. Our men took a great quantity of meat [this time], because in the [Mauvaises-Terres] we might not see much game.

The crew pushed [the keelboat with poles]. The mountains all around became higher and higher; they had extremely strange domes like pulpits [or] little towers [or] pastries set on their ridges, which were [also] often notched like saws. Navigation was much easier here than farther downstream, for there were no more swampy sandbanks into which the men sank, [thereby] constantly delaying us. Nor was the river water as dirty as before. The banks were high and steep, but the men on the cordelle usually had a path below, on which they could walk along the river.

With a brisk wind, we [began to] sail. The mountains before, behind, and beside us were now so altogether peculiar that we conversed about nothing else. I had never seen such high, sharp ledges, jagged on top, their mostly bare, gray masses without any vegetation, except for occasional spots of scattered, short [conifers]; qualified geologists must describe and investigate these [formations]. The domes, towers, [and] columns stood out most strangely against the blue sky. Unfortunately, we could not stay; destiny permitted us only to hasten through here.

We talked with Deschamps about Indian food sources. He told us [that] the Assiniboines, Crees, Ojibwes, and some northern Indians often suffered hunger and that whole families died [from] this sad misfortune. Therefore, they ate every living thing they could find, except snakes. They had few dogs, because they usually killed and ate them in emergencies. [Without sufficient] serviceable horses, they could not shoot enough buffalo, so they resorted to a kind of drive [see chapter 13]. The [other] Indians of the Missouri [fared better, for] they had more horses and more game in their territory.

Because the wind was gusty and unfavorable, the men were put on the cordelle again. But then the wind [changed] and we sailed on. The prairies along [both] shores were covered with bluish *Artemisia*. The peculiar high clay mountains everywhere formed the background. They became higher and higher, more gigantic, more massive, the domes like short towers, pavilions, Chinese [summerhouses], etc. In general they had the appearance of Säntis in Appenzell, or other Swiss mountains.

Black storm clouds had long since arisen, [and] as we were approaching a bend in the river, a thunderstorm broke. The crew worked furiously with the poles to move [us] on. Desjardins, one of our men, had severe abdominal pains and was very ill. This happens when people eat the now-very-fatty venison and then drink immoderate amounts of water in this great heat. Such cases occur frequently during Missouri keelboat journeys.

The very strong wind became favorable, [and] we sailed as swiftly as an arrow. Ahead of us mountain domes appeared that fully resembled white castles with brownish roofs. [We] had never seen such strange mountain shapes. [While] we were occupied observing the peculiar world of nature, the storm suddenly increased [and] the sail [was] torn to bits. We hurried to the left bank and secured the boat with hawsers. More storms gathered, [with] thunder, lightning, [and rain, all in] oppressive heat. They soon dispersed, however, [and] we had halted here for scarcely an hour before the men were again placed on the cordelle and the journey continued. We now approached the white mountain castles, as we called them; [when]

one gets close, the resemblance naturally vanishes, but from Mr. Bodmer's sketches one can easily see that from a distance there is a [remarkable] resemblance.

We put in at the left bank, about 300 to 400 paces from the place where we were during the storm. We visited a prairie dog village not far [away and] later saw a white wolf come down from the hills; it lay down in the level prairie. Dreidoppel and I crept toward [it] behind the bushes; the former shot it with a combination over-and-under rifle and shotgun. It was a white she-wolf, not large, [but] we grew very warm carrying [it] the long distance to the boat.

26 July: We cast off early, and [when] the river turned right [we saw] the formation referred to yesterday, which today we called the White Castles. Mr. Mitchell, Culbertson, and the hunters went hunting after breakfast; at ten o'clock Mr. Mitchell returned—he had not seen anything. We were aground for a while. When we were afloat again, we pushed upstream with poles in the middle of the river, then manned the oars and rowed to the left bank, where we continued by pulling the cordelle. On the prairies the *Gryllus* species were so numerous that the ground teemed with them. They hopped around in every direction and [made] a rattling and rustling noise where dry foliage remained on the ground.

The river became very narrow and made an extremely sharp, abrupt bend to the right. [The south] bank, [exposed to the force] of the water, was so strikingly eroded that the clay wall was split and torn into thousands of fragments, cones, pegs, and pyramids, which our men on the cordelle could struggle across only with the greatest difficulty. The heat was [intense]; the men had to drink, and [so] they lay down, endangering themselves, heads down and legs up in the air. In that steep bank, swarms of swallows nested, which my hunters shot at. Dreidoppel brought down the first one, and Mr. Mitchell was kind enough to send the dinghy for it. [It] was probably a young *Hirundo fulva*.

After a hot day, the sun set; the evening was splendid; the sky completely clear and calm.

27 July: Early in the morning Dreidoppel [and] I went on the left bank across the eroded clay hills toward a large wooded area. In the shady forest there were excellent grassy ravines and green areas; unfortunately, the mosquitoes were intolerable. We tracked buffalo everywhere but [found] nothing fresh. In the tall trees on the sparse, scorched and dry prairie, the big

[flycatchers] and blackbirds were very abundant, the latter with their young. We saw the keelboat arriving at the upper end of the forest, but since it was navigating along the other bank, we shot more birds, [including] *Hirundo bicolor,* one of the most beautiful swallows in America. We wandered for an additional half hour through the glowing prairie, then climbed through a ravine [down] to the river, sat on the bank, and cooled our burning thirst with excellent Missouri water. The dinghy fetched us.

At the place where we boarded the dinghy, or a few hundred paces before it, stood four Blackfoot hunting or war party huts; we were now in territory not inhabited by them [but] traversed by [their] raiding parties. The boat was pushed and pulled, partly along the right bank [and] partly in the middle of the river. [Later,] Messrs. Mitchell and Culbertson returned [from an excursion]. They had climbed the hills to the right and had had an incomparable view. To the west they saw the Little Rocky Mountains, like blue clouds in the distance. Among the mountains they surveyed [were] the so-called Bears Paw, which one [can] also see clearly from Fort Piegan (McKenzie).

We [continued until] it began to thunder and black clouds rose in the southeast [at] about four o'clock. We tied up on the left bank; the thunderstorm soon broke. The [rain] lasted scarcely half an hour, but the wind continued to blow hard. As a rule, during this dry season, thunderstorms are accompanied only by wind [and] seldom by significant rain. Our little ship was completely dried out from the intense heat; the deck joints [were] open, and hence we dreaded the rain, which got our beds wet. Several hours later the weather looked better. Because the wind had subsided, we put twenty-nine men on the cordelle [and] had them partially undress. We went farther up the river, now very shallow, [with] many sandbars. The crew, in the middle of the river, were up to their waists in water. We went 1 or 1½ miles farther and put in for the night on the left bank. The sky was dark and threatening; [it was storming again] by nightfall.

28 July: In the morning, gloomy sky, light rain, strong wind, cool. We continued navigating by poling. Dreidoppel and the hunters went out early to hunt.

The skulls (that [we] prepared with great effort) and other [specimens] had been deliberately thrown into the river. I had already lost two bear heads, an antelope head, a white wolf, and several other things in this manner—even though Mr. Mitchell threatened to punish such transgressions severely, they still occurred. [So,] despite all the interesting objects we had acquired, my collection remained quite insignificant.[M1]

The wind was favorable, [so] we hoisted the sail. Because of the light rain yesterday and during the night, the vegetation looked refreshed. [Farther] upstream, Mr. Mitchell, Culbertson, and I got out on the left bank, to visit the Musselshell River, which we thought to be not far [away]. We entered a tall, beautiful cottonwood forest with a dense underwood of rosebushes through which we had to force our way. The whole forest was full of elk lairs and fresh droppings. Among the roses, gooseberry bushes with black berries grew plentifully. The berries were ripe but somewhat sour; [they] can be used, dried or fresh, to make tasty dishes if sugar is added.

It began to rain rather heavily and we were very wet, so we called out to the skiff and returned to the keelboat. At eleven o'clock we reached the mouth of the Musselshell River, about 70 paces wide. This river flows parallel with the Missouri for [part of its course]. Its mouth is estimated to be halfway between Fort Union and Fort Piegan, which we will scarcely reach in less than seventeen to eighteen days. The river is more favorable for navigation upstream, however, [so] this goes more rapidly than the lower half.

We stopped briefly at the right bank, took on fuelwood, and rotated the men on the cordelle. After lunch we saw the half-Indian Deschamps returning with his assistant, Dauphin. He had shot a bison bull, a cow elk, and an eagle. The weather had cleared, but a rather strong and, unfortunately, totally contrary wind was still blowing. Bodmer and Dreidoppel went to the right bank to hunt. We pushed upstream with poles. Snags and other [obstacles] made the right [bank] not easily accessible. The crew was again put on the cordelle.

The river water was now much clearer. The [farther] one gets into the regions with rocky banks, the clearer it becomes. The forest on the left bank came to an end, [but that] to the right had especially tall, beautiful, slender cottonwoods. Bodmer and Dreidoppel came [down from the] hills, and the latter was carrying a huge, twelve-point elk antler [for] me. Because we had

---

M1 Regarding such barbarity, which in this respect still prevails in America, see Brackenridge (*Views of Louisiana*, p. 239[–40]), where it is said that Canadians called Nuttall, a naturalist of glorious renown, a fool because he undertook investigations into natural history. And Brackenridge reveals his own feelings in this regard when he says (p. [240]), "but [Nuttall] is unfortunately too much devoted to his favorite study." How could Nuttall be too devoted to this, the most splendid and preeminent of the sciences!

to move on and the antler was heavy, I called out to him to set it up on the elevation so that I could [get] it on the way back. This was done, and the antler could be seen from a great distance. Somewhat farther on, we put in for the night, [still within] sight of [that] antler. The evening was clear and beautiful, somewhat cool.

29 July: Warm early; sultry [by] eight o'clock. We pushed upstream with poles in the rather shallow river. The water was turbid today; it must have rained heavily farther upstream. The surrounding hills were flat on top and had no domes, as they did shortly before. The men were placed on the cordelle. Birds flew [over] the surface of the river: *Hirundo purpurea, fulva,* and often *bicolor,* and in some places *riparia.* About eleven o'clock, heavy rain, which penetrated our cabin at various places but fortunately did not last much longer than a good half hour. The region was attractive, with intermittent green wooded riverbanks, refreshed by the rain, and always mountains [as] a most picturesque background. We were now traveling along [a] clay and argillite wall; mica or micalike fossils had been washed out from [this] in many places and lay scattered, shining [and] glittering in the sun.

[Later,] we came to an island, long, overgrown with willows and cottonwoods, to our right. As we passed, we encountered such a powerful current that almost all the men had to be put on the cordelle. The rest pushed with poles. [The Missouri] turned left; [it] was very narrow here, only about 80 paces wide. The region ahead was pleasant and varied.

On the right bank we saw an impressive bison bull standing on a prairie. Papin, Deschamps, Saucier, and Dauphin quickly went ashore and tried to get closer, but the splendid animal watched us all for a long time [and] then galloped off. At dusk we landed on the left bank at the mouth of a small, [currently] dry creek. As usual, part of our crew slept on shore, where they carried their blankets and buffalo hides.

30 July: Pleasant, cool in the early hours; slightly overcast sky. The region was varied [and rugged in] appearance, [with forested banks and] mountains overgrown with grass and pines. We passed to the left of two islands. Perhaps [one was] Lewis and Clark's [Tea] Pot Island (an example of the ridiculous place-names assigned by those travelers). Summer flora were already appearing; *Solidago*'s golden rods bloomed here and there along the bank. A pleasant sailing wind came up, which propelled us a little; at the same time, our men pushed the boat with their poles. Beautiful butterflies, including the big, bright yellow *Papilio turnus* with its black stripes, flew in a tall,

sparse forest to the right. The yellow *Rudbeckia columnaris*, with its reflexed petals, was blooming, [too]. [It] grew abundantly in this upper region; I [had] not encountered it farther downstream. Grapevines and other climbing plants had already come to an end before Fort Union.

About twelve o'clock we put the crew on the cordelle [for the afternoon]. Between six and seven, while we were navigating in glorious evening weather, a canoe approached us, [carrying] the [Blackfoot] interpreter Doucette and two men from Fort McKenzie. They had left three days ago. A large number of Blackfoot Indians, about 150 tipis, were there now, and [others] were scattered along the Marias River. On the Judith River, about halfway between here and the fort, the Gros Ventres [des] Prairie were encamped, awaiting the keelboat. They had nothing to barter but were expecting gifts, and Mr. Mitchell did not have enough to [spare]. He expected nothing good from them. Those in the canoe had shot a very large bear today, not far from here, which we will find tomorrow and, if possible, hang up in a tree [so that I may collect] its skeleton on [my return] journey downriver. We navigated to the right bank and put in there for the night.

31 July: Early in the morning, nice, clear weather. We—Mr. Mitchell, Bodmer, Dreidoppel, Doucette, both Beauchamps, and I—got out on shore at the second bend of the river to search for the bear killed [yesterday]. After twenty minutes to half an hour, [we found that] magnificent bear. A buffalo had sunk into the mud below, and the bear had been eating it when Doucette approached with the canoe and shot a bullet through its chest. It had then climbed up the high bank and [died]. I measured this impressive bear and found it to be 6 feet 7 inches 3 lines, English measure. We immediately got to work, skinned it, cut the thickest flesh from the bones—this took a good two hours—[and] then pulled it up into the fork of an old cottonwood trunk stripped of its bark, where we fastened it with ropes to let it decay [so we could] take it along on our return from Fort McKenzie. The bear's skull was especially large and thick, its teeth rather worn. It had been rather fat.

When we were finished with this work, we followed the keelboat, which meanwhile had been pulled past us. Directly behind the forest, we found a prairie where there was a large prairie dog village *(Arctomys ludoviciana)*. [We] shot six of these little animals. They sat on their hills singly or in twos and made their squeaking noise. [We discovered that] the keelboat had hoisted [its] sail, and we had to walk for several hours in the intense heat before we saw it again. We made our way through rugged prairies and densely wooded promontories, [past] rough sandstone hills, [then down] to a sandbar, where they [finally] fetched us and took us on board. Today was Mr. Mitchell's birthday; we drank to his health. [That afternoon] the hunters [got three bison]. The evening was dark, the weather pleasantly cool and refreshing. We no longer saw many mosquitoes; we had probably outlasted them.

1 August: Two men were sent by land with a letter to Fort McKenzie. Each took only a woolen blanket and [a] gun. Men were put on the cordelle; [hunters went ashore and later returned], loaded with game. Bodmer came in from the right bank and brought a large snake *(Coluber eximus)*, 4 feet 2 inches 4 lines long.

[Difficulties were experienced in shallow water.] We navigated around a sandbar and tried to move up along the left side of the river. The hills to the right were strangely shaped: roundishly arched, breastlike, some with transverse sandstone strata. On top of them, organs, fortresses, small sentry boxes, columns, and furrowed ramparts. Hills and conic domes followed each other row on row. Some [were] deceptively similar to old castles on the Rhine. [All] were mostly bare, gray-brown or whitish gray, dried out and heated by the sun.

We were approaching the region called Mauvaises-Terres: tall, strangely shaped hills where the bighorn live.[3] The narrow strips of forest along [the banks would] soon come to an end, [and] the river course was much straighter than previously. The clay walls along [the] shore were mingled with big sandstone blocks. Before the hills, or rather mountains, there were level areas overgrown with light-bluish *Artemisia* bushes [and] old cottonwoods. A painter would have to stay here several years to sketch all the interesting mountain regions of the Missouri.

The wind here was brisk and cooling; we would have rapidly forged ahead, if only it had not been completely contrary. On the left bank, a prairie overgrown with thorn and *Artemisia*. Behind the prairie rose hills on which unusual formations stood. One looked like a house with a pair of gables. Heavy thunderstorms drew near so we made the ship fast, and the wind began, [but by] nine o'clock it was calm and beautiful.

2 August: In the early sunshine, we saw the singular clay and sandstone elevations all around us in beautiful illumination. Mr. Bodmer sketched several [of these]. There was a place at the right bank in the river here, exactly where there was just enough water for the boat, called *le premier rapide,* the first

rapid. Boulders on [the] bottom gave the river a little more fall or swiftness, and the men on the cordelle had to be assisted [by men poling].

The bare elevations became higher [as we came closer] to the rugged mountains called les Mauvaises-Terres. Throughout the entire stretch, there are no tributaries [or] brooks at all. [The] high, bare mountains are the principal haunt of the argali (bighorn, *grosses cornes*), which, to be sure, [could be] found earlier but not in such numbers. There was no longer any forest, and one could not expect any game other than bighorn. In the bend of the Missouri where we were now, the most unusual sandstone domes, mostly a yellow-reddish color, appeared along the mountains. [There were] protruding strata; round, smooth peaks marked with perpendicular fur-rows; as well as wall-like formations, in some places perfect imitations of the ruins of mountain castles. We saw [one exactly like] an old tower. The water was shallow, [and] the men on the cordelle were up to their waists in [it].

At twelve o'clock we reached an island without forest, undoubtedly more recent than Lewis and Clark's journey and unmentioned [by them]. We soon ran aground, and the crew worked strenuously to push the boat away from the bank. The wind was contrary, and the voyage proceeded very slowly. Incredible mountain elevations to the left, including one like a Brazilian church with a gable in front and several spires on the roof. We moved on, [passing] hills [with] isolated columns, each supporting a large block of sandstone; the column was ash-gray, the rock yellowish red. Such [formations] are extremely common here; they are remnants of eroded clay strata on which a sandstone stratum [once] rested.

Somewhat farther on, when the sun had set, we saw several bighorn standing silhouetted against the sky on top of the highest mountain [peak], about as high as the highest Rhenish hills. With the telescope one could see them clearly. Although it was already late, Mr. Bodmer immediately volun-teered to attempt the climb. Papin went ahead, and Dreidoppel followed but remained at the bottom of the mountain. Meanwhile Doucette discovered a beautiful piece of petrified wood on the shore; it was blackish and very solid, probably *Juniperus virginiana*. We smashed it with difficulty, and I took several fragments with me. Deschamps killed a rattlesnake *(Crotalus tergeminus)* close to the boat. At nightfall the hunters returned. They had seen three bighorn but got none.

3 August: During the night, some thunder and lightning; otherwise, beautiful

moonlight. In the morning, pleasant weather. The mountains were high, gray or whitish gray, strewn with yellowish brown sandstone boulders. Rubble lay everywhere; [it was, overall,] a picture of devastation and raw wilderness.

The hunters saw two bison and were set out early on the right bank. We hoped they [would] shoot some bighorn. To the left we now had high clay walls, completely barren; farther on, [there were] large sandstone masses [and stone columns] at the very edge of the river, only 40 paces from us: a most unique formation. On the opposite side of the river, our hunters appeared with meat; they had shot a bison bull. Fetching [them] cost us a full half hour. Deschamps had not seen any bighorn but did find their tracks. We were now approaching the most significant rapid, Dauphin Rapid, named after one of our crew, who fell into the water at this place last year.[4] On the left bank, on a very high hilltop, we saw two bighorn; one [was] a big ram. In shape, the bighorn is similar to the antelope but much thicker, sturdier, and heavier; full-grown, the ram weighs more than a deer. Its head is thick and, with the huge horns, very heavy. [Its underbelly] and hindquarters are white, the upper parts reddish brown. Its hair is hard and (like that of the antelope) brittle. Its meat resembles mutton.

The foothills rose by degrees, covered with short grass. These rugged deserts [were] totally devoid of people; even Indians [were] almost never seen here. It was much too difficult for them to travel through these steep mountains, since they mostly traveled on horseback.

We passed several [more] rapids—places where the river had more fall and hence a stronger current. The men on the cordelle had to pull with all their might. The view up and down the river [valley] was especially interesting [here]. The [river] no longer made big bends as it did before, moving in serpentine fashion between two [widely separated] hill chains. Here it was confined and flowed more straight ahead.

Bodmer returned [from hunting] with cactus thorns in his foot, not all of which could be extracted. The wind became strong and favorable, [so] we set the sail and moved swiftly. [When] we halted [that evening], we sat for a long time on [a] hilltop and viewed this remarkable region until it was veiled by night.

4 August: A stretch where the river had a rapid along the left bank delayed us a long time; the wind, too, was against us. On a tree to the right, two bald

eagles. From the right bank, the song of *Fringilla grammaca* reached us, short [and] flutelike.

Later, in the mountains, we heard Papin's shot, and Mr. Mitchell thought he saw him shooting a bighorn. It is very difficult to hunt them. One must climb terribly [high] in the steep mountains, [which] are entirely without water. The Alpine hunter in Switzerland finds cool springs and water everywhere; he has his brandy and good cheese. The mountain hunter here must endure great thirst; if he wants to drink, he must descend to the Missouri. Not infrequently, however, one can find bighorn in lower regions and can kill them without such great difficulty. These animals run and jump along the steepest walls with extraordinary agility. Indeed, one occasionally sees them standing like ibexes, with all four feet on a small rock. Even the young animals are difficult to catch in these mountains; Mr. McKenzie offered a horse to [any] hunter who brought [one] back alive but had not gotten any yet.

At twelve o'clock we reached an island overgrown with scattered cottonwoods and some prairie. There was a strong rapid there that required skillful work. We rested opposite the island, [then] pushed and pulled across [another] rapid along the left bank. [Soon] the prairie had a border of beautiful old timber; the forest indicated that we had passed the Mauvaises-Terres. [Later, after repairing a leak in the hull,] we navigated to the right bank and stopped there for the night.

5 August: The region was pleasant and pretty. At six o'clock we reached the mouth of the Judith River, which discharged on the left side; its banks were partially overgrown with woods. Just before the river mouth, in the prairie along the right bank, a large prairie dog village. It was the farthest upstream Mr. Mitchell had ever seen one. Today we [should] reach the camp of the Gros Ventres des Prairies; yesterday our hunters found fresh remains of buffalo killed by [them].

At 7:30 we put in at the right bank so the crew could have breakfast. At that moment we saw five reddish brown figures coming around a hill in the prairie through the whitish *Artemisia;* they were Indians. Their rifles flashed in the bright morning sun. They fired their guns and sat down near the forest opposite us. Mr. Mitchell went over to them with Doucette and Deschamps. Several women also arrived with a dog, which was pulling on a frame (dog train; *travois* in French). After a while, the Indians went along with [the men] in the dinghy, and Mr. Mitchell brought them to our boat.

There were four men and a woman, who carried a thick club in her hand. The men were rather tall and well built, not significantly different from the Assiniboines. They wore their hair hanging down to their shoulders, some-times [in] four or five braids. Most wore one or two large, thin iron rings of 2½ inches diameter in their ears. Their buffalo hides were painted reddish brown on the flesh side, as with all the northern Indians. Their weapons were guns and bows and arrows. They wore leather leggins; their upper bodies were bare. They sat in the cabin, smoking. Each was given a glass of whiskey mixed with water.

After they had been on ship for half an hour, [our guests] were put ashore and a chief was brought back. [He] had bound his hair in a knot in front, something only medicine men may do. He spoke Piegan or Black-foot somewhat, and thus Doucette could converse with him. We advanced with a good sailing wind and twenty-seven men on the cordelle, [but] the Indians alongshore moved [even] faster. Some rode ahead to inform their nation of our arrival; [others] ran swiftly. The reddish brown men, with their weapons, looked most unusual in the bluish prairie *Artemisia.* Mr. Bodmer sketched the chief. The Indians had told us that their entire nation was assembled several miles upstream; [this group] had assembled here to await the keelboat. We were not particularly pleased to see them, because they owned [few] articles for trade [but nonetheless] wanted merchandise. Not much good can be expected from any of these peoples; they are rather false and treacherous. If a dispute arose, [they could] easily massacre the fifty men on our boat. A favorable wind was of great benefit, for it swiftly drove us away from this dangerous band.

An hour and a half later, we reached a stony place on the left bank where there were several Indian women with [many] dogs, some pulling loads. The river deepened into a narrow gorge, barely 80 paces wide, and the poles had to be used. Another Indian swam through the river to the ship. He was completely naked except for a woolen breechcloth. [He] had marked his arm from top to bottom with big, parallel incision scars, one above the other. These scars [were] offerings [made] to the Lord of Life (Great Spirit) when some serious [undertaking was] intended—for example, stealing horses or going to war.

The river turned left. On the right bank, several more Indians had ar-rived; the sight of the reddish brown persons was most arresting. Through their chief, Mr. Mitchell indicated to the Indians that they should go to their village; we would put in [near] there, on the other side. He [would] send them the dinghy with presents of powder, lead, and some tobacco. [Around noon] we put in on the right bank by a rocky area to let [a] thunderstorm pass. A band of Indians sat alongshore near our men [and on] the other bank. Thunder roared [and] the contrary wind delayed us significantly. While we lay at anchor, a group of Indians moved in twos or threes back to their camp, which was no longer very distant; others were just now riding up to see us. The chief alone remained in the boat; [he] was bored and yawned hugely. Light rain continued, as did the unfavorable, excessively strong wind. Our patience was put to the test.

[When] we shoved off from shore, [the wind became unfavorable again] and the crew [had to] clamber over white stone walls. Several Indians also pulled on the [cordelle]. Others walked or rode alongside us.

When we came around the promontory, a very picturesque and strik-ing scene appeared. To the left was a high jagged, blackish mountain with whitish gorges [and] patches of grass; horses of all colors grazed on [its] foothills. To the right, along the river, unusual high white walls of sand-stone and clay. Before us the river vanished in a picturesque gorge. Near the gorge [and] far to the left, [on an extensive] green prairie, stood a large camp [of] over two hundred leather tipis of the Gros Ventres des Prairies, or Fall Indians. The chief's tipi stood near the front; beside it [was] a tall flagpole with the American flag, fluttering briskly in the wind. The entire plain was covered with reddish brown figures, innumerable dogs, and riders [on] horses—a most unusual sight.

We fired the cannon, and the Indians fired [their guns in response]. The keelboat landed opposite the village. [Accompanied by] the interpreter Doucette [and a few other men], Mr. Mitchell climbed into the dinghy and went over; he was the only one [with] pistols. Alongshore the red multitude of Indians formed a tightly crowded line. The chiefs sat completely alone on a mound near the river. Mr. Mitchell sat down beside them and after twenty minutes returned with eight chiefs. They took their places in our cabin and smoked the pipe. Most of them were big, strong men with expressive faces. They wore their hair long, like the Mandans and [Hidatsas], in many braids pasted with reddish clay. Their faces were painted red; several had streaked a few stripes [over] the red with a bluish metallic ore [from] the Rocky Mountains, [used and traded by] the Blackfoot and other tribes near those mountains. [They had metal and shell ear ornaments, but] apart from nice moccasins, they wore no fine clothing. One carried a war club made of elkhorn, which I bought from him. Their red stone pipes were of Dacota fabrication. Some of their tobacco pouches were attractive; one of them had [a pouch] made from the hide of a quite young bighorn, which he was not willing to sell.

Among these chiefs were several very good men, but one in particular, with a deceitful countenance, was known to Mr. Mitchell as a bad Indian whom he [had once] chased out of the fort, because [this Indian] had wanted to shoot him. Now [this man] assumed a friendly bearing and shook hands, even though in his heart he was scarcely so well disposed. He had tied his hair together in a thick knot on the front of his head. His name was Mexkemáuastan (Stirring Iron); [see pl. 16].

Scarcely were [the chiefs] on board when, although it was cold and raw, all the [other] men swam [across] the river, and in a short time the ship was [completely] full of slender young Indians. They all wanted tobacco, powder, [and] bullets but particularly whiskey, and [they] brought along [to trade] whatever they owned in the way of furs, tanned hides, dried meat, and the like. Those who had nothing to exchange begged. Soon we were crowded so close together that someone suggested to the chiefs that they should clear the ship. [In compliance] many [Indians] jumped into the water and swam away, but most, [when] driven from one end of the ship, climbed onto the [opposite end]. Fortunately, everything proceeded without incident.

The dinghy had remained on land to carry on some trade there. The Indians surrounded it and apparently did not want to let it go, [and] it remained there a very long time. Finally it arrived, loaded with Indians. [When we left] and the men pulled on the cordelle, perhaps as many as fifty Indians pulled along with them. The whole population moved alongside [us], and the [keelboat] was so full that it was moving low in the water. With this strange and unusual company, we navigated through a most remarkable area. Steep, high walls intermittently enclosed the river on both sides, the beginning of the region called Stone Walls.⁵ Mr. Mitchell told the chiefs that the dinghy was ready to [take] them to land, and after much talking, they were carried away in two loads. As presents they had been given two casks of whiskey (mixed with water) and tobacco. They were not satisfied with the first of these, [as] it was too little, whereupon someone suggested to them that they should come to the fort [to] get more.

Finally, we breathed more easily. Mr. Mitchell, when we put in on the right bank at dusk, drove all the remaining Indians ashore, [including] women, [who] were hidden in the beds of our crewmen. Several of the crew were missing things: one a wool blanket, another something else. Various things had been traded; we, too, had acquired a few trifles. Far more had been given than received.

6 August: The wind [was] strong and, [depending on which] way the river turned, sometimes favorable [for sailing]. The Indians [had] set out immediately for the fort, which they could reach in a day by land. All in all, we were very satisfied with their conduct, and Mr. Mitchell admitted that these Indians of ill repute had conducted themselves far better than others would have done in similar circumstances. [The Gros Ventres des Prairies] were compelled to be on good terms with American traders now, for they had completely forfeited the goodwill of [other] whites. Near the English frontiers, they had destroyed a fort, killed a clerk and eighteen men of the Hudson's Bay Company, and slain several whites in the Rocky Mountains. No one wanted any more dealings with them.

The region we passed through today was remarkable. The sandstone valley of the Missouri has greenish gray, moderately high hills, rounded off on top or flattened, and overgrown with clumps of low plants. White sandstone walls everywhere. In places where the turf cover has been washed away, one sees [fascinating] formations—perpendicular and horizontal ledges [topped by] strange figures [resembling] pillars [capped] with stone slabs like tables, [pipe] organs, pulpits, small towers, even men. Between eight and nine o'clock, the valley was especially curious, for on all sides one saw white, [bizarrely] formed sandstone sections, [those just mentioned, as well as] odd domes and turrets of all kinds. Every moment one saw new shapes; one could fill thick volumes with their description.

The bighorn live in these mountains. We [spied] six of [them] running up over the strange white sand[stone] walls. They stood on top, silhouetted against the sky. To the right, a [flock] of about twelve bighorn, [then another] seven to the right [and] five to the left—in short, these intriguing animals [were everywhere].

We halted on the left bank for a moment and took in the twenty-seven men who had been cordelling, because the brisk wind was favorable for sailing. Surrounded by this most singular—may I say, unique—world of nature, one forgot the cold weather [that] made drawing nearly impossible,

Fig. 6. Maximilian. Unusual rock formations. Ink. The prince and Bodmer both created dozens of sketches of these "singular" works of nature on the upper Missouri.

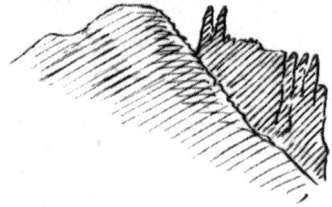

[although Bodmer created many fine sketches of these formations]. I have not yet read anything about this [fascinating area], and an exact description of it would certainly interest the European reader.

The region of the Stone Walls is about 12 to 15 miles long, [and] the river has a rather straight course [through them]. [Soon] we approached an un-usual [place where] the river seemed quite narrow. [On] the right side, the [white mountain walls], and opposite, [on] the left, a high, dark brown, narrow, pointed rock tower that the French engagés called la Citadelle [the Citadel]. We passed beneath this solid rock, which seemed to consist of argillite, graywacke, and a conglomeration of stone fragments in yellowish clay.

We put in behind the [Citadel] and the crew had lunch; then we continued the journey against [a] strong, wholly contrary wind. The region was [at first] more open, the hills much lower, only a few distinctive domes or rocks visible. [Later, on the right,] an indescribably strange, high rock wall, completely white, with short jagged points on top. Where the river seemed to enter a narrow gap, this wall reached the bank, as did another one from the left bank, and the [two walls] seemed to form a narrow gate. Beside us were the most regular walls, which looked as though they had been constructed from thick cubical stones, the joints as regular as [if they had been] hewn to size. On a hill stood a rock like an old Gothic chapel with a chimney. [See pl. 15.] We advanced toward

Fig. 7. Karl Bodmer. *Citadel Rock on the Upper Missouri*. Watercolor. This tall, dark, distinctive landmark, visible for miles on the upper Missouri, is at the approximate midpoint of the White Cliffs region of the river. 12⅜ × 7¾ in. 1986.49.191.

another [formation, high] on the right bank, that looked like a barracks, a long building, [with] corners [so] sharp [they might have] been regularly cut. A thick tower rock stood in the rocky wall of the left bank, [and] somewhat above it was a crescent-shaped cliff in which pines were growing. On one side, there was a cross-shaped figure, which could have been [man-made]. Our hunters had killed four buffalo on that side, [so] we crossed over and put in for the night at the prairie.

We climbed the incredibly strange hills, and I found the white sandstone so brittle that it could be pulverized in one's hand. The reddish stones, which here and there formed the [tops of the formations], were a little firmer. Cedars [were] stunted and strangely crooked [here]; the pines had grown up straight but were not over 40 feet high. Standing [amid] those strange rocks, one could believe one was in an old French garden, surrounded by urns, pyramids, obelisks, and the like.

7 August: In the morning we navigated past the blackish brown tower of the left bank. From [there] it was approximately 600 to 800 paces to the place that, from a distance, looked like a [gateway; beyond that,] both stone walls diminished in height, continuity, and regularity. A prairie extended along the right bank. The hills on both sides of the valley had [some] very unusual sandstone formations [but] not as magnificent and distinctive as those [observed] yesterday.

After eight o'clock it became very warm. We went up the right bank—Mr. Mitchell, Bodmer, Dreidoppel, and I—to climb the hills. The brittle white stone appeared everywhere, [and] strange figures surrounded us as soon as we reached the hilltops: mushrooms, tables, old fortresses, [etc.]. [From] the highest summit, the view was splendid. We were on a high plateau, dried out and yellow, like a stubble field in Germany after the harvest. In the distance the Bears Paw [Mountains] arose in the east-northeast; Fort McKenzie lay more to the northwest. On the prairie the grasshoppers were profuse; the earth was alive with them. The big lark (*Sturnella*) was common; I also saw a bird the size of a sparrow, with which I was not familiar. The droppings and trails of full-grown bighorn were quite fresh, and when one of them came [in view, Mr. Mitchell and I] immediately lay down on the ground. It would have come within shooting range, but at that moment Dreidoppel arrived and it caught wind of him, whereupon it galloped back to the summit. Having arrived below, we [found] the keelboat, which had hoisted its sail and had fifteen men on the cordelle.

At one o'clock we reached an island covered with tall cottonwood forest; at two o'clock, a second one. We ran aground on the tip of the last-mentioned island, where one had a fine view of the Bears Paw [Mountains], almost directly behind us. From the island we [headed] upstream to the right. The wind [became] favorable; we sailed briskly against the current. Farther on, in the south, we had [a] view upstream of the first chain of the Rocky, or Oregon, Mountains. They appeared as a distant blue [range and] soon vanished behind the banks of the river, which were lifeless [and] barren here. The hills, too, were covered with withered grass, completely without enlivening vegetation. [But soon a sparse] border of timber became denser and broader; we [stopped] briefly and put the men on the cordelle again. We navigated upstream for several more hours along the now-wide prairie. When the ship put in, I went out and saw a flight of *Lanius septentrionalis* and, in the air, a large number of *Caprimulgus americanus,* which flew closely around my head. On the river wild geese were calling, and in the tall trees along the bank, small falcons were extremely numerous. The evening was pleasant. The whole prairie was overgrown with *Artemisia* and a plant from the Syngenesia; [its] flower heads are boiled and drunk in this country as a remedy for venereal diseases. It is probably *Brachyris euthamiae.*

8 August: At daybreak [the wind was] contrary, [but by] 8:15 we had a good wind and sailed swiftly. On the left bank, [in] a strip of old, shady cottonwoods [and] willows, Mr. Mitchell, Culbertson, Dreidoppel, Doucette, Deschamps, and Papin got out to go hunting. The river [was] a beautiful light green color, its water almost completely clear. This is proof that Lewis and Clark were in error when they said the Marias River gives the Missouri its dirty color. At 10:45 we put in at the left bank. Dreidoppel [and] Mr. Mitchell came in; after twenty minutes we continued our journey. On the right bank, we followed steep, yellow-reddish bluffs; they receded, and prairie covered both banks of the Missouri. Farther on, [that] alternated with strips of timber along [the] shore. Those who climbed the hills saw the Marias River, not far from us, which the French call Marayon. A gunshot to the right caused us to assume that Indians were nearby, but we did not see any sign of them yet. Informed of our imminent arrival at the fort, Indians were gathering there, [and] we expected [to see] a large crowd.

In the forest on the left bank, we saw many birds, mostly big *Muscicapa* [and] *Quiscalus versicolor.* On the prairie, great numbers of big yellow-breasted larks. At four o'clock, nighthawks flew about everywhere in the intense heat, pursuing mosquitoes and other flying insects. The river turned to the right, [and we] saw a long chain of hills ahead; Fort McKenzie [lay] behind them. One could go there by land, over those hills, in half an hour. The Marias emptied on this side of that hill range, and beyond its outlet [were the] blackened [remains of] old Fort Piegan. Last summer (1832) it was abandoned, and the Indians [then] burned it down.

We saw two riders on the hills, undoubtedly Indians. As soon as they caught sight of us, [they] immediately sped off at full gallop, probably [to inform] the fort of the keelboat's arrival. We continued navigating [beyond the mouth of the Marias] until about dusk, when we put in beneath high hills along the left bank.

That evening Mr. Mitchell was amazed that neither Indians nor whites came from the fort to welcome us, [as had been typical of past arrivals. This, added to the treacherous and warlike nature of nearby] Indian tribes, who typically killed whites whenever they could annihilate them alone or in small groups, and who up to now had maintained peace at the fort solely for their own benefit, put our situation (at a considerable distance from the last white outpost) in a not very pleasant light. Strong watches were set up [for our camp, and] Mr. Mitchell decided to cross the hills [and see if all was well at] the fort. He took good marksmen, well armed, with him. I lent [him] my double-barreled gun—and a pair of European hunting shoes, for protection against cactus thorns [on] this nighttime [expedition]. We all stayed awake; Mr. Mitchell had told us to navigate downstream if he had not returned by midnight.

The [moonless] night was beautiful [and] dark. We clearly heard the [sound of] Indian drums [coming from] the direction of the fort. At 10:30 Mr. Mitchell returned with [some] of the men; two had set out once again to look for the fort—the whole group had lost their way [and] had reached the mouth of the Marias. [By] morning we had received no word about the situation at [Fort McKenzie].

9 August: Early in the morning we continued our journey [and] were [about to] navigate around a promontory when we saw five riders approaching at a gallop. All were whites [from Fort McKenzie]. They had good horses, the reins of which were colorfully decorated in the Spanish style with red, yellow, and multicolored cloth. Their apparel was wholly appropriate to this distant wilderness. They wore overcoats [made] of striped blankets; Indian leggins and shoes; shot bags decorated with red or blue; and guns on their

shoulders. They galloped up to the bank and fired over our heads. Thanks to them we were relieved of all worry; the rumor of disagreements with the Indians was unfounded—[they] were behaving very well and had deliberately [stayed away so they would] not delay our journey. After breakfasting, they rode back to the fort; we still had about 3 miles to go by water.

[We passed by steep bluffs;] spotted horses grazed on the prairie. The hilltops were all occupied by groups of Indians. Whole bands of brown children ran along beside the ship, and mounted Indians rode up and down the hills. A heavy rain fell, very unfavorable since the cannon had to be fired several times.

A unique, animated scene was revealed as we rounded the last bend of the river before the fort. A vast prairie extended along the right bank, on the point of which, near the river above a row of old trees, Fort McKenzie lay, built exactly like [forts previously described], with [a] flag waving on [its] flagstaff. A large number of Indian leather tipis were pitched on the plain, and the whole area was [thronged] with brown and brownish red [people] awaiting [our arrival]. About eight hundred Piegan men, drawn up like a well-ordered battalion, surrounded the fort. [Other] Indians sat on the fort's palisades and the roofs of its buildings. From time to time, white cannon smoke rose from the fort, and the rumbles that followed echoed in the adjacent hills.

We approached slowly, sent a boat to a sandbar at the right, [and] took aboard an Indian, who worked for the company. [Such men] are called soldiers (soldats), and at Fort McKenzie there were several from all the nearby nations and tribes: the Piegans, Bloods, Blackfoot, and Gros Ventres des Prairies. [Soldats] dressed partially in the European manner and served as a sort of guard; they were also employed for various dealings with the Indians. [This] one, White Buffalo, had an aquiline nose; [a] broad, bony face; and a [good-natured] expression. His dress [included] a kind of blue cloth overcoat, [a] round hat with a band of tin [and] a feather plume, Indian underclothing, and a wide scarlet band over his shoulders, decorated with bells [that] rattled and rang [as] he walked.

We moved closer and closer to this remarkable reception scene. Shots were thundering from the Indian multitude, and our men also began shooting. We saw three or four chiefs galloping around before the [battalion] of warriors. The most distinguished was Iron Shirt (la Chemise-de-Fer), called Mexkehme-Sukahs in his own language. He had a scarlet-red uniform with

blue lapels and braid; a round hat with four red and black plumes; and a saber in his hand. [He] rode an attractive light chestnut horse, which, without
stirrups, he deftly wheeled about in the midst of all the shooting. The most
highly regarded chief [at that time was] Spotted Elk, Kétsepenn-Núka in
[Piegan]. He was held in such high esteem because he had [recently] done
battle with the [Salish], in which forty-seven of the latter were killed. This
chief was a tall man with an ugly face. He had recently changed his name,
something they always do when they accomplish a [noteworthy] feat.[M2] He
wore a long green wool overcoat and a round hat decorated with feather
plumes and a tin band. Generally the chiefs looked outlandish on occasions
[like these], as [if] decked out from a junk shop; [they] all received such
apparel as gifts from the trading companies. Normally they went about in
their native dress, [their] hair hanging straight down, usually with just a
medal on their chests.

As we were about to land, the whites from the fort, drawn up in a row
alongshore, fired off a welcoming volley, and the Indians repeatedly fired
their guns. We went ashore and walked toward the fort through a colorful
crowd of striking figures. Big, strong men—faces painted vermilion-red,
[wearing] often beautifully decorated leather [clothing] and buffalo [robes],
coal-black hair hanging straight down and often over the forehead in three
braids, weapons in hand—stared at us in astonishment. The chiefs and
[other] prominent men welcomed us, and we shook their hands all down
the line—[at such times] one must look them straight in the eye. There were
130 Piegan leather tipis [nearby]; [more] were expected daily. We [walked
to] the fort, where, after a four-month journey from St. Louis up the Missouri, we [would] recover from the hardships of a long confinement. Our
journey had proceeded favorably and had been without incident; it had
lasted 34 days [since leaving Fort Union], and we had subsisted entirely on
game, [having shot 54 buffalo, 18 elk, and 39 deer, among other quarry].

M2 He no longer called himself Spotted Elk but Bear Chief, Nínoch-Kiáiu, in his
language. The other chiefs of the Piegans now present were 1) la Chemise-de-Fer,
Mexkehme-Sukahs, 2) la Vieille Tête, Otokuan-Nepó, now la Jambe-Roide, called
Haiesikate, 3) le Harangueur, called le Gros-Soldat, Ascháste, and 4) le Boeuf-Rouge,
Micutseh-Stomíck. Later the sixth chief, le Vieux Koutoné, Kutonápi, arrived.

XII

Description of Fort McKenzie

and First Stay There among the Indians

[FROM 9 AUGUST TO 13 SEPTEMBER 1833]

Fort Piegan, or as it is now called, Fort McKenzie, was built here in 1832 by
Mr. Mitchell to carry on trade with the three tribes of the Blackfoot (the
Piegans, the Blood Indians, and the actual Blackfoot [the Siksikas]), the
Gros Ventres des Prairies, the Sarcees, and [the] Kootenais, all of whom live
[in this area]. (In 1831 the American Fur Company [had concluded] a treaty,
drafted by Mr. McKenzie, [with the Blackfoot].)

[When] Mr. Mitchell first came here, he lived near the keelboat for a
long time. The Indians gathered in large numbers, probably four to five
thousand men (10,000–12,000 Indians altogether), and besieged him
[there]. A dangerous, unpleasant predicament [for the traders]. [Their] situation improved as soon as the fort was [built] and appropriate security
measures [could be] taken.

[Fort McKenzie] is situated 120 paces from the [west] bank of the Missouri. The fort is [square]; the outside length of each side is 45 to 47 paces.
On the upper corner facing the river, and on the one diagonally opposite,
there are blockhouses with firing slits and several small cannon; the entire
fortification is surrounded [by a wooden palisade, as are] all these forts along
the Missouri. About 800 paces behind the fort a hill chain extends from
south to north. Between the hills and the fort, the Piegans had pitched their
camps. The entire surrounding prairie was barren and dry, trampled down
by men and horses, and grazed bare. Everywhere one saw horses, [watched]
and herded by Indian boys on horseback. The fort had about twenty horses,
always guarded by four armed men. [Near] the fort [there] was a large island
called Horse Island, overgrown with grass and bushes, [where] the horses
grazed in winter. They never entered a stable and got nothing to eat but what
they found out in the open. [Fort McKenzie] was much smaller than Fort
Union. Before our arrival [there were] twenty-seven whites (and several Indian women married to them); we added fifty-three persons.

All the people living in this fort, except for the first table of six to eight persons, got nothing other than meat for food, and they were estimated to consume the meat of two buffalo daily. We had good hunters, [and] meat was [also] purchased from the Indians—twenty bullets and the corresponding amount of powder for the meat of one buffalo. [When] buffalo were numerous, the Indians received fewer bullets; if scarce, then as many as forty. For such a fort nearly one thousand buffalo a year were required. Considering the large consumption by Indian tribes who lived almost exclusively from these animals, one can imagine the enormous number of bison in the American interior.

The style of construction at Fort McKenzie was crude and flimsy, far behind Fort Union [in quality]. The houses were built adjoining the [interior face of the palisade and made] of thick cottonwood trunks squared on two sides and set against one another. They were one story [tall and] had small rooms with fireplaces, a door, a small parchment-covered window, [and] a very flat roof covered with sod, lower than the palisade. The flagpole stood in the middle of the courtyard. The gate was securely locked and strong; it was a double gate, and when trade with the Indians was fully under way, the inner one was closed [while] the entrance to the store between the two [gates] remained open to the Indians. A new fort was to be built a few miles up[river]; glass windows and all necessary parts had been brought here [on our keelboat]. Moreover, there were now a smith, cabinetmaker, and other necessary craftsmen here. There were people from all nations: Americans, Englishmen, Frenchmen, Germans, [and] Spaniards. Several of the latter were hunters.

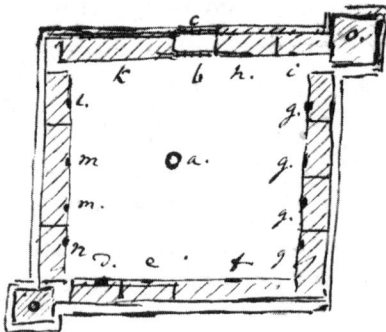

Fig. 8. Maximilian. Plan of Fort McKenzie. Ink. "'a' flagpole; 'b' inner gate; 'c' outer gate; 'd' Mr. Mitchell's quarters; 'e' our quarters; 'f' mess hall; 'g' four rooms for the engagés; 'h' stable; 'i' room; 'k' passage and trading house for the Indians at night; 'l' trading store for the Indians; 'm' stores (supply or warehouses); 'n' store for the whites; 'o' two blockhouses." For an exterior view of a larger but similar fort, see fig. 4, *Fort Union*.

On the first day of our arrival, after we entered the fort and our baggage was brought into the room assigned to us, we inspected the fort and the interesting animals it contained. There were three young bears running freely about in the courtyard. [Each] was about as large as a setter but very fat and ungainly. [They were] lively [and] not ill-tempered, always teasing each other, and keeping their distance from the dogs. A prairie fox *(Canis velox)*, a charming little animal, was very tame and completely trusting.

The [nearby] Indian camp [had] four sections, [with] large and small tipis intermingled. Piegan tipis were made like those of the Dacotas. Few were white and new; most were discolored from age; several chiefs' tipis [were] painted white and in colors. Packs of dogs and horses swarmed [about]. After lunch Mr. Mitchell and I were invited to the tipi of a Piegan chief, Iron Shirt. We [proceeded to] the center of the camp, where a large round space (which included some tipis) was encircled by a fence made of tree branches. At night the horses were driven into it [for safekeeping]; Indians are extremely fond of stealing horses and in this respect do not trust each other much. The chief's tipi was large and spacious, unlike any I had yet seen, a good 15 paces in diameter, very clean, and neatly swept. In the center, a fire in a stone circle. Without further ceremony we sat down on buffalo hides to the left of the chief. Men entered and took their places until the tipi was full. No women or children were to be seen. The chief, a big, powerful man, was naked except for his breechcloth. Scarcely were we seated when we were presented a tin dish [with] a serving of dry, finely grated meat and sweetish berries *(poires)*, which we ate with our fingers and found quite tasty. After we had eaten some, the chief took the dish and ate from it himself. Then, out of a sack he pulled a scarlet-red uniform [coat], with blue lapels and yellow braid, that he had received from the English and laid it in front of Mr. Mitchell as a gift. He also gave him six red and black plumes, a sheathed dagger, a colorful handkerchief, and finally, several beaver pelts. Mr. Mitchell accepted [the gifts] and [would now have to] present him [with] another costume, which is what the Indian wanted. When the chief began to fill his green stone pipe, we stood up and departed in the Indian manner, without saying anything or looking around. We crept through the small door, besieged by dogs.

In the afternoon the keelboat crew bestowed the *baptême* [baptism]—gunfire in the fort courtyard—on Mr. Mitchell and me, for which they were [traditionally] rewarded with whiskey. In the evening [we] heard Indian drums and chanting; [the drum] was beaten rapidly when medicine men were called to their patients (see [chapter 10] on the Assiniboines). They also used the *chichikué,* which the Blackfoot made from wood [and] leather, or a bladder, since they had no gourds. In our room [there was] such a large number of mice that they ran [over our feet] while we were writing. I had several traps, which caught the uninvited guests continually.

10 August: Preparations were made for trade with the Indians. The chiefs were in the fort off and on. In the afternoon the flag was raised. Two cannon were pulled into the center of the courtyard and loaded; one was fired as a signal to indicate that the Indians could commence trading. A half hour probably passed before [we] heard singing and shooting and saw Indians advancing from all sides. When Spotted Elk reached the gate, it was opened. Two cannon shots welcomed them, and three or four Piegan chiefs approached Mr. Mitchell with bowed heads and extended their hands to him, whereupon they were led into our mess hall [to take] their places. Soon another band approached; Mr. Mitchell walked toward them before the gate. They advanced in [platoons], the chiefs at the head; the [chiefs] always gave Mr. Mitchell some gifts—several beaver pelts and occasionally a horse. The chiefs then entered the fort, where they were received with two cannon shots. [They] sat down all around the mess hall. About thirty of the foremost warriors came in with them and sat down. Three or four bands advanced in this fashion, at a rapid pace amidst heavy firing and chanting; I went with Mr. Mitchell to meet them and was delighted with this remarkable sight.

Interesting, characteristically Indian [men] painted in every possible way, beautifully adorned, and in martial attire. Unfortunately, most of the chiefs wore uniforms acquired from the whites and hats decorated with plumes and tin [hatbands], like our German postillions. Spotted Elk wore an old green overcoat (made from a woolen blanket) with red lapels and collar, [and] a round, plumed hat; other chiefs had blue or red uniforms— indeed, even half red and half green, like carnival jesters—nothing but clothing given them by the Europeans. [Iron Shirt] had the most interesting Indian-style [attire]. His face [was painted] coal-black; [his] eyes, mouth, and two vertical stripes [on his] cheeks [were done in] vermilion.

[After] the Piegan bands [had been] welcomed, a band of the Blood Indians, Kaénna, came marching in, headed by their chief (medicine man), Natohs (Sun), [and] presented gifts. [Then] a [platoon] of sixty to eighty warriors of the Gros Ventres des Prairies appeared, who likewise presented a horse and beaver pelts, and some of them were admitted. Each [delegation] was welcomed with cannon shots; some handed over flags [they had] acquired from the English, which they carried in wholly military fashion on long poles in front of them. Mr. Mitchell [had tried] to dispense with the petty formalities and welcoming cannonade last year, but the Indians seemed to place great value upon [these things] and were even ready to withdraw if sufficient honors were not bestowed upon them.

When all the chiefs, about nine, [and] the foremost warriors, about thirty, had taken their places in the fort, whiskey was passed around, and they smoked their pipes. Meanwhile, Mr. Mitchell took Spotted Elk aside and presented him with a completely new half-red and half-green coat [trimmed] with silver braid; a red felt hat with many plumes; a new, double-barreled percussion gun—a complete outfit. This chief had always been loyal to the American Fur Company and had never traded [with] the English posts in the North, [so the company paid] him special honor. When he was dressed, he stepped into the courtyard. One could observe the unpleasant impression that his splendid attire (worth 150 dollars) made [on] the other chiefs. [Those] who had given gifts to Mr. Mitchell and not yet received anything in return, especially [Iron Shirt], could not conceal their feelings; [they] lowered their heads and seemed lost in contemplation. Mr. Mitchell had them told that the American Fur Company knew how to treat its friends with distinction. Could anyone say that they had ever received such fine clothes from the English? Some of them had traded with the English and sold them their beaver skins, [so] he could not give them big gifts. But he would give every chief a present. In the future, [if they] behaved like Spotted Elk, then he could give them big gifts, too. Spotted Elk was not popular; his situation was dangerous. He sat there with bowed head and finally went into Mr. Mitchell's room to separate himself from the others.

The chiefs [then] made [angry remarks]. The interpreter was not good, which certainly contributed to the misunderstanding. A fat old man, called Stiff Foot (Haiesikate), delivered a long speech, with vigorous gesticulations, in the fort's courtyard. He said to Spotted Elk, standing on the side, "Do not drink so much whiskey! That is my advice to you. And go home!" Because he was the chief's brother-in-law, that was to be regarded as good advice. The Blood Indians were offended [and] talked about shooting Spotted Elk. The latter's friends and relatives came and conferred with him. In the meantime, the other Indians were seated in semicircles before the fort gate. They sat on the ground, sang incessantly, [and] occasionally fired off their guns [while] whiskey mixed with water was brought to them.

These opening ceremonies and visits lasted until almost six o'clock, when the chiefs left and then returned with little whiskey kegs, which were filled for them as presents. Trading now began. They brought their beaver pelts, buffalo robes, and other objects. Whiskey, their idol, was always the principal thing for which they traded.

[Then] a tumultuous scene began. Our French engagés, who had drunk too much whiskey, began fighting. There were bloody noses. Harvey, the clerk, intervened [and] became involved in the fight; [he] struck someone on the head with his tomahawk, and the fight became very serious. This set a bad example for the Indians, who stood there quietly. After this unpleasant matter had finally been [resolved], we witnessed comical scenes. Some Indians who had drunk too much whiskey became extremely affectionate. There was no end of hand shaking, and they came up to embrace and kiss us cordially. They traded [and] begged continually for whiskey from all of us. Nevertheless, there were no quarrels among [them]. Very amusing was an old, almost decrepit Indian who brought a very tame, live bear into the fort to sell. He sat down on the ground with his pet [and] played [with] and kissed it repeatedly. The animal was delightful, completely tame, and I bought it on the following day for whiskey. Mr. Mitchell gave me a beautiful little male as well.

11 August: Very early in the morning, [there was a] rumor that the Blood Indians [planned] to kill the whites and take the fort. [Part] of the rumor was true: the Blood Indians, always very dangerous to whites, were infuriated and [would] withdraw, [although] several well-intentioned persons among them came into the fort and assured us of their friendship.

This morning Mr. Bodmer drew the Piegan chief, [Iron Shirt], who had [again] painted his face black and red. His leather shirt was [embellished] with rows of shiny buttons, trimmed on top with otter fur, [and] edged on the shoulders and arms with blue beads. His hair hung disheveled about his head; attached to the crown was a bunch of feathers from birds of prey [along] with white weasel skins, woodpecker heads and beaks, red cloth strips, etc.; [see pl. 18]. After lunch Mr. Mitchell suggested that we take the boat across the river to visit a Piegan chief who arrived there today. We [departed] at two o'clock. The river and its banks were teeming with Indians, mostly enjoying themselves swimming; they were all excellent swimmers. Beautiful, slender young people, their color a very darkly shining reddish brown.

We crossed the river in a big canoe. From the landing place, it was not far to a small ravine in a cottonwood thicket where we found several tipis. The chief, Kutonåpi (Old Kutonä), sat awaiting us; the [other] Indians fired their guns upon our arrival. We went into the small tipi and sat down on buffalo hides. The entire household—four or five men and a large number of women and children—crowded into the doorway to see us. The first thing we did was to shake hands with the men. Then someone handed us a wooden bowl with very fresh water, and we drank. Mr. Mitchell passed out some tobacco and gave the chief a small bottle of whiskey. When he received it, he immediately intoned a song or hymn to thank the Great Spirit, Natohs, whom they worship [as] the sun, for this precious gift. He drank and then gave the other men a swallow. [Next] a wooden bowl, with cooked beaver tail and *pomme blanche,* was placed before each of us. Beaver tail, cooked [till] quite tender, is regarded as a delicacy in the United States.

When we had finished eating, the chief presented nine beaver pelts to Mr. Mitchell. His son shook my hand and thanked me for having come from so far to visit them. They liked my double-barreled gun.

After the chief announced his [impending] visit to the fort, we returned [there, where] the bartering and bacchanalia were soon renewed. Indians arrived, each with a little keg, and gave every useful thing they owned for their favorite beverage. Many sang and danced and offered their women and girls for whiskey. Others brought horses [or] beaver and other pelts, and we witnessed indescribable scenes. In general it must be said that these Indians, even drunk, behaved better than all the others along the Missouri. As soon as they had whiskey, they went back to their camp, and [most] of them left today. During the evening, in and around the camp, we witnessed [many] comical scenes: they scuffled with each other [for] whiskey; young and old got something to drink—there were quite small children who could neither stand nor walk.

12 August: Last evening Spotted Elk brought another large whiskey keg to be filled. Mr. Mitchell had given him so many gifts that [the agent] flatly refused, [which] deeply offended this very self-important [chief]; [he] threw down his splendid new hat and left. This morning, however, he had it fetched. Mr. Mitchell knew that giving this man too many honors would excite envy,

but he did so deliberately to humiliate the other chiefs and draw them away from the English.

Toward noon the Piegan band of Kutonápi, the chief we visited yesterday, arrived amidst rifle fire. Kutonápi, with his foremost warriors, took their places in the space assigned them. A Piegan medicine man visited us and carefully unwrapped a big medicine pipe (*calumet* [in] French). It was decorated with feathers of all kinds, and Mr. Bodmer sketched him with [it] in hand. His name was Hotokáneheh, [Head of the Robe].

In the [late] afternoon we had a sad incident in the fort. A Blood Indian was sitting with several of the engagés in one of their rooms. Suddenly a shot rang out and Martin, a young man, was dead. The whites surrounded the startled Indian, [who] insisted that the pistol had gone off by accident. Since opinions were divided, and no one took immediate revenge on the [Blood] Indian, Mr. Mitchell had him taken out of the fort with instructions never to enter it again. Several hotheads among the whites insisted that the Indian should have been [killed]; this would have been the Indian way of revenge, but the initial moment was over.

Spotted Elk and Kutonápi seemed enraged at the Blood Indians. The [latter] delivered a fierce speech vividly setting forth the affronts of the Bloods to the whites and demanding that revenge [be taken]. But Mr. Mitchell stayed his course. Everyone remained calm.

At nine o'clock the interpreter Berger returned from [visiting] a Piegan band on the upper Musselshell River. It consisted of 250 tipis and would arrive here in a week.

13 August: The Indian with [the] big medicine pipe, [Hotokáneheh], was brought in again for sketching. The afternoon was peaceful and calm. I recorded words of the Kootenais and Gros Ventres des Prairies, [aided by Kutonápi, who was also known as] Hómach-Ksáchkum, la Grande Terre, [Big Earth]. In the Blackfoot camp, one found individual Indians of various nations. There were several Snake [(Shoshone)] Indian women here from beyond the Rocky Mountains; [they] had been taken captive. Most of the Indians were leaving, but new arrivals were expected daily.

14 August: Early in the morning a certain [James] Bird, who had formerly worked for the Fur Company and later went over to the Hudson's Bay Company, appeared on the hills with several Indians. Mr. Mitchell rode out with an interpreter and returned with Bird, [who] brought letters from Mr. McKenzie. Everything was going well at Fort Union. Bird rode off again toward noon;

he was not presently employed by any company but hunted and trapped for himself. He was half-Indian [and] looked brown, though his hair was crinkled. He spoke the [Piegan] language [and] lived with them constantly. [He] was a deceitful man who could be dangerous.

Spotted Elk was grievously offended again this evening, because he was refused whiskey when he demanded it for the fourth time. He [threatened] to withdraw immediately with all his people and demanded [his] gift of beaver back again; Indians can be silly, childish, and ungrateful. Mr. Mitchell remained firm and told him he should leave.

15 August: Early in the morning we had in our room the Gros Ventres des Prairies chief, Mexkemáuastan. He [was] mentioned [earlier, in chapter 11,] as a very bad Indian. He was naked above the waist, a strong, well-built man [5 feet] 10 inches in height, [Prussian measure]. His reddish brown buffalo robe left his right shoulder and arm free; on his back, sheathed bow and arrows; in his hand, a short gun with leather cover; leather leggins; hair tied together in front in a thick, protruding knot. Face [painted] vermilion and blue-violet with mineral color.

Two hunters were sent out this morning with a six-to-eight-man escort to get buffalo meat; they were expected back tomorrow evening. Today our large keelboat oars were sawed into pieces; they were hickory and were made into axe handles because there was no [suitable] wood here. The arrival of a Piegan band was announced; gunshots on the other side of the river confirmed this report. Our quarters were besieged all day by Indians, who were attracted by the drawing and writing. Whenever Mr. Bodmer produced an accurate portrait of a face, they said, "He can write very correctly."

In the evening we went onto the prairie to the Indians' tipis. There we saw many interesting sights—[such as a small child with] wide leather leggins that hung about his legs like big boots. We saw at least six women whose noses had been cut off; the Piegans and Blackfoot punished their women for infidelity [with] this hideous disfigurement. A Blood Indian, a fellow [of dubious reputation], visited us every day with his wife. This evening we were called to his tipi, which was new, clean, and spacious. He sat on a buffalo hide and leaned back on a mat of willow branches, set at an angle [and] covered with buffalo hide. The small fire in the center of the lodge [radiated] great heat. Dried berries were placed in front of us; we ate several. Isidor Sandoval, a Spaniard from Santa Fe and hunter here in the fort, served as interpreter. The evening was [quite] pleasant.

16 August: Mr. Mitchell suggested a ride to the place on the Missouri where he [planned] to build [a] new fort [to replace Fort McKenzie]. We crossed the prairie and climbed the range of hills stretching beyond it. On them a plateau extended to the deeply hollowed bed of the Teton River. This little river flows through a beautiful, shady cottonwood-filled valley and empties into the Marias River. On the elevated plain we saw two Indians riding, who caught sight of and galloped toward us. Because we were carrying our double-barreled guns in a horizontal position, the Indians had probably assumed that we were unarmed and meant to beg from or [frighten] us. They came rather close [and then] suddenly turned around and galloped away— they had spotted our guns. At a distance they stopped and [conferred]; one gave the other his weapons and came riding up to us. He was naked except for his buffalo hide and rode a thin white horse with nothing but a whip in his hand. Through sign language he told us that another young man had abducted his sister, the wife of the comrade riding with him. They [intended to find and] shoot him. He looked for tracks in the path we were riding on and then left.

We rode off and reached the edge of the hills, from which we had a beautiful view. To the right flowed the Teton River, named by the Indians for a pair of roundish mountains. Its valley, densely filled with the crowns of tall trees, created a fresh green strip in the brownish gray, bare region. Before us, somewhat [distantly] to the left, we saw the first range of the Rocky Mountains. From [there] it is about 60 to 80 miles to the highest and principal range, snow-covered [even] in summer. We [then] rode down toward the Missouri, through willows and dark thickets of cottonwoods, *Negundo,* and willows intermingled with buffalo berry, roses, *Cornus, Prunus padus, Ribes,* and several other bushes. A luxuriant growth of grass covered the ground. Men from the fort had made hay [from this] and raked it into stacks. We saw the big lark *(Sturnella),* many small falcons, a golden oriole, and several small birds. A pair of large ospreys [and] a flock of black crows flew up around the riverbank.

The place where the new fort was to be built [lay] at a bend of the river; Mr. Mitchell had selected a beautiful prairie on the right, or opposite, riverbank as the most suitable site for his purpose.

We had just reentered the shady woods [when] one of our men, Dauphin, came galloping up. The Bear Chief, [formerly called Spotted Elk,] had [threatened] to attack the Blood Indians, because they had killed his nephew. We returned [to Fort McKenzie and] were told that Bear Chief's nephew—a very good, quiet Indian—had ridden out that morning to look for a stolen horse and had been murdered by the Blood Indians. [Bear Chief] was furious, and several Blood Indians [who had] remained in the camp by the fort were immediately set upon; [one was] pursued across the river and shot at three times.

In the afternoon [Bear Chief] came to Mr. Mitchell with several Indians, to discuss what should be done. A reasonable man advised him not to make the matter public but to wait instead until he could kill one of the relatives. A call for whiskey concluded the discussion. The great chief was quiet and thoughtful. He wore a plain, poor robe; [he held] his new double-barreled gun in his hand. He had not cut off his hair, because, he said, his heart was too big and strong for [that]. The bloody quarrel between the Indians had arisen through the death of the engagé [Martin] who had been shot in the fort. At that time [Bear Chief] had taken the side of the whites and had struck several Blood Indians. Late in the evening the Bear Chief came once more and informed Mr. Mitchell that he must leave to avenge his [kinsman]. [To be sure it was] in good hands, he intended to give [his nephew's corpse] to Mr. Mitchell for burial. This gift could not readily be refused, since the man had died indirectly because of the whites, so it was accepted.

17 August: Early in the morning, the murdered man's corpse was brought into the fort on a travois, wrapped in a red blanket and a buffalo hide. A large number of Indians—women, children, and an old man—followed, crying and wailing. The chief's brother delivered a short speech to the lamenting Indians. He said, "Why are you crying? He has gone into the other country, and at least two Blood Indians must go with him to serve him there."

The corpse had lain in the open yesterday and all night and gave off a strong odor; it had to be quickly disposed of, and Mr. Mitchell gave the necessary orders. The dead Indian's brother, a boy, had also died last night; they presented his corpse [as well] to Mr. Mitchell. Because a child of [Mr. Mitchell's] had died at birth, we had three corpses in the fort; [they] were buried that morning. A grave was dug, [and] a piece of colorful cloth provided by Mr. Mitchell was placed over them. The grave was lined with boards. [The Indian man's] riding gear, whip, and the like were buried with him. In the afternoon Middle Bull's band arrived.

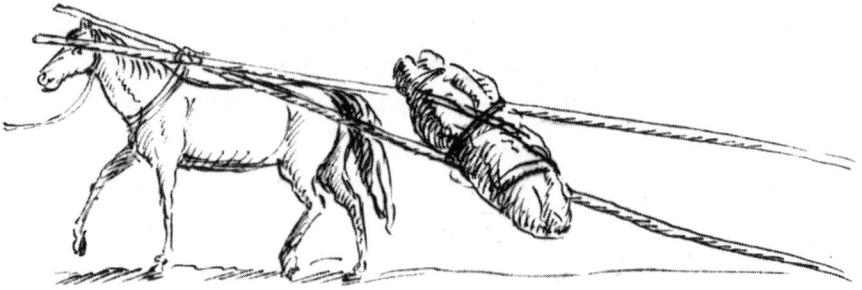

Fig. 9. Maximilian. Horse with travois transporting wrapped Piegan corpse. Ink. All manner of baggage and belongings were similarly transported on travois pulled by horses or dogs.

Today buffalo robes were packed, pressed and tied together into bales of ten pieces each. Cottonwood was stacked for the preparation of charcoal; [it] should be completely charred in six to eight days. We could not go [far] from the fort, since nothing good could be expected from the Blood Indians. Therefore our collections, except for the precious Indian curiosities, were sadly [curtailed].

18 August: The great Bear Chief, with his brother and friends, was in the fort very early. He wanted to go across the river, [to] a small band of Blood Indians, [and] shoot one of them to exact blood revenge. Perhaps then friendship could be restored among the Indians—or else the enmity would continue, and several more men would have to [die]. [However,] the Bear Chief hesitated and finally decided to stay here.

We went out onto the prairie, where I found sage *(Artemisia columbiensis)* in bloom for the first time. The yellow goldfinch and the finch with the striped head *(Fringilla grammaca),* as well as several *Muscicapa* and other small birds, were all [that we saw].

A Blackfoot Indian brought a horse and, in return for it, asked for a [uniform] and a postillion's hat, which he obtained; [it was] red and blue with silver braids. Bear Chief went about with a mustard jar, constantly begging for it to be filled with whiskey. One of his friends, to whom whiskey was given, embraced him and put a gulp of it into his mouth. This is the greatest demonstration of friendship one can show an Indian. Last year, when Mr. Mitchell had the entire Piegan band here, their principal chief, Middle Bull, was about to [leave with] his people. No one knew how to keep him, until an Indian suggested this. Mr. Mitchell took a small bottle of whiskey, went to [Middle Bull], and spewed it into the great man's mouth, whereupon he became affectionate, embraced him, and thought no longer of going away.

Indian women brought me a model of a leather tipi they had made for me; they got *rassade* (blue glass beads) for it.[1] I gave several bears' feet to one old woman for tanning. Since today was Sunday, the [fort's] people did not work. The young bears were more entertaining today than ever; they ran about very comically, especially [when] Indian boys teased and played with them; one would not be able to have fun [like that] with them much longer.

19 August: Mr. Mitchell had hides brought into the courtyard this morning for packing. One hundred pounds of beaver pelts make a pack. They have a machine in which folded pelts are [stacked]. Two heavy pieces of wood lie on top of them, on which [two men stand to] press the hides together. Buffalo hides [require] six to eight men [to] press [into] bales. We bought [four] bearskins, six wolf pelts, one wolverine, a species of marmot, and a lynx.

20 August: Several tipis close to the fort were taken down and moved into the woods near [the] Bear Chief. Yesterday and the day before, Mr. Bodmer drew the son of the old Kootenai, a handsome young Indian [called] Makúie-Póka (l'Enfant du Loup, [Wolf Child]). He was a very elegant, finely attired Indian, half Piegan, the tribe to which he considered himself to belong. The man with the big medicine pipe came, and some drawing was done. Bird had lunch with us, and we agreed that now was the most favorable time to shoot bighorn along the river, in the vicinity of the Stone Walls. Dreidoppel will probably leave tomorrow with a hunter [to] journey [there] by land. Bird told us much about the mountains and the Indians. Probably no one knows these people better than he, for he is a true Indian.

This afternoon there were between forty [and] fifty Indian [tipis close by]; from time to time we had sixty and more Indians in the fort at the same time, mostly women and children. In the evening it was a delightful sight when eight armed men drove the fort's horses home in a big herd at a trot or gallop. [This] cavalry arrived in a cloud of prairie dust.

21 August: At eight o'clock Dreidoppel and Papin, accompanied by a Piegan Indian, rode out to shoot some bighorn. They [were] prepared to stay out a night or two and took a packhorse. Papin had no great desire, so he said, to [participate in] this dangerous enterprise; if he were not obligated to the company, he would not have undertaken this ride for a hundred dollars.

I saw the shells, in their natural state, from which the Indians made their ear pendants. They are a *Dentalium,* probably from the [Pacific Ocean], beyond the mountains. An old man was drawn, Pioch-Kiáiu, [Distant Bear], who wore his hair tied together in a thick knot [on his forehead; see pl. 21].

The afternoon was very hot. Three to five Indians [were always] in our room. [I] constantly had to [light] their pipes; they were too lazy to get up.[2] The evening was very pleasant.

22 August: Bird was in the fort early; [he is] certainly a spy for the Hudson's Bay Company, [sent] to draw the Indians north, away from us. A chief sent word that they had killed twenty-eight buffalo; Mr. Mitchell should send packhorses [for] as much meat as he wanted. Unfortunately, the horses had all been put out to pasture, and there were none to be had.

Bird told me about the mountains [above] the sources of the Marias River, which are very high, [with] snow and ice in August. They are at least 150 miles away from the river's mouth. The valley woodlands are inhabited by the *orignal,* [moose] *(Cervus alces amer.),* and [deer]. One can comfortably ride there in ten to twelve days. [Bird] promised to send me his Ojibwe, [who] arrived at three o'clock, accompanied by a Piegan. He was a tall, good-looking, slender man, quite spirited. [He] spoke rapidly and loudly; with Deschamps' assistance I easily recorded his words. He promised to come again the next day and allow himself to be painted, for which he demanded a draught of whiskey. A crowd of Piegans listened to the words as they were pronounced and laughed at them. From [my] samples, one can see that many words, such as "Mississippi" and "squaw," were borrowed from this language.

It was very hot, even as late as five o'clock. The animals were panting for water. In our room the many Indians, who constantly demanded and smoked tobacco, made [it even warmer]. Dreidoppel and Papin returned late. They had killed a bighorn and had [its] skin. On the first day they had ridden until nine o'clock in the evening; they saw many antelope [and elk] but got none. [The next day] they rode farther downstream, shot this goat at six o'clock, and at nine o'clock [finally] stopped and ate; the Indian quickly butchered the animal and they roasted the meat. They suffered greatly from the heat.

23 August: At midmorning, Hotokáneheh, the man who owned the medicine pipe, went to Mr. Mitchell; Bird served as interpreter. Mr. Mitchell told him he should do everything in his power to help dissuade Bear Chief's family from taking revenge on innocent Blood Indians but only on the murderer's

family, if their honor necessitated [that]. [Hotokáneheh] should consider that it was disadvantageous not only for the whites of this fort but [also] for the Piegans, who could no longer hunt without exposing their wives and children to the gravest danger; [the Piegans] were much weaker than the Bloods and Blackfoot combined. He should remonstrate with Bear Chief about this matter. Hotokáneheh began to cry and said his family no longer had buffalo meat, and he had to try to live on venison. He could do nothing else but go up the Missouri to catch beaver; he hoped that they would be willing to lend him beaver traps, which he would faithfully pay for in pelts. Mr. Mitchell gave [Hotokáneheh] whiskey and tobacco and said he wished to give [him] the traps and whatever else he wanted. He knew that [Hotokáneheh] was a friend of the whites. He should go now and try to persuade [Bear Chief's] family.

Today Dreidoppel prepared the bighorn sheep, a task for which the great heat was not favorable—at twelve o'clock, 80°F in our room.

In the afternoon a man arrived with his wife and seven other Indians, who were greatly entertained by Mr. Bodmer's portraits. If they found a good likeness, they joyfully called out the name and clapped their hands. The young woman was very pretty and had a genuine Madonna-like countenance—beautiful eyes and fine features. Mr. Bodmer had the man informed that he wanted to draw [the man's] wife the next day; he finally agreed in return for red dye and blue glass beads.

Today an inventory was made of the goods, valued at about one thousand dollars, to [be taken on] an expedition to the Kootenais, which would depart in a few days. Tomorrow most of the Piegans [would] leave. The big band, as we learned today, was still very far away from here.

24 August: Clear weather, hot. At 7:30, 77°F. A guard called out that [wind-driven] fire was consuming the charcoal pile. Flames burst out and in a short time completely destroyed it; thus three or four days[' work] was completely lost. Bird and most of the Piegans had crossed to the other side of the river into the area recently selected [as] the site for the new fort. The Indian who was here yesterday with his wife brought her this morning. She had painted a few red stripes on her face and was sketched. Bear Chief, Nínoch-Kiáiu, came to Mr. Mitchell and announced that he was [leaving]. He was undoubtedly going where most of the Piegans and Bird went.

In the afternoon several Indians arrived from the distant Piegan [band] and told us their people would arrive in three days. They brought several beaver pelts to exchange. We again had numerous annoying visitors, attracted by the stuffing of [the] bighorn.

In the cool of the evening, we had a long conversation with Mr. Mitchell about the abuse of selling whiskey to the Indians, [which makes them] licentious [and] lazy, as well as dangerous. They neglect to sell the whites good hides and [other] products. The women, who know only too well that they will get nothing for their work—because the men buy whiskey and bring nothing substantial home—tan the hides only partially and poorly. The men neglect beaver trapping and become totally dissolute. In 1816 the government enacted [a] law forbidding the sale of whiskey to the Indians, and only so much was to be allowed into Indian country: [just enough] so that every man carrying on trade with the Indians (that is, working for the fur companies) had enough for his own needs, estimated at a half-pint a day of whiskey—but no drink for trade. This was recently changed, and no whiskey at all was to be imported.[3] The Indian agents (who are supposed to live among the Indians), as well as all military posts, were ordered to keep an eye on the importation of alcoholic beverages. But [the agents] not only do not live there, they [visit only] once a year [and] let everything go unpunished (some [agents] are related to principal men in the Fur Company). Yet the government pays them very well and every year, through them, gives the Indians substantial presents. If these gentlemen did their duty, the harmful use of whiskey among the Indians could largely be controlled. In the Fort McKenzie region, United States law [could] not be [effectively] introduced, for the Indians up here could obtain whiskey from the English. If they were not given any by the American Fur Company, trade [here] would totally turn to the English.

25–26 August: [On] Sunday I went with Dreidoppel [to collect plants on the prairie and Horse Island]; the mosquitoes were [terrible, and] we saw only a few birds. [On Monday] Marceau, our table attendant, [was feverish and had suffered] diarrhea for the [past] twenty-four hours. He had intense abdominal pains [and] cramps in his hands and feet, in short, an attack quite similar to cholera. He was given peppermint tea, put [in a] warm [bed], and massaged; soon he was better.

Toward evening Bird and a big, handsome Piegan arrived. His name was Mikotsótskina, [Red Horn]. He was the principal leader of war parties [and] had counted many coups. He was elegantly [attired]; on his chest [there were bits] of colored cloth, shiny buttons, glass beads, [and] a horizontal row of bear claws. He was lively [and] well built, [with] a friendly, good-natured expression. He had two white horses and rode [astride] a beautiful panther [skin, lined] with red cloth.

The evening was calm and pleasant, the moon nearly full. The hunters, Papin and Loretto, had shot an antelope and a deer. For days we had had nothing to eat but old, hard, dried buffalo meat and, at noon, Indian corn. Today an Indian sold [us] a beaver, the meat of which [we] ate this evening. It was tender and soft, though somewhat tasteless. Some of the Indians were suffering hunger. Mr. Mitchell gave them a large portion of the [old] dried meat, which the women and children eagerly contended for. The Indians who arrived today said that the big band, about two hundred [tipis], would arrive at the fort the day after tomorrow at the latest.

27 August: Last evening we were about to go to bed when we were invited to Mr. Mitchell's, because Mr. Culbertson, according to local custom, had married an Indian woman. He had paid goods worth one hundred dollars, and his Piegan wife had brought him a rifle; a horse was to follow. She was from White Buffalo's family.

Bear Chief, Nínoch-Kiáiu, was said to have [made] very ugly remarks [yesterday] about the fort and the whites. Bird was clearly inciting the Indians; he was certainly a spy for the Hudson's Bay Company, [set on] ruining the American Fur Company's Indian commerce. Yesterday an Indian woman [said] she had been told the Indians would demand double the usual price for their beaver, and if this were not given, they would kill all the whites. Even if such rumors were unfounded, they indicated a bad mood among the Indians. When the [expected] Piegan band arrived, we would be very weak, because tomorrow the expedition would leave for the Kootenais [with] two interpreters and several of [our] best men. We will retain only a few men who speak [just] a little Blackfoot and will often have difficulty making ourselves understood, especially when bartering.

Bird [asked] to buy a horse from Mr. Mitchell. He was told that a certain number of them were needed for the Kootenai expedition; these he could not have. But his choice always fell upon those [animals, and] therefore he was offended [and] resentful. Several new Indians arrived, including a jovial man who laughed loudly and with delight at the sight of [Bodmer's] portraits. Afterward he smoked with us. Mr. Bodmer's music box made a great impression on all who heard it. They regard this box as, next to the steamboat, one of the greatest medicines.

28 August: Today we had a serious alarm. There were about fifteen to twenty Piegan tipis near the fort—at the most, twenty to thirty battle-ready men, [who] had drunk much whiskey and [celebrated] all night. At daybreak, an Indian ran up and announced that enemy Assiniboines were advancing. Disorder prevailed everywhere. Most engagés had neither powder nor lead in sufficient quantity, nor did the Indians. When our men climbed onto the roofs of the buildings, where there was a [walkway] along the ramparts behind the palisades, they saw, on the hills behind the fort, everything red with Indians on foot and on horseback. All 580 of them quickly descended onto the plain and fell upon the Piegans in their tipis.[M1]

In a moment the Indians, frightened from their sleep, fled to the fort, [which] the Assiniboines surrounded. Many bullets struck the palisades, and arrows flew into the courtyard. The enemies were [at the] gate of the fort, [so] the interpreter Berger dragged [fleeing] women and children [to safety even as] they were being shot and thrust at from behind. Between the fort and the river, four women were shot to death; another [plus] three or four men were severely wounded, as [were] three or four children, who came into the fort pitifully injured. The back of White Buffalo's head had been badly grazed, and his brain seemed to be protruding into his hair. [One Blackfoot] had an arrow through his arm, another in his back, [plus] a lance wound and a shot in the groin. An old man was shot through the knee.

Upon the initial alarm Mr. Mitchell thought [that the] advancing [Indians] were coming in a large procession to trade and were firing in celebration, [so he] did not permit firing [in return]. Despite this, bursts of gunfire [came from] engagés and interpreters [at] every corner of the fort. When [most] Piegans were inside the [palisades], Mr. Mitchell called out to the right front blockhouse to fire a cannon [shot at] the enemy, but Piegans

---

M1 The 580 enemies included 100 Crees. They were led by the Assiniboine chief Minohánne (le Gaucher) [the Left-handed One]. Since then he has changed his name [to] Tatógan (Antelope). [Antelope is referred to later in Maximilian's journals as one of the "first chiefs" of the Assiniboines. The modern orthography for his first name is *Mína yuhána* 'Holds Knife'. Tableau 42, *Fort MacKenzie August 28th 1833* (*KBNAP*), Bodmer's action-packed re-creation of this attack for the *Reise*, has been both praised as a dramatic but realistic portrayal of intertribal warfare and criticized as a contrived artwork created in the artist's studio years after the event (Ewers, "Appreciation of Karl Bodmer's Pictures," 60; Ruud, *KBNAP*, 213).]

were still dispersed among them. As soon as the enemy received heavy fire from the fort, they withdrew somewhat; Piegans and whites followed them, firing [constantly].

We had been lying in our rooms fast asleep when Doucette stepped in, ran for his weapons, and shouted [over the sound of gunfire] that we had to fight. Just as we stepped into the courtyard, which was filled with horses and wailing women and children, several arrows wounded a trapper, Dupuis, in the foot, and his horse in the head. When we climbed onto the ramparts and took our positions, the Assiniboines had already been driven 200 paces [away]. Their fighters, many of them on horseback, withdrew more and more, finally retreating to the hills, where they concentrated in groups.

In the meantime there were pathetic scenes in the courtyard. White Buffalo, with his head wound, had such a fixed expression that I thought he would soon die, especially since he could not endure lying down. Later it turned out that he was still drunk from the previous night, and his women, screaming pitifully, gave him more whiskey—he was completely stone drunk. We [attempted] to bind up and attend the wounded, but there is no advising Indians. They shouted, gave whiskey to the sick ([which] raised their wound fever), rattled little bells, and shook their medicines. Outside the fort they had taken the scalp from [a] slain [enemy] and assaulted him with arrows, guns, clubs, and stones; the women and children vied with each other [in doing this]—they completely smashed certain parts of his body and cracked his head in two.[M2]

Riders had been sent to the big Piegan camp, and [reinforcements] were expected any moment. Nínoch-Kiáiu, Bird, and the remaining Piegans, [who were] camped farther upstream on the Missouri, had been attacked by another band of Assiniboines. Bird arrived about eight o'clock and demanded help from Mr. Mitchell. Hotokáneheh entered the fort and delivered a heated speech, whereby he reproached the whites for idly sitting around and not going out to do battle with the enemy. [Such] speeches irked Mr. Mitchell; he armed himself and rode out with several men and Indians toward [a skirmish between] about 150 or 200 Piegans [and] the

---

M2 The head of this dead Assiniboine, which I had hoped to acquire for [Professor] Blumenbach's collection, was completely destroyed. His lance and the plume from his head, however, I was fortunate [enough] to [acquire and take] down to Fort Union. [This observation, originally part of chapter 13, has been placed here for relevance.]

enemy, [who] were driven back to the Marias River, [where] they made a stand. Mr. Mitchell hurt his arm [when] his horse [was] shot high on its forequarters and fell down. The horse of an engagé, Bourbonnais, [was] shot through the neck; the rider dismounted and ran away. When he was close to the enemy, Mr. Mitchell shouted to the [Piegans, asking] why they now held back, since they had said the whites did not want to fight; now one could see who lacked courage.

Meanwhile, at the fort, more and more Piegans galloped in. Many stayed at the fort; [others] went chasing over the hills to the battle. Some were finely dressed in warrior attire: feathers hanging from their heads, medicines fastened on, bows and guns on their backs and in their hands. They whipped their horses and sang and shouted. [The Indians near the fort] believed they were safe now, [so] the wounded were carried to the tipis, [which] had been shredded and riddled by the enemy. A horse and several dogs lay dead. Old Pioch-Kiǎiu came to Mr. Bodmer, overjoyed, and told him that no bullets had hit him, undoubtedly [because] he had been sketched.

Mr. Mitchell returned after one o'clock. Many Piegans shook his hand, praised and saluted him as their friend and fellow warrior, and [offered] him horses as presents, which he did not accept. Altogether ten [Piegans were believed] to have been killed by the Assiniboines. Had the latter realized their advantage [and] occupied the high hills, they could have bombarded us terribly in the fort's courtyard. [Even so, everyone] agreed that the Assiniboines had shown far more courage than the Piegans.

In the afternoon more and more Piegans [arrived] on horseback; they approached like a caravan, and the dust from their horses rose from the prairie. In the afternoon the Indians sat in our room, where we gave them water for refreshment and let them smoke. Toward evening several men returned from the [Marias River], where the enemy was still being observed. By now the Piegans had gradually been reinforced [and] were as strong as the Assiniboines. They had shot several more of the latter but also had a few [of their own] wounded. We went into the tipis and bandaged five or six, had them washed, [and] cut off their hair around the head wounds. Instead of whiskey, [we] brought them sugar water, for they liked sugar very much. The whole courtyard was filled with Piegans, [some] finely [clothed]. One had an exceptionally beautiful feather ornament [like] a feather bonnet hanging down his back, which he had gotten from the Crows. [The warriors] announced [that] they would attack [the enemy] first thing in the morning. We thought the latter would not wait for morning but would withdraw during the night. The mutilated corpse in front of the fort had been burned. The fort, inside and all around, was filled with Piegans. One heard talk of nothing but the events of the day, everyone relating his deeds and [experiences].

When night fell, the Indians in the mess hall were given something to smoke; one of our pipes circulated among them, too. Although I lent it quite often, it was always returned. Mr. Bodmer's music box entertained them enormously; they stared at it in astonishment.

29 August: Piegans assailed us in our room very early. They had all slept in the open courtyard without blankets and had received nothing to eat, [so they] were sleepy and [hungry]. The Assiniboines had divided into three groups and withdrawn toward the Bears Paw [Mountains]; the [Piegans] had pursued the enemy and fired on them, but they had not responded—they were probably out of ammunition. They took several severely wounded and dead with them. Today we [expected to] learn more about the number of fatalities.

The fort was filled with Indians until eight o'clock. The principal chiefs [were] here during the night, and a chief of the Blackfoot (Siksikas), la Corne Basse, Ihkas-kinne, [Low Horn], was drawn by Mr. Bodmer today. He was a big, strong man with a deep voice. Most of the Piegans left [but] said they would set up camp at the fort today or tomorrow to begin trading.

Concerning the aforementioned Ihkas-kinne, Mr. Mitchell told me [about a] time when all the fort's horses had been stolen, undoubtedly by Blackfoot or Blood Indians. This man set to work, [found the horses,] and brought them all back except one. His outfit [then was] covered with pieces of mirror glass. Now, instead of mirrors on his war attire, he had fastened numerous bits of mother-of-pearl from mussels; [see pl. 19].

A goodly number of Blackfoot (Siksikas) had been present at the battle yesterday. The Indians had probably heard [what] was being said about them not wanting to attack. Therefore they told Mr. Mitchell their horses had been too tired, because they had ridden too far from their camp to the battle. This excuse was, in part, justified; but why did they not dismount and fight on foot? After all, the Assiniboines were mostly on foot. One heard the latter calling out to one another to advance and attack, and they did, something that the Blackfoot did not dare do.

This afternoon Bird left in great anger, because Mr. Mitchell did not want to sell him a certain horse. His pernicious influence [was] felt everywhere. An Indian told Mr. Mitchell in confidence that Bird had sent all the chiefs gifts of tobacco and strongly urged them not to sell their beaver here but to the English instead. Mr. Mitchell lectured [the informer at length] and [asked] if they [understood] that up north they would receive worse prices—they would go a long way for nothing. The Americans had sincere intentions; the Indians had seen that they did not even shun fighting beside them against the enemy. They should have confidence and consider that he certainly would not stay [here] if they sold even part of their furs up north. He would break off trading with them entirely, and then they would have to travel the long road north [and] get bad prices, because if no competition [came] from the Americans, the English naturally would pay even less. The chief responded [that] after the battle they had all agreed among themselves, seeing the whites fighting beside them, that they would not go north and [would] sell all their beaver pelts here. Before he had become offended, Bird told Mr. Mitchell, "The Indians have [decided] to sell only some of their beaver here, [enough] to obtain some whiskey. The principal portion they intended to sell up north to the Hudson's Bay traders." Therefore [Mr. Mitchell] should not give them whiskey, [Bird argued, and] he advised [Mr. Mitchell] not to pay as much [as usual] for the beaver. Mr. Mitchell easily saw through this man's web of lies. He was a bad man, devoted to the English.

30 August: The expedition to the Kootenais left at 7:30. It consisted of Doucette [and] Sandoval (both spoke Blackfoot) [and seven others], as well as nine packhorses with goods and bedding. They will [first] follow the Teton River and then go straight up toward the mountains in a northerly direction. If the Kootenais are in their usual territory, [the expedition] would get there in twelve days, but [they might] have to search for [the Kootenais]. [The leaders of the expedition] believe they will not return until winter. They were given instructions to bring back white mountain goat skins.

At nine o'clock I saw Piegans in large numbers approaching across the prairie. Toward noon a great many Indians arrived on horseback, and many [tipis] were pitched. Several [important] men came into the fort and asked when they could have whiskey. Mr. Mitchell was indisposed [and so] told them he could not begin trading today; they would not be admitted until tomorrow. Although only a few Indians were allowed into the fort today, there were always ten to twelve inside, and outside the gate, [many more].

In the afternoon Mr. Bodmer drew several Indians, including an old man with a very aquiline nose, who wore a round felt hat with colorful plumes. His name was Homachséh-Kakatóhs (la Grande Étoile), [Big Star]. After he was drawn and given tobacco, he stationed himself in the courtyard, and with nobility and dignity delivered a long speech, wherein, among other things, he stated that the chief from down below (Mr. McKenzie) should now treat [the Blackfoot] well [and] bring them good meat so that they would be happy, have a full belly, etc.

Toward evening a few chiefs came into the fort, including old Middle Bull and also Ihkas-kinne, [who made] a rather long speech. He [said, among other things, that he] did not have anything to trade. He had just returned from an expedition against the Crows, where they had lost two men. Without shoes, and with great exertion and deprivation, they had crossed vast stretches of prairie, [and] their feet were sore. He had nevertheless taken part in the battle, and no one had received anything. Mr. Mitchell responded that he would give the chiefs whiskey tomorrow. He felt [that] he had done enough, since he had distributed much powder and bullets and had [protected] people in the fort.

31 August: The Indian camp looked very picturesque today. It stood about 300 paces from the fort, the tipis close together in case of enemy attack (small bands [of] Assiniboines remained in the vicinity). At nine o'clock, when the cannon was fired as a signal for the Indians [to enter the fort for trading], about twenty-four Piegan chiefs and preeminent warriors, including one Blackfoot, came walking with slow steps from the camp; all the other men stayed behind. Women and children in large numbers assembled as spectators around the fort. Mr. Mitchell went to meet the chiefs. At that moment, on the hills beyond the Missouri, [we saw] a band of Blood Indians; they wanted to camp near the fort. But [then] Nínoch-Kiáiu appeared and declared that if these Indians came, he would shoot at them, [so] they were told [to stay away].

The Piegan chiefs, handsomely attired, entered in twos and threes and [were] led into the mess hall, where they smoked and drank whiskey. Their faces were painted red or with bluish metallic ore. They had very nice leather shirts, some decorated with many [strips] of ermine. Several—among others, old Middle Bull—were in Mr. Mitchell's room. Middle Bull spoke for a long time and said that it must not be believed [that] they were taking their furs north. It would be in their best interest to remain on good terms with the fort here, for the other was much too far away. If some talked about going to Hudson's Bay Company, these were merely attempts to obtain cheaper goods.

Old Middle Bull's face was thoughtful and serious. He was not large, [but] stocky. His [yellowish-white] leather shirt was the most beautiful of all. It was embroidered on the sleeves with blue flowers. On the right sleeve, long fringes of ermine fur adorned with little red feathers; on the left, long strands of black hair. Over his shoulders he wore a cape of otter fur and ermine. All the chiefs demanded whiskey, and each was to have a keg. They were seldom satisfied and [always] wanted more. Mr. Mitchell distributed over two barrels before trading began.

At about noon, [they] tried to get the chiefs out gradually. A [fight] broke out at the gate: an Indian struck a gatekeeper, who defended himself, and a knife was drawn. Fortunately, [a chief] and another Indian restored order by pushing the [offender] out. [After] lunch, singing, screaming, and scuffling at the gate [demonstrated] the effects of the whiskey on the Indians. Shots were fired near the fort; Piegans shot at Blood Indians, who [fired back]. Mr. Mitchell placed armed guards at the gate. The Blood Indians, on the tall bank opposite [us], could shoot into the fort. We were trapped inside like prisoners. Outside, a raging horde. Between the two gates the Indians were allowed passage into the room where trading was carried on, and there was continual pushing, exchanges of words, and fighting. Great patience is required to be in charge of such a post. [However], one seldom saw [violent] cases of intoxication among the Indians; they mostly became maudlin when drunk.

Toward evening the Blood Indians withdrew [and] camped somewhat farther away. The trading had [so far] proceeded rather calmly. The Indians all exchanged their beaver for whiskey. Several good Indians supported the gate [guards] and averted many quarrels. By about eight o'clock it [was] quiet. Probably most of the Indians were drunk. Beautiful, moonlit night.

1 September: Trade began again. Early in the morning I saw the Blood Indian chief's wife in the fort; she deplored the disagreements. Negotiations had [begun] with the Piegans to pay off the blood debt with gifts; perhaps they will be reconciled. The Blackfoot chief la Corne Basse [announced] that he and his people would hold themselves somewhat apart from the Piegans.

Many Indians came into the fort, and we exchanged various objects with them. I instructed a man to paint the recent battle on an elk hide. Several Sarcee Indians [brought news] that their entire band would soon [arrive] to sell their beaver.

This morning the Indians brought only a few beaver and even fewer buffalo robes [to trade]; [instead,] mostly large amounts of meat and several horses. The Indian from whom I bought the feather bonnet invited Mr. Bodmer into his tipi, where he was treated to three different kinds of meat. In the afternoon [this Indian] came and visited us. He was a pleasant person, and his attire [was] very elegant. He had received beautiful articles of clothing as gifts at [the] conclusion of peace with the Crows. Middle Bull came in poor, plain apparel. After he had been shown various pictures I asked him to let himself be drawn; to encourage him, I had someone tell him that it was striking that those we had drawn had not been killed or wounded. He was pleased to hear this and promised to come soon.

Toward evening the Piegan camp [appeared] greatly diminished; [after] finishing their trading, many had left to camp farther upstream along the Missouri or the Teton River, where there was forage for their horses. [We still saw] Piegans firing their guns at the charred [corpse] of the slain Assiniboine; women and children struck the [remains] with wood or stones. Their bitterness toward enemies has no bounds.

2 September: About seven o'clock we heard shooting, and Kutonápi's band advanced, about sixty to seventy men strong, three chiefs or principal men at their head. Mr. Mitchell took the latter into his room and gave them whiskey. While we were having breakfast, old Tátsicki-Stomíck, [Middle Bull], sat near us and [was given] coffee and meat. Later Bodmer drew him [and also] Nínoch-Kiáiu; [he] portrayed [both] very well.

In the meantime, six chiefs were with Mr. Mitchell, all [wearing new] red uniform overcoats with silver or gold braid, round red or black felt hats with colorful plumes, red trousers trimmed with little bells, [bright] calico shirts, [and] round mirrors hanging around their necks. They allowed themselves be dressed, like children, and it was most comical when attempts were made to press their enormous masses of long hair into hats that were sometimes too tight. According to company prices, one [such] outfit cost ninety dollars. Mr. Mitchell [told the chiefs] that they could see how the company [strove] to please them. He had still [more] goods [to give] if, this winter, after a good hunt, they traded their beaver here.

Trading continued on a small scale. Toward evening the Indians near the fort were very troublesome. Several attempted to shoot at the whites on the stockade and [had to be] restrained from doing so by others. They had broken in at various places and stolen [things]. In the rear blockhouse, they had taken a chest and attempted to steal a gun. Mr. Mitchell had the guns loaded with ball and ordered the sentry to keep a close lookout and to shoot immediately [if] any Indian climbed the stockade. He suggested to the chiefs that they might want to make their young men aware of this.

The Blood Indians [sent a message] that they wanted to come tomorrow to trade; Mr. Mitchell advised against this because Nínoch-Kiáiu was still in the vicinity, [and he said] they [should] come the day after tomorrow. After six o'clock all the Indians vanished, and guards were posted on the roofs with loaded guns.

3 September: In the morning, the Blood Indians shouted across the river that many Blackfoot were approaching. Kutonápi and a large group of Indians were already in the fort, [as was] Nínoch-Kiáiu, [who] again demanded whiskey. At 8:30 we heard shooting, and a Siksika war party of twenty to thirty men advanced. Several of the principal warriors were allowed into the fort. They told us that there were two powerful Blackfoot (Siksika) war parties on the move [but] the largest part of this nation was still up north. I bought a Piegan shirt decorated with hair and a beautiful cap with horns and ermine strands [that had been presented to the Piegans by] the Crows. An Indian gave Mr. Mitchell a fine leather shirt. Several offered horses for sale. The fort was full of Piegans and Siksikas, and [later], a Blood chief, regarded as a good Indian, also arrived.

At 5:30 [we] heard shooting and, on the hills behind the fort, saw a powerful Blackfoot war party advancing. They fired and then halted. There were 250 of them. They were turned away and not allowed in, because they had nothing to trade. The Blackfoot (Siksikas) and the Blood Indians catch few beaver and prepare few robes, because [they] are always at war. Of the three tribes, the Piegans catch the most beaver.

The evening was cool. Mr. Bodmer had guard duty from nine to eleven o'clock, Dreidoppel, toward morning, the most dangerous time for an Indian attack. Three men were always on guard duty and were relieved three times.

4 September: At 9:30 the band of Blood Indians moved close to the fort. The chiefs—la Dépouille de Boeuf^{M3} and a medicine man and chief of the same band, Pehtónista, [He Who Is Called the Eagle]—entered and sat down in the mess hall, where they were given whiskey and something to smoke. Soon the two Blackfoot war party leaders arrived. The first of [them] was a tall, handsome man, le Collier du Loup [or] Makúie-Kinn. Old Dépouille de Boeuf was a very good man who saved Mr. Mitchell's life last year when an Indian [tried] to kill him with his lance. He was the chief of a small band of Blood Indians that had been living near the Piegans for some time, and he wished to remain loyal to this fort. On his chest the chief wore a medal from President Jefferson. His face had a very pleasant, calm expression. He [regretted that] his son had shot young Martin to death in the fort and said, when Mr. Mitchell had him questioned about this matter, that it happened by accident and certainly was not deliberate. He said he [was sorry] that, because of Nínoch-Kiáiu's [anger], he could view the fort only from a distance. This evening he would strike camp and move to the Teton [to avoid this] quarrel with the Piegans. [These Bloods] did not have more than seventeen beaver and no robes to trade. They asked to have everything [the post] was willing to give them delivered today, since they would be leaving.

Deschamps and [two others] were ordered [to leave] tonight, as soon as the waning moon had risen, [and] take eleven or twelve horses from here down to Fort Union. They were to find their way on the [opposite] riverbank downstream along the Missouri. There was a rumor circulating that the Indians had plans [to steal] our horses. Perhaps this way one could forestall them. As long as [Indians] were nearby, we could not put the horses out to pasture, and there was practically no more hay.

5 September: [After Deschamps's departure, we had only] nine horses remaining, [and our forces were] greatly reduced—apart from us three Germans, they consisted of [just fifty-five men].

At 9:45 three Gros Ventres des Prairies arrived, declaring that they had eaten nothing in three days. They were allowed in; they smoked and rested in the mess hall and were given [food]. They were very crude. Naked down to the leggins and breechcloths, [they] wore only plain buffalo robes—they

---

M3 Stomíck-Sosáck. [This man, whom Maximilian referred to as Bull's Hide (la Dépouille de Boeuf), was more commonly known as Bull's Back Fat; see pl. 20 for Bodmer's portrait of this man.]

were poorly dressed because they were returning from a raid. We showed them portraits of several Gros Ventres [des Prairies], whom they seemed to recognize, since they were delighted and clapped their hands, but we could not understand what they said. Their language was very difficult—indistinct, short, barely audible sounds—and there was no interpreter. [Many Gros Ventres] spoke Blackfoot, but these three men did not know it very well.

Today, for the first time [in] a long while, the gates were open and one could go out. During the night there were just two men on guard duty.

6 September: Men were sent into the forest to cut wood for our mackinaw boat. We had decided not to travel to the falls of the Missouri [or the Rocky Mountains] but to proceed down to Fort Union as soon as our boat [could be] finished.[4] I deeply regretted not being able to see the falls, but when asked about our safety on such a journey, [Middle Bull,] the principal Piegan chief, told Mr. Mitchell that although the Piegans would do us no harm, he could not vouch for the Bloods and Blackfoot. In any case our horses would be in great danger, and [they] belonged to the company; I would have to pay for them. Besides, I had no interpreter, [and] I would not be able to stay there long (and thus could not make natural history collections or observations), [so] I decided to ask Mr. Mitchell to expedite the building of [a] mackinaw boat. He immediately took the necessary measures.

[We might] be attacked again by the Assiniboines any day, probably a more serious attack, so we were unable to go very far afield. We had learned as much as possible about the Indians of this region and had succeeded in making an interesting collection of portraits and drawings of them. We could not stay here all winter long, and if we [delayed] our return downriver, [it] would be cold and unpleasant. [The voyage would be] dangerous, but we planned to [travel by night] to evade our enemies, the Assiniboines. Weighing all these considerations, we hastened our departure as much as possible.

Since our food supplies were [inadequate], Mr. Mitchell sent a good hunter, Loretto, with a man and packhorses to get fresh meat. For a long time we had had nothing other than old, tough, dried meat, morning, noon, and night: in the morning, coffee with it and some bread; in the evening, tea with some bread; and at noon, corn boiled in the meat broth. But now this, too, was all gone, and we had nothing but hard meat. [Such a] way of life cannot be beneficial to one's health for very long—this [conviction] greatly contributed to our desire to leave.

In the afternoon Mr. Bodmer drew Marceau's wife, a Shoshone woman with a strikingly black color; she seemed to have a liver ailment. On the prairie I saw an uncountable number of grasshoppers *(Gryllus),* some engaged in mating. They were said to have been especially abundant this year; the whole earth seemed alive with them.

7 September: In the morning they worked on the ribs of our mackinaw boat; [it would be ready in a week].

At ten o'clock we saw several Indians over on the high bank. They soon came down to the river, and we discovered that they were Gros Ventres des Prairies: six men and several women, boys, and girls. They announced that fifty tipis of their people would be arriving shortly. An hour later several more arrived, their teeth chattering from the cold (they were very lightly dressed). At four o'clock about sixty men approached, perhaps twenty of them on horseback. Three hundred paces from the fort, they halted, dismounted, and gathered in front of their horses. Mr. Mitchell and the interpreter Berger went toward them and received a large, bony sorrel with only one eye as a present. In their poor traveling apparel, they followed us toward the fort, where the chiefs, four or five in number, were admitted and welcomed. The warriors remained at the gate. The chiefs smoked their pipes in the mess hall. [These visitors would] return today to their not-very-distant tipis, which would be pitched tomorrow nearer the fort. Several of the men were sick; they implored us to give them medicine. One had a severe venereal disease, another's eyes were badly inflamed, and both were most importunate, kissing and embracing us. Mr. Culbertson washed the eyes of one of them with lead acetate [and was given] a pair of leggins.

8 September: The fort filled up early with Gros Ventres, especially women and children. A band with about twenty-four horses arrived first, mostly pack-horses. The lodges were not yet here, and it was possible they would not come at all, because there was nothing for the horses to graze on. These Indians were badly prepared for trading. They had almost nothing other than some clothing to barter, not even meat, [of which] our stock was nearing an end; soon we would not even have any more jerky.

In the afternoon Mr. Bodmer went to the hills to draw the Bears Paw [Mountains]; Dreidoppel went along as his escort.[5] Although the Indians had [little] to sell, they remained all day, like flies. Indeed, one had to keep his door shut if he did not want to be overwhelmed by visitors [begging] for tobacco or sugar or the like. At six o'clock [our] hunters returned [but with no] buffalo meat.

9 September: Mr. Bodmer and I went to the hills behind the fort. By nine o'clock the heat was great in the arid prairie. When Mr. Bodmer opened his parasol and took a seat beneath it [to begin sketching the landscape], I went to the highest point of the prairie and soon saw a long line of Indians riding toward us. Because I did not know whether they were friends or enemies, we packed up our belongings and [returned] to the fort. Upon our arrival here, thirty men were just leaving to begin work on the new fort [upstream on] the Missouri. They had loaded their packs and tools on small, two-wheeled wagons. [They] took all our horses with them; [there was] no more forage here [for them]. This detachment would be away all week. In the afternoon great progress was made on our boat: the bottom was finished and all the ribs set up.

At four o'clock Loretto announced that he had seen a large group of Indians in the northeast along the right riverbank. If they were not Gros Ventres, then they must be a Crow war party. I went with Mr. Mitchell and two armed men [to] the hills behind the fort. We took a telescope with us. The Indians were no longer to be seen, [so] we returned to the fort. Because so many [unidentified] Indians had been sighted, the night guard was augmented with officers. We did not have more than twenty-eight men in the fort. [Then] a mounted Indian appeared at the gate, sent by the Gros Ventres to [say] that they had shot thirty buffalo and [would] give us as much meat as we desired.

10 September: I went with Mr. Bodmer to the hills, where [he resumed his] drawing, [while I] roamed over the parched prairie. I saw small flights of the [horned] lark (*Alauda alpestris* or *montana*) [and] shot one; its neck was a pale mixture of colors. Several Syngenesia and other plants with primarily yellow flowers were still blooming. It was very warm; at twelve o'clock, 66°F.

After lunch Mr. Mitchell [visited] the workers at the new fort, where he found a hundred pickets cut and the [site] marked out. The men were pleasantly situated in a beautiful forest [and] had built a small [fortified] shelter for the horses and themselves, in the event of an Indian attack. At two o'clock seven or eight Gros Ventres arrived with eighteen horses loaded with meat, for which they took whiskey, knives, and other articles.

11 September: The boat was finished and caulked today. The carpenter, Saucier, was making four new oars for it. I had someone show me a beaver trap, a spring

trap with two springs. [A] trap is laid in the water [with] willow branches on both sides, so that the beaver must go over [it] to reach the [bait] placed on a piece of wood. Similar, [smaller] traps are laid for muskrats.

12 September: They intended to launch [our new boat] in the river before noon. I went into the old cottonwoods below the fort and found a flight of magpies, which have a completely different call from that of the European ones. [Several colorful aster-like plants were in bloom;] *Artemisia columbiensis* had not yet opened its flowers. In the afternoon Mr. Bodmer went out again to draw, with Pierrot as a guard. Mr. Mitchell and I decided on the things we would need for [our] journey: two cooking pots, two metal plates from which to eat, forks and spoons, a coffeepot, three metal containers for drinking, 120 bullets and three pounds of powder for the crew, six flintstones, one-half gallon of alcohol, four pounds of salt, a quarter pound of pepper, four pounds of coffee, and eight pounds of sugar—a [total] value of fifty-seven dollars. The boat cost seventy-five dollars.[6]

13 September: Saucier worked on the bear crates. At seven o'clock several handsome, well-dressed Gros Ventres arrived with meat to sell. They said a Crow war party was near. Today I settled my account with Mr. Mitchell. [We were] packed. The boat [was ready], the rudder and other oars in place. The two bears were put into their crates; the small one went in willingly, the male with great resistance. Mr. Bodmer, while he was [out] drawing, had seen the smoke of an Indian camp rising not far away. The crew Mr. Mitchell picked [for] my boat were Henry Morrin (helmsman), Beauchamp, Urbin, and Thiébault. Night cool.

XIII

A Few Words Regarding the Blackfoot Indians,

[as well as the] Gros Ventres des Prairies

and Kootenais

The Blackfoot are a numerous nation divided into three tribes: the Piegans (usually called Piegans—they themselves say Piëkans); the Blood Indians,[MI] Kähnä (Kaénna); and the actual Blackfoot (Siksikas). The name Blackfoot, [however,] is applied generally to all of them by other nations. All together they can muster five to six thousand warriors and number about eighteen to twenty thousand, if one [conservatively] estimates three women, children, and old men per warrior. They live in and [near] the Rocky Mountains, [although] the Piegans [are] now down as far as the Marias River. [No explorer or scientist has yet provided accurate information about them.]

They trade with the English forts of the Hudson's Bay Company; sometimes with the American Fur Company, along the upper Missouri near its falls; and with the Spaniards near Santa Fe (as Spanish woolen blankets [and] crosses attest). Guns, rifles, compasses, and other objects [are] taken from slain whites. They are very dangerous to individual whites hunting and trapping beaver in the mountains; they usually kill and scalp them. In the vicinity of the fort, [these Indians do] keep the peace, especially the Piegans, [who] behave well there and are friendly toward whites. The Blood

---

[MI] This name has the following origin: before the Piegans and the [Blood Indians] divided into special bands, there were five or six tipis of [either] Kootenais or Sarcees encamped in the vicinity. There was talk of killing all of [them], which the Piegans voted against. But during the night [some men] attacked [the camp], killed everyone, took scalps *(chevelures),* dyed their faces and hands with the blood, and returned. A quarrel arose; the Indians separated, and the murderers had this name, [Blood,] imposed upon them, which they bear to the present day. They have always displayed a more bloodthirsty and rapacious character than the Piegans. [The modern orthography for the Blood, or Kaénna, Indians is *Káínaa;* for the Siksikas, *Siksiká.*]

Indians and Blackfoot, [however,] are trusted nowhere; they are masters at stealing horses, even near the fort.

In external appearance the Blackfoot do not differ significantly from other Indians of the upper Missouri. They [have] strong, well-built men and very pretty girls and young women. Some of the men are stocky and broad-shouldered, but more are slender and often [5 feet] 9 to 10 inches tall, Prussian measure. One Indian I measured was 5 feet 10 inches 2 lines tall, Paris measure (Mr. Kipp once measured a Blood Indian at 6 feet 11 inches, English measure). Their bodies are often strong and muscular; many have slender arms and legs; their calves are frequently leaner than those of the whites; hands and feet [are] mostly small [and] somewhat blackish brown with very prominent veins.

Their facial features are generally those of the other North American [Indians], hair long [and] coal-black. The beard and other [unwanted] hair growth is carefully pulled out, for which purpose they now mostly make use of a twisted wire or a piece of metal bent together. One sees no bald old persons, but [there are] many with gray hair. The color of these Indians is usually a beautiful reddish brown, often actually copper red. Children always have fat bellies and slender limbs, often a big navel.

The Blackfoot do not disfigure their bodies. Like all tribes along the Missouri, they do not perforate their nose and lips (except a tribe in the Rocky Mountains, the [Nez Perce]; they pierce their noses). They do have one or more small holes in their ears, in which they wear ornaments—strings of glass beads alternated with long, white shell cylinders [made from] *Dentalium* that they obtain from beyond the Rocky Mountains. Many do not wear anything in their ears, [which their] long, thick hair usually hides. I saw no tattoos, [but] many have parallel, scarred-over incisions on their arms, and most of them lack one or several finger joints (more on this below).

They paint their faces vermilion. The cinnabar (vermilion) that they get by trading [with] the whites is rubbed on with fat [so that] it shines. [Some] paint merely their eye rims and a few stripes on their faces. Others paint the latter yellow with clay. Still others paint their faces red, [then] the forehead and a stripe down over the nose or chin blue [with a shiny metallic earthen pigment] from the Rocky Mountains, [or they] paint their faces black, occasionally [with vermilion] eyelids and stripes [on] the black color. Women and children paint their entire faces red. Red paint is very expensive for them; the company sells a pound of vermilion in its stores for ten dollars, or 25 Rhenish florins.

Their hair hangs straight down, unadorned, often in disorderly fashion. Young people, who are more concerned with elegance, part it regularly and comb it smooth. A small white seashell is often fastened to a strand of hair on each side at the temples. Others wear a braid of hair wrapped with iron or brass wire on the left [or] both sides of their foreheads. A very few have the ornament observed among the Mandans and Hidatsas: [hairbows made of] two white bone or shell plates joined in the middle with yellow wire and blue glass beads and fastened on both sides above the forehead. Outstanding warriors [wear], on the backs of their heads, a tuft of owl or [other] raptor feathers, [or] occasionally weasel skins *(Mustela erminea)*, decorated with little bells, red strips of cloth, etc. Others tie their hair in back in a long braid, though [this is done] infrequently. Many, especially medicine men, wear it in the Mandan and Hidatsa style, distributed around [their heads] in thick braids, [which they] usually [bunch] together with a leather strap into a long, thick knot jutting out over their foreheads (see Mr. Bodmer's drawings).[1] Some have a smooth, flat, bluntly cut tuft of hair hanging down in the middle of their foreheads, down to the eyes or the tip of the nose. Many have a big grizzly bear claw fastened to their hair. Some wear a necklace woven of an aromatic variety of grass. [Others have] glass beads, for which they pay three or four dollars a pound and prize highly (especially women). Undoubtedly the finest necklace is that made of bear claws, seen only rarely among the Piegans, more frequently among the Crees and Assiniboines, and most frequently among the Crows, Mandans, and Hidatsas, because they are the most elegant.

They wear many brass rings on their hands, often on all five fingers, four or five on each one, [but] occasionally only one or two on the entire hand. They get them by the dozen from traders. They usually let their fingernails grow long, at least the thumbnail, [which] often [looks] like a claw.

Blackfoot [men's clothing] is prepared from tanned leather. The leather shirt [has] sleeves [with] long fringes hanging along the outer seam; long [locks] of human and other hair [are] often neatly stitched [to those seams] with [decorative] porcupine quills. [There is] usually a flap hanging down in back and in front at the neck, often lined with red cloth [and] decorated with fringes or with stripes of yellow or multicolored porcupine quills or sky-blue glass beads. [Sometimes the fringes are all] thin, pendant [strips] of white ermine fur; I saw [this] on several chiefs, but [such ornamentation] is very valuable and only seldom found—one can imagine how many small animals would be required. New leather shirts are usually a yellowish white color. [After being] worn a long time, they [can become] smoky and dirty [and are] often painted reddish brown. Some can be seen with one or two round porcupine [quill–embroidered] rosettes on the chest, but this is rare and does not appear to be genuine Blackfoot fashion.

As with the other Indian tribes, their leggins are trimmed with fringes of leather or human hair along the outer seam. The shoes of elk or buffalo leather are beautifully embroidered with porcupine quills; each shoe has a different primary color for its ornamentation—if one is yellow, the other is white. Farther downstream along the Missouri, the colors and designs of both shoes are the same.

A major [article of clothing] is the buffalo robe, usually painted, but less artistically than among some other nations. [They] usually have parallel black lines painted on the tanned side, with a few alternating figures painted black, yellowish red, and green, a kind of hieroglyphs representing their deeds in war (capture of prisoners, weapons, horses), horse stealing, scalps taken, wounds, and flowing blood. Such robes often have a transverse band, beautifully embroidered with porcupine quills and round rosettes, which divides a robe into two equal sections. Hides painted with hieroglyphs are found among all Missouri Indians; the most beautiful paintings [are] found among the Crows, Mandans, and Hidatsas. Such robes can be expensive; in the company's stores, they [may cost] six to ten dollars.

Buffalo blankets or robes are worn with the hair facing outward in summer, inward during winter. They wrap themselves in the ancient Roman manner, with the right shoulder and arm free. They go about clothed in the same manner in winter and summer, almost without any difference. One [might] say that in winter they were far too scantily clad, in the heat too warmly, but custom and acquired hardiness have [enabled] them to disregard that.

Women's garb consists, as among all Missouri Indians, of a long garment of tanned leather that reaches down nearly to their feet. It is tied around the waist with a strap or broad leather belt [and] is often decorated with many rows of elk teeth, shiny buttons, etc. [This] dress has short, wide fringed sleeves, [leaving] the lower arms mostly bare. The hem is fringed and scalloped. They decorate their festive clothing with dyed porcupine quills or wide bands of sky-blue and white glass beads *(rassade)*. Women are especially fond of [the latter]. Their taste in the [contrast] of colors is very good; they like to wear red in their black hair and prefer white or sky-blue and yellow on their brown skin. The women sew all these articles of clothing very skillfully. The men only make weapons and smoking equipment.

Blackfoot [tipis resemble those] of all the nomadic hunting peoples of the Missouri and the flat prairies of interior North America. The tipis last only a year and are made of tanned buffalo hides; initially they are nice and white, [but they] later [become] brownish from smoke [and] finally parchmentlike and transparent. Hence [it is] very light [on the inside]. Decorated tipis—painted and marked with figures of animals, men, and the like—are rarely seen; usually [only] a few chiefs have such tipis. Tipis are always surrounded by packs of big, wolflike dogs. [The Blackfoot] do not eat [their dogs], as the Dacotas do, but use [them] only as pack animals and for hauling.

Around the tipis the travois are placed upright [into] small, conelike [frameworks], like tipis, except they are not covered with leather. On [these frames] they suspend their shields, travel bags, horse gear, etc., [and] also—high up on strings so that hungry dogs cannot reach it—the thinly sliced meat of slain animals [to dry]. The medicine bag or magical apparatus is often hung or fastened on a special pole or above the door of the house. Household utensils consist of buffalo robes and [sometimes] woolen blankets for sleeping; various kinds of painted parchment bags, some crescent shaped [and] trimmed with leather fringes; wooden bowls, bighorn spoons, horn drinking vessels, pots, and occasionally metal containers, which they buy from the Fur Company, and other small items. In the middle of the tipi, a small fire burns inside a circle of piled-up stones.

One must also include horse gear among the household [goods]. The saddle consists of two broad, flat boards, placed at an angle against each other, that rest along the sides of the horse's back; hides [are laid over and] under the saddle; at night these [skins] serve as the Indian's bed. For luxury and pomp, the Blackfoot have nice caparisons, [for which] they love nothing more than a panther's hide, which they generally must get by barter from the mountains. Since such animals are already rather rare, they often pay a high price for a hide: a good horse, or even several. The panther hide is [lined] underneath with red cloth; the legs and the long, dangling tail form a broad fringe all around (see the illustration of the

Piegan on horseback, [Vignette XIX in the *Reise*]).

For men the pipe is a major article. Those they make themselves are not as beautiful as the red ones of the Dacotas, which the Blackfoot acquire by exchange and prize highly. Genuine Blackfoot pipes are made from a green or blackish nephrite [from] the Rocky Mountains. [Each has] a simple, smooth stem, 2 to 2½ feet long, of yellowish wood. The bowl is often pear- or urn-shaped. Among all the North American [Indians], the most beautiful pipes are those called *calumets* by the French: the medicine pipes, richly ornamented with woodpecker beaks [and red heads] and underneath with a fan of raptor feathers [and] long strands of horsehair dyed red, yellow, or green. These pipes are used for important occasions, especially at peace treaties, hence the name peace pipe. Blackfoot tobacco comes from a plant [that] grows in this region, called *sakkakomi* by the French and kócksinn by the Blackfoot.[2]

If one visits a Piegan in his tipi, one sits down silently, without ceremony, beside him; soon he will reach for his pipe, light it, and pass it to the left. [Each person] takes only a few puffs before passing the pipe to his neighbor. The last smoker in a row hands [the pipe] over to the person sitting opposite, and it goes to the left again. Before smoking, however, wooden bowls with food are usually placed before the guests; the [host] Indians eat only after [the guests] have finished.

As with most Missouri Indians, the Blackfoot get their nourishment from the yield of their hunting. They pursue buffalo on horseback [and] many are killed at once—sometimes forty, fifty, or more. They shoot with guns or bows and arrows. [They] often eat the raw kidneys and liver immediately, [then] cut the meat into narrow strips and dry it to preserve it and take it with them. They tan the hides of cows (bull [hides] are too thick) very well, [using] the well-known Indian method, and sell them to the whites or use them for clothing, tipis, blankets, bags, and straps. During the winter they make big "parks," into which buffalo herds are driven, with gradually narrowing constraints [built] of stone or wood on both sides,

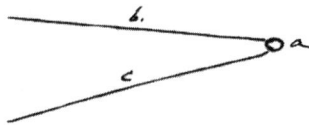

Fig. 10. Maximilian. Plan of buffalo park, or pound, showing the diversionary lines ("b," "c") that funnel the buffalo to the hunters hidden at "a." In a related ceremony (pages 298–99), "b" and "c" represent the lines of spectators, "a" the medicine lodge. Ink.

where hunters lie hidden and shoot [the running buffalo].³ They use nearly all parts of these animals: hide, meat, entrails, and sinews, with which the women and girls sew. They eat many other animals, [too]. In general, they stalk and shoot as we do, and [although] the Blackfoot are [often] said to be less skillful than whites with guns, their rifles and [flintlocks] are often poor. With bow and arrow, [however,] they are masters and very dangerous.

[For additional food,] the plant kingdom is rich in roots and edible fruits. The major role is played by the wild turnip, *Psoralea esculenta,* which the women and children dig out of the ground with a sharpened trowel-like piece of wood, and often sell to the whites. They boil [or] roast them and also eat them raw. Fruits include the *poire (Mespilus)* and cherries *(Prunus padus virginiana).* The former is tasty and readily digestible, sweetish sour; the latter, more tart, with a big pit and somewhat indigestible. These fruits are dried in large quantities for the winter. They also eat the sour red berries of the buffalo berry *(Elaeagnus argentea),* which are not edible until after a frost.

The Indians esteem whiskey above all else [and will trade anything] for it. They are never sold pure whiskey but only diluted—three parts water to one part whiskey. Even their women and girls [may be offered] for this drink of the gods. When intoxicated the Blackfoot are seldom bad[-tempered] but mostly cheerful, jovial, tender. Singing and dancing are the usual effects of this beverage, which is so deleterious to them. The chiefs receive gifts of whiskey and always keep their little kegs ready [for it]. In this regard they are troublesome beggars, a fault ascribed especially to this nation.

Women, [although] generally well treated [among] the Blackfoot, must do all the heavy work. They put up the tipis; cut sod and lay it around the lower edges of the tipis; cook; cut, split, and fetch dry firewood; tan hides (something they do swiftly and skillfully); [and] take care of clothing—in short, they are very busy. They dye feather and porcupine quills with lively colors, several of which they derive from materials [obtained from] the whites. They use a yellow moss for yellow dyeing; it grows on conifers in the mountains. Their vivid red dye [comes] from another plant. Like [other] Indians, they embroider attractive, colorful patterns with porcupine and feather quills on the tops of their shoes (I own some of these in great variety, including a Dacota pair on which a grizzly bear footprint or track is represented very accurately). They make leather supple with animal brains. They tan the hides [as] thin and light [as needed]. [On] hides intended for robes, the hair remains; it is removed from [the hides] used for tipis, clothing, straps, belts, shot bags, etc. For this work they have very suitable tools, particularly an animal bone or piece of wood [with] sharp teeth [set] at an angle; with [this] they scrape off all the fleshy parts from the hide. [The teeth are] often iron now.

[Many men] have six to eight wives, with whom they are very generous [in sharing with] the whites. They even offer little girls. However, they punish the infidelity of their women swiftly and severely; they frequently cut off their noses and cast them out—such women usually become prostitutes [or] support themselves by working or looking after [other people's] children. There have been instances when the man immediately shot such a woman to death. He [might] also revenge himself on her lover—take his horses and [other] objects of value—[and the lover] must [acquiesce].

Many whites—indeed, most of those at trading posts—have Indian wives whom they purchase, often paying one hundred, two hundred, or even three hundred dollars and offering one or more horses, fine costumes, glass beads, knives, powder, lead, rifles, etc. for them. These women are customarily abandoned [when the man] is transferred to another place. Most employees have women of this kind, often with children, at several trading posts simultaneously.

There are no marriage ceremonies among the Blackfoot; one pays for the woman and takes her home. The price is sent to [her] father through a friend or another man; if [the father] accepts it, he sends the woman, and the marriage is consummated. If the wife behaves badly, or [the husband] grows tired of her, she is returned, [without] argument. She takes her belongings and leaves; the children remain the property of the husband.

They have many children, sometimes eight to ten. (Nínoch-Kiáiu's old [uncle] had thirty children with different women.) They run around on the prairie and play and swim in the water. Their faces are painted red, and their ears are pierced [for] ornaments. Boys [go] naked until ten to thirteen. [At an] earlier [age,] girls get a small leather [dress], often nicely decorated with glass beads or elk teeth. The boys [learn to] shoot early with bows and arrows and become skillful. [The Blackfoot] apparently love their children very much but [seem to] entrust their upbringing to nature.

In their domestic life the Blackfoot, like all Indians, are calm and quiet. Quarrelling is seldom seen, although they are said to be more quick-tempered than other Indian nations. Duels and blood vengeance occur.

If one person kills another, the [victim's] family must take revenge [on] some member of the other family, preferably the murderer. Cleanliness is not particularly [common], although this [stems] in part [from] poverty; among [those better off], cleanliness and tidiness in the entire household are found to a higher degree.

The Blackfoot, even the worst of them—the Blood Indians—are very hospitable in their camps and tipis. When Mr. Mitchell visited a band of Piegans at the falls of the Missouri on a cold October night, the chief let [the trader] and all his people sleep in his tipi, [while] the Indians slept [outside]. It is easy for Indians to feed several white visitors, but [when] they visit the whites they demand the same treatment [for their much larger numbers]. They have often been told that there is a big difference here, but they do not understand it, and this [issue] is a major reason for Indian [animosity] against whites. Mr. Mitchell was once taught a lesson by the Dacotas on the Mississippi. They were eating in a tipi, and although he was a stranger, he did not get a bite to eat. The following morning the chief [said that Mr. Mitchell] must have ill feelings against [the chief for making him] go hungry, [but] recently the same thing had happened to [the chief] at Mr. Mitchell's, and [he] just wanted to make this clear so that [Mr. Mitchell] might never err in this way again.

They play all kinds of games. In one they sit on the ground in a circle. Several piles of glass beads or other objects are wagered, for which they play. One [player] takes several pebbles in his hand, which he moves rhythmically back and forth; another guesses [their] number, and [so] they win or lose items, often of significant value.

They have several dances: 1. *des maringouins*, 2. *des chiens*, 3. *des boeufs à corne fine*, 4. *des chiens de prairie*, 5. *de ceux qui portent le corbeau*, 6. *des soldats*, 7. *des vieux boeufs*, 8. *des imprudents ou téméraires*, 9. *de médecine*, 10. *de la chevelure* (Scalp Dance). [For information on the first seven, all associated with age societies, see page 300–301.]

The [Medicine] Dance does not take place every year. It is a women's ceremony, [although] men play a part. They build a large wooden lodge. The women dress beautifully and wear big feather bonnets. Men beat the drum (stohkimahtiss) and shake the *chichikué* (auanay). On the final day, they imitate a buffalo park, [and the dance spectators form] two diverging lines. Several men imitate buffalo bulls, whom the women initially drive back. Then [a] fire is started upwind, just as during a hunt; [once] they scent the fire, the women withdraw into the lodge, and this concludes the ceremony. They do this dance during the summer whenever they [want].⁴

The Scalp Dance. [Performed when enemies have been killed.] Women dress and dance like men and carry weapons. If a woman [took part in the expedition,] she paints her face black. Sometimes [one] woman carries a scalp, or several carry them, [or occasionally] an old woman dances alone. Drums and *chichikué*s accompany [the dance] chants.

Medicine men, superstitious ideas, and preconceptions generally play a major role among [the Blackfoot and other tribes]. Every Indian [has] an object, often an animal, which he regards as his guardian (a bear, for example), and [he] carries [pieces] of it on his person. They do not eat [this] animal. Nor [will] they stay in lodges where even part of [this animal, such as the hide] is found, without [performing] certain sacrificial rites. To bring him luck when he goes to war or out horse stealing, a Blackfoot first invokes his protective spirit [and] promises it [something] — a finger joint, for instance, or several. Often they have some trifling object, [such as] a nail, stone, piece of horn, or the like, wrapped in cloth or hide, which they reverently unwrap before an undertaking. These are frequently things gotten from the whites.

To [identify] a protective patron, they go to a solitary place, [where they] address the sun (their god, Nantóhs) in long speeches asking to be shown [the right] object or animal. They often spend several days [fasting] in solitude; their entire imaginative faculty is taken up with [this spiritual quest]. An animal or object [may] appear to them in a dream, or they [might] select the first animal they come upon; [this] becomes their protective spirit, or, as the Anglo-Americans and French Canadians call it, their medicine.

The Indians have many [items of] high [medicine] value that they will not give up for any price. A Blackfoot, asked if he is willing to sell such an object, replies, "I like it," and presses it to his chest. [When smoking] tobacco, many [will] first blow the smoke toward the sun and the earth. An old Piegan, who carried a bundle of large bells on a strap over his shoulder, rattled them vigorously before smoking. Noteworthy in this regard are the large calumet pipes. The owner [of one], who has chosen it as his medicine, has often paid a high price for it. [He] wraps it [carefully], carries [and] handles it respectfully; and when he smokes, he blows smoke on it, points it toward the sun, and speaks to it. If, after owning it [for] three or more years, he no longer wants it, then one night he lays it beside someone sleeping whom he knows is rich and will pay well for it. In most cases this person will (and should) take it, [although] many try to avoid such presents. If the medicine pipe is accepted, then large gifts—horses (as many as fifteen head), guns, powder, lead, woolen blankets, cloth, etc.—are given, and the protective device [lends the new owner] a certain authority.

The Blackfoot worship the sun (Nantóhs) and bring it [offerings]. They regard it as an important, high-ranking person or medicine, not as the creator of all things; they call him who created everything the Old One or Old Man (Nahpe) but do not venerate him. They invoke the sun [before] undertaking an important venture [and] sacrifice to it a beautiful white robe, a red blanket, etc., which they hang on a tree.

[There are] are certain associations or societies among the Blackfoot that have names and rules and serve in part to maintain law and order in the camp.[5] [The seven Blackfoot societies named to me] are based in part on age, and in [them] one can advance from the lower to the higher ranks. The lowest, or bottom, society is that of the

1. *Maringouins* [Mosquitoes] (Sohskriss). This society has no police function. [It] consists entirely of young people, many only eight to ten years old; several older people [see that] laws and regulations are upheld. This society carries out youthful pranks and swarms about the camp, pinching, nipping, and scratching men, women, and children as mosquitoes do. If somebody offends one of them, he will have them all on his back, because they stick together. They carry an eagle's talon on their wrists as a society symbol, [and they] have a special way of painting themselves and a specific song.

2. *Chiens* [Dogs] (Emitähks). Their [numbers and] symbol are not known to me. Their painting is varied. They consist of young married men.

3. *Chiens de prairie* [Kit Foxes] (Sähnipähks). This is a police association of married men. Like all the [societies], their dance has a different, [specific] song. Their symbol is a long, bent staff with feathers.

4. *Qui portent le Corbeau* [Raven-Bearers] (Mastŏhpate). Their emblem is a long rod with black feathers attached. They contribute to law and order.

5. *Boeufs à corne fine* [Thin-horned Buffaloes] (Ehtskinná). When they dance they wear horns on their bonnets. [In] disorders, they aid the soldiers (see the following).

6. *Soldats* [Soldiers] (Innakehks). The most highly respected men. [They]

exercise some policing power, particularly in camp. In public deliberations they [have] the deciding voice on whether to go hunting, move to another region, etc. [As] an emblem they carry a wooden war club, decorated with buffalo cow hooves [hanging from] the handle. [Their] dance music and manner of painting [are] different from the others. Occasionally they are forty to fifty men strong.

7. *Gros Boeufs* [Large Bulls] (Stomíck). These are the first in rank. When dancing, they carry a medicine with buffalo hooves, [which] they rattle. They are too old to exercise police power, have advanced through all the societies, and in a sense are retired.

The weapons of the Blackfoot are not significantly different from those of the other Missouri Indians; they are, however, not as beautifully and finely made as those of the Crows, Hidatsas, and Mandans. One does not find bows of elkhorn or bighorn among them, as among the Crows, but [only those] of ordinary wood. In their country they have no outstanding variety of wood from which to make bows; therefore, they trade for bow wood *(Maclura aurantiaca)* from the Arkansas River or [use] ash wood. Their quivers are of buffalo hide, although they prefer panther *(Felis concolor)* hide for this, for which they often pay a horse. I did not see lances among them; [I did see] war clubs, or head breakers, here and there, mostly taken as booty from the Salish. Many carry shields, cut from thick leather, round, usually painted green and red, and decorated with all kinds of medicines. Usually, when they intend to fight, they wrap their leather gun sheaths around their heads [like a turban]. Wolf hides are useful [when warriors] want to approach an enemy unnoticed; they wrap them around their heads [and] lie down behind a hill or uneven terrain, so that one might think a white wolf was lying in a ditch or behind an elevation.

Blackfoot medicine men are very inept. In our presence they constantly spat on the severely wounded with water that they took into their mouths, perhaps also with their saliva. The [28 August battle] wounds were not washed at all; only at our urging was [cleansing] finally done on the second day. As mentioned [in the previous chapter], they gave large amounts of whiskey to the injured and moved [them] incessantly from one place to another. That [even] the severely injured recovered [without proper care] demonstrates the [hardiness of these men]. The women supported the bullet-perforated limbs of the [casualties]; that was all that I saw of medical treatment, except for the drum and *chichikué,* which the medicine men employed daily in closed tipis. (The latter, however, occurs more in the case of illnesses, where they [try] to expel a tormenting spirit.) Mortally wounded children lay on the ground, uncovered and exposed to the blazing sun; they soon died. The Blackfoot are said to have [successfully] healed severe wounds. But [from] what I saw, I must ascribe such cures chiefly to the sound constitutions of these children of nature.

Several efficacious medicines are said to be found among these Indians—for example, a whitish root that grows in the Rocky Mountains. It causes vomiting and the opposite effect and tastes somewhat like our rhubarb. Another root is said to be especially effective against snakebite. [The Indians] have great confidence in the medicines of the whites; they often ask for such help. Many were devastated by old venereal infections and had let these diseases progress too far. If Indians are healed by their medicine men (who frequently [do] heal some illnesses, [like] coughs and colds, [with] steam and sweat baths in specially constructed huts, heated with hot stones), they are charged high fees.

When a Blackfoot dies, he is not buried in the ground: when possible, he is [dressed in] his best clothes; his face is painted red; he is tied up in his buffalo robe; and [he is] laid in an inaccessible place (ravines, forests, cliffs, high banks) with his best possessions. Because of the wolves, he is also occasionally covered with wood or stones. The relatives cut their hair [short and then] smear it, [their] faces, and [their] clothing with gray clay. Frequently they cut off a finger joint. They believe that the dead enter another land. [For] rich people, several horses are often killed on the grave; I was told of cases where twelve to fifteen horses were killed in this manner after the death of a chief.

Usually the dead [are disposed of] on the day they die. If someone dies at night, [the disposal is] the next morning. [If] an isolated spot cannot be found, the deceased remains aboveground in a kind of wooden hut. Sometimes they [are] compelled to inter [the corpse]. At Fort McKenzie they presented their dead to Mr. Mitchell. Following the [28 August] skirmish, six persons were buried in our woodcutting trench, so shallowly that a powerful stench arose.

[The three tribes (Piegan, Blood, Siksika) speak the same language, which] is not difficult for Germans to pronounce; they frequently have the velar 'ch' like 'ach' and 'och' in German. There is no article. They often place the noun before the adjective; they do not say "white buffalo," for example, but "buffalo white."

THE GROS VENTRES DES PRAIRIES, OR FALL INDIANS

The Blackfoot call these Indians Azäna; they call themselves Ahni-ninn.[6] They live in the vicinity of the Blackfoot and are neighbors of the Arapahoes, from whom they are said to be descended. Alexander McKenzie called them Fall Indians, because they lived along the falls of the Saskatchewan River when he found them.

They differ little in outward appearance and costume from the Blackfoot. Several wore large iron or brass rings (diameter 2½ inches) in their ears; some had eight to ten of them on the outer rim of the ear. Hair [dressed] like the Hidatsas and Mandans, in long, wide, flat [hanks] kneaded with reddish brown clay, or like many Dacotas—a single long braid of hair in back decorated with one or several brass rosettes. Their robes [have] attractive parallel stripes of mostly yellow or yellowish red porcupine quills [and bits of] sewed-on red cloth. Their tipis, household implements, and weapons are the same [as those of the Blackfoot]. I saw many war clubs made from elk antler tines. I bought an interesting dagger from them; the handle was the lower jawbone of a bear. One saw [similar weapons] among the Crees and Assiniboines.

In battles with the Crows, [the Gros Ventres des Prairies] have lost so many men that now the number of their women is much larger than [the normal] proportion. They are estimated at [perhaps] four hundred warriors and two hundred tipis. They have many pack dogs and more horses now than formerly [but] do not have as many as the Blackfoot.

At Fort McKenzie, they always behaved very well [and] supplied beautiful buffalo robes, which they prepared in the best and most perfect manner. All of them offered their women for whiskey and other articles. They are brave, good fighters.

Their language is one of the most difficult, [and] there is not yet a single interpreter for it. It consists entirely of short, abrupt sounds, so similar that often one can hardly distinguish them. Many Gros Ventres des Prairies speak the language of their neighbors and allies, the Blackfoot, and this is helpful. They often have the habit, like the English, of lisping.

[They] live on the other side of the mountains at the sources of the Marias River. The English and Anglo-Americans call them Kutnehä, the French, Koutanais; they call themselves Kutonáchä.[7] The Blackfoot know them by the name Kutanä. They are not numerous [and] do not count more than forty tipis. Among their ornaments they have many cylinders cut from mussels as well as dentalium, which they sell to neighboring nations. The Kootenais are at peace with the Piegans, enemies of the Kaénnas and the Siksikas. They [live on] roots, berries, beaver, splendid lake trout, and several other species of animals, especially the white mountain goats, the bighorn, and the *orignal*, [moose]. They raise strong, fine horses in large numbers. [They] are good Indians, well dressed, and excellent beaver trappers. Their language is difficult to learn. I wrote it down according to the pronunciation of an old Kootenai [called Big Earth], who pronounced words softly and indistinctly. They have many clicking [and] velar sounds.

XIV

Return Journey from Fort McKenzie to Fort Union

[FROM 14 SEPTEMBER TO 29 SEPTEMBER 1833]

September 14th: Bright, beautiful morning. Our boat was cleaned and loaded about eleven o'clock. It was too small; with the cargo [stowed], we could barely sit, much less find space to sleep. The larger of my two bears shrieked fiercely in [its] new [cagelike] crate, [which] was placed in the middle of the cargo, where it extended from one side of the boat to the other; it was too large and awkward and in this position could not be cleaned well. We took leave of our gracious host, Mr. Mitchell, and his sole companion, Mr. Culbertson, as well as of the other fort residents, [who] all accompanied us to the river.

We cast off at 12:30, a cannon was fired, [and] we glided swiftly down the Missouri. After half an hour, we reached the place where we had spent our final night on the voyage upriver on the keelboat. At 2:30 we reached the old fort [and] soon afterward navigated past the mouth of the Marias River. [Later on] we had [a] beautiful view of the Bears Paw [Mountains], which rose picturesquely above the prairie hills. Our bears roared wildly toward evening, an unwelcome situation [since we were] on guard against hostile Indians and [often] dared not light a fire [after dark]. Before dusk we put in at the right bank and cooked meat [and then] continued our journey well into the night. We [finally] fastened our boat under a steep wall and slept in it in a very awkward position; we were cold and soaked by heavy rain all night long.

15 September: During the night so much water had leaked into our boat that it was half full. We had not expected this and had not taken any precautionary measures—[it] caused much damage. We bailed water out of the boat [and] decided to navigate somewhat farther [before] halting and examining our [soaked] baggage. The sun was just rising [as we approached] the striking passage into the Stone Walls. When the sun was somewhat higher in the sky, we put in at the right bank, made a good fire, [and] took our wet buffalo robes and blankets ashore to dry them a little. We [discovered] that our pretty, tame, striped squirrel, which I had brought along in a cage, had

drowned [in] the high water in the boat. We warmed up with good coffee, ate our meat, and set out again an hour later.

At 9:30 we reached the beginning of the strange, astonishing Stone Walls. Large troops of bighorn stood crowded together [on] the grotesque formations: domes, hills, towers, jagged points, and isolated stones shaped like heads or tables. At [about] 11:30 we put in at the left bank to examine our baggage, since the sun was warm now and favorable for this task. We took all the crates and trunks on shore. How horrible! Not one of our things was dry: all the Indian and natural history collections, clothing, mathematical instruments, books—in short, everything—were completely soaked and drenched; one trunk was open at every joint and had become useless. [It] grieved me most of all that my entire botanical collection, assembled with effort and persistence during a journey of five to six months on the Missouri, now seemed completely lost. We opened all crates and packages, spread the contents out on the bank—they covered a sizeable stretch—and entrusted the hot sun to rescue at least part [of our belongings]. My extensive herbarium I placed in dry paper [out of?] the wind in a small gully on the bank, but soon it had to be repacked, and all the plants turned black and [moldy], a most distressing loss for me.

We left the baggage to dry all [afternoon] and, in the meantime, posted men on the heights [to] guard [against] surprise by Indians. Toward evening [we] cooked our meal, whereupon the fire was extinguished. At twilight a buck came close to us in the river, but to avoid any noise no one fired. The night was pleasant, [with] a little occasional moonlight. We maintained a double watch; [I was] matched with Thiebault from nine until eleven o'clock.

16 September: Cool in the morning, [then] magnificent weather. Our things dried quickly. We remained here all day, until about five o'clock, and went aboard after we had eaten. I [had taken] rock samples from the blackish stone walls and towers, on and between which the brittle white sandstone was found. This type of rock forms walls [seemingly] split into regular cubes as though hewed stones were intentionally placed one upon the other. We sailed past the tall [rock] called the Citadel, surrounded [by] grotesque, fantastic mountain [formations. When] night approached, we halted below a steep bank. I had the first watch and was entertained not a little by the howling of wolves [and] the melancholy "Hoo! Hoo! Hoo!" of the great horned owl.

17 September: We navigated early through the passage of the Stone Walls, where

we once more admired the white fortresses, turrets, old castles, churches, and rock pillars, to which we now had to bid farewell forever. The most striking ones [will] survive in [our] sketches [and] recollections of this remote, forgotten world of nature. Only trappers and the boats of the Fur Company observe these wonders, sometimes indifferently; a few dollars have greater value to them than all the marvels of nature combined.

About seven or eight o'clock in the morning, we halted on the left bank below a prairie. A fire soon blazed and warmed [us] cold travelers; we had breakfast. An hour later the journey was continued. At ten o'clock we reached the place where we had met the Gros Ventres des Prairies on our way upstream. Not a trace of them [was now] to be seen. At twelve o'clock we passed the mouth of [the Judith River]; since we suspected [that] Indians [might be nearby], we moved quietly and cautiously. Buffalo bulls frequently swam close to us through the river. They provided us with great entertainment. The huge, clumsy figures galloped [off] as soon as they [scented] us; if we had a good wind, we were able to get very close to them, for their sight and hearing are less acute. Farther downriver we saw a herd of about 120 buffalo, with many calves and cows; the bulls constantly gave forth their grunting roars.

At 4:30 we halted at a small ravine [in] the right bank above Dauphin Rapid, made a fire, and cooked our supper. Morrin used the time to stalk the numerous bighorn here and shot an old and [a] young female; we prepared the meat. I took one of the skulls with me.

Before dusk we continued our journey and [eventually] halted at the right bank [to sleep]. At ten o'clock, a splendid meteor appeared in the starlit sky, a long band of bright white light from east to west, very distinct; it lasted about an hour. Later it rained very heavily.

18 September: Everything around us was wet. We left [our] night quarters early. To the left under the high, steep mountains of the Mauvaises-Terres, we saw [buffalo] everywhere, [and numerous] bighorn; a troop of twelve elk with a big bull trotted through the river. Somewhat farther downstream in the river valley, surrounded by steep, whitish gray clay mountains, we got out to cautiously approach a large buffalo herd, but the unfavorable wind drove away the game. The animals galloped in the prairie along the river and then turned into a small lateral valley. We pursued them [there] for a while, but the entire herd climbed up a steep mountain to the highest precipices; we [were astonished that such] heavy animals could reach [that] height.

I described the mountains of the Mauvaises-Terres on the journey up-stream. Again we could not sufficiently admire their singularity. In several places they had brick-red domes, patches, and stripes, where the red clay appeared as perfectly baked as in a brick kiln.

At 9:30 we went ashore on the left bank and (in a very raw, cold wind) started a big fire and prepared our breakfast of coffee and bighorn meat, the remainder of which we saved for a cold lunch. At eleven o'clock we left this place [and] soon [ran] aground; the crew got into the water and pushed the boat. At 12:30 we wanted to stop to make a drawing of the Mauvaises-Terres, but the [presence of] buffalo herds and a gunshot, which we heard to the right in the mountains, led us to assume the approach of Indians. We decided to continue on. [Later in the afternoon] a herd of at least 150 buffalo crowded together moved into the river to drink. The view was most interesting: cows, calves, and bulls mingled; the latter bellowed mightily and drove the cows. We sat motionless, let the boat drift, and came within favorable rifle range, apparently without their noticing us. Scarcely 60 paces farther [along], [we saw] a troop of six cow elk on a sandbar near a small willow island; [they were] with a powerful bull, which emitted a bugling cry and three times covered a cow 300 paces directly in front of us. [Another] bull, which had been driven off [and] stood on the high bank of the prairie, got wind of us, and all of them, elk and buffalo, took flight. Today we saw more than several thousand buffalo, many elk, bighorn, and antelope; the journey certainly [was] unique for a hunting enthusiast.

We put [the hunters] Dreidoppel and Morrin ashore in the narrow chan-nel of [an] elk island on which we had shot so much game on the way up. The rest of us navigated up to the tip of the island, where we landed and started a fire. Morrin shot [a] white-tailed doe, which we immediately cut up and cooked. I combed a part of the island, found deer and buffalo rut-ting grounds in the tall grass, [and] heard bull elk bugling and buffalo bawl-ing. [As] night descended we agreed to take along the half-cooked meat and leave our campfire because of the Indians. We sailed until nine o'clock that night. The moon shone brightly; the weather and river were very beau-tiful. My watch duty lasted until eleven o'clock, when I woke Mr. Bodmer, who relieved me. We were terribly cold in our beds; the woolen blankets, drenched by the rain the previous night, were frozen solid in the morning.

19 September: We set out in the morning twilight, numb with cold. We soon saw elk in large number. Five head went through the river; a big bull followed,

bugling. Our rifles were ready to fire when, on the steep, 20-foot-high bank, an even larger bull stood majestically, bugling incessantly. Morrin, who was ready first, dropped him. We quickly landed and climbed the bank, where we found an indescribably magnificent animal. The bull was very old and large; his huge antlers had thick, tall prongs, long points, and carried, to use German hunter's jargon, an uneven 20 of them. The weight of both branches, sawed off at the base, was 24 pounds. The bull was [over] 7 feet long. The beautiful pale yellowish color of its body was nicely accentuated by the black-brown of its neck, belly, and legs. I decided to add [this impressive animal] to my zoological collection, and we immediately set to work removing the hide. Since some of our baggage was still wet, we [took advantage of] this halt to spread it out on bushes; the weather was very favorable for drying.

Our fire soon flared up among the young cottonwood trees, and after the splendid hunt, our breakfast was eaten in high spirits. We stayed until two o'clock. By then our bedding was dry and the elk hide somewhat cleaned.

After five o'clock we reached the prairie where we had killed the prairie dogs on 31 July. [We] did not halt, however, but sped our journey toward the wooded promontory on which we had fastened the large bear to a tree. We went ashore [expecting] to find a [fine] specimen, now completely freed of flesh — but what a disappointment! There was nothing [left] of the magnificent bear skeleton except several crunched and scattered bones. The bare, fork-shaped tree stump, into which we had hoisted and tied the bear with a rope, had been clawed all around by bears — they had inflicted this painful loss upon us. The rope still hung fast to the tree. We searched through the large trampled area [where] our treasure [was] destroyed; the skull was not to be found anywhere.

Regretfully we continued our journey rapidly down the river. Bull elk bugled in the woodlands but not as frequently as yesterday. We saw several wolves. In the evening bats swarmed over the surface of the river. [After] dusk, we sailed quietly and cautiously by moonlight, but the dark shadows cast [by] the tall, wooded banks were dangerous for us: the water rushed and raged past partly hidden snags, which we [could] steer clear of only with great caution. Fortunately our steersman, Morrin, understood these matters very well.

At nine o'clock we landed quietly at a large, flat sandbar off the right bank; only our bears could have betrayed [our presence] with their roars and scratching on the crate. During the second watch, about two o'clock, magnificent northern lights, but their beauty vanished after [just] half an hour.

20 September: Dense, cold fog on the river. At 8:30 we [stopped and] made a big fire in the cottonwood forest; two hours later we continued our voyage. Buffalo bulls moved close to us to the right and left along the water, some of them in the river. The common raven and black crow called out in the lofty blue sky; an eagle was perched on a dry pine. [Some time] later, at a bend of the river, we saw a large buffalo herd with many cows and calves. Morrin and Dreidoppel got out on the right bank, crept under the cover of the willow thickets toward them, and came within 20 paces of the herd, which had gone down a ravine to the river to drink. They shot and killed two fat cows, which supplied us with a large quantity of excellent meat.

The afternoon grew splendid and very hot. On a steep, bare bank of the prairie to the right there was a small flight of blue finches (*Fringilla amoena*), which were about to migrate. We put in to the right and cooked, [then] continued our journey. When the sun had set, we found ourselves at the place where, on 28 July, we had set up a large elk antler on the [far] heights of the left bank. We saw it, but it was too late in the day to get it. This was about 10 miles above the Musselshell River. [At] 8:30 [we] anchored for the night a mile [upstream of that river]. Our bears clamored terribly and put us in a far from trifling predicament. The night was not so cold as the previous one.

21 September: Shortly after daybreak we reached the Musselshell River and tied up at its lower tongue of land; the Musselshell [was] regarded as the halfway point to Fort Union. We continued on and saw buffalo everywhere along [the] shore. From our boat, Morrin shot a big calf. It was dark brown with [a] whitish mouth and short horns just breaking out. We started a fire, cut up the calf, and had breakfast. Our shooting and the odor of meat attracted numerous wolves; we saw twelve of varying [age,] size, and color, approaching one right after the other on the sandbar along the river. They came running at a gallop, saw us, and turned back somewhat. Most sat or lay down and struck up a doleful concert, howling in diverse tones. Around nine o'clock we left this place. Snags along the bank gave us jolts, but our helmsman found the course very well. The cottonwoods were already very yellow in this region; [the] old trees remain green longer and still were now; the thickets of young shoots are always the first to turn yellow. [Deer,

buffalo, elk, and various birds were observed.] At 11:15 several lone, fortress-like mountain domes on the elevations to the right. On the left bank, we saw a badger, which had probably swum through the river and [was now drying] itself. The American badger *(Meles labradorius* or *americanus)* has a beautifully marked head and longer ears than the European one; it was the first specimen of this kind that I obtained. Morrin shot it from the boat with the rifle, and we took it along.

Around a bend of the river, we again had fortresslike hills on the right bank; [these] were described on our upward voyage. Two buffalo crossed the river before us; an entire herd grazed on the hills to the right; among them on the sandbar stood five or six deer *(Cervus virginianus).* Several river bends farther on, we saw a bull elk with a cow. From the abundance of game in these regions, one could conclude that there were no Indians along the river.

At noon the heat was great, but on this journey I could not [easily] observe the thermometer. The elevations that rose before us bore a close resemblance to the Mauvaises-Terres. Somewhat farther on we halted at the left bank at the mouth of a creek to make a bed of cottonwood and willow branches for our bears in their crate. [By] six o'clock [we were not far above the white castles]. The sun had set, and coolness had replaced the day's heat. A solemn stillness prevailed in the vast world of nature; not a breath of air stirred; only the river [made] sounds. Our oars lay silent, [and] no one spoke, [so as] not to betray our presence to hostile Indians. Even our bears had been quiet since a [fresh] bed had been made for them; it was as though they were sharing in [the] calm [of] nature, so conducive to serious contemplation. Today we had not seen nearly as many buffalo as yesterday; on the other hand, we had counted more than twenty wolves, almost all of which appeared within rifle range on the bank. We continued navigating until ten o'clock by the brightest moonlight; the evening was incomparable. Unfortunately, during the night, we sailed past [and thus missed seeing] the beautiful white castles.

22 September: When daylight arrived, [we saw] unusual domes right and left [and,] in the distance, a [buffalo] herd moving hastily, spreading much dust, and we were afraid it might have been put to flight by Indians. Magpies fluttered around the boat, because it hung full of meat. Kingfishers, which we had not noticed while navigating upward, were on the riverbanks in great numbers here. At eight o'clock we put in at the left bank and made

a fire directly opposite a strange dome that Mr. Bodmer had sketched on the way up. At nine o'clock we continued. Along the bank and on wooded promontories, one frequently saw forts constructed from dry timber by Indian war parties; to our delight, we always found [these to be] empty. Whenever we passed them, we looked nervously to determine whether they might be occupied—our men were [in] great fear of the Indians. Whenever we halted, even for a moment, they expressed their displeasure. The river [was becoming] wider and wider, but the shoals and sandbars also began to grow more frequent and troublesome. In the clay hills and mountains, mica or isinglass-like fossils glistened here and there in the sun, like bright stars in the distance.

At 10:30 we found ourselves opposite the halfway pyramid [between the Musselshell and Milk Rivers]; it lay in a southerly direction from us. Somewhat farther downstream we found large sandbars in the river, which delayed us greatly, since one must swerve right and left to avoid them. [By] 12:30 we [were] opposite the place where Dreidoppel and I shot a buffalo [on 24 July]. In the afternoon a strong wind blew, lifting sand into the air.

The river was extremely shallow. On a sandbar, five elk cows; on the steep left bank, beaver tracks everywhere. At [a] bend of the river on a sandbar, [we saw] two magnificent snow-white cranes with black pinions *(Grus americana),* the whooping crane of the Americans, one of the most beautiful birds of this genus. Its plumage was dazzlingly white. I would have liked to possess [a specimen], but they were out of range. We continued on until it was very dusky and then halted at the right bank beneath steep hills. Evening magnificent, warm, and moonlit.

23 September: The river made big bends, so there was little current. The region was uniform: woods or steep prairie banks and mostly bare hills in the background. At 8:30 we put in on the right bank, started a fire, and prepared breakfast. We drank our coffee and ate buffalo meat on a fallen tree trunk. A strong wind arose, so we remained here all day. [Seated] on the trunk, I wrote in my journal. Dreidoppel brought the hide of our bull elk ashore to dry it. We set out guards facing the prairie and the forest. [By] five o'clock the wind had abated, [and] we continued on. Around [a] bend of the river, a two-year-old cow elk stood in the water. Morrin wounded [it] with the rifle, but it reached the forest. A wolf on the bank witnessed this scene and [must] surely have pursued the wounded animal. We navigated until nine o'clock by moonlight and ran aground several times; the men had to push

in the water. I [lost] my only hat in the river, [an] unpleasant experience.[1]

24 September: At seven o'clock [the next morning], on [a] promontory, we caught sight of an [impressive] bull elk [and] sprang ashore; I shot and killed [it]. We took the [twelve-point] antlers, a foreleg, and the canines as souvenirs. Somewhat farther [on], we found a flight of prairie hens *(Tetrao phasianellus)* sitting on the bank and on old driftwood; pheasants appeared on the left bank, a troop of antelope on the flat hills. At 8:30 we halted, [and] while our meal was being cooked, a wolf sat near the river and howled.

Departure at 9:45. Magnificent warm weather. In the ravines, autumn had painted the bushes in bright colors. Several short species of *Rhus* and roses replaced the scarlet-red staghorn sumac *(Rhus [trilobata])* here; cottonwoods [and] ashes, orange-yellow; *Prunus padus,* yellowish red; *Cornus sericea,* violet or purple.

At 2:30 we reached Milk River, now shallow, [and] sailed along close to its mouth. Below [that], we put in for a moment and cut green branches [and red buffalo berries] for our bears; they gladly devoured [the latter]. Substantial numbers of ducks, magpies, *Sturnella,* and blackbirds flew up along the bank. Everywhere one saw impressive elk bulls and cows. Since the [Marias River], Morrin had counted twenty-five beaver dens. [By] seven o'clock it was almost dark, and there was a nearly full moon. We continued on until 8:30 and then halted on a sandbar.

25 September: [Set off] at 5:30. Bull elk bugled in the thickets on the bank, and Morrin shot a very fat cow. The region ahead was flat, with sparse forest; behind [that, a] prairie, bordered by hills and overgrown with *Artemisia.* All the sandbars were crisscrossed with thousands of animal tracks.

At one o'clock, we let the boat drift, and [while] our men were eating, a wolf swam through the river before us. We saw many coots today; they were stopping [here] on their migration. [There was] little game, however; it was too hot, [and the animals] were resting. At 2:30 a severe storm rose suddenly out of the west-southwest. We saw it coming and had just [enough] time to swing the boat around [and fasten it behind a protective] trunk lying in the water at the right bank. The storm developed rapidly; we were afraid it would knock the trees down on our heads. It drove the dust from the sandbars, [and] we could not protect ourselves from it. Sparrow hawks, common ravens, crows, and blackbirds fled deep into the forest. The wind [was] very strong. For our protection we put up an Indian-style fortress of [fallen trunks and branches]. Toward morning the wind subsided.

26 September: Departed early. The river had big bends; at [one of these], a herd of buffalo grazed on open prairie. In many places the forest was a mixture of yellow, red, and green. [In the afternoon] the rain started and stopped at short intervals. At dusk we anchored at a wet, muddy sandbar; from seven to ten o'clock, I sat with Dreidoppel on our beds under [an] umbrella. At three o'clock the rain subsided; we got up; everything was soaked. A wolf circled us closely the entire night.

27 [September]: [The following morning, a] cold, contrary wind. About eleven o'clock we were opposite [Elkhorn Prairie, where we had stopped on 11 July]. Right after noon, torrential rain; we halted in the forest and attempted to build [makeshift] wooden shelters for ourselves. Two big fires were kept burning, [and] we spent a dismal, wet day [here]. The rain lasted until midnight, and [then there were] stars until daybreak.

28 September: The morning was somewhat better—cool wind, blue sky. The ash woodlands a fiery chrome-yellow. At 10:15 we reached the rugged mountain chain that extends to Fort Union. Dark clouds gathered again; the raw, completely contrary wind delayed us considerably, stirring up heavy waves on the river. On a sandbar some avocets (*Recurvirostra americana*) were fishing with their peculiar beaks, which they dip into the water, fishing against the current or snatching worms. We had not seen this interesting bird anywhere till now. When dusk fell we continued on [by moonlight until] one o'clock, [when] we stopped at a sandbar. Chilled to the bone, we slept until dawn, posting guards as usual.

29 September: Cranes woke at the same time we did, calling out loudly [and] soaring into the hazy, dawning sky. [In] a timber deposit on the left bank, we shot at prairie hens and found fresh Indian footprints. At 9:15 we landed and cooked our breakfast, though we had had no zwieback for a long time, [nor] any sugar for the coffee. The raw wind made our [remaining] voyage unpleasant, [but] at 12:30, [we saw] Fort Union in the distance. Renewed zeal seized our crew, [and] we reached the fort at one o'clock.

XV

Second Stay at Fort Union and Journey from There
to the Mandan Villages and Fort Clark

[FROM 30 SEPTEMBER TO 8 NOVEMBER 1833]

The appearance of the area had changed greatly since our stay in July. At that time there were many Indians here but now only one tipi inhabited by a half-breed Blackfoot. The prairie was barren and parched; plants bore seeds instead of summer flowers; the forests had turned yellow; nights [were] cool or cold; the river very low, with visible sandbars. Even inside the fort, it looked different. Mr. McKenzie had traveled with more than twenty men down to the [Bad River] and was not [expected] to return for two months. The population of the fort, therefore, was only about fifty persons. People were busy with a number of building [projects]. The entire stockade fence was being rebuilt and was almost completed. They had constructed a fine, solid powder magazine from large, hewn stones; it could hold 50,000 pounds of gunpowder.^{MI} Mr. Hamilton was in charge, [and] three clerks worked for him: Chardon, Brazeau, and Moncravie. More Indians were expected shortly, Assiniboines and Crees.

I had the opportunity and the space here to open all our damp boxes and crates on a dry and spacious floor and dry them out well. That kept us busy for several days. A comfortable, well-lit room [allowed] Mr. Bodmer to complete several drawings. Mr. Hamilton received us in a very friendly manner, and we were assigned the same living quarters [as last] summer, [where] I found the boxes [we] had left behind.

30 September: In the night, heavy hoarfrost. By 13 September, [Fort Union] had already heard from returning Assiniboines about the 28 August skirmish at Fort McKenzie. The Assiniboine [warriors] had grown to [an exaggerated

---

^{MI} On 4 February 1832, there had been an extensive fire at Fort Union. It would have destroyed the fort completely, had it reached the powder magazine. The buildings on the west side and five rooms burned down; fortunately, an east wind drove the fire away from the powder.

800], 100 Crees among them. I found Deschamps, too, [at Fort Union]. He had brought his horses safely [here from Fort McKenzie] in ten days and had been pursued by Indians (Gros Ventres des Prairies) only once. They probably wanted to steal the horses, but he managed to hold them off.

1–2 October: Strong, raw wind; frequent rain. Some Ojibwes arrived; several more will follow soon. Deschamps and others were sent out to hunt; there was no fresh meat left, and [the fort] badly needed it.

3 October: I went with Mr. Bodmer to the forest below the fort, where we found an enormous flock of *Quiscalus versicolor;* I shot [some of them]. When I came to the riverbank I saw a beautiful wild swan swimming in the river. I crept up and shot it. It took a lot of effort to get [the young male] out of the water.

4–5 October: Very unpleasant weather. Two men from Fort Cass on the Yellowstone came in the afternoon, traveling to St. Louis. I quickly finished a letter, [which] they took along. Afterward [I went on an] excursion through the lower forest onto the prairie, [where] I found interesting seeds.

6 October: It was Sunday, and people wore clean clothes. A beautiful, bright day. We worked at home. In the afternoon the [fort's] hunters returned. They had not seen any female buffalo but [had] shot ten bulls, six antelope, one elk, and one deer. Deschamps brought me a porcupine and a badger. The hunter, Antoine, returned from the lake [with] a *Grus americana* (the white crane) and a *Grus canadensis,* [which] the greedy engagés immediately plucked.

We visited Mr. Hamilton every evening to talk. He usually served us some kind of whiskey punch with sugar and hot water while we smoked our pipes. He read to us from his manuscript biography of old [Hugh] Glass, who, with two other white men, had been shot by Indians (most likely Arikaras) near the Yellowstone in spring 1833. During the previous winter, Glass had told Mr. Hamilton the story of his life, which would make an interesting book. For many years this old man led the dangerous life of a beaver trapper. He had numerous wounds [inflicted by] Indians. [He saw] many of his friends shot, [and] finally it was his turn. I own the scalp taken from [one of his] Arikara [murderers]; it was given to me by Mr. Chardon.

7 October: [The hunters brought me] several animals [along] with the buffalo meat. I described *Grus americana, Meles labradorius,* and *Hystrix dorsata.* Mr. Bodmer sketched the heads. In the afternoon I took a walk with Mr. Hamilton near the new fort [being] built by the Fur Company [of] Sublette

and Campbell. It [will] be called Fort William, situated on the Missouri a bit below the mouth of the Yellowstone. The Negro, Antoine, went hunting again today, hoping to bring new animals for us. We altogether forgot to read the thermometer today.

8 October: At seven thirty, 46°F. Last night Indian dogs killed some chickens belonging to the fort. They are like wolves and foxes; when starved, nothing is safe from them.

Deschamps told me today that, in our absence, the lower Assiniboines had made peace with the [Hidatsas]. Their principal chief, Uahktähno, [He Who Kills], had attended the peace ceremony. Deschamps brought his wife, a Cree woman, to have her picture drawn by Mr. Bodmer. She was a pretty woman, tattooed below [and at the sides of] her mouth toward her chin with bluish black lines. Chardon told me some words of the Osage language, and Deschamps a few [in] Assiniboine.

9–10 October: During the night [of 9 October,] two men of the fort deserted and took a boat with them. Chardon and Deschamps followed (only for a short distance) without catching up with them.

We were invited for lunch by Mr. Campbell at Fort William. The weather was incomparably beautiful and very warm—at twelve o'clock, 53°F. Mr. Hamilton, Mr. Bodmer, [and I went to] the new Fort William, located on flat prairie, about three-quarters of an hour from Fort Union. Two sections of [their] picket square were [done]; they had just dug trenches for the other two. Beside Mr. Campbell and two clerks, the crew consisted of fifty men, most of them absent [just then]. Mr. Campbell had a very good log house with glass windows and a clay chimney. In addition to the superintendent's house, two smaller buildings were ready for [occupation]. The other structures were yet to be built. Cattle, horses, hogs, chickens, and turkeys were the domesticated animals, as well as several dogs. Mr. Campbell told us interesting stories about his travels to the Rocky Mountains and the sources of the Columbia. Last summer he traveled there with Captain Stewart, the same man we saw in St. Louis [in March 1833]. We ate lunch at Fort William, took leave of our host at five o'clock, and arrived at Fort Union at nightfall. The necessary preparations for our buffalo hunt the next day had been made, [and] we were [scheduled] to leave on horseback after breakfast.

11 October: [It] was early [when we] brought the horses to the [river] and ferried [them] across. We landed [on a sandbar] and rode through the mud toward

the nearby high forest of old cottonwood, ash, elm, and [other trees], with a thicket of *Symphoria,* low rose bushes (now with red leaves), and buffalo berry, covered with light red berries. We had seventeen or eighteen horses and mules. Our hunting party consisted of Mr. Chardon; Bodmer; myself; the half-breed Cree Indians Deschamps, Marcellais, [and] Joseph Basile; Mr. McKenzie's Negro slave, Flemming; and additional men who loaded and drove the pack animals. [All] were on horseback and armed. Chardon, who had lived a long time among the Osages, entertained us with his lively descriptions of those Indians and their songs, war whoop, etc. On the other side of the forest, we followed along the river, [where] there was a pleasant meadow or plain with tall grass; a well-worn path meandered through [it]. Buffalo skeletons, some very fine and complete, were scattered everywhere; we could have stocked our anatomical collections with interesting pieces from that one area alone. From there we rode up hills of whitish sandstone, where we had a very nice view looking back at the Missouri valley [as] it disappeared from view. A few miles farther [on], the area [gradually] turned into a flat, undulating, arid prairie, covered with dried plants [that were] very short but still fed the buffalo well. There were whole stretches of dried-up roses, about a foot high; low *Solidago;* small asters; etc. The prairie inhabitants were *Arctomys hoodii,* the small prairie fox, and the wolf. The cute fox [was not] seen much at this time of year; despite this, we shot one. We saw flocks of common ravens and crows. Larks moved low above [the] ground. We spied one buffalo to the right but did not concern ourselves with it. One must ride twenty miles before reaching the area where there were always buffalo in sufficient numbers to feed the fort. Once every week the hunters were sent out; they shot nine, twelve, or fifteen buffalo [and] loaded the meat on packhorses.

About noon we reached a small creek meandering through [a] meadow; on its right (northern) side, a hill protected us from the wind. The packs were taken off the animals, and they were put out to graze. We lit a fire with buffalo dung and roasted a duck *(Anas boschas),* which a half-breed Cree Indian (who had been sent ahead of us) had shot. The creek, overgrown with tall grass, was partially dry but [had] water in a few places.

After resting a while, we continued. [Several] ridges were passed until we reached the last [and] highest one at about five o'clock; beyond that, buffalo could usually be found. We stopped on a hill and examined the surrounding areas with telescopes. We saw a few small [clusters] of bulls, four or five or six together, and decided to attack the largest group. Our horses trotted and galloped until we reached a gentle hollow between hills, where we saw buffalo close at hand to our left. Once all the guns were ready, we [charged, and] these heavy but fast animals stampeded. The shooters separated; I rode after a buffalo with a half-breed Cree and the slave Flemming. I could not get a good shot at it, but hunters used to this kind of hunting shoot very well in such situations. They stand up in their stirrups, extend the gun with both hands, bring it in line with their faces, ride close to the buffalo, and kill it—usually with one shot. They quickly throw powder into the gun barrel and [follow that with] bullets, which they hold in their mouths. They let one roll on the powder, where it sticks; no wadding. [In] this way they shoot ten to eleven [or] more animals, one after the other. We shot down almost the whole herd; buffalo lay scattered over the prairie. [My horse and I both] tired, I looked for the remainder of our party, [but] they had ridden after other buffalo, and I could see nothing of them. I rode a few miles through the barren prairie over gentle rises and hills. It was almost dark when [I] heard shooting and finally found Bathiste Marcellais, who had killed two bulls [and] was cutting one of them up. The second [bull] lay beyond a hill, and there I found Mr. Bodmer, who was sketching [it]. Later, we all rode back to [a] general assembly point [and] lit a fire with buffalo dung; to [further] feed [it], fat from the downed buffalo was thrown in. We put large marrowbones near the fire, as well as a kettle with meat, and retired very late. We slept well, even though it rained quite hard during the night.

12 October: The meat and marrow were ready early; we had breakfast and then saddled [the horses]. It was not cold, but [there was] a harsh, unpleasant wind. Deschamps loaned me his blanket coat because I had back pain. The pack animals, loaded with meat, followed us, and we went beyond the hills to a gorge with trees [and a spring, where] we lit a fire and roasted a few buffalo tongues and a creek duck shot by Flemming. The pack animals gained a big lead in the meantime. By noon we caught up with them in a gentle depression, where they were unloaded [to rest]. We ate some meat, [relaxed] for about an hour, and [left]. Approximately 4 miles from the fort, we noticed the foot tracks of an Indian war party, traveling in the same direction [we were, and] very recently. We rode fast and looked around carefully to avoid crossing paths with [them]. At three thirty we reached Fort Union; the pack animals with the meat of nine buffalo arrived before evening.

13 October: We had much work and kept busy at home. I had [a] mouse with

Fig. 11. Maximilian. Indian "letter" to a trader. Ink. Pictographic symbols were more typically painted on shirts and robes to depict a warrior's accomplishments; this is an unusual commercial use of the form.

long [cheek] pouches, [which was] not rare in the forest, and described it precisely. [Its] colossal pouches were filled with the seeds of small plants.[1]

Because today was Sunday, nobody worked. Mr. Hamilton [was pestered] terribly about brandy. The men almost always got it, too, and many were drunk. Several people from Fort William paid a visit to Fort Union. Antoine came back from the lake on the Yellowstone [with] thirteen muskrats and a large number of wild geese and ducks. He often caught 500 in one season, sometimes almost 1,000 or 1,500.

14 October: A cold, harsh east wind blew across the prairie. Müller, a German or Dutchman who had been drunk and tiresome yesterday, deserted this morning. Chardon and Deschamps rode after [and found] him. However, they contented themselves with asking Mr. Campbell at Fort William not to employ him, and they did not say a word to the deserter. He owes the company 100 dollars. Most likely Mr. Campbell will employ him, [causing] a rift between the two companies. In that case Mr. Hamilton will fetch Müller back by force.

15–16 October: The roofs were white with snow. Chardon was having a significantly larger boat prepared [to] trade for mine.[2] Mr. Hamilton gave me an interesting letter written by a Mandan, Dobchíhischi [Good Furred Robe] to Mr. McKenzie. [See fig. 11.] Explanation: In the middle, there is a cross, the Indian symbol for trade or bartering: the Indians cross the index finger of each hand [to make the X]. At the right side of the cross a beaver can be recognized, and above it a series of lines indicates the number of beaver pelts the writer wants to trade. Behind the beaver a rifle is drawn. He wanted to trade this, too, as well as everything to the right of the cross. For [all] that, he wanted a white buffalo skin and that of a fisher and an otter. The three animals are easy to identify in the drawing.

At five o'clock four Cree Indians arrived, among them a famous chief, le Sonnant. They brought news: the Assiniboines had shot a Gros Ventre chief, [and] two white men coming to Fort William had been robbed by the Gros Ventres. This was bad news for our travel plans. At seven o'clock we found three of the Cree Indians with Mr. Hamilton. The chief spoke long; Deschamps was the interpreter. He said he was poor and loved the white man. He had [nothing] to trade but was hoping they would pity him and lend or sell him a horse. He would pay for it later. They needed the horse to carry things to the fort occasionally. He [then] asked for some liquor to bring joy to his heart and enable [him] to lie down. He had actually received several [drams] already.

17 October: [Le Sonnant] came and Bodmer wanted to draw him. He had very sick-looking eyes and could not sit still, so the work was very difficult. He is a famous shaman in his nation. When men want to know [the future, a shaman will] use trickery. They appear without any ornaments, dressed only [in] a breechcloth. A small lodge is built with poles and covered [with] a blanket. [The medicine man's] hands are tied, and he is bound tightly to a post. The lodge begins to shake; one hears the cries of buffalo, bears, and other noises. They maintain, and sincerely believe, that the devil has come. Then [the medicine man] is found, still tied in the same position, and he makes prophecies. Once he was with the Mandans and predicted that a rider on a white horse would arrive the next day and be killed. This happened: a Cheyenne Indian came on a white horse, was taken prisoner, and was killed.

18 October: In the night, hoarfrost; [in the morning,] raw wind [and] driving snow. Later in the afternoon, some Assiniboines came and announced [that] 40 tipis of their tribe [would arrive] tomorrow. Today I read Morrell's [1832] work (A Narrative of Four Voyages to the South Sea) and found [information] about the Brazilian coastline. Unfortunately, this work has [nothing] about natural history. In the evening we finished [our notes] on the Osages.[3]

19 October: In the night, heavy frost. The whole ground solidly frozen. At breakfast it was very cold in the dining room. There was a fireplace, but no fire [was] lit. Eating in America is not viewed as a time for pleasure and conversation, as it is in Europe, but apparently more as a necessary evil. Everyone hurries, talks little, swallows hastily, and runs away.

At eleven o'clock, I went with Moncravie to the upper forest. We visited

Assiniboine tree graves. On one there were four warriors, among them a youth, thirteen to fifteen years [old]. Moncravie climbed up, opened the hides and robes, and cut off the head, which I carried home in my hunting bag. The skin and hair were still partially attached, but dried up. I hoped [the skull might] be featured in [Professor] Blumenbach's cabinet [collection of human skulls]. With snares, Deschamps' children caught two small prairie foxes in [their] burrows, one of them alive [and] very beautiful; I bought [it].

The afternoon remained cold. The snow did not melt in the shade. This is a cold region [with] a long winter. An Indian froze to death here on the prairie in May 1832. He was surprised by a heavy snowstorm; the girl who [accompanied him] lost a whole foot.

Several lodges of Assiniboines arrived [late in the day]. Mr. Hamilton, with whom I spent evenings, gave me a Dacota tobacco pouch made from the skin of an entirely white skunk—an interesting museum piece. Its feet and tail were trimmed with red and green cloth and glass beads; the eyes [were] two thick, blue glass beads.

20 October: Cold. In the dining room today they lit a colossal fire. Up to now [there had been none] at all, [but] today it was so [huge] that the house could have been set [ablaze] with it.

21 October: At seven thirty, 30°F. The thermometer could not be left hanging in the hallway today, because it had been stolen by the Indians once before, [and] we had to pay 10 dollars to get it back.

The Assiniboines were prowling everywhere. The clerks were dressed better this morning, because they expected many Indians [and] were said to be respected more by these people if they were well dressed.

Last night at Mr. Hamilton's, we [met] the Assiniboine chief General Jackson (Ajanjan) and two principal warriors. The first was called Man-tó-Uitkatt, [Crazy Bear]. All three were handsome men, tall and strong. The chief had an attractive but somewhat broad face, [a] friendly expression, [and] beautiful teeth. [He] was painted red and wore a colorfully striped shirt and an elegant waistcoat with little mother-of-pearl buttons. [Crazy] Bear was almost naked. The third man, Huh-Jiob, [Wounded Leg], was dressed the best and most characteristically. His face was red on top [and] black from his chin to his mouth; his hair was adorned with a horizontal strip of whitish skin. His chest was very heavily tattooed, marked with black stripes in different [but] regular directions. He wore shiny metal bracelets on his upper arms and wrists. All three [men] were from the [Assiniboine band called] Gens des Roches.

Today I packed my plant collection, [now dry, although] most of the specimens had turned moldy. At twelve thirty an Indian came rushing in on horseback, and in the distance we saw a whole troop marching toward us. Out in front was [Ajanjan] in a new white robe. [Wounded Leg] walked beside him, and after them followed 23 Assiniboines in one row. Travois [pulled by] dogs [and accompanied by] women and children arrived [next]. With Chardon, I went toward the Indians, and we shook hands with the important men, [who] were then led into the fort. The Indians, apparently already well fed at Fort William, were very merry, and one could hear singing everywhere. Tipis had been put up around the fort. Handsome men and women could be seen coming from the forest, where they fetched dry wood with their travois. At home I found a tall, handsome Indian called White Buffalo Cow (Pteh-Skah), whom Mr. Bodmer drew. He had true Indian facial features [and was] painted red; his teeth were very even and white.

Deschamps and other hunters returned with the meat of seven buffalo bulls. They had not seen any [buffalo] cows or other animals. Food provisions were poor at the fort; there were no buffalo in the vicinity on this side of the river. The Indians said that they wanted to go to the other side to shoot buffalo. If they did, they would destroy an important [food source] for the fort, and it would become a very difficult [situation]. Rarely does [the fort] have provisions for more than one week.

22 October: Slightly overcast. No frost. A crowd of Indians [were] in the fort very early. White Buffalo Cow came and wanted to be paid for being drawn. About 30 Indian tipis had been put up near the fort overnight. Indian dogs ran around in large numbers. Many of them came into the fort, and [their] howling drove us crazy.

My boat was being caulked. In the company store I bought a beautiful blackish wolfskin for a half dollar and a small Crow bow made from a bighorn for 3 dollars. I completed the [packing] of the herbarium.

Mr. Bodmer finished his drawing of White Buffalo Cow (Pteh-Skah), to whom he gave a neckerchief [and other items]. Moncravie bought an Indian woman today; after long bartering [he] paid perhaps 250 dollars for her. In the afternoon a group of the woman's relatives could be seen in a circle in the Indian camp, drunk and singing.

Mr. Bodmer and I roamed through the prairie. I found interesting seeds, among them those of the *Yucca angustifolia,* which grows on barren prairie hills. I bought a beautiful war whistle from an Assiniboine, nine and a half inches long, wrapped with bluish green and beautiful yellow feather quills, a fine ornament on the brown skin of an Indian warrior. The same man had an especially nice, colorfully adorned *chichikué* [rattle], which he did not want to sell, because it came from a fallen friend.

Dreidoppel went onto the prairie to pick sage *(Artemisia),* which he intended to pack with the birds, because of its pungency. We had crates made. [Our new] boat was caulked and will be on the river tomorrow. It will be equipped with a tent and a small oven, or stove. My [Fort McKenzie] boat will remain here in its place. Mr. Hamilton was very indisposed today, suffering from a liver ailment.

This afternoon I saw how the Indians mistreated [their] poor dogs. A lame dog [trying] to pull a loaded travois could not move [it]. He [was beaten] and howled pitifully; he was as emaciated as a skeleton. Another dog lay dead beside a tipi; he had doubtless died of hunger. These dogs gnaw on old hides, hard as wood — nothing is safe from their hunger. The fort's chickens were in constant danger.

The fort's billy goat, which had no female companion, [provided some] very comical scenes, paying court to a female dog, horse, or mule. It stood in front of them [and] pushed out its tongue, licking, and making the funniest noises. [There were other odd, amusing] scenes in the fort. A drunken Indian sat on the ground [while] two others hugged and kissed him. They probably reciprocally [put] brandy into each others' mouths.

23 October: There were still Indians in the fort. After nine o'clock [it] was stormy and dismal. In this country one cannot count on the same weather continuing for three days.

Four Assiniboines came into our room, among them a man who had been drawn full-figure, a relative of Deschamps; his name was Påsesick-Kaskutäu [Nothing but Powder]. They worked diligently on our boat. Soon after midday, however, the [weather] became so severe that [outdoor] work stopped altogether. We kept busy with packing. The storm increased toward evening; sparks from the fire flew across the fort's [court]yard, so it was very good that all the gunpowder was in the new powder magazine. The night was very unpleasant.

24 October: Deschamps' sons, [who were hunters,] quarreled with Chardon. They owed money to the company and did not want to turn in their beavers

[there], so they went to Fort William to sell them. As usual, we spent the evening at Mr. Hamilton's, who gave me some interesting [publications] of the Temperance Society.[4]

25 October: Weather calm [and] clear; at seven thirty, 34°F. About noon I went out to look for two markers (carved pegs) I made during my first stay at Fort Union [and placed] near clusters of *Cactus ferox* on the prairie. Unfortunately, we did not find either of them. In the afternoon [our] hunters returned, having [killed] five buffalo; one of the hunters brought me a large pack rat he had shot.

Shortly before dusk we saw Indians coming at a quick pace toward the fort. I counted 24 men, a war party. They were meanly dressed, most clothed entirely in leather, hides, [and pelts]. Some [had] coal-black faces (the ones who had counted coup); most [were] painted red. On their backs they carried bundles of possessions; in their hands some of them held lances [or] guns; on their backs, bows and arrows. Chardon went to meet this wild, fast-striding group, and they were led to the fort's Indian room. [Their] partisan [or leader] was Uatschin-Tönschenih, [Foolish]. [With them] was a young Indian, the son of Uïtschasta-Jutä, [Man Eater], a chief loyal to the Fur Company, who was [then] a six-day-journey [distant]. [The young man] came with a message from his father to Mr. Hamilton: another chief, insulted by the skirmish at Fort McKenzie, had moved 100 tipis north to the Hudson's Bay Company. Furthermore, a second Assiniboine war party was approaching Fort Union to steal the fort's horses. [The fort should] be on guard. The present war party intended to [mount] a campaign against the Hidatsas. [These war parties did not bode well for] our journey.

26 October: In the morning, gray sky, rain. The war party still remained here. After noon Mr. Campbell paid us a visit and stayed late, and we talked [at length] about travels to the mountains. [Our] boat was finished today.

27 October: The Indian war party left us this morning. Mr. Chardon [had persuaded] the partisan to give up his [Hidatsa raiding] plan, which [could have made difficulties for the fur company].

The forests [along] the Missouri stood completely leafless and winterlike. The wind drove sand high up from the sandbars; the air was filled with it. No living being could be seen on the prairie except for the fort's horses and dogs. Only a few Indian tipis were near the fort. In the afternoon, heavy driving snow started; [it was the kind of] winter afternoon [on which] one [likes to] snuggle up to the fireplace.

At six o'clock, during dinner, we found out that Moncravie's wife had abandoned her husband and left with Deschamps' son.

28 October: Morning bright, calm, cold. Light snow on the ground—for the first time I saw the prairie in its real winter coat. Smoke rose in the distance where the horses were kept. They [remained] outside all winter, [and] if there was deep snow, they went to the forest and lived only on bark. They were said to like cottonwood bark.

The weather turned almost nice during the day; beautiful sunshine. The hoarfrost that had covered the forests melted off toward noon. Because our departure was [imminent], we [completed] necessary preparations today. At noon Mr. Campbell ate with us. We talked at length about the Rocky Mountains. Mr. Campbell said that even now whites call certain Yellowstone [tributaries] by their Crow names, [like the] Bighorn River. He told [me] about the Snakes [Shoshones] and Flatheads [Salish]. He knew the [Great Salt Lake] very well.

[Our new boat had] a good tent in the middle [and] was much larger than [our] previous one—broad and spacious. However, we needed [a crew of five]: Henry Morrin (helmsman), Hugron, Louis Vachard, Beauchamp, and Bourgua.

29 October: In the morning, bright, calm, cold weather; light snow scattered across the prairie. At eight thirty we saw a substantial herd of antelope on the hills behind the fort—more than thirty. Dreidoppel attempted in vain to get close to them.

For the trip Mr. Hamilton provided us with many necessary and comforting articles: coffee, white and brown sugar, salt, pepper, mustard, red cayenne pepper, [and] some bottles of wine. I took 2 gallons of whiskey (16 dollars) and 2 gallons of alcohol (32 dollars)—one belonged to Mr. Bodmer.

I wrote a letter to Mr. Mitchell. Today the hunters rode out on a buffalo hunt; we will [not likely see] them again. The afternoon was calm and pleasant. [We] were busy with packing. Bullets were cast, which I had to distribute to my [crew]. Indians brought winter moccasins, the fur on the inside.

Every evening for three to four days, the medicine drum could be heard being beaten in an Indian tipi for a sick child. The parents [asked for] medicine from Mr. Hamilton, which he refused—first, because he could not heal [the child] of this [malady], and [second] because, if there was an unfortunate ending, the Indians would blame him.

30 October: The baggage was put in order early and distributed over the boat. [I discovered] that two of my men did not have [long] guns—Bourgua and Hugron, [although] the latter had a pistol. We took leave of Fort Union and its inhabitants at eleven o'clock in fine weather and navigated downriver. At twelve thirty the mouth of the Yellowstone River was to the right. Soon we put in at Fort William's landing-place, debarked, and [walked] toward the fort, 300 paces distant.

Mr. Campbell cordially received us and gave us letters for his clerk with the Hidatsas, Mr. [Joseph] Dougherty (brother of [John Dougherty,] the Indian agent). We received a small box of cigars [and] a prairie fox as presents; [the fox was] caught today in a steel beaver trap. At one thirty we continued our journey. It was afternoon, and our men had nothing to eat except awful old pork bacon fat. We looked greedily at a gaggle of wild geese on the riverbank. The rifles were loaded and put in order.

After an hour we lay to on a headland on the right [to prepare food]. A herd of seven [deer] *(Cervus virginianus)* came to the water to drink, [as did] two kinds of mice, whose cute little tracks were always visible in fours on the packed sand. Our men cooked their salt pork as well as some coffee. Dreidoppel did not feel well. All three of us had slight headaches, doubtless from the poor, fatty food.

We continued sailing until eight o'clock, when the night forced us to put in. Nobody stood watch.

31 October: Bright, beautiful weather; nothing noteworthy on the river. We lay to on a sandbar and lit a fire to prepare breakfast. Dreidoppel and Morrin went hunting [but by] ten thirty returned, having neither shot nor seen anything. We sailed on right away. The *Cornus* (red willow) on the edge of the forest formed a dark purple-red rim on the banks of the Missouri. Our men complained about the bad salt pork, and we looked everywhere to shoot something [to eat]. At eleven thirty we heard three shots, most likely [fired] by Assiniboines. We distributed powder. The hills here had a rugged, raw look. At one o'clock the men believed they saw Indians on the wide sandbars to the left, but [a view through] the telescope revealed them as lifeless driftwood.

At two o'clock we reached [hills] on the right bank, similar in shape and formation to [those] in the Mauvaises-Terres. We lay to on [a] steep forest bank. Morrin, Bodmer, Dreidoppel, and Beauchamp went to [search] for game. I watched over the boat and made notes about the views. Two eagles sat on high treetops; several magpies were in the forest. Today our small bear constantly and noisily scratched his crate. He lay mostly on his back and did not shy away from the nails we had driven in as deterrents. Resting near the bank, we did not hear anything but the unpleasant roar of waves breaking [on] snags and sandbanks collapsing near and far, often sounding like muffled [gunfire].

Finally, we happily heard two shots by the hunters, which raised new hopes in our people. Our animals were also very hungry; they did not want to eat salt pork. [But the men] came back [without] anything. At four o'clock we continued sailing. [When] we lay to on a sandspit, to cook for the evening, it was already late. We dispersed into the forest. Near the campground the sand was covered with doe and wolf tracks, [but] the only living animals I saw were crows, common ravens, magpies, and a flock of small linnets *(Fringilla linaria)*—unfortunately, I could not shoot one of them. Morrin and Dreidoppel also returned empty-handed. Our [crew] slept on land at the fire; [the three of us stayed] in the boat; nobody stood watch.

1 November: In the morning, very cold [as we set out]. When the sun came up, we saw a large number of prairie hens in the forest [and] flying back and forth across the river; also a bear in the hills. At eight o'clock we lit a fire on the right bank. The hunters went out. Morrin shot a female elk, [so] we now had meat for several days. When the game was brought to the ship, some of it was cooked and our hungry animals were fed. We sailed downriver; the hill chain was serrated with low, cone-shaped hills.

[By] ten o'clock, weather pleasantly warm; Indian summer. [At] twenty minutes past four o'clock, we put ashore on the right bank. [It] was steep, covered above with a thinned-out cottonwood forest and below with rose-bushes where innumerable tracks of game crossed, especially elk. I had never seen so many. We could not stalk, but [we] heard game walking, and Morrin claimed to have seen a herd of at least 200 elk. Mr. Bodmer went into the forest to the left, saw a deer, and walked into the distance. We waited a long time for him; it turned night, and he did not come back. Finally, very late, we heard two shots upriver; soon two more. We surmised that he must be lost. [When] we [fired a return signal shot, he] started to yell. Dreidoppel and Hugron walked toward him and brought him back at eight o'clock in total darkness. He had followed the deer, lost [sight] of the river, walked perhaps eight to ten miles, [and] gotten into terrible thorny thickets and a marsh. Finally, he saw a troop of twenty Indians on the prairie coming toward him. Thereupon he turned again toward the forest [and] shot six times, despite the Indians' proximity, because he was in peril. Luckily he [glimpsed] the river from a hill and worked himself [through the thickets] until he reached it. He was exhausted, overheated, and hungry. We gave him coffee and elk meat. We sailed on only about 300 paces [farther, to] a sandbar, where we slept.

2 November: The cold, raw wind was so strong that we [were soon forced to anchor and camp] the whole day in a cottonwood thicket.

At nine o'clock I left the fire [to explore] the thicket, where I found bear scat and tracks. The former contained whole heaps of undigested buffalo berry skins. Suddenly a shot was fired close by. It was Dreidoppel, [who] had just wounded a [young] deer. We followed the blood and finally shot it [and] its companion. Both [deer] were round and fat; some [crewmen fetched] the game and butchered it. It was dark at six o'clock; after nine the moon rose, and the wind abated toward midnight.

3 November: At dawn we sailed off. It looked as if it would rain. [The hills] here were far more significant than the ones seen earlier. The [formations] on the left bank [looked like] the Mauvaises-Terres, the same color and height; we reached them at eleven thirty. The hill chains soon retreated; a wide, flat area followed on both banks; to the left, forest, then prairie. The river was very wide here and carried more water than [upstream]. We lay to [at a prairie] on the right, and the [crew] cooked. It was overgrown in places with *Solidago* and some other plants. Mostly, however, large stretches alternated [between] *Symphoria* [and bushy] cottonwood, ash, and elm, surrounded [by] rosebushes. We roamed through these bushes and a mile farther [but saw only birds. The voyage continued, and] we sailed until about dusk, when we put ashore on the right bank. We lit a fire between high cottonwood trunks, two feet in diameter; [they] almost formed a circle. After we had eaten our dinner of meat, we stood watch for the first time. I had the first [turn]. A strong fire was maintained until [ten o'clock], then a lesser one. Night windy but not cold.

4 November: We sailed until eight o'clock and then [stopped] to prepare our breakfast. The forest was dense here, full of rose underbrush. I went into it with Morrin, and we soon saw six *Cervus virginianus;* only their white tails, as usual in an upright position, were visible [to us] in the dense bushes. We finished with breakfast at nine thirty, but Morrin did not want to leave

[then], on account of the wind. [We left later but at noon] stopped [again]; the wind was too strong.

We went out with guns. In the tall forest [there were] a few open areas with high grass, *Artemisia,* and other plants, now all yellow and reddish brown colored. Buffalo and deer tracks led in all directions. I followed one [trail], walked [around] and stepped over fallen trees, found shed deer antlers [and] the tracks of large bears, [and] saw prairie hens, some blackbirds that had not migrated, and a small flock of *Fringilla linaria.* We sensed game everywhere but [found nothing and therefore] sailed on. We saw no buffalo until Fort Clark, not a single one. After four fifteen [a] strong, raw wind blew again, and the air was full of sand. Slightly farther on, a beautiful view with several cone-shaped [hill]tops and some mesas. The day came to an end; the sky was very gray and seemed to foretell bad weather, [but] at midnight the sky cleared.

5 November: [A favorable day for travel, passing through a landscape similar to that observed earlier. At day's end,] the sun reddened the elevations in a marvelous, incomparable way with its last, fiery rays. We were not far from the mouth of the Little Missouri. At five thirty we put ashore on the right bank for the night.

The place was interesting, sandy with a cottonwood forest totally destroyed by beavers; they had felled a number of large trunks, forming a clearing. Besides beaver, fresh elk, deer, and wolf tracks were evident, also large bear prints. The night was dark but starlit; our fire shone brightly.

6 November: In the morning, bright and beautiful, cold, everything white with hoarfrost [as we set out]; at eight thirty we tied up on the right bank and started a fire in the tall forest. We watched eight elk walk away from the place. We separated to hunt. Morrin shot a fat fawn, which he carried back.

A bit downriver we saw [many] trunks, twice as wide as a man's body, gnawed off by beavers. There must have been a multitude of beavers in this area. Morrin counted 14 beaver lodges between Fort Union and here. Six, eight, and more animals lived in some [lodges]. We continued sailing, [and] after eleven thirty we were opposite the mouth of the Little Missouri River. [Later on,] we lay to on the right and looked for game. At two thirty we departed. [We had] a wide and broad view of the river. The elevations were rather low; everywhere on the bank, forests and willow bushes. To the left and behind us, a broad hill chain beyond the forest, with many brick-red, burned, conical peaks; some resembled miniature, inactive volcanoes. We sailed until dark and then put ashore on a savagely torn bank. The night was without starlight or moonlight [but] not so cold as yesterday. Wolves howled fiercely on both banks. At ten o'clock, when I finished my watch, I went down to the boat and woke Mr. Bodmer to relieve me.

7 November: We departed at dawn and [were] not even a quarter of an hour down the river when Indians called after us from our departure point. We had luckily but barely escaped [an] unpleasant encounter. When we were farther away, they fired a few shots.

After [noon] we saw a white horse in the distance at a turn of the river. Soon, near the bank, [we saw] an Indian; then three [were spied], with a whole herd of horses, at a watering place on the river. They had bare heads, reddish brown buffalo robes, [and] bows and arrows. A winter village of these Hidatsas was located in the [nearby] forest. They had moved [there] only a day or two [ago] from their summer villages. [The Indians] shouted at us, but we quickly moved past on the strong current. At the next wooded headland, we navigated again across the river. The bank was steeper there, [so the] water [was] deeper. We mostly sailed that way, [constantly] going back and forth. [We were] now in the true territory of the Hidatsas, [and] we expected to see them on both banks in great numbers. After the Missouri made a very large turn, [about a] mile downstream, we saw some Indians on the right bank, and soon to the left, [winter shelters] in the dense cotton-wood forest. A few men dressed like Europeans [appeared] nearby. Among them we recognized the old interpreter Charbonneau. They shouted to us; we put ashore and [saw] the brother of the Indian agent Major Dougherty, who was a clerk for Mr. Sublette and Mr. Campbell. [The latter two had] recently formed an opposition to Fort Clark, [and] the clerk had [moved] with [the Hidatsas] to their forested winter dwellings. [The traders] had only two temporary huts but were building a house in the forest.

I gave Mr. Dougherty a letter from Mr. Campbell. We ate with him in his small hut [and] also smoked; however, when we found out that gunpowder was stored there, [the smoking] ceased, for it was very dangerous [with a strong wind blowing into the hut]. We saw many Indians on horseback and on foot. [Some] sat with us around the fire and admired our long beards. The night was dark, stormy, and very cold.

8 November: In the morning we left early; Charbonneau accompanied us. After twelve fifteen we were opposite [a] Hidatsa village. There were Indians

on the bank, [and] at twelve thirty we were invited to come ashore. Char-bonneau advised us to [go]. A respected man, Íta-Widáhki-Hischá, [Red Shield], led us to his leather tipi above the riverbank. The lodge was new, white, spacious, warm, [and] very nicely decorated; at each side of the [en-try there] was a long, bright strip made of porcupine quills and glass beads. The host's brother and uncle, [as well as] young men, children, and women, were in the lodge. The host wore a beard that extended a little below his chin, like [that of] the Ponca chief Schudegácheh (see the illustrations by Mr. Bodmer [fig. 2]). [Íta-Widáhki-Hischä] had blackish blue stripes tat-tooed on his right breast. The old uncle had an ugly face [and was] fat, with a drooping chest and thick belly. His clothes were disheveled [and] his genitals bare. The woman of the house had a child on her lap with a big harelip. We received corn and beans, very well done, in a large bowl, and the three of us ate out of the bowl with spoons [made] from [horns of] buffalo and bighorn. [A] pipe was circulated (it was a Dacota pipe of red stone; [the Mandans and Hidatsas] made no good pipes). We talked to them through Charbonneau. Our [crew] received a kettle [of] boiled corn, for which we gave a present of some tobacco and [gun]powder.

At one o'clock we departed. To the right we saw the Hidatsa village called Awacháhwi (le Village des Souliers), [with] seventeen or eighteen lodges. At two thirty we reached Ruhptare, the first Mandan village to the right. When we [came] around a promontory, we saw in the distance the Mandan village of Mih-Tutta-Hangkusch, and soon Fort Clark became visible, too. At about three or four o'clock Mr. Kipp welcomed us at the bank and led us up to the fort. He was [an] American Fur Company clerk and administered Fort Clark.

XVI

Winter Sojourn at Fort Clark
among the Mandans and Hidatsas

FROM 8 NOVEMBER 1833 UNTIL 31 DECEMBER 1833

[8 November 1833:] Fort Clark had not undergone any important changes [since our June visit, when] the Yanktonais had [unsuccessfully tried] to make peace with the Mandans and Hidatsas. At the beginning of September, the Yanktonais finally achieved their goal. Two hundred tents of Yanktonais had camped on the prairie behind Fort Clark [for] three to four days. They had many festivities and dances, and Fort Clark was crowded with Dacota, Mandan, and Hidatsa Indians. Now it was quiet in the fort's surroundings. Some Indians had already moved into their winter quarters in the neighboring forest, but many still remained. In the fort itself, there were two interpreters: Belhumeur, an Ojibwe, for the Mandan language; [and] Ortubise, [now absent, for] Dacota. Mr. Kipp was more fluent in Mandan than Belhumeur. [Aside from] the interpreters, there were only six men.

Mr. McKenzie had [ordered a] house [to be built] in the fort for us. But there was a lack of workers, meaning craftsmen. The fort's store was well stocked [with] merchandise having a value of $15,000 in St. Louis, but with [the] large number of rats here, all supplies were in danger. There was always a large quantity of corn on hand, often 600 to 800 bushels. However, it can be assumed that, at the time of our presence, these rodents were eating five bushels of [it] daily.[M1] Mr. McKenzie took a physician upriver with [him, for fear of] the cholera that had caused great devastation on the lower Missouri this past August. At Bellevue and Mr. Cabanné's post, most people had died. Major Dougherty was almost the sole survivor of this frightful illness.

Because the new house [was not] finished, we all lived in Mr. Kipp's small room, where he slept with [his] wife and child; that [room] was constantly

---

M1 The rat that causes so much damage here is the one called Norway rat (*Mus decumanus*). It should be noted that a bushel of Indian corn weighed 50 pounds.

beleaguered by Indians. They sat down without further ado, wherever they could find a place, smoked, and frequently got food. Mr. Kipp's wife was a Mandan [with] nice facial features, rather white skin, [and] red cheeks. He had been here eleven years and knew perfectly all their manners and customs.

9 November: In the morning, I went onto the prairie and saw no living creature, [just] numerous holes in the ground, [made by] the *Arctomys hoodii* and prairie fox. Mandan women, loaded with bundles, [were] everywhere on the prairie, moving from their villages toward the forest.

I went behind the Mandan village Mih-Tutta-Hangkusch and found a strange arrangement. To make medicine (probably), they had stuck four poles [into the ground and] laid out four buffalo skulls [and], eight to ten steps farther back, a long row of twenty-six human skulls.[1] [I also saw] a white buffalo cow hide on a high pole, an item of high value for these people; the killing of such a cow [is] as important as killing an enemy, and they purchase [such] hides for high prices. Often the hides are dedicated to their gods [and] left to decompose.

A very recent [scaffold] grave was covered with red cloth. There was no lack of new graves. Many [people], particularly children and women, had died during an epidemic of a kind of whooping cough; [others] were still dying.

Several distinguished Indians visited us today, among them the Mandan chief Mató-Tópe, [Four Bears], who [admired] our Indian portraits [and] recognized several [subjects]. A proud and gallant man, [his generosity was great as his] glory in war. He campaigned with the Hidatsas against the Cheyennes. When [the warriors] met on the prairie, a Cheyenne chief rode forth and called, "Is Mató-Tópe among you?" [Four Bears] rode out right away. They fired at each other; [the shots] missed. Then they jumped from their horses. The Cheyenne tried to stab [Four Bears] with his knife, but the Mandan was faster [and] grabbed it, wounding his hand—[but] with [that knife he then] stabbed the enemy chief to death.

These Indians smoked Mr. Kipp's pipe every time they gathered; he handed out a few hundred pounds of tobacco yearly for this very purpose. A Mandan from Mih-Tutta-Hangkusch, named Síh-Chidä, Yellow Feather, invited Mr. Kipp and me to a feast. We went to the village. The lodge was spacious, rather bright, round (I measured one as 60 paces in circumference), [constructed of] poles [and] crossbeams on the inside, covered [on

Fig. 12. Karl Bodmer. *Mandan Earth Lodges*. Pencil. Maximilian makes numerous mention of this type of native village house. See especially chapter 18, the section on dwellings, and the color illustration of a lodge interior by Bodmer, PLATE 30. 3⅞ × 6 in. 1986.49.334.

the exterior] with turf, and made very tight. In the middle [of the roof there] was an opening [serving as a] chimney; below this opening, a small hole was dug for the fire. All kinds of implements were hung on or propped against the wall—[bullboats,] etc. We sat down on buffalo robes and received a wooden bowl with cooked corn and beans; another [contained] black berries [that] seemed to have come from a *Viburnum*. After we ate, our host lit a pipe and [handed it around] to the left for smoking. Thereupon we stood up and left without saying a word. Yellow Feather was the son of a famous man, les Quatre Hommes, [Four Men], who died not long ago.

10 November: In the morning, [windy]; light flurries. A distinguished Hidatsa warrior called Péhriska-Rúhpa (Two Ravens) visited us early. He was a big, handsome man who came quite often to the fort. We had [met] him [in June] on the *Assiniboine*.

Every day corn, beaver meat, and beaver pelts were brought in. Because of the competition with the Sublette and Campbell company, the price of beavers [was now] so high that a pound of [pelts] often cost seven dollars, causing a loss (the usual price was four dollars). [It] requires a lot of money to drive out competition.

11 November: Belhumeur rode [out] early with a man and two packhorses to hunt bison, because we had no fresh meat. After lunch Mató-Tópe came, also Péhriska-Rúhpa. They looked at the Indian portraits. The latter was in his nicest clothes, [obtained] from the Crows. He had a horse [equipped with] a colorfully ornamented bridle and saddle. A panther-skin quiver, like [those of] the Piegans, hung at the rear [of the saddle]. The bow was [backed] with elk [antler] or bighorn and was decorated with colorful cloth, white and blue [beads], and a tuft of sulfur-yellow horsehair. His clothes were rich and fine, [including] a beautiful bear [claw] necklace edged with otter skin around his neck. [His] leather shirt was reddish yellow with yellow porcupine [quill-embroidered] strips down the arms. Colorful [tufts of] horsehair [and] ermine and [locks] of long human hair [fringed the sleeves]. In his hand he carried a broad braid of scented grass, with which he occasionally wiped his mouth and nose. On each side of his forehead he had fastened the familiar [beaded hairbow] ornament of the Hidatsas. His leggins were rather plain. He did not stay long; [he] was said to be a great enthusiast of riding around.

12 November: Péhriska-Rúhpa visited us, as well as Mandans and [other] Hidatsas. The hunters returned; [they] had shot two bison bulls and a cow.

13 November: At nine o'clock, a Mandan [who looked] very concerned came and told us that there had been an extraordinary sign in the sky. Shooting stars had [soared] toward the west last night in unusually [great] numbers, by far more than usual.[2] This portended war or high mortality among humans. He asked what Mr. Kipp thought about it.

Later, other Indians came: Dipäuch (Broken Leg), Síh-Chidä, and another handsome man with noble features, Ah-Dä-Pússä (Striped or Spotted Arm).[3] All of them spoke about the meteor [shower]. Another Indian, Beróck-Itaïnú (Bull's Neck), appeared in mourning, poorly dressed and smeared with clay. A child of his had died [of] whooping cough, currently epidemic.

Mató-Tópe visited us with his wife and child, [who] was strong, round, [and] very cute, with beautiful, large eyes; he was completely naked. His name was Mató-Berocká (Male Bear). [Mató-Tópe] had a horse and baggage with him, also his medicine drum, black with red figures representing lightning and buffalo tracks. Almost every lodge has such a drum—a skin stretched over a broad hoop. [Four Bears] also brought along a lance, a beautiful bonnet of war-eagle feathers, and a few other things. He stayed a few hours. Later Yellow Feather came, too, [and] several others. They looked at the drawings with great enjoyment. [Yellow Feather] drew Mr. Bodmer and me; [he had] some talent.

They worked intensively on our dwelling [today], but [with no] carpenter; a common engagé did [everything]. A few wagons went daily to the lower forest to get wood; there was no supply of it [in the fort]. There were too few people here for the tasks [to be done].

14 November: Today they put glass windows in our house. The wind was so unpleasant and strong that they could not saw wood outdoors. At noon some men arrived with letters sent by Mr. Picotte at the Yanktonai trading-house. No letters from the lower Missouri had arrived yet, but [they] were expected any day. The Sioux were now dispersed across the prairies, but a rather good beaver trade had been conducted with them. Ortubise remained with Mr. Picotte.

A deaf-mute Mandan [arrived], sitting down like an automaton. He did not smoke tobacco. He was wrapped in a blanket and had [a] bow and arrows slung over his shoulders. He was a strong man; his height [was five feet] eight to nine Prussian inches. About evening, Wolf Chief (Chárätä-Numakschi) and a few other Mandans visited. The chief's leather shirt [was fastened] with a row of large, shiny buttons after the fashion of the whites. He stayed until we ate and [was given] meat, coffee, and corn bread.

15 November: In the morning, the Missouri carried ice for the first time; the sandbars were covered with [it].

Today Mr. Kipp's [men] took my boat out of the river to save it from the ice. Around ten o'clock the sun appeared; the weather turned pleasant. About noon I followed the creek that ran behind the fort, collected *Solidago* seeds, and found several types of grass. In shrubs of dry Syngenesia, a flock of *Fringilla linaria*—the first birds I had seen on [this] prairie.

After one o'clock Mató-Tópe came with his wife and child. He wore a blue and red uniform. Strips [embroidered with] white glass beads in the Indian fashion were attached to his [jacket] shoulders and [sleeves; the latter also had] fringes of black human hair. His face was painted yellow; the rims of his eyes [and the upper part of his forehead] were red.

In the afternoon I went with Mr. Bodmer to the area of the graves or scaffolds, about 300 paces from the fort, and he sketched a few medicines, among them the buffalo skulls and human skulls I mentioned [earlier; see

9 November and pl. 24]. The village was in the distant [background]. There were [other], different medicines [that] I shall describe [later]. [Among] the nearby graves, many [had] small boxes [placed] on scaffolds of four poles, in which, without doubt, children lay. Some were bound with hides. On other scaffolds we saw completely bleached skulls protruding from the hide [wrappings]. We inspected various skulls lying on the ground below the graves; I was reluctant to pick up any of them [because of] the Indians— [we were] so close to the village—but one could have easily made a highly interesting selection [of skulls] for Blumenbach's collection, choosing very differently formed [specimens]. Some were painted with three red stripes across the skull down over the temples. I decided to commit some thefts here in the future [to augment] the collection of that learned anthropologist. For that purpose the moon [would have] to shine brightly.

Mr. Kipp got his letters ready, because tomorrow he [planned to] send the men who had come with me back to the Yellowstone, and another man downriver to Mr. Picotte at the Yanktonais. That evening I wrote to Mr. McKenzie and to Chardon, asking the latter to buy me some additional Indian artifacts.

16 November: Mild frost. Morrin, Vachard, Hugron, Beauchamp, Bourgua, and Manyon went back on foot to Fort Union. They had two dogs [pulling] travois and intended to get there in seven days. Interpreter Ortubise's wife had received a message to join her husband. She loaded three [bullboats] with her luggage and traveled downriver, [a] trip [of] two and a half days.

Bodmer, Dreidoppel and I went hunting. We went down the steep slope from the high prairie to the wide, flat ground stretching between the Missouri and [the heights]. This plain was covered with willow thickets. The Mandans had cleared large stretches and planted corn, [squashes], various kinds of beans, and sunflowers (Helianthus). The corn, planted in hills, gets four [to] five [or] six feet tall. Between the cornstalks, long rows of tall

Fig. 13. Maximilian. Hidatsa women and bullboats. Ink. A bullboat was made by stretching bison hide over a wooden frame; Maximilian frequently called them "leather boats."

sunflowers were visible. [The Mandans] eat the seeds. Here and there, small [shelters] of poles, twigs, grass, and cornstalks, from which they watched over their fields at certain [seasons]. We went back about noon.

The evening was spent writing words of the Mandan language. Síh-Sä (Red Feather) corrected Arikara words for me. This young Mandan was a good person [and] accustomed to whites, because he was brought up by Mr. Kipp. He still watched the fort's horses, even though he was married. Síh-Chidä drew Indian figures [for] us. [Neither] Mr. Kipp [nor] I felt well. [He] took peppermint oil. The following morning I [took an herbal remedy].

17 November: Síh-Chidä had slept in the fort. He came inside early, got breakfast, and then continued his drawing.

At [noon] it turned much colder and the air [was] really snowy. Several Indians came [by, including] the tall, handsome Ah-Dä-Pússä, who spoke some Piegan. When we were at lunch, Charbonneau [arrived; he] had walked the whole distance up from [Joseph] Dougherty's [Hidatsa post]. Today was Sunday; [no one worked]. We hoped to move into our new quarters in three days. Doors, cots, and tables were [still] lacking. Síh-Chidä completed his drawing, representing himself in a blue and red uniform with a crown of feathers on his head; Mr. Bodmer gave him the colors. Indians are crazy about good, lively colors. Our fire burned poorly; a few Indian women, sitting in front of the fire in their heavy buffalo robes, took away from us the little heat we had.

In the evening Charbonneau had much [to say] about [Duke] Paul of Württemberg, with whom he had traveled. [Charbonneau] was lively but bragged a lot. He often [falsely claimed to have] shot buffalo and other animals. He [once] sold a horse to Mr. Kipp that he had already sold to Mr. Laidlaw. Similar [stories] have given him a bad reputation, but it was likely a bit too [harsh when] Sanford said [that] "he did not behave like a gentleman." He was strong, robust, a good rider and shot; and [he] ate [prodigiously]. Hunting was his main occupation. [Although] he could not hit buffalo from horseback, on foot he was an [able] marksman with rifle and shotgun. I did not feel well and went to bed early. Night cold.

18 November: Charbonneau left before breakfast. Mr. Kipp went with his gun and a man carrying goods to trade at Ruhptare. I wrote letters to Germany. They whitewashed our room today. In the afternoon Mató-Tópe came but did not stay long.

19 November: I [was] not well and took castor oil. The hunters rode out today

because we had no meat. The weather was pleasant, because there was no strong wind. Mr. Bodmer drew a view of Mih-Tutta-Hangkusch. Several Indians came into the fort—among them, [Mr. Kipp's father-in-law,] Medicine Bird, and three young people. Síh-Sä spoke about the great Medicine Rock of which Lewis and Clark tell (vol. 1 p. 224, [21 February 1805]). It is located on the bank of the Cannonball River, and one may get there on foot from the Mandan villages in two [to] three days. The rock, large as a house [and] round on top, [must] have consisted formerly of a soft mass, because on it one can see many impressions of animal and bare human feet; [there are] also travois tracks. The Mandans (who call it the medicine boulder, Mih-Chóppenisch) and the Hidatsas (who know it [as] Wíhdä-Katachí) [send] their war parties there. They do not [approach] the rock on the first evening but camp [nearby] and sacrifice a few items, like [bits] of cloth. The next morning they walk up to it and [someone, usually] the partisan, interprets the impressions and figures on the rock and predicts the outcome of their [proposed] venture. Then they smoke. [For more] about this subject see the history of the Mandans in [chapter 18].

We [made] frequent use of the long evenings to write down the Mandan, Hidatsa, Arikara, and Crow languages as correctly as possible according to Indian pronunciations. For all these languages, it was easy to find Indians here who spoke them fluently. All Mandans spoke Hidatsa; Mató-Tópe and others, fluent Arikara; but the Hidatsas seldom [knew] Mandan.

20 November: I was still not feeling well [and found my work] burdensome.

Dipäuch came and told us many things. He [wore] a mink fur cap with bells [and feathers] on it. His hair hung down naturally. His face was painted with many black, [vertical] stripes. On his chest he wore a silver gorget with a deer engraved [on it]. As usual, his upper body was bare, even in the harshest cold, as is customary among the Mandans and Hidatsas. He coughed a lot, as many of these Indians [did].

Several Hidatsas with big, beautiful bear [claw] necklaces visited us. Broken Leg came again, but he had taken off his fur cap and finery. Bodmer and Dreidoppel went hunting. [They built a drag] to haul rabbit viscera and other meat [as bait] for the wolves and predators, and then [waited]. They came back before dusk. Dreidoppel had seen a wolf and two red foxes. They only shot at the wolf. [Our] little [pet] fox ran away [twice] today and came back [both] times. The buffalo hunters returned; they had shot five bulls.

21 November: Several of us felt indisposed [in] our stomachs and intestines. Mr. Bodmer and I took medicine. This illness had affected many people the last few days.

The deaf-mute Mandan came early (Máhnu-Ningka, Turkey's Egg). He communicated fluently with Mr. Kipp [and] all his people by sign language. He was lively and liked to laugh. Síh-Sä mixed white clay with water and rubbed the tanned side of his buffalo robe with it—partly to remove dirt and partly to keep it clean. [The inner sides of] these robes are often painted completely white.

Our new [place] was completely finished. It was whitewashed yesterday with white clay [and] now had to dry out. Several young, handsome Indians looked in our windows [and] seemed to like the newly completed house. The young men were bare on the entire upper parts of their bodies, and their robes covered them rather carelessly. In the evening we finished [recording words of] the Mandan language.

22 November: We moved [to our new quarters, although] in some places the walls were still wet. It heated quite well [but was] very smoky when the wind blew from a certain direction. [The] clear glass windows [provided] excellent light to draw or write, [and there were] two small cottonwood tables and a few benches to sit on. The three beds were planks attached to the walls. The door could be locked. Stairs led to a small attic. [A smoky chimney] was the only problem.

At twelve o'clock, 25°F. Light flurries in the afternoon turned into a snowstorm with high winds. We had already set up our room and were working there. Síh-Sä had severe stomach pains and diarrhea today. Mr. Kipp gave him a strong dose of castor oil. Lower abdomen complaints were very common. Several Indians came, but we did not let them in.

23 November: The snow [had not been] more than half an inch. Mr. Kipp sent Síh-Sä back to the Mandan village, because he was very sick. We checked the fort's medicine and my own small [personal supply]. Unfortunately, we had neither peppermint, peppermint tea, nor tea of *Melissa [officinalis]*— nothing but a handful of lilac flowers and a bit more of the American chamomile, which tasted very different from ours. Luckily, the [ipecac] powder had been spared from the wetness on the boat.

I was informed today that, for the first time [this winter], the Missouri was frozen solid below the high bank of Mih-Tutta-Hangkusch. Strangely, it [happened] on the same day last year. I saw some Indian women on the

Missouri who had made holes in the ice, where they washed their heads, breasts, and upper bodies.

About ten o'clock Beróck-Itaïnú and Dipäuch brought a gray female wolf still showing [signs] of life. It had been shot in the head; some teeth on one side were destroyed. After lunch two Hidatsas brought 26 beavers that they wanted to sell; 22 of them were very large, 4 [were] half grown. Our wolf died wretchedly. I had paid two *tarquettes* of tobacco (a value of [sixty-four] cents) for [it]. Mr. Kipp got fourteen large beavers for one horse and red cloth. [The Indians] took back the rest [of the beavers], because they wanted another horse for them.

24 November: Because of all the rats, we put our tame prairie fox in the attic during the night, where a large amount of Indian corn was stored. He often chased the rats and made a lot of noise; we presumed that he caught some, too.

I gave Mató-Tópe a bear claw necklace to finish for me; I bought an otter skin and blue glass pearls in the store for this purpose. I [also] gave him colors and a piece of paper [so that he could] paint one of [his] skirmishes for me.

A few Hidatsas brought beaver pelts [and] wanted to [know] the price. Among them was the old chief Addíh-Hiddísch, who had caught more than fifty, including a spotted one. Tomorrow Mr. Kipp will buy close to 100 or 150 beaver pelts, having a value of a few thousand dollars.

Addíh-Hiddísch (Maker of Roads or Road Maker) sat the whole evening and smoked. He looked strange; he wore an old round hat, an old vest, [and] his hair [was] wild around his head; [see pl. 29]. [He was] said to be a very good Indian.

25 November: Our fire did not burn, [because] the wood was not dry; it was therefore uncomfortable in the room. I saw several hundred snow buntings (*Emberiza nivalis*) in the dry *Solidago* plants, picking the seeds. Indian boys had set up [many] snares of horsehair attached to a long stick; the stick was held down at each end by a rock. They sprinkled *Solidago* seeds around it and waited for success, [but I inadvertently] chased away the birds, whose white plumage flashed in the sun.

An Indian brought a well-preserved skin of a *[Centrocerus?] uropha-sianus,* which I bought for a mirror (worth seventy-five cents). In the skin of a prairie dog, he had large pieces of mica, which he [removed] and [then traded] me the skin for red [paint]. They burned mica and mixed it with water to make a very white paint.

Chief Kähka-Chamahän, [Little Raven], from Ruhptare, stayed with us a long time. He wanted to trade four beavers for a music box. [He had] a lame foot. In the evening Charbonneau [came and invited] us [to] the great buffalo medicine festival. This festival was held to attract buffalo and lasted four nights. The Mandans had already celebrated [it] a few days ago.

26 November: Breakfast was ordered earlier [than usual], because we planned to accompany Charbonneau to the Hidatsas eight hours away. At eight thirty we left the fort—Bodmer, Charbonneau, a Hidatsa, and I. We [started off] behind the first Mandan village, where [there were] several worn trails to Ruhptare. [The route] ran fairly straight, parallel to the Missouri, and along the [edge] of the [plateau above] the lowlands. [The summer village of] Ruhptare [was] entirely deserted. The medicines [and burial] scaffolds were the same as at Mih-Tutta-Hangkusch, except [there they] were even closer to the village. Crows sat on them. We walked through the village, which had at its center a round [plaza] with an ark, exactly like [Mih-Tut-ta-Hangkusch], [and] also the black[-faced Ochkíh-Häddä] in front of the medicine lodge.

Near [Ruhptare] we went down to the river and saw three Indians on the ice, whom we followed. They had marked [a safe] trail [with] a few stakes. The ice was rough; we walked carefully. [Then] the old chief Kähka-Chamahän came to us on the ice, and we followed him into dense willow thickets bordering a vast forest.

The winding trail continued to Ruhptare's winter village, located in thickets of willow, cottonwood, *Cornus*, ash, and elm. Here the chief said goodbye to us, because we could not stay [and accept] his invitation to his lodge. Everywhere we saw women, singly or several together, busy tanning hides [or] chopping or fetching wood. There was little old wood left [in the forest], [just] a dense [mixed] underbrush of [shrub and vine species]. There were open areas with high withered grass, [like] Fort Union. We followed the forest trail up to the hills. [Some were] strange hills of clay; springs frequently originated in them, [at that time all frozen solid]. Half an hour later, the hills retreated and there was a wide prairie [along] the Missouri. The prairie was covered with dry yellow grass. We followed the trail for several hours through this plain. Far ahead of us, we saw the hill chain [we had to pass through, and] when we reached a slight elevation, we saw that we had as much ahead of us as [behind]. We would have liked to travel on horseback, but Mr. Kipp could not give us any horses, because he had just yesterday sold five for beavers. I was wearing heavy boots, [and] my feet had become very sore. Mr. Charbonneau gave me [Indian] moccasins, and these helped, but [I] suffered much pain in my feet. When we reached the hilltops, Charbonneau led us to the left, away from the trail, passing below the hills, where our feet were [further] harmed by the hard ground, grass, and cactus thorns. The trail [finally went] into forest, and [we saw] women busy everywhere, cutting and hauling wood [in] large bundles on their backs.

We reached the forest village at dusk. The large lodges [were] built so close [together] that one could hardly pass between them. We heard crying and lamentation; a child had recently died. [Then] we saw Mr. Dougherty's [place], a log house with three rooms. He lived in the one farthest to the right; the store was in the center; and the room for the men was to the left. We were received [in a] very friendly [manner] and found many Indians congregated around the fireplace. Altogether lame, we went inside, after a difficult trek of at least nine hours, and rested. We learned that buffalo were near, [and] twenty Indians [planned] to hunt for them tomorrow. In preparation, this evening they [would] celebrate the buffalo medicine festival, the reason we had come. We ate, since we had not eaten anything since breakfast. At six thirty we went to the medicine festival.

In the middle of the village, between the lodges, there was an [elliptical] area 30 or more paces long, [enclosed by] a 10- to 12-foot-high fence built of willow branches and reeds. [There was] an entrance on the long side in front, [and] four fires burned inside. Old men sat somewhat to the right of the entrance; [these included] the elderly chief Lachpitzí-Síhrisch (Yellow Bear). His face was painted red in some places, and he wore a band of yellow skin around his head. Women sat around the fence, not directly at the fires. Children sat opposite them, [feeding] willow branches into the fire. The whole inner space was full of young, slender men, some nicely dressed, others poorly [so] or half naked.

When we arrived at this medicine lodge with Charbonneau, [a line of] six elderly men stopped in front of the entrance. They had been chosen by the young men to represent the buffalo bulls. They [all] carried long sticks with three to four black feathers on top, buffalo calf hooves hanging at intervals, [and] bells at the lower end. In their left hands, these men [held war clubs]; two [had] the badger [see below]. They stood, shaking their sticks, alternately singing and imitating the rasping, rattling sound of the buffalo bull with great perfection. Behind them walked a slim man wearing a fur-trimmed cap on his head, because he had been scalped in a skirmish (meaning he had been robbed of his hair [and] the skin of his head). He represented the leader of the bulls and [was] the head of the festival; [he] walked behind the bulls. They entered the lodge and sat beside the door. In front of them, a stuffed sack, which they called the badger, was beaten instead of a drum during the dance. Each of the buffalo bulls stuck his weapon into the ground in front of him; two of [these war clubs] had round heads with carved faces. We followed the bulls, and [were told] to sit to the right of chief Yellow Bear. Several young men distributed bowls, [some] with boiled corn, others with beans. The bowls were passed on after one had eaten something from them. Empty wooden bowls were often brought and set in front of us. I did not know what this meant [at first] but [observed] my neighbor, the old chief, [as] one of the food servers, a handsome, muscular young man, came to pick up an empty bowl. The old chief cupped his hand in front of his face, sang, and made a long speech, like a prayer, in a low voice. In [these prayers] they expressed good wishes for the buffalo hunt or war, and ask the heavenly powers to favor the hunters. Mr. Dougherty and I also made speeches, wishing [the hunt] well in German or English [while] making expressive gestures the Indians could understand. They were especially pleased by long speeches. The bowl-carrier replied with a few words of thanks. The eating ceremony continued for perhaps an hour. In the meantime the young men prepared pipes [and] offered them to the seated old men and [visitors]. Frequently the pipe was turned toward the cardinal points before it was received, and [many gestures] were made with it. In the meantime, behind their fire, the buffalo bulls continued beating a rhythm on the badger, singing, [and] shaking their medicine sticks. [Then] they stood up, leaned forward, and danced—meaning they jumped in the air with both feet, sang loudly and rattled at the same time. The singing consisted of loud sounds and exclamations. When they had danced for a while, they sat down again. After we had eaten and smoked for more than two hours, the women's role [began].

A woman approached her husband [and] gave him her belt and her undergarment, so she was naked, wrapped only in her robe. [She approached] the elderly men and with [her] right hand stroked a chosen man on his arm down to his wrist. Then [she] slowly left the lodge. The chosen man had to follow [her]. The woman led him a short distance through the forest to a secluded spot and lay down on the ground, expecting a certain tribute. One is not obliged to accept [the offer] but can do as one wishes, [offering a gift instead. After having done this on] our turn and returning to the medicine lodge, we again received [something] to smoke. The fires were burning low, and many Indians had left. We asked the chief whether we could retreat; [he reluctantly] permitted [us] to do so.

The night view of the medicine lodge was excellent. The high trees [and] closely packed lodges were illuminated by bright fires. Everywhere one heard singing, whooping, shouting, [and] drumming: the hustle and bustle prevailed the whole night in the forest and around our house. More interesting by far was the sight of the mass of red people in the medicine lodge, [their] strange garb and singular faces.

27 November: Beautiful, clear day. Very handsome men arrived—tall, with strong, muscular figures and expressive faces, often beautifully painted and adorned. The Hidatsas are generally taller than the Mandans.

Young people in the village were playing a [hoop and pole] game; [the] players had long poles and, running beside each other, threw them toward a small leather ring. Children played on the solidly frozen river. [Some] women [worked; others] played with a large leather [ball], tossing it onto their feet [and] kicking it up in the air.

28 November: Many Indians sat around our fireplace. A few brought beaver pelts, which Mr. Dougherty bought. Indian youths played—half naked!—on the frozen river.

I went with Charbonneau to Yellow Bear's lodge. Around the fire [there were] seats, flat on the floor, made of willow sticks. Yellow Bear, completely naked except for his breechcloth, sat on [one], painting a new buffalo skin with vermilion and black colors, which he had prepared on old [potsherds]. He dipped a sharp piece of wood in [the pigment] to draw the figures. The black and yellow colors both originated from [local] clay. They paint all [kinds of] objects on their hides, [indicating by repetition] how many [of these] they have given away; they become great and respected [when] such presents [are given in large] numbers: rifles, woolen blankets, whips (which signify horses), etc.

Today we had a long, hungry day, because there was no meat and we [had] to wait for the arrival of the hunters. In the afternoon a few Indians returned, their horses loaded with meat, [but we were] not brought [any] until late in the day. At seven o'clock Charbonneau sent news that [there was] a women's medicine dance in another lodge. We went right away. On the left side of the wooden door screen, a fire was burning. In front of it, hides were spread out on some hay, where five or six men sat in a row, one of them beating a drum with a stick; another had a *chichikué*. They outdid themselves in making noise; the drum was beaten vehemently. All of them sang. Elderly women sat around the lodge; one stood on the other side of the fire. She was the medicine woman, a tall, strong figure with a bony, broad, flat face. She was dressed in a garment of fringed yellow leather, trimmed in several places with pieces of red and blue fabric. We sat to the right of the men, Charbonneau beside me, children and onlookers behind us; a young man drove the children back with a stick whenever they pressed forward. The [medicine] woman pretended to have an ear of corn in her body, which she [intended] to drive out with her medicine and swallow again. When we arrived the ceremony was almost finished; the ear of corn had already been swallowed. But Charbonneau talked with them, [and after] a gift of ten sticks of tobacco, the performance was repeated. The purpose of the ceremony was to [make] the corn grow better in the coming year.

The music [intensified]. Four women began to move rhythmically, each [alone, and] in a different direction. They waddled like ducks, took small steps, kept their bodies straight, and swayed a little to each side. They moved in time with the rapid drumbeat, their arms hanging straight down. The medicine woman danced near the fire. Finally she began to shake, moving her arms forward and back [with increasing rapidity]. She held her head backward, and soon we saw the tip of a white corn ear filling her mouth and [steadily] moving outward. Her convulsions became more violent. Finally, when the ear of corn was almost half out, she [looked] as if she would collapse. A woman behind her grasped her body and sat her on the ground. [More] convulsions. The music crescendoed. Women grabbed sage branches and began to stroke them over her arms and breasts, whereupon the ear [of corn] slowly slipped inside again. The woman rose and danced a little. Another [conjuror] appeared. She repeated the same movements, and suddenly blood flowed from her mouth down her chin. She had a piece of liver in her mouth from which she pressed the blood. She, too, was awakened from her convulsions and then danced at the fire. After this scene seven women danced [in a line], and the festival ended. We took leave the Indian way: one rises and walks away suddenly without saying a word or looking around. The sight of that brown crowd [in] the firelight was most remarkable.

Almost all these people maintained that they had some kind of animal in their bodies, for instance, buffalo, deer, etc. One believed [he] had three lizards [inside]; he complained to Charbonneau that the animals hurt him. He was given a cup of coffee [and] asserted that the pain just became more severe. Then Charbonneau gave him a cup of tea and he was calmed. Superstitious ideas have overcome the whole soul of the Indians, and their beliefs are too deeply rooted to waste words [trying to] convince them otherwise.

29 November: I [had hoped] to return to Fort Clark today but could not get any horses. [It was noisy] all night long: whooping and singing in the village and the surrounding forest, [while] others bemoaned their dead. Everywhere females were visited by young men; almost all of them were loose, and this kind of [lusty] pastime was the principal Indian entertainment. Mr. Bodmer painted [figures on] buffalo robes for a few Indians—for one of them a cock, for another a horse. They hoped to become bulletproof this way. Durand arrived from the lower Mandan village. In the evening Bodmer, Durand, and Mr. Dougherty went to the medicine festival, repeated today to attract buffalo.

30 November: Mr. Dougherty had his horse saddled for me, and Durand accompanied us [on] his horse. He let Mr. Bodmer ride part of the way. At eight thirty we took leave from our pleasant hosts, Mr. Dougherty and Charbonneau, and reached the [Mandan winter] village at two or three o'clock. We passed over the [frozen] Missouri above Ruhptare, where the ice was rather smooth. Durand's horse, stiff and exhausted, could scarcely be brought across. It had no horseshoes and fell very dangerously several times.

We reached Fort Clark at dusk. During our absence the mail had arrived from St. Louis, but [there were] no letters for us. The news from there was generally good. The cholera had disappeared completely. Dreidoppel had gotten two species of mammals new to me: *Canis latrans,* the prairie wolf; and *Mustela vulgaris,* the small weasel. In the evening I wrote to Mr. Hamilton at Fort Union [requesting] some medicines, Assiniboine pipes, and Catlin's information about the Mandans.

1 December: Mató-Tópe brought me a drawing he had done for me, depicting him fighting with a Cheyenne chief. Afterward he attentively watched Mr. Bodmer drawing. In our absence Mr. Kipp had built a scaffold in the fort's [court]yard on which he [hoped to save] his Indian corn from the rats. The

ears [would be] covered [to protect] against moisture. The [uprights] were peeled smooth, so the rats could not climb them.

2 December: The corn was transported today through our room to the new scaffold, which drove us from our [quarters] for a while. Several Mandans came into the fort [with] beaver pelts again.

In the afternoon Mr. Bodmer went into Dipäuch's lodge at Mih-Tutta-Hangkusch and found it very well furnished and nice. He made a sketch of the round area in the village with the ark, the black[-faced] man, [and] the medicine lodge.

Dipäuch and Beróck-Itaïnú came and stayed in the fort that evening. To my delight, the former talked about the religious ideas and myths of his people, the most fantastic, silly stories. We were busy writing notes until after eleven o'clock.

3 December: [Wolf-hunting in the morning; two specimens obtained.] At four thirty we went to the [winter] village of the Mandans to watch the ceremonies celebrating the sale of the Soldier (Káua-Karakáchka) [society] to the [Raven] society. Before [we left], Mató-Tópe came and said [that] a troop of hostile Dacotas had been sighted in the prairie hills. Everyone was tense. Mr. Kipp loaded [the] horses, and [we] advanced quickly across the prairie along the Missouri. I cannot deny that the whole party looked left and right as we passed various gorges and small creeks to ensure [that] no enemies were hiding there. We reached the [winter village] at dusk. There were 70 closely packed lodges in the dense forest. The village was bustling; one heard singing, whooping, and calling everywhere.

We went to the lodge of Medicine Bird (Mandeck-Suck-Choppeníh), where we spent the night. The lodge was 20 paces in diameter [and] well furnished. A small [firepit, circled] with stones, [was at the lodge center]. In a square around this [hearth], willow branches were fastened to the floor, over which buffalo hides were [often] spread; the family [stayed by] the fire all day, engaged in various occupations. We smoked, sitting around the fire, and they [served] a large wooden bowl of sweet corn, which tasted a little like green peas *(petits poix)*.

Several drums could be heard in the village, calling together the two societies of Káua-Karakáchka [Soldiers] and Háhderucha-Óchatä [Crows or Ravens]. After seven o'clock Mr. Kipp gave the signal, and we went to the medicine lodge. Women sat around [by] the walls. We sat down at the place of honor, with some respected Káua-Karakáchka, in the center in front of the fire. This society [had] about 25 members. They were dressed in various ways, most very simply, bare on their upper bodies, covered only with their robes. Three men beat the drum very hard. Opposite the [line of] Káua-Karakáchka stood the men of the Háhderucha-Óchatä band, which today bought from the former the dance of the Half-Shorn Heads [and] all the apparatus and rights that go with it (see [chapter 18 on] the Mandan tribe). They have to ingratiate themselves to the former to gain permission for the purchase and must give them many valuable things: horses, guns, etc. They hold these festivities for forty nights, [offering] them tobacco, giving them food—and their women, as we would soon see. The Káua-Karakáchka had consented [to the transfer], and the festivities were carried out in the following manner. When we had taken a seat, the majority of the Káua-Karakáchka were not yet present. We suddenly heard their singing, accompanied by drumbeats, and they walked in with their insignia. [There were] four lances, probably seven to eight feet long; the tips were iron, similar to rapier blades. The [shafts] were tightly wound with broad strips of otter skin. Two were curved at the top; two were straight. The fifth insignia [was] a red-painted [war club] of the usual [gunstock] shape with a flat iron tip at the end, decorated with down and other feathers. Then [came] three [more] lances, decorated with hanging feathers, alternating black and white. [The] ninth [insignia was] a nicely decorated quiver and bow. The festivities began when the Káua-Karakáchka entered. They stopped at the entrance [to] the lodge, [behind] the wall [screening] the door. When they had stood, sung, and drummed for a while in this position, they stepped forward [and] took their seats.

The drums were beaten forcefully, struck with heavy mallets. The [men] alternately sang and whooped [a] war whoop, made by striking the mouth with the hand to produce a tremulous sound. This music was repeated over and over again with short pauses. Usually they began by beating the drums softly and swiftly, almost like a roll. Then they produced slower but stronger beats, the singing matching the drum. As this music continued, the purchasing society offered their pipes to each of us by bowing down and holding the mouthpieces toward us. Then they took a few puffs themselves and went to the next person on the left, but only to the strangers and the Káua-Karakáchka. Thus we continued to smoke, and [we] each also [got] a small cake of fat kneaded with sweet corn.

After about half an hour [of] this, two of the soldiers got up and danced toward each other. One was a tall, thickset man with a small, thin voice. [He had] a naked upper body and undecorated leggins. He grabbed the war club and held it firmly in his left hand, [while] his right hand hung down stiffly. He bent his upper body forward and jumped up and down to the rhythm of the music, keeping his feet almost even. The [second soldier] was beautifully adorned on his head and legs, but his upper body was naked, too. He grabbed one of the otter-skin lances and held it slanted above him with both hands. They danced toward each other as described above. After one or two minutes, the latter put the lance aside and sat down. The warriors did their whooping and war cries; the drums were beaten violently and then fell silent. The tall man with the war club then addressed the purchasing band [as] his sons and related some of his war coups. Then he offered them the war club. One of the Háhderucha-Óchatä called the presenter his father, stroked him with his hand downward over his arm, took the weapon out of his hand, and put it again in its place. The other dancer stood up, talked about his coups, and presented the lance to a member of the other band, who accepted it with the same ceremony and returned it to its place. They smoked, sang, and played the big drum. Then other soldiers stood up, spoke of their heroic deeds (how they had stolen horses or taken a medicine from an enemy), and handed over [an insignia] to the purchasing band.

When this had happened four or five times, the women rose. Four of them appeared, one after the other, completely naked, quickly grabbed the four lances, and [in succession] carried them outside and then back inside. They hurried to pass us, and some held their hands in front. This ceremony was repeated twice. The naked women approached the guests first, then the *soldats,* and invited them to follow, [just as in the recent Hidatsa medicine ceremony]. When they came in for the second time with their lances, Mr. Kipp rose; none of us waited for the second invitation. Some of the naked women were thick and fat, [while] a few [were] very young, one almost a child. We returned to Medicine Bird's lodge, smoked a cigar in his absence, and lay down in our clothes on the spread-out buffalo skins. The night was chilly. The Indians posted sentries against their enemies.

4 December: We left at seven o'clock [and arrived at] the fort at eight. Later a handsome, nicely dressed Mandan from the Káua-Karakáchka society visited us; [he] was the tallest man in this tribe, 5′ 10″ 2½‴. His name was Máhchsi-Karéhde (Flying War Eagle). In his hair he wore feathers spread like rays. [He had] a beautiful bear claw necklace and a reddish brown robe

well decorated with glass beads. [After agreeing] to [pose] for a drawing [he left], promising to return in four to five days.

5 December: Síh-Chidä, [having] spent the night at the fort, got dressed at our place and primped a long time in front of his small mirror.

This morning there was also one of those men whom the French call *bardaches* here in the fort.[4] They dress like and do the work of women: tan hides, paint skins, and make clothing. In short, they are altogether women. Indeed, it is even said that the young men chase after them and declare their love. Mr. Kipp asserted [that] it was a kind of vow these men made, like religious orders that take a vow of poverty. He did not see anything wrong in the lifestyle of the berdaches, [and] they were not despised or looked down upon. Others saw the matter from a somewhat different point of view.

Mr. Bodmer began to draw [Síh-Chidä full-]figure. A humid fog turned into full rain toward noon. If this wet, mild weather were to continue a few more days, the river would open up again.

[Two] mute Mandans returned from hunting [with enough] meat [so that] the fort received some, too. Our supply had been completely consumed, and [men] were eating corn boiled in water without any fat. My bears had not been getting anything but corn for a long time—in eight days almost a bushel, [costing] eight twists [of tobacco] (value: two dollars). Charbonneau stayed overnight and talked about Indians and his earlier life.

6 December: In the morning there was deep snow; [the wind] had blown all night long. [Last] evening we talked with Charbonneau about the dangers [presented by] Indians and agreed that, in this area, the Mandans were the most reliable. [But] it is always perilous to be among people possessed by superstitious ideas. The location of Fort Clark is especially precarious, because there are permanent Indian villages here that enemies [search out and] besiege. Several white men have been shot here. [However,] the number [attacked] by Blackfoot in the Rocky Mountains is by far larger—last year fifty-six, a few years earlier, more than eighty.

It snowed all day. I took care of my correspondence. Mató-Tópe visited us and viewed [Bodmer's] drawing of Síh-Chidä with great interest.

7 December: Snow covered the whole area, [but it seemed] warm. Dreidoppel [went hunting] early. There were three wolves on the river, and he even saw a fourth, a schähácká [coyote]. He shot at one of them, but it was still too dark. [Later, he] went [out again and] hit a schähácká and a fox; the latter

fled underground. Síh-Chidä was drawn. His wife was with him. He liked the [portrait and] wanted a copy of it.

8 December: Sunday. The snow [was] frozen; it crunched. Mr. Kipp had his cariole (a two- or three-seat sled) hitched and drove to the Hidatsa villages, because he had [no] meat [or] tallow. The latter was very necessary for candles. We were burning only one candle in the evening, and that was made from such bad, brown fat that we could hardly write by it.

Péhriska-Rúhpa visited us. However, when we spoke about drawing, he immediately left.

The drawing of Síh-Chidä was mainly completed. We gave him paper, pencil, and colors, and he returned with his wife to their village.

9 December: We ate the last meat for breakfast, [since] we expected [that] Mr. Kipp would bring some [soon]. An Indian stole an axe [from] the fort; Belhumeur sent a man after him. Most of them cannot keep from thievery.

Dreidoppel returned after lunch with three prairie hens; he had winged a fourth but did not get it. He saw [several bird species and collected] various kinds of plant seeds. Síh-Sä went out in the afternoon with the gun; we gave him [some] shot. Mr. Kipp came back toward evening. He had stayed overnight in the last Hidatsa village at old Bijou's place.

10 December: Mató-Tópe came early and brought me a small weasel in its snow-white winter coat, a very cute animal he had shot with an arrow. Fog covered the prairie hills and the forest, [so the] trees were encrusted in magnificent hoarfrost. Even the hair and heads of the Indians who came into the fort were white [with] frost. Mató-Tópe stayed a long time and looked at drawings, which [pleased him]. [We gave him] several little things, like tin cups for colors, red pencils [or crayons], and gum elastic.

Charbonneau came in the evening and announced [that] he had broken with Dougherty and wanted to return to the American Fur Company. The Mandans went buffalo hunting today.

11 December: In the morning, [dense] fog, [but] the sun soon dispersed [it]. At 11 o'clock I went out. [Although] tracks crisscrossed the snow in all directions, I saw nothing except a small flock of *Fringilla linaria,* of which I shot a single bird. I set up a mousetrap in a bunch of low-lying plants to see what species of mouse [made] the many trails we saw in the snow.

Mató-Tópe was with us in the evening. [He] said the Dacotas had stolen two horses from [his] village, which they chased ahead of them. Since they could neither capture nor mount them, they shot them dead. The Mandans found [the animals and] saw from the tracks that there had been only two enemies. Mató-Tópe slept in our room.

12 December: Mató-Tópe left before breakfast. At nine o'clock I went to my mousetrap; a wolf had picked it up, taken it a good 20 paces, and then dropped it. About evening we [spied] a wolf trotting on the prairie. An Indian ran after it, stalked [and] shot it, [and] brought it to the fort. It was a very large male wolf, unlike any [specimen] we had before. His head and neck were very thick, his ears short.

Some Dacota women arrived here late, bringing replacement horses for the Mandan [mounts] shot by members of their tribe.

13 December: Durand visited us. All the Mandans from his village went buffalo hunting today. In the forest across the river, Síh-Sä shot three birds very similar to waxwings (*Bombycilla garrula*?). An Indian sold me a wolf for a stick of tobacco (twelve cents).

14 December: We had [no] good meat [and] only a few tallow candles, so Charbonneau went to the Hidatsas today to procure some. I went out at nine o'clock to check on the mousetrap, [which] had been carried away again by a fox or wolf. I finally found it, full of snow, [with] a mouse inside, still warm. [So] the mouse [making all the tracks] in the snow here is *Mus macrocephalus,* similar to our large field mouse *(Mus sylvaticus)* but [with] a thicker head, shorter ears, and a shorter tail.

Some of the Mandan hunters returned [but] had shot only three bulls; [other] hunters had gone farther. Our meat would soon come to an end, and then we would have nothing but boiled corn and corn bread. We hoped to receive coffee and sugar from [Fort Union].

15 December: Early in the morning, [after heavy] snow the previous evening, a strong northwest wind blew down [our wooden] chimney guard. [It] was a strange [view from] the fort's gate, [like] seeing a terrible storm on the ocean. The wide, snowy expanse of the prairie was whipped up by the wind into a snow cloud, [and it] was so cold that one could not open an eye against the wind. We worked the whole day at home [as] the storm continued. In the afternoon Charbonneau returned; he had been blown over and could hardly see the trail. He got neither meat nor tallow [from] the Hidatsas; they too had nothing and were hungry. In the evening Dipäuch told us [Mandan] myths. The wind abated in the night; the sky cleared.

16 December: [Just] corn bread and coffee for breakfast. I went out along the

creeks. All the tracks were fresh: wolves, schähäckä, two species of fox, and a mink. Dreidoppel completed preparing a large wolf and a schähäckä, which we hung up in our room.

17 December: The Mandans returned from their hunt. Someone brought us meat. They had gone quite far [and] had shot fifty-four buffalo. Mr. Kipp's horse, which his father-in-law kept in the village, had been lost on this occasion—bridled and saddled, [it ran off with] a herd of buffalo. Two foals died [in] the [frigid] weather. The water had frozen a long time ago in the bucket in our room.

I went out; the snow was very deep and drifted in many places. I saw no animals except some shy snow buntings and a few *Fringilla linaria;* I could not get close to either [of them]. Mr. Kipp [went] to the Mandan village [and returned] with meat and tallow purchased at a high price. About dusk a severe storm rose from the east-southeast, [and the fierce wind] caused tremendous cold in our room, with [its many] open cracks. We could endure it only [by staying] close to the fireplace.

18 December: Glorious morning; sky clear and blue; no wind. At seven thirty, 12°F. I took a long walk, [and] it was so warm about noon that I perspired (23½°F). In the evening Dipäuch told us many curious things about his people.

19 December: The Missouri rose substantially and flowed over the ice in places. An Indian brought a white rabbit pelt, which I bought.

20 December: It snowed some about daybreak. Síh-Chidä visited us but did not stay; he said he had to return to the medicine dance. The forty nights when women were surrendered to the Káua-Karakáchka were not over yet. The moon was large in the sky at five o'clock, about ⅓ full.

21 December: Kipp and Charbonneau went by sled to the [farthest] Hidatsa village, where they would spend the night. Bodmer went to the Mandan village in the evening, where the last medicine dance was [being] celebrated. Several Indians visited us, among them a Káua-Karakáchka who wore nine to ten feathers in his hair, [signifying] that many coups.

22 December: Today was Sunday [so the men] did not work. Mr. Bodmer returned from the Mandan village about ten o'clock. Durand had housed and entertained him. In the evening he [attended] the medicine dance. At the end, the Foolish Dogs society came inside, naked, painted totally white, and danced. Mr. Bodmer wanted to leave but was advised to stay seated. Then a woman came, stroked [Bodmer's] arms and invited him to follow

her; he went outside with her, led her inside again, [and] then left [to] visit Síh-Chidä and Mató-Tópe.

Yesterday an Indian cut off and ran away with the tail of a wolf that I had bought. They wear these tails [trailing from] their heels as [symbols] of heroic [war coups]. Many Indians visited us and were very troublesome, [for] we could not watch them carefully enough [and] they stole various small things. Kipp and Charbonneau returned about four o'clock [with] only a little meat. There were many buffalo herds on the prairies, but all far away.

23 December: The snow was frozen hard. At twelve thirty we suddenly heard the beating of drums. A crowd of Indians came into the fort, fourteen men at the head, one with a drum, another with a *chichikué;* [it was] a medicine society from Ruhptare, As-Chóh-Óchatä. They [were going] to perform a medicine dance in [Mih-Tutta-Hangkusch]. They looked eccentric. Their hair was worn in long, flat braids that hung down from the top of their heads equally on all sides and completely covered their faces. It looked strange when the steam of their breath flew out between the hair braids. On their heads, they wore [upright] feathers of predatory birds, each [feather] with a white down plume [attached to] the tip. They kept their robes tightly closed and [each] held a bow-lance, decorated with feathers, colored cloth, and glass beads. They beat the drum, stood in a circle, and [made noises] like buffalo; [then they left for Mih-Tutta-Hangkusch]. The medicine dancers had scarcely left when the largest (physically) of the Mandans, Máhchsi-Karéhde, appeared [and] wanted to be drawn; the work began right away. [He] and two other men stayed until evening and looked at the drawings; one made witty remarks.

24 December: Severe, cold northwest wind. [The portrait of] Máhchsi-Karéhde [was continued]. Mató-Tópe stayed in the evening, gave me [information] about the Arikaras, and slept in our room. At midnight the engagés fired their guns to celebrate Christmas; about morning the shooting started [again].

25 December (Christmas): Several Indians came early, among them Medicine Bird and Péhriska-Rúhpa. Mató-Tópe did not get along well with Two Ravens, [so] he left immediately.

Later, Kähka-Chamahän visited us—a sarcastic, shrewd man. They expected to get whiskey today, but there was none in the fort. The deaf-mute came, and Durand with his Dacota wife and child. The room was full most [of] the time. Péhriska-Rúhpa [had an] especially beautiful robe, with a colossal sun (actually, a crown of feathers) [painted] on it.[5] In the adjoining room, the engagés [were noisy in their] French-Canadian jargon. They got slightly better food today. When we were ready to sit down at the table, there was a loud noise. The women's society of the White Buffalo Cow (Ptihn-Tǎck-Óchatä) performed their dance in the fort's courtyard. The band consisted of seventeen women, mostly elderly, and two men—one was the drummer and the other had a *chichikué*. An old woman [went first], wrapped in the hide of a white buffalo cow. In her right arm she carried a large bundle of brushwood, [with] down feathers at the top and, at the bottom, eagle wings and a metal container. Another woman had [a similar] bundle. The women all wore caps made from white buffalo skin, [except] two [who] wore skunk skins on their heads. All were painted alike: their left cheek and eye [were] vermilion; beside the right eye on the temple, two sky-blue spots. They arranged themselves in a circle. The music began with a fast rhythm. The men sang first, [and then] the women began to dance and sing in loud, high-pitched voices, as if stepping on the tails of cats. They danced, wobbling in place, stepping from one foot to the other. There was a pause [and] then the dance began anew. Most of these women were plain; a few had black, tattooed stripes on their chins.

The women had scarcely left when three engagés arrived, bringing mail from Fort Union. I received letters from Mr. McKenzie and Mr. Hamilton. The climate [there] had been very mild up to [December] fifteenth, when these [engagés] departed. The river was totally without ice, and no snow had fallen yet. I was invited to pay a visit, but in this extreme winter weather, my health was too [important to risk]. We were promised that the desired provisions (coffee, sugar, rice, and other things) would come shortly, by sled at the next opportunity.

26 December: In the morning, the wind drove the snow on the prairie into the air and clouded the atmosphere. At nine o'clock there was a rainbow in the east amidst the gray snow clouds with a sundog in the center, quite far from the actual sun.

I got letters ready [to send downriver tomorrow]. The packet contained letters to all my brothers and sisters, to Mr. Treviranus, Mr. von Schweinitz, Pastor Seidel, Mr. Krumbhaar, Mr. Gebhard, Mr. Thomas Say, and [others in Europe and America].

27 December: [Kipp sent off] the mail [to] the lower Missouri and St. Louis, with four men, two sleds, and a number of horses. Both sleds were loaded with

corn for the horses. Two [of the] men were supposed to return [from the Yanktonai post with] meat. We had [none]; we ate nothing but corn bread and biscuit for breakfast and dinner. We expected the men back in four days.

Síh-Chidä brought us a paper he [had] inherited from his father, the peace treaty concluded with the Mandans by General Atkinson and the Indian Agent, Major O'Fallon, when the troops were here in 18[25]. This instrument was in very large format, written in Hidatsa and English. Charbonneau doubtless gave the Indian names; they were mostly incorrectly written.

Síh-Chidä drew Bodmer's whole figure and took the picture along, perhaps as protection [against Bodmer's] portrait [of him].

28 December: They caught a wild dog in the fort, [intending to make it] pull a sled. It [resisted so violently] that it took a long time to catch it with snares [and then it died]. Dogs unaccustomed to it are not fit to pull sleds. If they are used to it, however, three strong dogs can pull a sled far better than the best horse. If the snow has a crust, they can run right across it, while [a] horse would fall through. [Dogs] have far more endurance. One can travel thirty miles a day with them, [and] if they lie on the snow for an hour and eat [just a little], one can drive on again. A horse needs sufficient fodder, frequent rest, [and] always a good place to water; if it is tired, one cannot make it go any farther. In winter buffalo hunting, when the snow has a crust, hunters can drive a light dogsled into the herd, [carrying a] sitting or kneeling archer.

About noon we heard drumbeats [and] went outside. The recently purchased society of the Half-Shorn Head Dance (Íschohä-Kakoschóchatä) came, dressed colorfully and elegantly. [There were] about twenty strong, slender, young men with their upper bodies bare, [having] cast [their] robes [aside. Some had] an eagle feather [or other] feathers stuck horizontally in their hair. Some [wore] bear [claw] necklaces, [or] foxtails on their [heels]. Their leggins of red cloth or leather were painted and occasionally trimmed with bells. [Each had] a mirror and various insignia in their hands. They arranged themselves in a circle.

Many [had] beautifully decorated lances, others bow-lances, still others, guns. One wore a large warbonnet with horns and [strips of] ermine fur; a broad piece of red cloth with eagle feathers hung all the way down his back. One, on horseback, wore an eagle feather upright in his hair; his entire upper body was smeared yellow, with red spots like bloodstains painted on his chest. The horse, a buckskin, was painted half yellow, including the mane and tail; the bridle was red. The three musicians were Káua-Karakáchka. They began to beat [the drum]; the Indians bent their bodies forward and jumped to the rhythm of the music. They held their guns as if they were ready to shoot. They danced this way about one minute, then did a loud whoop, paused, rested a little, and began the dance anew; [this] lasted about a quarter of an hour. [Spectators] threw them sticks of tobacco. [Then] they wrapped themselves in their robes and left for the Ruhptare [winter] village. They would sleep there and go to the Hidatsas tomorrow.

Mr. Kipp had received orders from Mr. McKenzie to come to Fort Union as soon as possible, [so] he [planned] to leave tomorrow with three or four men. [He] therefore bought Indian dogs, eighteen [in all]. There was hustle and bustle all day long. The dogs, locked up in the fort, howled unbearably.

29 December: At nine o'clock, Mr. Kipp [departed] with five [packed] Indian sleds, accompanied by Charbonneau on a horse sled.

Mató-Tópe visited us with his wife, who wore a beautifully painted buffalo robe portraying Mató-Tópe's heroic feats—he killed five Indian chiefs. It snowed rather heavily, [and] the snow blew through [our faulty] windows and door. Indians sat in our room and prevented us from doing anything.

Our little fox entertained us greatly with his friendly play. It was a lively animal [and] got into all kinds of things. The night was stormy, snowy, [and] very cold. We froze in our beds.

30 December: The strong wind roared. One could not see anything on the prairie because of the driving snow. We hoped that this weather [might force] buffalo herds closer, into the [riverine] forests. The area was strange to see. The wind whipped the snow into the air so that everything was cloudy and dark. [No] living being moved; neither animal nor human appeared willing to expose themselves to the fierce weather. Mr. Kipp was to be pitied, but perhaps he was waiting at the Hidatsas for better weather.

During [all] this, the fort's poor horses had to stay outdoors. They stood there quietly the whole night while snow piled high on their backs. Animals are subject to harsh treatment in America.

An old engagé who was assigned to [see to] our needs carried wood into the room, leaving the door slightly open. Mr. Bodmer's paint and brushes froze solid, [although] he had left them for only a moment. [He had to] use warm water for painting, thawing the paintbrushes [and] working quickly.

In the meantime I wrote near the fireplace. On one side [I] was burning hot, while [my other side] froze. I had to [move] frequently to warm up. Dipäuch and Berόck-Itaïnú visited and smoked a pipe at our place. [We heard that] that [the Mandans] desired to make war on the Saones and Yanktonais. When peace was made [before], [the Mandans wondered] how long [these Sioux] would keep the peace. [Not long]: they had shot two Mandan horses; stole seventeen Hidatsa horses; and [committed] other offenses.

31 December: An Indian brought news: buffalo were across the river, not far away; hungry Indians will soon pursue these animals in droves.

The frozen snow crunched loudly when we walked. For lunch, nothing but corn bread, corn cooked in water, and warmed-up bean soup.

XVII

Short Description of Fort Clark

and Its Surroundings

The famous travelers Lewis and Clark [were in this area] in 180[4] and 180[5]; they spent the winter in the vicinity of the Mandan villages. They built a fort on the left bank of the Missouri above today's fort, but the river has [shifted] so much that the site of [their] former fort is now in the middle of the river. Such changes in the riverbed of the Missouri are a common occurrence, [so] river charts remain correct for only a very short time regarding details such as islands, sandbars, small bends, [etc.]. Charbonneau, a French Canadian, was here at the same time as [Lewis and Clark]; he spent the winter in their fort and accompanied them to the Columbia. He came here thirty-seven years ago and has lived continuously with the Hidatsas, usually in the second Hidatsa village (Awatichai), excluding a few trips and short absences. He has become fully acquainted with their language, traditions, and customs.

In [1823] Mr. Kipp, a Canadian of [Dutch] heritage, came here in the service of the Columbia Fur Company.[1] At that time no fort existed [here]. Mr. Kipp began to build on the prairie in a location between today's fort and the winter [village] of Mih-Tutta-Hangkusch. This building phase was completed in November. [That same] summer, Colonel Leavenworth— with troops, cannon, and an auxiliary corps of Dacota Indians—had come upriver to the Arikara villages, [intending] to punish that nation, [who had recently attacked fur trader Henry] Ashley's keelboats, killing about eighteen men and wounding others. Missouri River residents [said] that [Leavenworth's] punitive force [was ineffective]; the troops [withdrew] without causing any serious damage. The Arikaras consequently became overconfident and killed many [more] white men. At the time of Lewis and Clark's [journey], this nation was friendly. Now they were the white man's bitterest enemy along the Missouri. [They] moved higher up[river] and settled in the forest [where] the Mandans now have their lower winter [village].

Mr. Tilton, the company clerk in charge of the fort built by Mr. Kipp, had only five men. [They] were in constant danger because the Arikaras resided so close to [them]. Indeed, one of their chiefs killed one of Tilton's men near the fort gate. [Then,] in the fall [of 1823], five men [from] a French fur company came upriver, [with a goods-laden boat,] to trade with the Mandans and the Arikaras. They met the latter in the vicinity of the Cannonball River. Charbonneau had advised [them of the] danger, but they did not believe it. They were discovered by an Arikara spy, who informed his [nearby] war party of sixty men. When the [warriors] approached, they called to the men in the boat [to] land. The helmsman begged [the Arikaras] not to kill [them and declared] that they would turn over all their goods. The answer was, "You talk very silly. The goods are ours anyway, and we have to kill you to salve our wounds with your fat. With [your] wares you will pay for our corn," [the latter statements] referring to Colonel Leavenworth's feeble attack, [which did] destroy various [resources] of the Arikaras and killed and wounded some of [their people]. A barrage of gunfire ensued, and the white men were [all] shot down.

[Mr. Kipp stayed] in Mih-Tutta-Hangkusch until the fort was completely finished. He lived in the lodge of a distinguished chief [and was thus] protected from any attack. At the beginning of December, Mr. Laidlaw arrived [from the Columbia company headquarters at] Lake Traverse with six loaded wagons, whereupon something like a peace treaty was made with the Arikaras. [But] they [only] came to the fort because they could not obtain merchandise anywhere else, [and] the peace did not last long. It [was] dangerous [just] to fetch wood [and] water. In spring [1824] Mr. Tilton went downriver to St. Louis with all his men [while] Mr. Kipp stayed behind alone. The Arikaras returned to their old villages, declaring they would not kill any more white men. Mr. Kipp did not see one white man the whole summer. He had the merchandise and the skins with him in the lodge of the chief whose son, Síh-Chidä, now about twenty-five years old, was mentioned in the preceding chapter. On 1 December [1824, eight men] from the Columbia Fur Company came with five wagons and stayed in the Mandan village over [the] winter. Mr. Kipp built a house beside the village, where they lived together.

On 4 April [1825], Jeffers went back to Lake Traverse. Kipp kept only two men. He had [them] chop off the [fort] pickets at ground level with axes [and] commissioned the Mandans to bring this wood to the village; [he]

also had the buildings torn down. Kipp expanded his house that summer by two rooms and set up all the salvaged pickets. Because he did not have enough merchandise to trade, he sent Charbonneau, who [had been] in the service of the Columbia Fur Company since Kipp's [arrival], with another man to Lake Traverse to get a wagonload of merchandise. Coming back, Charbonneau came across a troop of Assiniboines. He [and] his companion abandoned the merchandise, wagon, and horses and saved [themselves]. Everything was lost, so Mr. Kipp himself traveled with two half-breed Indians to Lake Traverse and brought back [sufficient] merchandise [to trade]. When he [arrived], General Atkinson had been to the Mandan villages with 500 to 600 men and had sailed as far up as Milk River. [Atkinson] returned that same summer, [1825,] and hostilities almost broke out between the Crows, who were near the Mandan villages, and the military. In [the] fall Mr. Tilton came [with more trade goods]. Kipp sent some men to the Assiniboines, Crees, and Ojibwes to invite their leaders here so that they might put together a peace and trade treaty. The troops had brought [Peter] Wilson upriver with them as an agent of the United States; [the Americans] wanted to draw [Indian trade away from] the British.

Messrs. Wilson and Tilton spent the winter in Mr. Kipp's fort but traveled back to St. Louis in April [1826]. Kipp remained at the fort with five men. In November Tilton returned on a keelboat with merchandise. Kipp moved upriver that same month to White Earth River, where he built a new fort to trade furs with the Assiniboines. He spent the winter there [but returned to the Mandan villages in the fall of 1828. Aside from temporary assignments at other company forts,] Mr. Kipp has [been at this post, which came to be called Fort Clark, since then and became] charged with supervising [it].

Trade with the Indians has mostly [remained] the same: sometimes better, sometimes worse. The merchandise [stays at] more or less the same price, except [when] increased through competition, [such as that] of Messrs. Sublette and Campbell.[M1] One must sometimes pay twelve dollars

---

[M1] Messrs. Sublette and Campbell suffered considerable losses this fall (1833). They sent a troop of about sixty men with merchandise into the mountains, and there was a misunderstanding with the Crow nation, who plundered from them nearly 150 horses and most of their merchandise. [The Crows] returned only some [undesirable] horses. The traders suffer [many] such adversities, even from nonhostile Indians.

for a good-sized beaver, but its worth is no more than four dollars in the United States. The Indians now demanded mostly horses [in exchange] for their beavers. Because Mr. Kipp did not have enough of them, he sent [a message] to [Fort Pierre] to have a few more delivered from there. Messrs. Sublette and Campbell have [placed a representative] in each village. Besides Charbonneau, Mr. Kipp had another trader [among] the Hidatsas, [who] visited the villages by sled in winter.

It is time to say something about the nation just mentioned. When Charbonneau came here thirty-seven years ago, he moved in with the Hidatsas in their central village. Three villages existed then, exactly as now. No trade had yet been instituted between here and St. Louis. Charbonneau obtained his necessities from the British traders in the north. In the year of his arrival, 1,300 to 1,400 Sioux, united with some 700 Arikaras, attacked the first Mandan village. About 1,000 Hidatsas rushed to the aid of the latter. They beat the enemy and killed more than 100 men. Since then the Arikaras have moved their villages farther downriver, where they are still to be seen. They have returned often since that time but never in such a mass. During Charbonneau's time another [Dacota] war party came to the hill chain on the other side of the Missouri and made challenging signs. There were only eighteen men in the large Hidatsa village (Eláh-Sá); the others were out hunting. But in the Village des Souliers (Awacháhwi), all the men were there, and the Mandans crossed the river with [the Hidatsas] on horseback to attack. They came to a ravine where they faced the enemy. The Dacotas shouted that they wanted to smoke with them, [but] at a distance. They all sat down [where they were], held their pipes toward each other, and smoked. When that was done, the Sioux partisan stepped forward and exclaimed [that] they were here to do battle. They knew they confronted men and therefore suggested fighting only in the open, avoiding the forest completely; this was accepted by the Mandans and the Hidatsas. They moved onto the plain and attacked each other. Two Mandans, Bídda-Apuckschá (Coal) and Itepan-Schüpischá (Black Cat), had an argument [over] who would fight the best.[2] The Sioux pushed back their enemies, who had already begun to retreat toward the forest. Coal retreated with them. Then Black Cat shouted that [if Coal] claimed to be so brave, did his actions [demonstrate] that contention? Bídda-Apuckschá pulled himself together and rode to Itepan-Schüpischá, gripped his arm, and said, "Well, we will die together!" They rode into the enemy. When the rest of their people saw

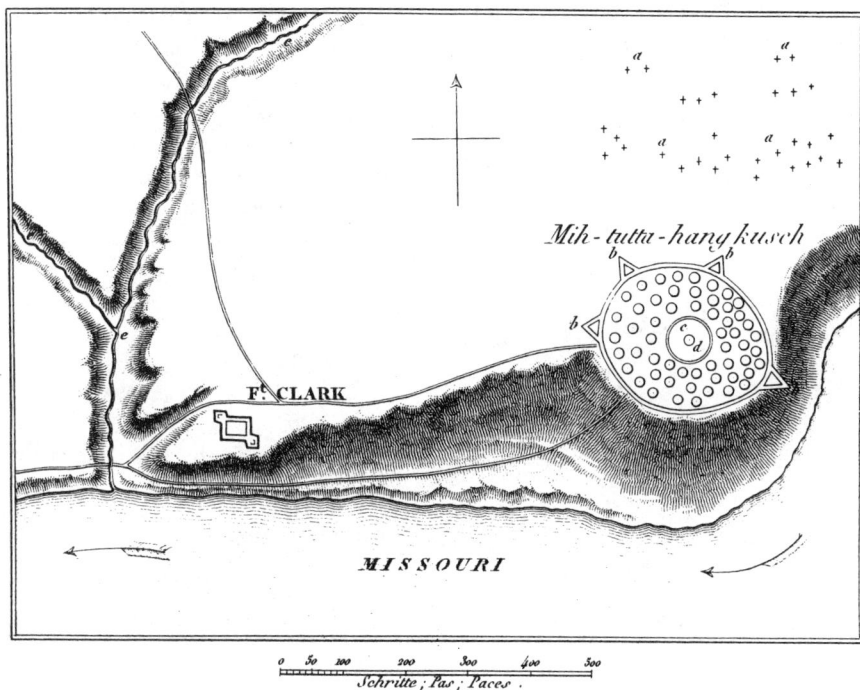

a. *Todtengerüste und Opferstangen.*   b. *Das Mandan-Dorf Mih-tutta-hangkusch.*   c. *Innerer Platz im Dorfe.*
d. *Die Arche des ersten Menschen.*   e. *Der Bach in welchem man die Schüsseln wascht.*

Fig. 14. Maximilian. Map: Neighborhood of Fort Clark. Woodcut. "'a' Scaffolds for the dead; offering poles; 'b' Mih-tutta-hangkusch; 'c' Village plaza; 'd' Ark of the First Man; 'e' Stream [Chardon Creek]." See Thwaites, *EWT*, 2:363.

this, they all turned around and attacked with newfound strength, and the enemy fled. Charbonneau knew both men.

[Enmity continues between the tribes; it] happens even now. Three weeks before our arrival at Fort Clark, three Assiniboines crawled to a point near the riverbank opposite the fort and made signs [asking] to be picked up. A man and two women went over in a [bullboat], and [the strangers] shot the former.

Fort Clark, as it presently exists, is located [not far from] the fort Lewis and Clark built in [1804] on the opposite riverbank. [It is] on a moderate elevation approximately 80 to 90 paces from the Missouri, which comes down from [the] northwest. The Mandan village Mih-Tutta-Hangkusch is located approximately 300 paces upriver from the fort on a steep, rather

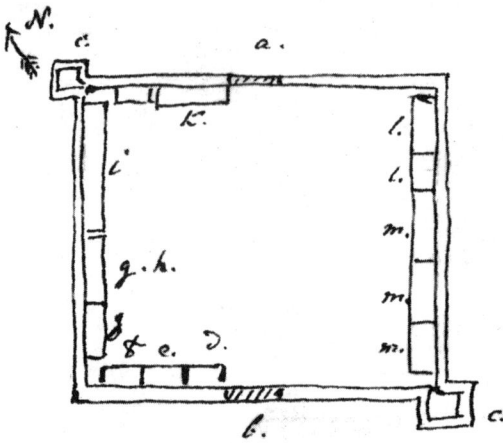

Fig. 15. Maximilian. Plan of Fort Clark. Ink. "'a' front gate; 'b' back gate; 'c' the two blockhouses; 'd' Mr. Kipp's quarters; 'e' clerks and interpreters' rooms; 'f' kitchen; 'gg' the new house; 'gh' our quarters; 'i' engagés' room; 'k' blacksmith shop; 'll' horse stables; 'mmm' stores for merchandise and the traded animal furs."

high, slightly protruding bank. A hill chain defines the background of the prairie and encloses the area on that side. About one hour below the fort, the Missouri turns east- or northeastward. Above the fort the path (mostly on the flat prairie) is unimpeded from Mih-Tutta-Hangkusch to the second Mandan village, Ruhptare; only a few small ravines with bushes break up the area.

Fort Clark is [laid out] as a quadrangle. Its front and back are 44 of my paces long, the sides 49 paces long. Two blockhouses, [in opposite] corners, defend the approach. The pickets are shaped like those of all the forts along the Missouri. The [one-story] buildings are located inside around the square yard. A [new] one, [just] built, [had] two bright, spacious rooms [and] glass windows (the others mostly had parchment shutters). Our living quarters were in the new building.

Three times daily, one-horse wagons (sleds when it snowed) went to the forest to get firewood, because there was none in storage. The disadvantage was [that] we always got green, somewhat wet wood. Mr. Kipp did not have sufficient men to cut firewood for storage. He also lacked a carpenter to [adequately] complete our quarters. Therefore, we had a room poorly insulated against the cold, where snow came in through the windows and the door, and a cold draft prevailed.

A small piece of land was cleared for a garden plot behind the fort. Close by, in the creek valley, a few Indians had set up small fields [for growing] Indian corn and squash. There was little hunting from the fort; the buffalo herds were usually at least twenty miles away, because of the many Indians, [and even they] seldom went far to hunt, because [only in large parties were they safe from] their enemies.

The [fort's few] horses were treated cruelly. They spent long winter nights in harsh snowstorms under open sky, standing in the fort yard without any cover, unmoving, backs often covered with snow or whitened by hoarfrost. When it was not too cold and the snow not too deep, the horses were driven out during the day; Síh-Sä was sometimes in charge [of that].

Fort Clark did not own any cattle or other domesticated animals except for about thirty chickens, which began to lay in March. A single tame cat in the fort did not help to lessen the plague of rats. These Norway rats were troublesome and numerous; [no] supplies were safe from them, especially the corn. The rats came here on the white men's ships. [They] did not presently exist in the Hidatsa villages, [but when] seven were seen on the trails [to the villages] from Fort Clark, all [were] killed; otherwise this plague would be there [shortly]. At first we had no rats in our new room, but they soon gnawed holes in the floorboards so we could enjoy their visits. We killed several, [but] they ruled undisturbed over the corn in the attic, until we put our small, tame prairie fox up there.

The only neighbors of the fort were the Indian villages, which will be described in the next chapters. They were surrounded by their scaffolds for the dead, a strange sight. The odors were neither pleasant nor particularly salutary, especially in [warm weather]. In summer the Indians, engaged in various activities, enlivened the prairie. But in winter the area [seemed] lifeless, monotonous, the wide snowy expanse animated by neither humans nor animals; at most, [there were solitary] roaming wolves. On the river ice there was usually more life, [as] the Indians [went] from their winter [lodges] to their summer village and the fort. Women, children, men, and dogs pulling small sleds could be seen all day long. Children from the fort went sledding on the ice, and the engagés ice-skated there sometimes on Sundays.

The climate was generally healthy. But spring, fall, [and] winter brought several minor indispositions. Completely lacking medical help, some died from these. Also, in the winter that we stayed there, [there were] several epidemics. Whooping cough took many children, [as did] diarrhea and stomach disorders. Because of the rapid and frequent changes of weather, catarrhs were frequent among the naked Indians, [although] fever was unknown. Spring usually brings bad weather: rain, storms, and snow—sometimes there were snowstorms in late May, [and] Indians died on the prairie. Last year a father and son perished in April. July is the only month when it does not freeze at all; [otherwise,] there is always frost during the night.M2

Extensive floods are rare. Since Charbonneau has been here, hence for thirty-seven years, there have been only two, but those were immense. During the first and worst one, they say the water level rose more than forty feet above average. Only the very tops of the high cottonwoods were visible. The second flood happened on 6 April 1826. Charbonneau lived in the central Hidatsa village. The water rose at daybreak so fast and so high that it forced him to flee two miles from the river and to climb onto a corn scaffold with a few of his possessions. He spent three days [on the scaffold], without fire, in a cold north wind and snow flurries. The water rose twenty-five feet.

Summer is generally dry and hot. The heat is not as onerous as on the Mississippi, although on the prairie it often gets quite oppressive. Summer brings a great misery—mosquitoes—but not [to] the same [degree] every year. In the hot season, the creeks dry up.

Fall is usually the most pleasant season: fair, bright days and moderate heat. Leaves fall in October. Often the fall change [is] fast and fierce. In one case there was clear, warm weather on 17 October, and on 18 October, such a snowstorm that two Indians froze to death on the prairie. Winter is long and usually severe. Most animal species leave; the winter fauna species are not numerous. The snow [depth] seldom measures more than two feet, but [it] stays on the ground till March. There are terrible snowstorms, when those lost on the prairie often lose their lives. A compass is then and in general an important, highly useful instrument [here]. The Missouri usually freezes in November. In winter 1833, the river stopped flowing in some areas on 23 November, [and] one could cross it a few days later at those places. Near the fort it is seldom frozen solid; usually [there is] an open but not [very] long channel. In the eleven years of his stay, Mr. Kipp remembers the coldest temperature as −36°F. Usually around New Year's, [there is] a frigid period of about a week, and this was the case during our [sojourn]. The winter of 1833–1834 was considered one of the most severe; for several days the temperature [was so low] that the mercury stayed [frozen] in the [thermometer] bulb.

M2 The [climatic] difference [in] a few days' travel downriver on the Missouri is often very significant. In some years in the Arikara villages, squashes are already being harvested when they are only blooming at the [villages of the] Mandans. The forest is blooming there, when leaves here are still in bud, and farther downriver it is naturally more and more so.

The water of the Missouri is cold, refreshing, and very healthy. In spring and summer it is usually murky; in winter, when frost occurs, it is completely clear. The creek water is usually bad, with some taste of salt. The soil in this area is said to be generally fertile on the plains, especially in the valleys between the hills, [where] there is a layer of humus more than two feet deep. But severe dryness in summer and winter causes some crops to fail. The almost unceasing wind dries out the soil, and the scant moisture [yielded by] rain immediately [disappears]. If one puts dung on the prairie, one will soon find it dried out, turned to dust, and blown away by the winds. The Mandans and the Hidatsas raise fine corn and never fertilize. When the field is exhausted after many years, they let it lie fallow and cultivate another piece of land, of which there seems to be a boundless [quantity] in this wide wilderness.

Concerning the natural formation of the soil, it likely consists mainly of clay, sand, and sandstone. The hill chains that traverse the prairies [are composed of much the same and contain] many impressions and fossils of shells and animal bones: mastodon, bivalve mussels, snails, etc. Twenty miles from the fort, there are places where [such things] lay visible on the surface. But access to this area is extremely dangerous, because of hostile Indians. The Indians [say] a petrified man [is located] three to four days' travel from the fort. The round head lies detached from the body; the skeleton is supposed to be intact. It doubtless belongs to a large prehistoric animal. It is regrettable that investigations on this land, so rich in objects of this kind, cannot be carried out freely and safely. I have already spoken occasionally about the extremely strange formation of the peaks bordering the upper Missouri in many places; geologists would certainly be rewarded by traveling through this area.

The wide prairies [and adjoining] hills are alive with numerous plants that have not yet been described. [John] Bradbury collected many plants in the vicinity of the Mandan villages. Perhaps my herbarium will add a few new specimens; I would be convinced of that if [so many] were not accidentally lost [to mold]. The protruding headlands [of the Missouri], and often other places on [its] banks, are wooded, mostly [with] tall cottonwoods (*Populus angulata*). In the young thickets on the bank, [these] are mixed with two kinds of willows (*Salix*); red willow (*Cornus sericea*); and a dense, thorny underbrush of roses, *Symphoria*, and a few other plants. Also growing in the upper Missouri woods are *Fraxinus; Ulmus; Acer negundo;* a type of oak; several kinds of currants *(Ribes); Prunus padus* (chokecherry); and in many places the buffalo berry [and] *poires* or serviceberries. [There are] several creepers, among [them] *Vitis, Clematis virginiana* (very common), *Celastrus scandens, Humulus,* etc. *Juniperus prostrata* forms black-brown spots on the barren hilltops; [other cedars] occur on some steep slopes. There are no conifers in the vicinity of the Mandan villages; one must travel farther upriver to find them. On the prairies in the vicinity of Fort Clark, some cactus species grow: *Cactus ferox* and a type related to the *mammillaris* that American botanists classify as the same, which, however, appears different to me. The grass [species] on the prairie are not as diverse as one might think. Several *Typha* [—] and *Arundo* [—] occur in ponds and marshes, the latter also near creeks and wet ditches. The prairie is overgrown with silver-leafed *Artemisia columbiensis* and colored whitish by it. Many plants, [such as] ferns, mosses, [and] fungi, are very rare; only a few occur.

Several officinal plants grow in the area of Fort Clark. The yellow-blooming, highly aromatic *Brachyris euthamiae* is especially common. The tea is extremely diuretic, and drunk with best results in the case of gonorrhea; for this purpose, whole blossoms are used, fresh or dried. A small handful suffices for one cup of tea. *Artemisia,* with a [strong] scent similar to that of European wormwood, is also officinal. It is bitter and makes a sudorific tea. The Indians use it for wounds and as a magic or medicine herb. *Mentha* tea is also supposed to be very pleasant, stomach soothing, and sudorific. There are many officinal plants on the upper Missouri but no doctors to apply them.

[Of the] several edible berries, serviceberry is likely the most healthy and best tasting. Currants and gooseberries are also fairly good to eat. They occur in great quantities in forest underbrush. Buffalo berries are very astringent, sour, [and] inedible until there is a freeze. The wild grapevines *(Vitis)* have only small insipid berries. In summer there are tasty strawberries in the forest. The so-called cherries (chokecherry), *Prunus padus virginiana,* are bad tasting, dry, and indigestible.

Around the Fort Clark area one can observe animals [native to] America's western prairies [and its] cold northern [regions]. Buffalo herds do not stay near Fort Clark, except during very severe winter weather, because the many Indians living here drive them away. However, during snowstorms, the animals seek shelter in the forests along the riverbanks;

then many are killed. Their bones and skulls cover the prairie everywhere. Elk *(Cervus canadensis)* can be shot about ten miles from here; elk skins are very valuable to the Mandans, [who] make their [moccasins] from them. The whitetail or common deer *(Cervus virginianus)* can be found in nearby forests in small numbers; they are more numerous 3 to 4 miles from the fort. The blacktail deer *(Cervus macrotis)* is a bit more distant, about 20 to 30 miles. The antelope *(Antilocapra)* lives close by all year long. Numerous in summer, [the animals] retreat in winter toward the mountains, where [they] find shelter from severe snowstorms. [They] return in April, when one can see their herds cross the Missouri. Then they disperse over the prairie to have their young. The bighorn *(Ovis ammon)* lives about fifty miles from here. The Hidatsas kill 100 or more of these animals in one hunting season, [on expeditions to] mountainous regions. The grizzly bear, *Ursus horribilis,* occurs about 4 miles from here; the Indians do not like to hunt it [but covet] the claws for necklaces and often pay high prices for them.

The variable wolf *(Canis variabilis)* is very common along the whole upper Missouri and can be found [with different coat colors:] wolf-gray, whitish, or all white. The animals are famished in winter, and some [get] extremely thin. They follow the buffalo herds and catch weak, sick, or young animals. When hunters come, it is [the wolves'] harvesting season. They recognize the sound of the gun so well that they come instantly when a shot is fired. Ravens also [do this] — hunters maintain that the wolves look to these birds to find the direction [in which] the prey is located. Any shot or wounded found by them is lost [to the hunter].

The prairie wolf, or schähäckä in Mandan *(Canis latrans),* is exactly in the middle between wolf and fox. The color and shape [are] more like the former. The red fox *(Canis fulvus)* is common but not nearly as numerous as the wolf. Its fur is beautiful [and] sought-after. The gray fox *(Canis cinerea argenteus)* is also found here. The prairie fox, or kit fox *(Canis velox),* is common. Foxes [and] wolves are caught during winter in traps.

The panther *(Felis concolor)* is now rare on the Missouri [although] Lewis and Clark shot one. The common lynx *(Felis canadensis),* called wild cat here, is scarce, but individual animals have been shot [nearby], and we tracked one in the snow. The fish otter *(Lutra canadensis)* that lives in the river is scarce because of the Indians. The mink *(Mustela vison)* is common. The large weasel *(Mustela erminea)* is numerous, and the Indians often hunt it with snares. They use it for adornments and [clothing]. The badger *(Meles labradorius)* is not scarce.

On the Missouri and its tributaries, the beaver *(Castor [canadensis])* is more frequent the farther upriver [one travels]. The Mandans and Hidatsas catch many of these sought-after animals, despite [a] significant decline in numbers. Nowadays, with the competition from Messrs. Sublette and Campbell, beaver pelts bring very high prices, as already mentioned. The muskrat *(Fiber zibethicus)* occurs on landlocked lakes and small brooks. The porcupine *(Hystrix dorsata)* is not rare, [nor are hares and rabbits]. The prairie dog *(Arctomys ludoviciana)* has villages here, a few miles away, [but] *Arctomys hoodii* is far more numerous. Bats are supposed to be here in rather large numbers, but I did not have the opportunity to obtain [many]. I have no doubt [that] there are several [other] species of small animals here [in summer].

The class of birds has many interesting species. The redheaded urubu (turkey buzzard) lives here in summer and [migrates] in winter, as [does] *Aquila leucocephala*. There are several species of hawks in summer, but in winter not a single one is seen. The great horned owl *(Strix virginiana)* is a hardy bird; it endures the whole winter here, as does another species of owl—I suspect *Strix asio*. The snowy owl *(Strix nyctea)* has been shot here on several occasions. In summer the burrowing owl *(Strix cunicularia)* has been found frequently in prairie dog villages. Hummingbirds *(Trochilus colubris)* come up to the Mandans in summer, but not in numbers or regularly. Wild pigeons are frequent in the forest during summer;[3] *Columba carolinensis* lives in small bushes on the prairie and in ravines. In winter almost all [these birds migrate]; so do the woodpeckers; only *Picus pubescens* endures. In addition to the blackbird (known here in four species—*Quiscalus versicolor, Icterus phoeniceus, Icterocephalus,* and a fire-colored and black [one] very similar to the Baltimore [oriole]), ravens and magpies are numerous. The waxwing *(Bombycilla garrula)* is said to live here in summer; in winter it is a visitor. The magpies stay the winter, mostly in forests. The bird that seems [able] to endure the most cold is the raven. The whippoorwill is found here once in a while in small numbers. Neither *Sitta* nor *Certhia* are seen in the forests in winter; on the other hand, *Parus atricapillus* withstands the severe winter. *Alauda magna* and *alpestris* live here in summer. The snow bunting and the linnet *(Emberiza nivalis* and *Fringilla linaria)* are [here] in winter [but not] summer. *Fringilla amoena* lives [here] in [the] summer in pairs in [the] forests, [as does] the goldfinch *(Fringilla tristis).* There is only one [galliform] species *(Tetrao phasianellus),* called prairie hen by the Americans; it stays in summer and in winter is numerous, but because of the many Indian hunters, it is very shy. There are marshes a few miles from the fort and a pond overgrown with reeds; [beyond] the opposite riverbank there are inland lakes, where a large number of waterfowl and marsh birds live in summer [and] especially in spring and fall. Numerous pelican flocks can be seen there and on the Missouri. The whooping crane—a splendid bird—and the sandhill crane are frequent in fall and spring migrations. These birds are eaten. Sandpipers live throughout the summer on the banks of the Missouri. The herons also move away in fall, because there is no open water where they can find food. In summer, *Numenius longirostris* lives on the prairies. The blackish coot *(Fulica* [—]) is common in summer and fall. Swans, ducks, and geese all leave in winter.

There are a few interesting amphibian species,[4] but unfortunately I did not get to see them alive in [their] natural habitat. A mud turtle *(Emys)* lives in the creeks, doubtless the same that I saw near Fort Union. [I was told there] are many species of lizards near the Mandans, [but] strangely, during our whole trip upriver on the Missouri, we did not see a single lizardlike animal. There were several species of snakes. *Coluber constrictor* is not found, but *Coluber proximus,* [in] its beautiful red-spotted variety *eximus,* a large beautiful snake, is very frequent. We came across only one species of rattlesnake: *Crotalus tergeminus,* frequent and large—I often saw it more than four feet long. There are several frog species, [including] *Rana halecina* [and] small tree frogs; after rain and storms, the ground is often completely covered with small frogs. Fish species in the Missouri are not numerous. There are two kinds of catfish, a species of pike *(Esox),* the goldeye, and sometimes the buffalo[fish]. There are doubtless other fish, [unnoticed by local] inhabitants.

Among the insects are several bothersome to humans, [such as] the numerous summer mosquitoes. On the prairie, [there is] a moderately large spotted grasshopper that eats plants quickly. Several species make noise when they fly but are not that destructive. Many animals feed on the prairie grasshoppers.

About mollusks and related animals, I [found little]. I [later] sent Mr. Thomas Say the *Unio* specimens I [collected on] the upper Missouri: a species from the Stone Walls [and another] from the creek near Fort Clark.

XVIII

Remarks on the Indian Tribe of the Mandans,
Actually Númangkake

The Mandans, as these Indians are generally called now, even though this is actually the Dacota term [for] them, were formerly a numerous nation that [once] inhabited thirteen [or] more villages. They call themselves Númangkake (the people, or humans). Smallpox and enemies reduced this nation so much that its total population found space in two villages: Mih-Tutta-Hangkusch (the southern village), about 300 paces above Fort Clark on the same bank of the Missouri, and Ruhptare.

Lewis and Clark, the famous travelers, spent the winter [of 1804–5] with the Mandans. They give [an essentially sound account], although the Mandan and Hidatsa languages were mostly incorrectly understood and written down. The information, names, and words given by me have all been recorded according to the statements of sensible and mature men of these nations. I attempted to write their language according to [its] true pronunciation. German or Dutch velar articulation aided me greatly, certainly more than English and French [would aid linguists. Velar articulation] is intrinsic to the Mandan and Hidatsa [languages] to the highest degree. Mr. Kipp and Mr. Charbonneau, who have lived for many years among these Indians, supported me at this task with patience and kindness.

[Ruhptare] is located 3 miles higher upriver than [Mih-Tutta-Hangkusch] but on the same bank. [It] has 38 lodges and 83 warriors. [Mih-Tutta-Hangkusch] counts 65 lodges and about 150 warriors. In both villages together there are about 300 horses.

The most important men in Mih-Tutta-Hangkusch are:
1. Chárätä-Numakschi (Wolf Chief)
2. Mató-Tópe (Four Bears)
3. Mato-Uaninächä (The One Not Shooting at Bears or Bear That Cannot Walk)

In Ruhptare:

1. Kähka-Chamahän (Little Raven)
2. Kipsandá-Tope (Four Turtles)

Later, under religious ideas, I will deal with the early history of the Mandans, since it is shrouded in darkness and mixed with fable and legend.

These Indians are a strong, well-built breed of men of medium height or taller; only a few could be called short. The tallest living man among them now, Máhchsi-Karéhde (Flying War Eagle), is 5 feet 10 inches 2 lines (Paris measure) in height. They are not as tall as the Hidatsas, however. Many are robust [and] plump; some [are] slender [with] rather thin limbs.

Their facial features are [like] most Missouri Indians, but they seem to have less aquiline noses and less heavy cheekbones than the Dacotas. The eyes are mostly long and narrow, blackish brown. The mouth is often large, broad, at times a bit thick; the cheekbones broad, slightly protruding. There are large variations in skull shape. I found the forehead [in general] no more receding than that of Europeans. [Of] the numerous skulls at burial places, many showed the forehead rising straight up, although [some were] lower and more receding.

Their hair is long, full, straight, [and] black, but seldom as jet-black and glossy as [that of] many Brazilians. There are whole families, for instance Síh-Chidä's, [whose hair] is gray or heavily mixed with gray and white. Like all Missouri [River] Indians, [Mandan] teeth are beautiful—strong, white as ivory, even, and tightly spaced. A defect or tooth gap is seldom seen, not even among old people, [although their] teeth [often] become worn (mainly attributed to chewing hard, dry meat).

Deformed individuals are rare, but there was a small hunchbacked man. Cross-eyed people are uncommon. One-eyed [persons], or [individuals] with a patch over one eye, occur frequently. There were several deafmutes—three siblings had this congenital trait: two brothers and a sister.

The skin color of these Indians is a beautiful reddish brown, which [might occasionally] be called copper; sometimes lighter, sometimes darker; in some individuals, more yellowish. If they clean themselves well, some have an almost white skin [and] even a red tint on their cheeks. They do not disfigure their bodies, [except] their ears; on the rim [at] the back they make two or three holes from which they hang glass beads, brass or iron rings of mixed sizes, or strings of shells traded from other Indians. They say, if asked, that [the shells] were brought from the Mönníh-Kärrä (the ocean). They are childishly vain, like all primitive people, and [greatly enjoy] adorning themselves. Young men always have a small mirror attached to their wrist. The mirrors are bought in cardboard cases from the traders but [are] immediately [fitted in] crude wooden frames that [the men] make [and lavishly decorate] themselves. They often look at themselves. After walking, especially [in the wind, which is so prevalent], they [check themselves in their] mirror, comb their hair, and put their clothing in order. Face painting is always done [with the aid of] this important article of toiletry.

Mandan [basic clothing] is rather simple; their heads demand more care by far. They wear their hair parted transversely across the center of the head. The hair in front is smoothed down and usually divided into three flat hanks. Two hang down [by] the temples and are typically braided in plaits. On [the plaits, at or above the temples,] they wear a [hairbow-like] decoration that consists of two pieces of leather or cloth connected in the middle with [a] winding of brass wire. [This ornament is] densely [sewn] with blue or white glass beads. Most times, a string [of] white dentalium shells, [attached to the hair bow,] hangs down past the chest to the middle of the body. Between these two strangely ornamented braids, a [lock] hangs down the middle of the forehead to the nose. It is smooth and flat, cut square below. The hair at the back of the head is separated into many long, flat skeins, about 1½″ to 2″ wide, that are kneaded or smeared with white or light brownish red clay. If their natural hair is not very long, they extend it with someone else's hair, attached with resin. If they are hunting or [traveling and] not in their best clothing, they often tie their long hair in a thick braid, wrap it with leather straps or ribbons of red cloth, and then bind it together above the forehead in a thick bun. [When] fully dressed, they [wear] various feathers in their hair. Often [these are from] birds of prey, set in a semicircle, like rays of the sun; or a tuft of raven tail feathers [worn] upright on the back [of the head]; [or] a thick bunch of great horned owl feathers (Strix virginiana); [or] small, round rosettes of raven feathers, trimmed short.

They also wear a large feather bonnet with horns (máhchsi-akub-háschka), ribbons of ermine, and in the back, a long, broad, trailing strip of red cloth. To this [strip], white and black war eagle feathers are attached. Only outstanding warriors, those who have counted many coups, can wear [this bonnet]. [They] have a high value, [since] one often pays 2 or 3 dollars for a war eagle feather.

Upper Missouri Indians like to wear necklaces of grizzly bear claws. In spring the claws are whitish and often more than 3 inches long. Only the claws of the front paws are used for this purpose. The necklace is trimmed with a strip of otter pelt, which hangs down the back, and is often lined with red cloth and [embroidered] with glass beads. The claws are [spaced] apart with [larger] blue glass beads, [and] the sides of the claws are painted red or yellow. It [is] a beautiful ornament for a warrior, [spreading] from one shoulder to the other [in] a wide, half circle! Such a necklace is very expensive for them: 10 to 12 dollars [or] more. They have all kinds of [other necklaces]: strings of colored glass beads, aromatic roots, or elk teeth (they can [exchange] a horse for 100 to 150 teeth), etc. These Indians usually have a bare upper body. The leather shirt of the Assiniboines, Crows, Blackfoot, and other [more northern] tribes is rare among them. Even in the most severe winters, their upper bodies are always naked, covered only with a buffalo robe. They paint the bare [parts of] the body reddish brown, [or] occasionally with white clay, and often make red or black drawings on their arms. Usually their faces are painted completely red with vermilion, sometimes yellow. There are no rules; the painting depends entirely on the [preferences] of the [individual] dandy, except for [traditions pertaining to] societies, certain dances, and war coups. At ordinary celebrations and dances they all paint themselves [deliberately] differently; [if] a young man sees [someone] painted like himself, [he] immediately leaves and [changes his paint], and this can happen [several] times at the same occasion.

At times, though seldom, their wrists and upper arms are ornamented with thin, polished steel bracelets that enclose the arm like a spring; these are obtained from traders. They wear many brass rings on their fingers; [these] are also sold to them. The main piece of clothing is the buffalo robe. The buffalo hides are worn with the hair on the inside when the weather is dry; if it is wet, [hair side] out. On the flesh side, [the robes] are painted white or reddish brown, and in the center, they are decorated with a horizontal band of blue or white beads, usually [including] three equally spaced, round, [beaded] rosettes (sometimes small, sometimes very large). [When] the horizontal band is made of colorfully dyed porcupine quills, it is narrower. [The quilled band] is the old style, worn before the Europeans sold them glass beads (*rassade*). [Some] robes are reddish brown on the tanned side [and] painted with black animal figures. Still others [have] a white background [painted] with representations of coups (heroic feats) in black or bright colors—[including] portrayal of slain enemies, blood streaming or spurting from wounds, numbers of scalps taken [or] horses stolen [or] weapons [seized] (guns, bows and arrows, battle axes)—everything drawn in outline in characteristic [native style]. Blood and wounds are red, [while] horses and people are often [done] in different, lively colors: black, yellow, green, and red.

Another type of drawing [found] on robes [depicts] objects given away, [always] represented in their correct numbers. The presents are often of great value; [the donors thereby] earn high standing among their compatriots. On such robes one might see long red figures, [each] with a black circle at the end, standing parallel above one another [and] painted across the hide in long rows. These represent whips given away—[actually,] the number of horses, since they always give a whip with a horse. Parallel horizontal stripes represent guns, often [also] drawn in complete outline. The sides are decorated with [locks] of human hair and horsehair ([the latter] in bright colors, especially yellow and green) and with glass beads. In the past such robes were painted with more care, and one was bartered for five bullets with gunpowder. [Even though] they are inferior now, they bring 8 or 10 dollars. A beautifully painted robe is worth as much as two unpainted [ones].

Their leggins, or trousers, are tied with leather straps to the belt. The outside edge [is decorated with] a one- to two-inch-wide vertical strip of porcupine quill [embroidery] in beautiful colors. Nowadays [the quillwork has often been] replaced with sky-blue and white glass beads. [There is] often also an edging of long leather fringes. The leather of the [leggings] is usually painted reddish brown or pale red [or at times] white; often [there are] black horizontal stripes below the knee. They use the so-called breechcloth, as do all North American [Indians]: a piece of woolen cloth, typically with narrow black and white stripes, that they pull between their legs and tuck through their belt at the front and back, where it hangs down with a broad [covering] surface. Their [moccasins] are of deer or buffalo leather and are usually simple and little ornamented. However, [for] their best finery, the [moccasins] are decked out with rosettes or stripes of porcupine quills or glass beads. Those who have counted coup wear a wolf's tail or strips of otter skin around their ankles that trail on the ground behind them.

Boys usually go naked; in winter [they are just] wrapped in a robe. The girls have leather clothing. The women's dresses [have] open sleeves, a leather belt around [the waist], and fringe at the bottom. They wear iron bracelets and strings of glass beads around their necks and often in their ears. Their trousers are short, from their feet to their knees.

Tattooing is fashionable but [not] a general practice. Usually only the right half of the chest and one arm are marked with parallel stripes and other figures, [as are] the forearm and individual fingers. Men's faces are free [of tattoos]. The women of the White Buffalo Cow society wear tattooed stripes on their chins. The [tattoo] needle pricks are colored blackish blue with willow bark [soaked] in water.

[After] the appearance of these interesting people, the first item attracting our attention is the way they arrange their dwellings, villages, [and] domestic life. Their villages are large settlements of earth lodges [arranged] in a roughly circular order but with no specific regularity. The largest of the Mandan villages is Mih-Tutta-Hangkusch, about [150–200] paces in diameter. Its outer perimeter was formerly surrounded by strong posts, like palisades; [these are] mostly missing now, burned [for fuel] in cold winters. The lodges stand close together, leaving a free round space [or plaza] in the center, about 60 paces in diameter, [where] the Mandans [have placed] the so-called ark (discussed later). It is a small cylinder made of planks about four to five feet high and open on top. The boards are stuck in the ground and bound with creepers or flexible branches to hold them together. On the north side of the plaza, the medicine lodge is located; certain religious celebrations and customs take place in it (discussed later). Attached atop a high pole is a figure made of skins; [it has] a wooden head, a black face, and a fur cap with feathers. It supposedly represents Ochkíh-Häddä, an evil [spirit or] person who once appeared among them and [then] vanished. They are afraid of him; he is what we call the devil.

The lodges themselves are of a round, gently vaulted shape. [At the] entrance, windbreaks protrude on three sides—from [each] side and above. The inhabitants block this entrance with brushwood and thorns when they are absent. The door opening is closed by a small, dried, stiff hide stretched on wooden poles [and] hung there. It is pushed aside when one enters. Above the center of the lodge there is a square opening [in the roof that serves] as a smoke vent; to [this, on the outside,] they attach [a] dome-shaped chimney [cover], made from sticks and twigs and [sometimes] covered with hides. The interior of the lodge is spacious, rather bright, and clean. Four strong pillars in the center, with several crossbeams, support the ceiling. The inner area of this lodge is made up of eleven to seventeen thick pillars, four to five feet high. Between [these pillars] stand slightly smaller ones very close together. On them rest pieces of wood slanted toward the center. [The exterior of the structure is] covered with [mats] made from willow sticks tied together with willow bark. This is the framework of the lodge on which hay and then earth is spread.

Lodge building, hunting, weapon making, war, and some of the harvesting are the occupations of men. All other jobs remain for the women, who, although they are generally well treated, have to do hard work. They carry wood from afar, cook, take care of planting and seeding, tan hides, make and maintain garments, and [perform] many other jobs.

In the center of the lodge there is a shallow, round pit for the fire. Above it, the cooking kettle hangs on a chain. Often this [hearth] is edged with upright stones. Around the inside [perimeter] of the lodge lies or hangs the luggage (sacks of parchment and skins, the former colorfully painted); saddles; horse harnesses; [and] dogsleds. Weapons [are] often hung on racks, as [are] meat and corn. The beds also stand [against the outer wall]. They are large, square boxes [made] of hide, [each] with a square entrance [and] spacious enough [to accommodate] several people. Inside, there are buffalo skins and woolen blankets on and underneath which they sleep. There is no bad smell in the dwellings at all. A wall or screen of willow branches covered with hides [placed] in front of the door keeps the draft out when the door is opened. The [hearth] is located in front of this screen and thus protected. [See pl. 30 for Bodmer's view of a lodge interior.]

The [text above describes] the summer lodges. In winter these Indians move with most of their belongings to the neighboring forests, where they have built villages consisting of similar but slightly smaller lodges. The departure [date] from the summer villages depends on the weather, usually toward the middle of November, and the move back again in spring falls in late February or [early] March. In the winter lodges, the horses have a separate compartment behind poles, where they are taken in the evening and fed corn. During the day, they graze on the prairie or in the forest, where they feed on cottonwood bark. The Mandans have a fair number of horses; most men have two, [although] several have none.

The Mandans are hospitable when one visits and often invite acquaintances.

They eat and smoke after sitting down on a buffalo robe beside the fire. The pipe is passed around from left to right. Their pipes are of red stone or black clay; the red pipes are usually obtained from the Dacotas. They also have wooden pipe bowls lined with stone. The stems are plain, long, and round. They smoke [a type of] tobacco [that] they raise themselves and [also] European [tobacco] mixed with red willow bark *(Cornus sericea)* or *sakkakomi* leaves. Pure European tobacco is too strong for them, [so] they do not particularly like to smoke cigarros.

[Mandan] meals are served in wooden bowls. Spoons are made from the horns of bighorn or buffalo. Their foodstuffs are diverse. They have an advantage over the migrating hunter nations in that they not only hunt [but also] take [great] sustenance from the fields, [a resource] upon which they [can] always fall back. They raise [nine kinds of] corn, [three of] squash, various beans, sunflowers (very similar to our [cultivar]), and tobacco. The tobacco of the Mandans, Hidatsas, and Arikaras—these three nations cultivate the same plants—seems to be a type of *Nicotiana*. The plant is raised without any care and grows in thick bushes. The smell and taste [were] somewhat unpleasant to us. They no longer raise much of this tobacco; it has been replaced by [the] white man's. However, [the native one] is still smoked during peace agreements and is therefore kept in the medicine bag.

Planting—each lodge or family has about 3 to 5 acres under cultivation—takes place in May. They throw individual kernels of corn in small holes arranged in rows and cover them with soil. During summer the plants are hoed and hilled three times [to improve] moisture access. Men, women, and children help with the corn harvest in October. For fieldwork, the women use wide iron hoes with curved wooden handles. Charbonneau remembers that [in the past] they used buffalo shoulder blades for that purpose. Their fields are never fenced but are completely free and open.

[Like] other nations, [the Mandans use] the wild plants of the prairie: *poires* (serviceberries), buffalo berries, currants, chokecherries or cherries, the *pomme blanche* and several roots, as well as the sweet, juicy sapwood of the cottonwood. They eat [squashes] freshly cooked [or] dry them [for future use]; several kinds of beans are mixed [and] eaten together. Corn is cooked in water [or] roasted; [it can] also [be] roasted, pounded, mixed with fat, pressed into small, round [cakes], and baked. Sweet corn is very tasty, especially when it is in the milk [stage, when] it is cooked, dried, and kept for [later] use.

The Mandans eat all kinds of animals: bear (especially when young and fat), wolf, fox, dog—everything except for horse. But only a few of them eat weasel. Among the birds, they find the turkey buzzard and the raven unpleasant because they eat the dead on the scaffolds. Turtles they eat; snakes they abhor. The buffalo is always the mainstay of their hunts. It supplies them with hides, meat, tallow, sinews, and [other items] for various needs (its hunt will be discussed later). Next to the buffalo [in importance] is the beaver, not only [for] its precious pelt but also [for its] tasty meat and fat tail—a delicacy. They do not often make pemmican, that favorite dish of the northern Indians that sometimes tickles olfactory organs uncomfortably.

Their only drink is water,[M1] because they receive absolutely no spirits at Fort Clark nor from the Fur Company of Messrs. Sublette and Campbell. Drunks, common [in] the more northern nations, hardly occur here.

Two, sometimes three, families typically live in each Mandan lodge, [usually] a father with his son or son-in-law. The number of wives varies, but they do not have more than four [and] usually only one. The [women] are very skillful. [They] paint robes very well. The colors [come from] various [sources]: red [from] the root of a plant called *savoyenne* by the French or from buffalo berries; yellow with a lichen from the Rocky Mountains; black from *Helianthus* and a certain black stone or clay; blue and green from European substances. Hides are tanned the same [way] as other nations; [it] is one of the women's main jobs [and] has been described many times [by others].

The Mandans and the Hidatsas in all five villages fire earthen pots and vessels of various shapes and sizes. The clay is slate colored and turns yellow-reddish when fired. They cook in [them]. Glazing is unknown.

They often have many children. Some families have up to ten, which causes much work during early childhood, when the [offspring] are still little. They love [their children] very much. Many die at a tender age. Because the mothers' work is in many instances hard, they frequently bear weak children. The births are usually very easy. The mother bathes immediately thereafter in the river, often even when it is ice-covered. It is said [that] the births of Indian children are much easier than those of whites and even [that] an Indian woman suffers more if the father of the child is white. After

---

[M1] They [do] like to drink well-sweetened coffee and tea.

ten days the child is considered to be safe; its most difficult time has passed. [Their] cradles [are] leather sacks hung by straps from a lodge crossbeam. They are not as elegant and beautiful as some we saw among the Dacotas and Assiniboines.

Mandan and Hidatsa children [are not] disciplined. They can do anything they please [and] are not told [they are] wrong! If the mother or father tells a boy something [and] the boy hits them in the face or kicks them, the father just lowers his head and says, "This [boy] will be an excellent warrior."

As stated, the women work hard and lead a difficult life. Some men treat them brutally. It is not uncommon [for such a woman to] walk out of the lodge and hang herself from a tree. [Women] receive little compensation for their continuous [labor]. They do not even have nice clothes — this European women's right is claimed here by the men.

Sisters have considerable power. All horses that a young man steals or takes in war belong to them. [If] he comes riding back from a raid and meets his sister, he will dismount immediately and hand the horse over to her. If, however, he needs something valuable that his sister owns, he just demands [it] — for instance, a nice dress: the sister takes it off at once and gives it to him.

If a young man wants to marry, he asks the girl for her consent [and] then goes to her father and seeks his permission. If he receives [it], he brings two [or] up to ten horses and ties them to the lodge of the father-in-law. The girl's father in turn takes other horses (if he does not have [enough] himself, relatives help out) and brings them to the lodge of the son-in-law. In such a case, an estimate is made beforehand as to how many horses the relatives of the woman have, because all presents received are reciprocated with the same number in return. As many horses are given as it is believed will be received in return. The bride cooks corn daily and brings a kettle or bowl of it to the bridegroom's lodge. After some time, the young man comes and sleeps with the bride, and the marriage is consummated. Frequently the young couple lives in the father-in-law's lodge; in some instances they build themselves a new lodge. Sometimes the two parties separate; this is not uncommon.

The women are anything but prudish; they often have two or several lovers. Unfaithfulness is often not punished. Only one woman had a piece of her nose cut off (this happened very frequently among the Blackfoot). A main occupation of young men is to try their luck with women and girls, and this, aside from [attention to] their finery, takes most of their time. They do not find many aloof beauties. In the evening, until late at night, they move around within their villages, [or] in the neighborhood, or from one village to another. They have a singular way to show off their great feats in these fields. They mark the number of conquered beauties with small, peeled sticks, painted red at [one] end, 2 or 3 feet long, and tied together at the lower ends in a bundle. Those of the Mandans are mostly without any further adornment, [but] among the Hidatsas there is usually a longer stick in the center [tipped with] a tuft of feathers. This longer stick denotes a favorite, and they tell each [sweetheart] that she might be the one.

If a man abducts a woman, the forsaken man avenges himself by seizing the abductor's goods, horses, and [other] items of value, and the latter has to accept it quietly. The woman is not taken back.

Some [Mandans] count their years [by] winters. In their medicine bundle or sack, they carry a piece of wood on which they mark the years, but only a few know their age precisely. The Mandans treat their elders very well. They do not let them suffer hunger, unless the elder has no more relatives at all.

Among the Mandans and the Hidatsas there are certain womanlike men called *bardaches* by the French. In the Mandan language they are míh-däckä, men who dress like women and do [the same work]. Young men treat them literally like women and have relationships with them. Mr. Kipp was not ready to believe this, but Charbonneau and several other men who have lived many years among the Indians all agree on this point. Charbonneau maintains [that] young men frequently prefer the berdache [over women] for certain activities. These types of womanlike men are found in many nations, for instance, the Ojibwes. There are not many berdaches among the Mandans, only one; among the Hidatsas, two or three. Frequently (actually usually), these people are children when they dedicate themselves to the libertine business discussed here; even now a few are emerging. They usually assert [that] a dream or inspiration, their medicine, [was the source of] this status and nothing can deter them from it. [Such] children have been treated harshly and beaten [and/or] given bows and arrows [and] nice men's (or warriors') clothes to encourage a desire in them for men's activities, but they have remained true to their intentions, and no one wants to interfere with [a] medicine or with another person's conscience.

These Indians lack neither reason nor intellectual abilities, and Harlan is not incorrect when he states in his *Fauna Americana* (p. 14), [regarding] the order of [the] five human races [described by] Blumenbach, [that] the American [Indian] should be placed immediately after the Caucasian. If [all] mankind have not generally received the same abilities from the Creator, I am convinced that [Indians] are not inferior to the whites in this regard. Some among the Mandans had much desire to learn, [a] considerable drive to find out about sophisticated matters. If they were not so attached to the prejudices and ways of thinking inherited from their forefathers, many of them would be easy to teach. However, the bad examples they see so frequently [among] white men, chasing after money in their country, do not inspire great respect [for or a] desire to emulate these white paragons. If they cannot be converted to Christianity, [Euro-American bad conduct] is a main reason, because [the Mandans] live more strictly by their rules than [do] the Europeans who call themselves Christians.

In many American and foreign works, the often accurate reasoning [and] correct judgment of Indians have been described, and it is unnecessary to repeat [these observations]. One is often at a loss [trying] to respond to their sharp, [perceptive observations]. They possess many impressive aptitudes for drawing, music, and so on. There were several Mandans who exhibited not only great enjoyment but also true talent in drawing. Some debated with genuine passion, even about sophisticated subject matter. The moon, the sun, the stars, and other objects [they] observed daily [but understood] only through silly fables—unsatisfactory even to them—they brought up for discussion, [wishing] to learn [from us]. Some considered our views far sillier than theirs; they laughed aloud when it was asserted that the earth was round or that it revolved around the sun. But others did not dismiss our views and thought [that since] the white men [could do] so much [that was] incomprehensible to them, then perhaps this could be correct as well.

[When] they cannot pursue their main activities—hunting and fighting wars—the men here are rather indolent. They sit near the fire all day long, smoke, eat, do nothing, and enjoy being waited upon. The Mandans and Hidatsas are not bad [people] in general. The Mandans, especially, have many dependable men who deserve only praise. [However,] there are thieving rascals among them. They do not kill white men if they come across an individual or a small number on the prairie, but they usually rob them. At

Fort Clark we had Indians [everywhere] all day long. Indeed, they some-times almost pushed out the rightful inhabitants, which was very irksome [considering the] winter cold and the small fireplace. It was especially up-setting because their big buffalo robes kept the heat away from the rest of the room. They always demanded to be fed, [and] they smoked more than 200 pounds of company tobacco a year, since one cannot deprive them of one of their greatest pleasures, the pipe. A few noble-minded Indians among the Mandans had more refined feelings; they usually left the din-ing room close to eating time. Most, who frequently had nothing but corn and beans during winter and were therefore greedy for meat, showed up at mealtime and waited impatiently [to be served].

Many are neat and clean. [They] bathe often, though their hands as well as their whole bodies are often dirty [or] at least smeared with colors. They usually wear their nails long. The women are typically dirty (especially their hands), because their hard work leaves them less time for cleanliness. They are very tolerant [of] vermin, [which] their heads and even their buffalo robes are generally said to be full of. They eat these [insect] guests with pleasure, pick[ing] them from each other's heads; men sometimes receive them from women as a present. They do not, [however,] like to eat lice from the heads of white men. The Indians bathe frequently, even in cold winter. The icy water in winter hardens them—even in severely cold weather, they walk naked beneath their buffalo robes.

As in most North American Indian tribes, there are certain associations or bands among them, societies that differ from each other in distinctive markings and certain rules. War or signal whistles (íhkoschka), [worn] hanging from their necks, [are among] the badges of the societies. The men are divided on the basis of age into six societies. The first is the Meníss-Óch-ka-Óchatä, [the] Foolish Dogs or Dogs Whose Names Are Not Known. The [members] are young men ten to fifteen years of age. They carry a small íh-koschka [fashioned] from wild goose wing bones. When they dance, three of them [wear] a long, broad piece of red cloth hanging from the neck to the floor. Like [every other] society, they have a special song for their dance. When boys below this age want to become men and enter this society, they talk to a [member, calling him] "father," [negotiating to] buy [from him] the position, the song, the war whistle, and the rank, [paying] with horses, blankets, kettles, cloth, and similar precious items. [The boy] then has the right to perform the song and the dance. The one who sold [the position] gives up his right to it, [and] he in turn buys into the next higher class. The dances of the different societies are the same, but the songs are different, [and] once in a while even the foot movement [as well]. Drum and *chichi-kué* are bought along with the other items.

The second society is called Háhderucha-Óchatä, the Crow [or Raven] Society, young men from twenty to twenty-five years [of age]. Often these young men are in no society for half a year. Then they approach [a member] of the Crow Society and say, "Father, I am poor, [but] I wish to buy from you." If he consents, they pay, as described above. They get the feathers that are worn by this society's members on their heads, a double íhkoschka with two goose bones tied together, drum, *chichikué,* song, and dance. Each society has a headman who decides on sales of rights and emblems. A festival is held in the medicine lodge lasting [from] four to forty nights. They dance, eat, [promote] the sale, [and] give the seller their wives every night until he has finally tired and closes the sale by giving up his [society] rights.

The third society, Chárak-Óchatä or Káua-Karakáchka, are the soldiers—the most outstanding warriors. They paint their faces red above and black below for their dance; their war whistle is made from a crane wing bone. Their insignia are two long, straight staffs (called mánna, "the wood") wrapped [in] otter skin with eagle owl feathers hanging from the shafts. When they go to war, they stick these staffs into the ground, face the enemy, and must not retreat. They have a similar staff with raven feathers; if [this is] stuck in the ground, they cannot desert it. [Their] metal *chichikué* [is] like a little kettle with a handle attached. Two pipes, smoked on special occasions, are entrusted to two men, [who] keep and carry them.

Those belonging to higher societies can be members of the Káua-Karakáchka at the same time; [i.e.,] its status can be bought additionally; however, all [soldier] society members have to agree [to] this purchase. If a single man votes [no], nothing comes of it. Individuals often do not give their consent, [in order] to drive up the purchase price and [thus also] the price of a later sale. The Káua-Karakáchka form a type of committee that directs all main activities, especially buffalo hunts (so important to the whole nation). If buffalo herds are close by, they do not allow anyone to scare, shoot at, or scatter them until a general hunt can be organized. The whites (waschí) living in their vicinity are subject to the same laws. They have taken axes away from the fort's woodcutters in the forest or forbidden them to cut wood, so they would not make noise.

The fourth society, Meníss-Óchatä, the Dogs, all wear a large warbonnet when dancing. It has black raven, magpie, and yellowish reddish and dark-striped eagle owl feathers [and is] decorated with colorful horsehair and strips of ermine. They have a big war whistle made from a swan wing bone. Three of the [dancers] wear a red cloth [trailer] hanging down their backs, like the first class, the Meníss-Óchka-Óchatä. If someone throws a piece of meat on the ground or in the ashes of a fire [and says,] "Here dog! Eat!" the men with the red cloth have to fall upon and consume it. The *chichikué* of this band is a stick, 1' or 1½' long, from which many animal hooves are hung.

The fifth society, Beróck-Óchatä, the Bulls, wear the skin of the upper head of a buffalo bull, [including] the long mane and horns, when they dance. Two chosen ones, the bravest among them (who afterward may never flee from an enemy), wear a [full mask]—a perfect facsimile of a buffalo head with its horns—set on their heads. They look out [through] its artificial eyes, [each] surrounded by a [metal] ring; [see pl. 28]. Only this society carries a wooden íhkoschka. There is a woman in this band who [carries] a bowl of water to refresh the bravest men ([the ones] with the bull's head [masks]). She wears beautiful clothing of bighorn leather, and her face is painted red. The dancers carry their weapons in their hands. The two men with the buffalo heads keep to the ends and behave like shy bulls, looking around in all directions and bellowing.

The sixth society, Schúmpsi-Óchatä, the Black-Tail Deer, is made up of old men [who are] above fifty years [of age] but still dance. All wear a wreath of grizzly bear claws around their heads [and symbols of] their heroic deeds on their [persons and their] clothing.

All these societies, as well as the following dances, are bought and sold. On these occasions, the buyer must always offer his wife (or wives if he has several) to the seller. A young man who is poor and has no wife will go to another village and [ask a] friend for his wife. This [friend] goes with him on the evening of the dance [to] offer his wives in place of the [buyer's lack]. Often someone brings three, four, or more wives to the scene and gives them to his "father" (the one from whom he buys); [this happens after] the dancing, dining, and smoking are concluded. Then one woman after another—as told in chapter XVI—strokes the arm of the man she wants to delight [and then] walks toward the entrance of the medicine lodge, where she waits [to see] whether he will follow her. Frequently he remains seated and [just] bows his head. Then the woman goes home, fetches valuable objects (guns, robes, blankets, and such), and places them in front of him, piece by piece, until he gets up and follows [her].

All these societies have other dances and songs that can be bought or sold. For example, a second dance of the Káua-Karakáchka—the dance of the Half-Shorn Heads, called Íschohä-Kakoschóchatä—[can be bought by a member of] a lower [society] before he is of age to buy [into] the Káua-Karakáchka. [This] dance was described in chapter XVI, [on 3 December].

The women are divided, similarly [to the men], into four societies according to age. The youngest is called the Gun Society, Erúhpa-Mih-Óchatä. They wear a few war eagle down feathers on the backs of their heads, paint themselves, and have their [own] dance. The next society into which they can buy is the River Society, Passan-Mih-Óchatä. When they dance they wear an eagle feather tied to their foreheads with a white ribbon [and] pointing toward the left. The third society is the Hay Women, Chan-Míh-Óchatä; when they dance they are dressed in their finest and sing only the Scalp Song. The fourth society is the women of the White Buffalo Cow, Ptihn-Tǎck-Óchatä. These are mostly old women; see the description in chapter XVI, [on 25 December].

The Mandans and Hidatsas have several games. The [hoop and pole game], called skóhpe, is played by two people with long poles [that are] often wrapped with long strips of leather and decorated with other items. They roll a small round hoop, 3″ to 4″ in diameter, on a long, straight, flat course or path. They run after [the hoop] and throw their long poles at it. Winning depends on the [players' previous] agreement on whether the pole should be thrown inside or to the right or left of the hoop or in what [other] place. The women are skillful in a game with a leather ball. They let it fall alternately on foot or knee, hurling it [up] in the air and catching it again in this manner for a long time; [it] may not touch the ground. They repeat this up to a hundred times and often offer prizes. Card games have not reached them yet. In summer the Indians often entertain themselves with races on the prairie near their villages; there are very fast runners among them.

The Mandans and Hidatsas are extremely superstitious. They hold bizarre ideas of nature. They believe in many different beings in the stars and celestial bodies, make sacrifices to them, [and] ask them for assistance—[they] cry, wail, fast, [and] undergo cruel penances, [all] so that these spirits will look favorably upon them. Some of their myths have similarities to revelations in the Bible—for instance, a belief in the great flood, when most of humanity perished and another part was saved in a wooden tower on a hill at the Heart River. To get [correct] information about these traditions we consulted Dipäuch, an Indian very familiar with all these beliefs; [this] respected man could have been chief a long time ago if he had wished. He told us the following in a serious, quiet, and conscientious manner. Mr. Kipp was the best possible interpreter for [our] evening conversations.

These nations believe in several higher beings, among them the Lord of Life, Óhmahank-Numákschi, the mightiest and most sublime, having created earth, man, and everything [else]. They believe him to have a tail [and to appear sometimes as] an old man, [sometimes as] a young man. Óhmahank-Chiká, the Evil of the Earth, is a wicked spirit who also has much power over human beings but not as much as God and First Man. Rokan-ka-Tauïhánka, who lives in Venus, protects human beings on earth; the human race would have perished long ago if not for his care. [Another] being (but with no power) is like the Wandering Jew on earth, always roaming about in human form. They call him Deceitful Prairie Wolf (Schähácká).

In addition to these, there is Ochkíh-Häddä, who [appears] in their legends as a kind of devil. They [fear and] make sacrifices to him.

They worship the sun, because they consider it the home of the Lord of Life. All their medicines or miraculous, magical, and protective rites are addressed exclusively to the sun, meaning to the Lord of Life.

In the moon, they say, lives the Old Woman Who Never Dies, to whom they also address sacrifices and presents. She has great power. She has six children, three sons and three daughters, who all live in certain stars. The eldest son is the Day (Kaschákosch). The second is the Sun, Máhap-Míhnang-gä, where the Lord of Life lives. The third son is the Night, Istúh-Hunsch. The eldest daughter is the morning star that rises in the east; they call her the Woman Who Wears the Plume, Míhhä Uahánkä. The second daughter is Kóhpuska, Striped Pumpkin, a star that circles around the north star. The third daughter, Kóhsedehä, Evening Star, [is] close to the sunset.

First Man, Numánk-Máchana, plays a leading role in the Mandan creation story. He is himself not a godly figure, but the Lord of Life bestowed great power on him, and they therefore revere and make sacrifices to him. [Dipäuch] told the story of the creation and the origin of the Mandan tribe in the following manner. Even though this story is foolish and tedious, the reader will not consider it out of place here, since it gives an idea of the intellectual state and the mythology of these people.

When the earth did not yet exist, the Lord of Life created First Man, [who] went about on the water and met a duck that alternately dove down and [rose] up. First Man said to the bird, "You dive so well, why not dive down and bring up some soil for me?" The bird disappeared and soon brought up some dirt. [First] Man took [this,] scattered it on the water, spoke an incantation, and [the earth] appeared. The new land was bare; not a blade of grass [was growing]. He walked around, believing [himself] to be alone, when he suddenly found a toad. He [exclaimed], "I believed [I was] alone, but you are here? Who are you?" It did not answer. "I do not know you, but I have to give you a name. Since your skin is rough and scaly, you are older than I; I will call you my grandmother." He kept on walking and found a piece of an earthenware pot. "I thought I was alone, but there must have been human beings living here before me." He picked up the shard and said, "I will give a name to you, too. Because you were here before me, I will also have to call you my grandmother." As he kept on going, he found a mouse. "It is obvious that I am not the first being," he thought; "I will call you my grandmother, too." A little farther on, he met the Lord of Life. "Oh, there is a man like me!" He went closer. "How are you, my son?" said Man to Óhmahank-Numákschi, who answered, "I am not your son, but you are mine!" First Man said, "I dispute your words." The Lord of Life replied, "No, you are my son, and I will prove it to you. Let us put our medicine staffs away and sit down. [He] who rises first is the youngest and the son of the other." They sat down and looked at each other a long time. Finally the Lord of Life turned pale, his flesh fell from his bones, and he collapsed. Man said, "You are certainly dead." They looked at each other in this manner for ten years. And when time passed, [not only had] all the flesh [fallen off] the Lord of Life's bones, [they] were in a weathered condition. Man stood up and said, "Well, now he is certainly dead," grabbed the staff of Óhmahank-Numákschi, and pulled it out of the ground. At that very moment the Lord of Life stood up and said, "Look, here I am and you are my son and I am your father!" And Man called him his father [and] they went away together. The Lord of Life said, "The land is not well formed. Let us make it better." The Lord of Life called the mink and told it to crawl into the ground and bring up grass. The mink did this. Then he told it to fetch trees; it soon brought [these] up. [The Lord of Life] divided the grass and the trees and gave half to First Man. This happened at the mouth of the Heart River.

The Lord of Life told Man to go and create the northern bank of the Missouri. He himself [made] the southwestern bank beautifully and appropriately, with hills, small valleys, and trees. Man, however, shaped all the land flat [with] a forest [some] distance away. The Lord of Life said, "Now we will go and see what you have done, Man!" They went, and the [Lord of Life] continued, "You did not do this well; it is all flat—one cannot stalk [and] get close to either buffalo or deer. Human beings will not be able to live here. They will be seen [by enemies] from far away on the plains and will not be able to withdraw, and [the parties will] destroy each other." Then he led Numánk-Máchana to the other riverbank and told him, "See, I put [in] springs and brooks, hills and valleys, and all kinds of animals and trees. Here one can approach [and hunt game] and live off their meat."

[Then] the Lord of Life led First Man to the mouth of the [Heart River] and said, "Let us make medicine pipes here." From the wood of ash trees, he made one [lined] with stone. Man made his from box elder. They set these pipes [together], and the Lord of Life said, "This shall be the heart—the center—of the world, and this river should be called Nátka-Pássahä" (Heart River). Each had his pipe in his hands, and when they came across any creature, the Lord of Life put his pipe down in front of it. They met a buffalo bull and did the same, but [the bull] said that it was no good, since they had nothing to smoke. "Then get something to smoke!" said the Lord of Life. The bull cleared an area with its hooves, urinated on it, and said, "When the time of the buffalo rut approaches, come here and you will find something to smoke." When this [season] approached, the Lord of Life sent someone to the place to get tobacco. But it was not yet dry [or] prepared [for smoking]. He therefore had the buffalo called; it spread the leaves [and] dried them, and the Lord of Life smoked [them] and found the tobacco good.

The Lord of Life and First Man [now] wished to create human beings. They started [this] near the bank of the Missouri. Human beings had to be able to multiply, too. [And they asked themselves,] "But where is the part needed for this supposed to be?" and they put the genitals on his forehead. A frog came out of the water and said, "A fine job you are doing! That part should be here!" He showed them the right place. "What right do you have to meddle?" said the Lord of Life, [and he] took his staff and hit the frog on its back. Since that time the frog has [had] a humped back. God told [man] to multiply but to live no longer than a hundred years, because otherwise there would not be [enough] space for everyone.

Once, a dead buffalo cow floated down the Missouri; wolves had eaten a hole into her side. A woman downriver saw it and said to her daughter, "Hurry, undress and bring that cow [here]!" First Man heard [this] and brought the cow. The girl ate the fat that Man gave her, and she became pregnant. She was ashamed and told her mother that she did not know how she got into this condition, since she had no contact with any man, and the mother, too, was ashamed. The daughter brought a boy into the world who grew rapidly [into] a young man [and] the greatest chief, or leader (numákschi), among humans. His first accomplishment was to build a canoe that understood what he said to it. He filled [the canoe] with people and told it to ferry them across and [then] come back. He sent it across in this manner several times. This chief was of the Númangkake (Mandan) nation.

People said that white men who owned large wampum shells lived at the edge of the great water (the ocean). Several times they had sent groups of fifteen to twenty men there, but they were all killed. The chief said, "I will send my canoe with eight men." The canoe arrived at the proper place and brought beaver to the white men, which they wanted very much. [The Indians] were well received in the [whites'] homes and [were] given food and tobacco. Each was [also] given buffalo skins full of wampum shells, and the canoe returned quickly. [When] the boat left for the second time, First Man went along. He was dressed very poorly and [carried] a large, hollow tube. [When] they arrived, [most men] went into the village, but First Man remained sitting near the boat, [where he had] excavated a deep hole over which he now sat. The inhabitants agreed [among themselves] to feed the strangers to death. First Man let the [excess pass] through his tube into the hole. The inhabitants were astonished [at the quantities consumed]. They [next tried] to kill [the Indians] with smoking. But First Man let the smoke pass through his tube, [so] their intentions were thwarted. Then they [attempted] to kill them with women and [sent] them [woman after] woman, without interruption. But First Man had a cow's tail and used that instead of his [own] natural part. The village inhabitants were very surprised at First Man's great lasting strength. They could not kill the strangers with food, smoking, or women. Therefore they gave [the Indians] as many shells as they could take and sent them back. [Later on], children [who] had heard that [this] canoe understood what it was told commanded it to sail down the river to the white people (waschí). [The canoe] obeyed and has never been seen since.

First Man told the Númangkake that he was going away [to the] west and [would] never return; however, when in peril, they could turn to him [for] support. [So when] their small village was surrounded [by enemies], they decided to appeal to their protector; but how [could they] reach First Man? One man suggested sending a bird, but it could not fly that far. Finally, someone observed that the mind would surely [be of] most help. He wrapped himself in his robe, fell down, [and] said, "I am thinking! I have thought! I am coming back!" He threw off the robe and was sweating all over. "First Man will come immediately." And soon he was there. He stormed against the enemies and they disappeared. [But] after that [the Mandans] never saw him again.

The Lord of Life [once] told First Man that "[any] Númangkake who crossed the river would be torn to shreds by wolves." [So] they killed all the old wolves [and] ordered the young [ones] not to eat any more humans but to limit themselves to buffalo, deer, and other game. They took the old wolves and threw them into the northern ocean, where they rotted; their hair floated on the water, and the white people originated from that.

When First Man infuriated the white men with his buffalo tail and his insatiability, they [made] the water rise so high that all the land was inundated. First Man told the ancestors of the Mandans [that] they should build a wooden tower on a hilltop, and the water would rise only to that point. They built this on the lower side of the Heart River, and part of the nation was [thus] saved. In each of their villages, they erected a small model in memory of that structure [or ark], and a festival [called] Okíppe is celebrated in [its] veneration; [see below].

Before the great flood, the Númangkake lived below ground,[M2] [although] a band of them came up earlier. They believe that there are four levels below the earth and four more above it. They live now on the fourth from below. The band that came up first, Históppä, The Ones with Tattooed Faces, mostly perished in the great flood. One day those who were living belowground saw light above them and sent up a mouse, [which] looked

---

[M2] Lewis and Clark ([*Travels,*] vol. 1, p. 138) gave the first (somewhat incomplete) account of the following legend. Catlin repeated it in his letters printed in the newspaper. I relate it here completely according to the narrative of the elders and other respected Mandans. [Catlin's 1832 letter, published in the *New York Commercial Advertiser* on 20 February 1833, contained a description of a Mandan origin myth.]

around, came back, and reported [that] it appeared just the same as down below. Then they sent up a white animal, the size of a mink, with black legs and facial stripes; this one told them that it seemed to be better above than below. The badger was [ordered to enlarge] the small opening, [and] they sent up a black-tailed deer; it ran around all day [and] ate serviceberries. Its tail was still white in those times. [When the deer] descended, at the moment when only its tail was aboveground, the sun went down—whereupon [its] tail turned black and has remained that way since then.

The [people] decided to go up. A chief went first. They climbed up on a grapevine, one after the other. When just half of them were up, and there was a corpulent woman at the middle of the grapevine, it broke. The rest of the Númangkake fell back [down]. [Those who had emerged went on] until they reached the Missouri, [which they followed upriver].

The chief divided his people into societies. First he created the society of Meníss-Óchatä (Dogs). He made four caps from crow feathers and instructed them to make more. He gave them íhkoschka and songs [and said] they should always be brave and in good spirits [and] never retreat from [arrows]. He also gave them strips of red cloth to hang down their backs. He said that if they followed his instructions, they would always be respected as brave and upright men. The chief then shaped two bent lances (mánna), wrapped [them] with otter skin, [and] gave them to the Káua-Karakáchka [along with] two additional [lances] with crow feathers. The former represent the sunflower, the latter the maize plant. He said, "Carry these symbols ahead of you when you move against the enemy. Stick them into the ground and fight to the last man—meaning never abandon them." [Next] he established the society Óchka-Óchatä (Small Dogs Whose Name Is Not Known). He called many young people together, instructed them to paint their faces black, gave them their own song with a war whoop at the end, and said he would call them Táchika-Óchatä (blackbirds).

The Númangkake moved up the Missouri until they reached [an area] opposite the Heart River (where a Mandan village was located for a long time.) An old Indian had begun to fish there when four men appeared across the river. He asked who they were. They answered that they were Hidatsas and asked his name, which he told them. He had an ear of corn with him, which he put on an arrow and shot across. [The Hidatsas] tried it and found it tasty. They shouted to him that in four nights there would be many people coming, so [the Númangkake] should prepare much food.

[The Hidatsas] returned to their camp and informed [the others] about the corn. They [had] tried many other things, but they found the corn to be the best. They broke camp and leisurely moved ahead. The Númangkake, [who] expected [the strangers] in four nights, cooked and prepared everything to receive them, but they did not come after the fourth night. Therefore [the Mandans] themselves ate all the cooked food. A year went by and the Hidatsas did not come, a second and third one, too. Finally, in the spring of the fourth year, all the hills turned black with people; the four days had been four years. All [these people] crossed the river and built a village near the Númangkake. The chiefs of the two nations came together and talked. The Hidatsa chief asked the other from whence they had [obtained] so much red corn. He answered, "When our enemies killed our women and children in the corn fields, it grew up mostly red." The Hidatsa chief [said] they wanted to assist [the Mandans] against their enemies. The next day many Cheyennes came and the combined nations attacked [them], killed many, and drove [the others away].

The Hidatsas remained united with the Mandans, [but] they were too numerous together—[they] did not have enough to sustain themselves. Therefore the Mandans said to [the Hidatsas], "Move up the Missouri. [But] do not cross the [Knife River]. If you go too far, there will be fights, [we will] make peace, and fight again. If you stay on this side [of the Knife], we will remain good friends." The Hidatsas moved there. However, they built one of their villages across the Knife River, and [so] they fought, made peace, and fought again. [Now,] for fourteen years, there has been uninterrupted peace and alliance between the two nations. At the time of the narrator's youth, the Arikaras lived close by and were fierce enemies of the Mandans. They fought them frequently, [and] also the Dacotas. If one of the allied nations fought alone, it came off second best; if they were united, they almost always won.

After the period of their first alliance with the Hidatsas, the Mandans are said to have inhabited eight to nine villages. [These] were located on both sides of the Missouri near the Heart River and farther up. Smallpox killed a great many people, and the Dacotas destroyed [the largest village] completely. Afterward, the [remaining] villages united in the two that still exist.

Now we will turn to current religious behavior. These Indians are possessed by prejudice and superstition to such a degree that they see spirits and miracles in all natural phenomena. They undertake nothing without first calling on their protective spirit, or medicine, revealed to them mostly in dreams. When they desire such a protective spirit—medicine, in their language chóppenih—they fast for three or more days, [retreat] to secluded places, do penance, sacrifice joints of their fingers, [and] shout and cry to the Lord of Life or First Man to reveal to them [a spirit or medicine]. In a feverish condition, they dream, and the first animal, or often the first object, that appears to them in their dream becomes their protective spirit. The strange man, or spirit, who appeared in their villages many years ago but never returned is supposed to have taught them this medicine worship. He was mentioned [earlier] under the name Ochkíh-Häddä.

In all uncommon natural phenomena, they look for miracles and intimations of coming bad or auspicious events. If shooting stars move frequently to the west, they predict war or the death of many people. They do not like to be sketched, because they believe they then must soon die. Kipp's Mandan wife exemplifies this. Mr. Catlin, a painter from New York, portrayed her in oil. [He] had just left when she got a serious nosebleed. She was not satisfied until her husband saddled his horse, rode after the boat, luckily caught up with it, and for 20 dollars bought back the picture. The same Catlin painted the profile of a Dacota [who], in a fight with another Indian, was shot in the part of his face that [Catlin], coincidentally, had just painted. Everybody blamed the painter, [and since] no one else [would] sit for a painting, [he] left.

When [Indians] go on important ventures, they carry [their medicines] with them, well wrapped or in special pouches. Each individual has his own beliefs, which the English and French term medicine.

They have special medicine pipes, or medicine stems, as the Americans call them, that are [shown] and smoked only on solemn occasions. The nation preserves a famous pipe of this kind as a sacred object that [they have] owned since primeval times, and no stranger sees it. I wished to make a drawing of it, but they demanded 100 dollars to show it to me. They preserve and consecrate such pipes at immense cost. Some of the necessary ornaments are not available here, for instance, the upper jaw and red cranium of the woodpecker *Picus pileatus,* a bird that does not occur [this] far up the Missouri. For each [pileated] head brought from St. Louis, they pay with a beautiful, large buffalo robe valued from six to eight dollars.

In the eyes of the Mandans and Hidatsas, the skin of a white buffalo cow is an important object and a great medicine. Anyone who has never owned one is not respected and worthy of pity. [If a man] has counted many coups but has never owned a white buffalo cow skin, an inexperienced young lad can say, "You have not even owned such a skin," [and the coup-counter will] hide his face in shame. If [a man] is not lucky enough to shoot a white buffalo cow himself, which is [usually] the case, [a skin can be] bought, often from far away. Other nations bring [these skins], because they [know their] value here. [Skins] must be from young cows no more than two years old. They pay from 10 to 15 horses for [one]. The Mandans do not wear such a skin as a robe, like the Hidatsas do. At most, a daughter or a wife wears it [once, and only] at an important festival.

The Númangkake have ceremonies for the dedication of [a] white skin. [As soon as] someone has obtained [one], he drapes it around [the shoulders] of a distinguished medicine man, who walks around the village in the direction of the sun and sings a medicine song. [The owner] often sacrifices the skin to the Lord of Life or First Man. [To do this,] he collects valuable objects for three or four years, [which are] rolled [into the skin with] sage *(Artemisia),* a medicine herb. Ears of corn are often also put inside. The bundle is hung on a high pole until it decomposes. At Mih-Tut-ta-Hangkusch, there was one in front of the village, next to the scaffolds of the dead, [and] Dipäuch had one on a tall pole in front of his lodge. When the dedication ceremony is complete, they often cut the skin into narrow strips, and family members wear them as narrow bands across the head or forehead when they are in full dress. Traders sell the Mandans [these] hides once in a while and [charge] up to sixty robes for them.

The Mandans have various medicine festivals. One of the most remarkable is Okíppe, the festival of penance or of the ark. It is celebrated in spring or summer, and unfortunately I cannot describe it as an eyewitness. A painter, Catlin, saw it himself and described it in the newspaper, but incompletely, because he did not understand it.[1] [So] I want to give an in-depth [account here that I] received from men initiated into the secrets of the nation.

First Man ordered the Mandans to celebrate this medicine festival each year. Once the village has [agreed on a time for the ceremony], they choose a respected, trustworthy man (in 1834, it was Mató-Tópe) to be in charge [of] the medicine. He is called Kauíh-Sächka. At the appointed time, he has the medicine lodge prepared [and] cleaned and [sees to] other necessary requirements.

[On the evening before the first day, the Kauíh-Sächka] enters the lodge at sunset [and] begins a fast that lasts four days. With him are six men who beat the so-called turtle, a vessel or parchment sack filled with water [that] is played like a big drum throughout the night. A man representing First Man comes before sunrise. He gets dressed in the medicine lodge: he fastens a wolfskin around his body [and] raven feathers around his head; he carries a medicine pipe in his arms [and some] pemmican in his robe; his face is painted red; [and] on his back [there is] a piece of wood to which a buffalo cow tail is attached.[M3] Early on the first morning of the festival this man goes into the villages and sings on the plazas. He is thrown various objects of value: guns, robes, woolen blankets, etc. He gives the people pemmican. [Then] he returns to the medicine lodge; he never speaks a word. Respected men come into the lodge, call [him] their uncle, and ask him, "How did you fare in the villages?" And he answers, "Very good, my nephew; I did not place my pipe on the ground even once," meaning he was well received and people showered him with [presents]. He says furthermore, "I saw many buffalo grazing on the prairie and drinking at the river!" These were horses, but he [is suggesting] that the medicine will attract buffalo in numbers.

All [those] who intend to subject their bodies to penance (to make themselves worthy of the Lord of Life and First Man) come to the medicine lodge [that first] morning. Their number is [sometimes] larger, [sometimes] smaller. [They] are naked [and] painted all over with white clay. [They] wear their robes with the hair to the outside and are completely wrapped up in them. In the lodge they take off the robes. On [this] day, they [go] out four times, wrapped in the manner described, and dance around the Mah-Mönnih-Túchä (the ark) in the plaza. The Kauíh-Sächka is at that time near the ark, wailing. All this happens [in the morning]. In the afternoon, everything is quiet, and [there is] no dance.

Second day: Early on the second day eight men appear, Berocki-Häddisch, representing buffalo bulls. They are naked [except for] aprons of blue-and-white-striped woolen cloth around their hips. Their bodies are painted black [with red and white markings]. They carry a [fan] of green branches in their hands. [On] their backs [they wear] a buffalo robe; the

---

[M3] The buffalo tail refers to the story told earlier about First Man, when he acted so gallantly with a cow's tail.

head [skin] with its long hair hangs down over their faces. These eight buffalo [dancers] walk in four pairs, stooped over, one after another, stretching
their robes [out] at both sides with their hands. At the same time, they hold
the fans of leaves upright [as] they dance right up to the ark. [They] divide
there—four going right, four to the left—[and go] around the plaza. They
unite again opposite the medicine lodge and then return to the ark, where
they continue to dance. They frequently imitate the voice of the buffalo.

When the dance starts, the six turtle drummers carry their instrument
out of the medicine lodge close to the ark and place it facing in an easterly direction. They beat it and sing a song [with] words like a prayer. The
Kauíh-Sächka stands precisely opposite the turtle; [he] leans on the ark,
his face turned down, and laments. He is completely naked except for an
apron of *cabri* skin. His whole body is painted yellow. Around his head
he wears a wreath of buffalo hair, bleached by rain and weather. The eight
[Berocki-Häddisch] dance around him [and then] proceed to the door
of the medicine lodge [and] form a kind of covered passage [with their
robes] through which the turtle is carried [inside]. This whole ceremony
is repeated eight times on this day—four times before and four times after
noon.

Third day: The same masks [as] yesterday dance twelve times this day.
They do not eat or drink, and many figures or masks are added:

1. Two men disguised as women join the dance [and] keep by the side
   of the eight buffalo. They wear bighorn leather dresses, women's
   [leggings], [and] robes with the hair to the outside. [Their] cheeks are
   painted red, [their] chins tattooed, [and their] heads adorned with
   glass beads [in] women's fashion.

2. Two other men represent a pair of swans. They are naked, carry a
   swan's tail in their hands, [and] are painted white all over, except [for]
   their noses, mouths (beaks), and the lower parts of their legs and feet,
   [which] are black.

3. Another pair of men represent two rattlesnakes. Their backs are
   horizontally striped black, their bellies yellowish, [and] a black stripe
   runs down from each eye across their cheeks. In each hand they carry a
   bundle of sage.

4. [One] man plays Ochkíh-Häddä (the devil). Two men from the village
   lead him, unobserved, to the river, where [they] paint and dress him.
   His whole body is painted black, [after which] he does not speak a

word. They put a cap with a black cockscomb on his head, [and he wears] a mask with white wooden rings around the eyeholes. They make big teeth for him from cottonwood fibers [and] paint a sun on his stomach, [a] half-moon on his back, and a white circle on each joint of his arms and legs. A colossal wooden penis, several feet long, is attached to him, [and] a buffalo tail to his back. A small stick with a ball of skin at the end is placed in his hands; a scalp, painted red underneath and supposedly representing the head of an enemy, is attached to [the ball]. When this monster is ready, they release him. He runs madly around the prairie, comes into the village, [and] climbs on [one] lodge [after] another, while the inhabitants throw him gifts. As soon as he notices this, he turns to the sun and explains through signs how well he has been treated and [that it seems] foolish for the sun to remain so distant. The Indians are very afraid of Ochkíh-Häddä, because they believe that anyone who sees him often or is touched by him must die. For this reason his role is not assigned to anyone; [the performer] must volunteer for it.

5. Two men represent bald eagles. They are painted blackish brown, [with] white on the head, neck, forearms, hands, and lower parts of their legs.

6. Two beavers wear robes with the hairy side outwards; a parchment beavertail is attached to the back of their belts; they are painted blackish brown.

7. Two birds of prey (shoulders painted blue, bellies yellowish and spotted) wear feathers on their heads [and carry] feet (with talons) in their hands.

8. Two or four bears, [each] wrapped in a bearskin (with head and claws), walk, mostly hunched over, around the dancers.

9. Two men represent the dried meat that is cut in narrow strips. They wear caps of white rabbit skin on their heads, [and] their bodies are painted with zigzag stripes. They have a belt of green branches around their bodies.

10. Perhaps forty or fifty Indians of different ages represent antelope. Their backs are painted reddish, their fronts white, noses and mouths black.

11. Two men represent the night. They are painted completely black [and] marked all over with white stars. On their backs each wears the setting moon, on their stomachs the rising sun. They dance twelve times with the other dancers, and when they return to the medicine lodge,

they are not allowed to sit down until the sun has set [and] then must remain seated until the next morning.

12. One or two wolves, painted white and wearing wolf skins, run after the antelope, which flee from them; if they catch one, the bears take it and eat it.

13. Two prairie wolves (painted white on the tops of their heads; faces yellowish red) wear dried herbs in their hair [and] carry a stick [with] reddish brown stripes. Originally only ten of these masks were [part of Okíppe]. In recent years [others] were added; these did not belong to the ancient observance of the festival.

During all these dances, the penitents remain in the medicine lodge, fasting, thirsting, [and] sitting quietly. The masks also assemble [there] in the afternoon. Then the [masks and] penitents walk together out of the lodge. The latter lie down on the ground on their bellies a little away from [and] forming a circle around the ark. The masks dance—to the beat of the turtle—around, between, and over [them]. Some of the penitents begin their torture now. They give a distinguished man or warrior a gift, so that he will inflict torments upon them.

Some have strips of their skin and flesh cut loose from their chests, arms, or backs in such a manner that [the strips] remain attached [to their bodies] at both ends. A strap is pulled through [the resulting openings], and [the penitents] are then thrown down [a] steep slope, where they hang suspended in the air. [Some] have a strap pulled through and [attached to] a buffalo skull that they drag behind them. Still others have themselves hung up from the flesh of their backs [or] from the skin above their stomachs, or cut off finger joints. Those tortured this day return to their lodges. However, [a few, those] who fast the longest, undergo their trials the next day.

Fourth day of the Okíppe: The penitents who could endure the four-day-long fast are assembled in the medicine lodge. The masquerades and dances of the previous day are [performed] sixteen times (eight times before noon and eight after noon), but they stop early. The torture candidates are cut at about two o'clock. After they have endured their torments, a large circle is formed. Two strong men who are not [part of] the festival take one penitent between them by his hands, the Kauíh-Sächka, too, and they move around in a circle at high speed. The exhausted, starving, tortured penitents fall down; [some] individuals faint. [When] released, [they] lie like the dead, stretched out on the ground.

Then the eight Berocki-Häddisch appear to perform the last dance, [while] First Man stands on one side of the plaza and invites the inhabitants to gather and go buffalo hunting. The men approach with bows and arrows, on horseback or on foot. The arrows have green leaves on the wooden points. The [Berocki-Häddisch] dance toward Numánk-Máchana, [who] pushes them back. [They] are shot at from all sides; they fall, roll on the ground, die, and lay there motionless. First Man then invites the inhabitants to take the meat from the buffalo. The [men's] robes have fallen off. They get up and walk into the medicine lodge, [where they exclaim] that they feel strong now. Some [vow] to kill their enemies, others [say] they will kill many buffalo, etc. The people leave [to] eat and rest; the festival is over.

Thick scars are evident on the backs, chests, and arms of most [penitents], especially among the Hidatsas. The [scars result] from the cuttings, piercings, [and trials described above]. The skulls that these Indians drag in pain, they keep afterward on the [roofs?] of their lodges; they can be seen everywhere. Some are medicines; these they bring into their lodges, stroke their noses, and serve them food. In general, the buffalo is a medicine animal—more or less sacred to them.

[Another] medicine festival is [like] the Corn Dance of the Hidatsas, described quite precisely and correctly by Say (see Major Long's *Expedition to the Rocky Mountains,* vol. 2, p. 58). There is actually neither dance nor dancing; it is a consecration of the crops to be planted. The Old Woman Who Never Dies, [who] causes crops to grow, sends the waterfowl in spring—the swans, wild geese, and ducks—as symbols of the field crops raised by the Mandans: the wild goose symbolizes the corn; the swan, the squash; and the duck, the beans. The Indians keep much dry meat ready to celebrate the women's spring Corn Medicine festival as soon as the birds arrive. This meat is hung on scaffolds [built] in front of the village, in [several] rows. Elderly women, as representatives of the Old Woman Who Never Dies, gather on a certain day near the scaffolds; [each] carries a stick on which an ear of corn is skewered. They sit in a circle [and] place their sticks upright in front of them. Then [they] dance in a circle around the scaffolds, taking their corn sticks in their arms. Old men beat the drum and rattle the *chichikué* in accompaniment. While the older women perform their medicine, younger ones come and put dry, pounded meat into the mouths of the former; in return, each [receives] a kernel of the medicine corn, placed in her mouth, which she swallows. They also [get] three to four kernels in their bowls, and these consecrated medicine kernels are mixed carefully with the seed corn, which [thereby] becomes fertile and brings success to the whole crop.

In the fall, the Corn Medicine is repeated, but this time to attract the buffalo herds and get meat. Each woman carries in her arms not a stick with an ear of corn but a whole corn plant torn out [of the ground]. They refer to the corn, as well as the birds that are the symbols of the field crops, by the name of the Old Woman Who Never Dies. [They] call out to her, "Mother, have pity on us. Do not send us severe cold too early! Do not let all the game move away, so that we have something for winter."

[The Mandans] believe in a gigantic medicine snake, which lives in a lake a few days' travel from here; sacrifices are made to it. They tell the story of this monster as follows: Two young men went downriver, noticed an opening in a rock, entered out of curiosity, [and] were surprised [to find] a beautiful land altogether unknown to them. Many buffalo herds grazed there. [They met giants and hunted buffalo and eagles with them; they then left] the giants, taking [many] precious feathers with them.

On their way back, they found the opening in the rock blocked by a colossal snake. At first they did not see a way to get by, but soon they piled up a large quantity of wood and burned the snake. One of the men [tasted] the roasted [snake] flesh, found it good, and ate some. [As] they continued walking, the head of the man who had eaten the meat began to swell and his face itched terribly. He begged his friend to lead him home. "Why did you eat the meat?" [his friend] asked, and led him to his lodge. On the second day, [the man who had eaten the meat] swelled up more and more. [He] became long, itched all over, and soon turned completely [into a] snake. He asked his comrade to carry him into the Missouri, and [the friend] labored for three days to get [him] there. As soon as [the snake] reached the water, it dove under [but] soon surfaced again and said, "There are many of my kind below, but they hate me. Carry me to the lake Mönníh-Háschka (Long Water)," three days' journey from the Missouri. And it happened. When [the snake] did not like it there either, [the friend] had to carry it to a second lake, Históppä-Numángkä (Place of the Tattooed Face), where [the snake] decided to stay. It asked the young man to bring it four objects: 1. a white wolf; 2. a skunk; 3. pounded corn; and 4. war eagle tails. He should then go to war four times and kill an enemy each time: that happened, too. The snake added [that] he would always be here, [as a] medicine, [and] if the Mandans desired something, they should come here, do penance, and entreat. They still do this [today,] attaching eagle tails, ravens, or similar [offerings] to poles on the lakeshore.

Another curiosity of this kind is the Medicine Rock, which [is described in the entry for 19 November, chapter 16]. They have many [other] kinds of medicine devices closer to their villages, all sacrifices to their gods. One, for instance, consists of four poles set up in a square. Between the two front poles, four buffalo skulls are set up in a row, and between the two poles in the back, 26 human skulls, some painted with red stripes. Behind this arrangement a few knives are stuck in the ground. On top of the poles rest bundles of brushwood and some kind of comb or rake of sharpened pieces of wood, painted red. [See pl. 24.] The Indians go to such places to make offerings or [pleas]; [they] cry and beg the Lord of Life, often [for] several days in a row. Dreams, as mentioned before, are usually the motivating force for such actions and penances. They consider what appears to them in dreams to be true. [For instance,] they did not yet have guns when one Indian dreamed of a weapon that could kill enemies from a long distance. Soon after, the white men brought them the first gun. They also dreamed of horses before they first obtained them.

Various superstitious ideas and prejudices prevail among the Mandans. They believe [that] whenever one [man] is negatively disposed toward another, he needs only to shape a figure from wood or clay and stick a needle [or] awl or porcupine quill in it. If this figure, which is supposed to be a likeness of the [adversary], is buried at the foot of a medicine device, then the man must die. Many, almost all, Mandans and Hidatsas believe that they have animals in their bodies. One of them [has] a buffalo calf; he claims to feel its kicking often. Others have a turtle, frogs, lizards, a bird, or the like. Owls are medicine birds for these people. They allege, for example, that they are able to talk to and understand them and therefore often keep them alive in their lodges as fortunetellers. They catch [other] birds of prey, also frequently [seen as] medicine.

The division of the year into moons agrees fairly closely with our months. They count the years by winters and say [that] so many winters have passed since [an] event; they count off the winters by numbers or with their fingers and hands. If we start with the beginning of the year, the first moon is

1. The one of seven cold days—Aschini-tächtä-mínang-gä. It corresponds to January.

2. Moon of the wolf rut—Chárätä-dúh-häminähki-mínang-gä. February.

3. Moon of the sick eyes—Ístippa-mínang-gä. March.

4. Moon of game; some call it [moon] of wild geese, ducks, etc.—Pattohä-ku-mínang-gä. April. This moon is also often called the one when the ice breaks up—Chódä-uáppi-mínang-gä.

5. Moon of seeding (corn) or moon of flowers—Wakíh-häddä-mínang-gä. May.

6. Moon of ripe *poires*—Mánna-puschákä-rátack-mínang-gä. June.

7. Moon of ripe cherries *(Prunus padus)*—Katáckä-rátack-mínang-gä. July.

8. Moon of ripe plums—Wáhkta-rátack-mínang-gä. August.

9. Moon of ripe corn—Makíruchah-mínang-gä. September.

10. Moon of falling leaves—Mánna-apä-haráh-mínang-gä. October.

11. Moon of freezing rivers—Chódä-áhke-mínang-gä. November.

12. Moon of little frost—Ischinin-takschúkä-mínang-gä. December.

[There are other names,] but these are the usual ones and [form] a natural and appropriate division.

The chief occupations of men are hunting and war (besides dressing, painting themselves, looking in the mirror, doing nothing, smoking, eating, and sleeping). The main game animal is the buffalo, or actually the buffalo cow. The men usually move out on horseback in numbers for this hunt, because they are safer from their enemies than if they go individually. In summer the buffalo herds are distant and dispersed on the prairie, but in winter the snowstorms sometimes drive them closer to the Missouri forest. Then they are killed in great numbers. [The Indians] stay for eight to ten days on such hunting trips; they [return] mostly on foot, because their horses are packed with meat. They usually shoot the buffalo with arrows at very close range, [the hunters] often riding [only] 6 to 8 paces away. If it is very cold and the buffalo remain distant on the prairie, as [happened] in the winter of 1833–1834, there is little hunting; they would rather starve or live on corn and beans than [suffer] frozen limbs.

The Mandans and Hidatsas do not use dogs for hunting. They shoot deer, antelope, and bighorn in the forest, on the prairies, and [in] the Black Hills or neighboring mountain ranges. For the antelope they establish parks but not for the buffalo; the Assiniboines are expert [at the latter]. The Hidatsas establish [such] parks more frequently than the Mandans. For that purpose a shallow valley (coulee) is located, [one] situated between hills with a steep drop-off at the end. On the tops of the hills, two converging lines approximately one mile long are marked out with branches. Below the drop-off, a fence is constructed with poles and brushwood, approximately 15 to 20 paces long. [The area is] covered over and filled with poles, brushwood, and hay. Riders drive the antelope between the ends of the two marked lines, [which are] distanced far apart. They ride quickly toward them, chasing them down through the valley between the marked lines. At the end, the animals plunge to the bottom of the hay-filled drop-off, where they are killed with [clubs] or captured alive.

There are not many bears in this area. They are not favored [as game by the Indians], because hunting [them] is often dangerous. Wolves and foxes are sometimes taken with a gun, as are rabbits. The first two are [also] caught in deadfalls. They now [get] beaver, in large numbers, with iron traps borrowed or bought from the white men; pelts and meat are equally important to them. They catch small animals like weasels with horsehair snares [set] in front of their lairs.

The hunting of birds of prey is said to be remarkable. The bird-catcher lies down lengthwise, completely hidden in a narrow dugout ditch that is covered with brushwood and hay. On its surface, pieces of meat are laid out, and a crow or similar bird is tied to it. The eagle or [other] predatory bird swoops down to get the meat. [When it lands] to eat, it is caught by its legs. I would not believe this if dependable men had not given their word on it. [In] this manner they catch the eagle with white and black tail feathers (called war eagle by the Americans). [The golden eagle, which I did not see,] is reputed to be common in the Rocky Mountains and the neighboring prairies and hill chains.

War is, to be sure, the Indians' main occupation. Seeking glory from achievements in war is their highest ambition. It is known that Indian bravery is very different from that of white men. In their eyes, to directly expose themselves to enemy weapons would be foolish. They seek [instead] to gain advantage over their enemies by trickery, slyness, spying, concealing their movements, and surprise attacks. [The man] who has killed many enemies without suffering harm himself is the best warrior. Counting coup is the most important matter of their lives. When a young man wishes to make a name for himself and count coup, he fasts [for] four to seven days, as [long] as his strength permits. He goes into the hills alone and cries to the Lord of Life [and] the gods for assistance; he eats nothing. Sometimes, in the evening, he goes home to sleep. A dream [suggests] his medicine. If the Lord of Life lets him dream of a piece of cherrywood or an animal, these are good omens, [and] if he counts coup, his name is established. [But] no matter how many coups he counts, if he does not make valuable gifts, he will not gain high respect. They [will] say of him that, [despite his] coups, he should be pitied as much as those he killed.

If a young man who has not yet counted coup is the first in a war party to kill an enemy, he paints a spiral line around his arm [in a] color of his choosing. He may [also] wear a full wolf's tail at one ankle or heel. If he kills or [is the] first to touch an enemy, then he [can] paint a slanted line around his arm and another [line] crossing the first in the opposite direction, with three diagonal stripes. After killing his second enemy, he [can] paint his left leg (meaning his [legging]) a reddish brown. If he kills a second enemy before another is killed by his comrades, he is entitled to wear two complete wolf tails. At the third coup, he paints two stripes lengthwise on his arm and three paired cross-stripes. This is the most valuable coup—after the third, no further marks are made.

In every large war party there are always four partisans (karókkanakah), sometimes up to seven. All partisans carry a medicine pipe (in a case on their backs); other warriors are not permitted to have [these]. To become a chief, [warriors] must have been a partisan and have killed an enemy during a raid when not a partisan. If one follows another partisan for a second time, discovers the enemy first and kills one of them, [and] then, in addition, acquires the skin of a female white buffalo with its horns in perfect condition—then one becomes a chief. The source of this information, Dipäuch, has done all this and is a man respected by his people. However, he has never used the title of chief.

If a young man wants to become a partisan, he [first] attempts to earn the affection and trust of the young men through presents and other demonstrations of friendship. [Then] he consecrates a medicine pipe, a very simple, undecorated pipe stem. He spends four days and four nights at an isolated place—for instance, in the prairie hills—where he dedicates his pipe [and beseeches] support [from] the Lord of Life, the sun, First Man (Numánk-Máchana), and all celestial relatives; [he] neither eats or drinks. [Afterwards,] if sufficient participants are found, and a raid is decided upon, [the men] dance, eat, and amuse themselves for several nights in the village medicine lodge, from which they also make their departure, usually during the night. Women are never present at such dances. When [the men] leave, they are [plainly] clothed [and] not painted. They do not leave the village together but [either] singly or a very few at a time. When they are a short distance away from the village, they stop on a solitary hill, sit down in a circle, [and] open the medicine pouches and small bundles. The partisan unwraps his medicine pipe, and they smoke from it. He spreads his medicine objects on the ground or hangs them up, and from them foretells the future. All this takes place ceremonially.

When warriors return from a raid and have counted coup, they often paint their faces and even their bodies black. They carry the scalps on tall poles. The women and children come to meet them, and they enter the village performing the Scalp Dance. This dance is performed for four consecutive nights in the medicine lodge. Later they also dance it in the village center on the open plaza. If the raid took place in spring or summer, and no tribal member was killed, they perform the dance until [autumn]. If [the raid] was in the fall, they dance until spring. In the meantime, if one of them is killed, all festivities immediately cease. At the Scalp Dance, [the participants] paint themselves in various colors, form a semicircle, and dance [by moving] forward and backward with singing, drum, and *chichi-kué*. The wives of the men who took the scalps carry them on long poles.

Every outstanding [deed by] a war party brings honor to the partisan. All scalps belong to him, as do all captured horses. [Any] man who kills an enemy is brave and counts a coup, but the partisan rises the highest, even if he saw none of the slain enemies. When he comes home, the old men and the women assemble and sing the scalp song for him; they receive valuable presents from him in return. He gives away all the captured horses and valuable articles. Afterward he is a poor man, but his name is great. Successful partisans [can] become chiefs and are honored by their nation. Young Indians participate in war as early as age fourteen to fifteen.

Occasionally the Mandans and Hidatsas go as far as the Rocky Mountains against the Blackfoot. Their other enemies are [the] Saones (Dacotas), the Arikaras, the Assiniboines, [and] the Cheyennes. They are at peace with the Crows.

The weapons [of the] Mandans and Hidatsas are, first, [well-made bows and arrows with metal points] (when Charbonneau arrived on the Missouri, he found individual arrowheads still being made from flint). Almost all Mandans and Hidatsas [also] have guns, [ramrods, and shot bags], often nicely decorated. Their war clubs and battle-axes are of various kinds. Some have a thick, egg-shaped stone attached to a stick with leather straps. [Others] have small iron axes but not the tomahawks with pipes attached. We were told that the Mandans use lances in battle. All carry a knife on their belts in the back; this is indispensable to them in hunting or war. Some make the knife handle from the jawbone of a bear, retaining the large [canines]. The bow is still esteemed nowadays by all nations living along the Missouri, [who] are very good archers. The Mandans and Hidatsas are said to [fight well], and [instances] of individual bravery and determination are not rare. One of their most outstanding warriors is Mató-Tópe (Four Bears), of whom [some characteristics] are mentioned elsewhere. He killed more than five chiefs of foreign nations. Mató-Tópe's father, whose name was Suck-Schih (Pretty Child), played a trick very similar to that of the Hidatsa chief Kokoáhkis, about whom Say writes (see Long's *Expedition*, vol. 2, p. 30) In the evening, while wrapped in his robe, he went into the lodge of an Arikara enemy, the way young people from the villages are often in the habit of doing, and with his face covered, laid down with a woman. When his business was finished with her, he cut off a tuft of her hair and left. He could have killed the woman, as [Kokoáhkis had], but he refrained.

Among the Indians, wounds are said to heal wonderfully easily. In many cases an arrowhead remains in the body, [but] if the arrow can be pushed completely through, this danger is eliminated. Often men who are scalped in skirmishes become conscious again later and recuperate. There are two such men among the Hidatsas, who always have their heads covered and do not like their bare skulls to be seen.

The Mandans and Hidatsas often suffer from eye [problems]; some of them are one-eyed or have a skin [film?] on one eye. When they have eye infections, they are in the habit of scratching the inner eye with a sharp, sawlike blade of grass, which causes much blood to flow and may cause the loss of an eye.

Rheumatism, cough, and the like occur frequently, because [people] walk half-naked in the severest cold and jump into icy water. They [have a] kind of sweat bath, [taken] in a small, specially constructed, tightly closed hut. Inside it they [heat] stones in an intense fire and then pour large quantities of water on them, producing a hot, almost suffocating steam. They sweat [heavily], go outside quickly, and roll around in the snow or jump into the ice-covered river; [they] do not return to the heat, as Russians [do].

Some [Indian bathers] have apparently dropped dead on the spot.

Another cure for various illnesses and complaints is treading [on] the body, especially the belly. [The treatment is] so severe that hardening of the intestines, or ulcers, especially of the liver, often occur. Spitting of blood [is seen] frequently, but not actual consumption. Gonorrhea is very common. They maintain [that] all venereal evils have come from the Crows. When they have such diseases, they sit over a heated pot and almost burn themselves. Buboes they cut open with a knife, and then they run a few miles as fast as they can. Yellow jaundice does not occur. They do not know any emetics, but if they feel sick in their stomachs, they often thrust a feather down their throat to induce vomiting. They have laxatives from the plant kingdom. Sunstroke is unknown here. Poison-vine *(Rhus radicans)* often causes swellings, particularly in children. They rub frozen limbs with snow. Snow blindness is very common in March; [as a remedy] they dissolve gunpowder in water and bathe their eyes in it. Bloodletting is often done with a [sharp] flint or a knife. They frequently ask white men for medicine.

When a Mandan or a Hidatsa dies, he is not left for long in the village. They place him on a narrow scaffold as long as a man; [the scaffold,] resting on four poles about 10' high, [is erected] several hundred paces away from [the village]. [The deceased is laid there] after his body [is wrapped] and tied in buffalo robes and his woolen blanket. His face is painted, and [he] lies facing the sunrise. A number of these scaffolds stand near the villages. They themselves say this custom is detrimental to their health, but they do not abandon it despite [the health hazard]. Ravens can usually be seen sitting on the scaffolds, and [the people] do not like these birds, because they eat the flesh of the deceased. If somebody asks a Mandan why they do not bury their dead in the ground, the answer is, "The Lord of Life told us we came from the earth and should return to it. But not long ago we began to leave the dead aboveground, because we love them and weep at the sight [of them]."

They believe that in every human being there are [several] spirits: a black one, a brown one, and a light-colored one; the latter is the one who returns to the Lord of Life. They think that after death they will go south, where there are several villages visited frequently by the gods. The good and the brave go to this village of the good, the cowards and the wicked to another one. They live there the same as here—food, hunting, and war are the same. The more good done here, the better they will live there.

They mourn a whole year for their dead. They cut their hair and smear their entire bodies with white or gray clay. [They] often make incisions in their arms and legs from top to bottom with a knife or a sharp flint, [cut] beside [cut], so that they seem to be covered with blood. In the first days after a death, there is crying and lamentation. Often a relative or [friend] comes to "cover the dead," as they say here. He buys one or several woolen cloth blankets—red, blue, green, or white—and after the body has been placed on the scaffold, he climbs up and covers [the deceased] with them. To such a person the bereaved family gives a horse.

The Mandan language is easier for Germans or Dutchmen to pronounce than for [the English or French]. I collected many words [and attempted a grammatical study as well].[2] An old man assured [me] that in his youth the languages of the Mandans and the Hidatsas differed much more than they do today. They understand each other better now and have borrowed words from each other. Formerly the languages were entirely different, [and] they still [are] in major aspects. Time will have its influence here even more. [The] Indian nations on the Missouri are said to have no curse words [such as] the European [languages have]; the Mandans have [only] the word wáhchi-kanaschä, which means "bad people." With the kind support of Mr. Kipp, I collected many more comments about the Mandan language that would take too much space. Still, [here are] a few comments about their names, which always have meaning, sometimes equivalent to whole phrases. All objects in their [world] are possibilities for names, and [names] are frequently very smutty. Here [are] some strange examples: Bear That Is a Spirit—Mató-Manóchikä; Bull That Is a Spirit—Beróck-Manóchikä; Little Hawk Whose Foot Is Full of Blood (Arikara)—Starapat; I Hear Coming—Kuhá-Handéh; There Are Seven of Them Married to Old Women—Taminsickä-Kúhpa-Kohä-Chihä.[3]

XIX

A Few Words about the Two Tribes of the Mönnitarrís (Gros Ventres) [Hidatsas] and the Arikaras

This nation is called the Mönnítarris ("the ones who have come across the [river]") by the Mandans and most other [Indian] nations; by the French and the Americans, Gros Ventres. They call themselves or their nation Biddahátsi-Awatíss.[1] They are close neighbors and for a long time have been allies of the Mandans, whom they call Arabúcku.

In one place in his description of his trip to the Mandans, Brackenridge uses the expression "the Mandans, or Gros Ventres," as if he considered both nations to be one and the same (*Views of Louisiana,* p. 77). But later it appears that he did not assume this, [since] he claims [that] the languages of these nations are entirely different, which is quite correct. He [also says] that the Hidatsas lived in five villages (in 1811). This is wrong because, when Charbonneau came to them thirty-seven years ago, they had no more than three villages, the same as now. The lowest one, located on the left bank of the mouth of the Knife River, which flows into the Missouri, is called Awacháhwi (Village of the Mountains); the French call it le Village des Souliers, after an old chief, Itáchpa-Süpihähsch, les Souliers Noirs, [Black Shoes]. It contains about eighteen lodges. The central village, Awatichai-Ächpú, Village on the Hill, is also located on the left bank of the Knife. They usually call it simply Awatichai; it contains about forty lodges. The uppermost village, located on the right bank of the Knife, is called Eláh-Sá; it is by far the largest of the three villages, [with more than] eighty lodges. From all three villages together there might be about 350 warriors. At the present time, the chiefs in the three villages are the following:

At Eláh-Sá:

1. Lachpitzí-Síhrisch (Yellow Bear)
2. Itsicháichä (Monkey Face)

   At Awatichai:

1. Ahji-Süpischä (Black Horn Buffalo)
2. Wóharusiss (Catches Fish)

   At Awacháhwi:

1. Addíh-Hiddísch (Maker of Roads)
2. Atischíäss (Bad Lodge)
3. Lachpitzí-Wáh-Kikíhrisch (Hunts Bears).[2]

The Hidatsas reside permanently now in these three villages. They formerly roamed, as the Pawnees, Omahas, and other prairie tribes [still do], following the buffalo herds after their planting (corn, beans, squash, and tobacco) was done. In the fall they returned, [but] once the harvest was completed, they hunted again. On their travels they used leather tipis; some of these can still be found in good condition. The larger part of their former nation, the Haideróhka, or Crows, have remained a hunter nation and do not plant anything at all. The Hidatsas are not significantly different from the Mandans, but strangers do notice that they are generally taller. The women look much like the Mandans; some are tall and strong, [but] most are short; many [are] heavy. One can see a few pretty faces among them.

They have lived [close to] the Mandans for so long that [they] wear the same traditional attire, but perhaps it can be stated that the Hidatsas generally pay more attention than the Mandans do to nice clothes and ornaments. Their bear claw necklaces, which they may pay dearly for, are large and flawless. [They] often consist of forty frontal claws [and] reach in a wide semicircle across the chest from one shoulder blade to the other. The hair ornament that is worn [in the hair] beside the temple is very long and often decorated beautifully on the lower end with colorful small feathers or strips of ermine skin. They wear their hair quite long in smooth braids hanging down the back; [it] forms a broad surface [to be] smeared with reddish brown clay and, if not long enough, [is] often extended with false hair attached with pine tar. They allegedly often take that hair from slain enemies. To [represent] their coups, they put a circle or tuft of feathers from birds of prey or ravens into their hair. They seldom wear leather shirts like [those of] the Crows, Assiniboines, and Blackfoot. Most of the time their upper bodies are bare, [although] their arms and often their whole bodies are painted. Their leggins are [like] the Mandans, [as are] the breechcloth [and belt. Moccasins] are decorated in various ways, frequently with a long stripe or an elegant, round rosette of colorful porcupine quills. Almost everything [here duplicates the] discussion in the Mandan [chapter].

In this nation there are many men with tattoos, especially on one side of the body. For instance, the right side of the chest and the right arm [might be adorned] with various stripes, sometimes down to the hand. Indeed, the old chief Addíh-Hiddísch had his whole right hand striped. The tattooing procedure is like [that of] the Mandans, [as is] the manner of painting the body.

The Hidatsa villages are arranged similarly to those of the Mandans, except [there is] no model ark of the great flood or a figure of Ochkíh-Häddä. However, at Eláh-Sá [there is] a figure of a woman atop a long pole, doubtless the grandmother (Makóh), discussed below.

I described the interior of lodges in chapter [16 and] our [28 November] visit to the Hidatsa lodge of chief Lachpitzí-Síhrisch. [Hidatsa lodges] are furnished like Mandan [lodges]. In winter the Hidatsas, like the Mandans, move into the forests on both sides of the Missouri, where they have shelter and [firewood].

Their domestic life differs little from the Mandans. They have approximately 250 to 300 horses in their three villages, about as many as the Mandans. They have a moderate number of dogs, like the Mandans. They use them in [the same] manner—that is, only to carry loads; they do not eat them.

When these people have a feast, each [guest] brings his own bowl. It is filled for him, and he must empty it. If he cannot, he passes it to his neighbor (with a small piece of tobacco as a gift), [who must] empty it by eating everything. At gun and war festivals, [each guest] must eat everything that is served.

When they name their children—it cannot be called baptism—they have the following custom: The father goes buffalo hunting and brings back much meat. In the village he may load ten to twelve large slabs of meat on his back [and his] child on top [of that]. He walks, bent by the weight, into the lodge of a medicine man, who bestows the name [on the child]. The meat is a present or reward for [the bestowal].

Like the Mandans, the Hidatsas have several bands, or societies, which each have different [insignia], dances, [and] songs, and [members] can sell their rank and insignia. They are the following:

1. The Stone Society, Wíwa-Óhpage, boys from ten to eleven years of age; [they] wear feathers on their heads.
2. The Society of the Large Sabers, Wírrachíschi; [they] are fourteen to fifteen years old and carry sabers in their hands when they dance.
3. The Crow [or Raven] Society, Haideróhka-Ächke, [consists of] young people from seventeen to eighteen.
4. The Society of the Small Prairie Foxes, Éhchoch-Kaïchke, wear otter and wolf skins on their bodies when they perform.
5. The Society of the Small Dogs, Waskúkka-Karíschta, wear feathers on their heads and broad strips of red and blue cloth draped down [from] their shoulders.
6. The Society of the Old Dogs, Waschúkke-Ächke, wear feathers on their heads, the above-mentioned strips of cloth over their shoulders, [and] a wolf skin around their bodies. They carry a [rattle] in their hands, a stick with buffalo calf hooves [attached to it]; a war pipe whistle hangs from their necks.
7. The Society of Bow-Lances, Sóhta-Girakschóhge, wear feathers on their heads and carry bow-lances—very big, long bows [with] a large iron spear tip at one end [and] trimmed overall with colorful cloth, glass beads, [and] feathers. This is the same society or dance [that] the Mandan call Íschohä-Kakoschóchatä.
8. The Society of the Enemies, Máh-Iháh-Ächke, carry guns in their hands and are the equivalent of the Mandan Káua-Karakáchka, the soldiers.
9. The Society of the Bulls, Kädap-Ächke. On their heads [they] wear the head skin of a buffalo with horns attached; around their bodies and on their legs, strips of cloth [ornamented with] bells; [they carry] spears, guns, and shields.
10. The Society of Ravens, Pehriskäike. [These] are the oldest men. Each carries a long pole covered with red cloth and hung with raven feathers. They wear beautifully decorated clothing [and], on their heads, feathers and war-eagle-feather bonnets.
11. The Society of Hot Water, Máhsawähs, is the same as [the Stone Society]. They dance around naked and take meat from a pot of boiling water.

Women's societies exist here as among the Mandans:

1. The Society of Wild Geese, Bíhda-Ächke. When they dance they carry
   [sage] and an ear of corn in their arms. A feather is attached horizontally to their foreheads. This band consists of the oldest women.
2. The Society of Enemies, Máh-Iháh-Ächke. They wear long pendants of
   shells and *rassade* attached to the sides of their foreheads and a feather
   horizontally on their heads.
3. The Skunk Society, Chóchkäiwi. On the backs of their heads, they wear
   a tuft of erect feathers painted black, [and on the face,] a white vertical
   stripe (like a skunk).

Besides these societies the Hidatsas have two [other] distinct dances:

1. Táiruchpahga, the Dance of the Old Men. At this dance the men appear
   almost naked with no adornments. Only old men perform it, [those
   who] no longer go to war.
2. Zúhdi Arischí, the Scalp Dance, [performed by] the women. [They]
   carry scalps on poles [and weapons] in their hands. Men play the
   drums and the *chichikué* while the war party stands in a line, moving
   their feet in rhythm [to the music]. See the description [in chapter 20].

The games of the Hidatsas are the same as those of the Mandans.

The skin of the white buffalo cow has great value for [the Hidatsas] as
well as the Mandans, who say that the Hidatsas adopted the worship of the
white buffalo cow from them. They will pay for one with fifteen horses,
guns, kettles, cloth, woolen blankets, robes, and items of significant value.
[The owner] keeps the skin [for] about four years after announcing its ac-
quisition to the village from the top of his lodge. Family members sometimes wear the robe at ceremonial events. Small, narrow strips are also cut
off and worn as decorative bands across the head. When [the allotted] time
has passed, the skin is given as a sacrifice to one of the deities. A medicine
man is hired to perform the necessary ceremonies. A bundle of brushwood
is attached to the top of a long pole, which is then wrapped with the beautiful white skin and set up in a place chosen by the owner, where it [is left]
to decay. For his services, the medicine man often receives 150 robes and
various other valuables—some of which he distributes among [ceremony]

spectators. Sometimes the owners choose to ride onto the prairie with their skin [and lay it] on a red or blue blanket on the ground. They hobble a horse, tie up its mouth, and leave it [there as a] sacrifice. If someone were to steal that horse, they would say, "He is a simpleton or a fool to steal from the Lord of Life!"

Their medicines and superstitions are closely related and [so] intertwined with their religious myths and the traditions of their history that it [is] necessary to [relate] these first. [In] the beginning, only water existed and no earth. A large bird with a red eye dove below the surface and brought up soil. The Man Who [Does] Not [Die], or the Lord of Life (Éhsich-kawáh-hiddisch, translated literally as First Man), who lives in the Rocky Mountains, sent down the large bird to fetch [the] soil.

Another being worthy of veneration is called Old Woman. They also call [her] Grandmother (Makóh). She roams the whole earth. She had a small share in the creation; she created the mole and the toad. She [also] gave the Hidatsas a few pots, which they have preserved as sacred objects, used on certain occasions as medicines. She told [the Hidatsa] ancestors to keep the pots and to remember the great water, too, from which all animals had come "dancing," as the old storyteller expressed it. The [bird] with red shoulders (Icterus phoeniceus) appeared at that time from the water, as well as all the different birds that can still be heard singing on the riverbanks; they consider [them all as] medicine for the corn planting. When these birds sing, [the Hidatsas] must fill the sacred pots with water, be happy, dance, bathe, and remember the great flood. When a serious drought threatens their fields, they celebrate a medicine festival with the [sacred] pots, asking for rain; [it was] for that [purpose] that they were given the pots.

The sun, or as they say it, the Sun of the Day, is an important medicine for them. They do not know what it actually is but are well aware that it serves to preserve and warm the earth. They make sacrifices to it when [planning some enterprise]. The same applies to the moon, which they call the Sun of the Night. The morning star, or Star of the Day, is the child of the moon and an important medicine, [for] it is the grandchild of Makóh. The evening star is the same. They call the Milky Way the Path of Ashes, but [they] do not know what it actually is. Thunder is the noise [made by] the wings of the large bird that causes rain. Lightning is created when that bird looks around, searching [for something].

When First Man created the Hidatsas they [were] one and the same nation with the Haideróhka, or Crows. A medicine woman among them had three sons. The oldest was called Aíhla-Wirasass, meaning Black Circle Around His Face; the second, Itáhschi-Íhsakiss, Robe with Beautiful Hair; and the third, Ahjipsass, Straight Horn.[3] Each built a village. The oldest went down the Missouri with his people, and no one knows what became of them. The second [took] his people to the mountains and founded the Haideróhka tribe, [and] the third established the tribe of the Biddahát-si-Awatíss, [who] later built the three villages that exist today on the Missouri. The uppermost village was [first] called Biddahátsi-Awatíss, but a medicine man called it Eláh-Sá, the Village of the Big Willows, because [even when] the willows were cut down by ice, [they] always grew again. Awacháhwi was earlier located farther down the Missouri in the vicinity of the Butte Carrée; the inhabitants moved upriver to [join] the rest of the nation. The [tribe] at that time was less than 1,000 men strong.

The Hidatsas consider their medicines as important as the Mandans [do]. All wolves and foxes, especially the former, are medicine to them. When they go to war, they wear a strip of wolfskin, including the tail, which hangs down their backs. They make a lengthwise cut in this skin and thrust their heads through in such a manner that the wolf head hangs down their chests. Buffalo heads are also medicine. In one village they preserve buffalo neck bones [to keep] the buffalo herds from moving too far away.

Like the Mandans, they have medicine trees and stones, where they sacrifice red cloth, red paint, and other objects to the heavenly powers. [They also] do penance to please and be supported by the gods in achieving their purposes. Say wrote about the Hidatsa, Wolf Chief, who sat for five days on an isolated boulder without eating (see Long's *Expedition to the Rocky Mountains,* vol. 1, p. 257)—the same prairie hill [to which] the Mandans go with the identical intention. They endure there as long as their physical powers permit and at night crawl into a nearby hole to sleep. Say [also] states that the ancestors of the Hidatsas lived belowground (ibid., p. 258), but [the Hidatsas] do not say this; it [is a Mandan] legend—[see] the preceding chapter.

The Hidatsas have numerous medicine festivals. [Their] Corn Dance, or more correctly, the ceremony for the consecration of the crops, is celebrated in the manner [I recounted for] the Mandans. In chapter XVI I described the great medicine festival to attract the buffalo herds, which we observed [on 26 November].

They also celebrate the great penitence festival that the Mandans call Okíppe, but with a few differences. As stated, there is no ark on the plaza in their villages; instead [they have] a pole set in [the ground] with a fork on top. In May or June, when partisans [plan] a raid, these preparations are combined with the penance festival, [held for] youths who want to [become] braves. A large medicine lodge is built, open above, with a partition in the center where the penitence candidates take their places. [There are] usually two elongated, rectangular pits excavated for the partisans, in which they lie [for] four days and four nights, naked and stretched out, with only a piece of leather tied around their hips. There are always young people ready to endure bodily tortures as proof of their bravery and determination. They fast for four days and four nights and become weak and faint. Some start their tortures on the third day, but the fourth is the [usual] day set for [this purpose]. An old man is chosen to [oversee] the tortures, which are like those of the Mandans. On the day of the tortures, [the penitents, like] the partisans, are covered completely with white clay [paint]. No one dances but the penitents, and there is no music other than a dried buffalo skin that is beaten with willow rods. No remedies at all are applied to the wounds [suffered during the tortures]. The [resulting scars] grow like thick calluses, rising quite high—far larger and more pronounced than those on Mandans. Indeed, I saw many Hidatsas whose chests had three to four crescentlike ridges standing almost an inch high [across] the whole width of [their torsos]. Horizontal or vertical scars can be seen on their arms, often [covering the entire limb].

The Hidatsas, like the Mandans, make pilgrimages to the Medicine Rock, [described in chapters 16 and 18]. Another remarkable medicine device of the Hidatsas is the sweat lodge. If a man desires to undertake something, [such as a war party,] and to implore assistance from above, he builds himself a small sweat lodge with branches and makes it airtight [by covering it with] buffalo robes. From the entrance, a straight path 40′ long and 1′ wide is constructed by digging up sod that is [then] piled at the end opposite the lodge. Beside this pile a fire is lit, in which thick stones are heated to glowing. On the path, two [long] rows of shoes are lined up, one behind the other, sometimes thirty to forty pairs. When the stones are hot, they are carried into the [sweat] lodge and placed on a hearth [there]. The whole [village] sits on both sides of the path as spectators; many bowls with prepared food—cooked corn, beans, meat, etc.—are set up there. An old medicine man is asked to perform the [ceremony]. He goes from the [sod pile] to the sweat lodge [by walking on] the lined-up shoes, [carefully placing] his feet [only] on them. The young man for whom the medicine is performed stands naked, except for his breechcloth, in front of the sweat lodge and laments and cries there for some time. The medicine man comes out of the sweat lodge with a knife or arrowhead and cuts off a joint of [the young man's] finger, which he throws away as a sacrifice to the Lord of Life or to some other medicine in which the young man has placed his trust. The old medicine man [next] takes a willow switch, walks to the food bowls, dips the switch in each of them, and throws [a bit] of their contents to the four [cardinal] directions, the Lord of Life, the fire, [and other] medicine beings. The food is then distributed among the spectators. The older men go inside the sweat lodge. Women cover the outside carefully. [In the lodge,] water is sprinkled onto the hot stones with bundles of wormwood. [All] those present break into heavy sweat. They sing in rhythm to the *chichikué*. When they have perspired enough, they call to the women to take down the hides. Someone carries a buffalo head, its nose pointing forward, over the rows of shoes to the small pile of sod and places [the head] on top [of the pile]. The medicine is now completed. The young man gives the robes with which the lodge was covered—sometimes sixty to eighty in number—as payment to the medicine man, who [then] gives some of them to those present.

The Hidatsas occasionally make sacrifices to the big snake that lives in the Missouri. The reason [for this] is explained in a tale similar to the Mandan [legend in chapter 18, about a warrior who eats of and becomes a powerful medicine snake]. The Hidatsas firmly believe this story.

Owls (doubtless *Strix virginiana*) can be found occasionally in [Hidatsa] lodges, kept [there] as prophets; they claim to understand [the owls'] voices and interpret them. They also keep the war eagle (*Aquila* [—]) alive to get its tail feathers, which they consider very valuable.

[There is] a certain Hidatsa [who, when he] smokes his pipe, [does so] very slowly. [While he smokes,] no one is allowed to talk or move, except to accept the pipe. Neither women nor children are permitted to be in the lodge at that time; someone constantly watches the door so no woman, child, or dog may enter. If there are, however, exactly seven persons present for smoking, then all precautionary measures are dropped, and the pipe can be smoked quickly. [When] the pipe is cleaned out [and] the contents are thrown into the fire, [it] flares up high. It is likely that [this man] put gunpowder or something similar in the bottom of the pipe beforehand. If somebody has a diseased or painful spot on [their body], [he] places his pipe there and smokes. He asserts [that] through his smoking, he is pulling out the illness, [which] he finally grabs with his hands and throws into the fire.

The Hidatsa division of the year according to the moons is not significantly different than [that of] the Mandans, [nor are their customs of] hunting and war. The Hidatsas are peaceful toward the white men in this area at present, but if one encounters a war party on the prairie, one is usually robbed. They are often inclined [to be] hostile toward the white men and half-breeds living on the Red River in the north. Their true enemies are the Blackfoot, Gros Ventres des Prairies, Assiniboines, Dacotas, Pawnees, Arikaras, Cheyennes, Crees, [and] Arapahoes.[M1] Their allies are the Mandans [and] the Crows.

Unlike the Mandans, the Hidatsas [appear] to know few real [medical remedies]. The drum, the *chichikué,* and the song of the medicine man [often suffice as] healing [treatments]. For wounds, they singe fragrant grass over coal [and] hold their hands [first] in the smoke, then over the wound, [and finally] lay tallow on it. [At the time I visited] there were two men among these people who had recuperated from being scalped in skirmishes. [That and] the many large scars [one sees] on their bodies prove the healing power of their strong constitutions.

From time immemorial they have placed their dead on scaffolds. Because the Lord of Life does not like [people] to quarrel and kill each other, those who do are buried in the ground, so [they] can no longer be seen. However, a buffalo head is placed on the grave, so that the buffalo herds will not stay away (because if they scent the wicked, they might leave and not return). Good people are laid upon scaffolds so [that] the Lord of Life can see them.

The Hidatsa language is very different from Mandan and is much more difficult to pronounce correctly; the difficulty lies mainly in the accent.

[M1] All these Indians treat the bodies of their slain enemies barbarously. They mutilate them and carry or throw individual pieces around. [Once,] after shooting an Assiniboine, they brought us just his hand, hanging from a stick. Charbonneau [said that] in one of the Hidatsa villages, they kept a [dead] Assiniboine for several months in winter and propped him up during the day to use for target practice.

Words are sometimes very shortly and suddenly cut off [and are] often pronounced very softly and indistinctly. What can be expressed in German and French with a few words usually requires several in Hidatsa, which bespeaks the poverty of the language.

THE ARIKARAS

The Aríkkarras, Ríkkaras, or Rees, are a Missouri [River] tribe that separated from the Pawnees many years ago. At that time [they] settled on the Missouri [in] two villages. [When] Lewis and Clark [and later] Brackenridge visited them, they behaved peacefully. Not long afterward, [though, they began to attack] the keelboats of several trading companies—killing, among others, seventeen to eighteen of General Ashley's men. [Action] against [the Arikaras] was not very vigorous. Especially damaging, people say, was [the outcome of] Colonel Leavenworth's [1823] expedition. [Leavenworth] came upriver with a significant number of troops, cannon, and Dacota allies. He could have destroyed the [Arikara] villages completely [but] left without accomplishing anything. He supposedly had no orders to attack. The Arikaras must have considered [Leavenworth's] behavior a weakness; afterward [they] were worse than ever [and] killed many whites. With no further prospects for trade on the Missouri, and [other] ensuing [difficulties], they left their villages in the fall of 1832. [They] are said to have settled [at a distant place] above the sources of the Platte. Because this nation has been often mentioned, I [will] report some of the information I have received about them.

They call themselves or their nation Sáhnisch (people, humans). They are strong, well-built men—a few are almost six feet tall. Their physiognomy [resembles] that of neighboring nations, especially the Mandans and Hidatsas; their women are reputedly the prettiest on the Missouri (but also the most dissolute).

Their dress is not essentially different from the Mandans. They have abandoned the attire and most customs of the Pawnees.

They inhabited two villages on the Missouri, Nahokáhta [and] Hóhka-Wirátt (also [called] Achtárahä, according to old Garreau). They numbered about 500 warriors when they left the Missouri and had many horses and dogs. Now said to number 600 valiant men, [they remain] a warrior nation, very dangerous to white men. The most extensive information I have about this nation is given by Brackenridge, [but it] is rather sparse. I will [include] here what I learned from a few Mandans who lived among the Arikaras a long time, especially chief Mató-Tópe. The architecture of their lodges is no different than the Mandans and Hidatsas. [Brackenridge] states [that] the Arikara villages were very dirty and compares them with some older European cities. Because one must assume that Mr. Brackenridge never saw European cities, where there is probably more order enforced by police than [that which] prevails in American cities, his comparison is very inappropriate. In European cities, hogs never run in the streets as [they do] in the largest American places.

When the Arikaras left the Missouri, their chiefs in both villages were the following:[4]

At Nahokáhta
1. Starapat [Bloody Hand]
2. Pachkúnehoch, Old Head
3. Chátschisch-Schauatá, White Horse

At Hóhka-Wirátt
1. Nescháhni-Sanách, Crazy Chief
2. Warúch-Tháhka, White Hair
3. Honníhtatta-Káhrach, Bad Brave

Arikara agriculture was the same as it still is among the Mandans and Hidatsas. [But] the upbringing of children is said to have been far better. Little [rascals] received a good thrashing.

Like most Indian tribes, the Arikaras have several bands, or societies, [and] also special dances (see Brackenridge). Their [six] societies are not very different from those of the Mandans, [but they] have at least seven [additional] dances, [including] the Dance of the Little Bird, Hunúchka ([the dancers] wear the skin of the screech owl, *Strix asio,* on their foreheads); the Dance of the Ghosts, Naníschta (they wear a large owl feather bonnet [that] hangs down [their] backs and wraps around their bodies, [and] war whistles on their necks); [and] the Dance of the Stretched Robe, Tschiri-Wakáh. [The latter dancers] dress as if going to battle, [and] only the most outstanding warriors [may participate]. When one of them accepts a present, another [participant] — who has counted [even] more coups — comes, pushes him aside, [and] recounts his own deeds; then yet another one does the same; and thus it continues until the bravest [one] has finally [taken all] the gifts.

They use the same coup [representations] as the Mandans, [and] their partisans observe the same customs, except an Arikara partisan usually wears a wrapped corncob on his chest; corn is as an important Arikara medicine. Arikaras fight better [in smaller rather than larger parties]. No [other] nation has killed as many whites as the Arikaras [have]. The Pawnees [formerly] tortured their prisoners [but] don't any longer, because of Petalesharo's [influence]. The Arikaras gave up this custom when they separated from the Pawnees.

The Arikaras are said to have the same religious ideas and traditions as the Mandans. They call the Lord of Life Pachkátsch, like the prairie wolf *(Canis latrans)*; First Man [is] Íhkochu or Sziritsch; this is also the name of the wolf. Ochkíh-Häddä, or the devil, they know by the name of Nachskunachkoch, meaning Small Hairy One. They formerly venerated the ark of First Man, but they gave it up. Medicine festivals and superstitions of all kinds prevail here as with the other Missouri [River] Indians. They do not actually have the Okíppe but [do] perform penances, though not as extended [or severe]. All kinds of animals are medicine to them; they choose these as other nations do [but in the process] do not fast as long as the Mandans and Hidatsas—at the most, one day. [It is through generosity that a warrior or hunter] becomes a respected man. The Lord of Life told the Arikaras [that] if they gave to the poor and carried burdens, they would always be lucky and blessed in their ventures.

They have remained true to one of their greatest medicine festivals, the Napáhruchte, or the medicine of the bird-case. They esteem this medicine as highly as Christians do the Bible. It is their general rule and law, [and] they act in accordance with [it]. In their villages, this [sacred item] is mounted high in the medicine lodge, and it travels with them [whenever] they move. It is a narrow, quadrilateral parchment box, 6' to 7' long, [that] opens at one end. On top of the case, seven [red-tufted bottle gourd] *chichikués* are attached in a row. In the case are all kinds of stuffed bird skins [from those] that live here in summer. Besides these, the box contains a famous medicine pipe, Napáhruchti, that is smoked on extraordinary occasions and [ceremonies]. If an Arikara has killed, even his own brother, [if he] has first smoked from this pipe, all [animosity toward] him must be forgotten. They perform medicine with this [case] after the crops are seeded and the first squashes are ripe. The [squash] blossoms are watched, and as soon as the first fruits ripen, distinguished braves are [bidden to] come. Articles of value are tossed to them, [and] the first fruits are cut and given to [them] to eat. In return they must take down the bird-case [and] open [it]; medicine songs are sung, and the big pipe is smoked.

The Arikaras have many fantastic [tricks], juggleries, and masquerades. They perform remarkable magic, tricks said to have [been learned from] a famous juggler among them. They have medicine festivals where complete comedies are [staged]. [A man], for example, plays a bear. [Wearing] a bearskin with head and claws, [he] imitates the movements and voice of the animal so well that an observer believes [he/she] is seeing a bear. [The bear] is shot; blood flows; [it] falls down; dies; is skinned—and the man appears unscathed. [In] another performance, they chop off a man's head with a saber and carry it outside. The body lies there, bleeding, [yet] this headless man soon [begins to] dance around. The head is replaced [but] facing in the wrong direction. He dances again. A short time later, the head is resecured firmly to the body [in the right position], and the man dances unscathed. [Such] scenes are, of course, intended to thoroughly deceive the spectators. Most white men, especially the French Canadians, firmly believe in [these] marvels.

God told the Arikaras they were created from earth and must return to earth again. They therefore bury their dead in the ground. Distinguished men are occasionally [buried with] several objects to accompany them; they are dressed in their best clothes [and] their faces painted red. In some instances, a good horse is killed on the grave. If the deceased has a son, he receives his father's medicine apparatus; if not, they put it in the grave with [the dead man].

Their manner of name giving is [like] that of [other] Indian tribes on the Missouri, the surrounding prairies, and the Rocky Mountains. They take the names of animals [or of] other objects [in their] surroundings and [also names reflecting] the different conditions and activities of living creatures. These names are frequently melodious. As with all these nations, [names] are often changed. They usually get their first names as children [and] change them upon reaching manhood or [to mark an] outstanding achievement.

XX

Continuation of the Winter Sojourn at Fort Clark

1 January: In the morning, clear; at seven thirty, −8°F. Three of our woodcutters had [frostbitten] faces: two, their noses; and one, his nose and cheeks. Belhumeur locked me out of the fort by accident, and I had to call and knock for a long time before they heard me. I was half frozen. In our miserable room, everything froze that was not immediately in front of the fireplace. We were burned in front (our clothing, literally) and frozen behind.

2 January: In the morning, we could scarcely bear it until the fire [was started and] burning. I [could not] write; the ink was a frozen lump. [We learned today] that Kipp, [who had set out for Fort Union on 29 December,] would stay with Bijou in the [farthest Hidatsa] village, waiting for milder weather to complete his trip.

   We had no meat. Our shoes and boots were frozen solid in our room; we could not put them on. Charbonneau's wife, an Arikara, gave birth yesterday in the lower [Hidatsa] village. Today she came to the fort, [a journey of] one and a half hours on foot, in the severe cold, [her newborn] on her back.

3 January: The mercury [froze] in the bulb, meaning [the temperature was] lower than −30°F. Everything in our room was solid [ice] — [and there was] no more wood in the fort. The men had to fetch supplies daily in that severe cold. Moreover, the houses were so poorly constructed that one could hardly endure [the cold] inside, even with a tremendous fire in the fireplace. [There were] strong drafts in every corner.

   At eleven thirty an engagé I had sent out brought some meat on a sled from [Ruhptare]. We finally had meat again! The sun was blinding on the white prairie. No living creature could be seen except for small flocks of snow buntings *(Emberiza nivalis)* near Mih-Tutta-Hangkusch.

4 January: At nine o'clock or nine thirty, we [saw] two of Picotte's engagés with horse sleds on the ice, loaded with merchandise and dry, hard meat. They had spent the two coldest days in the forest, where the wolves stole some

of the meat. Mr. Picotte wrote [that] he did not think Kipp's horses, [sent downriver with men and sleds on 27 December,] were [strong enough], so he did not load much [on them]; he would send more shortly. In the evening [it was a] fairly [comfortable] temperature in Kipp's room, where we all gathered—Belhumeur, Charbonneau, and de l'Orme, in addition to us three strangers. Máhchsi-Karéhde visited us with a pretty woman he supposedly kidnapped [just] for today. They slept in our room on the floor and froze [there].

5 January: About eight o'clock, −9°F [outside]; it [felt] far colder in our room. The tall Mandan, Máhchsi-Karéhde, was measured: 5′ 10″ 2‴ Parisian measure in height.

At one o'clock [we saw] two sun dogs fairly distant from the sun in the hazy air; they were weak and irregular. No drinking water was available in the fort; the water [in the] barrel in our room was frozen solid down to the bottom. Many Mandans showed up during lunch today. Mr. Picotte had sent, from the Yanktonai post, a small barrel of wine for the Mandans as a present from Mr. McKenzie. It was given to the chiefs for distribution.

The Mandans intended to hunt buffalo tomorrow. For that purpose they had seized two horses from the fort without asking, [and in the] dark, Síh-Sä was sent after them. In the evening old de l'Orme told me words of the Ojibwe language. The French call this nation Sauteurs or Sauteux.

6 January: In the morning, snow flurries, mild weather, 29°F. About noon the snow was mixed with rain, and water [leaked] through the ceiling onto our books and papers. We were [just] happy to be able to work again after the long interruption [caused] by the cold; we had not been able to do anything for about a week. An Indian boy brought us snow buntings today that he caught with snares. My little prairie fox stole one of them right away and began to eat the head. He [really] likes birds. In the evening, it was so unusually warm that in bed we could leave our hands above the covers.

7 January: Despite the recent severe cold spell, the river had an open area on the side opposite the fort, about 200 paces in length but very narrow.

The Yanktonai (Psíhdjä-Sáhpa, [Black Swallow]) came to us and, after much encouragement, [agreed] to be drawn. Síh-Chidä convinced him. Soon Mató-Chihá (Old Bear) came, too, and promised to have himself drawn. In the afternoon I had to help [Belhumeur] weigh several metal kettles, because he could not read, write, or differentiate the numbers on the weights. Not a single one [of the fort's men] could read or write. I had to write everything whenever a note [was needed], and if they received letters, I had to read their secrets to them. [That night] Síh-Chidä slept at our place. After he undressed he lay on his robe and made a speech—a kind of prayer to the Lord of Life—of which we understood some. He said [that], among other [needs], the Lord of Life should send them buffalo so they would not starve. He spoke rapidly, in a low voice, with no gesticulations.

8 January: Dreidoppel went hunting [but] saw nothing except prairie hens. In the forest the snow was too deep, [and] he could not move easily. Mató-Tópe visited and brought a completed bear claw necklace that I had asked him to make [on 29 November].

At twelve o'clock I went to look at the thermometer, [but] it had been stolen by Indians. Síh-Chidä left and soon sent the lost instrument back. He [had] found it in the possession of a woman.

La Chevelure Levée, [meaning scalped man] (a Hidatsa; his real name is Bídda-Chóhki [Sparse Forest]), came with a Mandan from Ruhptare and stayed overnight in the fort. We wrote down his language, but he was not in a very good mood, because he got no brandy.

9 January: The deaf-mute Mandan came into our room very early. La Chevelure Levée allowed himself be drawn, but it was too cold in the room and the work soon stopped. Because brushes and colors froze while painting, we had to keep warm water constantly [available].

10 January: Few Indians came to the fort today. A tall man, Nátka-Númpä ([Two] Hearts), came to us and offered to be drawn. He was a lively, friendly man [who] laughed and talked a great deal. He told us about his love affair with a Negro woman who came upriver on the *Assiniboine* last summer; we were on the same [steamboat]. Very fine snow in the afternoon. Mató-Tópe visited us but did not stay. He had reconciled with Péhriska-Rúhpa, for whom he bought a green blanket as a present. We kept a strong fire in the fireplace, as usual, when we went to bed. We estimated that we would burn at least six cords of wood a month in the fireplace if it stayed this cold.

11 January: After Indians were drawn, they returned often; [they] believed we should be grateful to them. Usually we kept the door bolted and did not let many in. That evening we heard Máhchsi-Karéhde call in front of the fort's [gate], "Káwa-Kapúska! Káwa-Kapúska!" [Painter?] (that is what they called Bodmer). [He was allowed] inside and slept at our place.

12 January: Big Máhchsi-Karéhde was drawn at midmorning. Cháratä-Numakschi

(Wolf Chief) visited us and smoked our pipes, which he did not [ordinarily] do.

13 January: Durand told us that a wolf had attacked three women in the forest; they defended themselves with their axes. Síh-Chidä visited and returned a small bow to Bodmer that he had [taken and] decorated neatly with *rassade,* cloth, and ermine.

14 January: Toward noon, the thermometer in our room showed −12°F; −8½°F outside. Wind blew directly into our room, causing severe cold. About evening [it] abated, however, and it was not as cold. Tomorrow the Indians planned to send people to find the buffalo herds, [and] then they would go hunting. It was highly necessary for us to get fresh meat, because the dry meat sent to us by Picotte, hard and tough as leather [and] almost impossible to eat, was almost gone. We had nothing left but corn and beans, miserably cooked the same way every day. The engagés, who had to go out repeatedly for firewood, complained bitterly about the cold; the cause of [their distress] was the piercing wind, which they had to face head-on. In this country there is almost always wind, [and it] increases the cold exceptionally.

15 January: Towards noon Mató-Tópe came with many Indians. One of them wore a long, trailing bonnet of white and black [eagle] feathers. This beautiful headdress, [called] máhchsi-akub-háschka, had about 40 eagle feathers attached to a broad red strip of cloth. They [were going] to Ruhptare to adopt a medicine son and to dance the medicine pipes.

Mató-Tópe was beautifully dressed. In his hair he had [symbolized] all his wounds with small wooden sticks: four yellow, one red, and one blue. I had precise copies made. On the right side of his head, he also wore a knife made of wood, painted partly red as a sign that he had killed a Cheyenne chief with [just such] a knife. On top of each wooden [stick], a yellow nail was driven in, like a little button. On the back of his head, he wore a large tuft of eagle owl feathers, a symbol of the Meníss-Óchatä; eagle feathers were stuck radially upright in his hair. I lent him my bear claw necklace, and he took an ornamented eagle's feather belonging to Máhchsi-Karéhde that was at our place and stuck that in his hair, too. One eye was painted yellow, the other red; his forehead and the lower part of his chin [were] red. His body and arms were marked with reddish brown vertical stripes, and his coups [were] indicated by horizontal stripes on his arms. On his chest a [painted] yellow hand that indicated he had taken prisoners.[MI] In the afternoon the Yanktonai came and roasted ears of corn on the fire.

16 January: In the night [a] very severe wind blew the ashes out of the fireplace into the room, heavily [coating] all tables, books, and papers. There were no Indians of importance in the fort, only a few women. The Dacota wanted to eat corn in our room again, but we kept quiet with the door closed. In the afternoon Mató-Tópe came back from Ruhptare and said that he had enumerated his coups and no one could better him. In the evening we had meat that was inedible—all fat—[and] tomorrow [will be] the last [of that]. In the evening old Garreau told me about the Arikaras, with whom he had lived for a long time. He said he was living only on corn; he [did not] look well. They had no meat in the Hidatsa village near Dougherty's, either. It gets worse here every year for game. The white man brought all this misery. When Garreau first came, game was abundant. Beavers were heard every-where in the evenings, [slapping] their tails in the small brooks and rivers.

17 January: Snow in the night and early morning. At nine o'clock the sky cleared, [and] Dreidoppel went out with his gun for the first time in a long while but soon returned empty-handed. I bought a beautiful magpie from an Indian boy. Mató-Tópe, whose portrait was to be drawn, first painted himself in front of the mirror, probably for two hours, [in] highly original reddish brown, red, and yellow [colors], as described above. He sat [for the portrait] quite motionless, his battle-axe in his hand.

Charbonneau had gone to the Hidatsas to look for meat, of which we had none. Our lunch consisted of corn boiled in water mixed with beans and cornbread.

18 January: The Missouri, frozen solid, [was a] white expanse [with] trails [made by] Indians and our woodcutters. It snowed [but] only for half an hour—it was too cold.

Today the inhabitants of Mih-Tutta-Hangkusch went buffalo hunting on horseback. Mató-Tópe stayed here for [his portrait work]. Charbonneau

[MI] Mr. Bodmer portrayed this interesting man (who has a very high opinion of himself) in [all] this attire very truly and correctly. [Bodmer's three-quarter watercolor portrait of Four Bears shows this regalia quite clearly; it is reproduced here as pl. 26. The replicas of the wooden coup symbols that Maximilian commissioned from the chief are in the Wied Collection at the Linden-Museum in Stuttgart (36076a–f; Schulze-Thulin, *Indianer der Prärien*, 45).]

came about evening and brought some fresh meat. The old Hidatsa chief, Road Maker (Addíh-Hiddísch), told us the history of his people.

19 January: Today we had meat all day long. Mató-Tópe left us. Old Addíh-Hiddísch related much [more], which I recorded with Charbonneau's aid.

20 January: [The] weather about noon [was] pleasant—meaning cold but clear and calm. Durand visited us. Charbonneau gave me some information about the Hidatsas.

21 January: Everything froze in our room during the night. The surrounding area was covered with fog, or haze, in [which] the sun formed two beautiful crescents, [or sun dogs], large and high, [widely flanking] the sun, and whitish yellow, bright in the dim haze, like the sun itself. The snow was frozen so solidly that one could break it into large, hard pieces that gave off a [ringing?] sound when kicked. The [sunlit] air glittered, filled with thousands of small ice particles. The Indians hacked holes in the icy surface of the Missouri, from which they fetched water. [The holes] were marked with twigs and surrounded with buffalo robes.

Three Yanktonais came to invite the Mandans to [participate in] a raid against the Saones. But [the Mandans declined] the invitation.

22 January: A few Indians arrived, [their] hair frozen white, covered with hoarfrost. As we were sitting at dinner, which consisted of cornbread and coffee, someone knocked on the fort gate. An Indian called out that he had a message for Belhumeur. They unlocked [the gate], and Dipäuch's son stepped inside to announce that buffalo herds were not far from the lower village, about 6 miles [away]. The Mandans would ride out tomorrow [and asked] whether [we] desired to send hunters, too. Belhumeur wants to [do so]. The Arikara, present by chance, offered to shoot for the fort if they gave him a horse.

23 January: Three engagés, together with the Arikara, rode out early to hunt buffalo. After breakfast Charbonneau traveled to Bijou [at] the Hidatsa village to look for meat.

24[–25] January: The Arikara and the [engagés] returned in the night. They had shot two cows and a young bull; the Mandans likely shot 50 [head]. Two of the three slain animals were brought to the fort, [so] we had meat again.

[The following day] the Arikara invited us to Belhumeur's room for lunch, or as they say here, for a feast. He had cooked buffalo cow meat. We sat around the fireplace. Three Arikara women and [a] Mandan were present. Men worked all day long in the [central] yard of the fort to remove the deep snow [that had] blown in [and] frozen hard. At four o'clock Charbonneau returned with meat and some buffalo tongues. The night was stormy.

26[–27] January: Sunday. Strong northwest wind; very cold. We worked at home. Síh-Chidä came in the afternoon. [Night] clear, cold, [and] bright like daylight, with the most beautiful full moon and stars. [Next] morning, at seven thirty, –3°F. Síh-Chidä left us.

28 January: After breakfast Charbonneau went to the uppermost Hidatsa [village]. I asked him to bring me an [antelope], if possible. Dreidoppel went across the river into the forest but found a lot of snow there: sometimes [it] supported him, sometimes [he] broke through. He saw nothing but a few titmice *(Parus atricapillus)*.

29 January: In the morning, the sun had two short, beautiful, [rainbow-like parhelia] on both sides. Charbonneau returned, [with] no meat; the Hidatsa hunters had not yet come back from their hunt.

At three o'clock we heard a drum. Lo and behold, the women of the White Buffalo Cow [Society] from Ruhptare marched in. They were dressed like the ones [we] recently saw from Mih-Tutta-Hangkusch. On their caps they [wore] eagle owl, crow, and a few red-colored feathers. Two wore skunk skins around their heads, [and] one wore the skin of a white buffalo cow. The music was played by three men, [who] also wore white buffalo caps. After they danced they received tobacco, *rassade,* and a knife, [and] they left. Síh-Chidä spent the night in our [quarters].

30 January: About four [thirty] in the afternoon, Mr. Kipp returned with three [or] four sleds, sled dogs, [and] six men. They were covered with ice; their noses and cheeks all [looked frostbitten. After a] four-day stay with the Hidatsas, Mr. Kipp took twelve days [to get] to Fort Union. At the beginning they had nothing to eat, and his dogs starved for nine days—[so deprived] that they staggered. [Since the dogs] could not be loaded down, [the travelers] had to make the trip mostly on foot. [Mr. Kipp] met a small war party of nine Assiniboines; some ran away; he sent the others out to hunt. [This provided] buffalo meat for several days; his men also shot deer and elk. At Fort Union the thermometer supposedly registered –45°F for more than fourteen days. There were no buffalo nearby; the fort's hunters [were out] for twenty-nine days and took only two bulls, two cows, and one calf. People were starving this winter along the Missouri from Fort Clark on upriver, [although] there was no news yet from Fort McKenzie. Mr. Hamilton wrote to me that they could not send me the items [I] requested, because the sleds

were overloaded, but everything would be [taken care of] in spring. Kipp's return trip took eleven days, mostly on foot again. When he arrived, his dogs had not eaten for three days, [yet] they got [only] some cut-up buffalo skins, because there was no meat.

31 January: In the morning, half-clear sky, very warm, 22°F; [we were] scarcely able to stand the fire. At noon [or] twelve thirty, 33°F, [a] complete thaw. [Such] unusual temperatures cause colds.

1 February: Today Mr. Kipp sent three engagés with two dogsleds downriver to Picotte, to get meat and a few other things. They [were] ready early [and] hitched the dogs, who howled pitifully, because their feet were still bloody and sore from the last trek [and now] they had to leave again. Animals, dogs as well as horses, are terribly maltreated in this country.

Mr. Bodmer went into Dipäuch's lodge in the [summer] village to draw its interior precisely. Mató-Tópe visited us and stayed through noon. Charbonneau traveled to Bijou at the Hidatsa [villages]. For lunch we had nothing but corn soup and cornbread; we will have no meat for at least four more days.

2 February: At seven thirty, 37½°F. Our indoor thermometer had been below the freezing point in the morning for 59 days, since 5 December. [There was a] significant thaw, [with] much water on the river [ice].

One of the sleds sent to Picotte returned; it had broken down because they had to occasionally travel over sand and soil. Charbonneau came back from the Hidatsas, from whom the Assiniboines had stolen three horses last night. One hundred fifty Hidatsas saddled up to pursue and kill the thieves.

3 February: The change in the weather [and] the [appearance] of the whole area was quite remarkable. Over half the snow was gone. The prairie and the hills were only spotted with snow; large stretches were bare of [it]. Rarely have I experienced such a fast change. At seven thirty, 39°F. The magpies and ravens [flew] again on the open prairie, looking for food.

News came at noon that the pursuing Hidatsas had killed one Assiniboine, whom they found asleep. They woke him with whiplashes, killed him, and continued their pursuit of the other Assiniboines.

The Assiniboines are a fearless, bold people. They approach the Mandan and Hidatsa villages in [all seasons] and occasionally shoot people in or near [them]. An Assiniboine shot into a group of young men who stood at a village stockade fence and killed one of them. The others ran into the village and sounded an alarm. During that time the Assiniboine ripped off the scalp of the [man] who was shot, [then] ran down the steep bank to the river [and] through the midst of many people bathing [there]. Other Assiniboines stole eleven horses from a Hidatsa lodge in a village, and only [as the thieves took] the last one did [the Hidatsas] notice. [And] lately, in the Hidatsa villages, arrows have been seen stuck in [door]jambs and lodges — where Assiniboines lying in ambush had shot at people walking from one lodge to another in the evening.

4 February: Early in the morning, a young Indian came [to the fort]. He was carrying a hand [tied] to a stick [with a] piece of string; [the hand] had been cut off the Assiniboine shot yesterday. A crowd of children surrounded him. Síh-Sä took the barbaric trophy away from him and [then] happily carried it around [himself]. Belhumeur went buffalo hunting on horseback with three men and eight horses. At twelve o'clock, 54°F; the snow diminished more and more.

Charbonneau was absent again today. This 75-year-old man was always chasing women.

5 February: It froze a little during the night, [but] the snow [cover] was greatly diminished everywhere; horses grazed on the prairie again. The wagons went out to get hay. The creek behind the fort flowed rapidly, [although] ice was still visible in places.

At dusk Belhumeur returned without [even] half an ounce of meat. He had not come across any buffalo at all. Now we have neither meat nor [tallow for] candles. One of the two deaf-mutes, who had pursued the Assiniboines with the Hidatsas, walked around the fort with his face blackened to show his pride in the heroic feats of others.

6 February: A thin layer of ice had frozen over the small water channels on the river. About nine o'clock the wind turned and blew anew out of the north; dark clouds rose in that direction, and it became raw.

A tall, handsome Mandan (Upsichtá, or Great Darkness) came to us and was willing to be drawn. [His visage] was captured extremely well. Later Mató-Tópe came, too. In the evening, in our room, we could hear the loud, high-[pitched] bark of schäháckäs [near] the fort. This evening Kipp wrote to Picotte at the Yanktonai post, [asking him to] send us meat and fat for candles as soon as possible; today we used almost the last [of the] tallow candles. These things [could be gotten from Picotte] in four to five days at the earliest.

7 February: At daybreak, the three engagés selected for the mission to Picotte

started moving out. They had two horse sleds loaded with corn and were supposed to bring back meat, fat, and perhaps other things. Old De l'Orme and Papin accompanied them to pick up their things [at Picotte's]; [they will] return afterward. Charbonneau lent them his sled (cariole). When we were at breakfast, news came that there were buffalo herds a short distance away across the river. The Indians in the lower forest village were informed by [men] from Ruhptare; [the latter] had made the discovery and wanted [everyone to] go hunting together. At Mih-Tutta-Hangkusch, [people] could be seen driving their horses [in] from the prairie. Mató-Tópe [visited us and,] about ten o'clock, Upsichtá [as well]. This tall Indian had counted many coups. He killed three Assiniboines in a skirmish, [and] in 1822 he caught [an Assiniboine] in the water and held him under until he drowned.

8 February: The hunters, Belhumeur and F. Contois (from Fort Union, a half-breed Cree) and another engagé, moved out very early to hunt buffalo with the Mandans and Hidatsas. They had excellent weather [for this].

Old Addíh-Hiddísch stayed in the fort today. He wanted me to [give him] salt, for telling me so many words. He was tattooed with bluish black horizontal stripes, not only on his chest, arms, and hands, but on his legs as well. I had never seen such a heavily tattooed American [Indian]. Upsichtá did not go hunting [but instead] came to our room.

Today they cleaned the crate of the larger bear; [this was difficult] work because he was angry and did not [appreciate the attention]. It was thawing significantly again, and water was running in the creek. The ground was muddy on top, but the soil was frozen many feet deep. Today we have been at Fort Clark for exactly three months—[this should be] over half of our stay here, God willing!

Belhumeur and Contois returned in the afternoon. [While] they were riding [in pursuit of buffalo], they saw an Indian on the distant hills; [he] fired his gun to [indicate that] he had something to tell them. It was Bull's Neck, who said [he] had seen about 300 Sioux and had therefore turned back. Our hunters also returned because of [the Sioux, so] again we got no meat.

9 February: (Sunday). The sun shone very warmly. It was thawing on the surface everywhere, and water was running in the creeks and ravines. Many women carried loads, especially wood, from the lower forest village to Mih-Tutta-Hangkusch. They had to cross a recently formed channel on the ice [near] the fort. It was covered with thin ice, [which] they broke with poles

and [then] waded through. It was noteworthy to see how they put [such] heavy loads on their backs. The wood lies on the ground, tied together. The woman lies down with her back on [top of the bundle], and another person lifts the wood up with her until she can lean forward and stand up [under the weight]. The frozen river was covered with individual women carrying [burdens] to the village. The Indians [had decided] to move back because they were too scattered [and] enemies [were near].

The deaf-mute with the blackened face, Máhchsi-Níhka (Young War Eagle), was drawn full-figure. On his head he wore the tail feather of a cock [and] nine wooden pegs representing wounds received or shots into his clothing; [his] face [was painted] black. He and his two deaf-mute siblings belong to a prosperous family; his brother is a berdache and works [hard]; he is a strong man. I met Dreidoppel on the prairie about noon; he had not seen anything. We looked for the lost mousetrap, [the one set on 11 December,] but there was still too much snow. Charbonneau [arrived] from Ruhptare, where all the inhabitants had already [left] their forest [village] because they were afraid of early ice drift and high water. In Mih-Tutta-Hangkusch, perhaps twenty families moved in today.

10 February: In the morning, the ground was lightly covered with snow. The wind out of the north was strong, cold, and raw, as it had been all night long. Our room [was] full of smoke. Two of our men came back from Picotte's with two dogs and one sled. They brought news that many buffalo and Indians were in the region. It had been colder [there] than anyone could remember for many years. The thermometer indicated −30°F and −40°F for a long time. Three of Mr. Laidlaw's men had frozen terribly as they traveled. Two froze their legs up to their bodies [and] would surely die.

I wrote a letter to Mr. McKenzie this afternoon, because tomorrow men would leave for Fort Union. In the evening Kipp [had to] take care of the papers he needed to send, so we returned to our room early. We had candles again.

11 February: [The men] left early [for] Fort Union, [carrying] letters to Mr. McKenzie. The whole fort filled gradually with Hidatsas—tall, strong men, mostly with black-painted faces [but occasionally] some red, too—[all] well dressed. La Chevelure Levée (Bídda-Chóhki) and [Red Shield] arrived as well. The latter is the man who offered his wife to us at the buffalo medicine [ceremony] in Dougherty's village. [From] these people we learned that their buffalo hunters had fought with the

Assiniboines; the skirmish outcome was not yet known.

The rooms were all full [of] Hidatsas, who took the best places at the fire; [they were] not as well behaved as the Mandans. We kept quiet in our room with the door bolted and admitted only a few Indians. After two o'clock [eighteen Hidatsa] women came, accompanied by many children and a few Mandans. [The] women moved in pairs in a close column into the yard of the fort, [taking] slow, short steps. Seven men from the Dog Society supplied the music: three had drums; four [had] *chichikués,* short sticks about one foot long, hung densely with animal hooves. The women marched up in a semicircle. [Their] faces were painted: some black, some red, some red and black striped. Most wore robes; some, colorful woolen blankets; a few, white buffalo skins. On their heads most wore an upright war eagle feather; one [had] a long trailing crown of feathers. They carried battle-axes or guns decorated with red cloth and [clipped] black feathers. [They were,] in short, dressed like warriors.

The wife of a chief, Itsicháichä, stood on the right wing. In her right hand she carried a long, thin pole. A scalp [was] hung from the top, [and] above that, a stuffed magpie with its wings spread; a second scalp, a lynx skin, and many feathers were hung farther down the pole. Opposite her, another woman carried a third scalp on a similar long pole. After they had arranged themselves in a semicircle, the music began. The men sang with a tremolo and [vigorously] drummed and rattled. The women began to dance, [taking] short steps, like ducks. [The two] ends of the semicircle moved [first] toward and [then] away from each other. [While dancing,] they sang in clear, piercing voices, [sounding] like mistreated cats. This lasted a while, then they rested a bit, and [then] the dance continued for perhaps twenty minutes. Mr. Kipp had [someone] throw to them, on the ground in the center of the circle, tobacco, knives, and small mirrors from the store. They danced once more, in a faster rhythm; the event thus came to an end, and they departed for the lower Mandan village.

All the Hidatsas left the fort [that] afternoon, so we were completely without Indians in the evening. Snow, more than an inch, fell during the night.

12 February: Garreau, a deceitful old man, asked the deaf-mute Mandan why he had allowed himself to be portrayed in such poor attire, since all the other Indians who were [painted] were dressed up. This upset [his] limited mind, [and] he complained [to us] with violent gestures. All our efforts to make

him understand that we wanted to draw him in his simple warriorlike attire were in vain. Bodmer made a copy of the drawing; he planned to show it to the Indian, tear it up, and throw [the pieces] into the fire to pacify him.

This morning for the first time in four weeks I saw a small flock of finches near the fort, *Fringilla linaria*. About ten o'clock, the fort was filled with Hidatsas, who were on their way back [from the Mandan village]. The chiefs and the most respected men sat in Kipp's room, where they smoked and ate. Almost none of them could speak the Mandan language. [Itsicháichä], a sly, [unreliable] Indian, wore a red, round white man's hat. He was the leader, and when he left, almost everyone else followed him. [Red Shield and] his family sat in our room. They looked at Bodmer's drawings and listened to his music box. Every one [of them] demanded something, and they would have stolen [anything] if we had not watched them constantly. All of them asked for [food]. We directed them to Kipp, as we had nothing to eat ourselves, whereupon they went home.

In the afternoon, three sleds with meat from Picotte arrived. De l'Orme and Papin had changed their minds and stayed downriver.

13 February: Máhchsi-Karéhde's brother, Mándeh-Páhchu (Eagle Nose), came early and brought a flute [that he wanted to trade] for a European dog whistle and some red [paint]. We agreed to the exchange. [That afternoon,] our room was filled with Hidatsas; Síh-Chidä, who joined us, did not seem to be very pleased about this company [and] soon left. Charbonneau had gone to Ruhptare, [and] without him we could not cope very well with the many Hidatsas. They stayed [a while] and then left for Ruhptare. Dipäuch visited us and told [us] about various animals. We were able to make ourselves fairly well understood with the aid of signs. [Later], in Kipp's room and with his help, [Dipäuch] gave me an extensive description of the Okíppe festival. I wrote it all down; this lasted till late [in the evening].

14 February: Northwest wind. With the snow blown off it, the ice was very slippery everywhere. We saw several Indian women fall. Máhchsi-Karéhde's brother came in the afternoon. The music box greatly entertained [him]. He thought there was a little waschí (a white man) sitting in it who made the music.

15 February: It snowed a little. Durand [and] several Indians visited us. Mr. Kipp [said] the buffalo herds were still almost a three-day trip distant, too far away to hunt. The Hidatsas found a dead buffalo cow on the prairie. [It] smelled strong, but despite that [they] ate all the meat.

I went with Dreidoppel to Mih-Tutta-Hangkusch. A few flocks of snow buntings and *Fringilla linaria* swarmed around there. The wind was so cold that it would have damaged our ears if we had stayed [out very] long. In the evening we wrote down Hidatsa words [given by a] young Indian.

16 February: At midmorning the whole river was covered with Indian women dragging wood to Mih-Tutta-Hangkusch. Evening clear, calm, very cold; at nine o'clock, −2°F.

17 February: At daybreak, the water had frozen in our room, but not the ink. [A rise in the river meant] paths had to be found for the sleds [transporting] firewood across the ice to avoid the water. It snowed heavily in the afternoon. In the evening, Dipäuch told us a long story about the Corn Festival.

18 February: The sun rose brightly. The woodcutters brought such poor wood yesterday that [our room was not] warm at all; I was hardly able to write, [even] close to the fire. Today they went out early to the lower forest and were supposed to bring better firewood. Síh-Chidä slept at our place and was numb with cold. I gave him a small magnifying, or burning, glass in a green case, which made him very happy.

19 February: The sky that [at first] promised a bright day [became] cloudy. The wind changed from west to south several times. Dreidoppel returned from a hunt [with] a fine red fox *(Canis fulvus)*. He had lured [it], and when it came close, he shot it. It was different from the European [animal].

A few Hidatsas came and stated [with certainty] that the Assiniboines had shot one of the two engagés sent upriver to the Yellowstone by Mr. Dougherty (of the Sublette and Campbell Fur Company). The Arikara's son brought me a kind of mouse *(Arvicola)* that I did not know yet. [In the] evening the report of the dead engagé was withdrawn. The Indians often conveyed false news.

20 February: Kipp had to send a horse-drawn wagon to the Hidatsa [winter] village to pick up [Bijou's] merchandise and belongings, because [the Hidatsas had] moved back into their three [summer] villages.

21 February: Toward morning it became very cold. For the first time in a long time, the ink froze, and I had to thaw it.

An old Hidatsa chief, Kíhrapä-Süpischá (Black Buffalo [Bull]), was [here] this morning. He is one of the most respected men of his nation, a famous partisan and warrior. His robe was painted with all his heroic deeds: how many horses he had stolen, how many times he had been partisan, how many scalps he had brought home from [raids], how many enemies he had killed, and so on. I bought it from him for a new, white robe that cost me 5 dollars in the fort's store. Dreidoppel completed [preparing] his fox.

22 February: In the morning a large flock of snow buntings [was] near Mih-Tutta-Hangkusch. Many Indians went after them [and] caught several in horse-hair snares. At ten o'clock the sun on the snow glared [so intensely] that we could scarcely see. Dreidoppel therefore made Esqimaux snow-goggles from cottonwood to use while hunting.

Five Hidatsas knocked and were let into the room, although we did not know who they were. They were unpleasant guests, because they planted themselves in front of the fire with their thick robes and [appropriated what] little heat there was. [Despite] their pride and their contempt for white men, they begged at every opportunity. Today they demanded to-bacco, shirts, whiskey, Indian corn, etc. Many Mandans were present during lunch, among them Old Bear, or as he is now called, Mató-Óchka, [Crazy Bear]; [he] had somewhat red and inflamed eyes, which Kipp [treated with drops of] lead acetate.

In the afternoon thirty Indians could be counted walking back and forth on the ice at the same time. [Red Shield] visited us with two women but luckily did not stay long. He had a hand crippled [by] an Assiniboine gun-shot. (Most of these Indians had wounds; some [had] many and serious [ones].) On his chest he had four thick, parallel, horizontal [scars from] the cuts [made] during the penitence festival, [the incisions] through which straps were pulled.

The [deaf-]mute Mandan returned from hunting with six horses packed with buffalo meat. They had been away four to six days.

23 February: In the morning, the sun [was] a dim, yellowish spot in the fog. Neither animals nor people were to be seen, except for a few Indians who drove horses onto the prairie and a few dogs that followed them. About nine o'clock light snow fell. Máhchsi-Karéhde and Dipäuch visited us and smoked their pipes. We worked at home with ice-cold feet and hands. The [deaf-]mute Mandan brought fresh meat today, [which] we had for lunch, an event that had not occurred for a few months.

The afternoon [was] bright [and] cold. I heard a very loud scream in front of my door, and when I opened [it], I found the tall Arikara's child, who had touched the rail of a sled runner with its tongue and was im-mediately frozen to it; [the child] had already torn itself loose, but the skin remained stuck and [the] tongue was covered with blood. The child screamed terribly.

24 February: At daybreak, −27°F. In our room everything had frozen. Our blankets and robes [were] covered with hoarfrost, [and] the hair and eyelashes of the Indians who came into the fort [were coated in] ice. We had fresh meat again this morning, but our sugar will run out soon—we will have to drink molasses with [our] coffee. Several Indians, including Mató-Tópe, sat all morning in our room.

About noon, Kiäsax, the Piegan who had traveled with us to Fort Union and then returned [to Fort Clark] again by steamboat, visited us for the first time. We told him [about our journey] and showed him the Piegan portraits, which he found very entertaining. Then other Indians came; in short, our room was full all day long. The black[-faced] deaf-mute brought me the machtóhpka, the gopher with large cheek-pouches.

25 February: The sun rose brightly. [It was] very cold, the air filled with ice particles. Chárätä-Numakschi came into the fort early; Mató-Tópe [arrived] later. I described the gopher. The evening [was warmer]; at nine o'clock, 30°F.

26 February: Today two men cut ice on the river for the ice cellar. Mató-Tópe came for a moment to get paints; he was drawing something for me. At noon there was already much water on [the river ice; it was] 38½°F. In the afternoon whole Indian families moved back to the [summer] village. They all had three to four horses; even the foals [were] saddled, and some were loaded. The wind turned raw and cold.

27 February: They cut [more] ice on the river. Indian women also carried ice into the village to melt water from it. About ten o'clock Durand visited [and] said someone claimed to have seen ducks yesterday. Síh-Chidä [brought] his five-year-old child. Mató-Tópe came, [with] an interesting drawing he had done, [depicting] some of his feats. [After] lunch, we [entertained] Máhchsi-Karéhde, and soon Kähka-Chamahän [as well], a funny, intelligent, elderly man, with large, lively eyes. He cracked all kinds of jokes.

The prairie snow was almost gone. Scattered horses grazed everywhere, as far as the distant hills. About evening Indian boys played, [sliding] down the snowbanks, frequently [on] a piece of a buffalo backbone with four to five or six ribs [still] attached; they sat down in this and [shot] down as fast as an arrow.

28 February: [A Hidatsa] partisan arrived to be pictured and was drawn full-figure.

Síh-Chidä came for a moment. Mató-Tópe came in the afternoon. He wore a strange headdress that would have better suited an old woman. A strip of wolfskin, the long hairs standing apart like rays, was wound around his head and trailed far down his back. Single feathers, pointing outward, were attached to the wolf hair. [They] had been stripped, except at the tips of the vanes—the bare shafts were painted red.

Toward evening, two men sent upriver by Picotte arrived with completely unexpected mail from St. Louis. I received a letter from Germany that contained enclosures [dating] from July, August, and September 1833. Family news, all very good. Happily, [my niece] Luitgarde gave birth to a son.

1 March: In the night [there was a] severe storm that let up a little about morning. Mató-Tópe and Old Bear were in the fort early. Then the two great soldiers and comrades [arrived], Dipäuch and Beróck-Itaïnú. In the afternoon, the Hidatsa, Biróhkä, was drawn with his white buffalo cap. The Mandans call him Páhchub-Háschka (Long Nose). He demanded a black silk neckerchief [to sit] for the drawing, which he did not like at all. Síh-Chidä and Mahchsi-Berrockä came. The former had done some drawings for me; the latter, a native Crow, gave me words of his language. Kipp's [pregnant] wife, a Mandan, left him [to go back to her village]. [Dipäuch] gave me Cheyenne words in the evening, [which was] calm [and] starlit.

2 March: The forests [were] covered with hoarfrost, [but] the day turned warm [by] noon. Síh-Chidä fetched some buckshot and shot a sipúska, [a grouse or prairie chicken,] for me. About noon Belhumeur and Hugron departed with a dog travois [and] letters to Fort Union; they will return at the end of March with my canoe guides.

Now that all the Indians had moved to their summer villages, Mr. Kipp employed four respected men as protective guards against the women and children.[1] They are called the soldiers (les soldats) of the fort. Today Dipäuch and Beróck-Itaïnú (Bull's Neck), the oldest brother of the three deaf-mutes, [served] that function. Tomorrow it will be Mató-Tópe's and another man's turn. They get food but no pay.

The sunset was beautiful. Our room was a guesthouse for the Indians. We had to keep a lot of tobacco ready.

3 March: Bodmer went with Síh-Chidä to Ruhptare, where the Meníss-Óchatä were dancing. The great soldat, Dipäuch, said that I should go and talk to Kipp. There I found out that [Dipäuch planned to] perform a medicine ritual with his pipe and was collecting gifts for this purpose. I gave

him a knife, and he was much pleased.

Kipp had a discussion with [some] Indians, including Dipäuch, who was very eager for knowledge and liked to talk about scientific matters. Kipp asserted that the earth is round, which they tried to refute in several ways. Dipäuch smirked pityingly, [and] Beróck-Itaïnú laughed aloud at the simple-mindedness of the waschís. Only two were of the opinion that white men likely knew better, since they understood so much.

[When] Bodmer returned, he brought a beautiful male *Fringilla linaria* with a very red breast but a little too much riddled with shot. In the evening Mató-Tópe explained the drawings he had made of his heroic achievements.

4 March: The weather [was] singularly beautiful till nine o'clock, [and] then [there was a] strong raw wind. I took a walk to the creek but still could not find my mousetrap. I saw no living things other than ravens and horses grazing [on] the prairie. Síh-Chidä came [in the afternoon]; I drew soldiers for him. Máhchsi-Karéhde slept at our place.

5 March: Snowstorm about daybreak, sky heavily overcast. Máhchsi-Karéhde was here almost all morning, [but] in the afternoon we were without any Indians [as we] worked at home.

6 March: Mató-Tópe came and brought the Arikara, Pachtüwa-Chtä, who was to be drawn. He was a well-dressed and handsome [but] wicked [fellow] who had shot or killed many white men.

Dreidoppel went to the forest across the river, but there were so many women there [gathering wood] that he [saw no] animals, except for a few prairie hens. For Mató-Tópe, [Bodmer] had to draw a [bald eagle] holding a scalp in its bloody claws. About four o'clock it started to snow. The weather was too changeable; no two days [were] the same.

7 March: In the morning, cold, the whole area covered with 2 to 3 inches of snow. Chárätä-Numakschi and a few other Mandans [were] in Kipp's room, Máhchsi-Karéhde and the Arikara at ours. In the afternoon it snowed heavily again. I had to draw a bear for the Arikara and a hussar for Máhchsi-Karéhde. The Arikara wanted a forest on his picture. [When] I assured him I was not capable of doing that, they said among themselves [that trees must] be my medicine.

About evening the Ruhptare Dog Society (Meníss-Óchatä) danced at Mih-Tutta-Hangkusch. Bodmer went to see it. [Later, those dancers] marched to the fort, a crowd of people swarming around them. We heard their war whistles outside the gate. Twenty-seven to twenty-eight men formed a circle. All of them were dressed in their best—some in beautiful robes, a few with bighorn shirts, others in red cloth shirts or European uniform overcoats, yet others with bare upper bodies on which [their] coups and wounds were painted in reddish brown. Four of them—the leading, or real, Dogs—wore enormous bonnets or caps on their heads, [made] of densely arranged raven tail feathers, [with] small down feathers attached [to each raven feather] tip. In the middle of [each] mass of feathers, the beautiful white and black tail of a war eagle stood upright, attached in a line reaching from front to back. When they danced, the feathers rocked up and down. Two other men wore bonnets just as enormous as [those of] the real Dogs [but made] of eagle owl feathers, and one wore the large, beautiful máhchsi-akub-háschka. All others wore thick tufts of feathers on their heads. They all [had] war whistles [and carried] weapons—guns, bows, etc.—[and] the *chichikué* [of] this society, decorated with blue and white *rassade* and festooned with animal hooves. From the tip [of the rattle], a single war eagle feather was usually hung, either left white or tinted red.

They set a drum on the ground in the circle, beaten by five seated men. Beside them stood two additional men, each one beating a small drum similar to a tambourine. The Dogs accompanied the intense, rapidly repeated drumbeats [with] their war whistles, [blowing] short, repetitive notes.

They suddenly began to dance, dropping their robes behind them on the ground. Some danced in the center of the circle; the others danced around them in no particular order, facing the inside [of the circle]. They were crowded close together, and once in a while they all lowered their heads and upper bodies, whistling together on their war whistles [while] the drummers beat concurrently [and] intensely; the *chichikués* were rattled at the same time. The view was extraordinary and novel: the head-feathers bouncing up and down, the wild noise, the whistling [and] drumming, the colorful, diverse masquerade—a remarkable scene for a stranger!

8 March: The Indian boys caught snow buntings again, as they had on previous days, but we could not get any [birds] from them, because they were too hungry and ate them immediately. Our coffee was so weak this morning that we could hardly drink it. Our provisions of this good plant were meager; we had to be very economical. The Indians stayed till about three o'clock. I wrote down Arikara words. Máhchsi-Karéhde brought red willow wood for tobacco. Crazy Bear brought his shield (that Catlin had painted very miserably for him in oil) and laid it down in our room. Dreidoppel,

[out hunting again,] shot two white rabbits near the hills [and] set snares for [other animals]. Charbonneau was with the Hidatsas. The buffalo were supposed to be en masse not far away, and [the Hidatsas] all wanted to go hunting.

9 March: Dreidoppel checked his snares early. [A] fox had been caught [but got away because] the wire was no good. Mató-Tópe, Dipäuch, Beróck-Itaïnú, Péhriska-Rúhpa, and Máhchsi-Karéhde were in our room. The latter was drawn. It [began] to snow heavily and continued the whole afternoon. To-day we ate rabbit twice; game [was] an agreeable change for our stomachs. In the afternoon I had to draw soldiers for Máhchsi-Karéhde. Síh-Chidä sketched Ochkíh-Häddä [in] pencil, [then] wanted to draw [this figure] in color. At nine o'clock [that evening] there were two [gun]shots close to us. I found out later that the engagés had shot rats in their room.

10 March: Mató-Tópe and the Arikara came, [and the drawing of the latter] was completed in the afternoon by three o'clock.

[This morning] most of the Mandans went buffalo hunting; they will likely stay [out] fourteen days. Another party went to the other side of the Missouri. Two of Picotte's men arrived with letters, dried meat, and a dog-sled. One was [temporarily] snowblinded and [had to be] led by the other man.

11 March: All of us have felt rheumatic pain for two days, and I had a [badly] swollen knee. Kipp had severe headaches for several days; Bodmer alternately had toothaches and headaches; Dreidoppel had frequent pain in his knees, back, and head.

Today, on my good sister [Louise's] birthday, we were in a very sad state. We had weak, horrible coffee for breakfast. Instead of sugar we had honey, [of which only] 20 pounds [was] left, and when this ran out in about ten days, we would have just molasses. We had no wine or other spirits to drink a toast to [Louise].

We were extremely tired of life in this dirty fort. Filth everywhere was the disgusting order of the day. Because the Negro, our cook (Alfred), suffered from a serious venereal disease, we had another slovenly cook and waiter, Boileau, who wore a fur cap on his head. He sat down with us and reached for cups and plates with his disgusting fists after having cleaned his nose in the fashion of our farmers. The clerk of the fort, Kipp, and his wife and child, behaved similarly. They threw things around and wiped their fingers on the first available object. The little boy had an opening in the front and the back of his pants, so that he could relieve himself instantly on the floor of the room—and this often happened during meals. The indolence and indifference of this otherwise quite good man went so far that he relieved himself beside the fort in front of everyone. He did not even have a privy built for this purpose. In short, the sojourn here was a difficult test, especially [considering] the severe cold in our "smokehouse," open [to the weather] on all sides.

At nine o'clock the wind rose again. Mándeh-Páhchu came with his father, Mahchsi-Berrockä; [he was] nicely dressed and [was] drawn.

12 March: Old Addíh-Hiddísch did not want to be drawn. He was going beaver hunting soon, [and after he] returned, would be better dressed. This was likely only an excuse. The [deaf-]mute Mandans brought fresh meat again—they were good, hard-working hunters.

Mándeh-Páhchu came to be drawn, but Péhriska-Rúhpa [arrived] far better dressed, [so] he was sketched; [the portrait session continued through] the afternoon.[2] The ground thawed a little on the surface. In the evening the wind abated; it was pleasant and not cold. Kipp wrote letters until late in the night, because he intended to send Picotte's [engagés] back tomorrow.

13 March: Picotte's two men went back downriver with letters. Today we had fresh meat for breakfast, an exceptional rarity, [and] even a few eggs, because the chickens were laying [again]—a sumptuous breakfast! Péhriska-Rúhpa came early to be drawn. His toilette took at least an hour. The ground was not frozen anywhere this morning, but the thaw was [slow] because there was no sunshine. Mató-Tópe visited us; [he] left after lunch, and Dreidoppel [went] hunting. In the afternoon the homely wife of Péhriska-Rúhpa appeared; [she] sat by our fire, stuck [there] like a burr. Few Indians came to the fort now; most had gone buffalo hunting and would not likely return before the end of March.

Today we saw the first ducks winging up the Missouri, doubtless *Anas boschas*. The evening was rather warm and pleasant, windless, and the sun was still shining at sundown. All the young people gathered next to Mih-Tutta-Hangkusch to play. In the evening we drank tea with sugar in place of our daily honey, which did our stomachs much good.

14 March: This morning we had the last of the dried meat. Mr. Kipp heard the first male prairie hen today, performing its courtship [display].

In the afternoon Péhriska-Rúhpa took a long time to dress in the outfit of the Dog Society. For that purpose he wore the large, black bonnet of magpie tail feathers with a beautiful wild turkey tail in its center. Around his neck [there was] a war whistle, [and] down his back, two broad strips of cloth, a red one on his left shoulder, a blue one on his right—[they] came together in front and hung down low in the back; [see pl. 27].

Dreidoppel brought back seeds that he found lying on the [pads?] of a cactus plant in the prairie hills. [He also] fetched a nice buffalo skull, which we [were] lacking.

15 March: Our meat was completely gone. We breakfasted on coffee with honey. Luckily, each of us received two fresh eggs and indigestible cornbread. The weather was pleasant. Indian youths played around the fort [with] a woven [netted] disk; they rolled it and [then] thrust or tossed a stick through it. Whoever hit the right spot or got closest won. Mató-Tópe [arrived] and told us there were many buffalo near the Hidatsa villages. We gave him buckshot to shoot other game that was expected to also be there.

We had nothing for lunch but corn boiled in water and cornbread; Kipp, who does not like corn, remained hungry.

16 March: Early [today] we saw a swan flying in a northwesterly direction. Birds arriving now could not stay here, because they would find no open water. [It] was Sunday; therefore, as a rare exception, we had rice soup and cornbread for lunch. In the evening [they served] *crêpes* (thin pancakes with flour and fat but no eggs or milk) [and] molasses, [with] weak coffee and honey to drink. I stayed at home and did not eat.

17 March: Heavy snow fell for an hour and a half, [and] then the weather cleared. The blacksmith sent his wife away, because she spent time with other men; in her place he took a horse into his small hut. The Missouri was rising, [but] the ice could not be expected to disappear [just yet; the water level would] soon subside again. When the Rocky Mountain snow[melt] comes, the ice cover breaks, and the drift ice usually passes within three to four days.

18 March: Windy and raw all day long. Our lives were pitiful—we had nothing [to eat] but corn; for the sick and on Sunday for the others, [there was] a little rice. My condition [remained] the same, [and I] left neither room nor bed.

19 March: Síh-Chidä brought his shield to have a bird painted on it. Kipp received—what a miracle!—a buffalo tongue. In the afternoon we heard that there were many buffalo about two hours from Ruhptare. Unfortunately, most of the Indians were away with their horses.

20 March: The river was still rising. No one walked across the ice anymore. Kipp

sent Síh-Sä out on horseback to look for buffalo today. Mándeh-Páhchu came to [be] drawn. Mató-Tópe and Péhriska-Rúhpa arrived in the afternoon. They had shot five buffalo and gave away most of the meat. Kipp received some, [and] we [got] two [buffalo] tongues. Síh-Sä, with other Indians, shot a [buffalo]; he also brought meat.

21 March: Early in the morning, bright, strong east wind. The Hidatsas returned with a great deal of meat; Charbonneau went to the villages. Someone saw the first [bald] eagle today.

22 March: Heavy snow fell. Mató-Tópe and Péhriska-Rúhpa came [and] stayed a long while with us.

23 March: The river rose overnight, [perhaps] one foot. Síh-Sä was drawn today. The Hidatsas reportedly came across a Sioux tent and killed all [the] inhabitants. I spent today and yesterday in bed. [In the] afternoon, snow. Evening calm.

24 March: The ice was moving and had piled up in some areas of the river. The Mandans arrived with meat. Kipp's wife delivered a daughter this morning at Mih-Tutta-Hangkusch. I had a bad day.

25 March: Overcast in the morning; [that afternoon,] snow until five o'clock. Mató-Tópe was in our room. Dougherty visited us as well. [Later on], I began to treat my foot with moist heat and sage, which made it worse. The news about the Dacota lodge [was] corrected—[just] one person was supposed to have been murdered.

26 March: In the morning, clear, cold. At eight o'clock, 16°F. They believed [that] the river [ice] would break [up] soon. Addíh-Hiddísch was drawn. It snowed intermittently all day long. I [treated my foot with heat and] sage.

27 March: Addíh-Hiddísch's [portrait was continued]. It was cloudy, and at twelve o'clock, 41°F. In the afternoon, the Crazy Dogs danced in the fort, and at dusk a man from Ruhptare who had argued with Kipp over the price of a beaver trap broke a window in the room adjoining ours. They pursued him unsuccessfully.

28 March: In the morning, winter; heavy snow. Kipp's wife returned from the village today with her [newborn] child.

29 March: The river dropped more than 3 feet. I did not have a good day. The night [was] calm.

30 March: (First day of Easter.) The Mandans went hunting again, as buffalo were said to be not far away. At ten o'clock we saw the first flock of wild geese migrating up the Missouri. Some Mandans returned without

anything; others continued to hunt.

31 March: We saw a flock of ducks early. The wind blew stormily all day. Much ice [near] the riverbank broke loose. News came that Assiniboines had killed [some] beaver-hunting Mandans and captured a woman.

1 April: Mató-Tópe came early, then Péhriska-Rúhpa, who [sat] until evening, stuck [to us] like a leech. The news of the Assiniboine attack was confirmed: the Hidatsas and Mandans had abandoned a poor woman who was [then] captured by the enemy. Today the Mandans shot the first wild geese. Pieces on the edge of the ice broke loose; their color [was] blackish.

2 April: Today the Mih-Tutta-Hangkusch women celebrated the corn festival, or the dedication of the corn. [By] eleven o'clock, the festivity was finished, [but] three women remained near the offerings all day. The young people held races.

3 April: Bright sunshine in the morning. Síh-Chidä visited us, and I gave Péhriska-Rúhpa a buffalo skin to be painted [for me]. Today, ducks and geese [were seen] in fair numbers, [and] we saw the first crows (Corvus corone americana). Large sheets of ice broke loose in the river. We looked forward to the impending departure of the ice. Kipp [assigned] someone to guard our boats [from the rising water] during the night. The band of Íschohä-Kakoschóchatä from Mih-Tutta-Hangkusch danced in the fort.³ Mató-Tópe led them on horseback and wore the máhchsi-akub-háschka on his head. The [dancers] were given knives, mirrors, and tobacco.

4 April: At eleven o'clock the river started [to flow] but soon stopped again. A broad channel opened, clogged up, [then] opened again. The water level was low and little noise was heard. [There were] many ducks and geese and a curlew on the ice in the afternoon. Bodmer drew the blacksmith's Arikara wife.

5 April: About midday [the river] suddenly rose by three to four feet, and at twelve o'clock the upper ice broke loose; [it was] 68°F, [with a] strong south wind.

6 April: Clear [and] calm this morning; a little frost during the night. There was already less ice floating on the river. It dropped one foot last night and was still dropping. Today I received two Arctomys hoodii. Dreidoppel found the big lark on the creek. At twelve o'clock, 78°F, at nine o'clock [that evening], 55°F.

7 April: Only a little ice floated on the river now; [the level had] dropped somewhat during the night. Two swans were seen today. The wind was very strong.

8 April: We saw a flock of 26 swans moving upriver. The Hidatsas danced a Scalp

Dance in the fort today. [Then,] at one o'clock, [there was] a huge ice drift that carried many tree trunks downstream, endangering our boats. The Indians landed much wood [and] a drowned elk, already [decomposing], which they ate. Our blacksmith fetched some meat from it for himself. The drift ice had diminished greatly by evening, [but] some men who had planned to go downriver to Picotte now had to stay here.

9 April: Almost all the ice [was] gone. Seven men [left for Picotte's] in [bullboats]. Mató-Tópe came in his most magnificent clothing. The Indians [continued to] fish quantities of wood out of the river. An anemone was blooming, actually a *Pulsatilla,* that the Indians call—in [English] translation—the red calf flower, because buffalo calves are born at this time [of year].

About evening nine men of the band Beróck-Óchatä (Bulls) appeared in the fort and fired their guns. Only one of them wore the whole buffalo head (see [chapter 18]). *Picus auratus* was shot today.

10 April: Bright, beautiful, [and] calm; the river dropped 3 feet last night. The Mandans have [gone off with] the Hidatsas on a raid. The night was stormy.

11 April: The Hidatsas [had] plundered some [white] beaver hunters, taking their horses, traps, beavers, [and] bedding. On the other hand, the Assiniboines stole 34 horses from [the Hidatsas], though [they] lost a man while doing it.

12 April: Mató-Tópe was drawn full-figure. The men [we] expected from Fort Union could not travel, because of the storm.

13 April: [An] even more severe storm during the night and in the morning; [again] we could not expect any men [from Fort Union]. Today Síh-Chidä took leave of us forever, because he was [going out] with a war party [and we would soon be departing].

14 April: About midday three men from upriver [appeared and] announced the [impending] arrival of Chardon and his people, [including Belhumeur,] from Fort Union. They brought letters and news from Forts Union and McKenzie; Doucette had been shot by Blood Indians. Now we had to wait for Picotte, whose men [would assist in] caulking our boat.

15 April: At ten o'clock Picotte's boat arrived with about twenty men. It was unloaded and [then] reloaded, [mostly with] corn.

16 April: Overcast, fog, cold. Our boat was readied for departure. Dreidoppel went with Charbonneau to the [nearby] site of Lewis and Clark's old [winter camp, Fort Mandan]. Toward evening, Picotte sailed for Fort Union.

17 April: [Work on] our equipment continued. It rained heavily the whole day, [but the winds were] calm.

18 April: Weather calm, bright, and nice. My [swollen] foot [was] like the day before. I had coffee, two eggs, and cornbread for breakfast. Kipp handed me the bill [for our stay].[4]

Chardon would travel with us to the [Bad River]. The crates for the bears [were prepared]. Mató-Tópe gave me a large, beautiful war whistle of swan bone. I gave him presents in return.

At midday, nice weather; calm; light wind. At twelve o'clock, 58½°F; the boat was loaded.[M2] After lunch, at about three o'clock, we took leave from Mr. Kipp and the inhabitants of the fort. Mató-Tópe, Péhriska-Rúhpa, and other Indians shook our hands. Our boat was equipped with a leather tent, where I stayed. I was led [on board], still quite lame.[5] A few cannon shots were fired in our honor.

We slid down the river. Now and then we could see just a little green on the prairie. We saw single ducks, wild geese, swans, and a few pelicans. Bodmer bagged a wood duck. Toward evening [the weather was] cool [and] windy; we lay to on the right bank. The boat was [secured] with ropes, a fire was lit in the forest, [and we] cooked.

[M2] At Fort Clark I left behind seven large crates with interesting natural history specimens and ethnographic objects; the [crate] numbers [were] XX, XXI, XXII, XXIII, XXIV, XXV, [and] XXVI. They were all lost [because of] the fire on a steamship. [Maximilian refers to the loss of the American Fur Company steamboat *Assiniboine* in July 1835. Jackson, *Voyages*, 112; Barbour, *Fort Union*, 244n40.]

XXI

Journey from Fort Clark to Cantonment Leavenworth

19 April: Our tame little prairie fox had unfortunately [escaped in the night]. After cooking [breakfast,] we set off. The wind was favorable and moderately strong. At twelve o'clock we reached the Heart River. The boat sprang a leak, which held us up for a long time. My men included the helmsman Fecteau, the Canadian Bourgua, the American Melone, and a Pole. At two thirty we reached Picotte's winter quarters and stopped there. Today we observed *Anas boschas, Anas acuta, clangula,* and teal, also paired prairie hens, a few woodpeckers, many birds of prey, robins, [and] turkey buzzards. [Stormy] night; rain [mixed] with snow.

20 April: Everything snow-covered; cold. Three hunters went out [but] saw nothing. I stayed on the boat, and my breakfast consisted of coffee, two egg yolks, two small potatoes, and cornbread. Unfortunately, I no longer had any greens to eat; my foot [bothered me].

Because of the [weather], we stayed on the bank, [where] our men found little protection in the sparse forest. About four o'clock it stopped snowing, [and] the wind abated in the evening. During the night we were alarmed by some game or a wolf; [we] believed Indians [were] close by. Chardon posted sentries.

21 April: Departure at five o'clock; at seven thirty, we sailed past the Cannonball River. Today we saw nothing green, [un]like yesterday, when some willows and roses were already green. At twelve o'clock, 51°F. Northeast wind; a little sunshine. Ahead of us we saw some antelope herds, [numbering] ten to twelve [animals each]; one [herd] was just crossing the river. We hurried but [were] too late. We saw individual buffalo bulls and a small herd of about fifty cows, but they were far away. Shortly before dusk we put in on the right bank; snow during the night.

22 April: A storm forced us to stay put; the boat was well tied down. Dreidoppel and Melone went hunting, [as did] Bodmer and Chardon. Toward noon the sky was clear [and] the sun shone, but the strong wind threatened to tear our poor-quality leather tent apart. [By] evening, calm.

23 April: In the morning, clear and nice. [Occasional] shrub thickets [showed] a slight greenish coloring, that is, new leaves; some bushy willows were already all green. We saw antelope on the prairie, turkey buzzards in the air, and the first turtledoves on the riverbanks. At twelve o'clock, we reached the two abandoned Arikara villages [and] landed immediately below them [on the west bank]. We lit fires and heated the cooked corn. Mr. Chardon and Bodmer went into the villages to look for skulls and to collect prairie onions for me. They found some graves opened by wolves [and] brought back two nicely bleached skulls. We then continued on. A few hours later, rain [drove us temporarily] ashore almost opposite the Grand River, 10 miles [downstream] from the Arikara villages.

[Another] severe storm out of the north at dusk; snow mixed with rain; the boat battered by such waves that it sprang a leak and took on much water. The men [camped on shore] had no shelter or firewood. We stayed awake all night long and frequently bailed water out of the boat. Toward midnight the [storm] let up, [but] then it froze hard.

24 April: In the morning, all [our] wet objects were frozen solid. Departure at six o'clock. [Later that morning], on the right bank, we saw [many] antelope and [other] game [but] could not go ashore and had to travel half an hour farther. Finally the hunters [could] disembark and attempted to approach the antelope. [However,] we got nothing, [although Dreidoppel] found a large prairie dog village and shot one of the animals. The evening [was] clear but cold. We put in on a steep bank opposite the mouth of Little Cheyenne [Creek].

25 April: Early departure at five o'clock. We saw two boats ahead of us and caught up [with them about nine]. They had lit fires on the bank, and we stopped a while, too. Ortubise and his wife were there [with some other company men], and their square skin boats were loaded with [hides, pelts, and/or furs]. [They] gave us some game and a swan. Dreidoppel collected [green] onions. We departed about eleven o'clock. I took along a certain Crenier, who had injured his hand, as well as a few Indian women. The heavily loaded leather boats, one of them steered by Ortubise, soon fell behind.[1]

[That] evening we stopped 15 to 20 miles above Fort Pierre. The leather boats joined us, and we bivouacked together. Night clear, calm.

26 April: We left early. The area was bare and monotonous. We [quickly] put the leather boats (which had left even earlier) behind us. The river had many

sandbars here, [and] we ran aground several times before the last turn to the right [toward] Fort Pierre. The men pulled and pushed in the water. There was still snow in the ravines on the hilltops [and] hardly any green on those bare elevations. About two o'clock we reached the Fort Pierre landing area [and] immediately went to the fort, where we were welcomed with a few cannon shots.

Fort Pierre was in good condition, neat and clean. The whole plain was covered with scattered Dacota tents—mostly Tetons [but] also several Yanktonais. We got a good room. Our boat was unloaded, because one could not trust the Indians, [who] might easily kill our bears out of hunger.

There was a considerable lack of fresh food, because here, too, there were no buffalo that winter. For today, Mr. Laidlaw bought an Indian dog for twelve dollars. Because of the lack of [alternatives], they had to eat dogs every day, so these were expensive and hard to obtain. However, they [otherwise] lived very well; bread, potatoes, cabbage, beets, various preserved fruits, rice, coffee, sugar, and tea rendered life far more bearable here than at [Fort Clark].

Today we (Mr. Laidlaw, Chardon, Papin, the interpreter Dorion, and us) were invited to a celebration in an Indian tipi. After we sat down on a new buffalo robe decorated with porcupine [quills], dog meat was taken out of the kettle. More and more Indians arrived and sat in a circle. The meat was very fat and looked blackish, like mutton. It was delicious, and [any] prejudice [against eating dog] was quickly overcome. Afterward there was smoking, [and] Mr. Laidlaw was given the robe that we sat on as a present. The host made a speech before we ate [in which] he talked about his devotion to the whites, and for that Mr. Laidlaw expressed his thanks through Dorion. We returned to [our quarters]. A large group of Dacotas stayed in Mr. Laidlaw's spacious living room the whole day. They came mainly to see us. Among them we found our friend Wáh-Menítu, happy to see us again and extremely friendly. Usually Mr. Laidlaw did not tolerate Indians in this room.

27 April: We looked at the company stores, where eighty thousand dollars worth of merchandise was housed. I bought several interesting Indian curiosities: 1. Dacota painted leather shirt, 6 dollars; 2. matching Dacota leggins, 3 dollars; 3. five pipes, 5 dollars; 4. raw pipestone, 1 dollar; 5. a large decorated medicine pipe, 10 dollars; 6. a pair of Indian pistol holsters, 1 dollar; 7. two long pipestems, 6 dollars; 8. a bow, arrows, and a pipe from Dorion,

5 dollars; 9. a Dacota woman's skirt, 12 dollars; 10. a Dacota quiver, 1 dollar; and 11. a medicine drum (for a knife from the store, 1 dollar).

In the afternoon I took a walk on the prairie. My health permitted this because of [my recent, improved] diet, although I was still weak. The prairie was pleasantly green. We did not see any birds other than the large lark (*Sturnella*), which sang. In the plain of the river valley, the bushy plum trees (*Prunus*) bloomed beautifully; [they looked] like [they were] covered with snow. A little reddish white flower covered the prairie everywhere. The Indian horses [grazing there] had ample fresh fodder. They recover quickly from the hunger of the severe winters [in] this harsh region.

[Now that we had] become so closely acquainted with the Mandans, Hidatsas, and other nations farther up the Missouri, the differences in the Dacota physiognomy were very evident to us. [The Dacotas] have by far less pleasant features, usually [including] stronger, protruding cheekbones, and their stature is seldom as tall and strong. On the other hand, their facial expression is [generally more] kind and good-natured.

28 April: We packed our luggage. Our men received several days' [supply of] corn, which they simmered in lye to remove [the hulls]. They call this *lessirer le maÿs*.[2] For six dollars I bought a swan from the interpreter Ortubise; he had preserved it very well.

Wáh-Menítu and several Dacotas visited us [that] afternoon and looked at our drawings. A skin tipi we received here was set up on the boat. Mr. Laidlaw let me have zwieback, onions, some potatoes, rice, apples, turnips, dried meat, preserved red beets and pickles, fresh butter, and a loaf of fresh bread, for which I was charged very little. We packed a large box with Dacota curiosities and natural history specimens, [stored] here since our first stay, in which a few mice had built nests and caused some damage. Mr. Bodmer did a few sketches—a view of the fort from the hills and [one] of an interesting [burial] scaffold with a curved, woven basket; [under this, wrapped] in a red blanket, were the bones of a Dacota warrior, carried from afar [and] laid here to rest.

29 April: A troop of men, including the Arikara interpreter Lachapelle, got ready for a trip to the Mandan villages to fetch corn. Two oxcarts [hauled our] crates and boxes [to the riverbank to be] loaded on [our] boat.

[A storm delayed our departure, but by] five thirty the wind had abated. Mr. Laidlaw gave me a good, capable man, Dauphin from Carondelet, a

Fig. 16. Karl Bodmer. *Sioux Scaffold Burial.* Pencil. Scaffold burial, on an erected platform or on the limbs of a tree, was a common Plains Indian practice. The skeletal remains might later be buried in the earth. Maximilian found the vaulted framework here unusual; perhaps it provided extra protection from scavenging birds or other predators. 10 × 12½ in. 1986.49.248.

better helmsman than Fecteau. A certain Descoteaux asked for passage to St. Louis; in return, he would row. He had about 120 beaver pelts to sell downriver. Besides those [already] mentioned, I took along a [sick] young man, so that we were ten persons aboard. We took leave forever from the inhabitants of the fort. Mr. Laidlaw accompanied us to the river. The evening was pleasant, and we glided rapidly down[stream]. Soon we passed the mouth of the [Bad River], where Messrs. Sublette and Campbell—the competition of the American Fur Company—had a fort. We could not [stop there but] landed for the night about 6 miles below Fort Pierre.

30 April: Very heavy rain all day long, but we sailed on, putting ashore [occasionally, so that] the men could make a fire and warm and dry themselves a little. We [made our night camp] early in the evening; the night was nice and clear.

1 May: At six o'clock we reached Big Bend, where Dreidoppel and Dauphin got out to hunt. Everywhere the trees were in their new green, [and] the plum bushes were white, covered with flowers. After noon we found our hunters again at the other side of the bend. They had come across three *Charadrius* and shot one, as well as a prairie dog, but no antelope. They [saw] several Dacota lodges, and some Indians on horseback.

At noon it was hot, 64°F. About three or three thirty, we reached the Sioux Agency, Major Bean's post. Inside the fort, we found the interpreter Cephir and three [other] men, who had little food. They had had no buffalo all winter and had lived off antelope meat and a little salt pork. They were impatiently awaiting the arrival of Major Bean with the steamboat *Assiniboine*. About thirteen Dacota tipis were camping in the area. Others had been here, waiting for the steamboat, but [they left to] hunt antelope and had just sent [one] to the white men. Wahktágeli, whom Bodmer drew [last year, came] and gave repeated assurances of his faithfulness to the white men (see pl. 8). After half an hour we sailed on. The evening was pleasant [and] cool.

2 May: We sailed past the White River this morning. [The] wind became so strong that we put ashore, and I [went on] an excursion. I saw *Picus auratus* [and] *Fringilla grammaca* on the creek, [where there were] some green bushes. On the hills, *Yucca angustifolia* were numerous. Old antelope and [other] game trails were often visible. *Cactus ferox* grew beside the creek, which was almost dry.

The severe southeast wind dashed the boat so hard against the rocks [on] the riverbank that it began to leak. The [men] tied pieces of tree trunks to [the boat] to hold it back from the bank. The wind abated in the evening but rose again in the night, so we still could not depart.

On 3 May, [our flora and fauna observations continued.] Orioles *(Icterus)* appeared in flights on the high, steep riverbank. We saw the yellow-headed *Icterus icterocephalus,* and Dreidoppel found a defoliated tree, probably porcupine *(Hystrix dorsata)* [feeding damage]. In the dense creek thicket, I found a white-headed finch I had never seen before [and several other bird species].

About eleven o'clock we continued on, since the wind [had] abated. We had not gone far when [a] very heavy rain [began]. After a few miles, we put in again on the left bank, [where] we lay fairly protected, not quite one mile above [the] Bijou Hills; we saw them [looming] before us in the misty atmosphere. At nightfall the storm became very severe. Mr. Bodmer pointed out a large, heavy tree [obliquely] angled directly above the boat. [It] seemed to have very few roots, [and] the storm could easily have toppled it, smashing [us]. He suggested that we spend the night on land in the [downpour]. However, I preferred the danger on the boat where we were [covered and dryer], and the tree did not fall.

4 May: [That morning], on the left side of the river, we saw water [cascading] over the banks into the Missouri from the [rain-]flooded prairie. We were stuck for a long time on a sandbar opposite Bijou Hills. The prairie here was a fresh, bright green; after the rain [there] were also such spots on the hills — the beautiful young green of May. A little farther downriver, we saw the first swallows, *Hirundo* [—]. The cottonwoods and willows here [were] already completely green. In the afternoon we stopped at Cedar Island and heated some food. The hunters roamed through the rugged, woody island, a dark, wild forest of cedars mixed with *Prunus padus* [and] *Celtis;* the former had flower buds. [A] mixture of cedars and deciduous trees is very attractive. An agreeable fragrance was spread by the cedars, [a] [recognizable] scent [that] dominated the forest. We found elk and deer tracks crossing in all directions. After a stop of about an hour, we left beautiful Cedar Island, [and we] put in on the left bank [later that] evening.

5 May: The sail was hoisted, [but by] about eight o'clock, the wind [was] too strong, [so we stopped at] a large island. Taking the shotgun, I went off with Dreidoppel and Dauphin, and we spread out. I [would] shoot birds; the two others [were after larger] game with the rifle. This island [had] an airy forest of high, slender cottonwoods that creaked mightily as they moved in the wind. [It] was bordered by a rim of willows *(Salix angustata),* and the ground was densely overgrown with tall, dry plants — *Xanthium strumarium* and other three- to four-foot-high, burrlike herbage — so densely grown that it made walking extremely arduous. Birds sought shelter [in the] undergrowth from the present storm: *Turdus rufus* (very shy); *Troglodytes aedon* singing charmingly; woodpeckers; and *Fringilla erythrophthalma* in the willow border on the riverbank. When I returned to the boat, Dauphin had shot an elk doe, and our men went to carry the venison back. [When they] returned, we wanted to embark immediately, but Melone protested vehemently that he would not leave until he had a good meal of venison. After a harsh exchange of words, this unpleasant man had to embark nonetheless, since his comrades did not share his rebellious spirit. We navigated

down through the channel alongside the island, but when we arrived at its tip, the storm hit us [so hard] that we lost our sail. We put ashore [until] about five o'clock, [when] the wind abated. We left [and] navigated past the mouth of Ponca [Creek], and as the sun set, [we saw] three Ponca tipis on the right bank. We were informed of the proximity of the steamboat *Assiniboine;* we would [see it] tomorrow. The Ponca Indians here looked poor and dirty, having suffered much hunger. We continued on [and later camped] opposite the mouth of the [Niobrara River].

6 May: Before daybreak, [we heard] a wild turkey cock gobbling very loudly (to court [possible mates]), [and] later [we spied] a whole flock of pelicans. About eleven o'clock we saw the *Assiniboine* ahead of us. It was moored on the left side and apparently did not have enough water [depth to proceed]. Its funnel showed no smoke. My men claimed [that] we could not get [to the steamboat] because of sandbars and strong wind. We therefore put ashore opposite the *Assiniboine.* The steamboat's woodcutters were about one mile above the place where we landed, cutting wood. At noon we saw a boat bringing some of [the cutters] back across the river. The rest, who had seen our smoke, came looking for us. When the *Assiniboine's* boat [came for them], it brought along a note from Captain Bennett asking [if] I was on the mackinaw boat [and] welcoming us aboard the steamboat. The [crew] offered to bring my barge across undamaged, and that task was carried out immediately. About ten to twelve men lent a helping hand; we conquered the turbulent river and easily avoided the sandbars. We had hardly arrived on the [opposite] riverbank when we saw our old travel companions [approaching] — Mr. Sanford, Major Bean, and Captain Bennett — happy to see us and to receive news from the upper Missouri. Our conversation was lively. They kept us for lunch and dinner. After that, we took leave to sleep on our [own] boat.

On board the steamboat we also found the Ponca chief Schudegácheh, very friendly and glad to see us again. There was also a second chief [and] some Ponca men and women. Schudegácheh was exceptionally well dressed, completely in otter skin. [He had] an otter[-skin] cap, a tobacco pouch of [the same material, and] a shirt, [again] of beautiful otter fur, with a round, red cloth collar. [These garments] excellently suited the handsome, interesting Indian. He had a long conversation with Major Bean, the agent for this tribe, and before the conversation began, with the aid of [an] interpreter, the Indians took off all their clothes and gave them to the agent as a present; [they were] completely naked, except for their breechcloths. But Bean returned everything to them; they had to put on their clothes again, except for Schudegácheh, who did not want to take back his otter clothing. The village of these Indians, about 100 lodges, was presently located about four days' [travel] up [the Niobrara River]. When we returned to our boat, Dauphin seemed to be the only one sober.

7 May: Today we were exactly two years absent from Neuwied. We [pushed off] early; Melone, Descoteaux, and Fecteau were still drunk and made much noise. About eleven o'clock, we passed [the James River]. We put in on the right side, because the wind was again very strong, but our position [had no] shelter.

Dreidoppel and Dauphin went to look for waterfowl. I went through a dense thicket of narrow-leafed willows [and wild] roses, far onto the now verdant prairie. I saw a red fox *(Canis fulvus)* [and several birds:] two or three kinds of swallows gliding above the plain, a *Cypselus,* a large lark, the yellow-headed *Icterus icterocephalus,* [and] a pair of hawks with white uropygia. In the willows [were] *Picus auratus, Corvus corax* and *corone; Papilio plexippus* and *Libellula* flew in the warm upwind.

At the [camp]fire, we had no [discipline]. Most of the men were lying around drunk in the high grass. Melone, a former United States soldier, a native of Liberty on the Missouri, [and] a wicked man, [had tried] to persuade the others to leave. He assumed [they agreed, so] he carried all his belongings off the boat [and] demanded that the others abandon us. When they did not, he [abusively insulted] them. He finally gave up and asked me for passage, which I categorically refused. He could build his own boat. About six o'clock the wind abated, [so] we continued on; Melone remained, alone.

We made about twelve to fifteen miles, [and] when the sun had set, we put ashore at a nice, secure place, [and] our fires soon blazed brightly. Whippoorwills deafened our ears with their calls [as they] flew around the [flames at just] three paces away. A few were shot. They frequently sat on tree branches; it made them easy to shoot down. From here on downriver, whippoorwills were common.

8 May: Not far above the mouth of the Vermillion, we encountered large sandbars on which we noticed avocets *(Recurvirostra)*; our hunters pursued them in vain. Beautiful [forested] hill chains adorned this region. Many Sioux were said to have [recently] moved down into this area to hunt.

On the steamboat we were told [that] a beaver [trapper, Johnson] Gardner, the [foremost] pilot of the Missouri, had gone downriver ahead of us, [but] we would catch up with him because he had a poor, heavily loaded canoe. I was advised to take him on with his load, since we would then have a very reliable helmsman. About noon we saw Gardner's canoe ahead and soon caught up with it, [a] square leather boat loaded with furs. I suggested that he bring his cargo on board our boat and take over the helm, a proposal he accepted with pleasure, because he had little trust in his [own vessel]. He had two oarsmen with him and was returning from a beaver hunt. We put ashore on the left bank [for] the [cargo] transfer. In the meantime we went out [hunting in the forest]. On the ground we believed we saw a mouse running [near] the roots of a tree. We followed, [shot it, and] discovered that it was a simply but extremely prettily colored *Fringilla acutipennis* that we saw today for the first and last time.

[In the afternoon, wind and sandbars hampered our progress.] The evening was calm and beautiful. We lit our fire on the beach, and Gardner told me about his various dangerous expeditions into Indian country and his skirmishes with Indians. He was the one who killed the two Arikaras (I have the scalp of one). The day before [he did so], the [Arikaras had] killed old [Hugh] Glass and his two companions, [who had been] beaver hunting on the Yellowstone River. As they crossed [it], all three were shot, scalped, and robbed by a war party of about eighty Arikaras. From there these Indians — so dangerous to the white men — moved to the sources of the Powder River. It so happened that Gardner, with about twenty men and thirty horses, was camped [nearby that night]. While the Americans sat at several fires, the Indians appeared suddenly, greeted them in Hidatsa, surrounded the fires, and dried their shoes. Gardner, a man experienced in dealing with Indians, took safety precautions right away, especially since a Hidatsa woman with him informed him that the strangers were Arikaras. Gardner had his men gradually assemble at one of the fires and keep their weapons ready. He feared for his horses; some were already missing. He [also] sent out [a few men] to build a so-called fort from [fallen?] tree trunks for the night.

The Indians have a custom that, when they [intend] to steal horses, they suddenly make a sign, whereupon they all run off, scatter the horses, and drive [the animals] away with them. Gardner anticipated this [and] watched the enemy closely. When they sped away, [Gardner and his men] seized three of them and tied them up. The Arikaras saw this, [so] several came back, [feigned] innocence about the disappearance of the horses, and pleaded for their comrades. But Gardner said that if they did not immediately return the horses, the prisoners would die. In the meantime, one of [the prisoners], who had hidden his knife, cut his ropes and escaped. The Indians negotiated a long time but were sent away. The prisoners, foreseeing their deaths, intoned their death songs and told of their heroic feats, [declaring] that they were great warriors. One of them had old Glass's knife; the rifles of the murder victims had also been seen in the group [of Indians]. The horses were not returned. The prisoners claimed the necessity [to relieve themselves] and were led aside. In the dense thicket they attempted to escape, but one of them was stabbed to death on the spot; several shots were fired at the other, [and he was mortally] stabbed as well. Both [were] scalped, and I now own one of these scalps. Gardner had all the fires extinguished. [He and his men] remained vigilant overnight in the just-completed wooden fort, expecting an enemy attack at any moment, but everything stayed quiet. They discovered the following morning that [the Arikaras] had left with their loot, having sacrificed the prisoners for the horses. I received the scalp mentioned above later from Mr. Chardon of Fort Union.

9 May: In the morning we [could soon see] the hill chain [near the mouth] of the Big Sioux on the left bank [of the Missouri]. [After passing that in the afternoon,] we reached Floyd's Grave. At the next turn of the river, [perhaps] a few miles onto the prairie, an Omaha Indian village was located, containing about 50 lodges. We could not visit it, [since we] had neither guide nor interpreter; we also needed to take advantage of the nice [weather], because we had [earlier] lost so much time during the frequent storms.

In the evening we stayed overnight on the left bank.

10 May: Good, clear, weather; hot early; at seven thirty, 72°F. We saw many wood ducks, pelicans, and geese. At nine thirty we put ashore across from the grave of the great Omaha chief Waschínga-Sáhba, where we found many game trails. The hills on which Blackbird's grave is located (described [on 7 May 1833]) appeared nicely green. We departed [but] after one to two hours put in again, because we had [entered] an area with a great many snags, which could be dangerous to [navigate] in [strong] wind. [When] the wind [finally] abated, we wound through [the] threatening snags without hitting anything, because Gardner steered our boat so admirably. About sundown

we sailed by the mouth of the Little Sioux River. Approximately three miles below [that], we put ashore for the night. The evening was fair, [and] ducks called nearby.

11 May: Pleasant morning. We stopped on the left bank for a quarter of an hour. In the almost impenetrable new [growth] of the dense willow thicket [there] were many interesting birds—the rust-colored thrush, the multivoiced *Icteria viridis,* with its magnificent lemon-yellow throat, the beautiful *Muscicapa ruticilla, Sylvia aestiva,* and others. We saw an extraordinary number of wood ducks. Pairs of the beautiful white *Falco furcatus* (which we had seen yesterday) glided above the high forest. At noon we had much wind [and] moored on a high bank with a willow thicket. In many places within the thicket there was a dense underbrush of *Lonicera* or *Symphoria, Cornus,* and the like, where *Icteria viridis* [were] hidden. The magnificent Baltimore [oriole] flew around in pairs; *Sylvia aestiva* [was] very numerous; [an] olive-gray flycatcher was very common. In the neighboring forest the ground was densely overgrown with two- to three-foot-high rushes *(Equisetum hyemale),* [each] as thick as a finger. At about four thirty we departed. Around six o'clock we reached the Soldier River and landed in a secure bay on the left side.

12 May: In the morning [we saw] a pair of cormorants; the female settled in the forest. Dreidoppel got out, crept up with his rifle, and shot this bird (new to us) down from its high seat.

Around ten o'clock we passed by Council Bluff and the ruins of the cantonment formerly located there. A flock of *Sterna hirundo* winged upriver, and Dreidoppel shot a nice specimen. In the afternoon we reached [Boyer River], from which it was three miles to Pilcher's trading post; about one o'clock we sighted [it] and half an hour later landed there. Mr. Pilcher received us cordially, and we stayed all day. A lawyer was there to investigate a criminal case; an engagé had recently coldly and intentionally shot a comrade.[3]

At this moment not many Indians were [at the post], but there were some Otoes, Omahas, Missourias, and Iowas, [and] the great Omaha chief Óngpa-Tánga (Big Elk) was expected any day. Mr. Bodmer drew an Omaha and an Otoe Indian. The two nations do not differ in customs and traditions, [and] their appearance is fairly similar. Mr. Pilcher's house seemed more orderly than before. The store had been moved. It was now on the upper floor, where we found a significant supply of pelts and skins, among them 24,000 muskrats, the packs [neatly] tied together in squares. Many beaver pelts and buffalo robes were also stacked there.

I made an excursion after lunch. The surrounding hills and forests displayed lush foliage. [Many colorful birds] enlivened a beautiful valley [with] a path to the Omaha villages. [Various] fine trees and bushes grew [here, such as] oak, elm, ash, *Celtis* (its trunk one and a half feet in diameter), and maples. I shot several interesting birds. Close to [Pilcher's place, I saw] good cattle, many hogs (some also roam in the forest), and chickens. Not far from the buildings there were extensive corn and potato fields. Mr. Pilcher gave us some provisions. There was cholera here late last summer, but not as many people died of it as at Dougherty's agency, because Mr. Pilcher [had] medicine. We took leave from our gracious host in the evening and slept on our boat.

13 May: At eight o'clock [we made] a short stop at a lovely prairie on the right bank with pretty clumps of bushes and many scattered tall trees. Several birds appeared, among them the beautiful black and white hawfinch with a red breast *(Loxia ludoviciana),* of which we shot several specimens. At noon we reached Bellevue, Major Dougherty's agency, but unfortunately, Dougherty was not expected until July. When cholera paid a visit last summer, seven of ten people living here died within 24 hours, and one person had to bury them all while feeling sick himself. There were no ill people in this area now. We found the Bellevue vicinity very pleasant and particularly interesting to naturalists. The forest hills had shady gorges and small valleys where many large-leafed linden trees grew, [as well as] oaks, ash, elm, *Celtis,* [and many other trees; also] *Staphylea trifolia,* creeping *Vitis, Humulus, Smilax,* [and] *Hedera,* all with lush foliage. On the ground, as [we also saw] yesterday, sky-blue phlox bloomed magnificently, [as did] numerous strawberries. We did not see many [other] flowers yet—only the bright vermilion *Aquilegia canadensis.* The bushes were animated by many birds [and] beautiful butterflies. [At the agency] we received a few provisions and milk, which is supposed to be a mainstay against scurvy. Near Mr. [Lucien] Fontenelle's house I saw [and] bought a small pig that we took aboard after [our] long stop at Bellevue. Mr. Fontenelle had not yet returned from his excursion last year to the Rocky Mountains. We departed after two o'clock.

Papillion Creek [was soon] on our right. They say it is 24 miles from Pilcher's house to Bellevue, [and] six miles from Bellevue to the mouth of the [Platte]. [When] the sun [was ready] to set, [we] camped on the right bank of the Missouri. I went ashore [and followed] a long, narrow, reedy marsh overgrown with *Typha;* raccoons had carved [out] very flat, passable trails there. Beyond the marsh the green hill chains stretched, overgrown with trees and bushes where the Baltimore [oriole] was seen and *Icteria viridis* was extremely common. Its song, similar in some strophes to that of the nightingale, resounded everywhere; these birds are very mobile and restless, especially toward evening.

14 May: Nice, bright morning. We passed Weeping Water [Creek]; a little farther [there was] a small creek on the right bank where we heard turkeys calling. We landed; four hunters fired at and missed the sought-after birds. The spot where we came across them was beautiful. The creek made a sharp bend that formed a level, shady basin, lushly green with grass and tall trees, [their] crowns touching. We continued on and after ten o'clock, put ashore on the right, where we pushed into a magnificent virgin forest. Caterpillars made these dense forests unpleasant, especially the willow thickets. [One's] clothing was immediately covered with them. [Vines] entangled everything; [this and the many] bushes and fallen trees made walking difficult, [but] we found a great number of [bird] species. After half an hour, we sailed on [but] soon ran aground: [another] delay. We noticed the first parakeets that afternoon. Gardner had [seen] these beautiful birds before we came across him, therefore, at about the [Niobrara River]. We navigated [through heavy snags and] landed about one mile below the mouth of the Little Nemaha [River]. As soon as the [camp]fire was burning, Dauphin went fishing and caught a white catfish [weighing] about fifteen pounds.

15 May: Bright morning; fog on the river. [It was] five miles from our night quarters to the mouth of the Nishnabotna, [which we reached] at eight o'clock. Two *Cervus virginianus* stood opposite us in front of the willows. One of them was hit, [and the hunters] followed the blood but did not get it. We shot several small birds here, among them *Troglodytes aedon* and a swallow with a white belly.

Farther on, we [stopped briefly again], and cooked lunch. [After four o'clock, we passed the mouth of the Big Nemaha River and then set up our evening bivouac about six miles above the Wolf River.] Everywhere [there were] unbelievable numbers of caterpillars.

16 May: Dense morning fog [delayed our departure]. Between twelve and one o'clock [we passed] the mouth of the Nodaway. Magnificent, primeval forest scenery—in that rich foliage we could recognize (even from the boat)

the vermilion-red tanager *(Tanagra rubra)* and the beet-red cardinal, which glowed like flames [in the] bushes.

About four o'clock we reached the beautiful Blacksnake Hills, and nearby, the [Joseph] Robidoux trading house, picturesque when viewed from the river. Fine cattle grazed on the plain, and behind the [white-painted] dwellings [there] were large, fenced-in cornfields. Mr. Robidoux and his son were away. Unfortunately, the coarse engagés there would not grant our request to visit the neighboring Indians: an Iowa village about 6 miles [away] and a Sauk village, downriver. These Indians got [plentiful] spirits from the outermost American settlements, 15 miles distant. Easy [access] to cheap [liquor] is highly pernicious to the Indians and [is] more and more the ruination of these people. We were told that it would not be advisable to visit the villages at this time because Indians [there] had done nothing for days but drink [liquor] and [thus] were dangerous. We saw several Indians [near the post], most on horseback, some with four to five casks of their favorite drink hanging on their horses.

We remained [tied up to] the bank overnight.

17 May: Hot day. We navigated between the wooded banks against the wind; [when it] became a little brisk, we put in on the right bank and went deep into the forests to hunt. The countless caterpillars had completely defoliated the young cottonwoods on the bank. They lay en masse on the trunks; the ground was literally covered with their excrement. If we walked into the bushes, [even] for a moment, we were covered with caterpillars.

We shot the gray squirrel, *Fringilla cardinalis, Icteria viridis,* [and] the red-eyed flycatcher *(Muscicapa* [—]). The glorious forest that extended in front of the hills [consisted] of *Platanus,* various oaks, walnut trees, ashes, elms, maples, *Celtis, Cercis,* [and] cottonwoods; their spreading crowns and colossal trunks [cast] dark shadows. [There were] a great many nice plants, [including] yellow-flowered *Cypripedium* [and] purple *Phlox.* We departed at four o'clock. The wind was still strong [but] very warm.

Soon after [six] we reached Cow Island; from there, it was still 9 miles to Cantonment Leavenworth. On the island we saw grazing cattle that belonged to the military post. We put in on the right bank for the night. Several of our men, Gardner among them, went ahead to Leavenworth.

18 May: [At] nine o'clock we shipped off for the military post. [When we arrived, a] sentry, [his gun] at full cock, compelled us to stay [close] together and be led by him, [marching] as if we were prisoners, to the commander, Major

Riley. The major received us fairly politely in his house and gave orders [that] the requested provisions, including meat and bread, be supplied to us.

The site of the cantonment was pleasant. About ten to twelve neat houses, with galleries or verandas around [them], accommodated two companies of the 6th [Infantry] Regiment—only 80 men, including ten officers. The rangers who had been stationed here earlier had withdrawn, [purportedly to] be replaced by cavalry. We would have seen the place better if there had not been a heavy rain falling.

A certain (Major) Morgan owned the store here, where most necessary merchandise could be found. He had fur trade [business] with Gardner, who therefore [decided to] stay here. We departed at four o'clock [in the] rain. Some of our people were drunk; [so was] Gardner, who had to unload his merchandise in the rain and mud.

XXII

Journey from Cantonment Leavenworth

to St. Louis and Stay There

18 May: [We headed downriver but] put in before dusk. The rain lessened, but the forest was terribly wet, the sky very cloudy.

19 May: Heavy rain [again; when] the weather cleared, we continued the journey. [By] eleven o'clock the mouth of the [Kansas] River was to our right. High, magnificently freshly green forest covered the banks. In the forest, small, isolated log houses [and] grazing cattle. We put ashore near a few houses called Portage d'Independence. Independence, [Missouri], was located about three miles inland, a fine, substantial town. In one of the houses [at Portage], we found Mr. [Milton] Sublette, laid low by an old foot wound. He had [long been involved in] the fur trade [and] was eager for news from us about the upper Missouri. A retired soldier asked for passage [on our boat], and I took him along.

After five o'clock we reached the landing place of Liberty but did not stop. Toward evening, we [camped] for the night at the left bank, a little below [some] houses. While a fire was lit on the beach, I explored the fields in a little valley surrounded by hills covered with high forest. The Baltimore [oriole] and the vermilion tanager *(Tanagra rubra)* with black wings and tail immediately caught my eye at the edge of the forest. In the surrounding areas, frogs croaked; we [also] heard tree frogs [and saw] an animal just like our European black- and yellow-striped salamander, probably a related species. A *Rubus* with large, snow-white flowers bloomed beautifully in all these woodlands. [Eventually,] the dusk drove me home. It rained part of the night.

20 May: The sky cleared. We stayed moored here to dry our wet [belongings]. I roamed the woodlands even more thoroughly than yesterday; [the vegetation] left not even the smallest spot free. A single roadway along the bank led from one plantation to another. The forest had glorious trees [and] a great variety of birds, [including] the cuckoo, the large *Picus pileatus,* [and]

Sitta carolinensis—we had not seen [either of the latter] for a long time. The soldier [we had] taken along yesterday found whiskey in the [settlement] and got a few of my men drunk. All [the] neighboring planters came to see my grizzly bears, [which caused] more sensation here than in any other area of the United States. In the afternoon I went in a different direction down along the river. I found a beautiful, romantic [wilderness]. Pawpaw trees were blooming. There was a dense cover of ferns on the valley floor. Everything [was] thickly leaved, luxuriant in lush greenery. A clear brook meandered [through] the grass, and the houses of several planters stood in the shadows on the hills.

In the evening several plantation owners visited, among them some men of the religious sect called Mormons. A wise, elderly man gave us an idea of their teachings, to which he seemed very [devoted]. He complained bitterly about the treatment their congregation had received. They [once] lived on the [opposite] Missouri bank but were driven away by their neighbors. Their plantations were destroyed, their houses [were] burned, and some of them were killed. Why? I could not find out. We were told it was because they purportedly have some wrong customs in respect to the female gender. According to this man, they believe in the Old and the New Testaments; they consider the [Book] of Mormon as the most important revelation, [and] from that their name was taken. [He] maintained [that] their sect was harmless and would never hurt other people; [it seems] inconceivable that they have been unable to have their rights recognized.

Our possessions were of great interest to these backwoodsmen, especially our double-barreled shotguns and combination over-and-under rifle/shotguns. The day had been nice and hot, [enabling us] to dry our luggage completely. We prepared to leave early the following morning.

21 May: Departure at seven o'clock; [uneventful travel downstream]. Toward three o'clock we had the Lexington ferry on the left [and], a little farther on the right, a steam [saw]mill. In the evening we put in at the right, and [the crew] cooked. On the nearby meadow, tall grass [and] a beautiful sky-blue or light violet-blue iris grew. There were not many birds, but the hour was late.

22 May: Very warm. We stopped about seven o'clock [and] bought milk, butter, and other items at a settlement with extensive plantations. At eleven o'clock we met the steamboat *Ioway*, which was [attempting to] travel upriver [but] had insufficient water. We put ashore, and Mr. Bodmer went to the

steamboat to get news from St. Louis. [He] found old [Joseph] Robidoux from the Blacksnake Hills on board. [Robidoux] had recently bought the trading house there ([the one] we [had] just visited) from the American Company, fully equipped, for $5,000.[1] Now [he] was going back to it. We stopped here for a few hours. Toward five o'clock in the evening, we passed the Grand River, and [we camped] 6 miles below it at a plantation on the right bank after sundown. The good, friendly people who lived there could let us have only a little food. The surrounding forest was lovely.

23 May: The hunters went out very early but unfortunately returned empty-handed at breakfast. [There] was a young female black bear *(Ursus americanus)* in the neighborhood, which I had brought to me; [I] bought it. Departure at six thirty. At noon we reached Chariton.[2] [Not long after,] we heard a strange scraping beneath our boat. Our skipper assured us that it originated from a fish with spiny fins, which produces that sound [by rubbing those] fins on the bottom of a boat. This fish weighs up to five [or] six pounds and is called the buffalo[-fish] by the Americans. After sundown, the old village of Franklin was on the left; on the right, Boonville. We put ashore for the night below the latter town. Two Negroes from Boonville, [who had been] felling trees, [stopped] and stared in wonder at our bears. One of them carried a four- to five-foot-long metal speaking tube in his hand; they used it to call [fellow workers] together in the forest. The Negroes of this area were all slaves.

24 May: Beautiful rocks and uninterrupted forest adorned the banks all day long. About six o'clock [we arrived] at Jefferson City, the capital of the state of Missouri, where Governor [Daniel Dunklin] lived. Hogs and cattle [roamed] between the houses of this town, which was [still] in the process of being built. We stopped here for a while to buy provisions but got just salt pork, biscuits, and whiskey. [There] were only a few schoolbooks in the so-called bookstore. After half an hour, we sailed on. We [camped] overnight opposite the Osage River.

25 May: In the morning, heavy fog; we had to put ashore again soon [after leaving our camp]. At seven thirty the fog dispersed, [and] we [went] past Cote Sans Dessein. At noon we reached Portland, a village founded two years ago. The mouth of the Gasconade River became visible a little farther downriver. Beautiful elevations and magnificent forests characterize this area.

26 May: Hot day. At seven thirty, 75°F; no wind. At nine o'clock we put in near the isolated house of a certain Porter. [He] owned a young bear, which he sold

to me and [sent to have] it fetched from the neighborhood. We had to wait about two hours [for delivery]. This man requested that I name the bear after him—Porter.

[Sometime after] five o'clock [we passed] the rather sizable town of St. Charles. We put ashore [on the opposite bank] at a settlement of five to six homes where a certain Chauvin kept a stage inn, [offering] passengers the most direct route straight overland to St. Louis. Today's stage had [already] left, so we had to stay overnight. Very heavy rain made the ground completely sodden.

27 May: In the morning, cloudy, very warm. [Mud] everywhere. Because no stage was leaving early, we hired a farm wagon, open on top and pulled by three horses. Dreidoppel left early with [our?] boat down the Missouri [and expected to] reach St. Louis today.

We departed between seven and eight o'clock. Colossal sugar maples, honey locusts, elms, and oaks covered a hilly area near the road, which extended nineteen miles straight through the country to St. Louis. Everywhere in the tall forest, the ground was covered with interesting plants [attracting] large, beautiful butterflies. Frequently [seen] among the blooming plants [were] a pale red (flesh-colored) *Monarda; Tradescantia virginica;* a large, beautiful blue iris, in a marsh [and] on flat meadowlands; and a dark blue *Delphinium.*

A multitude of *Papilio ajax* flew about with many other species. The partridge *(Perdix virginiana)* was [common] in this forest; its two-[part] whistle resounded everywhere. These cute birds—the male, with its white- and dark-striped head, is exceptionally charming—were not shy at all. They often let us drive by very close. *Cervus virginianus* and wild turkeys were said to be numerous here. We noticed various interesting birds: woodpeckers, the blue jay, the yellow-headed parakeet, the cardinal, the red-eyed finch, and many others. From time to time we came across settlements in the forest, the houses built of wood boards, [with shingled] roofs [and] brick chimneys.

Among the interesting plants in the St. Louis area is the ginseng *(Panax [quinquefolius]),* which also grows in the state of Illinois and other areas. It is still gathered and exported, but the demand for it [varies annually]. The root is bulbous [and] strangely shaped. Several other officinal plants grow here, for example, *Frasera walteri,* which furnishes false columbo root for the trade (See Coxe's *American Dispensatory,* 8th edition, p. 310). *Mentha piperita,* originally brought from England, now grows everywhere in the United States, [making it] unnecessary to import this article. *Myrica cerifera* grows in the south from New Orleans along the whole coast up to New Jersey; fragrant green candles are made from its wax (the berries are cooked, and the wax is skimmed off the top).

Among the timber of the forests, the oak needs to be specially mentioned. White oak furnishes excellent building timber. Red oak, with its deeply carved, sharply lobed leaves, is used, particularly in St. Louis, for dyeing and tanning, [as is] black oak *(Quercus tinctoria)* bark; [the latter is also] is exported to England.

At noon we stopped at a solitary inn on the edge of the forest and the [adjoining flat or gently hilly areas locally] called prairies. From here it was 6 to 7 miles to St. Louis; we reached [the city that afternoon].

St. Louis had not been overtaken by cholera, as we had been told everywhere along the Missouri, but some cases did occur on a few New Orleans steamboats.

At the American Fur Company office I found letters from Germany dated 2 March, as well as one from Mr. Say in New Harmony dated 15 April. I wrote right away to Germany [and] to New Harmony to inform Mr. Say of our imminent visit there. The gentlemen of the Fur Company were very gracious. We were invited to Mr. Lamont's and made the acquaintance of his family. He lived in a nice house in the upper part of the city. Mr. Chouteau [lived on] the main street [by] the river, [in a] spacious, elegantly furnished house.

I had four new crates made in St. Louis for the live bears, for which I paid $41. I packed seven new boxes with natural history specimens; the eighth was still in Mr. Edward Tracy's store. The numbers of the seven new boxes were XXVII–XXXIII. I visited Major O'Fallon [at his home, where] we saw a large collection of Indian paintings by the artist Catlin. They were mostly inferior. All [were] painted very lightly; a few were interesting and [resembled their subjects].

1 June: We took a trip to the other side of the Mississippi to visit the Indian mounds. We crossed over on a steam ferry that had room enough for our gig and horse. On the opposite side, [there were] houses shaded by tall trees, a few inns, and stores. Fish and various turtles, as well as vegetables and the like, were taken daily from here to the St. Louis market.

[We followed] a road through low marshes [and] open, bushy areas to the edge of the prairie. We refreshed ourselves [at] an inn called Prairie House. As soon as we left the woods along the Mississippi, [we saw] a row of flat, ancient Indian mounds [laying] parallel to the river. Another row cut through the prairie at an angle with the former. [The second row] had a few higher mounds; the largest (about 60′ high) was located at the corner where the two [rows] met. It is called Trappist's or [Monks Mound], because several years ago French monks of that order lived there; [they] have since left the area.

From the river it was 6 miles to [Monks Mound]. It was overgrown with grass and [isolated] tall trees; a few new wooden houses were located on it. A herd of cattle rested under a copse of tall cottonwoods on the prairie. We left the wagon there, [although] the bull that reigned [over the place initially] disputed our right to [do so]. The [50 to 60] Indian mounds were interesting—some [were] in pairs, most [were] isolated. A few were still cone-shaped, others [quite] flattened. Mr. Bodmer hurriedly sketched a few. We returned [to St. Louis] shortly before two o'clock. Many mounds [such as those at Cahokia were once] located [near] St. Louis; [although] most have been destroyed by construction, some still exist. These old remains offer an intriguing field for research, [a mystery] difficult to fathom.

After I had given my crates to Mr. Edward Tracy, we took leave of our friends [and made ready] to embark the following morning.

XXIII

Journey from St. Louis through Indiana to Portsmouth on the Ohio

FROM 3 JUNE TO [20 JUNE 1834]

3 June: About noon we went on board the steamboat *Metamora* [and went] swiftly down the beautiful Mississippi, the riverbanks now clad in the most sumptuous green; we passed Chester, [Illinois], before nightfall.

4 June: Along the bank, tall forests full of creepers; lush, densely leafed pawpaw trees; *Gleditsia;* and many *Platanus,* all young. We [heard] that the New Orleans steamboat *Napoleon* sank recently; it hit a snag; all passengers were saved.

At eight forty-five we reached the mouth of the Ohio, that is, its confluence with the Mississippi. We stopped there. The Ohio water [level] was [currently] too shallow for the large New Orleans boats. Therefore, boats from St. Louis, always smaller, waited there to pick up passengers traveling to Cincinnati, Louisville, or Pittsburgh—an inconvenient [and lengthy delay] for us; we went into the neighboring forest.

Papilio ajax and *turnus* were very numerous there; we caught many. Mr. Bodmer found a *Tanagra mississippiensis* nest [and] shot several specimens of [it] as well as the fiery-colored Baltimore [oriole and] several other attractive birds. At about three o'clock in the afternoon, the ship's bell summoned the passengers, who were scattered in the forest. Two big New Orleans boats came toward us. The *Mediterranean* (the largest boat on the Mississippi) sailed upriver to Smithland, [Kentucky, where it would] leave passengers for us. It was a 600-ton ship with 13 boilers and 40 firemen. At four o'clock we continued up the Ohio, stopping at midnight at Paducah, [Kentucky].

5 June: At midday we reached Smithland [and] took on board many passengers [from] the [*Mediterranean* and other] New Orleans [vessels]. The day was very hot and windless. The view of the Ohio [was] beautiful and splendid. Toward evening we passed close to Cave-in-Rock, [Illinois]. [We] traveled through the night, and by daybreak [on]

6 June reached Mount Vernon, where we left the *Metamora* [and] had breakfast at an inn while the innkeeper readied his dearborn to [drive] us to New Harmony, 16 miles [away]. The most beautiful trees and interesting plants grow [here]. The blooming *Frasera walteri* (false columbo root) was often 4′ to 5′ high; ginseng *(Panax)* also grows on the Wabash, [and] the slippery elm (*Ulmus* [—]); the bark [of the latter proved useful] during the cholera [epidemic and was] now stocked as a powder in pharmacies. The wood of the catalpa, so characteristic of these forests, furnished very good posts [and] excellent shingles. Tulip tree *(Liriodendron tulipifera)* wood was used everywhere by cabinetmakers in place of our fir. The sassafras was very common; its leaves furnish an aromatic, blood-cleansing tea.

On our journey through the glorious forest to Harmony, we entertained ourselves with beautiful butterflies, catching many of them. The gray squirrel *(Sciurus cinereus)* was very numerous; our coachman [hoped for] a meal from these little animals with the help of his rifle, but he was not successful. We caught a large, beautiful colubrid [snake] that we put inside the coach — alive, not exactly at the pleasure of our coachman.

About noon we reached Harmony. Mr. Say was very happy to see us again, as [were] our [other] friends, all of whom we found [present and] in good health, with the exception of Mr. Richard Owen, who had moved to Cincinnati with his wife. Mr. Robert Dale Owen lived here now with his family. Previously he wrote [for] a newspaper in New York, [the] *Investigator,* [and authored] several publications. Two of his brothers and a sister [also] lived here. [They were all] learned people.

In General Twigg's home, I found Mr. Lesueur, who still intended to travel to France, but [I think he] will probably not see his fatherland again. We spent several very cheerful days with these friends. Mr. Say worked diligently on his study of American [mollusks], of which issue six had appeared. The description of many new North American insects occupied the rest of his time. Mr. Lesueur had been in New Orleans since [we saw him last] and had left his friend Barrabino very ill; [he subsequently] died. Mr. Lesueur was now particularly engaged in the observation of a few turtles. He had brought very interesting [items] from New Orleans, including fine gopher specimens. We were in continual motion [as] our friends made [every] effort to make our sojourn enjoyable.

7–8 June: Mr. Bodmer went back to Mount Vernon to get our luggage, because we had changed our travel plans and now intended to go to Vincennes. Mr.

Lesueur promised to accompany us. [I] ordered a dearborn with two horses for [9 June], and we took leave of our friends.

9 June: We had breakfast early at Mr. Twigg's house. Mr. Lesueur went with me [in the carriage]; Messrs. Twigg and Bodmer made the trip on horseback. The whole area that we traveled through was uninterrupted forest, except very close to the Wabash near Vincennes. Settlers' dwellings were located in [the forest] on both sides of the roadway, mostly log houses [but also] some better wooden ones and occasionally brick. The fields were fenced everywhere. The [very dry] heat was [irritating,] the dust even more so. [However,] there was no lack of refreshing clear water on our way, because almost every house had a well or a spring. We usually mixed [our] water with some of the brandy we brought along.

The field crops looked good in this area, even though the spring had been very dry. The corn was still small. Many cattle grazed in the forest; hogs were quite numerous. About noon we reached Owensville, a small village. We [paused] for lunch and gave our hot and thirsty horses some rest. In the afternoon we traveled again through tall forests where tree frogs were heard in large numbers. Before evening we reached Princetown, where we stayed overnight in a good inn.

10 June: Early departure. We traveled through forests even taller and more [densely wooded] than yesterday. The catalpas were now in full bloom. At noon we reached an open place in the forest on a creek where a large sawmill had been erected. An inn was located nearby; stages stopped [there] for lunch. We got squirrel meat, green onions, and coffee. In smaller places like this, the coachman usually eats at the same table.

From the sawmill it was about three miles to the White River, [where] we were ferried across for 25 cents. On the opposite bank, the area changed considerably, and from [this point] on, [we saw] sandy soil [and] more or less the same plants as on the prairie near St. Louis. It was [about 12 more] miles to [Vincennes].

[As] we approached [the town, we saw] the so-called Warriors Hill, [from which] the Americans observed the enemy in [1779], when they took Vincennes from the British. It was flat, like most old Indian mounds, and densely overgrown with oaks. Soon we saw Vincennes, scattered on the plain before us, on the bank of the Wabash. This town is one of the oldest settlements in the West, about as old as Philadelphia. The French built it, and at the time, it was one of the posts that formed a secure line of [French] communication in this wilderness. It was named after a French officer of that time, [François Marie Bissot, sieur de Vincennes], who settled here; he was a friend of the Indians, from whom he received land as a gift. Very old buildings could still be seen, [along with] many fairly nice, new brick houses. There were numerous descendants of the old French settlers; they were coarse, uneducated, superstitious, and [not part of] the better-educated segment of the population. Many Americans had settled here and had established some nice shops. [There was once] a bookstore, but it did not survive; we found it closed. The house of the former governor was nicely located in an open space near the river with a very shady [grove] of trees in front.[1] It formerly had a lovely—almost a botanical—garden that the present owners had let fall into complete disrepair.

We stayed in Clark's Hotel in Vincennes. The stages departed from there, and we wanted to leave the next morning. But the owner told us rather laconically that we had by far too much luggage for the small, six-seat stage leaving on the morrow. We had to wait for the next one, which caused us two days' delay.

13 June: At three [in the morning] the travelers were awakened in the [hotel], and at four o'clock we drove off on the stage. The coachman had blown [his] metal horn in the streets, and we had said goodbye, perhaps forever, to the honorable old Lesueur. Six persons were in our carriage. They did not make significant conversation. At first we traveled through a mixed landscape of meadow or prairie and bushes. [After] scarcely one or two miles we were deep into the uninterrupted forest that lends Indiana its principal character. About eleven o'clock we reached Washington, a small town 20 miles from Vincennes, where we changed horses. The farmers were plowing their fields, in which isolated trees often remained standing; [these] gave no shade, because fire had killed them long ago. They grew all kinds of grain in Indiana, but it was generally held that this state was among the most difficult to cultivate, because of the extremely strong, deep tree roots of the primeval forests and the dense vegetation. The land in Indiana, except for areas along the Wabash and White rivers, was said to be not as fertile as in Illinois. Around Springfield, Illinois, it was hardly necessary to plow; [one just] hoed the ground, and it produced fine crops: 60 to 80 bushels of corn and 50 bushels of wheat per acre.

Frost [damage] was visible everywhere on the trees as we traveled through the forests—there would be no fruit and silage this year. The field crops were about as far along as those on the Rhine at this time [of year]. We ate lunch in a house where there were some good books, particularly on geography, lying around. From [there] we drove directly downhill to the bank of the [east fork] of the White River, which flowed through sublimely beautiful woodlands. A ferry took us across, and beyond the river we traveled through a dark, tall, almost purely beech forest; [we] enjoyed the large [trees] and the refreshing [shade]. [When] we reached the highest elevation in the area, we saw wild woodland scenes: romantic, rugged valleys [so] filled with tall forest trees [that] the blue sky was hardly visible [from the valley floor]. The height of the majestic trunks was impressive, and their diverse mixture highly picturesque. I had never [before] seen such forests in North America! That evening we stopped [at an isolated inn] surrounded by good farm buildings and encircled by fields in a lonely, rugged forest area. We had not expected to find such good accommodations, but everything was very well set up—it was extremely clean and the food [was quite] good. We rested splendidly after the exhausting stage travel in great heat.

14 [June]: [We traveled] 6 miles to the town of Paoli, [suffering] many sharp jolts on the rough road. The forests became more sparse. [At] Greenville, a small, poor village, there [was] a gathering of many country people; an election was being held. The heat was high and the dust very troublesome. [Several miles beyond,] we again found a gathering of many farmers, drinking a lot of whiskey; the assembly was very noisy and lively. They, too, had come together for the election of a councilman. The crowd was very inquisitive; they pressed around the coach and wanted to know where we came from.

We climbed to the end of a limestone hill chain, the summit of which we [had gained] gradually and without noticing. [From] its southern slope, we had an incomparable view into the valley, or rather, into the vast plain of the Ohio. As far as the eye could see, a dark forest covered the broad land, and the beautiful river cut through it like a silver stripe. In the distance we saw the houses of New Albany and Louisville, stretching out on both sides of the Ohio.

[At] New Albany [our stage] crossed the Ohio on a steam ferry in order to drive to Louisville, a few miles [away, where] some cholera cases [had been reported], but people had become rather indifferent to this serious illness. Our stay in Louisville was very short this time. The steamboat *Paul Jones* was [scheduled] to leave for Cincinnati in just a few hours. We had our luggage brought on board right away [and] departed at about five o'clock. [Our] course was very fast, but during the night, something broke in the steam engine, and we had to stop until two or three o'clock the [following] afternoon.

15 [June]: Rain all day, but in the afternoon it cleared up slightly, and we could admire the glorious Ohio forests; the colossal *Platanus* were especially outstanding. [We] even saw natural history curiosities on our boat. The clerk owned a young live lynx that was rather tame, [and] Mr. [William Backhouse] Astor from New York had brought along some prairie hens *(Tetrao cupido)* from St. Louis that were doing very well.[2]

Toward evening we reached [Madison, Indiana], a charming town, [where] we took on some passengers. Before dusk, the mouth of the Kentucky River was on our right. According to Flint (see *Indian Wars*, p. 49), the name "Kan-tuck-kee" should mean, in the Indian language of this area, the dark and bloody ground.

As night approached, the steam engine that had been repaired broke down for the second time, and we had to stop again.

16 [June]: During the night they repaired the engine at Vevay, and we then continued [on]. Vevay was established by Swiss [immigrants] from the [canton of Vaud]. In Cincinnati I sampled wine [made in Vevay] and found it very good. It had the color of a Madeira [and] a somewhat similar taste, only not as strong and alcoholic. At seven o'clock in the morning, we reached Rising Sun, [Indiana], with a few fairly attractive houses. [After noon] we reached Lawrenceburg, [Indiana], and then approached the city of Cincinnati. Settlements, houses, and country homes [increased] in its vicinity. [At] Cincinnati we disembarked at a large place [paved] with cobblestones on the riverbank, where [we met] numerous German emigrants. Many of the [drivers] who took travelers' luggage to the inns were Germans, almost all of them from Rhenish Bavaria, Baden, or Württemberg.

17 [June]: I looked around [the area] and mailed a few letters. Cincinnati is an imposing city, regularly [laid] out with broad streets crossing [at right angles], full of life and traffic [and a] great many fine stores and manufactories. [Their location on] the Ohio facilitates a far-reaching trade to the west, the south, and upriver, as well as a very lively communication [system, which] flourishes through the steamboats. Of these [latter] the following were anchored here: *Caledonia, Erin, Blackhawk, Tom Jefferson, Emigrant, Science,* U.S. Mail *Guyandotte,* [and others]. I visited the so-called Western Museum of [Joseph] Dorfeuille,[3] to whom I had a letter from Mr. Say. I found several

interesting artifacts there, although all these American museums are dedicated not to science but more to making money. [This one was] illuminated every evening starting about eight o'clock. Music, mostly played by foreigners (especially Germans), could be heard, and [there was] a small bubbling fountain, surrounded by benches. Gentlemen as well as riffraff sat around, as is customary in America, [with] their feet on the benches, admiring the marvel.

Mr. Dorfeuille is a man [with] a real feeling for science and would gladly do more for it, but his museum [attracted few] visitors until he opened an exhibition on hell: grottos where numerous skeletons move [about], the devil among them. This silly performance attracts the rabble. It is sad that in this country one must resort to such means to promote the interests of natural science, the sublime study.

Among the acquaintances I looked up was Mr. Richard Owen. I [also] had the [pleasure] of meeting [an] outstanding North American physician, Dr. [Daniel] Drake, known for various publications. His *Picture of Cincinnati* shows that he did not neglect the study of natural science. He had the kindness to inform me about several writings on cholera, among [other subjects]. At Captain Culbertson's I had to deliver a letter from Mr. Culbertson on the upper Missouri. In return I received very interesting Dacota artifacts from the [Minnesota] River, among them red stone pipe bowls [and] war clubs, as well as a large calumet stem.

At the booksellers in Cincinnati, I searched thoroughly for natural history works and North American travel accounts. But I found nothing except the second volume of Nuttall's *Ornithology,* published [during] my trip along the Missouri, as well as the latest Ohio and Mississippi [river guide]. In the bookstores here [there were mostly] *belles-lettres,* usually fashionably bound to attract buyers.

18 June: I was told [that] Dreidoppel had traveled through here [on his way] to Portsmouth a few days ago with the live animals. (I had been obliged to leave him behind in St. Louis, because the luggage was not yet in good order.)

19 June: At midday, eleven o'clock, we left the city of Cincinnati on the United States Mail boat *Guyandotte.* The weather was hot, [but it was] pleasant on the river. The steamboat *Lady Scott* [set out] at the same time as we did but soon [was] far behind our mail boat. The *Guyandotte* was a very fast boat and, like most Cincinnati vessels, had a largely white crew, since there were no Negro slaves in the state of Ohio.

There are three of these mail boats that alternately carry government dispatches. They only [do this] occasionally, because they receive no more than 5 dollars in compensation for [each] service. However, only the fastest boats are chosen for [this duty], and [they] then can [display] the inscription U.S. Mail in red on their wheel cover. At nightfall we were near the town of Ripley, [Ohio].

20 June: Early in the morning, [we had] a view of a chain of beautiful green, forested mountains that stretched along the river. Large, flat, square boats loaded with cut timber awaited the steamboats everywhere. If a skipper needed to buy wood, a [flatboat] was attached [to the steamer], unloaded while the journey continued, [and] released as soon as the wood was transferred. We put ashore at Portsmouth [at about half past noon].

XXIV

Voyage on the Ohio Canal via Lake Erie to Buffalo

Portsmouth is a rather unprepossessing town located in the angle between the Scioto and Ohio [rivers]. I found Dreidoppel here with our bears. [He] had already spent almost a week here and was delighted at his [imminent] deliverance. The inn was miserable, so I hurried to [book] the first [available] canal boat.

To get to the point of embarkation, we had to cross the Scioto and then drive a few hundred paces over sandy ground to a saloon [on] the canal, in front of which several boats were moored, including ours.[1] The length [of these boats was about] 77′ to 80′, width 14′. There were two kinds [on the Erie Canal in New York]: freight boats and packet boats, [both] pulled by horses. However, on the Ohio Canal, [the boats] were of one type only, [taking] passengers and freight together. They had a long space in the middle for freight [and] two small cabins [forward]—one for ladies [and] one for gentlemen. There were upholstered benches on the walls, where beds were made up [at] night; if there were more passengers than space, the floor was used. At the rear of the vessel, near the helm, was a small room where meals were taken.

We paid 18 dollars for the bears to Lake Erie. Our passage (three persons with much luggage) amounted to [——]. Among the passengers, we found Dr. [Zina] Pitcher ([a] physician in the United States Army) and his family, whom we had met on the steamboat from Cincinnati to Portsmouth, [a man knowledgeable about] natural history. He was coming from Fort Gibson on the Arkansas [River, in Oklahoma, and] had interesting specimens. I received a horned lizard from him, seeds of *Maclura aurantiaca* and *Sapindus saponaria,* [and] letters of recommendation to Dr. Edwin James of Albany and Dr. [Samuel George] Morton in Philadelphia. Our voyage began at approximately six o'clock in the evening, and beautiful weather favored us.

21–22 June: Splendid forested hills on each side of the canal: first, tall maples, then magnificent beeches. Our hunters shot the kingfisher *(Alcedo alcyon)* that was numerous here and [also] a kind of songbird. We [had been] following the Scioto River [since] yesterday and frequently saw [it] close beside the canal. About an hour and a half from Chillicothe the canal turned away from the Scioto and [crossed] the picturesquely beautiful Paint Creek. The aqueduct over which the canal flowed was wide, [with] three arches and two stone piers; paths with railings were provided on each side of [the aqueduct] for the draft horses and pedestrians.

Near six o'clock we caught sight of the town of Chillicothe lying before us in the flat area of the broad valley. The canal passed through [it]. Chillicothe is a sizeable [place] (currently 2,000 to 3,000 inhabitants) in a very nice area experiencing significant growth. We had a long stopover until dusk [and then traveled overnight].

[Next] morning, we passed several locks [and approached] the rather extensive town of Circleville, [which] received its name from [and was originally built within] an old, circular Indian fortification, or earthwork. The courthouse now stood at about the center of the circle, [the grass-covered, earthen walls of which once encompassed] 17¾ acres.[2] The canal boat made a stop here [lasting] three-quarters of an hour. It was Sunday. We used [the time] to look for remains of the Indian circle, but [our search was unsuccessful and] we returned quite displeased, seeing that all such [sites] were being destroyed [in this country] without regard for history. This was the case at Marietta, Cincinnati, St. Louis, and many [other] places. Instead of sparing [these] highly interesting documents of antiquity (there was sufficient space to build nearby), [the Americans] chose precisely these locations [to build, demolishing] [al]most everything [in the process]. The typically scanty descriptions of [these sites] are all that remain for us. In this way the Americans, with irresponsible selfishness and callousness, [not only] have driven out the native populations between the ocean and the Mississippi [but also] were destroying these last records of historic remembrance.

In this area of the canal, we saw meadows with grazing cattle, forest, and wooded hills, [all] alternating pleasantly. Iris, now without flowers, grew frequently on the banks. The area along the canal here was generally low bog land with many rushes and reeds where *Icterus phoeniceus,* the red-winged blackbird, swayed on the stalks in full splendor.

[Later, we passed through] eight locks near the small town, or village, [of] Lockbourne, [one of the many places where] we changed horses. The canal rose perhaps one hundred feet here and continued level at that elevation for a long way. During the night we passed Baltimore and Millers[port]. About morning we reached [a high] point of the canal, where it was laid through a deeply cut hill; we had passed 51 locks from Portsmouth up to this high place.

23 June: [After sunrise] we reached a town on the canal called Hebron, founded in November 1825 [and] located on the major, so-called National Road, [which comes] from Cumberland, [Maryland], and [passes] through the states of Ohio, Indiana, and Illinois. [At] Newark (999 inhabitants in 1830), we [stopped] for an hour and bought books about the area in a [shop] fairly well stocked for this part of the country. Seven miles from Newark the canal emptied into the Licking River [in] a beautiful, rocky forest valley, overgrown with conifers and deciduous trees, [that would] offer interesting [vistas to] a landscape artist. We left the Licking River [as] the canal turned to the left [and passed a number of small settlements before coming to] Nashport. On [each] side we always had forest, [but it was] no longer as tall and upright as that on the Ohio [River]. The fields were all surrounded by fences, just as decorative here as in Pennsylvania and [other] states. [On] a lock gate, I found a tree frog (*Hyla* [sp.]) sitting on the damp wood [and] caught it easily.

The evening was very pleasant, [and] during the night we followed the Tuscarawas, which [occasionally] flowed beside the canal.

24 June: [In the afternoon, we came to] Dover, about 80 [miles south of] Cleveland. From Dover we went on to Zoar, a charming settlement of German [religious] separatists who had come here from Württemberg. [Kilbourn's] *Ohio Gazetteer* (p. 510) states that the place was laid out originally on an area of 4,000 acres purchased [by the settlers] in the year 1818. A large part of this land is now under excellent cultivation. [The residents also] own two vineyards and various factories. We stopped [at] a long wooden bridge across the canal and the river. A shepherd was driving a considerable flock [over it]. I talked to him, and he answered in authentic Swabian [dialect], *"Freili sei mer Dütsche!"* [Naturally, we are Germans!]. He was dressed [exactly like] German shepherds, [in] a gray coat of thick material, a broad leather bandoleer with brass figures on it, and a flat round hat.

25 June: [When we got to] Akron (a significant town [with] many nice wooden houses, stores, factories, etc.), the valley began a steep descent. To bring the boats down from this considerable height, many locks [were built close]

together, [becoming] more and more distantly spaced as [one moved] farther down [the canal]. In a distance of 2½ miles we counted 21 [locks], of which about 10 to 12 followed each other directly within Akron.[3] [We eventually] reached the Cuyahoga River, which [flowed beside us all the way] down to Lake Erie.

26 June: About nine or ten o'clock [next morning], we reached Cleveland, bustling with people, life, and food. It had several thousand inhabitants, numerous churches, a school academy, a jail, inns, shops, and stores. Trade here was extremely lively, due to the Erie Canal and lake shipping. Many canal boats and schooners plied the lake, [and] steamboats departed daily, [though] none was present at the moment of our arrival. The beautiful, oceanlike view of Lake Erie pleased us and [made us think of] our imminent return to our native shores.

While I was [sightseeing around the harbor], the [steamer] *Oliver Newberry*, scheduled to sail to Buffalo, [arrived]. We went aboard immediately and departed at twelve noon. The view back toward Cleveland was [impressive]; we saw how the town extended along the shore, up the hill, and [then] across the plain. Our steamboat did not steer far from the lake's southern shore. [Lake Erie] is 290 miles long from southwest to northeast, and 63 miles [at its widest point]. The southern shore belongs to the United States, the northern to England.

27 June: [Next morning,] land appeared on both shores; we were already approaching the end of this beautiful lake, [and the] sizable city [of Buffalo] soon [appeared] before us. Magnificent steamboats—more than thirty [currently] sailed on this lake—passed us with flags flying and [crowded] with passengers. Buffalo is a [lively] city. [There were about] 12,000 inhabitants, [whose numbers had] increased exceptionally in a short time. Thanks to its location, [the city] promises to become an important commercial center. The Erie Canal begins here, a fine, fast connection to the cities of New York, Boston, and Philadelphia. The remarkable Niagara Falls are [not far away and] attract large crowds of tourists and foreigners—who also visit Buffalo. [There are] several fine public buildings, all enumerated in small booklets written [for] tourists (see, for instance, *The Traveler's Guide through the Northern States* and similar works).

We stayed only half a day in Buffalo and [that] afternoon visited [a] Seneca Indian village southeast of the city. They lived in the woodlands, [among] their scattered fields and plantings, in small wooden houses built in the fashion of the whites. A pretty little church [was at] the approximate center of this Indian colony. The Senecas living here were engaged in agriculture and had cattle [and] horses. Their clothing was almost the same as that of white men. The facial features, skin color, and hair of many of these people did not differ significantly from Missouri Indians (essentially the same facial features can be found [among] all American [Indian] nations). Some spoke English, [while] others [did not], and all used their old Indian language when they talked among themselves. Originally 900 Indians were said to have been settled here, but they are no longer that numerous. We returned in the evening to Buffalo, mourning the destruction of all of these highly interesting native peoples of eastern North America. Dreidoppel put our live bears aboard an Erie Canal freight boat, on which he would sail the following morning. Only with much effort did we succeed in getting the bears aboard a boat; the skippers would not agree to anything at first.

XXV

Journey to Niagara Falls and Visit with the Tuscaroras near Lake Ontario

FROM 28 JUNE TO [1 JULY 1834]

28 June: We left Buffalo on the stage at about eight o'clock in the morning and drove up along the Erie Canal, which flows parallel to the beautiful Niagara River here. The river originates at the eastern end of Lake Erie and has the same magnificent, bluish green water. [Not far from the lake is] a large island called Grand Island, which the Seneca Indians sold to the state of New York in 1815. The state paid 1,000 dollars and an annuity of 500 dollars.[1] The island is said to be 12 miles long and 2 to 7 miles wide. [There are other,] smaller islands [in] the Niagara, which is 35 miles [long]. In that distance, it creates the glorious large falls about which so much has been endlessly written already [that] I will only describe the impression they made on us. About twelve thirty we approached the village of [Niagara Falls], built next to the falls. The banks of the Niagara [River] are mostly rock walls picturesquely overgrown with broad-leafed trees and conifers. A certain [Samuel] Hooker lived opposite our inn in Niagara. For a fee, he acquainted tourists with all the [local] curiosities. He owned a small collection of minerals, petrifactions, stuffed animals, and Indian curiosities [for sale]. I bought an outstanding specimen of *Strix nyctea* (it sometimes stays here in winter), as well as several items made by the Senecas and Tuscaroras, especially birch bark baskets trimmed with porcupine and colorful bird quills. After lunch we went to look at the falls.

The river, [flowing over] a rocky bed, begins to break up before [it reaches the] village. Its whole surface turns into a rapid—a wildly foaming body of water [descending in] five- to six-foot-high cascades. Even from a distance, we could hear the raging and roaring of the falls, and we saw high columns of white water vapor rising into the sky. From the village we [walked] to the rapid just described and [crossed over] the end on a wooden bridge to a small island called [Green Island]. A house here collected a bridge toll of 37½ cents, [allowing] one to pass free for the duration of one's stay. The toll collector [offered] refreshments and a good collection of local fossils [and] Indian artwork from the tribes of the Seneca, Cayuga, Tuscarora, etc. We crossed a second bridge from [Green Island] to the large, [thickly] forested Goat Island. A comfortable path [went] along the shore of the island, through the forest, and [then] abruptly up to the steep rim [overlooking] the colossal torrent of the right river branch. [The river] is divided by Goat Island into two main branches forming two large cascades. The view was more grand by far than I had imagined it from various descriptions. The broad, magnificent river, with its lively, bluish green water and snow-white foam, drops, boiling, 170 to 180 feet vertically into the depths, dissolving halfway down into mist, rain, fog, and clouds; astonished eyes can follow it only to the vapor and not down to the [bottom of the abyss]. The chasm was filled with [this] mist; columnlike clouds [of it rose] high into the air. At the edge of Goat Island, we walked down a somewhat steep slope, where we could sit on the trunk of a thick old birch bent down to the ground. [This] placed us at the edge of the right falls, where we enjoyed a splendid view. It was awe-inspiring!

We returned from there to the top of Goat Island and followed a path through the dark shadows of the forest along the front edge of the island. After 400 to 500 paces, or a little more, we reached an exceptionally imposing vista of Horseshoe Falls. They cross the entire, colossally wide riverbed [and] are 150 feet high; the raging torrent of water plunges downward, dissolving into mist that partially shrouds the wooded banks, [which could] be only half seen through the veil. We walked down a steep [incline] to a wooden tower [with] a spiral staircase. [From] the circular gallery [at] its top, [as well as from] windows [placed] at different levels, we could view the magnificent scenery from [different] elevations. [At the bottom,] beneath the rock face of the island, we walked to the right [to American Falls] and to the left [to Horseshoe Falls]; one could step into the dark shadows under the torrents of water, if one did not mind the soaking rain and strong wind. Both locations were indescribably imposing.

We went up the stairs again and continued to walk [around] the edge of the forested island to a small house with several partitions, [each space] open and unobstructed in front [so that] we could sit and enjoy the magnificent scenery. Thousands of names from all countries are written and carved there, and their numbers increase daily — a bad custom found in all parts of the world, wherever the Europeans have taken it.

[After exploring further] we went back to the village [and] down to the ferry. Although it is hardly more than three to four hundred paces below the falls, the water is [not] very choppy, and we soon landed on the Canadian, or British, bank. The falls were right in front of us, and Mr. Bodmer made a sketch; [see pl. 31].

We climbed up an [easy] trail along the rock face and reached a house on top, where refreshments were to be had. A guide [then] led us to the so-called museum. An Englishman there had quite an interesting natural history collection, which he showed for a fee.

From there we went to [the vantage point named] Table Rock, where one could survey both falls; many tourists prefer this view to that on the American side. I must say, however, that each has its merits, and travelers [should] visit both. Filled with the great scenery of nature, we returned home in the evening.

29 June: Sunday. Mr. Bodmer went out to sketch the falls. I drove to the meeting (church service) of the Tuscarora Indians, who were settled [on a reservation] 8 miles from Niagara, toward Lake Ontario. When I [arrived], I saw scattered, individual wooden Indian houses, constructed European style, [and] the small, white-painted church of the Tuscaroras. [It] was completely filled with Indians. The clergyman, a young man who had been here only since last spring, was already at the pulpit. [He] gave a sermon in English, as he did not yet understand the Indian language. Next to him on the right stood an interpreter, who repeated all his phrases. When the sermon, [followed by a prayer and singing], was over, I followed the clergyman outside. He told me [that his] Tuscarora congregation [numbered] 300 souls. They were Presbyterians. They resembled [the Senecas] in language and appearance. However, I found less authenticity among the Tuscaroras than among the Senecas near Buffalo. Their features, color, and hair seemed to have suffered more from mixing with the whites. I could not obtain any books in the language of this nation.

30 June: Sunshine. [After seeing waxwings and a rainbow on Luna Island near the American Falls,] I explored Goat Island a long time this day and found all kinds of interesting plants in the shadow of its tall forest: *Podophyllum, Trillium, Asarum, Juniperus virginiana,* [and] *Thuja occidentalis.* Several species of *Rhus* were very common. [There were] *Betula lenta,* beech trees, sugar maples, elms, [and other] tall, slender trees.

1 July: At about nine o'clock we left Niagara on the stage for Tonawanda and the Erie Canal. A [canal] packet boat, with three horses hitched to it, arrived at Tonawanda after eleven o'clock, and we went aboard.

XXVI

Voyage on the Erie Canal to Albany

FROM 1 JULY TO 4 JULY [1834]

[1 July:] These boats were furnished for passengers only and not for freight, [and so] the whole inner space was divided into several quite nicely furnished cabins, [including] two rooms for ladies. We could not take as much luggage, [however].

Twelve hundred [passenger and] freight boats navigate the Erie Canal. Its construction cost 7 million dollars; the Ohio Canal is said to have cost only 4 million. The difficult stonework was said to have been the cause [of the higher cost].[1]

At [first] we followed Tonawanda [Creek], with woods and cultivated fields on its [banks]. About 5 miles from the village [of Pendleton], the canal had been cut through a bed of graywacke, at first 4, [then] 5, 8, 10, [and finally] 15 feet above the water. We noticed boreholes for blasting everywhere.

[When] we approached a place, someone would blow a type of Kent horn, [a bugle,] to [alert] those who wished to travel. We put ashore in the shadow of a broad, high bridge at Lockport, [where] we had to descend from a significant elevation, [requiring] five locks to get the boats down. The summit was at least 60 feet high, [and] the view from it was very fine! About evening [we passed] Middleport, a village.

2 July: [We landed at] Rochester early in the morning, an imposing city [with] a quite well-stocked bookstore. We embarked on a new boat and continued [our voyage]. [At] Pittsford, which had a few good brick houses and a church with a steeple, we changed [canal boat] horses. We saw beautiful small forests, almost purely oak, in this area, [also] many turtles and blooming roses. We encountered several canal boats loaded with European emigrants. Our horses trotted constantly; a packet boat like ours could cover 100 to 104 miles in 24 hours.

[We passed nearby] forests heavily mixed with firs. *Thuja* grew here in numbers, tall and strong, also the Ohio larch *(Larix), Platanus, Cercis,* several kinds of walnut, oak, elm, maple, willow, and *Rhus.* The magnificent dark of the forest and its excellent scent were enjoyable and refreshing. Clearings and extensive fields followed on gentle elevations to the left. Discounting the [numerous] fences and the somewhat different look of the bushes, the area showed a similarity to Germany. After twelve o'clock we reached Palmyra, a small place with considerable trade, mills, and factories. The trumpet summoned passengers, and fresh horses were hitched. In the afternoon we passed the village of Lyons, and approximately an hour later, Clyde, an impressive town [with] a glass pane factory.

3 July: At daybreak we were at Syracuse, a large [place with] more than 500 houses, among them very handsome ones; several inns; a few nice churches; a bank; [and] many good stores. Syracuse did not exist twenty years ago. At that time, a single, old house stood on this place. Now the wide, flat, fertile valley is heavily cultivated. The land was purchased from the Onondaga Indians; we saw several in the town of Syracuse—they did not differ significantly from the Senecas and Tuscaroras. After a stop of about an hour, our boat continued its voyage; several new passengers came aboard at Syracuse, and the boat was very full. Because it is a custom in America—even among gentlemen—to chew tobacco, all these boats kept large, round, tin containers with an opening in the sunken upper part. Less than lovely brown liquids were spat into these [cuspidors].

We [passed] Manlius [and] Chittenango [and] at twelve o'clock came to Oneida, [built] on both sides of the canal with one irregular street. Here we saw perhaps more than one hundred Oneida Indians, whose lands, given to them by the government, were located not far to the south. Part of this nation was about to embark from here to settle at Green Bay.[2]

In the brightest sunshine, at about five thirty, we reached Whites[boro] on the left canal bank, a charming, productive place. The White family started this town, i.e., they were the first settlers here. A certain Henry White, who gave me this information, was on our boat. His grandfather had been one of the first settlers, and the place was named after him. When the Messrs. White settled here, the Oneida Indians lived in the whole area. Their revered chief at the time was Skenandoah. He visited the White family often, and a very good relationship existed. Mr. Henry White's oldest sister, a child two years old at the time, was [well liked] by the Indians. One day they asked [her parents] if they would let her go home with them into their forests. This question alarmed the parents, who discussed what should be done. They considered the matter and found it politically expedient not to arouse any distrust, so they let her go. The Indians were very happy. [A date of return was agreed upon, when] the Indians punctually brought the child, who had been given small gifts, attached to her clothing. [The Indians] were very grateful for this proof of trust.

The whole Whitestown area (in general, the entire Mohawk River valley) is highly attractive, the most beautiful and friendly I saw in North America. The Mohawk nation formerly lived in this area. [Many] were, however, enemies of the United States and took the side of the British [in the American Revolution], so they were later resettled in Canada.

Utica was soon before us. The canal was crowded with boats near this sizable, bustling place.

4 July: Fog in the morning. [The canal went through] the town of Canajoharie, [and by the time] we passed Glen [and] several locks, [we were] 59 miles [past] Utica. The Mohawk flowed hidden between shaded bushes. Herds of horses grazed on the meadows of the flat valley floor, where some very nice barley fields were located. Then, on the left bank, [we saw] Amsterdam, 16 miles [from] Schenectady, [which] we reached about three o'clock. Carriages stood ready there to [take] passengers 16 miles to Albany on the [Mohawk and Hudson Railroad]. We [boarded one of these large, comfortable] stages. The luggage was packed in covered, locked baggage cars hitched to the stage. These wagons ran on grooved wheels on railroad [tracks]. A single horse pulled [each] wagon a few hundred paces [until we reached] a gently rising elevation. [The horses] were then unhitched. Ropes were attached to the wagons. [Stationary] steam engines on the top of the eminence [pulled] the wagons uphill. [After] arriving at the summit, the row of wagons was connected to a steam [engine]. Everything slowly started to move. But the steam quickly had its full effect, and we rolled along on the railroad as fast as an arrow. The distance of 16 miles was covered in an hour, [and] we reached our destination [when it was] still early in the afternoon.

Albany, where we now were, [had] 26,000 inhabitants, handsome buildings, and wide, regular streets full of good, diverse shops. I [will not] repeat here what can be read in any traveller's guide about the city, [but it] was a great day when we [arrived there]: 4 July, [the] Day of Independence, the same day we reached America exactly two years ago.

I made use of a letter [of introduction] from Dr. Pitcher to Mr. Edwin James, the geologist of Major Long's expedition to the Rocky Mountains. I found him [to be] a very courteous man. He is a great friend of botany, but his herbarium was not set up well—[it had] inferior, small specimens. He has occupied himself [lately] with Indian languages, particularly that of the Ojibwes. He resided among this people for a long time. He kindly gave me a schoolbook written by him in this language and a long list of [Ojibwe] words, as well as a letter of recommendation to Mr. DuPonceau in Philadelphia. I spent the evening in the company of his family, [and] I hope to have gained [in Mr. James] a [useful] American correspondent, [for] the true value of my journey will be seen in [times ahead].

XXVII

Journey from Albany to New York
and Stopovers There and at Philadelphia

FROM 5 JULY TO 16 JULY [1834], UNTIL THE VOYAGE TO EUROPE

5[–7] July: At seven o'clock we boarded the fine steamboat *Albany,* which sailed
to and from New York. We made the 144-mile [trip] in one leisurely day.
The river was at least twice the width of the Rhine. The [Catskills] were
without question the loveliest place I saw along the picturesque Hudson,
and [the scenery] is to be recommended to [any] landscape painter. [After
passing through a narrow gorge, we saw] West Point, [home of] the United
States Military Academy, located in scenic, forested mountains. About one
hour from West Point, we were opposite Sing Sing on the [eastern] bank—a
handsome, sizable [but] scattered town with white houses;[1] [there was] a
penitentiary on the river below [it], a large, barracks-type building. We
reached New York before evening.

After I had called on and seen our friends on 6 and 7 July, I went to
Philadelphia.

8–10 July: We [traveled by steamboat and stage to Philadelphia] and arrived at
about four or five o'clock.

I immediately visited Mr. Krumbhaar, as well as Dr. [Richard] Harlan,
who introduced me to Mr. DuPonceau, a learned researcher in the Indian
languages. Unfortunately, I had very little time to [take full advantage of]
these acquaintances. Dr. Harlan owned [John James] Audubon's large ornithological work, which I had not seen so complete, as well as an interesting collection of skulls [including] many from different Indian nations.
Later, Dr. Harlan kindly showed me the collection of the Geological Society
[of Pennsylvania] and that of the [Academy] of Natural Sciences; [the lat-
ter] society owns items from all the branches of natural history, and I received a copy of their writings in exchange for my illustrations of Brazilian
animals, which I promised to send to them.

Some of my remaining time was spent in the museum of Mr. Titian

Peale, where I found very interesting objects.[2] Peale's collection of Indian artifacts was very rich. There were particularly nice pipes with figures [carved] in relief [that] I had never seen before. I visited Mr. Isaac Lea; his conchylia collection was remarkable, [with] magnificent *Unio* species and American river and saltwater crustaceans.

My last business in Philadelphia was the purchase of many books necessary for [my research] in Europe. Mr. Krumbhaar had been so kind as to order them for me from Mr. Dobson, one of the best book dealers. I took a full wooden crate along with me to New York.

11 July: We [returned to] New York. Our tasks here had piled up, but the Messrs. Gebhard and Schuchardt assisted us in every respect. Prussian Consul Schmidt kindly invited us [once more] to his comfortable home, where we saw Mr. William Astor and his wife. Mr. [John Jacob] Astor, [William's] father, was in New York, and I made his acquaintance. He was constructing a very large inn [on Broadway], a massive stone building [that] will become an ornament of the city.[3]

I booked passage on the packet boat *Havre,* Captain Stoddart [commanding], that was to sail on 16 July, [and] we arranged everything for the impending voyage. Our passage [costs] per person came to 140 dollars, which included wine and drinks. Dreidoppel was charged 70 dollars, and my four bears also [cost] 70 dollars.[4]

On 15 [July], I made my farewell visits. The ship on which we embarked [was large and well equipped, with a crew of 27 men]. [On board it] had a milk cow with a calf, many small pigs, wethers, turkey hens, peacocks, ducks, and chickens as provisions to be slaughtered [as needed]. The menu was excellent—daily beef or mutton, fresh pork, chicken, duck, or goose, ham, fresh green peas, potatoes, beans, lentils, onions, various cooked and preserved fruits, pies, fancy cakes, and [other] items of this kind. [Also,] good wines such as Bordeaux, Graves, champagne, Madeira, sherry, and others, [plus] good port, ale, soda water, [and] lemonade—in short, passengers could order what they wished. At eight o'clock we ate breakfast: coffee, wine, corn mush, pancakes, waffles, anchovies, ham, smoked tongue, and so on. At twelve o'clock luncheon [was served:] cooked fruit, cold meats, wine, smoked salmon, and the like. At four o'clock [we ate dinner], a meal of considerable variety, always ending with several wines, nuts, and dried fruits as dessert. In the evening, [we had] tea after seven o'clock—cold, light foods served with tea and wine. Milk, fairly fresh, was available at every meal. Radishes were grown in [wooden] boxes on the ship.

[There were twenty registered passengers on this ship (listed by name), and,] in addition, Mr. Bodmer, Dreidoppel, and myself.

XXVIII

Sea Voyage to Europe

16 July–24 July: At ten o'clock we went aboard a steamboat that [ferried] passengers to the *Havre,* in the middle of New York's fine harbor basin. [The first days were relatively uneventful; several ships were sighted, as were *Physalia,* petrels, and much *Fucus vesiculosus.* By the afternoon of 24 July,] we were not far south of Newfoundland's [Grand Banks].

25 July: In the morning, some rain, then the sky was slightly cloudy. Someone saw a shark. One of my American blue finches *(Fringilla cyanea)* flew away, and we neither saw nor heard it again. Dolphins jumped high out of the water and often loudly slapped the surface with their tails. Rain in the night.

26 July–5 August: [With a] good, brisk wind, we moved fast. In 24 hours we sailed through approximately five degrees [of longitude], precisely following the [record-setting] course of the *Columbia,* which made the voyage to New York in fifteen days [in 1829]. [By 30 July] we had already covered a little more than half the distance [to Europe].

6 August: We sighted [several] vessels, [mostly] from afar, [but one] three-masted ship [came] within [hailing] distance. We called to [those on board] with a speaking tube. It was the *Congress* out of New Orleans, which had come from there in 48 days and was bound for Liverpool.

7 August: We had sailed by Lizard [Point] during the night and were now in the middle of the Channel, approximately 38 miles from the English coast. The tips for the stewards were collected; each passenger contributed 20 francs.

At three o'clock someone saw land from the mainmast: the island [of] Guernsey. [Later] the French coast [and Cap de la Hague] were clearly visible. The wind was very strong, the sky dark, and everything led us to expect a bad night, particularly [since it appeared that] we could not take a pilot aboard this evening; the Channel is dangerous when shipping during a storm. Finally the Captain shouted that he saw a pilot boat, and very soon we could see the small red, white, and blue flag flying at the top of its foremast. We hoisted [our] foremast flag right away, as a signal for the pilot. The pilot boat fought fiercely against the waves; there were only three men on it.

Finally it was beside us. We hung thick [padded?] balls overboard to buffer the impact of the [vessels]. [Ropes were thrown from the *Havre*,] which the pilots tied down and [then] pulled themselves [close to us]. One of [the pilots] threw a bundle across and jumped on board. The ropes were immediately released, and our vessels distanced themselves from one another. We raised our sails and sped away.

The pilot [told] me there were 41 pilots at [Le] Havre. Yesterday [they] celebrated Jour du Saint Sauveur, the only holiday for pilots; he said that was why one saw so few pilots on the seas today.

8 August: At daybreak we were [just off Le] Havre. We had to lie there until ten thirty, when there was enough water [depth] to enter the harbor. The wind was blowing at gale force, so we carried only [a] few sails. We saw perhaps 30 to 40 smaller ships in the Channel. All passengers were busy putting their luggage in order, and we exchanged addresses, since we had made many pleasant acquaintances.

Finally the pilot checked his watch and called out that we [would now] go in. The sails were quickly set, and our ship hurried toward the harbor [in a rough sea]. The harbor entrance at [Le] Havre—like all harbors on the Channel—is narrow and can be entered only at high tide. It does not compare with the magnificent, wide harbors of America, [with] plenty of space and deep water everywhere. At eleven thirty the *Havre* dropped its anchor. We were now securely in Europe, after having been absent from these shores for two years and two months.

XXIX

Journey through France and Holland to Germany

[Le Havre] is a lively commercial city of 35,000 inhabitants. The harbor and the docks are quite extensive and busy with ships from all nations. The American traffic is especially strong. Many English people were settled here; therefore, there were several very English inns as well as English steamboats sailing regularly. We [had difficulty] finding accommodations [but] finally [found a room] in the London Hotel; it was not particularly good.

I called on Mr. [Alexandre] Eyriès (the brother of the well-known translator), who lived very comfortably near [Le] Havre. I gave him news and regards from his friend [Mr.] Lesueur in [New] Harmony, which made him very happy. He himself was an expert in and enthusiast of botany and cultivated many beautiful plants [in an extensive,] terraced garden [and a] greenhouse. [He] owned a nice cactus collection [and] liked to trade [specimens].

Dreidoppel put my bears aboard a boat bound for Dunkerque and left with them in the night of 9 August; I paid 65 francs for the passage.

On 11 August, we embarked on a French [steamboat] to [go] up the Seine to Rouen. The boat was fairly loaded with passengers; the cabin [was] very small and dark. We sailed past Harfleur [and then] Honfleur. In the afternoon, the [broad] river [became more] narrow; in its lower regions, the Seine [has shifting] shallow spots and sandbanks, making shipping dangerous and arduous. Small flags mark these places. As night came, we saw ahead of us the numerous lights of Rouen, where we moored at the *quai* directly in front of the Hotel Rouen and disembarked.

Rouen, an imposing city of 100,000 inhabitants, [is] built in the old style with tall houses [and] narrow streets. There is much commerce and ship traffic; various factories; fine, diverse stores; many large, old churches; a city hall with a public promenade; and shady avenues. Very much worth seeing is the old Gothic cathedral with its two tall towers, truncated on top. From its platform there is an incomparable view down toward the mass of houses [in] the old city.

I found only one dealer in natural history objects, who had only a small cabinet. He also functioned as a barber.

13–14 August: We departed at eight o'clock on the *diligence* [(stagecoach)]. The roads were good, but the area was very hilly. Beyond [Neufchatel], the harvest was under way everywhere. All the farmers were in the fields, bringing in the crops. We reached Abbeville at twelve o'clock that night and stopped at the Hotel d'Angleterre.

Early [the next] morning I visited my old ornithological correspondent Mr. [Louis Antoine François] Baillon and saw his interesting collection. He [now focuses just] on waterfowl [and] owns [a] very complete [collection of those].   I dined at Mr. Baillon's and got acquainted there with a man who had [collected the] nests of all the birds he had been able to reach. [Some nests] were in tall glass cabinets, arranged [on] moss. I promised him additions.

15 August: We left Abbeville [on] the [stagecoach and traveled all day and night, arriving] at Dunkerque at daybreak. We learned that the steamboat had left for Rotterdam the previous evening. We had arrived too late and had to stay here [for days, waiting for] a Dutch steamboat.

The booksellers I visited were very poor. The only natural history institution was [one personal] collection, quite nicely [and] daintily stuffed and exhibited, [with] a few interesting pieces.

20–21 August: At [noon] the bears were brought to the steamboat; the rest of our luggage came later in the afternoon. We stayed nearby until ten thirty that night, when we embarked. Our ship, a small steamboat, had perhaps 20 passengers. In the morning, cloudy sky, strong wind, and high seas. Except for me, most of the passengers [were] seasick. At ten o'clock we had a view of the coast of Holland far to the right; at eleven the pilot came aboard [to] steer the ship between the buoys and poles that marked the shallows; and shortly before dusk, we moored at the Boompjes in Rotterdam. Our passports were checked aboard the ship. Then we [took] our luggage to a nearby inn. Because the bears had to be weighed and transit customs duties had to be paid for them, Dreidoppel stayed in Rotterdam. But I went with Mr. Bodmer on the morning of 22 August on board the steamboat *Zeuw*, [bound] for [Nijmegen], [which we] reached about four o'clock in the afternoon. [After an overnight stay, we made an] early departure on 23 August. About ten o'clock we reached Emmerich [and the] Prussian border.

We handed in our passports but were not checked, got away after one hour, [and sailed on].

24 August: In the morning, we reached Cologne [and] disembarked, [and] I went by carriage to Bonn, where we arrived at four o'clock [and spent the night].

25 August: I took a carriage and drove to Remagen [and] from there to Hammer-stein, and [I] reached Monrepos about noon, [where I] surprised my family, [who were] all completely healthy.[1]

Editorial Notes

Editorial Procedures

1. The three large *NAJ* volumes are thoroughly annotated with identifications of geographic and geological phenomena, historical events and people, etc. A small percentage of Maximilian's footnotes have been moved into his text, typically where they expand on his text discussion. The twenty-first-century editorial notes have been largely eliminated in the condensation. In most instances, readers will either be familiar with a person, place, or thing or will be able to quickly look the name up in readily available printed or online sources (including this condensation's cast of characters; see page xxxi). When an item might not be generally known or easy to research, a footnote has been provided. Maximilian's remaining footnotes, designated by M1, M2, etc., are printed on the page with which they are associated; editorial footnotes, designated by Arabic numerals only (1, 2, etc.), are grouped by chapter at the end of the entire narrative.

2. Maximilian, in his author's preface to *Travels in the Interior of North America,* as reprinted in Thwaites, *EWT,* 22:26.

An Introduction to Prince Maximilian of Wied and His Expedition to North America

1. Letter to Michael L. Hall, National Endowment for the Humanities, October 20, 2005. Gary Moulton is the editor of *The Journals of the Lewis and Clark Expedition.*

2. Maximilian, Prince of Wied's *Travels in the Interior of North America, 1832–1834,* author's preface, as reprinted in Thwaites, *EWT,* 22:25–27. Maximilian, in his introduction to his 1839–43 publication on his North American journey (intended for a largely European readership), did credit the report on the expedition of Meriwether Lewis and William Clark and James's report on Stephen Long's expedition but lamented the dearth of natural history data in them.

3. Details of Prince Maximilian's life are taken largely from Paul Schach, "An Introduction to Maximilian, Prince and Scientist," *NAJ* 1:xxxv–xlii.

4. Karl Viktor Prinz zu Wied, "Maximilian Prinz zu Wied," 17.

5. Huppertz, "Textkritische Analyse," 75.

6. Ernst Schwendler to Maximilian, 9 March 1832, MBC, JAM.

7. Captain von Mühlbach to Maximilian, 25 February 1832, MBC, JAM.

8. Forty-five thalers would have been about $30.00 in 1834 (Grund, *Merchant's Assistant*); in 2014 dollars, as calculated by the Consumer Price Index, that would be just under $1,000 (www.measuringworth.com/uscompare/ [accessed 24 September 2015]).

9. Details of Bodmer's life before and after the North American expedition are from Orr, "Karl Bodmer," the most complete biography in English. For reproductions of Bodmer's original North American drawings and watercolors, see Hunt et al., *KBA*, and Wood et al., *KBSA;* for the prints, see Ruud et al., *KBNAP.*

10. David Dreidoppel (also spelled Dreydoppel; 1793–1866) served Maximilian on his earlier Brazilian expedition as well. Evidently an expert marksman, he was also a skilled taxidermist. For a biography, see Schmidt, "Hofjäger David Dreydoppel."

11. *NAJ* 1:10nM1.

12. International Institute of Social History, Royal Netherlands Academy of Arts and Sciences, www.iisg.nl/hpw/calculate2.php (accessed 23 September 2015).

13. *NAJ* 1:97.

14. *NAJ* 1:261nM165.

15. Wied, *Reise,* ix.

16. *NAJ* 2:196, 198.

17. *NAJ* 2:525. Fort Union was located close to the junction of the Yellowstone and Missouri Rivers, near the border of present-day North Dakota with Montana; Fort McKenzie was in north-central Montana, close to the mouth of the Marias River and northeast of modern Great Falls.

18. *NAJ* 2:321.

19. The French translation of the *Reise, Voyage dans l'interieur de L'Amerique du Nord, exécuté pendant les années 1832, 1833 et 1834,* was produced by Arthus Bertrand in three smaller-format volumes in Paris. The abridged, single-volume English translation, *Travels in the Interior of North America, 1832–1834,* was published by Ackerman in London. For information on the complex history of Bodmer's production of the accompanying eighty-one engravings, which were produced in both black-and-white and color versions, see Ruud et al., *Karl Bodmer's North American Prints.* These prints, highly sought by collectors today, are among the earliest, finest, and most accurate of nineteenth-century depictions of the American western landscape and Plains tribesmen.

20. This material remained in storage at the Wied estate in Neuwied for nearly a century after Maximilian's death in 1867. Through the efforts of Josef Röder (1914–75), a German museum official and an acquaintance of the Wied family, a small selection of Bodmer watercolors and drawings was exhibited in United States Information Agency Amerika Haus facilities in German cities after World War II. A traveling exhibition of 116 Bodmers was subsequently circulated in the United States by the Smithsonian Institution (1953–58). In 1959, the Wied family sold the art and archives to M. Knoedler and Company, a well-known New York City gallery. The Smithsonian Bodmer exhibition had been shown at Joslyn Art Museum in 1954; the museum's director, Eugene Kingman, and its board chairman, John F. Merriam, keenly understood the significance of Maximilian and Bodmer for America, particularly for the Plains region. In 1962, Omaha's Northern Natural Gas Company, of which Merriam was the corporate chairman, purchased the North American collection from Knoedler and placed it at Joslyn on long-term loan. The company, which in 1980 changed its name to InterNorth Inc. and later to Enron Corp., donated the entire assemblage to the museum in 1986.

21. For other types of items in the MBC, see *NAJ* 1:xxvii–xxviii.

22. *NAJ* 1:371. Volume 1 of the manuscript journals ends with chapter 6; volume 2 ends with chapter 14.

23. *NAJ* 3:265&n33.

24. Another indication of the class difference between Dreidoppel and Bodmer in Maximilian's eyes is reflected in the fares he purchased for them on the Atlantic crossings; in both instances Bodmer traveled with the same amenities as the prince, while Dreidoppel's fare (and presumably the quality of his berthing and meals) was much less. *NAJ* 3:405n25.

25. Quoted in Bradley, "Affairs at Fort Benton," 206–7.

26. The first quotation is from a letter to James Kipp; the second is from a missive to P. Chouteau, Jr., both written in December 1833 and included in Abel, *Chardon's Journal*, 353, 366.

27. Thwaites, *EWT*, 22:20.

Chapter I. *[Journey] from Europe to Boston*

1. On the Réaumur temperature scale (hereafter abbreviated as "R"), water freezes at 0° and boils at 80°. To convert to Fahrenheit, use Réaumur degree × 9/4 + 32, and to Celsius, Réaumur degree × 5/4, or use the conversion tool at www.csgnetwork.com/tempconv.html. In this instance, 13.5°R = 62°F.

2. The "Paris foot," or *pied*, is equivalent to about 12.79 English or U.S. inches (32.48 centimeters in metric terms). The *pied* was divided into twelve *pouces*, or inches, themselves subdivided into twelve *lignes*, or lines. Six French feet would equal 6.39 English feet.

Chapter II. *Stay in Boston, New York, and Philadelphia*

1. New York City's first case of cholera was recorded on 26 June 1832. The city had about 3,500 cholera fatalities in the following two months. City University of New York, "Cholera in 1832," www.virtualny.cuny.edu/cholera/1832/cholera_1832_set.html.

2. John Scudder's American Museum was then located at Broadway and Ann Street. P. T. Barnum purchased the museum in 1841 for $10,000. Haberly, "American Museum." Rubens Peale's New York Museum was at 252 Broadway. Barnum acquired the Peale collection in 1843 and moved it to the American Museum. See Sellers, *Mr. Peale's Museum*.

3. Dr. James McDonald (1803–49) was director of the Bloomingdale Insane Asylum in 1832. *Appleton's Cyclopedia*. The location was in today's Morningside Heights neighborhood. Columbia University's Buell Hall is the last building that survives from the old asylum. Columbia University, "Columbia University in Morningside Heights: A Framework for Planning," http://neighbors.columbia.edu/pdf-files/ch6.pdf (accessed 8 June 2006).

4. Thomas McKenney and James Hall's *History of the Indian Tribes of North America*. For its complex publication history, see Tyler, *Prints of the West*, 38–45.

5. Maximilian traveled under the pseudonym Baron von Braunsberg.

Chapter III. Sojourn in Bethlehem, Pennsylvania,
and Excursions into the Surrounding Region

1. Maximilian and Dreidoppel could have been suffering from mild cases of cholera.

2. The Lehigh Coal and Navigation Company was the proprietor of the Mauch Chunk coal mines, and the company's railroads there were gravity operated at the time of Maximilian's visit. Thwaites, *EWT,* 22:123n48; Mathews and Hungerford, *History,* 662–65. The name Mauch Chunk is a corruption of the Lenni-Lenape term meaning "Bear Mountain"; the town today is called Jim Thorpe. Mathews and Hungerford, *History,* 656. Mauch Chunk was a major tourist destination from the 1820s until World War I. Sears, *Sacred Places,* 191–208.

3. According to Duke Bernhard, the town's name originated as a "joke concerning the great fertility of its citizens." Jeronimus, *Travels,* 206. The German verb *hecken* means "to breed (livestock)."

Chapter IV. Journey from Bethlehem in Pennsylvania
to New Harmony on the Wabash

1. Maximilian's information on the number of slaves and free blacks in Pennsylvania is from an undated newspaper clipping from the *United States Gazette,* a Philadelphia newspaper (JAM, MBC).

2. Economy, now a National Historic Landmark site known as Old Economy Village, was the third and final American home of the Harmonists (or Rappites), a communal Pietistic sect led by George Rapp (1757–1847) that fled religious persecution in Germany. Arndt, "George Rapp's Harmony Society"; Pennsylvania Historical and Museum Commission, "Old Economy Village Historical Overview," www.oldeconomyvillage.org (accessed 23 October 2006).

3. Maximilian's route here followed the National Road, the first federal highway, authorized by Congress in 1806. Only a few fragments of the sandstone monument to Clay survive, and they are now housed in the Oglebay Mansion Museum, Wheeling. See *West Virginia,* 515–18; and Smithsonian Institution, American Art Museum, "Inventories of American Painting and Sculpture," americanart.si.edu/search/search_data.cfm (accessed 23 October 2006).

4. The source appears to be the same clipping mentioned in note 1, this chapter. The prince made mistakes in transcription and addition; corrections are in brackets.

Chapter V. Four-and-a-Half Months' Stay in New Harmony

1. The Rappite cemetery in New Harmony contained stone slab-lined Indian graves typical of the Mississippian culture (AD 1450–1650); burial mounds are more characteristic of the earlier Middle Woodland culture (ca. 200 BC to AD 400) in this region. Muller, *Archaeology,* 4–5.

2. Maximilian obtained a copy of this guide and made frequent reference to it on his

subsequent travels on the Ohio and Mississippi Rivers.

3. The Indian Removal Act of 1830 empowered the federal government to force the migration of southeastern Indian groups to Indian Territory (present-day Oklahoma). States such as Georgia and Mississippi were already engaged in efforts to dispossess Indians there at the time of Maximilian's stay in New Harmony; see, for example, Galloway and Kidwell, "Choctaw in the East," esp. 516.

4. The Wabash River has changed course since Maximilian's time. The Cutoff River is now the main channel, while the former main channel is labeled Wabash River (Old Channel) on modern USGS maps. The Fox River (a bayou of the Wabash, not a separate river) meets the Old Channel about two miles west of New Harmony. Cutoff Island is now called Ribeyre Island. Fox Island is a short distance northwest of New Harmony.

5. The post at Council Bluff was Camp Missouri, later called Fort Atkinson, near the present-day town of Fort Calhoun in Nebraska (not to be confused with the modern city of Council Bluffs, Iowa). In March 1820 the Stephen Long expedition was in winter quarters near there. Roberts, *Encyclopedia,* 481; Thwaites, *EWT,* 14:282.

6. Maximilian guessed Lesueur's age as seventy; the French scientist was fifty-five at the time.

7. Invitations to New Harmony dinners, dances, and celebrations of Christmas and George Washington's birthday were addressed to Baron Brownsburg or Braugnsberg (variations on Baron von Braunsberg, Maximilian's travel pseudonym), Mr. Bordman, and Mr. Treiteppel (JAM, MBC).

Chapter VI. Journey from New Harmony on the Wabash to St. Louis on the Mississippi and Stay There

1. Now more commonly called Tower Rock, this rocky island in the Mississippi River is part of Perry County, Missouri, and lies opposite the town of Grand Tower, Illinois.

2. This is the first of many times Maximilian expresses height as a number of inches. The number should be understood in Prussian measure: five feet plus the given number of inches. Thus, a 6′ height would be five Prussian feet, or 1.57 meters (about 5′ 2″ in English measure), plus ten Prussian inches; a Prussian inch equals 1.03 English inches. For further explanation, see *NAJ* 1:373n121; and Schmidt, *Prussian Regular Infantryman,* 10.

3. The *Yellow Stone,* constructed by the American Fur Company at McKenzie's suggestion, was the first steam-powered vessel to ascend the upper Missouri River. Jackson, *Voyages.*

4. Maximilian obtained a set of thirty-four maps from O'Fallon, detailing the Missouri River from the vicinity of present-day Omaha, Nebraska, to a point near modern Great Falls, Montana, as well as the area near the Three Forks of the Missouri and much of the Yellowstone River. These were copied from Clark's 1804–06 route maps. Wood and Moulton, "Prince Maximilian." The "Clark-Maximilian" maps, published in Moulton, *Atlas,* are part of the MBC at Joslyn Art Museum.

Chapter VII. Journey from St. Louis to the Borders
of Settlements along the Missouri

1. *Engagé* is a French term used to describe most fur-trade employees, except clerks and managers. McDermott, *Glossary,* 73. For a general description of the duties, obligations, and compensation of engagés, see Barbour, *Fort Union,* 117.

2. This is the first of several instances where Maximilian refers to distances by water from the mouth of the Missouri. He apparently took the information from at least three handwritten sources: two are tables that he compiled and placed in the addenda to manuscript journal volume 2 (*NAJ* 2:525); the third is a list found at the front of the set of Lewis and Clark 1804–06 map copies he obtained from General Clark. The data in the three tables are not identical.

3. The tribal self-name in modern orthography is *Kką·ze.*

4. The modern orthography for the Crow Indian self-designation is *Apsaálooke.*

5. Modern engineering has closed off the original mouth of the Osage and diverted the river's flow; the current mouth is several miles downstream on the Missouri.

6. Indian pictographs in this area are described in Denny, "Lewis and Clark," 3–26. The pictograph Maximilian mentions may have been among those dynamited during the construction of a railroad line along the bluffs.

7. Water depth was measured with a rope attached to a lead sinker.

8. This is the Platte of northwestern Missouri, not to be confused with the larger Platte River in Nebraska.

9. On Maximilian's *Reise* map, Fox Prairie is shown on the south bank of the Missouri east of Lexington. The battle Maximilian describes took place in 1794. Schweitzer, "Otoe and Missouria," 448.

10. The tribal self-name today is *Wažáže.*

11. Six Osage Indians toured Europe in 1827. Leavelle, "Osage in Europe."

12. Maximilian consistently used the German word for "leather" in contexts where someone today, familiar with American Indian material culture, would use "hide" or "skin" or a comparable term.

13. The original western boundary of the state of Missouri was a line running due north and south from the confluence of the Kansas and Missouri Rivers; six northwestern counties of present-day Missouri were not part of the state at the time of Maximilian's journey. Aron, *American Confluence,* 229–30.

14. The present tribal self-name is *Báxoje.*

Chapter VIII. Journey from Cantonment Leavenworth
to the Grand Bend and [Fort Pierre]

1. Joseph Robidoux (1783–1868) operated this trading post at what later became St. Joseph, Missouri. Mattes, "Joseph Robidoux."

2. The Nishnabotna River mouth has shifted considerably since Maximilian's time; it was then farther downstream on the Missouri, likely near the line between Atchison and

Holt counties, Missouri. Moulton, *Journals,* 2:379n7.

3. This island may have been a few miles upstream of present-day Brownville, Nebraska; it no longer exists. Moulton, *Journals,* 2:386n2.

4. Maximilian refers to the 1830 Treaty of Prairie du Chien; for the complete treaty, see Kappler, *Indian Treaties,* 305–10.

5. Fort Atkinson, named after Colonel Henry Atkinson, was built in 1820 near what is now the town of Fort Calhoun, Nebraska. Lewis and Clark named the site Council Bluff, after their council with Otoe and Missouria Indians in August 1804, and recommended that a fort and trading establishment be located there. The post was abandoned in 1827. Roberts, *Encyclopedia,* 481; Moulton, *Journals,* 2:438–42, 443n11.

6. The hill containing the chief's grave site, now known as Blackbird Hill (singular), is on the Omaha Indian reservation in Nebraska, southeast of Macy.

7. The modern orthography is *Dakhóta* 'Sioux; Indian', 'friends/allies'. The Indians described as those "along the Mississippi" were likely Mdewakanton Santees. For an overview of the historic Sioux divisions, see DeMallie, "Sioux until 1850," 729.

8. This is another reference to the Treaty of Prairie du Chien. See note 4, this chapter.

9. The bedrock here is shale, possibly overlain by limestone. Diffendal and Diffendal, *Lewis and Clark,* 20. Maximilian often used the term "argillite" to describe various shales found near the Missouri River.

10. The topography of this area was much changed by the construction of Gavins Point Dam in the 1950s. Only a portion of Calumet Bluff now remains in Cedar County, Nebraska, about four miles west and a little south of Yankton, South Dakota.

11. Maximilian's *Reise* map shows two islands with the name Cedar Island, one of which is the island Maximilian describes here (now inundated by Lake Francis Case). The other is upstream of the Big Bend of the Missouri River.

12. Sources differ as to which of two brothers, Joseph or Louis Bissonet, both of whom commonly used the surname "Bijou," was the namesake for the hills. The latter is most likely the Bijou mentioned here and elsewhere in Maximilian's journal. See Bissonet in the "Cast of Characters," p. xxxii.

13. Big Cedar Island, later known as American Island, was located opposite Chamberlain, South Dakota; it is now inundated by Lake Francis Case. William Clark described the island as "about a mile long" in 1804. Moulton, *Journals,* 3:87, 88n2.

14. Maximilian describes a native instrument, common on the plains, called a dewclaw rattle. Both Bodmer and Maximilian depicted one in their portraits of the Hidatsa warrior Two Ravens dressed in the regalia of the Hidatsa Dog Society (for Bodmer's watercolor, see page 141). For illustrations of Sioux dewclaw rattles, see Densmore, *Teton Sioux Music,* pl. 46. The term *chichikué* was used by Maximilian in reference to other types of rattles as well.

Chapter IX. Journey from Fort Pierre on the Teton [Bad] River to Fort Union on the Yellowstone River

1. This description, possibly the earliest known, is of the remains of a Sioux Sun Dance arbor with its center pole and crosspiece of brush.

2. Maximilian generally used the term "Yanktonan" when referring to the Yanktonai Sioux tribe, as they are called in the *North American Journals* and the present concise volume. He used "Dacota" sometimes in a general sense, encompassing all the Sioux tribes, and sometimes more specifically, in reference to the tribes known today as Eastern or Santee Sioux. Because of that ambivalent usage, the editors of the *NAJ* followed Maximilian's "Dacota" terminology rather than substitute modern names.

3. When describing human hair or hairstyles, Maximilian often used the German words for "braid" or "tress" where a contemporary English speaker might use "lock."

4. In modern orthography, the tribal self-names are *Sichą́ǧu* 'Burned Thigh'; *Oglála* 'Scatters One's Own'; *Saóni,* meaning unknown; *Sihá Sápa* 'Black Foot'; and *Húkpapha* 'Head of Camp Circle Opening'.

5. A bullboat is made from bison hide stretched over a frame. Maximilian called these "leather boats" or "leather canoes." See fig. `13.

6. The Square Buttes, several conspicuous flat-topped buttes in southeastern Oliver County about fifteen miles north of Mandan, North Dakota. Maximilian's name, "la Butte Carrée," is singular.

7. This is the Mandan village site now known as Double Ditch, a North Dakota state historical site about ten miles northwest of downtown Bismarck. For a site description, see Will and Spinden, *Mandans.*

8. The modern orthography for the first name is *Thathą́ka Kté* 'Kills Buffalo Bull'; for the second, *Yawicakha* 'Speaks Truth'.

9. Maximilian frequently used the German word for "jacket" where an English speaker would use "shirt."

10. The modern orthography is *Rų́wą́k-a:ki* (lit. 'Person[s]-atop [earth]').

11. Maximilian used several variant spellings of this tribal self-name, all probably corruptions of *Mirahací* 'Willow [People]' or *Hiraacá* 'Hidatsa'. Awatíss *(awadíš)* means "village."

12. The modern orthography is *Piikáni.*

13. This location (the French name translates to "Dancing Bear") was in Mercer County, North Dakota, opposite the future site of Like-a-Fishhook, the last earth lodge village occupied by the Mandan, Hidatsa, and Arikara Indians, which may have been chosen, in part, for its proximity to this ceremonially important locale. Smith, *Like-a-Fishhook Village,* 5–6. It is now inundated by the Garrison Dam.

14. The modern orthography for Kiäsax is *Kiááyiisaksi* (*Kiááy(o)* 'Bear' + *Isaksi* 'Exit'); the French version of his name literally translates to "Left-handed Bear." For Matsókuï, the modern orthography is *Mattsokóyi* (*Mattsi* 'Crazy' + *okoyi* 'Wolf').

Chapter X. Stay at Fort Union, Description of the Fort and the Surrounding Area and the Assiniboine Indians

1. The modern orthography for Nahíâak is *Ne·hiyaw(ak);* for Maskepetoon, *Ma·skipiton* 'Crippled Arm'.

2. For more about buffalo parks, see note 3 in chapter 13.

3. The modern orthography for this name is *Nąp'éšį* 'No Flight' (also the name of a men's society).

4. Maximilian sometimes used the old French Canadian term *parflèche*, as he did here, to mean a shield and occasionally employed its broader sense in applying it to other articles made of rawhide. Today the anglicized term "parfleche" usually refers to the large folded and brightly painted envelope-like storage containers of the Plains Indians. See pl. 11 for Bodmer's portrait of this young warrior, in the regalia described by Maximilian, including the shield.

5. Ajanjan, in modern orthography, is *Aóžąžą* 'Shines'. Fur trader Edwin Denig rendered the Assiniboine name in English as "The Light." Denig, "Of the Assiniboines," especially 86–87.

Chapter XI. Journey from Fort Union to Fort Piegan, or McKenzie

1. On his *Reise* map Maximilian located the "horn pyramid" on the south side of the Missouri between "Indian Fort Creek" (probably Nickwall Creek) and the Porcupine (now Poplar) River. Some scholars have suggested that the structure may not have been of Indian construction but rather had been built as a marker by members of the expedition led by Colonel Henry Atkinson and Indian agent Benjamin O'Fallon in 1825. Steven Moffitt, cited in Wood et al., *KBSA*, 15. However, this explanation does not account for the red stripes noted by the prince.

2. Although Maximilian implies that the bear was her personal medicine, the woman's refusal more likely reflects the Blackfoot belief that only those who had power from the bear spirit had the right to handle bear hides; anyone lacking that power who undertook the tanning of a bear hide would be punished with sickness or death. See Schultz, *My Life*, 110.

3. Maximilian's Mauvaises-Terres, or Badlands, are now known as the Missouri Breaks; much of the region is managed by the federal government as the Upper Missouri River Breaks National Monument in Montana.

4. Located about thirteen miles below the mouth of the Judith River, these rapids were "considered the most dangerous in the Upper [Missouri] [R]iver." They were reportedly named for "an Antoine Dauphin, who died of smallpox in 1837." Historical Society of Montana, *Contributions* 10:298n264.

5. This area is now commonly called the White Cliffs of the Missouri.

Chapter XII. Description of Fort McKenzie and
First Stay There among the Indians

1. In Mississippi Valley French, beads "for the Indian trade" were called *rassades*. McDermott, *Glossary*, 133. Maximilian used the singular form of the word.

2. The observation reflects a cultural misunderstanding. In commenting on Blackfoot interactions with traders, Alexander Henry remarked, "All having taken a few whiffs of the trader's pipe, the chief produces his own, which he fills and presents to the trader. . . . The compliment is greater if the chief presents the pipe to the trader to light." Henry et al., *New Light*, 2:729.

3. From 1802 until 1832, section 21 of the Trade and Intercourse Act of 1802 was the basic law governing alcohol importation into Indian territory; it authorized the president to "prevent or restrain" such trade, which left some discretion to the executive branch. An 1822 amendment to the act allowed the search of traders' baggage and the confiscation of unauthorized liquor. Congress passed an outright ban on importing liquor into Indian territory in 1832. Prucha, *Documents*, 21, 35, 62.

4. To compensate for not seeing the falls, Maximilian copied and placed here a lengthy passage from "Mr. [David] Mitchell's" personal diary describing his own journey there and the beauty of "the highest [fall] of any on the Missouri," in the estimation of Lewis and Clark. *NAJ* 2:412–13.

5. Several references are made on this and subsequent manuscript journal pages to Bodmer's September excursions, on which he sought to capture on paper what Maximilian called the "first chain" of the Rocky Mountains and "Bears Paw Mountain" (actually the Highwood and Little Belt Mountains). What they saw is preserved today in two watercolor landscapes (see pls. 22 and 23) and Tableau 44 in the *Reise (KBNAP)*. For a modern description of the same scenes, see Wood et al., *KBSA*, 17.

6. Expenditures related to this trip also included "2 Large Boxes for Bearz [*sic*] and Plants," $9.00 (Fort McKenzie ledger sheet, JAM, MBC).

Chapter XIII. A Few Words Regarding the Blackfoot Indians, [as well as the] Gros Ventres des Prairies and Kootenais

1. Among Bodmer's several portraits of Blackfoot men wearing their hair in this style, the profile of an unidentified individual inscribed "Piegan medicine man" most clearly shows the leather binding (watercolor and pencil, JAM, MBC, *KBA* 251). For an idea of the hairstyle, see fig. 3 and pls. 16 and 21.

2. *Arctostaphylos uva-ursi,* bearberry. Spelled as *sacacomi* or *saccacomi,* the Mississippi Valley French term could refer either to the plant or to the smoking mixture made from it. McDermott, *Glossary,* 135.

3. Maximilian's park is more commonly called a pound, a reference to the corralling or impounding method of hunting that he describes; for an overview of northern Plains buffalo hunting, see Arthur, "Introduction to the Ecology." For a diagram, see fig. 10.

4. The ceremony described here is the Blackfoot form of the Plains Sun Dance. See Dempsey, "Blackfoot," esp. 616.

5. Variously referred to in the literature as age, military, or warrior societies, these male organizations were common on the northern plains. They provided personal social benefits to the members, who in turn carried public, community responsibilities. For the Blackfoot, see Dempsey, "Blackfoot," 615; for a concise Plains summary, see Lowie, *Indians of the Plains,* 105–14.

6. The modern orthography for the tribal self-name is ʔɔʔɔ́ɔ̌niinénnɔh 'White Clay People'.

7. The modern orthography for the tribal self-name is *Ktunaxa.* This is the official tribal name in Canada; it remains Kootenai in the United States.

Chapter XIV. Return Journey from Fort McKenzie
to Fort Union

1. Maximilian's first recorded purchase upon his arrival at Fort Union on the afternoon of 29 September was a "Hat $10" (Fort Union ledger sheet, JAM, MBC).

Chapter XV. Second Stay at Fort Union and Journey
from There to the Mandan Villages and Fort Clark

1. *Perognathus fasciatus,* olive-backed pocket mouse, bears the scientific name given to it by Maximilian, who published the first scientific description of the species in 1839. Wied, "Über einige Nager."

2. The exchange of boats cost Maximilian $30, billed to the American Fur Company account of Baron Braunsberg (Maximilian's traveling pseudonym) (JAM, MBC, Fort Union ledger sheet).

3. Maximilian's essay on the Osage Indians, based on information supplied by Francis Chardon, appears in the addenda to volume 3 of the manuscript journals; see *NAJ* 3:446–55.

4. These publications may be issues of the *Temperance Recorder,* published by the New York State Temperance Society, held in the Maximilian-Bodmer Collection at Joslyn Art Museum. Two, dated 3 July and 6 November 1832, are devoted largely to a discussion of the relationship of cholera epidemics to intemperance.

Chapter XVI. Winter Sojourn at Fort Clark among
the Mandans and Hidatsas

1. Bodmer's detailed watercolor depiction of this shrine is reproduced in this volume as pl. 24.

2. The Leonid meteor shower of 12 November 1833 was visible throughout North America, and the event figured prominently in many of the Plains pictographic calendrical records called "winter counts."

3. Maximilian translated the name Dipäuch as both Broken Arm and Broken Leg. The modern orthography is *Rip 'U:x* 'Broken Marrow'.

4. French traders and missionaries applied the term *berdache* to individuals they perceived as homosexuals. But Plains berdaches were later described as alternative or third-gender roles that included women warriors and men who preferred women's work and dress. Berdaches often had distinctive religious and healing powers as well. See Wishart, "Berdache"; for a discussion of more complex usages of the term, see Jacobs et al., *Two-Spirit People,* 4–6. Maximilian's spelling, "bardache," was a common variant used by Americans. McDermott, *Glossary,* 22–23.

5. A Bodmer portrait of Two Ravens (JAM, MBC, *KBA* 329) shows him wrapped in a spectacular robe painted with this design. George Horse Capture explores "crown of feathers" as the most logical meaning of this design in "The Warbonnet: A Symbol of Honor."

The watercolor portrait was reproduced as Tableau 17 *(KBNAP)*.

Chapter XVII. Short Description of Fort Clark and Its Surroundings

1. Kenneth McKenzie's successful Columbia Fur Company merged with Astor's American Fur Company in 1827. Lamar, "Kenneth McKenzie."

2. The modern orthography for these names is *Mirá'bugša* 'Embers' and *Iidubáà Šibíša* 'Black Panther (large feline)'. These are Hidatsa, not Mandan, names.

3. Maximilian used the German word *Tauben,* which can be translated as either "pigeons" or "doves." *Ectopistes migratorius,* passenger pigeon, very likely reached North Dakota in Maximilian's time and was a forest-dwelling bird. It is now extinct.

4. Maximilian's "amphibian" here contradicts modern usage: snakes, lizards, and turtles are reptiles, not amphibians.

Chapter XVIII. Remarks on the Indian Tribe of the Mandans, *Actually Númangkake*

1. Catlin gave a more detailed description in his *Letters and Notes,* first published in 1841. For a contemporary general summary of the Okippe, or Okipa, which has much in common with the Plains Sun Dance, see Wood and Irwin, "Mandan," 357–59.

2. Maximilian seems to have felt that his language work was incomplete; a lack of time and his increasingly poor health during the winter of 1833–34 were doubtless the main problems. He nonetheless amassed extensive vocabularies, particularly for the Mandan language; see the appendices to his *Reise* (2:454–645) and to his manuscript journal *(NAJ* 1:395–99, 2:475–505, 3:461–72).

3. The modern orthography for the Mandan names is *Wątó-Wąřų-xik* 'Spirit Bear'; *Wřók Wąřų-xik* 'Spirit Bull'; *Kuh E* 'Hears Returning'; and *Ta-w·:h Ř·-sik-kúpa-ko-xihxih* 'Your Brothers-in-Law Are/Have Seven Crones'. For the Arikara name, the modern orthography is *Štaanapaa'At* 'Bloody Hands'.

Chapter XIX. A Few Words about the Two Tribes of the Mönnitarrís (Gros Ventres) [Hidatsas] and the Arikaras

1. See note 11 in chapter 9 for Maximilian's "Biddahátsi-awatíss."

2. The modern orthography for the following Hidatsa names is Monkey Face, *Icixéèxe* 'Monkey'; Black Horn Buffalo, *Aai ibía* 'Black Horn'; and Hunts Bears, *Naxbichí Maagigîr* 'Bear Seeking Something'.

3. The modern orthography for the third name is *Aaibcá* 'Young Buffalo' (lit. 'sharp horn', referring to a two- to three-year-old buffalo).

4. The modern orthography for the following names suggests translations different from Maximilian's: Warúch-Tháhka, *WaRUxtaáka* 'White Rabbit'; Honníhtatta-Káhrach, [?] + *Karax* 'Formidable'.

Chapter XX. Continuation of the Winter Sojourn at Fort Clark

1. The corresponding passage in the nineteenth-century British translation of the *Reise* describes these men as "a guard against the importunities of the women and children." Thwaites, *EWT*, 24:73.

2. There are two known Bodmer depictions of Two Ravens. In one, he is a veritable Plains fashion plate, clad in a scalplock-fringed shirt, a stunning painted robe, and an impressive bear claw necklace. In the other, perhaps the best-known and certainly the most beautifully dramatic Indian portrait of the early nineteenth century, he is arrayed in all the dazzling accoutrements of a principal Dog Dancer. See JAM, MBC, *KBA* 329 and *KBNAP* Tableau 17; the second portrait is reproduced here in pl. 27.

3. For a description of the Half–Shorn Head Dance, see chapter 16, the entry for 28 December.

4. See fig. 16.11, *NAJ* 3:75, for an account sheet of Maximilian's expenses at Fort Clark, which totaled $205.57½ for supplies (nails, tobacco, coffee, etc.), goods (otter skins, buffalo robes, calico, etc.), and services (e.g., $6.00 to Garreau, possibly for information given to the prince about the Arikaras).

5. Maximilian is rather vague in his journal regarding his health, which deteriorated rapidly in early 1834. He is more explicit in his publication: "At the beginning of April I was still in a hopeless condition, and so very ill, that the people who visited me did not think that my life would be prolonged beyond three or, at the most, four days. The [Fort Clark] cook, a negro from St. Louis, one day expressed his opinion that my illness must be the scurvy, for he had witnessed the great mortality among the garrison of the fort at Council Bluff, when several hundred soldiers were carried off in a short time. . . . On that occasion, at the beginning of spring, they had gathered the green herbs of the prairie, especially the small white flowering [wild onion], with which they soon cured the sick. . . . Indian children accordingly furnished me with an abundance of this plant and its bulbs . . . and I ate [them]. On the fourth day the swelling of my leg had considerably subsided and I gained strength daily. The evident prospect of speedy recovery quite reanimated me" (Thwaites, *EWT*, 24:81–82). He nevertheless remained weak well past the day of his departure.

Chapter XXI. Journey from Fort Clark to Cantonment Leavenworth

1. The "leather boats" (Maximilian also calls them "leather canoes") used by the fur traders were similar to but larger than the bullboats made by upper Missouri Indians (described in *NAJ*, 2:183n66). They were made of more than one hide, sewn together with sinew and stretched over a frame (sometimes as large as a wagon frame); the seams were caulked. Alfred Jacob Miller pictured such a boat, loaded with a mind-boggling array of goods and passengers. Ross, *West*, 180.

2. A rough translation would be "to wash or leach the corn." It is how hominy is made.

3. Louis Penault fatally shot Louis Blay on Christmas Day 1833. No court records regarding this incident are known to be extant. Sunder, *Joshua Pilcher*, 106. The American Fur

Company, fearing exposure of its illegal liquor sales to Indians at its Missouri River trading posts, ensured that none of its employees would be available in St. Louis as witnesses in the case. The accused murderer was acquitted for lack of evidence. Chittenden, *History*, 1:42–44.

Chapter XXII. Journey from Cantonment Leavenworth to St. Louis and Stay There

1. In the *Reise* (2:358), the purchase price is given as $500.
2. The now-extinct town of Chariton was located near the former mouth of the Chariton River in southeastern Chariton County; the Chariton and Missouri rivers have both shifted significantly in this region since Maximilian's time.

Chapter XXIII. Journey from St. Louis through Indiana to Portsmouth on the Ohio

1. William Henry Harrison (1773–1841) was the first governor of Indiana Territory (1801–12) and later the ninth president of the United States (1841). The mansion, Grouseland, is now a National Historic Landmark. Grouseland Foundation, "Welcome to Grouseland," www.grouselandfoundation.org/Grouseland/Home.html (accessed 22 July 2010).
2. John Jacob Astor's son, William Backhouse Astor, had likely been in St. Louis to represent his then ailing father in closing the recent sale of Astor's fur trade interests to his former partners, effective 1 June 1834. Madsen, *John Jacob Astor*, 225–26.
3. See chapter 4, note M2.

Chapter XXIV. Voyage on the Ohio Canal via Lake Erie to Buffalo

1. The canal is the Ohio and Erie Canal, which connected the Ohio River with Lake Erie and was completed in 1832. The southern terminus was Portsmouth; the northern was Cleveland. Ohio Department of Natural Resources, "History of Ohio's Canals," http://parks.ohiodnr.gov/canals (accessed 1 August 2006).
2. The Circleville earthworks are attributed to the Hopewell culture. They were completely destroyed by the growth of the town of Circleville. Ohio Historical Society, "Circleville Earthworks," Ohio History Central, www.ohiohistorycentral.org/entry.php?rec=2413 (accessed 1 October 2010).
3. These are likely the "staircase" locks in central Akron, some of which are preserved in Cascade Locks Park. The descent from the Akron summit was the steepest portion of the Ohio and Erie Canal. Hannibal et al., "Maximilian," 22n62, 23n64.

Chapter XXV. Journey to Niagara Falls and Visit with the Tuscaroras near Lake Ontario

1. This purchase actually applied to all islands in the Niagara River "within the jurisdiction of the United States," of which Grand Island is the largest. Hauptman, *Conspiracy of Interests*, 137.

Chapter XXVI. Voyage on the Erie Canal to Albany

1. That work included a seven-mile deep cut on the western section of the canal, near Lockport, two miles of it through solid rock. Shaw, *Canals for a Nation*, 41–42.

2. In 1788, the Oneida nation controlled approximately 300,000 acres in what are now Madison and Oneida Counties. Various treaties reduced these holdings drastically. Between 1822 and 1838, many Oneidas moved to Wisconsin, where a large portion of the Oneida people reside today. Only 200 Oneidas remained in New York by 1848. Hauptman, *Conspiracy of Interests*, 27–28, 74; Campisi, "Oneida," 484–85.

Chapter XXVII. Journey from Albany to New York and Stopovers There and at Philadelphia

1. The village of Sing Sing changed its name to Ossining in 1901; New York State still maintains a penitentiary known as Sing Sing nearby.

2. Maximilian also visited the Philadelphia Peale Museum on 17 July 1832. Titian Peale, a son of the founder, Charles Willson Peale, was the museum's curator, not its sole proprietor; other family members were also involved. *NAJ* 1:69&n88, 1:71.

3. Astor's hotel opened in 1836 as the Park Hotel but was later known as Astor House. Its construction cost over $400,000––a colossal sum of money at the time. "John Jacob Astor," *ANB*.

4. As a retainer of the prince, and thus not a "gentleman" in his own right (unlike Bodmer), Dreidoppel presumably did not have access to the same amenities aboard the ship and was therefore charged a lower fare. Correspondence (JAM, MBC) with the Rotterdam firm that arranged the party's passage to Boston in 1832 indicates similar treatment for Dreidoppel on that voyage.

Chapter XXIX. Journey through France and Holland to Germany

1. Built between 1757 and 1772, Monrepos was the summer residence of the Wied family near Neuwied. The original eighteenth-century building no longer survives. An early twentieth-century house on the grounds is now the home of an archaeological museum. City of Neuwied, "Schloss Monrepos," www.neuwied.de/schloss-monrepos.html (in German, accessed 9 March 2010).

Bibliography

Maximilian's references are marked with an asterisk.

Abel, Annie Heloise, ed. *Chardon's Journal at Fort Clark, 1834–1839.* Reprint ed. Lincoln: University of Nebraska Press, 1997.

American National Biography. Edited by John A. Garraty and Marc C. Carnes. New York: Oxford University Press, 1999. (Cited in notes as *ANB.*)

Appleton's Cyclopedia of American Biography. Edited by James Grant Wilson and John Fiske. New York: D. Appleton and Company, 1888–89.

Arndt, Karl J. R. "George Rapp's Harmony Society." In *America's Communal Utopias,* edited by Donald E. Pitzer, 57–87. Chapel Hill: University of North Carolina Press, 1997.

Aron, Stephen. *American Confluence: The Missouri Frontier from Borderland to Border State.* Bloomington: Indiana University Press, 2006.

Arthur, George W. "An Introduction to the Ecology of Early Historic Communal Bison Hunting among the Northern Plains Indians." *Archaeological Survey of Canada* no. 37 (1975): 1–136. National Museum of Man Mercury Series.

Bailey, Martha J. *American Women in Science: A Biographical Dictionary.* Denver, Colo.: ABC-CLIO, 1994.

Barbour, Barton H. *Fort Union and the Upper Missouri Fur Trade.* Norman: University of Oklahoma Press, 2001.

Barry, Louise, comp. "Kansas before 1854: A Revised Annals. Part Seven, 1833–34." *Kansas Historical Quarterly* 28, no. 3 (Autumn 1962): 317–69.

*Barton, Benjamin Smith. *New Views of the Origin of the Tribes and Nations of America.* Millwood, N.Y.: Kraus Reprint Company, 1976. Reprint of original 1798 publication.

Beckwith, Paul Edmond. *Creoles of St. Louis.* St. Louis: Nixon-Jones Printing, 1893.

*Blunt, Edmund. *Northeastern Coast of North America from New York to Cape Canso Including Sable Island.* New York, 1828.

*Brackenridge, Henry M. *Views of Louisiana.* Pittsburgh, 1814.

Bradley, James H. "Affairs at Fort Benton." In *Contributions to the Historical Society of Montana,* vol. 3, 201–87. Helena, Mont.: State Publishing Company, 1900.

Campisi, Jack. "Oneida." In Sturtevant, *Handbook of North American Indians,* vol. 15 (1), *Northeast,* edited by Bruce G. Trigger, 481–90 (1978).

Cartography Associates, David Rumsey Map Collection. "Map to Illustrate the Route of Prince Maximilian of Wied . . . in North America." 2005. www .davidrumsey.com/luna/servlet/detail/RUMSEY~8~1~3703~360043:Carte-itineraire -de-Prince-Maximili (accessed 3 March 2016).

Catlin, George. Letter dated 12 August 1832 published in the *New York Commercial Adver-tiser,* 20 February 1833. Clipping available from National Anthropological Archives, papers related to the Smithsonian Office of Anthropology (E 78 c36 SOA), Museum Support Center, Suitland, Md.

———. *Letters and Notes on the Manners, Customs, and Conditions of the North American Indians.* Reprint in 2 vols. New York: Dover, 1973. Republication of the original 1844 London edition, replacing 257 of the line drawings with paintings reproduced from the Catlin Collection of the Smithsonian Institution.

Chittenden, Hiram M. *The American Fur Trade of the Far West.* Reprint in 2 vols. Lincoln: University of Nebraska Press, 1986.

———. *History of Early Steamboat Navigation on the Missouri River: Life and Adventures of Joseph La Barge.* 2 vols. Reprint, Minneapolis: Ross and Haines, 1962.

*Cumings, Samuel. *The Western Pilot.* Cincinnati: N. and G. Guilford, 1829.

*Darton, William, Jr. *Darton's Pocket Tablet of Christian Sects.* London, 1816.

*Davison, Gideon Miner. *The Traveller's Guide through the Middle and Northern States and the Provinces of Canada.* 6th ed. Saratoga Springs, N.Y.: G. M. Davison, 1834.

Deloria, Vine, Jr. *The World We Used to Live In: Remembering the Powers of the Medicine Men.* Golden, Colo.: Fulcrum Publishing, 2006.

DeMallie, Raymond J. "Sioux before 1850." In Sturtevant, *Handbook of North American Indians,* vol. 13 (2), *Plains,* edited by Raymond J. DeMallie, 718–60 (2001).

Dempsey, Hugh A. "Blackfoot." In Sturtevant, *Handbook of North American Indians,* vol. 13 (1), *Plains,* edited by Raymond J. DeMallie, 604–28 (2001).

Denig, Edwin Thompson. "Of the Assiniboines." In Ewers, *Five Indian Tribes of the Upper Missouri,* 63–98.

Denny, James M. "Lewis and Clark in the Boonslick." *Boone's Lick Heritage* 8, nos. 2–3 (June–September 1997): 3–26.

Densmore, Frances. *Teton Sioux Music.* Bureau of American Ethnology Bulletin 61. Wash-ington, D.C.: Smithsonian Institution, 1918.

Dictionary of American Biography. 11 vols. New York: C. Scribner's Sons, 1994, 1964. (Cited in notes as *DAB.*)

Dictionary of Canadian Biography. Toronto: University of Toronto Press, 1966. (Cited in notes as *DCB.*)

Dictionary of Scientific Biography. Edited by Charles Coulston Gillispie. New York: Scrib-ner, 1970–80. (Cited in notes as *DSB.*)

Diffendal, R. F., Jr., and Anne P. Diffendal. *Lewis and Clark and the Geology of Nebraska and Parts of Adjacent States.* Lincoln: University of Nebraska–Lincoln, 2003.

*Drake, Daniel. *Natural and Statistical View, or Picture of Cincinnati and the Miami Coun-try.* Cincinnati: Looker and Wallace, 1815.

*Elford, J. M. *Elford's Marine Telegraph, or Universal Signal Book etc. Being also the Key to the Patent Telegraph, Invented by the Author, Capable of Making 9330 Progressive Changes, by Using the Figures from 1 to 6 Only.* Charlestown, S.C.: Archibald E. Miller, 1823.

Ewers, John C. "An Appreciation of Karl Bodmer's Pictures of Indians." In *Views of a Vanishing Frontier,* by John C. Ewers, Marsha V. Gallagher, David C. Hunt, and Joseph C. Porter, 51–93. Omaha: Joslyn Art Museum, 1984.

———, ed. *Five Indian Tribes of the Upper Missouri.* Norman: University of Oklahoma Press, 1961.

———. "Folk Art in the Fur Trade of the Upper Missouri." In Ewers, *Plains Indian History and Culture,* 150–65.

———. *Plains Indian History and Culture: Essays on Continuity and Change.* Norman: University of Oklahoma Press, 1997.

———. *Plains Indian Painting: A Description of an Aboriginal American Art.* Palo Alto, Calif.: Stanford University Press, 1939.

———. "When the Light Shone in Washington." *Montana: The Magazine of Western History* 6, no. 4 (Autumn 1956): 2–11.

Fairchild, Herman L. *A History of the New York Academy of Sciences, Formerly the Lyceum of Natural History.* New York: published by author, 1887.

Fletcher, Alice C., and Francis La Flesche. *The Omaha Tribe.* 2 vols. Reprint, Lincoln: University of Nebraska Press, 1972. (First published in the *Twenty-Seventh Annual Report of the Bureau of American Ethnology to the Secretary of the Smithsonian Institution,* 1905–06. Washington, D.C.: Government Printing Office, 1911.)

*Flint, Timothy. *Indian Wars of the West: Containing Biographical Sketches of Those Pioneers Who Headed the Western Settlers in Repelling the Attacks of the Savages, Together with a View of the Character, Manners, Monuments, and Antiquities of the Western Indians.* Cincinnati: E. H. Flint, 1833.

Galloway, Patricia, and Clara Sue Kidwell. "Choctaw in the East." In Sturtevant, *Handbook of North American Indians,* vol. 14, *Southeast,* edited by Raymond D. Fogelson, 499–519 (2004).

*Godman, John D. *American Natural History.* 3 vols. Philadelphia: Carey and Lea, 1826–28.

Gray, John S. "Honoré Picotte, Fur Trader." *South Dakota History* 6, no. 2 (1976): 186–202.

Grund, Francis J. *The Merchant's Assistant, or Mercantile Instructer* [sic]. *Containing a Full Account of the Moneys, Coins, Weights and Measures of the Principal Trading Nations and Their Colonies; Together with Their Values in United States Currency, Weights and Measures.* Boston: Hilliard, Gray and Company, 1834.

Haberly, Loyd. "The American Museum from Baker to Barnum." *New-York Historical Society Quarterly* 43 (July 1959): 273–87.

Hafen, LeRoy R. "Joseph Bissonet, dit Bijou." In Hafen, *Mountain Men,* 9:27–32.

———, ed. *The Mountain Men and the Fur Trade of the Far West.* 10 vols. Glendale, Calif.: Arthur H. Clark, 1965–72.

———. "Toussaint Charbonneau." In Hafen, *Mountain Men,* 9:53–62.

Haines, Aubrey L. "Johnson Gardner." In Hafen, *Mountain Men,* 2:157–59.

Hamy, E. T. *The Travels of the Naturalist Charles A. Lesueur in North America, 1815–1837.* Edited by Hallock F. Raup; translated by Milton Haber. Kent, Ohio: Kent State University Press, 1968.

Hannibal, Joseph T., Sabina F. Thomas, and Michael G. Noll. "Maximilian, Prince of Wied's Trip along the Ohio and Erie Canal in 1834: An Annotated New Translation." *Ohio History* 116 (2009): 5–25.

Hanson, Charles E., Jr. "J. B. Moncravie." In Hafen, *Mountain Men,* 9:289–98.

*Harlan, Richard. *Fauna Americana: Being a Description of the Mammiferous Animals Inhabiting North America.* Philadelphia: A. Finley, 1825.

Harris' Pittsburgh Business Directory for the Year 1837. Pittsburgh, 1837.

Hauptman, Laurence M. *Conspiracy of Interests: Iroquois Dispossession and the Rise of New York State.* Syracuse: Syracuse University Press, 2001.

Henry, Alexander, David Thompson, and Elliott Coues. *New Light on the Early History of the Greater Northwest: The Manuscript Journals of Alexander Henry, Fur Trader of the Northwest Company, and of David Thompson, Official Geographer and Explorer of the Same Company, 1799–1814; Exploration and Adventure among the Indians on the Red, Saskatchewan, Missouri, and Columbia Rivers.* 3 vols. New York: Francis P. Harper, 1897.

Hill, Edward E. *The Office of Indian Affairs, 1824–1880: Historical Sketches.* New York: Clearwater, 1974.

Historical Sketch of the Moravian Seminary for Young Ladies. Bethlehem, Penn.: Moravian Publication Office, 1876.

Historical Society of Montana. *Contributions to the Historical Society of Montana.* Vol. 10. Reprint, Boston: J. S. Canner and Company, 1966.

History of Tioga County, Pennsylvania. Harrisburg, Penn.: R. C. Brown and Co., 1897.

Holmberg, James J. "The Life, Death, and Monument of Charles Floyd." In *Exploring with Lewis and Clark: The 1804 Journal of Charles Floyd,* edited by James J. Holmberg, 5–34. Norman: University of Oklahoma Press, 2004.

Horse Capture, George P. "The Warbonnet: A Symbol of Honor." In *Visions of the People: A Pictorial History of Plains Indian Life,* edited by Evan M. Maurer, 61–68. Minneapolis: Minneapolis Institute of Art, 1992.

Hunt, David C., Marsha V. Gallagher, William H. Goetzmann, and William J. Orr. *Karl Bodmer's America.* Lincoln: Joslyn Art Museum and University of Nebraska Press, 1984. (Cited in notes as *KBA.*)

Huppertz, Josephine. "Textkritische Analyse und Vergleichzwischen schriftlichem Nachlass und Reisewerk." In Röder and Trimborn, *Maximilian Prinz zu Wied,* 32–79.

Jackson, Donald. *Voyages of the Steamboat "Yellow Stone."* New York: Ticknor and Fields, 1985.

Jacobs, Sue-Ellen, Wesley Thomas, and Sabine Lang, eds. *Two-Spirit People: Native American Gender Identity, Sexuality, and Spirituality.* Urbana: University of Illinois Press, 1997.

*James, Edwin. *Account of an Expedition from Pittsburgh to the Rocky Mountains, Performed in the Years 1819, 1820.* 3 vols. London: Longman, Hurst, Rees, Orme, and Brown, 1823.

Jeronimus, C. J., ed. *Travels by His Highness Duke Bernhard of Saxe-Weimar-Eisenach through North America in the Years 1825 and 1826.* Translated by William Jeronimus. Lanham, Md.: University Press of America, 2001.

Johansen, Gregory J. "'To Make Some Provision for Their Half-Breeds': The Nemaha Half-Breed Reserve, 1830–66." *Nebraska History* 67, no. 1 (Spring 1986): 8–29.

Jones, A. E., ed. *In Memoriam: Cincinnati 1881, Containing Proceedings of the Memorial Association, Eulogies at Music Hall, and Biographical Sketches of Many Distinguished Citizens of Cincinnati.* Cincinnati: Printed at the Western Methodist Book Concern, 1881.

Kappler, Charles J., comp. and ed. *Indian Treaties, 1778–1883.* Reprint, Mattituck, N.Y.: Amereon House, 1972.

Kellogg, Elizabeth R. "Joseph Dorfeuille and the Western Museum." *Journal of the Cincinnati Society of Natural History* 22 (April 1945): 3–29.

*Kilbourn, John. *The Ohio Gazetteer, or Topographical Dictionary.* 11th ed. Columbus, Ohio: Scott and Wright, 1833.

Lamar, Howard R. "Kenneth McKenzie." In *New Encyclopedia of the American West,* edited by Howard R. Lamar, 671. New Haven, Conn.: Yale University Press, 1998.

Larousse, Pierre, ed. *Grand dictionnaire universel du XIXe siècle.* Vol. 7. Paris: n.p., 1870.

Leavelle, Tracy N. "The Osage in Europe: Romanticism, the Vanishing Indian, and French Civilization during the Restoration." In *National Stereotypes in Perspective: Americans in France, Frenchmen in America,* edited by William L. Chew, 89–110. Amsterdam: Rodopi, 2001.

Lecompte, Janet. "Charles Autobees." In Hafen, *Mountain Men,* 4:21–37.

*Lewis, Meriwether, William Clark, and Thomas Rees. *Travels to the Source of the Missouri River and across the American Continent to the Pacific Ocean . . . in the Years 1804, 1805, and 1806.* 3 vols. London: Longman, Hurst, Rees, Orme, and Brown, 1815.

Liberty, Margot P., W. Raymond Wood, and Lee Irwin. "Omaha." In Sturtevant, *Handbook of North American Indians,* vol. 13 (1), *Plains,* edited by Raymond J. DeMallie, 399–415 (2001).

*"Long's Expedition." When Maximilian refers to this publication about Stephen Long's exploration, he means to cite James, *Account of an Expedition,* q.v.

Longworth's American Almanac, New York Register, and City Directory for the Fifty-Fourth Year of American Independence. New York: Thomas Longworth, 1829.

Lottinville, Savoie, ed. *Travels in North America, 1822–1824.* Translated by W. Robert Nitske. Norman: University of Oklahoma Press, 1973.

Lowie, Robert H. *Indians of the Plains.* New York: American Museum of Natural History with McGraw Hill, 1954. Reprint, Garden City, N.Y.: American Museum Science Books, 1963.

Luttig, John C. *Journal of a Fur-Trading Expedition on the Upper Missouri, 1812–1813.* Edited by Stella M. Drumm. New York: Argosy-Antiquarian, 1964.

Madsen, Axel. *John Jacob Astor: America's First Multimillionaire.* New York: John Wiley and Sons, 2001.

Mathews, Alfred, and Austin N. Hungerford. *History of the Counties of Lehigh and Carbon in the Commonwealth of Pennsylvania.* Philadelphia: Everts and Richards, 1884.

Mattes, Merrill J. "Joseph Robidoux." In Hafen, *Mountain Men,* 8:287–314.

Mattison, Ray H. "Alexander Culbertson." In Hafen, *Mountain Men,* 1:253–56.

———. "Alexander Harvey." In Hafen, *Mountain Men,* 4:119–23.

———. "Francis A. Chardon." In Hafen, *Mountain Men,* 1:225–27.

———. "James A. Hamilton (Palmer)." In Hafen, *Mountain Men,* 3:163–66.

———. "John Pierre Cabanné, Sr." In Hafen, *Mountain Men,* 2:69–73.

———. "William Laidlaw." In Hafen, *Mountain Men,* 3:167–72.

Maximilian-Bodmer Collection. Joslyn Art Museum, Omaha, Nebraska. (Cited in notes as JAM, MBC.)

McDermott, John Francis. *A Glossary of Mississippi Valley French.* Washington University Studies—New Series, Language and Literature no. 12. St. Louis, Mo.: Washington University, 1941.

Morgan, Dale L., ed. *The West of William H. Ashley: The International Struggle for the Fur Trade of the Missouri, the Rocky Mountains, and the Columbia, with Explorations beyond the Continental Divide, Recorded in the Diaries and Letters of William H. Ashley and His Contemporaries.* Denver, Colo.: Old West Publishing, 1964.

Morgan, William N. *Prehistoric Architecture in the Eastern United States.* Cambridge, Mass.: MIT Press, 1980.

*Morrell, Benjamin. *A Narrative of Four Voyages to the South Sea, North and South Pacific Ocean, Chinese Sea, Ethiopic and Southern Atlantic Ocean, Indian and Antarctic Ocean.* New York: J. and J. Harper, 1832.

Moulton, Gary E., ed. *Atlas of the Lewis and Clark Expedition.* Vol. 1 of *The Journals of the Lewis and Clark Expedition.* Lincoln: University of Nebraska Press, 1983.

———, ed. *The Journals of the Lewis and Clark Expedition.* 13 vols. Lincoln: University of Nebraska Press, 1983–2001.

Muller, Jon. *Archaeology of the Lower Ohio River Valley.* New York: Academic Press, 1986.

Myers, John. *The Saga of Hugh Glass: Pirate, Pawnee, and Mountain Man.* Lincoln: University of Nebraska Press, 1976.

Nieuw Nederlandsch Biografisch Woordenboek. Leiden, 1911–37.

Noll, Michael G. "Prince Maximilian's America: The Narrated Landscapes of a German Explorer and Naturalist." Ph.D. diss., University of Kansas, 2000.

Nunis, Doyce B., Jr. "Milton G. Sublette." In Hafen, *Mountain Men,* 4:331–49.

*Nuttall, Thomas. *The Genera of North American Plants.* 2 vols. Philadelphia: printed for the author by D. Heartt, 1818.

* ———. *A Manual of the Ornithology of the United States and of Canada: The Land Birds.* Cambridge, MA: Hilliard and Brown, 1832.

Oglesby, Richard E. *Manuel Lisa and the Opening of the Missouri Fur Trade.* Norman: University of Oklahoma Press, 1963.

Orr, William J. "Karl Bodmer: The Artist's Life." In Hunt et al., *Karl Bodmer's America,* 349–76.

Pitzer, Donald E. "The Original Boatload of Knowledge down the Ohio River: William Maclure's and Robert Owen's Transfer of Science and Education to the Midwest, 1825–1826." *Ohio Journal of Science* 89, no. 5 (1989): 128–42.

Prucha, Francis Paul, ed. *Documents of United States Indian Policy.* 3rd ed. Lincoln: University of Nebraska Press, 2000.

Roberts, Robert B. *Encyclopedia of Historic Forts: The Military, Pioneer, and Trading Posts of the United States.* New York: Macmillan, 1988.

Röder, Josef, and Hermann Trimborn, eds. *Maximilian Prinz zu Wied: Unveröffentliche Bilder und Handschriften zur Vöolkerkunde Brasiliens.* Bonn-Hanover-Stuttgart: F. Dümmler, 1954.

Ross, Marvin C. *The West of Alfred Jacob Miller: From the Notes and Water Colors in the Walters Art Gallery with an Account of the Artist.* Rev. ed. Norman: University of Oklahoma Press, 1968.

Ruud, Brandon K., Marsha V. Gallagher, and Ron Tyler. *Karl Bodmer's North American Prints.* Lincoln: Joslyn Art Museum and University of Nebraska Press, 2004. (Cited in notes as *KBNAP.*)

Schmidt, Arno. "Hofjäger David Dreydoppel, der Reisebegleiter des Prinzen Max zu Wied." In *Heimat-Jahrbuch 2010 des Landkreises Neuwied,* 250–56.

Schmidt, Oliver H. *Prussian Regular Infantryman, 1801–15.* Oxford, U.K.: Osprey Publishing, 2003.

Schultz, James Willard. *My Life as an Indian: The Story of a Red Woman and a White Man in the Lodges of the Blackfeet.* Boston: Houghton Mifflin, 1907.

Schulze-Thulin, Axel. *Indianer der Prärien und Plains: Reisen und Sammlungen des Herzogs Paul Wilhelm von Württemberg (1822–24) und des Prinzen Maximilian zu Wied (1832–34) im Linden-Museum Stuttgart.* Stuttgart: Linden-Museum, Staatliches Museum für Völkerkunde, 1987.

Schweitzer, Marjorie M. "Otoe and Missouria." In Sturtevant, *Handbook of North American Indians,* vol. 13 (1), *Plains,* edited by Raymond J. DeMallie, 447–61 (2001).

Scoville, J. A. *The Old Merchants of New York City.* New York: Carleton, 1863.

Sears, John F. *Sacred Places: American Tourist Attractions in the Nineteenth Century.* New York: Oxford University Press, 1989.

Sellers, Charles Coleman. *Mr. Peale's Museum: Charles Willson Peale and the First Popular Museum of Natural Science and Art.* New York: W. W. Norton, 1980.

Shaw, Ronald E. *Canals for a Nation: The Canal Era in the United States, 1790–1860.* Lexington: University Press of Kentucky, 1990.

Smith, G. Hubert. *Like-a-Fishhook Village and Fort Berthold, Garrison Reservoir, North Dakota.* Anthropological Papers 2. Washington, D.C.: U.S. Department of the Interior, National Park Service, 1972.

Stroud, Patricia Tyson. *The Man Who Had Been King: The American Exile of Napoleon's Brother Joseph.* Philadelphia: University of Pennsylvania Press, 2005.

Sturtevant, William C., gen. ed. *Handbook of North American Indians.* 20 vols. Washington, D.C.: Smithsonian Institution, 1978–.

Sunder, John E. *Joshua Pilcher: Fur Trader and Indian Agent.* Norman: University of Oklahoma Press, 1968.

Taylor, Alan C. "John Bradbury." In *Early American Nature Writers: A Biographical Encyclopedia,* edited by Daniel Patterson, 70–76. Westport, Conn.: Greenwood Press, 2008.

Thorne, Tanis C. "Black Bird, 'King of the Mahars': Autocrat, Big Man, Chief." *Ethnohistory* 40, no. 3 (Summer 1993): 410–37.

Thrapp, Dan L., ed. *Encyclopedia of Frontier Biography*. Glendale, Calif.: Arthur H. Clark, 1988.

Thwaites, Reuben Gold, ed. *Early Western Travels, 1748–1846: A Series of Annotated Reprints of Some of the Best and Rarest Contemporary Volumes of Travel, Descriptive of the Aborigines and Social and Economic Conditions in the Middle and Far West, during the Period of Early American Settlement*. 32 vols. 2nd ed. New York: AMS Press, 1966. (Cited in notes as *EWT*.)

Trottman, Alan C. "Lucien Fontenelle." In Hafen, *Mountain Men*, 5:81–89.

Truettner, William H. *The Natural Man Observed: A Study of Catlin's Indian Gallery*. Washington, D.C.: Smithsonian Institution Press, 1979.

Tyler, Ron. "Alfred Jacob Miller and Sir William Drummond Stewart." In *Alfred Jacob Miller: Artist on the Oregon Trail*, edited by Ron Tyler, 19–45. Fort Worth, Tex.: Amon Carter Museum, 1982.

———. *Prints of the West: Prints from the Library of Congress*. Golden, Colo.: Fulcrum Publishing, 1994.

Van Ravenswaay, Charles, and Candace O'Connor. *St. Louis: An Informal History of the City and Its People*. St. Louis: Missouri Historical Society Press, 1991.

Wager, D. E. "Whitesboro's Golden Age." In *Transactions of the Oneida Historical Society at Utica, 1881–1884*, 65–144. Utica, N.Y.: Oneida Historical Society, 1885.

Waldman, Carl. *Who Was Who in Native American History*. New York: Facts on File, 1990.

Warren, Leonard. *Constantine Samuel Rafinesque: A Voice in the American Wilderness*. Lexington: University Press of Kentucky, 2004.

West Virginia: A Guide to the Mountain State. New York: Oxford University Press, 1941.

Who Was Who in American Art, 1564–1975: 400 Years of Artists in America. Edited by Peter Hastings Falk. Madison, Conn.: Sound View Press, 1999.

Wickman, John E. "James Bird, Jr." In Hafen, *Mountain Men*, 5:39–43.

Wied, Karl Viktor, Prinz zu. "Maximilian Prinz zu Wied: Sein Leben un seine Reisen." In Röder and Trimborn, *Maximilian Prinz zu Wied*, 13–25.

Wied, Prince Maximilian of. *The North American Journals of Prince Maximilian of Wied*. Edited by Stephen S. Witte and Marsha V. Gallagher; translated by William J. Orr, Paul Schach, and Dieter Karch. 3 vols. Norman: University of Oklahoma Press in cooperation with the Durham Center for Western Studies, Joslyn Art Museum, 2008, 2010, 2012. (Cited in notes as *NAJ* 1, 2, or 3.)

Wied, Maximilian, Prinz zu. *Reise in das innere Nord-America in den Jahren 1832 bis 1834*. 2 vols. with picture atlas. Koblenz: J. Hoelscher, 1839–41. (Cited in notes as *Reise*.)

———. *Reise nach Brasilien in den Jahren 1815 bis 1817*. 2 vols. Frankfurt: H. L. Brönner, 1820–21.

———. *Travels in the Interior of North America, 1832–1834*. Translated by Hannibal Evans Lloyd. London: Ackermann, 1843. (Reprinted as vols. 22–25 in Thwaites, *EWT*, q.v. Cited in notes as *Travels*.)

———. "Über einige Nager mit äusseren Backentaschen aus dem westlichen Nord-America." *Nova acta physicomedica academiae caesareae Leopoldino-Carolinae naturae curiosorum*, 365–84. Breslau and Bonn, 1839.

———. *Verzeichniss der Reptilien, welche auf einer Reise im nördlichen America*. Dresden: E. Blochman and Son, 1865.

———. *Voyage dans l'interieur de L'Amerique du Nord, exécuté pendant les années 1832, 1833 et 1834*. 3 vols. Paris: Arthus Bertand, 1840–43.

Will, George F., and Herbert J. Spinden. *The Mandans: A Study of Their Culture, Archaeology, and Language*. Papers of the Peabody Museum of American Archaeology and Ethnology 3, no. 4. Cambridge, Mass.: Harvard University, 1906.

Wilson, Gilbert L. "Hidatsa Eagle Trapping." *Anthropological Papers of the American Museum of Natural History* 30: 99–245. New York: American Museum of Natural History, 1928.

Wischmann, Lesley. *Frontier Diplomats: Alexander Culbertson and Natoyist-Siksina' among the Blackfeet*. Norman: University of Oklahoma Press, 2004.

Wishart, David J. *An Unspeakable Sadness: The Dispossession of the Nebraska Indians*. Lincoln: University of Nebraska Press, 1994.

Wood, Richard G. *Stephen Harriman Long, 1784–1864: Army Engineer, Explorer, Inventor*. Glendale, Calif.: Arthur H. Clark, 1966.

Wood, W. Raymond. "James Kipp: Upper Missouri River Fur Trader and Missouri Farmer." *North Dakota History* 71, nos. 1–2. Bismarck: State Historical Society of North Dakota, 2011.

Wood, W. Raymond, and Lee Irwin. "Mandan." In Sturtevant, *Handbook of North American Indians*, vol. 13 (1), *Plains*, edited by Raymond J. DeMallie, 349–64 (2001).

Wood, W. Raymond, and Gary E. Moulton. "Prince Maximilian and New Maps of the Missouri and Yellowstone Rivers by William Clark." *Western Historical Quarterly* 12, no. 4 (October 1981): 372–86.

Wood, W. Raymond, Joseph C. Porter, and David C. Hunt. *Karl Bodmer's Studio Art: The Newberry Library Bodmer Collection*. Urbana: University of Illinois Press, 2002. (Cited in notes as *KBSA*.)

List of Flora and Fauna

This list is limited to the Latin binomials appearing in the concise volume and their modern equivalents as of 2008. Only the common names used by Maximilian are cross-referenced here. For a full understanding of Maximilian's biological observations, consult the flora and fauna indices for volumes 1–3 of his *North American Journals.*

Acalypha virginica, three-seeded mercury

Accipiter spp., hawks

A. striatus, sharp-shinned hawk

Acer spp., maples

A. eriocarpum. See *A. saccharinum*

A. negundo, box elder

A. nigrum, black maple

A. pensylvanicum, striped maple

A. saccharinum, silver maple

A. saccharum, sugar maple

Acipenser fulvescens, lake sturgeon

Actaea racemosa, black snakeroot

Adam-and-Eve. See *Aplectrum hyemale*

Aesculus glabra, Ohio buckeye

Agama sp. See *Sceloporus undulatus*

Agaricus spp., mushrooms

Agelaius phoeniceus, red-winged blackbird

Agkistrodon piscivorus, water moccasin, cottonmouth

Aix sponsa, wood duck

Alauda alpestris or *montana.* See *Eremophila alpestris*

A. magna. See *Sturnella magna*

Alcedo alcyon. See *Ceryle alcyon*

Alces alces, moose

Allium spp., onion/wild onion

Allogona profunda, broad-banded forest snail

Alnus spp., alders

Amelanchier spp., *poires,* serviceberries

A. alnifolia, western serviceberry

Amorpha fruticosa, wild or false indigo

Anas spp., ducks

A. acuta, northern pintail duck

A. boschas and *boschas fera.* See *A. platyrhynchos*

A. clangula. See *Bucephala clangula*

A. crecca, green-winged teal

A. moschata. See *Cairina moschata*

A. platyrhynchos, mallard

A. rufitorques. See *Aythya collaris*

A. sponsa. See *Aix sponsa*

Andromeda paniculata. See *Leucothoë racemosa*

Anemone patens, pasque flower

Annona triloba. See *Asimina triloba*

Anodonta spp., freshwater mussels

Anolis bullaris. See *A. carolinensis*

Anolis carolinensis, green anole

Anser canadensis. See *Branta canadensis*

Antelope. See *Antilocapra americana*

Antilocapra americana, pronghorn antelope

Antilope furcifer. See *Antilocapra americana*

Antirrhinum linaria. See *Linaria vulgaris*

Apalone mutica, smooth softshell turtle

A. spinifera, spiny softshell turtle

Aplectrum hyemale, Adam-and-Eve

Apocynum spp., dogbanes

Aquila chrysaetos, golden eagle

A. leucocephala. See *Haliaeetus leucocephalus*

Aquilegia spp., columbines

A. canadensis, American columbine

Ara spp., macaws

Arabis bulbosa and *rhomboidea.* See *Cardamine rhomboidea*

Aralia nudicaulis, wild sarsaparilla

Arborvitae. See *Thuja* spp.

Archilochus colubris, ruby-throated hummingbird

Arctomys hoodii. See *Spermophilus tridecemlineatus*

A. ludoviciana. See *Cynomys ludovicianus*

A. monax. See *Marmota monax*

Arctostaphylos uva-ursi, bearberry

Ardea herodias, great blue heron

A. virescens. See *Butorides virescens*

Argali. See *Ovis canadensis*

Aristolochia macrophylla, Dutchman's pipe

A. serpentaria, Virginia snakeroot

A. sipho. See *A. macrophylla*

Artemisia spp., sagebrushes

A. cana, silver sagebrush, dwarf sagebrush

A. columbiensis. See *Artemisia cana*

Arundinaria gigantea, giant cane

Arundo phragmites. See *Phragmites australis*

Arvicola xanthognatha. See *Microtus* sp.

Asclepias spp., milkweed

A. syriaca, common milkweed

Ash, white. See *Fraxinus americana*

Asimina triloba, pawpaw

Asio otus, long-eared owl

Aspen. See *Populus tremuloides*

Aspidonectes ocellatus. See *Apalone spinifera*

Aster acuminatus, whorled aster

Athene cunicularia, burrowing owl

Aureolaria pedicularia, annual false foxglove

A. virginica, smooth false foxglove

Aythya collaris, ring-necked duck

Badger, American. See *Taxidea taxus*

Baeolophus bicolor, tufted titmouse

Baltimore [oriole]. See *Icterus galbula*

Bartonia ornata. See *Mentzelia decapetala*

Basswood. See *Tilia* spp.

Batschia canescens. See *Lithospermum canescens*

Battus philenor, pipevine swallowtail butterfly

Bear. See *Ursus* spp.

Bear, American black. See *Ursus americanus*

Beaver, American. See *Castor canadensis*

Beech. See *Fagus grandifolia*

Belle dame. See *Chenopodium* spp.

Betula spp., birches

Betula lenta, sweet birch, black birch

B. nigra, river birch

Bighorn. See *Ovis canadensis*

Bignonia crucigera. See *Doxantha capreolata*

B. radicans. See *Campsis radicans*

Birches. See *Betula* spp.

Bison bison, American bison

Blackbird, red-winged. See *Agelaius phoeniceus*

Blackbird with a yellow head. See *Xanthocephalus xanthocephalus*

Blackfish. See *Globicephala* spp.

Black-tailed [or mule] deer. See *Odocoileus hemionus*

Bladder wrack. See *Fucus vesiculosus*

Bluebird, eastern. See *Sialia sialis*

Blue jay. See *Cyanocitta cristata*

Bombycilla spp., waxwings
B. garrula. See *B. garrulus*
B. garrulus, Bohemian waxwing
Bombyx cecropia. See *Hyalophora cecropia*
Bonasa umbellus, ruffed grouse
Bow-wood. See *Maclura pomifera*
Box elder. See *Acer negundo*
Brachyris euthamiae. See *Gutierrezia sarothrae*
Branta canadensis, Canada goose
Broussonetia papyrifera, paper mulberry
Brown thrasher. See *Toxostoma rufum*
Bubo bubo, Eurasian owl (resembles North American *B. virginianus*)
B. scandiacus, snowy owl
B. virginianus, great horned owl
Bucephala clangula, common goldeneye
Buckeye, [Ohio]. See *Aesculus glabra*
Buffalo. See *Bison bison*
Buffalo berry. See *Shepherdia* spp.
Buffalo[fish, bigmouth]. See *Ictiobus cyprinellus*
Bulbostylis capillaris, reed, [sedge]
Bullfrog. See *Rana catesbiana*
Bunting, snow. See *Plectrophenax nivalis*
Buteo jamaicensis, red-tailed hawk
B. lagopus, rough-legged hawk
Butorides virescens, green heron

Cabri. See *Antilocapra americana*
Cactus ferox. See *Opuntia polyacantha*
C. mammillaris. See *Coryphantha* spp.
C. opuntia. See *Opuntia humifusa, O. polyacantha*
Cairina moschata, Muscovy duck (domesticated)
Calcarius pictus, Smith's longspur
Calidris minutilla, least sandpiper
Callinectes sapidus, blue crab
Campephilus principalis, ivory-billed woodpecker
Campsis radicans, trumpet creeper

Cane. See *Arundinaria gigantea*
Canis cinerea argenteus. See *Urocyon cinereoargenteus*
C. fulvus. See *Vulpes vulpes*
C. latrans, prairie wolf, [coyote]
C. lupus, gray wolf [includes white and reddish phases]
C. variabilis. See *C. lupus*
C. velox. See *Vulpes velox*
C. vulpes. See *Vulpes vulpes*
Capra montana. See *Oreamnos americanus*
Caprimulgus americanus. See *Chordeiles minor*
C. vociferus, whippoorwill
Cardamine rhomboidea, spring cress
Cardinal. See *Cardinalis cardinalis*
Cardinalis cardinalis, northern cardinal
Carduelis flammea, common redpoll
C. tristis, American goldfinch
Carpinus caroliniana, hornbeam
Carpodacus purpureus, purple finch
Carya lacinosa, shellbark hickory
C. ovata, shagbark hickory
Cassia marilandica. See *Senna marilandica*
Castanea spp., chestnuts
C. dentata, American chestnut
C. vesca. See *C. dentata*
Castor canadensis, American beaver
Catalpa speciosa, northern catalpa
Catbird. See *Dumetella carolinensis*
Cathartes aura, turkey vulture
Cattails. See *Typha* sp.
Ceanothus americanus, New Jersey tea
Cedar tree, cedars. See *Juniperus* spp., possibly *Thuja* sp.
Celastrus scandens, bittersweet.
Celtis occidentalis, hackberry
Cemophora coccinea, scarlet snake
Centrocercus urophasianus, sage grouse.
Cerasus spp. See *Prunus* spp.
Cercis spp., redbuds

Cercis canadensis, eastern redbud
Certhia americana, brown creeper
C. familiaris. See *C. americana*
C. varia. See *Mniotilta varia*
Cervus alces americanus. See *Alces alces*
Cervus canadensis. See *C. elaphus*
C. elaphus, wapiti or elk
C. macrotis. See *Odocoileus hemionus*
C. virginianus. See *Odocoileus virginianus*
Ceryle alcyon, belted kingfisher
Cetaceae, an order of marine mammals including whales, dolphins, and porpoises
Chaetura pelagica, chimney swift
Charadrius spp., plovers, including the killdeer (*C. vociferus*)
Chelone obliqua, purple turtlehead
Chenopodium spp., lamb's quarters, goosefoot
Chestnut. See *Castanea* spp.
Chestnut, American. See *Castanea dentata*
Chipmunk, eastern. See *Tamias striatus*
Chlidonias niger, black tern
Chokecherry. See *Prunus virginiana*
Chondestes grammacus, lark sparrow
Chordeiles minor, common nighthawk
Choromytilus chorus, mussel
Chrysemys picta, painted turtle
Cicada septem-decem. See *Magicicada septendecim*
Circus cyaneus, northern harrier
Cirsium spp., thistles
Cistudo clausa. See *Terrapene carolina*
Cladium mariscoides, twig rush
Claytonia virginica, spring beauty
Clematis spp., clematis
Clemmys guttata, spotted turtle
Cnicus spp. See *Cirsium* spp
Coati. See *Nasua nasua*
Coccyzus americanus, yellow-billed cuckoo
C. erythrophthalmus, black-billed

cuckoo
Colaptes auratus, northern flicker
Colinus virginianus, northern bobwhite, quail
Coluber coccineus. See *Cemophora coccinea*
C. constrictor, blue racer, eastern yellow-belly racer
C. eximus. See *Lampropeltis triangulum*
C. flaviventris. See *C. constrictor*
C. porcatus. See *Storeria occipitomaculata*
C. proximus. See *Thamnophis proximus*
C. proximus, red-spotted. See *Pituophis catenifer sayi*
C. saurita. See *Thamnophis sauritus*
C. sipedon. See *Nerodia sipedon*
C. sirtalis. See *Thamnophis sirtalis*
Columba carolinensis. See *Zenaida macroura*
C. migratoria. See *Ectopistes migratorius*
Comptonia asplenifolia. See *C. peregrina*
C. peregrina, sweet fern
Condor. See *Vultur gryphus* or *Gymno-gyps californianus*
Conuropsis carolinensis, Carolina para-keet (now extinct)
Convallaria [majalis], lily of the valley
Coot. See *Fulica americana*
Coragyps atratus, black vulture (the one "with a reddish head")
Cornus spp., dogwoods
C. florida, flowering dogwood
C. mas, Cornelian cherry (a European species of dogwood)
C. mascula. See *C. mas*
C. sericea, red osier dogwood
Corvus brachyrhynchos, American crow
C. corax, common raven
C. corone americana. See *C. brachyrhynchos*
C. cristatus. See *Cyanocitta cristata*
C. pica. See *Pica hudsonia*

Corylus americana, American hazelnut
Coryphantha spp., pincushion cacti
Cottonwoods. See *Populus* spp.
Cow bunting. See *Molothrus ater*
Crabapple. See *Pyrus coronaria*
Crane, sandhill. See *Grus canadensis*
Crane, whooping. See *Grus americana*
Crataegus spp., hawthorn
C. monogyna, one-seeded hawthorn
C. oxyacantha. See *C. monogyna*
Cristaria coccinea. See *Sphaeralcea coccinea*
Crotalus tergeminus. See *C. viridis* or *Sistrurus catenatus tergeminus*
C. viridis, prairie rattlesnake
Crow, [American]. See *Corvus brachyrhynchos*
Cuckoos. See *Coccyzus* spp.
Cuculus carolinensis. See *Coccyzus americanus*
Cucumber tree. See *Magnolia acuminata*
Culicidae, mosquitoes
Curlews. See *Numenius* spp.
Currants. See *Ribes* spp.
Currant with yellow flowers. See *Ribes odoratum*
Cyanocitta cristata, blue jay
Cygnus spp., swans
Cygnus americanus. See *C. columbianus*
C. columbianus, tundra swan
Cynomys ludovicianus, black-tailed prairie dog
Cyperus spp., sedges
C. strigosus, umbrella sedge
Cypripedium spp., lady-slipper orchids
Cypselus pelagius. See *Chaetura pelagica*

Danaus plexippus, monarch butterfly
Datura sp. See *D. stramonium*
D. stramonium, jimsonweed
Deer. See *Odocoileus* spp.
Delphinus delphis, common dolphin
D. phocaena. See *Phocaena phocaena*

Dendrocopus major, European spotted woodpecker
Dendroica petechia, yellow warbler
D. striata, blackpoll warbler
Dentalium spp., dentalium scaphopods, tusk shells
Dicentra cucullaria, Dutchman's breeches
Diervilla canadensis. See *Lonicera canadensis*
Diospyros virginiana, persimmon
Dodecatheon meadia, shooting star
Dogwoods. See *Cornus* spp.
Dolichonyx oryzivorus, bobolink, ricebird
Dove, American. See *Columba migratoria*
Doxantha capreolata, cross vine
Dryocopus pileatus, pileated woodpecker
Duck, butter. See *Bucephala clangula*
Dumetella carolinensis, catbird

Eagle, bald. See *Haliaeetus leucocephalus*
Eagle, golden. See *Aquila chrysaetos*
Eagle owl. See *Bubo bubo*
Echeneis spp., shark suckers and slender remoras
Ectopistes migratorius, passenger pigeon (now extinct)
Elaeagnus argentea. See *Shepherdia argentea*
Elanoides forficatus, swallow-tailed kite
Elder. See *Sambucus canadensis*
Eleocharis ovata, ovate spike rush
Elk. See *Cervus elaphus*
Elm, red or slippery. See *Ulmus rubra*
Elms. See *Ulmus* spp.
Emberiza nivalis. See *Plectrophenax nivalis*
E. oryzivora. See *Dolichonyx oryzivorus*
Emys biguttata. See *Glyptemis muhlenbergii*
E. concentrica. See *Malaclemys terrapin*

E. geographica. See *Graptemys geographica*

E. picta. See *Chrysemys picta*

E. punctata. See *Clemmys punctata*

E. serrata. See *Trachyemys scripta*

Eptesicus fuscus, big brown bat

Equisetum spp., rushes

E. hyemale, horsetail, scouring rush

Eremophila alpestris, horned lark

Erethizon dorsatum, North American porcupine

Eriophorum spp., cotton grass

Ermine. See *Mustela erminea*

Esox lucius, northern pike

Eupatorium coelestinum, mistflower

E. purpureum, purple joe-pye weed

Euphagus carolinus, rusty blackbird

Euphorbia corollata, flowering spurge

E. maculata, spotted spurge

Fagus grandifolia, American beech

Falco borealis. See *Buteo jamaicensis*

F. cyaneus. See *Circus cyaneus*

F. furcatus. See *Elanoides forficatus*

F. gutturalis. See *Circus cyaneus*

F. haliaëtus. See *Pandion haliaetus*

F. peregrinus, peregrine falcon

F. sancti-johannis. See *Buteo lagopus*

F. sparverius, American kestrel

F. velox. See *Accipiter striatus*

Felis rufus. See *Lynx rufus*

F. concolor. See *Puma concolor*

Fence mouse. See *Tamias striatus*

Fiber zibethicus. See *Ondatra zibethicus*

Fir, Canadian. See *Tsuga canadensis*

Fireflies, several genera and species

Fisher. See *Martes pennanti*

Fox, gray. See *Urocyon cinereoargenteus*

Fox, kit. See *Vulpes velox*

Fox, prairie. See *Vulpes velox* or *V. vulpes*

Fox, red, cross, silver. See *Vulpes vulpes*

Fragaria spp., strawberries

Frasera caroliniensis, American columbo

F. walteri. See *F. caroliniensis*

Fraxinus spp., ash trees

F. americana, white ash

Fringilla acutipennis. See *Calcarius pictus*

F. amoena. See *Passerina amoena*

F. canadensis. See *Spizella arborea*

F. cardinalis. See *Cardinalis cardinalis*

F. cyanea. See *Passerina cyanea*

F. erythrophthalma. See *Pipilo erythrophthalma*

F. graminea. See *Poöecetes gramineus*

F. grammaca or *grammacea.* See *Chondestes grammacus*

F. hudsonia and *hyemalis.* See *Junco hyemalis*

F. indigofera. See *Passerina cyanea*

F. linaria. See *Carduelis flammea*

F. melodia. See *Melospiza melodia*

F. pennsylvanica. See *Zonotrichia albicollis*

F. purpurea. See *Carpodacus purpureus*

F. tristis. See *Carduelis tristis*

Fucus vesiculosus, bladder wrack, sea wrack, rockweed

Fulica americana, American coot

Fulmarus glacialis, northern fulmar

Fumaria sp. See *Stylophorum diphyllum*

Gadus morhua, Atlantic cod

Galium spp., bedstraw

Gannet. See *Sula sula*

Geothlypis trichas, common yellowthroat

Gerardia pedicularia. See *Aureolaria pedicularia*

G. quercifolia. See *Aureolaria virginica*

Gerbillus canadensis. See *Zapus hudsonius*

Ginseng, [American]. See *Panax quinquefolius*

Gleditsia triacanthos, honey locust

Gleditsia triacanthos var. *inermis,* thornless honey locust

Globicephala spp., pilot whales

Glycymeris siliqua, clam

Glyptemis muhlenbergii, bog turtle

Gnathodon cuneatus. See *Rangia cuneata*

Goldeye. See *Hiodon alosoides*

Goldfinch [American]. See *Carduelis tristis*

Gooseberries. See *Ribes* spp.

Gopher. See *Spermophilus tridecemlineatus*

Goura cristata, Western or blue crowned pigeon, a New Guinea species

Grape, fox. See *Vitis labrusca*

Graptemys geographica, common map turtle

Grasshoppers. See *Gryllus* spp.

Grebe, pied-billed. See *Podilymbus podiceps*

Grindelia squarrosa, curlycup gumweed

Ground berry. See *Mitchella repens*

Groundhog. See *Marmota monax*

Grouse, heath hen. See *Tympanuchus cupido*

Grouse, ruffed. See *Bonasa umbellus*

Grouse, sharp-tailed. See *Tympanuchus phasianellus*

Grus americana, whooping crane

G. canadensis, sandhill crane

Gryllus spp., crickets (Maximilian included grasshoppers in this genus as well)

Guillemot. See *Uria aalge*

Gum, black. See *Nyssa sylvatica*

Gutierrezia sarothrae, broom snakeweed

Gymnocladus [dioica], Kentucky coffee tree

Gymnogyps californianus, California condor

Hackberry. See *Celtis occidentalis*

Haliaeetus leucocephalus, bald eagle

Hamamelis virginiana, witch hazel

Hawfinch, red-breasted. See *Pheucticus ludovicianus*

Hawthorn. See *Crataegus* spp.

Heath hen. See *Tympanuchus cupido*

Hedera quinquefolia. See *Parthenocissus quinquefolia, P. vitacea*

Hedyotis caerulea, bluet

Helianthus spp., sunflowers

Helix profunda. See *Allogona profunda*

Hemlock [eastern]. See *Tsuga canadensis*

Heteranthera reniformis, mud plantain

Heterodon spp., hognose snakes

H. nasicus, western hognose snake

H. platirhinos, eastern hognose snake

Hibiscus syriacus, rose of sharon

Hickories. See *Carya* spp.

Hiodon alosoides, goldeye

Hirundo bicolor. See *Tachycineta bicolor*

H. fulva. See *Petrochelidon pyrrhonota*

H. purpurea. See *Progne subis*

H. riparia. See *Riparia riparia*

H. rustica, barn swallow

Hognose snake. See *Heterodon platirhinos*

Hornbeam. See *Carpinus caroliniana*

Houstonia caerulea. See *Hedyotis caerulea*

Hummingbird, [ruby-throated]. See *Archilochus colubris*

Humulus sp., hops

Hyalophora cecropia, cecropia moth

Hydrangea arborescens, American hydrangea

Hydrobates pelagicus, European storm petrel

Hyla spp., tree frogs

Hylocichla mustelina, wood thrush

Hypericum spp., Saint-John's-wort

H. corymbosum. See *H. punctatum*

H. ellipticum, pale Saint-John's-wort

H. mutilum ssp. *mutilum,* dwarf Saint-John's-wort

H. parviflorum, probably *H. mutilum* ssp. *mutilum*

H. perforatum, common Saint-John's-wort

H. punctatum, spotted Saint-John's-wort

H. sphaerocarpum, Saint-John's-wort

Hystrix dorsata. See *Erethizon dorsatum*

Ichthyomyzon castaneus, chestnut lamprey

Icteria virens, yellow-breasted chat

I. viridis. See *I. virens*

Icterocephalus sp. See *Xanthocephalus xanthocephalus*

Icterus agripennis. See *Dolichonyx oryzivorus*

I. baltimore. See *I. galbula*

I. galbula, Baltimore oriole

I. icterocephalus. See *Xanthocephalus xanthocephalus*

I. pecoris. See *Molothrus ater*

I. phoeniceus. See *Agelaius phoeniceus*

I. spurius, orchard oriole

I. strigilatus. See *Dolichonyx oryzivorus*

Ictiobus cyprinellus, bigmouth buffalo fish

Impatiens capensis, spotted touch-me-not

I. fulva. See *I. capensis*

Ironwood. See *Ostrya virginiana*

Juglans spp., walnuts

J. alba. See *Carya ovata*

J. cinerea, butternut, white walnut

J. nigra, black walnut

Junco hyemalis, dark-eyed junco

Juniperus spp., junipers

J. horizontalis, creeping juniper

J. prostrata. See *J. horizontalis*

J. virginiania, eastern red cedar, juniper

Kalmia spp., laurel

K. latifolia, mountain laurel

Kingbird, eastern. See *Tyrannus tyrannus*

Kingbird, western. See *Tyrannus verticalis*

Kingfisher. See *Ceryle alcyon*

Lamb's quarters. See *Chenopodium* spp.

Lampropeltis triangulum, milk snake

Lanius spp., shrikes

L. excubitor, northern shrike

L. septentrionalis. See *L. excubitor*

Larix spp., larches

Lark, mountain. See *Eremophila alpestris*

Lark, yellow-breasted. See *Sturnella* spp.

Larus canus, mew gull

L. eburneus. See *Pagophila eburnea*

L. ridibundus, black-headed gull

Lasiurus borealis, eastern red bat

Laurus benzoin. See *Lindera benzoin*

L. sassafras. See *Sassafras albidum*

Lepus americanus, snowshoe hare

Leucothoë racemosa, sweetbells

Liatris sp., blazing star

Libellula spp., dragonflies

Linaria vulgaris, butter-and-eggs

Linden, probably *Tilia americana*

Lindera benzoin, spicebush; Maximilian's spicewood

Linum spp., flax

Liquidambar styraciflua, sweet gum

Liriodendron tulipifera, tulip tree

Lithospermum canescens, hoary puccoon

Lizard, spine-headed [short-horned]. See *Phrynosoma hernandesi*

Lobelia cardinalis, cardinal flower

L. inflata, Indian tobacco

L. siphilitica, blue lobelia

Locust, black. See *Robinia pseudoacacia*

Locust, honey. See *Gleditsia triacanthos*

Lonicera canadensis, American fly honeysuckle

L. sempervirens, trumpet honeysuckle

Lontra canadensis, northern river otter

Lophodytes cucullatus, hooded merganser

Loxia cardinalis. See *Cardinalis cardinalis*

L. ludoviciana. See *Pheucticus ludovicianus*

Ludwigia alternifolia, square-pod water primrose

L. macrocarpa. See *L. alternifolia*

L. nitida. See *L. palustris*

L. palustris, common water purslane

Lupa hastata. See *Callinectes sapidus*

Lutra canadensis. See *Lontra canadensis*

Lynx, northern. See *Lynx canadensis*

Lynx canadensis, Canada lynx

L. rufus, bobcat; in Maximilian's usage, wildcat

Macrochelys temminckii, alligator snapping turtle

Maclura aurantiaca. See *M. pomifera*

M. pomifera, Osage orange or bow-wood

Magicicada septendecim, cicada

Magnolia spp., magnolias

Magnolia acuminata, cucumber tree

Magpie, [black-billed]. See *Pica hudsonia*

Malaclemys terrapin, diamondback terrapin

Mallard. See *Anas platyrhynchos*

Malva spp., mallows

Maples. See *Acer* spp.

Marmota monax, woodchuck, groundhog, marmot

Marten. See *Martes americana*

Martes americana, marten

M. pennanti, fisher

Medusa pelagica (in Maximilian's time, either a jellyfish or a man-o-war)

Megascops asio, eastern screech owl

Melanerpes carolinus, red-bellied woodpecker

M. erythrocephalus, redheaded woodpecker

Meleagris gallopavo, wild turkey

Meles americanus. See *Taxidea taxus*

M. labradorius. See *Taxidea taxus*

Melissa officinalis, common lemon balm

Melospiza melodia, song sparrow

Menobranchus lateralis. See *Necturus maculosus*

Menopoma spp., salamanders

M. alleganensis. See *Protonopsis horrida*

Mentha spp., mints

M. piperita, peppermint

Mentzelia decapetala, stickleaf

Mergus cucullatus. See *Lophodytes cucullatus*

M. merganser, common merganser

Mespilus spp. See *Amelanchier* spp.

Mice, jumping. See *Zapus hudsonius*

Microtus sp., vole

Miegia macrocarpa. See *Arundinaria gigantea*

Mimulus alatus, sharpwing monkey flower

Mink. See *Mustela vison*

Mitchella repens, partridgeberry

Mniotilta varia, black-and-white warbler

Molothrus ater, cowbird

Monarda spp., bee balm

M. fistulosa, wild bergamot

Morus rubra, red mulberry

Mosquitoes. See Culicidae

Mountain goat. See *Oreamnos americanus*

Mountain lion. See *Puma concolor*

Mulberry, paper. See *Broussonetia papyrifera*

Mulberry, red. See *Morus rubra*

Muscicapa spp., flycatchers

M. crinita. See *Myiarchus crinitus*

M. ruticilla. See *Setophaga ruticilla*

M. tyrannus. See *Tyrannus tyrannus*

Mus decumanus. See *Rattus norvegicus*

M. macrocephalus. See *Peromyscus maniculatus*

M. sylvaticus, field mouse (European species)

Muskrat. See *Ondatra zibethecus*

Mustela erminea, ermine, white weasel

M. nivalis, least weasel

M. pennanti. See *Martes pennanti*

M. vison, American mink (Maximilian thought this was identical to *M. lutreola,* the European mink)

M. vulgaris americana. See *M. nivalis*

Myiarchus crinitus, great crested flycatcher

Myosotis arvensis, field forget-me-not

Myrica cerifera, wax myrtle

N. advena. See *Nuphar advena*

Nasua nasua, coati

Necrophorus grandis. See *Nicrophorus americanus*

Necturus maculosus, mud puppy

Neotoma spp., wood rats, pack rats

Nerodia sipedon, northern water snake

Nicotiana spp., tobacco

Nicrophorus americanus, giant carrion beetle

Nighthawk, common. See *Chordeiles minor*

Nightjar. See *Chordeiles minor*

Norway rat. See *Rattus norvegicus*

Numenius spp., curlews

N. americanus, long-billed curlew

N. longirostris. See *N. americanus*

Nuphar advena, cow lily or spatterdock

Nuthatches. See *Sitta* spp.

Nymphaea spp., water lilies

Nymphalis antiopa, mourning cloak butterfly

Nyssa sylvatica, black gum

Oaks. See *Quercus* spp.

Oak, black. See *Quercus velutina*

Oak, blackjack. See *Quercus marilandica*

Oak, live. See *Quercus virginiana*

Oak, red. See *Quercus rubra*

Oak, scrub. See *Quercus ilicifolia, Q. prinoides*

Oak, white. See *Quercus alba*

Oak, willow. See *Quercus phellos*

Oceanodroma leucorhoa, Leach's storm petrel

Odocoileus hemionus, black-tailed deer, mule deer

O. virginianus, white-tailed deer

Oenothera spp., evening primroses

Ondatra zibethecus, muskrat

Onion, wild or prairie. See *Allium* spp.

Oporornis formosus, Kentucky warbler

Opuntia spp., prickly pear cacti

O. humifusa, prickly pear

O. polyacantha, plains prickly pear

Oreamnos americanus, mountain goat

Orignal. See *Alces alces*

Oriole, golden and striped golden. See *Icterus galbula*

Osprey. See *Pandion haliaetus*

Ostrea edulis, flat oyster (European)

Ostrya virginiana, ironwood or hop hornbeam

Otter, northern river. See *Lontra canadensis*

Ovis ammon. See *O. canadensis*

Ovis canadensis, bighorn sheep

Owl, burrowing. See *Athene cunicularia*

Owl, great horned. See *Bubo virginianus*

Owl, eastern screech. See *Megascops asio*

Owl, snowy. See *Bubo scandiacus*

Oxalis spp., wood sorrel

O. acetosella, northern wood sorrel

Pagophila eburnea, ivory gull

Panax quinquefolius, American ginseng

Pandion haliaetus, osprey

Panther. See *Puma concolor*

Papilio ajax, green swallowtail butterfly

P. antiopa. See *Nymphalis antiopa*

P. glaucus, tiger swallowtail butterfly

P. plexippus. See *Danaus plexippus*

P. turnus. See *P. glaucus*

Parakeet, [Carolina]. See *Conuropsis carolinensis*

Parthenocissus quinquefolia, Virginia creeper

P. vitacea, woodbine

Partridge, usually refers in Maximilian's usage to *Colinus virginianus*

Parus atricapillus. See *Poecile atricapillus*

P. bicolor. See *Baeolophus bicolor*

Passenger pigeon. See *Ectopistes migratorius*

Passerina amoena, lazuli bunting

P. cyanea, indigo bunting

Passiflora caerulea, blue passionflower

Pavia lutea. See *Aesculus glabra*

Pawpaw. See *Asimina triloba*

Pediomelum esculentum, pommes des prairies, pomme blanche, Indian breadroot

Pelecanus erythrorhynchos, American white pelican

Pelican. See *Pelecanus erythrorhynchos*

Perdix virginiana. See *Colinus virginianus*

Perognathus fasciatus, olive-backed pocket mouse

Peromyscus maniculatus, North American deer mouse

Persimmon. See *Diospyros virginiana*

Petrochelidon pyrrhonota, cliff swallow

Petromyzon cinereus. See *Ichthyomyzon castaneus*

Phalaena cecropia. See *Hyalophora cecropia*

Pheasant, used by the prince for several species of game birds

Pheucticus ludovicianus, rose-breasted grosbeak

Phlox, blue. See *Phlox divaricata*

Phlox divaricata, blue phlox

Phocaena phocaena, harbor porpoise

Phoradendron serotinum, American mistletoe

Phragmites australis, common reed

Phrynosoma spp., horned lizards

P. hernandesi, short-horned lizard

Physalia [physalis], Portuguese man-of-war

Physocarpus opulifolius, ninebark

Phytolacca americana, pokeweed

P. decandra. See *P. americana*

Pica hudsonia, black-billed magpie

Picoides pubescens, downy woodpecker

P. villosus, hairy woodpecker

Picus auratus. See *Colaptes auratus*

P. carolinensis or *carolinus.* See *Melanerpes carolinus*

P. erythrocephalus. See *Melanerpes erythrocephalus*

P. major. See *Dendrocopus major*

P. pileatus. See *Dryocopus pileatus*

P. principalis. See *Campephilus principalis*

P. pubescens. See *Picoides pubescens*

P. varius. See *Sphyrapicus varius*

P. villosus. See *Picoides villosus*

Pigeon, blue Indian crowned. See *Goura cristata*

Pike, [northern]. See *Esox lucius*

Pine, Weymouth. See *Pinus strobus*

Pine, white. See *Pinus strobus*

Pinus canadensis. See *Tsuga canadensis*

P. rigida, pitch pine

P. strobus, white pine

Pipilo erythrophthalmus, eastern towhee

Piranga rubra, summer tanager

Pituophis catenifer sayi, bullsnake

Planorbis lentus, ramshorn snail

Platanus spp., sycamores

P. occidentalis, buttonwood, sycamore, American plane tree

Plectrophenax nivalis, snow bunting

Plum trees. See *Prunus* spp.

Podiceps. See *Podilymbus podiceps*

Podilymbus podiceps, pied-billed grebe

Podophyllum peltatum, mayapple

Poecile atricapillus, black-capped chickadee

Poires. See *Amelanchier* spp.

Poison ivy. See *Toxicodendron radicans*

Pokeweed. See *Phytolacca americana*

Polygala verticillata, whorled milkwort

Pomme blanche, pomme de prairie. See *Pediomelum esculentum*

Poöecetes gramineus, vesper sparrow

Poplars. See *Populus* spp. (Maximilian also applied this common name to *Liriodendron*, tulip tree)

Poplar, Lombardy or Italian. See *Populus nigra* "Italica"

Populus angulata. See *P. deltoides*

P. deltoides, Plains cottonwood

P. nigra "Italica," Lombardy poplar

P. tremuloides, quaking aspen

Porpoise. See Cetaceae

Prairie chicken or hen. See *Tympanuchus* spp., *Centrocercus urophasianus*

Prairie dog. See *Cynomys ludovicianus*

Prairie wolf. See *Canis latrans*

Prenanthes alba, rattlesnake root

P. rubicunda. See *Prenanthes alba*

Procellaria glacialis. See *Fulmarus glacialis*

P. leachii. See *Oceandroma leucorhoa*

P. pelagica. See *Hydrobates pelagicus*

Procyon lotor, northern raccoon

Progne subis, purple martin

Protonopsis horrida, hellbender

Prunus spp., cherry, plum

P. padus, P. padus virginiana. See *P. virginiana*

P. spinosa, blackthorn (a Eurasian species)

P. virginiana, chokecherry

Psittacus carolinensis. See *Conuropsis carolinensis*

Psoralea esculenta. See *Pediomelum esculentum*

Pulsatilla sp. See *Anemone patens*

Puma concolor, mountain lion

Pycnanthemum sp., mountain mint

Pyrethrums, now included in *Chrysanthemum* spp.

Pyrus coronaria, crab apple

Quercus spp., oaks

Q. alba, white oak

Q. banisteri. See *Q. ilicifolia*

Q. bicolor, swamp white oak

Q. chincapin. See *Q. prinoides*

Q. coccinea, scarlet oak

Q. ferruginea. See *Q. marilandica*

Q. heterophylla, a hybrid of *Q. phellos*, willow oak

Q. ilicifolia, scrub oak

Q. macrocarpa, bur oak

Q. marilandica, blackjack oak

Q. montana, mountain chestnut oak

Q. monticola. See *Q. montana*

Q. obtusiloba. See *Q. stellata*

Q. phellos, willow oak

Q. prinoides, chinquapin oak

Q. prinus. See *Q. montana*

Q. rubra, red oak

Q. sempervirens. See *Q. virginiana*

Q. stellata, post oak

Q. tinctoria. See *Q. velutina*

Q. velutina, black oak

Q. virginiana, live oak

Quiscalus ferruginea. See *Euphagus carolinus*

Q. quiscula, common grackle

Q. versicolor. See *Q. quiscula*

Raccoon. See *Procyon lotor*

Raja spp., skate

Rana catesbeiana, bullfrog

R. esculenta, a common European frog species

R. *halecina*. See *R. pipiens*

R. pipiens, northern leopard frog

Rangia cuneata, Atlantic rangia

Ranunculus spp., buttercups

Ratibida columnifera, prairie coneflower

Rattlesnakes. See *Crotalus* spp. and
    Sistrurus spp.

Rattus norvegicus, Norway rat

Raven, common. See *Corvus corax*

Recurvirostra americana, American
    avocet

Redbud. See *Cercis canadensis*

Regulus calendula, ruby-crowned
    kinglet

R. satrapa, golden-crowned kinglet

Rhexia virginica, meadow beauty

Rhododendron maximum, great laurel

Rhus spp., sumacs

R. glabra, smooth sumac

R. radicans. See *Toxicodendron radicans*

R. trilobata, aromatic sumac

R. typhina, staghorn sumac

R. typhinum. See *R. typhina*

Ribes spp., currants, gooseberries

R. odoratum, golden currant

Rice, wild. See *Zizania palustris*

Ricebird. See *Dolichonyx oryzivorus*

Riparia riparia, bank swallow

Robin, American. See *Turdus
    migratorius*

Robinia pseudoacacia, black locust

Rockweed. See *Fucus vesiculosus*

Rosa spp., roses

R. nitida, swamp rose

Roses. See *Rosa* spp.

Rubus spp., blackberries, raspberries

R. odoratus, flowering raspberry

Rudbeckia spp., coneflowers, black/
    brown-eyed susans

R. columnaris. See *Ratibida columnifera*

R. purpurea, purple coneflower

Rumex spp., dock

Rushes. See *Equisetum* spp.

Sage. See *Artemisia* spp.

Sagittaria hastata. See *S. latifolia*

S. latifolia, arrowhead

Sakkakomi. See *Arctostaphylos uva-ursi*

Salamandra aurantia. See *S. salamandra*

S. salamandra, salamander

Salix spp., willows

S. angustata. See *S. eriocephala*

S. babylonica, weeping willow

S. eriocephala, diamond willow

S. purpurea, red osier

S. sepulcralis, weeping willow

Salpa spp., tunicates

Sambucus spp., elderberry

S. canadensis, common elderberry

Sapindus saponaria, soapberry

Sarsaparilla, [wild]. See *Aralia
    nudicaulis*

Sassafras albidum, sassafras

Savoyenne, possibly *Sanguinaria
    canadensis*, bloodroot

Scalopus aquaticus, eastern mole

S. canadensis. See *S. aquaticus*

Sceloporus undulatus, fence lizard

Schähäckä, coyote (Mandan)

Schoenus mariscoides. See *Cladium
    mariscoides*

Sciurus carolinensis, eastern gray squirrel

S. cinereus. See *S. carolinensis*

S. hudsonius. See *Tamiasciurus
    hudsonicus*

S. macrourus. See *S. niger*

S. niger, eastern fox squirrel

S. rufiventer. See *S. niger*

S. striatus. See *Tamias striatus*

Scolopax minor, American woodcock

Scomber spp., ocean-dwelling mackerel

S. scomber. See *S. scombrus*

S. scombrus, Atlantic mackerel

S. thynnus. See *Thunnus thynnus*

Sea wrack. See *Fucus vesiculosus*

Seiurus aurocapillus, ovenbird

Senna marilandica, southern wild senna

Serviceberry, [western]. See *Amelanchier alnifolia*

Setophaga ruticilla, American redstart

Shave grass, [scouring rush]. See *Equisetum hyemale*

Shellbark [hickory]. See *Carya lacinosa*

Shepherdia argentea, silver buffalo berry

S. canadensis, russet buffalo berry

Sialia sialis, eastern bluebird

Silpha spp., carrion beetles

Sistrurus catenatus catenatus, eastern massasauga rattlesnake

S. catenatus tergeminus, western massasauga rattlesnake

Sitta spp., nuthatches

S. carolinensis, white-breasted nuthatch

Smilax spp., briars

Solidago spp., goldenrod

S. ciliaris. See *S. juncea*

S. juncea, early goldenrod

Spanish moss. See *Tillandsia usneoides*

Sparrow, song. See *Melospiza melodia*

Sparrow hawk. See *Falco sparverius*

Spermophilus richardsonii, Richardson's ground squirrel

S. tridecemlineatus, thirteen-lined ground squirrel

Sphaeralcea coccinea, red false mallow

Sphyrapicus varius, yellow-bellied sapsucker

Spicewood. See *Lindera benzoin*

Spiraea opulifolia. See *Physocarpus opulifolius*

S. salicifolia, meadowsweet

S. tomentosa, hardhack

Spizella arborea, American tree sparrow

Squirrel, eastern gray. See *Sciurus carolinensis*

Squirrel, red. See *Tamiasciurus hudsonicus*

Squirrel, rust-bellied. See *Sciurus niger*

Stanleya pinnata, prince's plume

S. pinnatifida. See *S. pinnata*

Staphylea trifolia, bladdernut

Sterna spp., terns

S. hirundo, common tern

Storax. See *Liquidambar styraciflua*

Storeria occipitomaculata, northern red-bellied snake

Strawberry. See *Fragaria* spp.

Strix spp., owls

S. asio. See *Megascops asio*

S. cunicularia. See *Athene cunicularia*

S. nebulosa, great gray owl

S. nyctea. See *Bubo scandiacus*

S. otus americana. See *Asio otus*

S. virginiana. See *Bubo virginianus*

Sturnella magna, eastern meadowlark

S. neglecta, western meadowlark

Stylophorum diphyllum, celandine poppy

Sugar tree, *Acer saccharum* or *A. saccharinum*

Sula alba. See *S. sula*

S. sula, red-footed booby

Sumacs. See *Rhus* spp.

Suslik. See *Spermophilus* spp.

Swans. See *Cygnus* spp.

Sylvia aestiva. See *Dendroica petechia*

S. calendula. See *Regulus calendula*

S. formosa. See *Oporornis formosus*

S. sialis. See *Sialia sialis*

S. striata. See *Dendroica striata*

S. trichas. See *Geothlypis trichas*

Symphoria spp. See *Symphoricarpos* spp.

Symphoricarpos spp., snowberries

Syngenesia, a term no longer used in modern taxonomy; included members of the family Asteraceae

Tachycineta bicolor, tree swallow (similar to *T. thalassina*, violet-green swallow)

Tamiasciurus hudsonicus, red squirrel

Tamias striatus, eastern chipmunk

Tanagra mississippiensis. See *Piranga rubra*

T. rubra. See *Piranga rubra*

Taphozous rufus. See *Lasiurus borealis*

Taxidea taxus, American badger

Teal (ducks). See *Anas* spp.

Tern, black. See *Chlidonias niger*

Terrapene carolina, eastern box turtle

Testudo clausa. See *Terrapene carolina*

Tetrao cupido. See *Tympanuchus cupido*

T. phasianellus. See *Tympanuchus phasianellus*

T. umbellatus. See *Bonasa umbellus*

T. urophasianus. See *Centrocercus urophasianus*

T. virginianus. See *Colinus virginianus*

Thamnophis proximus, western ribbon snake

T. sauritus, eastern ribbon snake

T. sirtalis, common garter snake

Thrush, fox-colored or rust-red. See *Toxostoma rufum*

Thryothorus ludovicianus, Carolina wren

Thuja spp., cedar, arborvitae

T. occidentalis, northern white cedar

Thunnus thynnus, bluefin tuna

Tilia americana, American linden or basswood

Tillandsia usneoides, Spanish moss

Titmouse, can refer to many small birds of the family Paridae, especially of the genus *Parus*

Towhee bunting. See *Pipilo erythrophthalmus*

Toxicodendron radicans, poison ivy

Toxostoma rufum, brown thrasher

Trachemys scripta, pond slider

Tradescantia spp., spiderwort

T. virginica, Virginia spiderwort

Trifolium spp., clover

Tringa spp., sandpipers, yellowlegs

T. pusilla. See *Calidris minutilla*

Trionyx sp. See *Apalone* spp.

Trochilus colubris. See *Archilochus colubris*

Troglodytes aedon, house wren

T. hyemalis. See *T. troglodytes*

T. ludovicianus. See *Thryothorus ludovicianus*

T. troglodytes, winter wren

Tsuga canadensis, eastern hemlock

Tulip tree. See *Liriodendron tulipifera*

Turdus aurocapilla. See *Seiurus aurocapillus*

T. felivox. See *Dumetella carolinensis*

T. migratorius, American robin

T. rufus. See *Toxostoma rufum*

Turkey, wild American. See *Meleagris gallopavo*

Turkey buzzard, turkey vulture. See *Cathartes aura, Coragyps atratus*

Turnip, wild. See *Pediomelum esculentum*

Turtledove. See *Zenaida macroura*

Tympanuchus cupido, grouse, heath hen, prairie hen

T. phasianellus, sharp-tailed grouse

Typha spp., cattails

T. latifolia, common cattail

Tyrannus tyrannus, eastern kingbird

T. verticalis, western kingbird

Ulmus spp., elms

U. rubra, slippery elm

Unio spp., mussels (Maximilian's term now encompasses many genera and species)

Uria aalge, common murre

U. troile. See *U. aalge*

Urocyon cinereoargenteus, gray fox

Ursus americanus, American black bear

U. arctos horribilis, grizzly bear

U. ferox. See *U. arctos horribilis*

Urubu. See *Cathartes aura* or *Coragyps atratus*

Vaccinium spp., blueberry or cranberry

Verbascum spp., mullein

V. thapsus, common mullein

Vespertilio ursinus. See *Eptesicus fuscus*

Viburnum spp., a genus of well over one
  hundred species of shrubs and small
  trees

V. lentago, nannyberry

Viola spp., violets

V. pubescens, downy yellow violet

Vireo olivaceus, red-eyed vireo

V. solitarius, blue-headed vireo

Virginia creeper. See *Parthenocissus
  quinquefolia*

Viscum sp. See *Phoradendron serotinum*

Vitis spp., grapes (wild and
  domesticated)

Vulpes velox, swift fox

V. vulpes, red fox

Vultur gryphus, Andean condor

Walnut. See *Juglans* spp.

Water moccasin. See *Agkistrodon
  piscivorus*

Waxwings. See *Bombycilla* spp.

Whippoorwill. See *Caprimulgus
  vociferus*

Wildcat. See *Lynx rufus*

Willows. See *Salix* spp.

Willow, Babylonian. See *Salix babylonica*

Willow, gray, also red. See *Cornus sericea*

Willow, weeping. See *Salix babylonica*
  and/or *S. sepulcralis*

Wolf, gray, red, white. See *Canis lupus*

Wolf, prairie. See *Canis latrans*

Woodchuck. See *Marmota monax*

Woodcock. See *Dryocopus pileatus*

Wood duck. See *Aix sponsa*

Woodpecker, golden-winged or yellow.
  See *Colaptes auratus*

Woodpecker, pileated. See *Dryocopus
  pileatus*

Woodpecker, redheaded. See *Melanerpes
  erythrocephalus*

Wood rat. See *Neotoma* spp.

Wood thrush. See *Hylocichla mustelina*

Wormwood. See *Artemisia* spp.

Xanthium strumarium, cocklebur

Xanthocephalus xanthocephalus, yellow-headed blackbird

Yucca angustifolia. See *Y. glauca*

Y. glauca, yucca or soapweed

Zanthoxylum americanum, prickly ash

Zapus hudsonius, meadow jumping
  mouse

Zenaida macroura, mourning dove

Zizania palustris, interior wild rice

Zonotrichia albicollis, white-throated
  sparrow

Zostera marina, eelgrass

Index

Page numbers in italics indicate illustrations. Common names for plants and animals are in some cases given as supplements to Maximilian's terminology.

Antelope (*cont.*)

190, 213; items made from, 111, 180, 213, 216; in Maximilian's collection, 234, 240, 433; observed, 172, 182, 272, 308; symbolism of, 401, 402

Arapaho Indians, 303, 422

Arctomys monax (groundhog, woodchuck, marmot), 24, 152, 271

Argillite, 163, 170, 172, 190, 222, 242, 252, 511n9

Arikara Indians (Rees), 187, 191n, 423–26; Dacotas and, 189, 191, 192, 361, 423; enemies of, 191, 364, 396, 409, 410, 422; at Fort Clark, 432, 440, 441, 444, 446; fur trade and, xxxv, xxxvii, 361–62, 423; horses and, 423, 462–63; interpreters for, xxxv, 190, 339, 340, 431, 456; subsistence practices of, 368n, 381, 424, 426; territory of, 189, 191, 192, 193, 423; villages of, 191, 423, 454, 512n; violence and, xxxv, 170n, 174–75, 462, 463; warfare and, 189, 423; whites and, 191, 196, 212, 316, 423, 426, 427, 444, 462–63

Arrows, 378; attacks using, 276–77, 410, 435; boys and, 217, 297, 384; in ceremonies, 403; flint (chert) points for, 84, 409; hunting with, 296, 353, 406; in Maximilian's collection, 158, 185, 455; in myth, 395; ubiquity of, 84, 158, 206, 209, 213, 248, 325, 331, 337. *See also* Quivers

Artemisia spp. (sagebrush), 270, 289, 370; ceremonial uses of, 347, 398, 400, 417; as medicinal plant, 370, 449; observed, 184, 204, 221, 223, 226, 227, 230, 234, 235, 236, 238, 244, 248, 255, 313, 330; as packing material, 324

Asclepias spp. (milkweed), 49, 184, 227

Ash trees (*Fraxinus* spp.), 88, 163, 164, 168, 169, 171, 184, 221, 301, 314, 318, 329, 343, 392, 465, 467

Ashworth, Charles Howard, xxxi, 159, 160, 173

Assiniboine (steamboat), 104, 163, 165, 168–88, 193, 203, 429; captain of, xxxii, xl, 168, 174, 460; cargo of, 178, 188, 210, 211; fire on, 204, 452n; fur trade and, 187, 458; Indians aboard, 196–97, 198–99, 200, 201–2, 203, 205, 206, 335, 460; keelboats with, 167, 170, 175; woodcutting for, 171, 460

Assiniboine Indians, xxii, xxxi, 67n, 124, 125, 209n, 210, 214, 238, 323–25, 348; attack on Fort McKenzie, 276–79, 286, 315, 325; Blackfoot and, xxiii, 279; bows of, 206, 209; burial practices of, 225, 322; clothing of, 322, 325, 377, 414; Crees and, 276; described, 205–6, 209, 212–13, 214, 217, 248, 292, 322, 323; dogs and, 213, 238, 323; face painting of, 125, 212, 214, 217, 322, 325; at Fort Union, 208, 212–13, 214, 315, 321, 322–25; fur trade and, 363, 440; Hidatsas (Gros Ventres) and, 214, 317, 321, 325, 365, 422&n, 434–35, 437–38, 441, 451; hunting by, 209, 433; language of, 103, 206, 210, 212, 220; leaders of, 217, 219, 276n, 322, 325; Mandans and, 214, 409, 434, 436, 450; medicine devices/shrines of, 126, 211, 217; Piegans and, 276–79, 283; territory of, xliv, 204, 209, 212, 223; tipis of, 127, 208–9, 217; women of, 213–14, 217, 218

Asters, 39, 49, 318

Astor, John Jacob, xxvii, xxxi, xxxviii, xl, 15–16, 188, 217, 497, 516n, 518n, 519n

Astor, William Backhouse, xxvii, xxxi, 480, 497, 518n

Atkinson, Henry, xxxi, 93, 94, 358, 363, 511n, 513n

Awacháhwi (Village des Souliers, Village of the Mountains), 201, 202, 332, 364, 413, 414, 419

Awatichai (Village on the Hill), 201, 202, 361, 364, 413, 414

Badger (drum). *See under* Music

Badger, 173, 311, 316, 372; in myth, 395

Badlands. *See* Mauvaises-Terres

Bad River, 155, 182, 215, 315, 457

Barrabino, Joseph, xxxi, 75, 77, 79, 476

Battle-axes, *140, 143,* 168, 198, 202–3, 204, 378, 410, 431, 438. *See also* Tomahawks

Beads (glass), 298, 322, 332, 400; on ceremonial items, 356, 416; on clothing, *132, 134,* 203, 205, 274, 292, 294, 297, 337, 351–52, 377; as earrings, 185, 198, 205, 375; for hair ornaments, *131,* 157, 198, 202, 376; on neckbands and necklaces, 185, 292, 342, 377; *rassade,* 271, 294, 377, 417, 430, 513n; as trade goods, 99, 185, 271, 273

Bean, Jonathan: as Indian agent, xxxii, 97, 102, 114, 166, 167, 175, 177, 178, 458, 460–61; Maximilian's party and, 149, 181

Bear Chief (Nínoch-Kiáiu; formerly Spotted Elk), 258n, 262–63, 265, 271, 275, 277, 283, 297; Assiniboine attack and, 277–78; Blood Indians and, 266–69, 270, 272–73, 281, 284, 285

Bear claws, 16, 205, 232, 274–275, 292, 388, 401; necklaces of, 198, 205, 292, 336, 340, 342, 351, 358, 371, 377, 414, 429, 430, 517n

Bears (*Ursus* spp.): black *(Ursus americana),* 29, 30, 147, 231, 471; bones of, 309, 410; cubs, 165, 188; as food, 30, 382, 455; foods of, 231, 232, 234, 243; at Fort McKenzie, 261, 264, 271; grizzly *(Ursus arctos horribilis),* 127, 185, 192, 198, 205, 214, 217, 231, 292, 296, 371, 377, 388, 470; habitat of, 147, 230; heads/skulls of, 30, 240, 243, 309, 401; hides of, 15, 29, 86, 232, 235, 271, 426, 513n; Maximilian's, xxiv, 30, 188, 264, 289, 305, 309–311, 313, 328, 352, 436, 452, 455, 470, 471–72, 473, 483, 487, 497, 501, 502; tracks of, 225, 296, 329, 330; trapping, 30, 33

Bears Paw Mountains, 240, 254, 255, 279, 287, 305, 514n

Beauchamp, David, 243, 289, 326, 327, 338

Beaver *(Castor canadensis),* 158, 195, 320, 342, 372, 401, 431; depletion of, 75, 150, 190–91; as food, 275, 304, 335, 382, 407; lodges of, 190, 230, 313, 330; in myths, 393; tails of, 265, 382; tracks of, 312, 330; trapping and hunting, 197, 205, 273, 274, 288–89, 290, 316, 342, 407, 447, 449, 450, 451, 461, 462; trees gnawed by, 161, 196, 330. *See also* Hide, beaver

Beeches, 24, 30, 34, 42, 46, 49, 53, 479, 484, 490

Belhumeur, Michel, 333, 336, 427, 428, 432, 435, 436, 443, 451

Bellevue Agency, Nebr., xxii, xxxii, xliv, 112, *121,* 155, 156, 157, 183, 333, 465

Bells, 91, 99, 159, 257, 340, 344, 358, 416

Bennett, Andrew, xxxii, 105, 181, 460

Berdaches, 352, 384, 437, 515n4

Berger, Jacob (Jacques), xxxii, 195, 219, 266, 276, 287

Bernhard, Duke of Saxe-Weimar-Eisenach, xxxii, 37, 58, 92, 98, 508n3

Beróck-Itaïnú (Bull's Neck), 198, 202, 336, 342, 349, 360, 436, 443, 444, 446

Bethlehem, Pa., xix, xx, xli, xlv, 19–20, 21, 22, 34, 38, *116*

Biddahátsi-Awatíss. *See* Hidatsa Indians

Bighorn sheep *(Ovis ammon),* 17, 207, 246, 254; habitat of, 206, 230, 244, 245, 247, 251, 306; hides of, 201, 205, 250, 388, 400, 445; horns of, 201, 246, 301, 332; range of, 205, 237, 308

Big Sioux River, 155, 156, 162, 180, 463

Bijou (Bijoux), Joseph and/or Louis, xxxii, 175, 353, 427, 432, 434, 440, 511n12

Bijou Hills, 175, 176, 458, 459, 511n12

Birches (*Betula* spp.), 42, 48, 488, 489, 490

Bird, James, Jr., xxxii, 266–67, 271–75, 277, 280

Bison *(Bison bison)*, 17, 81, *142*, 196, 210, 228, 233, 234, 236; bears and, 232, 243; bones of, 165, 171, 192, 195, 204, 211, 236, 318, 381, 442; bulls, 195, 216, 307, 308, 310; butchering, 230, 236, 319; ceremonies associated with, *142*, 298–99, 388, 399–400, 403, 419; dung of, 318, 319; as food aboard *Flora*, 173, 224, 228, 234–35, 237, 241, 242, 254; as food for fur trade posts, 174, 207, 208, 219, 260, 267, 366; fur trade and, 295, 398; habitat of, 224, 230–31, 242, 307; hair of, 233, 400; head of, 388, 399–400, 416, 419, 421, 422, 451; herds of, 229, 307, 308, 311, 318–19; hooves of, 301, 344, 416; horns of, 187, 226, 300, 332, 358, 388; hunted by Indians, 92, 126, 156, 180, 192, 196, 212, 238, 247, 298, 387, 392, 406; importance of, 296, 382; in myth, 392, 404; range of, 170, 175, 186; scarcity of, 206, 209; skulls of, *126*, *138*, 165, 171, 184, 195, 211, 334, 337–38, 402, 403, 405, 448; swimming, 228, 307, 310; tail of, 393, 394, 399&n, 401; tongue of, 433, 448, 449; tracks/trails of, 204, 228–29, 239. *See also* Hide, bison

Blackbird. *See* Waschínga-Sáhba

Blackfoot Indians, 67n, 102, 262, 290, 294–96, 302, 513–4nn2–5; appearance of, *131–35*, 291–94, 297, 514n1; ceremonies/dances of, 295, 298–301; clothing of, *131–35*, 270, 292–94, 377, 414; customs of, 240, 295–96, 298, 301–2; fur trade and, xxiii, xxxii, 203, 205, 243, 257, 284, 290, 294; horses and, 185, 279, 290–91, 294, 295, 297; interpreters for, 243, 280; language of, 103, 195, 248, 302–3; leaders of, 282, 285, 300–301; other Indians and, xxxii, 187, 201, 249, 273, 276, 279, 286, 303, 304; pipe

smoking and, 295, 299, 513n; territory of, xliv, 103, 240; tipis of, 294, 297, 298; trade with, 270, 290, 291, 297; tribes/bands of, 259, 279, 290, 302; violence and, 174, 297–98, 300–301; weapons of, 290, 296, 297, 300, 301; whiskey and, 296, 301; whites and, 286, 290, 297, 352; women, 235, 267, 291, 293–94, 295, 296–97, 298–99, 383. *See also* Blood Indians; Piegan Indians; Siksika Indians

Black Hawk, xxxiii, xxxvi, xlii, 89, 93–94

Blankets (wool), 90, *131*, 157, 165, 167, 168, 251; as bedding, 178, 222, 242, 294; as clothing, 177, 196, 217, 262, 337; as gifts, 300, 346, 386, 389, 399, 417; mourning and, 200, 411; Spanish, 131, 205, 290

Blood (Kaénna) Indians, 259, 266–69, 290&n, 302–3, 304; fur trade and, 257, 263, 284, 285; leaders of, *134*, 262, 285; Piegans and, 269, 270, 272–73, 281, 282, 285; theft of horses by, 279, 291; whites and, 264, 286, 290–91, 451

Bluebird *(Sylvia sialis)*, 19, 22, 76, 153, 159

Blumenbach, Johann Friedrich, xvii, xviii, xxxiii, xxxviii, 63, 80, 277n, 322, 338, 385

Bobcat, wildcat, 65, 70, 216

Bodmer, Karl, xviii–xix, xxvii, xxxiii, 53, 65, *146*, 149; assisting Maximilian, xxvii, 76, 97, 243, 470–71; bird specimens collected by, 53, 62, 63, 102, 475; ceremonies witnessed by, 343–46, 355–56, 443, 444; as hunter, 64, 154, 188, 235; hunting, 49, 83, 106, 109, 113, 231, 221, 223, 245, 318, 327, 340, 453; illness/injury of, 3, 4, 6, 38, 49, 58, 66, 341, 446; in Indiana, 68, 477; music box of, 275, 279, 439; New Orleans excursion of, xxi, xxxi, 71, 75, 76–78; painting robes, 348; portrait of, 358; portraits by, xxiv, 77, 267, 273, 275, 278, 283, 286, 323, 353, 358, 438–39; specimen sketches by, 80, 316

Bodmer, Karl (artworks by): *Addíh-Hiddísch, Hidatsa Chief, 143*; animals and birds sketched by, 8, 22, 23, 65, 232, 233; Arikaras drawn by, 446, 450; *Assiniboine Camp, 127, 219; Assiniboine Medicine Sign, 126, 211*; Assiniboines drawn by, 124, 125, 214, 217, 323, 324; *Bellevue Agency, Post of Major Dougherty, 121*; Blackfoot drawn by, 133, 134, 135, 278, 279, 281, 285n, 514n; *Chan-Chä-Uiá-Te-Üinn, Teton Sioux Woman, 123, 185*; Choctaws drawn by, 78; *Citadel Rock on the Upper Missouri, 254*; Crees drawn by, 317, 321; Crows drawn by, 447; Dacotas drawn by, 179; *First Chain of the Rocky Mountains above Fort McKenzie, 136, 514n; Fort MacKenzie August 28th 1833, 276n; Fort Union at the Mouth of the Yellowstone River, 208, 218, 219*; fur trade forts sketched by, 136, 276n, 456; Gros Ventres des Prairies drawn by, 130, 248, 250; *Head of a Buffalo, 233*; Hidatsas drawn by, 143, 429, 442, 443, 447–48; *Ihkas-kinne, Siksika Blackfoot Chief, 133, 279; Interior of a Mandan Earth Lodge, 144, 434; Janus, 10; Junction of the Yellowstone and the Missouri, 128, 218, 219; Kiäsax, Piegan Blackfoot Man, 131, 205; Leader of the Mandan Buffalo Bull Society, 142; Mandan Earth Lodges, 335*; Mandans drawn by, 140, 142, 352, 353, 356, 429, 431&n, 438–39, 447, 449; *Mandan Shrine, 138, 337, 349, 515n; Mató-Topé, Mandan Chief, 140, 431&n, 451; Mexkehme-Sukahs, Piegan Blackfoot Chief, 132; Mexkemáuastan, Gros Ventres des Prairies Chief, 130, 250; The Missouri below the Mouth of the Platte, 120*; New Harmony sketches by, 57, 61, 64, 68; *Noapeh, Assiniboine Man, 124, 214*; Otoes and Omahas drawn by, 464; *Péhriska-Ruhpa, Hidatsa Man, 141, 447–48, 515n, 517n*; Piegans drawn by, 132, 135, 266, 271, 278, 283, 295, 514n; *Pioch-Kiäiu, Piegan Blackfoot Man, 135, 278; Pitätapiú, Assiniboine Man, 125, 214, 217*; Poncas drawn by, 165, 166, 167, 332; scenes sketched by, 26, 29, 61, 78, 81, 118, 226, 236, 239, 244, 251, 287, 288, 289, 340, 474; *Schudegácheh, Ponca Chief, 166, 332*; Shoshone drawn by, 287; Sioux drawn by, 122, 123, 179, 185, 428; *Snags on the Missouri, 119; The Steamboat Yellow Stone, 118; Stomíck-Sosáck, Blood Blackfoot Chief, 134, 285n*; towns sketched by, 4, 19, 20n, 23, 83; *The Travellers Meeting with Minatarre Indians near Fort Clark, xxii–xxiii, 146; View of Bethlehem on the Lehigh, 116; View of New Harmony, 117; View of Niagara Falls, 145, 490; View of the Bears Paw Mountains from Fort McKenzie, 137, 514n; View of the Stone Walls, 129; Wahktägeli, Yankton Sioux Chief, 122*; Yanktonais drawn by, 122, 428

Boston, Mass., xix, xxi, xlv, 7, 11–12, 13–14, 486

Bourgua (engagé), 326, 327, 338, 453

Bow-lances, 125, 198, 214, 358, 416

Bows, 141, 160, 198, 206, 209, 296, 248, 350, 384, 409–10, 445; horn/antler and, 201, 301, 323, 336; in Maximilian's collection, 185, 323, 455; ornamentation of, 201, 219, 336

Box elder (*Acer negundo*), 102, 163, 169, 369

Brackenridge, Henry Marie, 191, 241n, 413, 423, 424

Brazil, xviii, 90, 230, 245, 321, 496

Broken Leg (or Arm). *See* Dipäuch

Buffalo. *See* Bison

Buffalo berry (*Shepherdia* spp.), 163, 169, 171; fruit of, 296, 313, 381, 382

Buffalo parks, 212, 238, 298–99, 406–7, 514n3

Bullboats, 224, 335, *338*, 365, 451, 512n5, 517n1

Bunting, snow *(Emberiza nivalis)*, 342, 355, 372, 427, 428, 440, 441, 445

Butte Carrée, 195, 196, 419, 512n6

Cabanné, Jean (John) Pierre, xxii, xxxiii, xl, 157, 158, 188, 217, 333

Cactus, 246, 256, 344, 448, 501; *Cactus ferox*, 219, 236, 325, 370, 458; *Cactus mammillaris*, 218, 225, 370; *Cactus opuntia* (prickly pear), 177–78, 211, 218

Campbell, Robert, 326; at Fort William, 317, 325, 327; fur company of, xxxiii, xxxv, xli, 111&n, 320, 331

Canals, 40, 41, 42, 43, 483–86, 487, 492–94, 518nn, 519nn

Cannonball River, 193, 195, 340, 453

Canoes, 107, 111, 155, 170, 192, 243, 512n5, 517n1

Cantonment (Fort) Leavenworth, Mo., xxii, xxxvii, 111, 113, 151, 159, 467–68

Cardinal *(Loxia carolinensis)*, 68, 467, 472

Catalpa, 57, 68, 476, 477

Catbird, 18, 193, 194

Catlin, George, xxxi, xxxiii, xxxviii, 73–74, 95, 348, 394n, 397, 398, 445, 473, 516n1

Cattails *(Typha* spp.), 24, 370, 466

Cave-in-Rock, Ill., 84, 85, 475

Cedar Island (S.Dak.), 171, 172, 182, 511n

Cedars, 85, 163, 168, 171, 172, 182, 189, 190, 254, 459; *Juniperus virginiana*, 104, 169, 245, 490; *Thuja* spp., 490, 492. *See also* Junipers

Celtis sp. (hackberry), 169, 171, 173, 459, 465, 467

Cephir (interpreter), 181, 458

Chan-Chä-Uiá-Te-Üinn, *123*, 185&n

Chárätä-Numakschi (Wolf Chief), 198, 337, 374, 419, 429–30, 442, 444

Charbonneau, Toussaint, 146, 427; experiences of, xxiv, 352, 361, 362, 364, 368, 409, 413, 422n; at Fort Clark, 203, 436, 451; fur trade and, 353, 359, 362–63, 434; Hidatsas and, 331, 332, 348, 354, 356, 358, 364, 431, 432, 432, 433, 446, 449; as interpreter, xxiv, xxxiv, 198, 200, 202, 331, 332, 374, 439; Mandans and, 381, 437; Maximilian and, 343–44, 346–47, 352, 428, 431–32

Chardon, Francis A., 317, 318, 455; American Fur Company and, xxxiv, 320, 324; Assiniboines and, 323, 325; Fort Clark and, xxxiv, 212, 339; Fort Pierre and, 452, 453, 454; Fort Union and, 315, 451; Maximilian and, 338, 384, 463

Cherokee Indians, 66–67&n, 77

Cherries, wild, 192, 208, 296, 381, 406

Cheyenne Indians: enemies of, 201, 321, 334, 348, 396, 409, 422, 430; horses of, 187, 321; language of, 103, 443

Chichikué (rattle). *See under* Music

Chickadee, black-capped *(Parus atricapillus)*, 61, 177, 372, 433

Children, 23, 148, 213, 271, 323, 332, 344, 409, 415, 426, 443; adult societies and, 286–87; appearance of, 156, 291, 297; babies, 218, 265; behavior of, 40, 269, 277, 283, 383, 424, 517n; care of, 297, 382; death and illness of, 334, 338, 367, 382, 411; education of, 20, 72, 297; Maximilian and, 517n; mixed-blood, 105, 188, 206, 297, 382; mythological, 390, 393, 396; playing, 44, 271, 297, 346, 367, 442, 447; poverty/hunger and, 50, 93, 275; as spectators, 168, 202, 257, 265, 281, 287, 347, 435, 438; violence against, 148, 273, 276, 302; work done by, 296, 322, 381

Chippewa Indians, 67n, 161. *See also* Ojibwe Indians

Choctaw Indians, 66–67&n, 77

Chokecherry, 153, 164, 168, 171, 208, 268, 296, 313, 370, 381, 406, 459

Cholera, xix, xx, 16, 23, 54, 508n1, 515n4; in Europe, 62; medicines for, 333, 465, 476; in Missouri Valley, 333, 465; in New Orleans, 66, 69, 73; in New York, 14, 17, 37, 507n1; in Ohio Valley, 40, 50, 51, 60, 479; in St. Louis, 60, 65, 348

Chouteau, Pierre, Jr., xxxiv, xl, 92, 95, 97, 98, 99, 100, 102, 111n, 188, 217, 473

Cincinnati, Ohio, xxv, xxxiv, xxxv, xlv, 47, 50n, 51, 82, 475, 479, 480–81

Citadel Rock, 252, 254, 306

Clark, William, xxxiv, 92–93, 159, 505n2, 509n4, 510n2, 511n5; as superintendent of Indian affairs, xxi, xxvi, xxxiv, xxxviii, 92, 93, 94, 96, 97

Cleveland, Ohio, xxv, xlv, 486, 518n

Columbia Fur Company, xxxvi, xxxvii, xxxviii, 361–63, 516n1

Columbia River, 102, 112, 202, 317, 361

Coots (Fulica americana), 62, 313, 373, 374

Cordelle, 221–25, 230, 233–35, 237, 238, 239, 242, 245, 249, 250

Corn (Indian), maize, 81, 333n, 367, 383, 441; in ceremonies, 347, 398, 403, 417, 419, 425; farming of, 71, 103, 156, 162, 167, 191, 192, 338, 366, 369, 381, 406; as food, 275, 333, 349, 352, 354, 358, 386; in myths, 395–96, 418; preparation of, 286, 332, 335, 337, 345, 350, 360, 381, 456, 517n; storage of, 333, 342, 348–49, 380; as trade good/commodity, 59, 60, 335, 362, 436

Cornus sericea (red willow), 163, 164, 169, 171, 313, 369, 380

Cote Sans Dessein, Mo., 105, 108, 110, 471

Cottonwoods (Populus spp.), 87, 100, 310, 459, 467; bark/pulp of, 223, 326, 380, 381; branches of, 181, 311; for charcoal/firewood, 192–93, 270; felled by beavers, 190, 330; flooding/ice drift and, 190, 222, 368; items made from, 341, 401, 441; along lower Missouri River, 101, 106, 148, 151, 157, 160, 162, 163, 164, 169, 170, 172, 175; for lumber, 207, 260, 341; shelter provided by, 226, 265, 309, 310, 329, 331, 343, 474; along upper Missouri River, 184, 189, 193, 221, 227, 235, 236, 241, 242, 244, 247, 255, 313, 318, 328, 369

Council Bluff, Nebr., 78, 147, 150, 159, 216, 217, 464, 509n5, 511n5, 517n5

Coup, counting, 274, 277, 325, 377, 398, 407, 409, 424–25, 436

Coyote (prairie wolf, schähäckä) (Canis latrans), 348, 352, 355, 371, 402, 425, 435; as mythological person, 390, 425

Cranes (Grus spp.), 56, 65, 80, 108, 312, 314, 316, 373; bones of, 387

Crataegus spp. (hawthorn), 41, 149, 153

Cree Indians, 110–11, 211–12, 220, 238, 292, 318, 319, 436, 512n1; attack on Fort McKenzie and, 276n, 276–79, 315–16; fur trade and, xxxii, 321, 363, 443; leaders of, xxxvii, 321; other Indians and, xxiii, 209n, 276n, 422; population of, 67n, 212; territory of, xliv, 212

Crops: barley, 71; buckwheat, 37, 39, 71; clover, 25, 39; corn (grain), 39, 72, 73, 156, 158, 207, 466, 478; cotton 78, 88; fruit orchards, 25, 40, 45, 50, 58, 63, 478; garden produce, 3, 18, 71, 207, 366; hay, 52; of Native Americans, 338–39, 381, 403; oats, 52, 71; onions, 456, 477, 497; rye, 71; squash, 192, 338, 366, 368n, 381, 403, 414, 426; strawberries, 3, 13; sunflowers, 338–39, 381, 382, 395; wheat, 71. See also Corn (Indian); Tobacco

Crow, American (Corvus corone), 61, 73, 151, 177, 268, 310, 313, 318, 328, 343, 450, 461; feathers of, 395, 433

Crow Indians, 103, 198–201, 292, 419, 510n4; bows of, 201, 219, 301, 323; clothing of, 203, 212, 293, 336, 377, 414; horses and, 198, 201; language of, 103,

Crow Indians (*cont.*)
326, 340; other Indians and, 174, 201,
281, 283, 284, 409, 411, 414, 418–19,
422; warbonnet of, 187, 278; war party
of, 288, 289; whites and, 363
Culbertson, Alexander, xxvii–xxviii,
xxxiv, 220, 240, 275; hunting by,
222–23, 229, 239, 255; Maximilian and,
221, 241, 305, 481
Cumings, Samuel (author, *Western Pilot*),
xxi, 60, 85, 86, 509n2

Dacota (Sioux) Indians, xxii, 67n, 103,
162, 178, 179n, 180&n, 183, 186, 298, 322,
337, 397, 511n7, 511n1, 512n2; appearance
described, 179, 184–85, 186, 203, 375,
456; Arikaras and, 189, 191, 192, 361;
burial practices of, 178, 180–81, 183, 187,
210, 456, *457*; clothing of, *122*, *123*, 179,
197, 296, 455; counting coup, 186–87;
dogs and, 180, 184, 294; fur trade and,
xl, 333, 349, 455; horses and, 170, 180,
187, 353, 354; hunting by, 170, 461;
Indian agencies and agents of, xxxii,
xxxix, xliii, 102, 178, 180, 458; language
of, 206, 212; Mandans and, 195, 196,
197, 198–99, 200, 353, 354, 360, 374, 396,
409, 436; other Indians and, 161, 166,
175–76, 209, 210, 364, 422, 449; pipes
of, 158, 162, 250, 332, 481; territory of,
149, 162, 175, 220, 458, 461; tipis of, 178,
179–80, 184, 187, 199, 261; whites and,
178–79; women of, 180, 187, 201. *See
also* Saone Sioux; Teton Sioux; Yanktonai Sioux; Yankton Sioux
Dances: bear dance, 203; buffalo dance,
344–45; men's societies and, 300–301,
351, 356, 359, 388–89, 416, 424–25,
445; Scalp Dance, 299, 409, 417; Sun
Dance, 511n1, 514n4, 516n1; women's
societies and, 298–99, 357, 417, 438
Dauphin, Jean Baptiste, 241, 242, 268,
456–57, 459, 461, 466, 513n

Dauphin Rapid, 246, 307, 513n
Dead Buffalo (Tatánka-Ktä), 196–97, *197*
Deer (*Cervus* spp.), 15, 45, 65, 216, 230,
236, 388, 472; antlers of, 27, 29, 31, 67,
76, 330; as food, 195, 207, 224, 258, 275,
308, 316, 329, 433; habitat of, 230, 272,
371, 406; hides of, 111, 216; hunting, 28,
103, 170, 194–95, 204, 222, 223, 227, 228,
392, 406, 466; moccasins and, 224, 378;
in myths, 392, 394, 395; observed, 224,
228, 310–11, 327, 329; tracks/trails of, 63,
147, 162, 171, 226, 330, 459
Delaware (Lenni-Lenape) Indians, 27, 38,
84, 112, 508n2
De l'Orme [Pierre], 428, 436, 439
Dentalium spp., 271–72, 291, 304, 376. *See
also* Wampum
Deschamps, François, 223, 232, 241–42,
245, 318; family of, 317, 324, 326; at
Fort Union, 285, 316, 320; as hunter on
Flora, 223, 226, 228, 229, 230, 231, 241,
255; hunting bison, 242, 318–19, 323; as
interpreter, 247, 272, 317, 321; Maximilian and, 221, 234–35, 316, 319
Dipäuch (Broken Arm/Leg), 198, 202,
340, 408, 432, 443, 515n3; at Fort Clark,
336, 342, 444; information from, 349,
354, 355, 390, 408, 439, 440, 443; lodge
of, *144*, 349, 398, 434; visiting Maximilian, 340, 360, 439, 441, 443, 446
Dogs: as draft/pack animals, 180, 184,
209, 212, 248, 294, 303, 415; as food,
180, 192, 238, 294, 382, 455; in fur trade
forts, 261, 317, 325, 359; hunting and,
30, 65, 68, 358, 406; of Indians, 199,
201, 213, 217, 249, 423, 441; sleds and,
215, 358, 359, 367, 380, 433, 437, 446;
travois and, 212, 213, 247, 323, 338, 443;
treatment of, 278, 324, 434
Dog Society (Blackfoot; Hidatsa;
Mandan), *141*, 300, 388, 416, 430, 438,
443–45, 448, 511n14, 517n2. *See also*
Meníss-Óchatä

Dogwoods (*Cornus* spp.), 41, 46, 101, 268, 343, 464; red willow, or red osier *(C. sericea)*, 163, 171, 184, 210, 225, 313, 327, 369, 381, 445

Dorfeuille, Joseph, 50n, 82, 480–81

Doucette (engagé), 255, 277, 280, 451; as interpreter, 243, 247, 248, 249; Maximilian and, 243, 245

Dougherty, John, 111, 113, 333; experiences of, xxxiv, 95, 108, 150; hunting by, 109, 153–54; as Indian agent, 97, 102, 121, 148–49, 155, 327, 331; Indian culture/languages and, 103, 105, 108, 152; specimen collecting by, 151, 154; traveling with Maximilian's party, 96, 100, 102, 104

Dougherty, Joseph L., xxxv, 449, 465; fur trade and, 327, 331, 339, 344, 345, 346, 353, 440; Hidatsas and, 345, 348, 431, 437

Dreidoppel, David, xxv, *146*, 205; bird specimens and, 57, 58, 62, 63, 74, 102, 162, 188, 196, 239, 464; Bodmer and, 241, 287, 328; explorations by, xx, 56, 254, 437; at fur trade forts, 284, 429, 431, 433, 451; as hunter, xix, xxxv, 113, 167, 231, 328, 440, 506n10; hunting for food on river journeys, 221, 228, 240, 255, 453; hunting game birds, 42, 353, 461; hunting large game animals, 229, 236, 245, 271, 272, 308, 310, 329, 459; hunting small animals, 154, 445–46, 454; hunting with Maximilian, 224–25, 236, 239–40, 243, 312; hunting wolves, 340, 352; illness of, xx, 4, 6, 23, 37, 64, 327, 446; as Maximilian's employee, xxvii, xxviii, 16, 21, 69, 80, 83, 85, 97, 472, 481, 487, 497, 501, 502, 507n24, 519n4; observations of animals by, 193, 226, 444, 450; taxidermy by, 24, 273, 312, 355

Ducks, 48, 58, 62, 65, 68, 73, 79, 403, 406, 453; hunting, 58, 68, 76, 80, 153, 318, 320; mallard *(Anas boschas)*, 73, 76, 318, 447; migrating, 48, 65, 79, 373, 406, 447, 450; in myths, 391, 403; observed, 62, 149, 160, 162, 164, 177, 222, 313, 452, 463; on upper Missouri River, 442, 447; wood duck *(Anas sponsa)*, 58, 62, 81, 147, 154, 464

DuPonceau, Pierre Etienne (Peter Stephen), xxxv, 70, 495, 496

Durand [or Durant], Alexis, 348, 354, 355, 356, 430, 432, 439, 4422

Eagles, 199, 300, 310, 327–28, 357, 404–5; bald eagle, 74, 107–8, 234, 246–47, 372, 401, 444, 449; feathers of, 158, 203, 358, 376–77, 389, 407, 416, 421, 430, 438, 445; hunting, 241, 407; war eagle, 336, 376, 377, 389, 404, 407, 416, 421, 438, 445

Easton, Pa., 22, 25, 39

Economy, Pa., xx, 44, 46, 508n2

Eláh-Sá (Village of the Big Willows), 201, 202, 364, 413, 414, 415, 419

Elk *(Cervus canadensis)*, 17, 45, 165, 309; antlers/horns of, 17, 86, 191, 196, 201, 226, 227, 241–42, 301, 310, 313, 513n1; bones/marrow of, 158, 224, 236; herds of, 307, 308; hides of, 216, 283, 309, 371; range of, 190, 371; teeth of, 293, 297, 313; tools made from, 250; tracks of, 162, 171, 194

Elkhorn Prairie, 226, 227, 314, 513n1

Elms *(Ulmus* spp.), 48, 62, 65–66, 153, 163, 164, 168, 171, 184, 221, 318, 329, 343, 465, 467, 472, 476, 490, 492

Engagés, xxii, 154, 155, 161, 251, 428–29, 432; appearance of, 111, 177, 224; behavior of, 220, 356, 446, 466; as Canadian, 100, 104, 152, 426, 453; canoes and, 155, 192, 243, 443; diet of, 152, 228, 230; drunkenness among, 100, 264, 461, 468, 470; French speaking, 111, 252, 356–57; fur trade and, xxii, 207, 215, 276–78, 357, 510n; Indian scalps and, 100, 102–3; mixed-blood, 100, 111,

Engagés (*cont.*)
161, 215, 221; violence against, 266, 269, 285, 440, 464, 517n; whiskey and, 261, 274; work done by, 430, 434, 435–36

Erie Canal, xx, 483, 486, 487, 488, 491, 492, 519n1

Erie, Lake, xxv, 483, 486, 488, 518n1

Ermine. *See* Weasel

Euro-Americans, nationality of, 206, 260; English, 27, 67, 159, 299, 304, 490; French, xxxiii, xxxv, 17, 26, 49, 81, 87, 88, 89, 98, 102, 105, 108, 111, 148, 181; German and Swiss, xx, xl–xli, 17, 19, 20, 27, 32, 33, 41, 43, 45, 53, 57, 60, 88, 96, 111, 320, 480; Spanish, 77, 148, 161, 267

Feathers: of birds of prey, 186, 212–13, 264, 292, 295, 300, 336, 344, 350, 445; 356, 357, 389, 407, 414, 416, 424; on caps, *143*, 211, 340, 395, 445; dyed or painted, 296, 443; fans made of, 202, 219; in hair, 90, *122*, *132*, *135*, *140*, 158, 179, 186, 202, 212–13, 264, 351, 358, 376, 414; on headdresses, *115*, *141*, 158, 159, 213, 298, 356, 387, 399, 416, 417, 424, 430, 433, 438, 443, 448; on lances and bow-lances, 91, *125*, *142*, 356; as ornamentation, 203, 218, 282, 384; painted on robes, 356–57, 515n; on warbonnets, 187, 278, 358, 376–77, 388. *See also under* Eagles; Owls; Turkeys

Fecteau (engagé), 453, 457, 461

Ferries, 72, 470, 473, 479, 490

Finches: *Fringilla* spp., 61, 68, 462, 467; *F. erythrophthalma* (eastern towhee), 29, 154, 173, 184, 459; *F. indigofera, amoena, cyanea*, 22, 229, 310, 372, 499; *F. linaria* (linnet), 188, 328, 337, 353, 355, 372, 439, 440, 444; *F. tristis* (goldfinch), 22, 229, 373; hawfinch (*Loxia ludoviciana*), 465. *See also* Sparrows

First Man: Íhkochu or Sziritsch (Arikara), 425; Numánk-Máchana

(Mandan), 365, 390–94, 397, 398, 399&n, 403, 408

Fish, 8–9, 10, 11, 46, 154, 181, 208, 230, 373, 466, 471

Flatboats, 48, 59, 85, 109, 482

Flathead Indians. *See* Salish Indians

Flora (keelboat): cargo of, 228, 243; cordelle crew of, 221, 233, 240, 241, 242, 248, 251, 254; cordelle for upstream journey, xxiii, 223, 225, 230, 234–35, 237–39, 244, 245, 255; crew of, 234, 246, 261; described, 221, 222; dinghy/skiff of, 247; food for, 228, 234, 236, 237, 244, 245, 258; Indians aboard, 247–48, 249, 250–51; Indians on cordelle, 249, 250; passengers on, xxiii, 221, 222; poling upstream, xxiii, 222, 234, 237, 238, 239, 240, 241, 242, 245, 248; sail used for upstream journey, 223, 228, 232, 233, 234, 237, 238, 241, 242, 243, 246, 248, 251, 254, 255

Floyd, Charles, xxxv, 161, 463

Flycatchers, 188, 194, 226, 240, 255, 270, 464, 467; kingbirds (*Muscicapa tyrannus*), 160, 194; *Muscicapa ruticilla* (American redstart), 22, 24, 172, 177, 464

Fontenelle, Lucien, xxxv, 155, 156, 157, 183, 215, 465

Foolish Dogs Society, 355, 395. *See also* Meníss-Óchka-Óchatä

Fort Cass [Mont.], xxiii, 174, 201, 207, 316

Fort Clark [N.Dak.], xliv, 197–98, 352, 365–66, 442, 446–47; and American Fur Company, 197–98, 315, 332; cannon at, 197, 452; dances performed at, *142*, 356, 357, 358–59, 449, 451; dogs at, 358, 359, 433, 434; employees at, xxxix, 333, 337, 338, 339, 355, 357, 366, 427, 428–29, 451; fauna near, 367, 368, 370–73; firewood at, 337, 366, 387, 427, 429, 430, 440; flora near, 369–70; food at, xxiii–xxiv, xxv, 335,

352, 353, 354, 355, 358, 360, 366, 367, 386, 427, 430, 432, 455; fur trade at, 342, 343–44; horses at, 339, 359, 339, 343–44, 366–67; illness at, 333, 334, 341, 517n5; Indians at, 131, *139*, *146*, 198, 199, 331, 333, 336–37, 340–43, 351–54, 356–59, 385–86, 428, 447, 448; Kipp at, xxxvi–xxxvii, 332, 333, 357, 447; mail at, 337, 338, 339, 348, 357, 437, 443, 447; Maximilian's party at, ix, xix, xxii, 332, 386, 436, 452&n, 517n4; Maximilian's quarters at, xxiii, 337, 339, 341, 348–49, 351–60, 427; medicine devices at, 337–38; rats at, 333, 342, 348, 367, 446; severe cold at, xix, xxiii, 359–60, 427–30, 442; store of, 333, 366, 441; Sublette and Campbell and, 331, 440; surroundings of, *365*, 367–73, 374; theft at, 353, 356; whiskey and, 356, 382

Fort McKenzie [Mont.], xxiii, xxvii, xxxviii, xliv, 137, 182, 207, 267, 284, 433, 451, 506n 17; Assiniboine attack on, 276–78, 315–16, 325; burials at, 302; cannon at, 259, 262, 263, 276, 281; dangers at, 256, 271; described, 257, 259, 260; food at, 260, 275, 286, 272, 275, 283, 286, 287, 288; fur trade at, 221, 260, 262–63, 270, 271, 273, 280, 283–84; horses of, 182, 259, 271, 275, 316; Indian tribes at, 243, 257, 259, 261, 262–63, 264, 266, 278–79, 284, 285, 287; Indian-white relations and, 130, 263, 265–66; interpreters at, 263, 275; intertribal relations at, 263, 269, 272–73; landscape surrounding, 259, 268, 288–89; transportation to, 225, 241, 244; view from, 240, 256, 268; violence at, 264, 266, 282, 284

Fort Osage, Mo., 108, 109, 110

Fort Piegan, 220, 256. *See also* Fort McKenzie

Fort Pierre [S.Dak.], xxxix, xliv, 183–88, 198, 364, 454

Fort Union [N.Dak.], xxiii, xxxvii, xliv, 128, 207, 210, 212, 213, 315n, 317, 320, 327, 359, 433, 506n; and American Fur Company, xxiii, xxxix, 128, 174, 206, 207–8; employees at, xxvii, xxxviii, xxxix, 206, 315, 316, 317, 318, 338, 443, 451; food at, 207–8, 210, 219, 316, 323, 324, 354, 357; Indians at, 126, 174–75, 250–51, 315, 316, 321–24, 325, 442, 463; mail delivery and, 348, 357; Maximilian and, xxiii, xxvii, 221, 315–17, 321–24, 325, 348, 463; surroundings of, 314, 315, 343, 373; transportation to, 128, 241, 258, 286, 338

Fort William [S.Dak.], 316–17, 320, 321, 323, 325, 327

Fossils, 36, 45, 80; of large animals, 50–51, 95, 159, 369

Four Bears. *See* Mató-Tópe

Foxes, 210, 216, 317, 354, 355, 382, 419, 441; gray or silver (*Canis cinerea argenteus*), 216, 371; hides of, 165, 210, 216, 419; hunting/trapping, 322, 327, 352–53, 407, 446; Maximilian's pet, 261, 340, 342, 359, 367, 428, 453; men's societies and, 300, 416; prairie or kit (*Canis velox*), 261, 318, 334, 371; red (*Canis fulvus, C. vulpes*), 27, 65, 340, 371, 440, 461; tails of, 213, 358

Fox Indians. *See* Meskwaki Indians

Fox River (Ind.), xx, 58, 62, 63, 67–69, 81, 509n4

Fringilla spp. *See* Finches

Frogs, 22, 24, 33, 75, 89, 114, 235, 373, 469, 477, 485; in myth, 392

Fucus (rockweed), 8, 9, 499

Fur trade, xxii, xxxiv, 206–7, 209, 215–16, 251, 320, 361–64, 468; clothing and, xxxi, 132, 196, 197, 208, 257, 261, 262, 270, 283; Indians and, 262–64, 297, 361, 423; mixed-bloods and, 318, 319; whiskey and, 264, 274, 280. *See also* names of specific companies and posts

sparverius), 29, 226, 227, 236, 313; kite *(F. furcatus)*, 464; northern harrier *(F. gutturalis, cyaneus)*, 184, 188; osprey *(F. haliaëtus)*, 24, 58

Heart River, 180, 195, 390, 391, 392, 394, 395, 453

Hedera quinquefolia (Virginia creeper), 41, 46, 53, 68, 465

Hemlocks *(Tsuga canadensis)*, 28, 29, 30, 42

Herons *(Ardea* [and *Butorides]* spp.), 24, 56, 65, 373

Hickory trees *(Juglans* spp.), 39, 41, 68, 267

Hidatsa (Mönnitarrí, Gros Ventres) Indians, 201, 367, 384, 413; appearance described, 201, 202–3, 346, 375, 414, 415, 420, 422; Arikaras and, 174, 175, 201, 409, 422, 423, 462; Assiniboines and, 214, 317, 321, 325, 365, 409, 422, 434–35, 437–38, 440, 441; beaver trapping by, 342, 372; beliefs of, 389, 418–22; berdaches among, 384; bison hunting and, 415, 419, 422, 446, 449; burial practices of, 411, 422; clothing of, 201, 203, 293, 332, 336, 337, 340, 347, 398, 414–15; Dacotas (Sioux) and, 201, 409, 422, 436, 449; deities of, 418; elderly among, 332, 344, 347, 403, 416, 417; face and body painting and, *141*, *143*, 198, 202, 337, 344; "festivals" of, 344–48, 403, 415, 418, 419–20; food of, 332, 345, 420–21, 431, 439; at Fort Clark, xxii, *146*, 198, 199, 437, 438, 439, 441; fur trade and, xxxv, 327, 339, 353, 354, 355, 364, 440; games of, 346, 417; horses and, 199, 348, 415, 417, 418, 434, 435; interpreters for, xxiv, 198, 200, 340, 432, 439, 440; language of, 374, 411, 413, 422–23; leaders of, *143*, 335, 344, 410, 414, 415, 438, 439, 440; lodges of, 332, 415; Lord of Life (First Man) and, 418, 421, 422; Makóh

(Grandmother, Old Woman) and, 415, 418; Mandans and, 103, 199, 201, 359, 364, 395–96, 413, 414, 415, 417, 419, 422, 439; Medicine Rock and, 340, 420; men's societies of, 141, 415–16, 447–48; other Indians and, 333, 334, 409, 418–19, 422; partisans of, 420, 442; penitence practices of, 403, 419–21, 425, 441; personal adornment of, *141*, 292, 414–15, 416, 417, 419; pipe smoking by, 332, 345, 364, 421–22; portraits of, 442, 443; Scalp Dance of, 417, 450; scalped men of, 410, 422, 450–51; subsistence practices of, 103, 369, 381, 406, 414, 418; territory of, xliv, 201, 331, 413; villages of, 103, 199, 201, 202, 332, 361, 364, 368, 413–14, 415, 419, 512n; warfare and, 143, 385, 410, 414, 422; weapons of, 202–3, 331, 409–10, 416; white buffalo and, 397–98, 417; whites and, 195, 353, 361, 422, 451; winter villages of, 331, 344, 440; women of, 200–201, 344, 345–47, 348, 440; women's societies of, 417, 438

Hide, beaver, 165, 168, 382, 457, 465; fur trade and, 210, 215, 216, 264, 271, 273–74, 283, 284, 285, 320, 324–25, 337, 346, 349; as gifts, 261, 262, 263, 265, 267; prices of, 263, 275, 335, 342, 343, 344–45, 363–64, 372; whiskey and, 280, 282

Hide, bison, 212, 341, 357, 399–400, 382; as bedding and padding, 178, 222, 242, 261, 267, 294, 351, 380; decoration of, 219, 455; fur trade and, 185–86, 210, 215, 216, 250, 270, 271, 283, 465; as gifts, 399, 421; painted, *123*, *127*, 185, 198, 248, 293, 294, 341, 348, 359, 377–78, 382, 440–41, 450, 515n; price of, 397, 398; as robes, 122–25, *130*, *143*, 156, 157, 165, 167, 179, 196, 206, 212, 285, 296–97, 377, 386; for shields, *125*, *142*, 214; for tipi furnishings, 180, 267, 335, 349; for tipis

Hide, bison (*cont.*)
(lodges), *127*, 168, 294, 297, 420–21;
white, 197, 198, 320, 334, 357, 397–98,
408, 417, 433, 438, 441; wrapping
corpses in, 302, 411
Hides, pelts, skins, 166, 216, 271, 510n; for
caps and hats, *115*, 211; for ceremonies,
401, 438; for clothing, *122–25*, *131*, *132*,
134, *143*, 172, 201, 205, 209, 297, 388; as
containers, 380, 393, 398; decoration
of, 351–52; for moccasins, 166, 224,
378; painted, *123*, 180, 185, 198, 214,
248, 283, 346, 356; prices of, 363–64,
372; for quivers, 158, 301, 336; of small
mammals, 216, 271; tanning, 185, 235,
274, 295, 296, 382; uses of, 111, 342, 379.
See also under specific animals
Horses, 41, 52, 174, 203, 297, 355, 418; canal
boats and, 484, 491, 492; captured, 351,
378, 409; feed for, 71, 326; at Fort Clark,
199, 339, 343–44, 359, 427–28; at Fort
McKenzie, 256, 272, 285; at Fort Pierre,
182, 183; at Fort Union, 206, 207, 285,
326; as gifts/prizes, 218, 247, 275, 287,
300, 350, 386, 411, 417; horsehair, 90,
115, *141*; for hunting, 187, 219, 232, 238,
319, 406–7, 428, 435; Indians and, 160,
187, 200, 212, 382, 383, 405, 415, 423,
462; packhorses, 208, 215, 271, 280, 287,
318, 319, 321, 349, 359, 406, 441, 442;
pasturing of, 259, 283, 285, 287, 288,
380, 442; quality of, 52, 199; sleds and,
353, 357, 359, 366, 427, 436; tack for, 185,
198, 294, 336, 359, 380; theft of, 174, 217,
261, 269, 279, 285, 293, 316, 325, 360,
434, 435, 440, 451, 462–63; as trade
goods, 201, 283, 284, 301, 342, 343–44,
364, 398; for transportation, 66, 170,
175, 215, 246, 343, 348, 478; travois and,
269, *270*; treatment of, 367, 380, 434;
wagons and, 366, 494; as wealth, 180,
187, 302, 346; women and, 383, 384,
448; wounded in attacks, 277, 278

Hotokáneheh (Head of the Robe), 266,
272, 277
Hudson River, xx, xlv, 15, 496
Hudson's Bay Company, xxiii, xxxii, 251,
266, 272, 274, 275, 280, 282, 290, 325, 364
Hugron (engagé), 326, 327, 328, 338, 443
Hunting, 75, 430; of antelope (pronghorn), 173, 189, 191, 192, 203, 204, 216,
229, 275, 316, 406–7; of bear, 30, 205,
231–33, 407; of bighorn sheep, 216, 245,
307, 406; of bison, 92, 126, 175, 180,
212, 216, 224, 228, 229, 231, 237, 242,
244, 246, 295, 310, 358, 435, 514n; of
deer, 27, 28, 62, 108, 170, 194–95, 203,
224, 227, 228; of elk, 150, 170, 191, 192,
194, 195, 205, 224, 226, 230, 241, 313;
of game birds, 42, 62, 68, 76, 109, 149,
153, 154; along Missouri River, 108, 147,
153–54; of rabbits, 108, 109, 111, 152; of
raptors, 58, 69, 79; shelters/camps for,
108, 170, 196, 227, 240; of small birds,
24, 53, 74; of small mammals, 152;
for specimens, 64, 70, 151; steamboat
travel and, 112–13; of turkeys, 62–63,
67, 69, 70, 73, 75, 108; of wolves, 75, 216

Ihkas-kinne (Corne Basse, Low Horn),
133, 279, 281, 282
Insects: ants, 153, 236; beetles, 27; butterflies,
11, 39, 102, 222, 224, 233, 236, 242, 465,
472, 476; cicadas, 40, 43; cockroaches,
54; crickets and grasshoppers, 40, 65,
236, 239, 254, 287, 373; mosquitoes, 161,
173, 190, 196, 211, 224–26, 235, 236, 239,
244, 256, 274, 368, 373; moths, 64
Iowa Indians, 105, 106, 148, 510n14; other
Indians and, 148, 156, 157, 158; territory
of, 106, 113, 147, 149–50, 152; trade
with, 158, 464, 466
Iron Shirt. *See* Mexkehme-Sukahs
Íschohä-Kakoschóchatä (Half-Shorn
Heads) society, Mandan, 358, 389, 416,
450

Íta-Widáhki-Hischä (Red Shield), 332,
437, 441
Itsicháichä (Monkey Face), 414, 438, 439

James, Edwin, xxvii, xxxvi, 156, 483,
494–95, 505n2
Janus (ship), xix, xxxvi, 3, 4, 5, 10, 11, 13
Jefferson Barracks, Mo., xxvi, xxxi, 89,
93, 94, 159
Jewelry: bracelets, 165, 202, 322–23, 377,
379; earrings, 248, 249, 272, 291, 303,
375–76, 379; gorgets, 340; necklaces/
neckbands, 292, 377, 379; rings, 292,
377; shell plates. *See also* Bear claw
necklaces; Medals
Judith River, 243, 247, 307, 513n4
Junipers (*Juniperus* spp.), 10, 245, 370. *See
also* Cedars

Kaénna Indians. *See* Blood Indians
Kähka-Chamahän (Little Raven), 343,
356, 375, 442
Kansa Indians, 67n, 103, 112, 148, 510n3
Keelboats, 255, 259, 261; attacks on, 361,
423; dinghy/skiff for, 205, 225, 234,
236, 237, 240, 241, 247, 249, 250; food
for, 222, 223–24, 230; fur trade and,
xxiii, 207, 363; on Missouri River, 111,
153, 167; steamboats and, 170, 182,
188; upstream travel of, 221, 222, 223,
231; wrecked, 229–30. *See also Flora;
Maria*
Keokuk, xxxvi, 91, 93, 94
Kiäsax (L'Ours Gaucher, Bear on the
Left), 131, 201, 203, 205, 442, 512n14
Kingfisher (*Alcedo alcyon*), 68, 101, 311,
484
Kipp, James, xxiii, xxiv, xxxvi, 291, 334,
339, 352, 361, 446; family of, 333–34,
340, 355, 397, 443, 446–47, 449; at Fort
Clark, xxiii, xxxvi–xxxvii, 202, 203,
332, 338, 348, 363, 366, 368, 433–35, 437,
446–49; at Fort Union, 359, 427, 433;

fur trade and, 339, 342, 343–44, 349;
Hidatsas and, 353, 355–56, 433, 438–40;
as interpreter, xxiv, 333, 374, 390, 411;
Mandans and, 334, 336, 339, 349, 351,
355, 362, 384, 443–44; Maximilian and,
450, 452; medicine given by, 341, 441
Knife River, 201, 202, 396, 413
Knives, 13, 405, 410; as emblem, 140, 430;
as gifts, 433, 438, 444, 450; as trade
goods, 99, 288, 297, 456; ubiquity of,
100, 177, 410; utility of, 96, 174, 411, 412,
421, 463; as weapons, 107, 175, 282, 334
Kootenai Indians, 259, 290n, 304, 514n7;
expedition to, 273, 275, 280; language
of, 266, 304. *See also* Kutonäpi
Krumbhaar, Lewis, xxxvii, 17, 21, 23, 357,
496, 497
Kutonäpi (old Kootenai, Hómach-Ksáchkum, Big Earth), 258n, 265, 266, 271,
281, 283, 284, 304

Lachapelle, David, xxxvii, 190, 192, 195,
212, 456
Lachpitzí-Síhrisch (Yellow Bear), 344,
345, 346, 414, 415
Laidlaw, William, xxxvii; at Fort Pierre,
183, 184, 186, 187, 456–57; fur trade
and, 339, 362, 437, 455; Upper Missouri
Outfit and, 188, 217
Lamont, Daniel, xxxvii, 182, 186, 188, 217,
473
Lances, 91, 277n, 285, 325, 336, 350–51,
356, 358, 395; bow-lances, 125, 198, 214
Larks (*Alauda* spp.), 188, 288, 372
Lead deposits, 89
Leavenworth, Henry, xxxvii, 361, 362, 423
Leggins, 158, 172, 455; decoration of, 186,
198, 203, 205, 209, 293, 358, 378; as
standard element of clothing, 157, 165,
177, 179, 248, 256, 267, 336
Lehigh River, 20, 22, 25, 30, 34, 37
Lenni-Lenape Indians. *See* Delaware
Indians

384, 386, 406, 442; horse tack of, 198, 359; illness among, 334, 336, 341; interpreters for, xxiv, xxxv, 200, 333, 339, 340, 390, 412; language of, 374, 412, 413; leaders of, xxxviii, *140*, 200, 202, 334, 337, 343, 374–75, 408; medicine devices and shrines, *138*, 200n, 334, 336, 343, 365, 379, 390, 394, 397, 399, 402, 405; medicine lodge of, 343, 349, 379, 387, 388, 398–403, 408; medicine pipes of, 392, 397, 399, 408; Medicine Rock and, 340, 405; men's activities, 380, 385, 406–10; men's societies, *142*, 349–51, 358–59, 386–89, 395, 408–9, 444–45; music of, 357, 387, 399, 400, 403, 409; Ochkíh-Häddä (devil) and, 379, 390, 397, 400–401; Okippe festival of, 398–403, 516n1; origin story of, 390–96; other Indians and, 333, 396, 409, 411, 430, 432; partisans of, 340, 408–9; penitence practices of, 389, 397, 398, 399, 402–3, 405, 425; personal adornment of, 292, 375–77; personal hygiene among, 386, 406; pipe smoking by, 332, 381, 386, 392, 397; pottery of, 382, 391; subsistence practices of, 338–39, 368n, 369, 403–4, 406–7; territory of, xliv, 395–96; U.S. government and, 102, 358; villages of, 103, *139*, 193, 194, 195, 197, 199, 201, 202, 332, 334, 374, 379, 512nn; warbonnet of, 187, 336, 376–77; warfare and, 407–10; weapons of, 301, 378, 409–10; white buffalo and, 197, 397–98, 408; whites and, xxxiii, 175, 195, 352, 385, 387; winter (forest) villages of, 333, 343, 348, 349, 359, 361, 367, 380, 437, 442; women of, 200–201, 334, 341–42, 343, 349, 351, 367, 380, 382–83, 386, 388–89, 398, 436–37; women's societies of, 357, 379, 389, 433, 450. *See also* Medicine Rock
Mandeck-Suck-Choppeníh (Medicine Bird), 340, 349, 351, 355, 356

Mándeh-Páhchu (Eagle Nose), 439, 447, 449
Maples (*Acer* spp.), 30, 41, 42, 53, 55, 465, 467, 483, 492; sugar maple *(Acer saccharum)*, 104, 147, 472, 490
Maria (keelboat), 167, 170, 175, 177, 178
Marias River, 243, 255, 256, 272, 278, 290, 304, 305, 313, 506n17
Mató-Óchka (Crazy Bear, Old Bear), 441, 443, 445
Mató-Tópe (Four Bears), xxxviii, 340; as artist, 342, 348, 353, 442, 444; described, 198, 337, 430; family of, 336, 337, 359, 410; headdress of, 187, 443; information from, 349, 353, 356, 424; as Mandan leader, 336, 374, 398, 450; Maximilian and, 342, 353, 356, 429, 452; other Indians and, 356, 424, 429; portrait of, xxxviii, *140*, 431, 451; as *soldat* for Fort Clark, 443; visiting Maximilian, 336, 339, 352, 354, 429, 432, 434, 435, 436, 442, 446, 447, 449, 450; as warrior *(soldat)*, 334, 348, 349, 359, 410, 431&n, 444
Mauch Chunk, Pa., 20, 24, 30, 34–37, 508n2
Mauvaises-Terres (Badlands), xxiii, 237, 244, 245, 247, 307, 308, 311, 327, 329, 513n3
Maximilian Alexander Philipp of Wied, xxvii–xxviii, *146*, 344; as artist, xiv–xv, xviii, xxvi, 95, 96, *197*, 203, 244, 251, 252; banking of, 76, 78, 79, 97, 99; as Baron von Braunsberg, 507n5, 509n7, 515n2; boats of, 286, 287, 288–89, 305, 320, 323, 324–26, 337, 451, 452, 454, 458, 460, 515n2; books of, xix, 38, 64, 66, 85, 96, 232, 306, 428, 497; family of, xvii, xviii, xxv, xxvii, xliii, 4, 73, 80, 443, 519n; fur company account of, 219–20, 514n6, 515n1, 517n4; illness and indisposition of, xx, xxiv, 20, 23, 41, 58, 62, 64, 107, 319, 327, 339, 340, 341, 446,

Maximilian Alexander Philipp of Wied
(*cont.*)
448, 449, 452, 453, 456, 508n1, 517n5;
Indian women and, 346, 351; language
studies of, xiv, xxiv, 91, 106, 266, 272,
339, 340, 341, 516n; *Tagebuch* (journal)
of, xiii, xiv, xv, xix, xx, xxi, xxv–xxvi, 4,
89, *115*, 312. See also *Reise in das Innere
Nord-America*

McKenzie, Kenneth: experiences of,
151, 205, 215–16, 247, 303, 315; at Fort
Union, 207, 266, 333, 437; as fur
company principal, xxxvii, xxxviii,
93, 96, 97, 100, 111n, 113, 172, 188, 192,
259, 516n; Indian relations and, 166,
170, 212, 218, 281, 428; Indian women
and, 186, 187; intertribal negotiations
and, 196, 197; Maximilian and, xxviii,
94–95, 99, 102, 104, 110–11, 177, 181,
219–20, 333, 338, 357; steamboats and,
167, 509n; Upper Missouri Outfit and,
188, 217

Measurement units: French measure
("Paris foot"), 428, 507n2; Prussian
measure, 158, 179, 267, 291, 337, 509n2;
Réaumur temperature scale, 507n1

Medals (medallions), 122, *134*, *143*, *166*,
179, 200, 211, 217, 258, 285

Medicinal plants, 27, 65–66, 171, 255, 302,
370, 398, 411, 472–73

Medicine: for abdominal pain, 274;
alcohol as, 5, 277, 301, 321; calomel as,
64, 66, 110; castor oil as, 339, 341; for
cholera, 333, 465, 476; enemas, 66;
gunpowder as, 411, 421–22; herbal
remedies and, 339, 341; ipecac as, 341;
lead acetate as, 287, 441; Spanish fly
plaster as, 148

Medicine Bird. *See*
Mandeck-Suck-Choppeníh

Medicine Rock, 340, 405, 420

Melone [Maloney?] (engagé), 453, 459,
461

Mentha spp. (mints), 66, 339, 341, 370

Meskwaki (Fox) Indians, xxxiii, 90–92,
107, 110, *115*; territory of, xlv, 84, 147, 152

Mexkehme-Sukahs (Iron Shirt, Chemise-
de-Fer), *132*, 257, 258n, 261, 263, 264

Mexkemáuastan (Stirring Iron), *130*, 250,
267

Mice, 151, 262, 327, 456; in myths, 391, 394;
Perognathus fasciatus (olive-backed
pocket mouse), 319–20, 515n1; trapping, 262, 353, 354, 437, 440, 444

Middle Bull (Tátsicki-Stomíck), 269,
270–71, 281, 282, 283, 286

Mih-Tutta-Hangkusch (Mandan village),
139, 201, 332, *335*, 362, 379, 398, 436;
activities at, 431, 447; burial scaffolds
near, 334, 343; Missouri River and,
341–42, 366, 374; surroundings of, 199,
361, *365*, 427, 440, 441; winter lodges
and, 334–35, 437

Milk River, 209, 232, 234, 236, 312

Mink *(Mustela vison)*, 69, 355, 371, 391;
hides of, 216, 340

Minnesota River, xxxvii, 175, 176, 180n,
195, 220, 481

Mirrors, 279, 283, 342, 358, 376, 438, 450

Mississippi River, xxi, xxvi, xlv, 60, 82,
86, 98, 100, 180&n; flora of, 58, 87, 104;
steamboats on, xxvi, 71, 75, 76–77, 78,
87, 88, 93, 475

Missouria Indians, 103, 107, 150n, 465,
511n

Missouri Fur Company, xxxiv, xxxiv,
xxxv, 155, 210

Missouri River: appearance of, 100, 112,
119, 120, 147, 150, 155, 190, 242, 255, 318;
banks of, 106, 111, 114, 150, 152, 160,
162, 190, 191, 194, 207, 223, 224, 225,
234, 237, 239, 241, 242; bends in, 234,
245, 366; Big Bend of, 181–82, 458,
511n; bluffs along, 152, 157, 160–61, 163,
164, 168, 169, 170, 172, 190, 192, 193,
206, 222, 223, 255, 257; canoes on, 107,

111, 155; confluence with other rivers, 98, 100, *128*, 206, 207, 218, 225, 268; distances along, 101, 102, 181, 182, 204, 236, 241, 258, 465, 467, 510n2; drinking from, 238, 240, 247; exploration and, xvii, 61, 361; falls of, 182, 286; fishing in, 101, 154, 163, 181, 208, 230, 466; flooding of, 106, 368, 451; fossils of, 159; frozen, 139, 215, 234, 341–42, 343, 346, 348, 367, 368, 406, 431, 432, 436–37, 442; fur trade and, 95, 98, 215; health and, xxiv, 103–4; ice on, 190, 232, 337, 448, 450; Indian agencies along, xxxiv–xxxv, 97, 178, 179n, 181; Indians of, 74, 103, 112, 113, 148–49, 150&n, 152, 155, 156, 157, 161, 180n, 209, 212, 283, 361, 413, 423, 425; keelboats on, 111, 153, 167, 225; maps of, 95, 164, 242, 245, 361, 509n4; in myths, 392, 395, 396, 404; navigation of, xxiii, 98, 101, 107, 108, 112, 148, 152, 153, 154–55, 157, 161, 163, 172, 226, 228, 234; steamboats on, xxii, 98, 101, 107, 108, 118, 128, 152, 153, 163, 165, 167, 171, 181, 225, 509n; Stone Walls [White Cliffs] of, *129*, 513n5; western exploration and, xxi, xliv–xlv, 73, 89, 101, 102, 361, 365

Mitchell, David Dawson, 244, 285; Assiniboine attack and, 277–78, 302; engagés and, 222, 240, 247; experiences of, 205, 223, 229–30, 231, 240, 241, 514n4; at Fort McKenzie (Fort Piegan), xxxviii, 130, 182, 220, 260, 266, 284; fur trade and, 271, 280; gifts given by, 185, 243, 249, 270–71, 273, 283–84; gifts offered to, 261, 262, 263, 278, 284; hunting by, 222–23, 225, 229, 235, 239, 255; Indian customs and, 263, 265, 269, 302; Indians and, 186, 222, 249, 250, 251, 256, 267, 275, 280, 281, 287, 298; intertribal relations and, 265–66, 268, 272–73; Maximilian and, 221, 229, 234–35, 241, 243, 254, 264, 286, 289,

305, 326; new fort planned by, 268, 273, 288; prairie dogs and, 188, 247

Moccasins ("Indian shoes"), 111, 166, 208, 212, 249–50, 326, 420–21; cost of, 208, 224; decoration of, 179, 185, 296, 378, 415; hides for, 224, 371, 378; Maximilian's use of, 344

Moncravie, Jean (John) Baptiste, xxxviii, 315, 321–22, 323, 326

Mönnitarrís. *See* Hidatsa Indians

Monrepos, 503, 519n1

Moose *(Cervus alces)*, 272, 304

Moravian Brethren (American Moravian Church), xli, 19, 20, 21, 37, 38

Morrin, Henry, 234, 329, 338; as helmsman, 289, 309, 310, 326, 330; as hunter, 307, 308, 312, 313, 327, 328

Moser (botanist), 21, 22, 28, 30

Mountain goat *(Oreamnos americanus)*, 272, 280, 304

Mountain lion, panther, 15, 371; hides of, 275, 294, 301, 336

Mount Vernon, Ind., xxi, 54, 60, 69, 71, 75, 76–77, 78, 83, 476

museums. *See under* American culture (of Anglo-Americans)

Music: "badger" (drum), 344, 345, 346; bells, 96, 159, 277, 344; for ceremonies, 344–47, 350, 351, 356, 357, 359, 387, 389, 399, 403, 409, 417, 420, 438, 445; dancing and, 70, 71, 82, 159; drums, 70, 71, 82, 159, 213, 219, 262, 298, 299, 301, 326, 336, 357, 456; drunkenness and, 82, 70, 264, 296; as entertainment, 3, 20, 44, 45, 110, 481; for festive occasions, 70, 82; in healing ceremonies/treatments, 218, 301, 326, 422; instrumental, 104, 131, 188, 219, 387, 445; music box, 275, 279, 342, 439; rattles *(chichikué)*, 141, 180, 262, 298, 299, 301, 347, 357, 388, 425, 511n; singing/chanting, 188, 212, 214, 262, 299, 344–45, 346, 350, 357, 400, 438; "turtle," 399, 400, 402

Muskrat *(Ondatra zibethecus, Fiber zibethecus)*, 23, 71, 81, 372; hides of, 216, 464; trapping, 289, 320

Mussels: fossils of, 82, 114; decorations from shells, 279, 304; *Unio* spp., 46, 56, 59, 63, 235, 373, 497

Musselshell River, 225, 235, 236, 241, 266, 310, 312

National Road, 485, 508n3

Native Americans. *See names of specific American Indian groups*

Native American women, 93, *123*, 148–49, 220, 389; appearance of, 90, 158, 185, 191, 201, 217, 273, 291–92; artistry of, 111, 271, 294, 296; as captives, 266, 268; ceremonial roles of, 388, 403–4; clothing of, 293–94, 339, 400; drunkenness among, 213–14; mixed-bloods and, 317, 318; pregnancy, childbirth, and children of, 171, 213, 218, 261, 427; societies of, 298–99, 357, 379, 389–90, 417, 433, 438, 450; violence and, 276, 277; white men and, 188, 200–201, 207, 221, 251, 259, 275, 297; work done by, 185, 209, 217, 235, 248, 296–97, 352, 380–82, 386, 436–37, 441

Negroes. *See* African Americans

Neuwied, xxiv, xxvii, xxviii, 3, 23, 73, 506n20

New Harmony, Ind., xlv, 72, *117*, 508n1; description of, 55, 56, 59, 65; founding of, xx, xxxix, 44, 58–59; Indian mounds near, 60, 63, 75, 508n1; Maximilian in, xx, xxi, xxiv, 55, 56–82, 476–77, 509n7; residents of, xx, xxiv, xxxv, xxxvii, xl, xlii, 56–57, 79, 473, 476; surroundings of, xxi, 57, 59–60, 61–62, 65, 68–69, 73, 76, 80, 83

New Orleans, La., xlv, 53, 86; Bodmer's trip to, xxi, xxxi, 71, 75, 76, 77–78; cholera in, 66, 69, 73; as shipping and transportation center, 49, 59, 71, 75, 80, 83, 93, 98, 99, 475, 499

New York City, xix, xxi, xxxvi, xxxix, xli, xlv, 13, 15–16, 19, 24, 99, 145, 486, 489, 497, 499; cholera in, 14, 17, 37, 507n1

Niagara Falls, N.Y., xxv, *145*, 486–90

Nicolet, Mr. (banker), 76, 78, 79, 99

Nighthawk *(Caprimulgus americanus)*, 193, 255

Nínoch-Kiäiu. *See* Bear Chief

Niobrara River, 156, 165, 167, 168, 461, 466

Nishnabotna River, 113, 150, 152, 466, 510n2

Noapeh (Troop of Soldiers), *124*, 213, 214

Númangkake. *See* Mandan Indians

Nuttall, Thomas, xxxviii, 72, 177, 241n, 481

Oaks *(Quercus* spp.), 23–24, 27, 34, 39, 41, 42, 53, 55, 57, 68, 101, 114, 152, 163, 370, 465, 467, 472, 473, 477, 492

Ochkíh-Häddä (Mandan evil spirit), 343, 349, 379, 390, 397, 400–401, 415, 425, 446

O'Fallon, Benjamin, xxxiv, xxxviii–xxxix, 95, 358, 473, 509n4, 513n1

Ohio [and Erie] Canal, xxv, 483–86, 518n3

Ohio River, xlv, 83, 86, 518n1; navigation of, 60, 85, 475; settlements along, xlii, 43–44, 47–55, 475, 479; steamboats on, 47, 49, 52, 53, 479–80, 481–82; transportation and, xxi, 98, 480, 483, 518n1

Óhmahank-Numákschi (Mandan Lord of Life), 390–92, 394, 397

Ojibwe Indians, 100, 175, 272, 316, 333, 363, 384, 428, 494

Okíppe, Mandan ceremony, 394, 398–403, 420, 425, 439

Old Kootenai. *See* Hómach-Ksáchkum

Omaha Indians, xxii, xxxviii, 102, 155, 156–59, 165–66, 465; Iowas and, 148, 156, 158; leaders of, xxxii, xlii, 78, 161, 463, 464; subsistence practices of, 103, 414; territory of, xliv, 149–50, 156, 165, 463, 511n6

Oneida Indians, xli, 493–94, 519n

Óngpa-Tánga (Big Elk), xxxii, xxxviii, 78, 161, 464

Orioles, 458; Baltimore *(Icterus baltimore)*, 227, 268, 372, 464, 466, 469, 475

Ortubise, Pierre, xxxix, 191, 192, 194, 196, 206, 333, 337, 338, 454, 456

Osage Indians, 67n, 103, 108, 110, 317, 318, 321, 510ns10–11, 515n3

Osage River, 104, 110, 471, 510n

Otoe Indians, 102, 103, 155, 156, 157, 464, 511n5; territory of, 107, 149–50, 150n, 152

Otter, river *(Lutra canadensis)*, 16, 63, 71, 371; hides of, 91, 133, 168, 216, 264, 320, 342, 350, 377, 378, 395, 416, 460–61, 517n

Owen, Richard, xxxix, 57, 476, 481

Owen, Robert, xx, xxxvii, xxxix, 44, 58, 60, 61, 70, 82

Owls, 58, 62, 65; "eagle owl," 387, 430, 433, 445; feathers of, 158, 376, 387, 388, 430, 433, 445; great horned owl *(Strix virginiana)*, 306, 372, 376; as medicine birds, 405, 421; screech owl *(Strix asio)*, 424

Painting, body, 152; black, 399, 400, 401, 409; for ceremonies, 300–301, 377, 389, 399, 400–402, 409; counting coup and, 430, 445; by midwestern Indians, 84, 92, 94; pigments for, 135, 342, 399, 420; red, *140*, *141*, 198, 377, 445; with spots and circles, 359, 401; with stripes and spirals, 158, 167, 401, 408, 415; white, 158, 355, 377, 399, 400, 401, 402, 420; yellow, *140*, 359, 400, 401

Painting, face: black, 90, *132*, *141*, *143*, 262, 264, 291, 299, 325, 387, 395, 409, 437; blue, *130*, *135*, 249, 267, 281; for ceremonies, 387, 388, 399, 438; counting coup and, 409; of the dead, 302, 411, 426; with dots and circles, 185, 357; by

midwestern Indians, 90, 91, 92, 94; with stripes, 157, 211, 249, 262, 273, 340, 417, 438; vermilion/red, 90, 91, *115*, *122*, *125*, *130*, *131*, *132*, *134*, *138* [skulls], *140*, *141*, *143*, 152, 157, 158, 179, 185, 186, 198, 199, 201, 202, 203, 209, 211, 212, 217, 249, 258, 264, 267, 281, 291–92, 297, 322, 323, 325, 344, 357, 377, 400, 430; warfare and, 325; white, 156, 157; yellow, *140*, 214, 337, 377, 402

Palmer, James A. Hamilton. *See* Hamilton, James A.

Papin, Jos. (hunter), 436, 439, 455; on the *Flora*, 223, 224, 228, 229, 230, 231, 255; as hunter, 232, 235, 242, 245, 247, 271, 272, 275

Parakeet *(Psittacus carolinensis)*, 55, 58, 62, 63, 64, 65, 72, 74, 81, 106, 113, 466, 472

Paul Wilhelm, Duke of Württemberg, xxxix, 101, 339

Pawnee Indians, xxxix, 67n, 102, 103, 152, 155, 414; other Indians and, 166, 191, 192, 423, 425

Pawpaw trees *(Asimina triloba)*, 48, 49, 148, 470, 475

Peale, Charles Willson, xxxix, 80, 519n2

Peale, Titian Ramsay, xxxix, 17, 496–97, 519n2

Peale museums, xxxix, 15, 17, 80, 507n2, 519n2

Péhriska-Ruhpa (Two Ravens), 198, 356, 429, 449; described, 335, 336, 356–57; Maximilian and, 335, 446, 447, 449, 450, 452; portrait of, *141*, 353, 447, 448, 511n, 515n, 517n

Pelican *(Pelecanus)*, 152, 373, 452, 460, 463

Petalesharo, xxxix, 78, 103, 425

Philadelphia, Pa., xix, xxi, xxv, xxxv, xxxvii, xxxviii, xxxix, xlv, 17, 19, 21, 24, 483, 486, 495

Phlox, 103, 104, 152, 156, 465, 467

Picotte, Honoré, xl, 337, 338, 427–28, 434, 435–36, 437, 439, 443, 447, 451, 453, 467

Piegan Indians: as Blackfoot, 259, 290&n, 514n; Blood Indians and, 266, 269, 272–73, 281, 282, 285, 290n; clothing and adornment of, *131, 132*, 257–58, 262, 281, 282, 284; depicted, *131, 132, 135*, 514n1; at Fort McKenzie, 257, 272, 273–74, 275, 280–82; horses and, 258, 261, 269, 275; language of, 248, 302–3, 339; leaders of, *132*, 258&n, 264, 266, 269, 274, 281–82, 286, 442; other Indians and, 276–79, 281, 283, 284, 290n, 304; tipis of, 257, 258, 261, 298

Pigeon, passenger *(Columba migratoria)*, 10, 27, 73, 113, 516n3

Pilcher, Joshua, xl, 100, 102, 112, 157, 159, 464, 465

Pines *(Pinus spp.)*, 28, 30, 31, 87, 104, 242, 254, 310; pine resin, 104, 414

Pioch-Kiäiu (Distant Bear), *135*, 272, 278

Pipes, 175, 180, 185, 186, 197, 200, 206, 213, 217, 261, 263, 295, 299, 381, 387, 421–22, 430; as gifts, 218; in Maximilian's collection, 185, 455, 481; medicine pipes and calumets, 91, 92, 218, 266, 271, 272, 295, 299–300, 392, 397, 399, 408–9, 425, 430, 455, 481; pipe-tomahawk, *115, 122*, 179; Sioux (Dacota), 158, 162, 200, 250, 295, 332, 381, 455, 481

Pitätapiú, *125*, 214, 217

Platanus (sycamore), 22, 48, 49, 53, 55, 68, 85, 87, 100, 108, 467, 475, 480, 492

Platte River (Mo.), 106, 113, 120, 510n8

Platte River (Nebr.), xliv, 155, 156, 161, 465, 510n8

Pocono Mountains, 27, 28, 31

Poires (*Mespilus* spp., serviceberries), 192, 208, 261, 267, 296, 370, 381, 396, 406

Poison ivy *(Rhus radicans)*, 154, 411

Pomme de prairie (pomme blanche) ("wild turnip," edible root), 169, 170, 171, 173, 192, 265, 296, 381

Ponca Indians, xxii, 102, 103, 165, 167, 460; appearance described, 165, *166*, 168, 460; lodges/tipis of, 165–66, 168; territory of, xliv, 165, 170, 461

Porcupine *(Hystrix dorsata)*, 316, 372, 458. *See also* Quills

Portsmouth, Ohio, xxv, 49–50, 481, 482, 483, 485, 518n

Poultry, 27, 152, 497; chickens, 50, 86, 151, 208, 317, 324, 367, 447

Prairie, 65, 168, 408; fauna of, 67, 163, 164, 173, 210, 230–31, 406; flora of, 165, 170, 171, 173; of lower Missouri River, 107, 110, 150, 155, 156, 157, 160, 162, 182; of upper Missouri River, 114, 369–73

Prairie dog *(Arctomys ludoviciana)*, 173, 177, 243, 372; hunting, 309, 458; skin of, 342; villages of, 168, 188, 239, 243, 247, 454

Prairie hen. *See* Grouse

Pratte, Bernard, Jr., xl, 174, 188

Pratte, Bernard, Sr., xl, 188, 217

Prunus spp. (cherry, chokecherry, plum), 101, 102, 408, 456, 458; chokecherry *(Prunus padus)*, 153, 164, 168–69, 171, 268, 313, 459; fruit of, 192, 208, 296, 370, 381, 406

Quills, porcupine (sometimes bird), 405; in ornamentation, 111, 179, 186, 203, 206, 209, 211, 214, 218, 292, 293, 296, 303, 332, 336, 377, 378, 415, 455, 488

Quivers, 156, 158, 185, 199, 203, 267, 301, 336, 350, 456

Rabbits and hares, 24, 73, 108, 109, 111, 113, 372

Raccoon *(Procyon lotor)*, 42, 63, 64, 69, 72, 151, 152, 154, 466

Railroads, 34, *35–36*, 494, 508n2, 510n6

Rapp, George, xx, 44–45, 58, 60, 81, 508n2

Rassade. See under Beads (glass)

Rats, 333&n, 342, 348–49, 367, 446

Raven *(Corvus corax):* as carrion eaters, 371, 382, 411; feathers of, 376, 387, 388, 399, 405, 414, 416, 445; men's societies and, 300, 349; observed, 310, 313, 318, 328, 372, 434, 444, 461

Redbuds *(Cercis canadensis),* xxii, 100, 101, 102, 103, 104, 112, 147, 149, 467, 492

Red Shield (Íta-Widáhki-Hischä), 332, 437, 439, 441

Rees. *See* Arikara Indians

Reise in das Innere Nord-America . . . (Maximilian zu Wied), xiii, xvi, xxi, xxv, xxvi, 124, 134, *146,* 276n, 295, 506n15, 506n19, 510n9, 511n11, 513n1, 514n5, 516n2, 517n1, 518n1

Rhus spp. (sumacs), 25, 33, 41, 48, 68, 153, 163, 313. *See also* Poison ivy

Ribes spp. (currants, gooseberries), 102, 163, 225, 229, 241, 268, 370, 381

Robidoux, Joseph, xl, 467, 471, 510n1

Rocky Mountains: exploration of, xxxvii, xxxix, xli, 56, 95, 102, 155, 317, 326; fauna of, 17, 407; fur trade in, 111, 112, 215, 251, 465; Maximilian's plans to journey to, xxiii, 286, 514n4; ores and pigments in, 249, 291; snowmelt in, 194, 448

Roses, wild *(Rosa* spp.): blooming, 221, 229, 492; in fall, 313, 318; in spring, 102, 173, 184, 453; as undergrowth, 223, 225, 227, 241, 268, 328, 329, 369, 461

Ruhptare (Mandan village), 374; Fort Clark and, 427; Hidatsas and, 429; Indians of, 343, 375, 439; mentioned, 201, 202, 332, 339, 366, 436; winter (forest) village and, 343, 348, 437

Rushes *(Equisetum* spp.), 58, 101, 106, 147–48, 153, 454

Russel (hunter), 62, 64, 65, 67, 69, 70, 79

Sac Indians. *See* Sauk (Sac) Indians

Sage, 347, 398, 400, 417, 449. See also *Artemisia* spp.

Sakkakomi *(Arctostaphylos uva-ursi),* 295, 381, 514n2

Salish Indians, 258, 301, 326

Sandoval, Isidor, 267–68, 280

Sanford, John F. A., 159, 168, 339; on *Assiniboine,* 167, 211, 460; hunting by, 108, 109, 111, 153–54, 173; as Indian agent, xxxviii, xl, 101, 102, 198, 200; Indian women and, 186, 187; Maximilian's party and, 100, 102, 104, 181; specimen collecting by, 151, 154

Saone Sioux, 187, 360, 402, 432

Sarcee Indians, 259, 282, 290n

Saucier, L. (carpenter), 226, 242, 288, 289

Sauk (Sac) Indians, 67n, 90–93, 110, *115,* 160, 466; Black Hawk War and, xxxiii, xxxvi, xlii, 89; other Indians and, 107, 161; territory of, xlv, 147, 152

Sawmills, 28, 31, 49, 59, 108, 470, 477

Say, Lucy Way Sistaire, xl, 56, 59

Say, Thomas, 66, 77, 178; ethnographic observations by, 70, 74, 78–79; faunal studies of, xxxi, 55–57, 59, 61, 63, 64, 67, 71–73, 76, 81, 373, 476; Long's expedition and, xl, 56, 61, 403, 410, 419; Maximilian and, xx, xxiv, xxvii, 57, 58, 60, 62–65, 69, 71, 80, 95, 96, 117, 357, 473, 476; travels of, 81, 82, 156

Saynisch, Dr. [Lewis?], xl, 20, 22, 23, 24, 28, 34, 36, 38, 42, 45, 46, 62

Scalp Dance, 298, 299, 409, 417; performed, 438, 450–51

Schudegácheh ("He who smokes"), 165, *166,* 167, 332, 460–61

Schweinitz, Lewis David von, xli, 21, 23, 38, 357

Scientific societies. *See under* American culture (of Anglo-Americans)

Scurvy, xxiv, 78, 465, 517n5

Seidel, Charles F., xli, 20, 21, 23, 37, 38, 357

Seneca Indians, 486–87, 488, 490

Serviceberry. See *Poires*

Shawnee Indians, xlii, 84, 112, 113

Shells, 15, 9, 56, 80, 165; collections of, 20, 44, 57, 59, 64, 71; as ornamentation, 133, 214, 249, 271–72, 291, 292, 376, 417. See also *Dentalium* spp.; Wampum

Shields, *125, 142, 144*, 184, 185, 214, 217, 294, 301, 416, 445, 448, 513n4

Shoshone Indians, 67n, 266, 287, 326

Shrikes (*Lanius* spp.), 188, 233, 255

Síh-Chidä (Yellow Feather): as artist, 337, 339, 353, 358, 443, 446; Bodmer and, 334, 355, 356, 358, 430, 443; family of, 335, 362, 375, 442; Maximilian and, 334–35, 336, 355, 358, 429, 433, 439, 440, 443, 444, 448, 450, 451; other Indians and, 428, 429; portrait of, 352, 353, 358

Síh-Sä (Red Feather), 339, 340, 341, 353, 354, 367, 428, 435, 449

Siksika Indians, *133*, 259, 279, 284, 290&n, 302–3, 304. *See also* Blackfoot Indians

Sioux Agency and agent [S.Dak.], xxxii, xxxix, xliii, 102, 178, 179n, 180, 181, 458

Sioux Indians. *See* Dacota Indians; Saone Sioux; Teton Sioux; Yanktonai Sioux; Yankton Sioux

Skulls, human, xxxiii, xxxviii, 63, *138*, 322, 334, 337–38, 375, 405, 454, 496

Skunks, 22, 69–70, 157, 159, 227–28, 322, 357, 404, 417, 433

Smallpox, xxxviii, xlii, 157, 161, 166, 167, 374, 396, 513n4

Snake Indians. *See* Shoshone Indians

Snakes, 63, 75, 76, 171, 516n; *Coluber* spp., 23, 109, 154, 155, 156, 173, 174, 195, 244, 373, 476; as food, 238, 382; hognose (*Heterodon* spp.), 113, 148, 153; in myths, 404–5, 421; rattlesnakes (*Crotalus* spp.), 28, 29, 31, 32, 34, 153, 158, 163, 168, 219, 223, 227, 235, 245, 373, 400; skins of, 201, 219; snakebite and, 27, 302

Solidago spp. (goldenrod), 39, 242, 318, 329, 337, 342

Specimens, faunal: loss of, 240–41, 305, 452n; packing, 37, 38, 58, 69, 70, 79, 80, 99, 185, 456, 473; preservation of, xxii, 22, 28, 73, 74, 96–97, 113, 153, 195, 273, 274; shipped to Europe, xxiv, 38, 71, 74, 80, 83, 99, 211

Specimens, floral: botanical paper and, 96, 106; loss of, 232, 306, 323, 452n; packing, 58, 69, 70, 99, 185, 323, 473; preparation of, xxii, 74, 103, 323; shipped to Europe, xxiv, 71, 74, 99

Spotted Elk. *See* Bear Chief

Square Buttes. *See* Butte Carré

Steamboats/ships: animals frightened by, 157, 172, 193, 203; cannon and, 186, 187, 191; cholera and, 54, 473; cordelle and, 109, 204; crew of, 109, 151, 161; descriptions of, 14, 47, 53, 84, 85; in Europe, xix, 3, 501, 502–3; explosions and fire on, 69, 204, 452n; firewood for, 81, 86, 88, 102, 103, 107, 148, 155, 162, 482; food on, 151–52, 154, 172, 181, 204; keelboats and, 167, 170, 177, 182, 188; on Mississippi River, xxvi, 71, 75, 76–77, 78, 86, 87, 89, 98, 475; on Missouri River, xxii, 98, 104, 105, 108, *118*, 128, 152, 165, 167, 181, 225, 442, 470; on Ohio River, xxi, xxv, 47–51, 52–55, 83, 84, 85, 98, 475, 479–80, 481–82; as public spectacle, 86, 100, 105, 106, 113, 167–68, 178, 183, 198, 202, 203, 206, 211, 275; repairing, 49, 53, 104, 107, 109, 110, 151, 480; transportation in East via, 14, 16, 18, 19, 50, 66, 486, 496, 499. *See* also *Assiniboine*; *Yellow Stone*

Stewart, William Drummond, xli, 95, 96, 97, 317

St. Louis, Mo., xxi–ii, xlii, 80, 100, 101, 104; cholera in, 60, 65, 348, 473; flora and fauna of, 472–73, 476, 477; fur trade and, xxxiii, 157, 182, 207, 333, 362, 364, 397, 457, 471, 473, 517n5, 517–18n3; Indian mounds of/near, xxiv, 75, 99,

Winnebago Indians, xlii, 67n, 85, 89
Wolf, prairie. *See* Coyote
Wolves *(Canis lupus)*, 65, 73, 240, 342,
382, 401, 425; behavior of, 193, 229, 312,
371, 430; burials and, 178, 302, 454;
food of, 234, 393; near Fort Clark, 367,
427; hides of, 210, 216, 301, 323, 399,
416, 419, 443; howling of, 306, 310,
313; hunting, 349, 352, 354, 407; along
Missouri River, 147, 160, 182, 309, 311,
331; in myths, 394, 404; tails of, 213,
356, 378, 408, 419
Woodpeckers, 42, 63, 68, 102, 177, 237, 372,
453, 459, 472; beaks of, 91, 264, 295;
northern flicker *(Picus auratus)*, 27, 61,
193, 451, 458, 461; pileated woodpecker
(Picus pileatus), 42, 53, 68, 105, 397,
469; redheaded woodpecker *(Picus
erythrocephalus)*, 19, 25, 172, 173, 193

Yanktonai Sioux, 197, 512n2; fur trade
and, xl, 337, 338, 358, 435; at fur trade
forts, 185, 333, 428, 431, 455; Mandans
and, 196–97, 333, 360, 432; territory of,
xliv, 180n; whites and, 197, 337
Yanktonan Sioux. *See* Yanktonai Sioux
Yankton Sioux, xliv, *122*, 149–50, 179n,
180&n, 185
Yellow Feather. *See* Síh-Chidä
Yellow Stone (steamboat), xxii, xxxi,
xxxii, 99, *118*, 172, 186, 509n3; amusement on, 104, 177; cannon on, 178, 183;
cargo of, 109–10, 152, 185–86; in St.
Louis, 93, 94, 96, 100
Yellowstone River, xliv, 73, 170, 320; confluence with Missouri River, *128*, 206,
207, 218; Fort Cass on, 201, 207, 316;
fur trade and, 95, 462; Maximilian's
party and, 95, 327